WORKING WITH

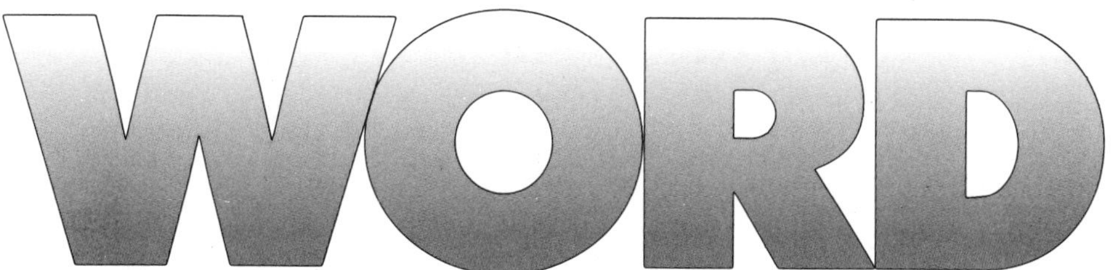

WORD

WORKING WITH

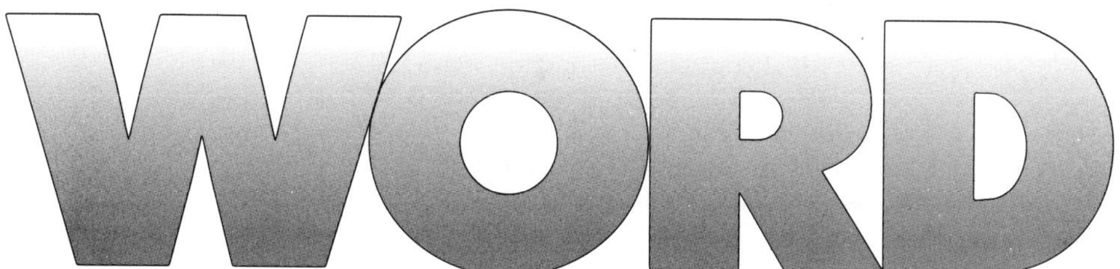

The Definitive Guide to Microsoft® Word on the Apple® Macintosh™

Chris Kinata
Gordon McComb

PUBLISHED BY
Microsoft Press
A Division of Microsoft Corporation
16011 NE 36th Way, Box 97017, Redmond, Washington 98073-9717

Library of Congress Cataloging in Publication Data

McComb, Gordon.
Working with Word.
Includes index.
1. Word processing. 2. Microsoft Word (Computer program)
3. Macintosh (Computer)—Programming. I. Kinata, Chris.
II. Title.
Z52.5.M52M36 1988 652'.5 87-5466
ISBN 1-55615-032-6

Printed and bound in the United States of America.

1 2 3 4 5 6 7 8 9 MLML 8 9 0 9 8

Distributed to the book trade in the United States by Harper & Row.

Distributed to the book trade in Canada by General Publishing Company, Ltd.

Distributed to the book trade outside the United States and Canada by Penguin Books Ltd.

Penguin Books Ltd., Harmondsworth, Middlesex, England
Penguin Books Australia Ltd., Ringwood, Victoria, Australia
Penguin Books N.Z. Ltd., 182–190 Wairau Road, Auckland 10, New Zealand

British Cataloging in Publication Data available

To Lydia and Jonah—bright stars both

Chris Kinata

To Eli Hollander and Jim Bierman

Gordon McComb

Contents

	Acknowledgments	ix
	Introduction	xi
SECTION 1	**Laying the Foundation**	
1	Word-Processing Concepts	3
2	Word Fundamentals: Creating a Two-Page Document	35
SECTION 2	**Building the Framework**	
3	Organizing Through Outlining	63
4	Writing and Editing Techniques	79
5	Automatic Text Entry with Glossaries	125
6	Using the Spelling Checker	145
7	Character Formatting	163
8	Paragraph Formatting	191
9	Working with Style Sheets	239
10	Section Formatting	275
11	Headers, Footers, and Footnotes	295
12	Document Formatting and Printing	323
SECTION 3	**Adding the Final Touches**	
13	Creating a Table of Contents and Index	369
14	Documents with Tables and Lists	385
15	Transferring Text and Graphics	405
16	Merge Printing	447
SECTION 4	**Blueprints for Projects**	
17	Blueprints	475
SECTION 5	**Appendixes – Toolbox**	
A	Setting Up Word	519
B	Table of Character Sets	527
C	Using PostScript	537
D	Mathematical Typesetting	561
	Index	567

Acknowledgments

It's chronically amazing that so many people can lend their influence to the preparation and marketing of a book such as this. We owe our thanks to:

Rebecca Pepper, one of the most caring and thoughtful editors who has ever put hand to manuscript.

Copy editor Lee Thomas, whose eagle eyes spot errant commas at hundreds of yards. This project would not have materialized without her aid—we owe her a great debt, for both her discipline and her high spirits.

Proofreaders Marsha Wright and Mike Perry gave their close attention.

Sylvia Hayashi, Rob Howe, and David Dressler of Product Support read the manuscript and made many valuable suggestions.

Reviewers among Word's development team: Chris Mason, Patriarch of Programming and Breeder of Digital Rabbits; and David Luebbert, The Style King. Their unflagging endurance under our merciless interrogation and their patience for our silly questions are an inspiration for teachers everywhere.

Philip Boulding of *Magical Strings* for the picture of his Concert Oranmore harp, which led to the scanned image on page 477, and Todd Laney, developer of the raytracing graphics routines that resulted in the wonderful PostScript image in the Introduction.

Eli Hollander, for portions of his screenplay for the movie *Out.*

Darcie Furlan and Becky Geisler-Johnson, artists who applied their highly refined æsthetic instincts to the design and layout.

Jim Brown, Theresa Mannix, and Karen Meredith of Marketing, for being patient.

Finally, Larry Anderson, who shepherded chapters like little beasts through the gates of the L300, and went out of his way to rescue the strays.

Introduction

Microsoft Word 3.02 for the Macintosh, the latest version as of this writing, is at a crossroads in the development of word-processing software. In the dark ages of word processing—perhaps five years ago—you were restricted by the limitations of the hardware you used. There were no mice then, and so you had to use the keyboard to place markers at the beginning and end points of text you wanted to edit. Text came in only one size, and you were lucky if your combination of program and printer could produce "special effects" such as boldface and underlining.

Meanwhile, people in the publishing trade have been working with a much more sophisticated set of parameters for measuring and formatting the text in books and other printed media. They are accustomed to kerning, letterspacing, font families, font sizes, rules, and graphics. Moreover, they place these elements on a page accurate to units of a point (1/72 inch). Unfortunately, the equipment needed to produce books, newsletters, and magazines by these methods is expensive and requires extensive training to use. So much training, in fact, that few have sufficient experience to command the entire range of tasks necessary to produce high-quality results.

Word represents a meeting place for these two viewpoints. Many come to Word with a background colored by "traditional" word-processing programs and may not realize how far word processing has come. In fact, it helps to get another perspective on Word by considering this: Word is not a word processor.

What is it then? To the extent that you can manipulate outlines with Word, you could call it an idea processor. To the extent that you can easily enter and modify text, you could call it a text editor. You could even call it a page-layout program, using this book as evidence: Everything between its covers was printed from Word.

Word is the most successful of the new documenting environments in combining the ease of simpler word processors and the power of traditional typesetting systems. It's the one environment that supports the entire range of tasks involved in creating a document, whether you're interested solely in the process of writing or charged with producing beautiful designs in print.

It's easy to learn enough about Word to produce well-formatted and well-designed documents. However, to reach the outer limits of the effects you can create, you'll need to become familiar with some publishing concepts and terms. In this book we try to give you the complete range of experience you'll need to push Word to its limits—there's a lot of ground to cover!

To give you an overview of the process for creating a document in Word, Section 1, "Laying the Foundation," presents two tutorials: one for entering and editing a business letter, and one for an internal document a business might use.

Section 2, "Building the Framework," concentrates on the essentials of outlining, editing, formatting, and printing documents.

Section 3, "Adding the Final Touches," covers embellishments you can add to your document: indexes and tables of contents, other types of tables and lists, graphics, and merge printing.

Section 4, "Blueprints for Projects," presents some projects that show what kinds of documents are possible in Word, with comments on how you might adapt them for your own needs.

Finally, Section 5, "Appendixes – Toolbox," contains appendixes you may find helpful: setting up your Word disks, a table of the character sets for six fonts, a short tutorial on using PostScript in your documents, and another tutorial on typesetting mathematical formulas.

Each chapter has the following elements:

- ❑ Where appropriate, numbered lists of steps to follow.
- ❑ Tips important for you to know, or tips of an advanced nature, which are shaded in the text, setting them off from surrounding material.
- ❑ Summary sections at the end of most chapters, which outline the chapter's main points; numbered procedures and tables of mouse and key sequences are listed for future reference.

Before you Continue...

As you read through this book, keep these points in mind:

- To simplify matters, we assume you're using the mouse. If you prefer to use the keyboard, refer to the summary sections for listings of keyboard equivalents. Word has key sequences for nearly every operation and often has more than one set for a given command.
- Some menu commands are single step: You choose the command, and Word immediately carries out your request. Other commands present a set of options within a dialog box.
- Step-by-step mouse movements to select a command or complete an action are omitted. Instead, the text indicates generally what to do, such as "Choose Open from the File menu" or "Click the Cancel button."

Before you begin to use Word, take the time to make backups of the Program and Utilities disks and arrange Word's files in a way that best suits your system. Appendix A gives details for creating working copies of your master disks. After you do this, don't be afraid to experiment. If something happens to the copy, you still have the original. After playing for a while, check out the next two chapters, which introduce the vast world of Word.

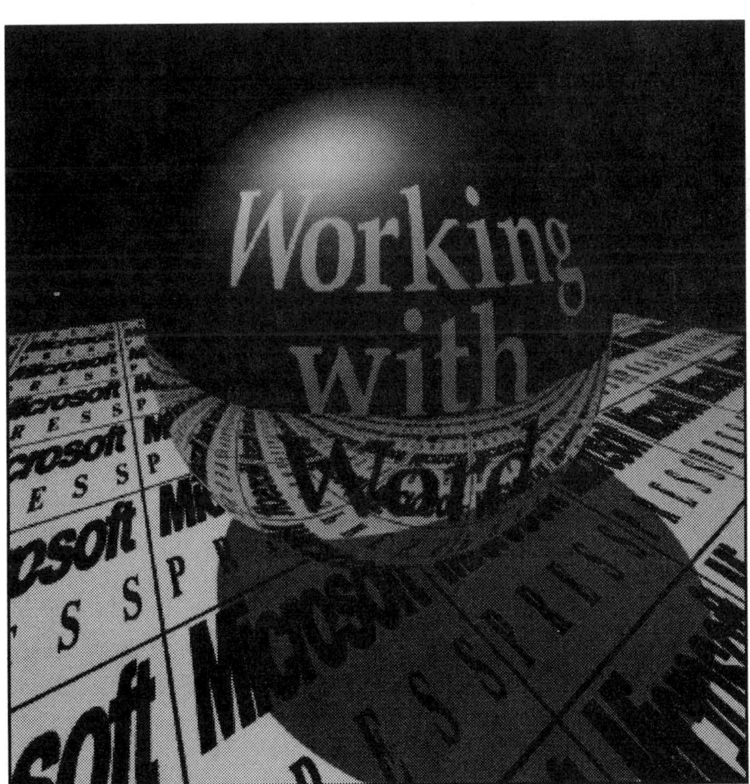

SECTION 1

Laying the Foundation

Word-Processing Concepts

Word version 3.0 is a sophisticated, multifeatured program that enables you to produce professional-looking documents easily and quickly. You won't master all of Word's possibilities in a few hours, of course, but you can productively use the program almost immediately with some background information and a little practice. This chapter offers both: The first half contains a primer of basic word-processing concepts and introduces some of Word's features. The second half presents a hands-on tutorial in which you'll create a simple one-page letter.

Because the Macintosh and the mouse are such natural companions, many of the exercises and explanations in this book use mouse terminology such as drag, click, and double-click. Not every writer or typist is mouse friendly, however. Many nimble-fingered keyboardists become annoyed when they have to use the mouse to perform such simple tasks as cutting and pasting. The programmers of this latest version of Word have taken great pains to please the most demanding of keyboard virtuosos. Almost every mouse-performed operation can also be accomplished with a key sequence, whether you are using an unenhanced 512K Mac, a Mac Plus, a Mac SE, or a Mac II. At the end of each chapter you'll find tables of handy keyboard shortcuts for your machine.

Start Word by double-clicking the Word icon. The Document view window appears, ready to receive text. (Figure 1-1 shows the window with a document displayed.) Drag down a command menu—for example, the Edit menu. Although you see only one set of commands, all the menus in Word except the Search menu actually comprise two sets: Short Menus and Full Menus. (See Figure 1-2.) The Short Menus set contains commands for routine word-processing tasks; the Full Menus set contains the Short Menus commands and additional commands for more advanced tasks. If Word is in Short Menus mode, you'll see the Full Menus command at the bottom of the Edit menu—choose it to switch to Full Menus. If Word is in Full Menus, you'll see the Short Menus command on the Edit menu—choose it to switch to Short Menus. This ability to switch between modes is called *toggling*.

Now that you are acclimated to Word's basic environment, you're ready to learn about word processing in general and about Word in particular.

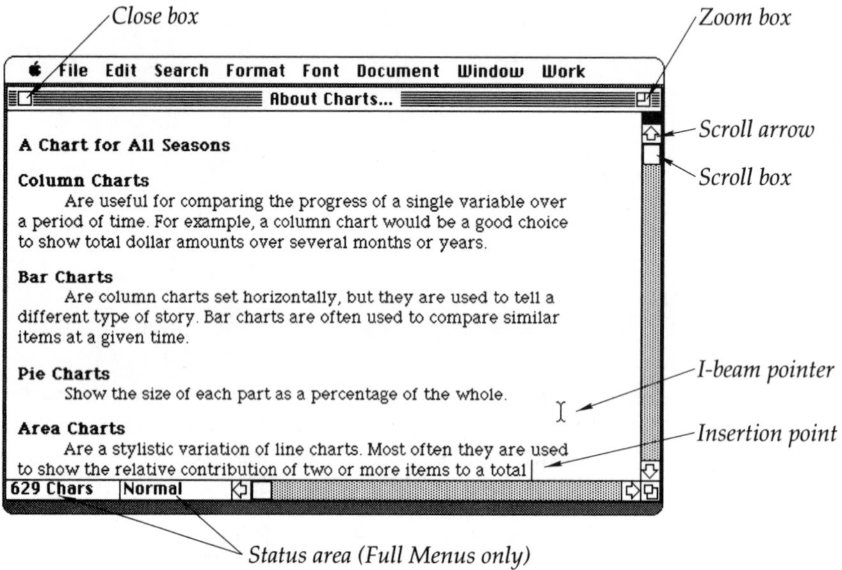

Figure 1-1
The Word desktop and a document displayed in Document view.

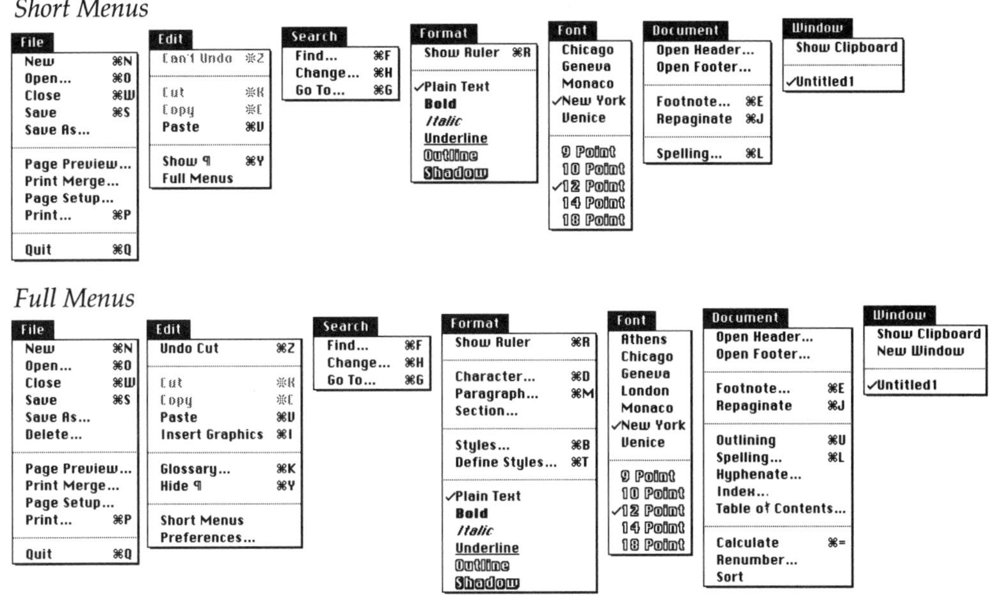

Figure 1-2
The two sets of commands: Short Menus and Full Menus.

Creating a document on a word processor involves five steps or functions: entering, editing, formatting, saving, and printing, as depicted in Figure 1-3. The first part of this chapter gives an overview of how you accomplish each of these steps in Word.

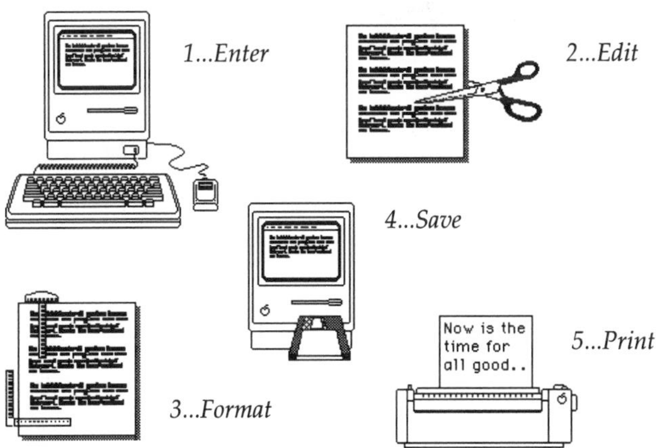

Figure 1-3
The five word-processing steps.

You won't necessarily use the entire set of steps every time you create a document, and you might not perform the functions in exactly the order presented. For a quick note to yourself, you might simply enter the text and print it. For a longer document, you might enter some text, save it, enter some more, pause to format a word (in italics, say), then edit a phrase, and so on. In Word, all five functions are available to you at all times.

■ *Entering*

The first step in creating a document is to enter text by simply typing on the keyboard. In Word, you usually enter text by typing in *Document view;* however, you can create raw material for your documents in other ways as well. Among Word's features are tools to produce outlines and to insert already existing text or graphics into your work.

Outlines

When you work in *Outline view,* Word displays each topic and subtopic in the familiar indented style common to outlines, as shown in Figure 1-4. This feature lets you clearly see the overall plan of a document—more clearly than when you scroll through the document in Document view. An added benefit is that you can easily manipulate the topics in the outline. You can, for instance, move an entire topic and its associated text and graphics to another place in the document with a few clicks of the mouse button.

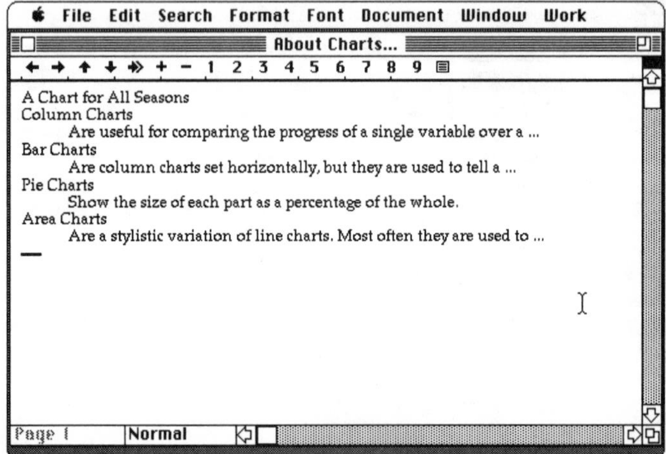

Figure 1-4
The same document as in Figure 1-1 displayed in Outline view.

Boilerplate Text and Graphics

In the old days when steam boilers were common, manufacturers found that they could use the same basic metal sheets—known as boilerplate—to construct boilers of all sizes and types. The term *boilerplate* was later used in the newspaper industry to mean any journalistic material in readily available form, usually columns or syndicated features that were already typeset.

In word processing, *boilerplate text* means any collection of characters—terms, short paragraphs, even whole documents—that you can easily insert into a document. You can save generic documents as boilerplate and then call them up as needed, or you can copy sections from a boilerplate document to the document you are creating. In Word, you can store boilerplate text in *glossaries*. A Word glossary is not a miniature dictionary, but is rather a collection of pieces of boilerplate text or graphics, each of which you can call up by entering the name that you assign it.

The glossary feature provides the easiest way to import boilerplate material into a document, but you can insert material in other ways, too. You can copy material to the Scrapbook and then paste it into a document, and with Word's QuickSwitch feature and the Switcher you can transfer material between documents even if they were made by different applications. For example, you can create an illustration in MacDraw or a table in Microsoft Excel and then insert it into a Word document. Unlike text, however, graphics cannot be edited in Word. You must go back to the original application used to create the graphic and edit it there. You can, however, indicate the exact placement of the graphic in the document, and you can size or crop the graphic as desired. (For more information on this subject, see Chapter 15, "Transferring Text and Graphics.")

■ *Editing*

After entering text, you can edit it: correct spelling, typographical errors, and grammar, or simply change your mind and write something else. Unlike a typewriter, a word processor lets you make changes painlessly; you don't have to commit your work to paper until you're satisfied with it. Even after printing the document, you can recall it and further alter it if you've saved it on disk. Word has two features that make the editing process even easier: a search-and-replace function and a spelling checker.

Search and Replace

Let's say you write a letter in which you consistently spell your client's name *Thomson* instead of the correct *Thompson*. You could go through the document and make each change manually, but a quicker approach is to use the Change command from the Search menu to replace the text. Simply enter both the old and new spellings, and Word automatically corrects each occurrence of the name. You can change phrases and complete sentences in the same way. You can also search for a word or phrase without changing it, using the Find command; at each occurrence, Word stops and displays the text.

Spelling Checker

Nothing detracts more from a professional document than misspellings and typographical errors. Other than hiring a copy editor, the best way to avoid these embarrassing mistakes is to use a spelling-check program. Word's built-in spelling checker contains a dictionary with 80,000 entries. By comparison, the typical vocabulary of a college-educated adult is fewer than 10,000 words, including slang. In fact, Word's dictionary includes many slang terms, so the spelling checker helps with many kinds of writing. You can even create your own dictionaries containing a total of about 64,000 words.

■ *Formatting*

New users of word processors often confuse text and formatting. The difference is important. Text consists of the individual typed characters—the content of the document. Formatting is the way the content appears on the page—the "look" of the document, including type, paragraph indents, margin widths, and so on. This distinction is maintained in Word; that is, manipulating content and determining appearance require separate actions.

Like many word processors—and unlike typewriters—Word can determine much of the page and document formatting for you. For a start, it lets you enter text without concerning yourself with line endings and page endings. When a word won't fit on the current line, it is dropped to the line below; this is called *wordwrap*. The only time you press the Return key when entering text is to begin a new paragraph. When you run out of space on the current page, Word starts a new page. In practice, it's as if you were writing on a continuous scroll of paper; you may not even be aware of where the pages break until you print the document.

In Word, formatting involves four format domains: *character, paragraph, section,* and *document*. Basically, character formatting determines what the characters in your document look like; paragraph formatting controls the appearance of the lines of characters that form a paragraph; and section formatting specifies how blocks of text are arranged. These first three domains are represented by commands on the Format menu (in Full Menus mode). The document domain is a special case, as discussed below.

WYSIWYG User Interface

WYSIWYG (pronounced "wizzy-wig") is an acronym for "what you see is what you get" and refers to the faithful reproduction on screen of the text as it will appear on paper. Word is almost entirely WYSIWYG. Text appears on the screen in the same font, size, and style used for printing. Margins and text alignment are accurately reflected as well. A space of one inch on the screen translates almost exactly as a space of one inch on the printed copy.

Some formatting options, such as multiple columns, are not usually displayed on the screen, but you can see the formatted result without printing the document by choosing Page Preview from the File menu. The Page Preview command saves time and paper because you can check the layout of each page before printing.

Character Formats

Character formats affect such attributes as the font (typeface), font size, font style (for example, boldface or italic), and letterspacing. Spaces, created with the Spacebar, and tabs, created with the Tab key, are considered characters and can have formats, too. Although these characters—and thus their formats—conventionally are invisible, you can see them by choosing the Edit menu's Show ¶ command. (This subject is discussed further in Chapter 7, "Character Formatting.")

Paragraph Formats

Some formatting options, such as indents, tabs, and line spacing, affect an entire paragraph. If you make a line-spacing change to a character in a paragraph, for example, the entire paragraph is altered, not merely the character or the line that contains the character. Some paragraph formatting options appear when you choose Paragraph from the Format menu. (This command appears only when you are in Full Menus mode.) The Word Ruler, displayed when you choose Show Ruler from the Format menu, lets you set tabs, indention, line spacing, and alignment. It is shown in Figure 1-5.

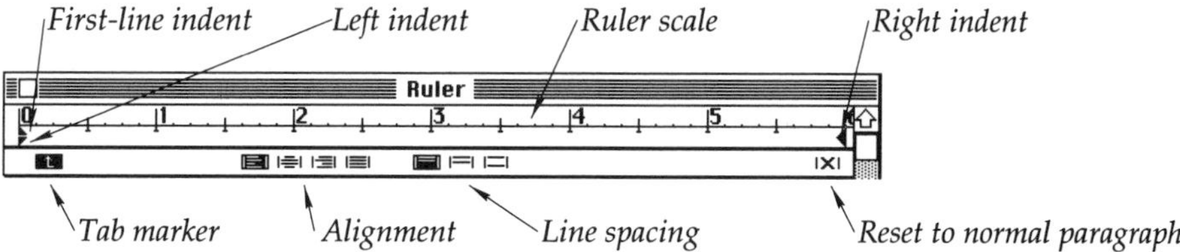

Figure 1-5
The Word Ruler, Short Menus version.

Indents

Word lets you create various kinds of paragraph indents. Many people indent the first line of each paragraph one-half inch (about five characters) from the left margin and set subsequent lines flush with the left margin. Word allows you to enter first-line indents either one by one, by pressing the Tab key, or in any number of paragraphs at once, by dragging the first-line indent marker (the upper of the two small triangles at the left margin in the Ruler) the desired number of spaces to the right.

Word also allows you to create hanging indents, in which the first line of a paragraph is flush left and the rest are indented. This style of indention is often used in bibliographies. To create a hanging indent, you drag to the right the lower of the two triangles in the Ruler. Figures 1-6a, 1-6b, and 1-6c show three types of paragraph indents; other types are possible. Indenting is discussed in more detail in Chapter 8, "Paragraph Formatting."

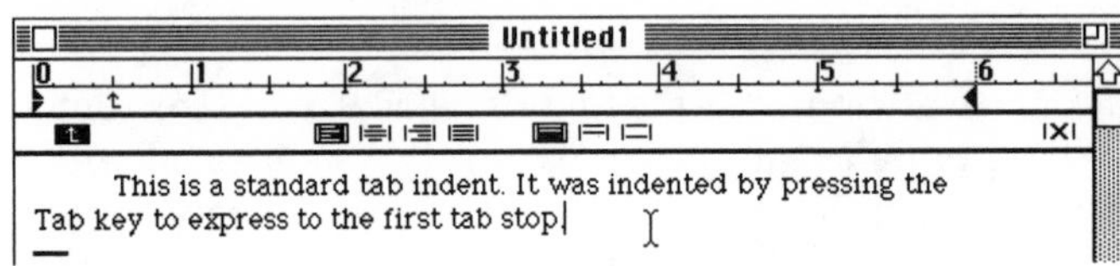

Figure 1-6a
A standard (user-entered) indent.

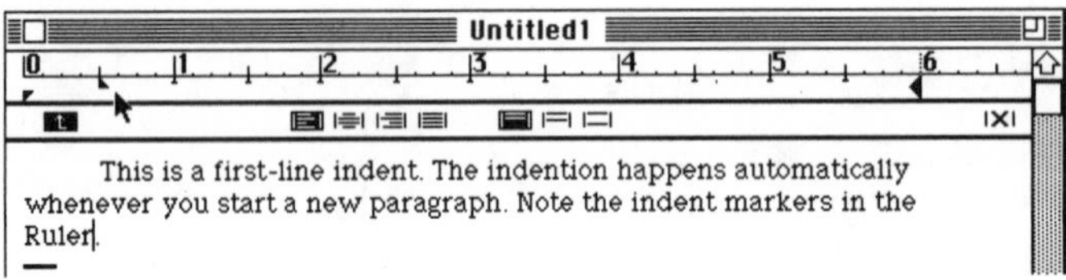

Figure 1-6b
A required (automatic) indent.

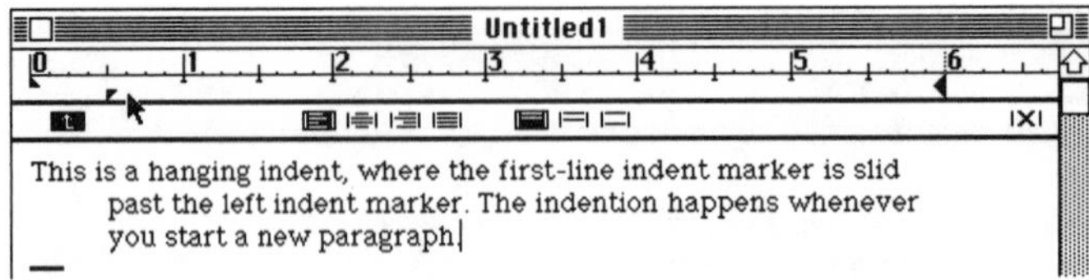

Figure 1-6c
A hanging indent.

Alignment

Alignment determines how the lines are placed between the right and left indents. Lines can be flush left (aligned on the left indent), flush right, justified (aligned on both indents), or centered between the indents. Figures 1-7a, 1-7b, and 1-7c show the same text with three different alignment formats. Notice that each paragraph is terminated with a paragraph mark, created when you press the Return or Enter keys and made visible when you choose Show ¶ from the Edit menu.

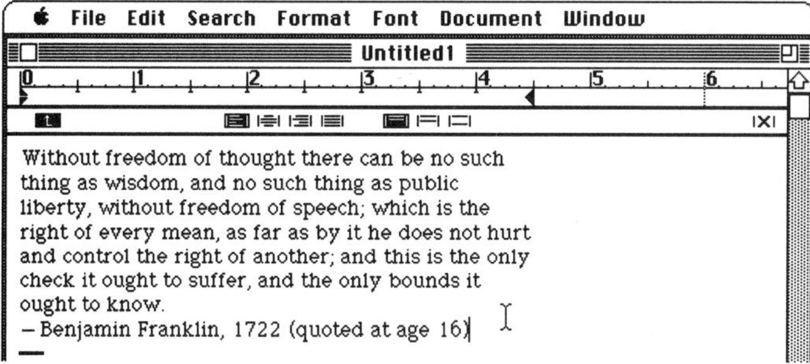

Figure 1-7a
Flush-left paragraph.

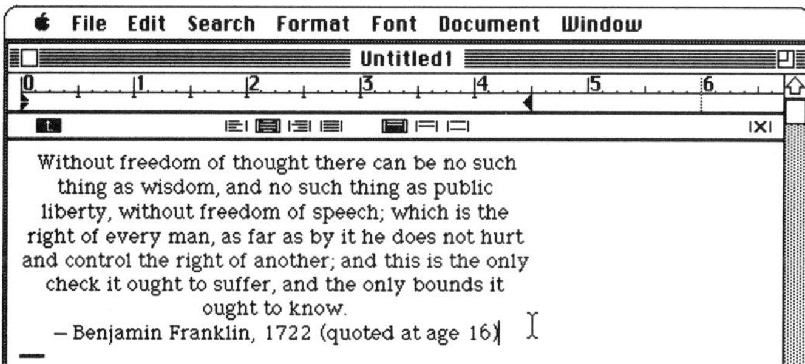

Figure 1-7b
Centered paragraph.

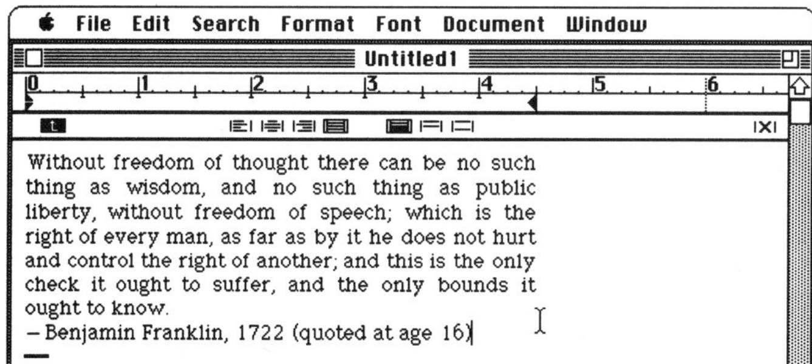

Figure 1-7c
Justified paragraph.

Styles and Style Sheets

In Word 3.0 the term *style* denotes a collection of character and paragraph formats that has been given a name and applied to one or more paragraphs. Format and style are closely related, but there are differences between the two. A style can be made up of a variety of character and paragraph formatting options, given a name, and applied to blocks of text using the Styles command from the Format menu. (This command is available in Full Menus mode only.) A format is a single attribute, such as line spacing or font size.

When first started, Word uses a standard block-letter style, called the *Normal* style. It calls for the 12-point New York font, indents set at the page margins, single line spacing, and flush-left alignment. Figure 1-8 shows a document in *Normal* style.

You can alter the *Normal* style at any time, even after you enter the text. When you change a style, every paragraph that was labeled with that style changes. You can even group styles together to form style sheets, a powerful feature unique to Word. When you want to reformat a document, you simply edit the style sheet or import a style sheet from another document, and the document instantly takes on a completely new look. You're saved the time and trouble of going through the text and reformatting it paragraph by paragraph. Best of all, once you get the hang of it, the style sheet feature is easy to use.

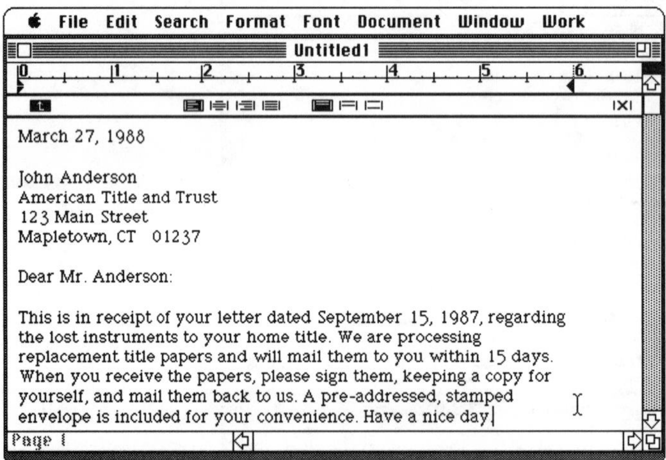

Figure 1-8
Word's *Normal* style.

Section Formats

Section formatting lets you determine certain overall layout features for any text that you define as a separate part of your document—that is, as a section. A good analogy for sections are the chapters in a book. For example, you might format one part of a document in two columns and leave the rest in one column, or you might create a running head that appears on every page of the document except the first page of each chapter. If a document has only one section—the default condition—Word applies the section formats you set to the entire document.

Headers, Footers, and Footnotes

Word greatly facilitates the use of headers and footers—repeating text that appears at the top (head) or the bottom (foot) of every page or of pages within desired sections. You need enter the text only once; Word then prints it on every designated page. Word also prints footnotes at the bottom of the appropriate page or at the end of a section or document, as you request, and even keeps track of the numbering for you. For example, if you insert a new footnote, the program renumbers all subsequent notes and their in-text references.

Columns

Newsletters, brochures, menus, and many other types of documents are conventionally set up in two or more columns. Word lets you format a document with as many columns as there are characters on a line, but the practical maximum for an 8.5-by-11-inch page is four columns. The columns do not appear alongside one another as you enter the text (and therefore are not WYSIWYG), but they do appear this way when you use Page Preview.

Auto Numbering

Certain documents, such as outlines, legal documents, screenplays, and technical manuals, use numbering to identify lines and paragraphs. Word can number lines and paragraphs, freeing you from this time-consuming task. The program can also renumber lines and paragraphs if you move, add, or delete blocks of text.

Document Formats

The fourth format domain, that of the document itself, controls the overall design of each page, including attributes such as page size, the placement of page headers and footnotes, and page margins (although you can use paragraph formatting to change the "margins" for particular paragraphs—in Word these are called indents). Document formatting options do not have a command on the Format menu but are represented in typical Macintosh style by the Page Setup command from the File menu and by commands from the Document menu.

■ *Saving*

You probably already know that all files that you intend to keep must be saved on a disk. Once saved on disk, files can be recalled for subsequent editing or printing. When you save a file in Word with the Save or Save As command from the File menu, it is not erased from the screen, and thus you can continue working with it. This is useful because with Word, as with most other Macintosh programs, you should save each document at frequent intervals (every 15 minutes or so), as well as before you close the document's window or quit a session. Turning off the machine without saving the document erases all your work.

Word lets you save documents in various data formats. You'll probably save most Word files in regular Word 3.0 format, but you can also save files so that they can be read directly by Word version 1.0, MacWrite, and Microsoft Works (all for the Macintosh) and by Word 4.0 (for the IBM PC). Finally, you can save files in RTF interchange format (used by some Mac, IBM PC, and UNIX applications) and in ASCII (text only) format, with or without line breaks. This wide range of options lets you more easily export data for use with other applications, telecommunicate your Word documents to other Macs, and transfer Word documents between the IBM PC and the Macintosh.

■ *Printing*

Although technology pundits have long foreseen a paperless world in which all letters and other documents are distributed electronically, printed documents are still the norm rather than the exception. Word has several major features that help you get your work on paper the way you want it.

Page Preview

Before you print a document, it is often helpful to see exactly what it will look like. Word's Page Preview command, in the File menu, provides this view of your document. (Page Preview is a third view, other than Document and Outline views.) In Page Preview mode, an example of which is shown in Figure 1-9, you can adjust the positions of running heads, the width of margins, and the placement of page numbers. You can also change *page breaks* so that important headings appear at the top of a page.

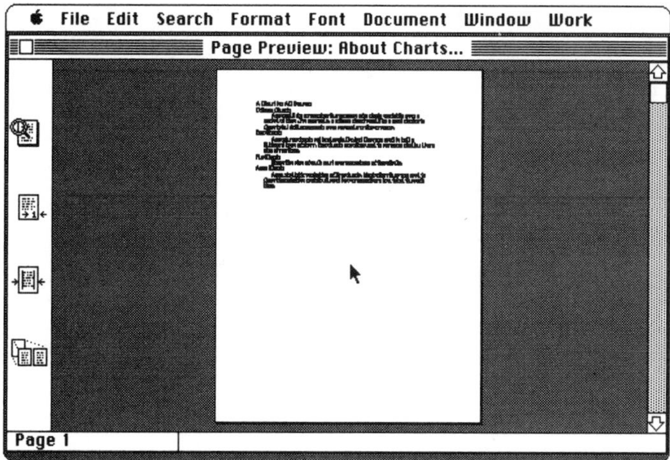

Figure 1-9
The same document used in Figures 1-1 and 1-4 in Page Preview mode.

Pagination

Pagination is the process of breaking text into pages and of numbering these pages. You can have Word break pages for you, or you can do it manually. You can also have Word number pages, and you can specify on which page to begin the numbering, where on the page to place the number, and what kind of numbering to use: Arabic numerals, Roman numerals (uppercase or lowercase), or letters.

Hyphenation

Word's built-in hyphenation feature, accessible from the Hyphenate command in the Document menu (Full Menus mode only), lets you correctly hyphenate almost every word in the English language. Hyphenation can improve the appearance of your copy by helping you avoid particularly unequal line lengths in ragged-right (flush-left) text and unsightly word spacing in justified text.

You can have Word hyphenate the entire document automatically or have Word pause before each word it wants to hyphenate so that you can confirm the placement of the hyphen. With the latter method, when the program encounters a word that is too long to fit on the current line but can be hyphenated, the word is displayed in a dialog box and marked at one or more proper hyphenation points. (See Figure 1-10.) You can then decide if and where the hyphenation is to occur.

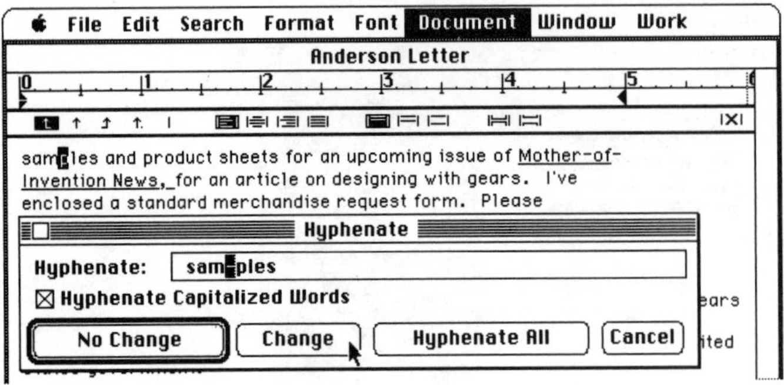

Figure 1-10
The hyphenation feature.

Merge Printing

The process of merge printing, often simply referred to as merging, is similar to using boilerplate or glossary text. You simply merge the main document—perhaps containing names and addresses and other "personalizing" information. Word then prints a different version for each chunk of data in the data document: With a form letter, it prints a different copy for each name. (See Figure 1-11.)

October 15,	October 15,	October 15,	October 15, 1987
Joan Foxwor	Robert Temp	Jessica Stu	Melvin Crooks, CPA
1025 Maple :	15-23 Expre	634 Flower	876-A Main
Moretown, N.	Niagara Fall	Granger, MN	Del Mar, CA 92014
Dear Joan:	Dear Bob:	Dear Aunt Je	Dear Mel:
We're movin	We're movin	We're movin	We're moving again! We've outgrown our
larger accon	larger accon	larger accon	larger accommodations. We've found a be
Island and w	Island and w	Island and w	Island and will be moving there by the 10
new phone nı	new phone n	new phone n	new phone number are listed below. I'll t
of November	of November	of November	of November, and I hope you can come!
Best,	Best,	Best,	Best,
Alex, Beth, ε	Alex, Beth, ε	Alex, Beth, ε	Alex , Beth, and Mikey

Figure 1-11
Merge printing.

■ *Concepts into Action: Creating a Letter*

Theory goes only so far. In this section, you'll learn how to apply the five basic word-processing steps—entering, editing, formatting, saving, and printing—to create a basic one-page letter, using only the Short Menus commands. But first, you need to set up your program so that what you see on the screen matches the descriptions in this tutorial.

Setting Up

If you haven't already started Word, do so by double-clicking its icon. A blank Document view window appears. Word will store your settings (such as Short Menus versus Full Menus) from session to session so that you don't have to reconfigure the program to your liking each time you start it. Thus, before beginning the tutorial, do the following to make sure that your settings are the same as the ones used here:

1. **Choose the Short Menus mode.** Pull down the Edit menu. If the Short Menus command shows near the bottom of the Edit menu, choose it. You are now in Short Menus mode. If the Full Menus command appears at the bottom of the Edit menu, you are already in Short Menus mode.
2. **Hide the formatting marks.** Pull down the Edit menu. If the Hide ¶ command is near the bottom of the menu, choose it. Word now hides all formatting marks. If Show¶ appears instead, the formatting marks are already hidden.
3. **Display sizes in inches.** Choose the Show Ruler command from the Format menu. The Ruler should be graduated in inches, as shown at the top of Figure 1-12. If the Ruler shows centimeters or points, change it:

    ❶ Choose Full Menus from the Edit menu.

    ❷ Choose Preferences from the same menu.

    ❸ In the dialog box that appears, click Inch. Then click OK.

    ❹ Choose Short Menus from the Edit menu.

    ❺ Choose Hide Ruler from the Format menu.

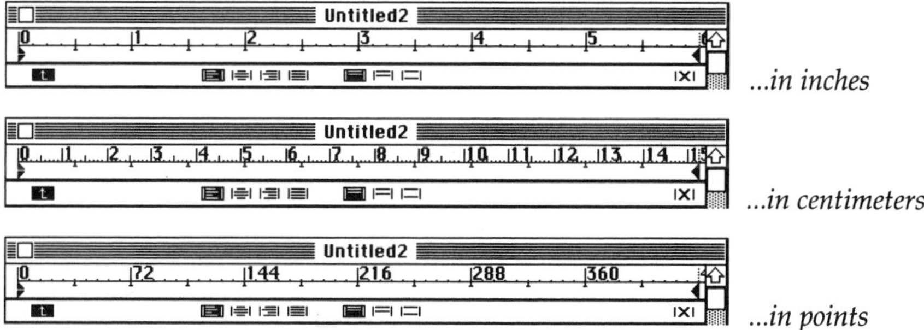

Figure 1-12
The three types of Ruler graduations.

If you were to quit Word right now, these settings would be saved. You would not need to repeat the procedure of setting them up unless someone changed them on your working copy of Word. In Chapter 4, "Writing and

Editing Techniques," you will learn more about setting preferences and saving them in the Word Settings file.

Entering the Text

Type the following text into the blank window. (When you see ¶, press the Return key.) Notice that you don't have to press the Return key after each line. Word places ("wraps") words that won't fit on the current line onto the next line. If you make a typing mistake, press the Backspace key (the Delete key on some keyboards) to erase characters to the left of the blinking insertion-point marker.

January 15, 1988¶
¶
Michael Fox, Associate Editor¶
MOTHER-OF-INVENTION NEWS¶
5690 Sunset Drive¶
Hollywood, CA 91500¶
¶
¶
Dear Mr. Fox:¶
¶
Thank you for your letter concerning our new line of high-impact plastic gears. We understand that you would like samples and product sheets for an article on designing with gears in an upcoming issue of Mother-of-Invention News. I've enclosed a merchandise request form. Once we have the form, we can send the samples to you.¶
¶
Please don't hesitate to write or call if you need assistance. I can, if you wish, put you in touch with our engineers, who can answer any specific questions you may have.¶
¶
Sincerely,¶
¶
¶
¶
David A. Buxton¶
Public Relations Specialist¶
enc.¶

The text of the letter doesn't quite fit in one window on the screen. You can scroll back to the beginning of the document by dragging the scroll box on the right side of the window or by clicking the up arrow in the scroll bar, as shown in Figure 1-13. The horizontal scroll arrows on the bottom of the window are not activated in Short Menus mode, so if you click them now, nothing happens. Later on, you will see how to use the horizontal scrolling feature to pan back and forth to see all of an extra-wide document.

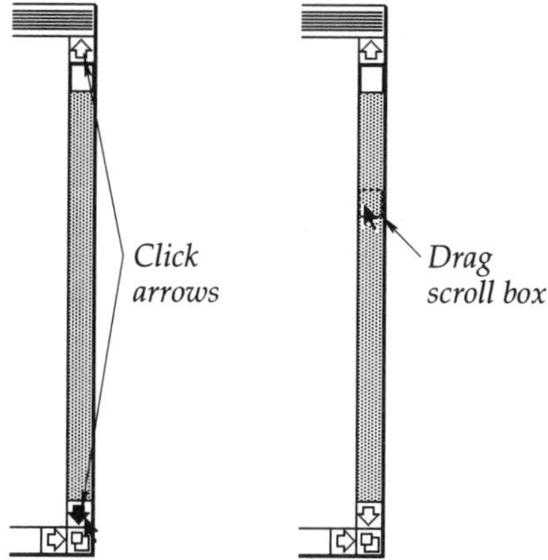

Figure 1-13
Vertical scrolling in a document.

Editing the Text

You can add characters, words, or sentences to the body of your letter. Add some text after the sentence *I've enclosed a merchandise request form* by following this procedure:

1. Set the insertion point immediately to the right of the period at the end of the sentence by moving the I-beam pointer there and clicking the mouse button.
2. Press the Spacebar once (or twice if you prefer two spaces between sentences).
3. Type this text:

   Please complete it and send it back to me at your convenience.

As you add the new text, Word pushes the characters beyond the insertion point to the right. Repeat the procedure to add a single word in the next paragraph:

1. Set the insertion point immediately after the word *specific* in the second paragraph.
2. Press the Spacebar once.
3. Type the word *technical.*

If the two words run into each other, set the insertion point between them and press the Spacebar. If there are too many spaces between the words, set the insertion point immediately to the left of the second word and press the Backspace key to delete the unwanted spaces.

Adding Paragraphs

Once you have typed the letter, you can go back and add any amount of text anywhere you like. Practice adding more text by entering the following paragraph in the letter.

1. Set the insertion point after the last period of the second paragraph, at the end of the sentence ending *questions you may have.*
2. Press the Return key twice to start a new paragraph and insert a blank line.
3. Type this text:

As you may know, we have been making high-grade gears for more than 50 years. In the early years, Anderson Gear had three employees: John Anderson, his wife Loretta, and his younger brother Ted. The company now employs more than 220 people and has sales offices around the world. In addition to the new line of affordable high-impact plastic gears, Anderson Gear manufactures and markets a complete line of stock gears made with brass, nylon, steel, aluminum, and fiber-reinforced plastic.¶

Editing Words

Now change a word in the letter. Locate the term *high-grade* in the first sentence of the third paragraph. "High-grade" sounds like crude oil, not a precision-machined part, so change it to *fine-grade.*

1. Set the insertion point immediately to the left of the hyphen.
2. Press the Backspace key four times to delete the word *high.*
3. Type the word *fine.*

That was easy. Now try a different method to change a word. Locate the word *people* in the middle of the third paragraph (in the sentence *The company now employs...*).

1. Place the pointer on *people* and double-click. (You don't need to set an insertion point first to select an entire word.)
2. Without doing anything else, type *men and women.* Word replaces the selection (*people*) with the new text (*men and women*).

To see what the letter would look like if you printed it now, choose Page Preview from the File menu. What you see should match Figure 1-14. To return to editing the letter, click the close box in the upper left corner of the Page Preview window.

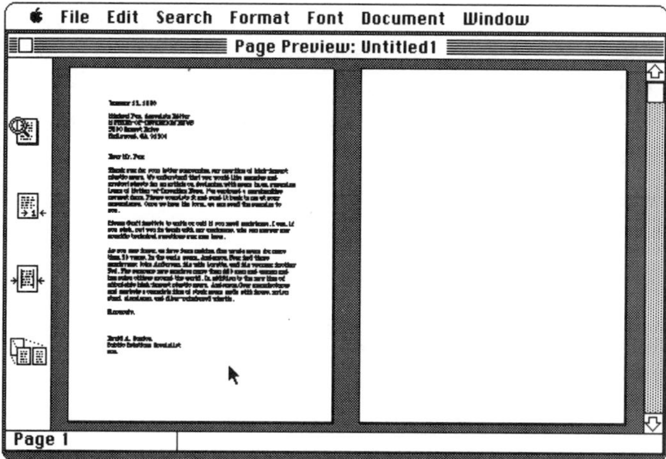

Figure 1-14
Using Page Preview.

Moving Paragraphs Within the Document

In the original text, the paragraph beginning *Please don't hesitate to write or call* closed the letter. Because you added a paragraph to the end of the text, however, this closing statement moved to the middle of the letter. Instead of retyping the paragraph, cut and copy it using the Clipboard.

❶ Scroll the window so that the *Please don't hesitate to write or call...* paragraph is in view.

❷ Place the I-beam pointer on the paragraph, and slowly move the pointer to the left. Just before you reach the edge of the window, the pointer will change to a right-pointing arrow, as shown in Figure 1-15. This means that the pointer is now in the *selection bar*, an invisible strip that runs along the left edge of the document window. The selection bar is useful for selecting lines, paragraphs, and even the entire document.

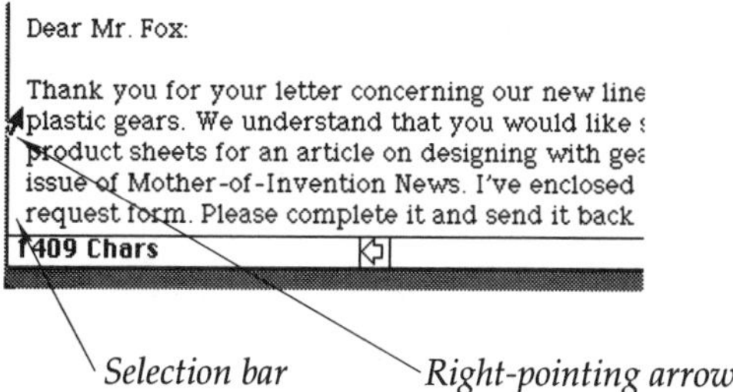

Figure 1-15
The pointer points to the right when in the selection bar.

3. Double-click while the pointer is in the selection bar to select the paragraph. The entire paragraph should be highlighted. If not, go back to Step 2 and try again.
4. Choose Cut from the Edit menu. The selected text is removed from the document and placed in the Clipboard.
5. Press the Backspace key (the Delete key on some keyboards) once to remove the extra line between the paragraphs.
6. Set the insertion point on the line after the paragraph ending *fiber-reinforced plastic.* Press the Return key once.
7. Choose Paste from the Edit menu. The previously cut selection is pasted into the document at the insertion point.

Checking for Errors

Word's built-in spelling checker scans your documents, looking for words that you misspelled or typed incorrectly. Word knows how to spell about 80,000 words and, if you want, presents the correct spelling for you, saving you from having to look up entries in the dictionary. You can also enter the correct spelling from the keyboard and have Word use it to replace the incorrect text. You have full control over when and where Word alters the spelling of text. To check the letter for spelling:

1. Set the insertion point at the beginning of the document.
2. Choose Spelling from the Document menu. The dialog box shown in Figure 1-16 appears.
3. Start the spelling check by clicking the Start Check button or pressing the Return key. (You can always select bordered buttons in Macintosh dialog boxes by pressing the Return key.)
4. Word may present another dialog box asking you to verify your choice. Answer by clicking the OK button.
5. The first suspect word in the letter is *Michael*—that is, if you didn't make any mistakes before the word. It is shown after Unknown Word in the Spelling dialog box and is also highlighted in the text. This word is spelled correctly, but the spelling checker has noted it because it isn't in Word's dictionary. (Nor are any proper nouns, although you can add them—as well as other words—to your own dictionary file, as explained in Chapter 2.) Click the No Change button and proceed.
6. Assuming that you haven't made any typographical errors, the next suspect word is *Loretta.* Again, the word is spelled correctly but isn't in Word's dictionary. Click No Change to skip past it.
7. If a word is flagged as suspect and is indeed spelled incorrectly, change it by entering the proper spelling in the Change To box. Then click the Change button or press the Return key.

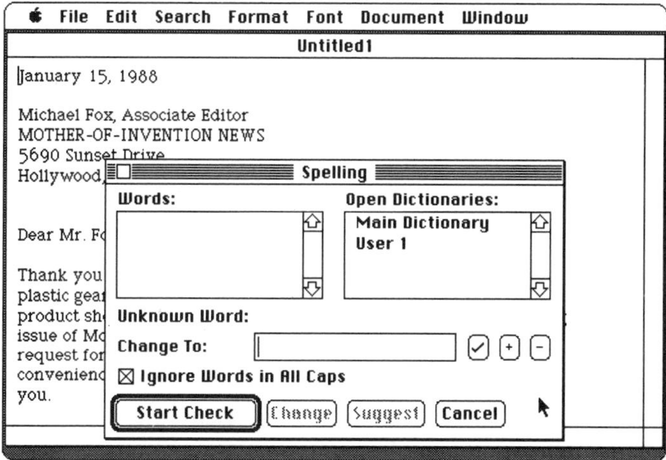

Figure 1-16
The Spelling dialog box.

❽ Continue through the rest of the letter, clicking the No Change button for properly spelled words and entering the new text and clicking the Change button for improperly spelled words.

❾ After the letter has been checked, Word presents a dialog box saying *End of document reached.* Click OK. (If you started the spelling check at a point other than the beginning, Word asks if you want to start over at the beginning. In this case, click OK to check the entire document.)

You can have Word analyze a suspect word and come up with a list of potential correct spellings by clicking the Suggest button. Alternative spellings appear in the Word list box. (See Figure 1-17.) The first word in the list is highlighted and also appears after Change To. Scroll down the list if necessary, click on the suggestion you want, and then click the Change button.

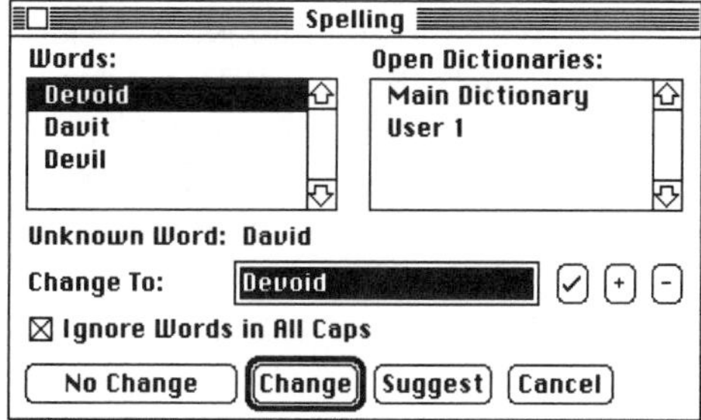

Figure 1-17
Using the Suggest feature.

Formatting the Text

Formatting in Word is a fascinating and complex subject; in fact, several later chapters are devoted to the topic. This exercise gives you only a glimpse of the possibilities.

Formatting Characters

You can change the font, font size, and style of any character in a Word document. For now, try underlining a few words. Locate the text *Mother-of-Invention News* in the first paragraph.

❶ Select the text as follows: Move the pointer just to the left of *Mother*. Press the mouse button and, holding it down, drag the mouse until the pointer is after the *s* in *News*. (Don't select the period.) Then release the mouse button. The phrase *Mother-of-Invention News* should be highlighted.

❷ Choose Underline from the Format menu. The selected text is underlined.

❸ Click anywhere in the document window to deselect the text.

Font styles can be mixed and matched. You can combine underlining with boldfacing, for example, or you can combine shadow, outline, and italic styles in the same text. The effect isn't always pretty, but you can experiment until you get the look you want. To combine styles, select the text and then choose each style. A check mark appears beside the styles you have activated. You can cancel any style by choosing it again. (The check mark goes away.) To return to regular text, choose Plain Text.

Creating a Letterhead

The sample letter is designed for use with preprinted letterhead stationery. You can incorporate a standard letterhead into the document and print it with the rest of the text. The letterhead can consist of text or graphics.

First, "shrink" the document a bit to accommodate the extra space taken up by the letterhead. Word normally starts up with the 12-point New York font. The letter can be substantially reduced in size by the use of 10-point New York. To change the font and size for the entire document, press the Command key and click in the selection bar at the left margin of the document. Choose 10 Point from the Font menu. Deselect the document by clicking anywhere in the window.

Text Letterhead

You can type the letterhead text directly at the top of the document.

❶ Set the insertion point at the very beginning of the document, before the *J* in *January*. Press the Return key once, then click in the new first line to set the insertion point there.

❷ Choose the Show Ruler command from the Format menu.

❸ Click the Center icon in the ruler (the second icon from the left in the alignment icons; see Figure 1-5). The text you enter will now be centered between the left and right indents.

❹ Type this text. (Remember to press the Return key where you see a ¶.)

Anderson Gear Company¶
121 Pike Avenue South¶
Urbaneville, NJ 01111¶
(201) 555-1265¶
¶

You can make the name of the company stand out by selecting it and choosing Bold from the Format menu. Choose the Page Preview command to see how the document looks. It should resemble Figure 1-18.

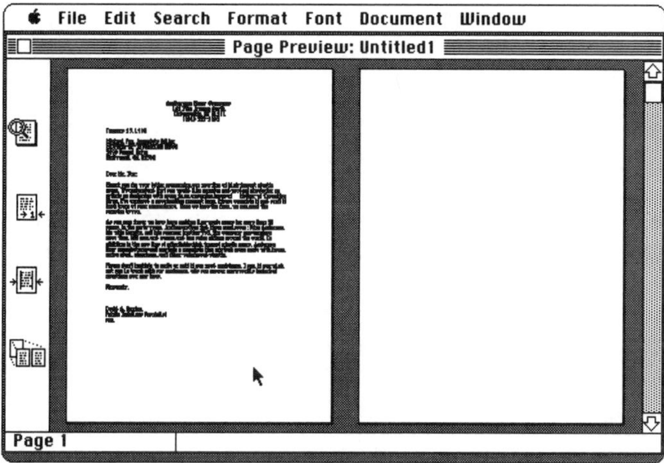

Figure 1-18
Letter with text letterhead.

Notice that the date is too close to the letterhead. To correct this, return to Document view by clicking the close box, and then do the following:

❶ Position the insertion point immediately to the left of the *J* in *January.*

❷ Press the Return key twice. Each time, the text moves down one line.

Saving Your Work

You'll probably want to save most of the documents you write with Word. To save the letter:

❶ Choose Save As from the File menu.

❷ Enter *Reply Letter* as the name of your sample letter, and click Save.

If you want to save the letter on a disk other than your Word Program disk (the name of the disk appears in the upper right corner of the Save dialog box), click the Eject and Drive buttons, as you do in most other Macintosh applications.

Note that the letter remains in the window so that you can continue working with it. When you are through making changes to a document, save it and then close the window by clicking the close box. If you forget to save the changes first, Word will remind you by displaying a dialog box.

The times you need to use the Save As command are when you are saving a new file for the first time, when you want to save an existing file under another name, or when you want to save the file on another disk or in another file format. Otherwise, you can simply choose the Save command or press Command-S. Word then saves the file under the old name. If the disk that contains the document is not in a drive, Word asks you to insert it.

It's a good idea to save your documents at frequent intervals as you work with them. Otherwise, if a power outage should occur as you're writing, your work would be lost. By saving often and regularly, you decrease the chance of having to redo a document from scratch.

Previewing and Printing the Letter

Printing is one of the more straightforward tasks you do with Word. Before printing, however, again check the document in Page Preview mode to be sure it looks all right. Choose Page Preview from the File menu; the letter appears in miniature form on the left page of the Page Preview window, as shown in Figure 1-19. Note the four Page Preview icons at the left side of the window. Here's how they work:

- ❑ Magnifying Glass: Click the icon, move it to the part of the document you want to magnify, and click again. You can then use the scroll bars to display different parts of the page. Click the top icon (it will have changed to the page-view icon) to redisplay the full page.
- ❑ Page Number: Click the icon, and then click on the page to set the position for the page number.
- ❑ Margin Set: Click to set page-specific margins and page breaks.
- ❑ One-page display: Click to switch between one-page and two-page display. In a one-page display, the image is somewhat larger.

You can't edit the document while in Page Preview, but you can change margins and set the position of page numbers. (These techniques are explained in depth in later chapters.)

To return to Document view, click the close box in the upper left corner of the Page Preview window, or choose the Page Preview command again.

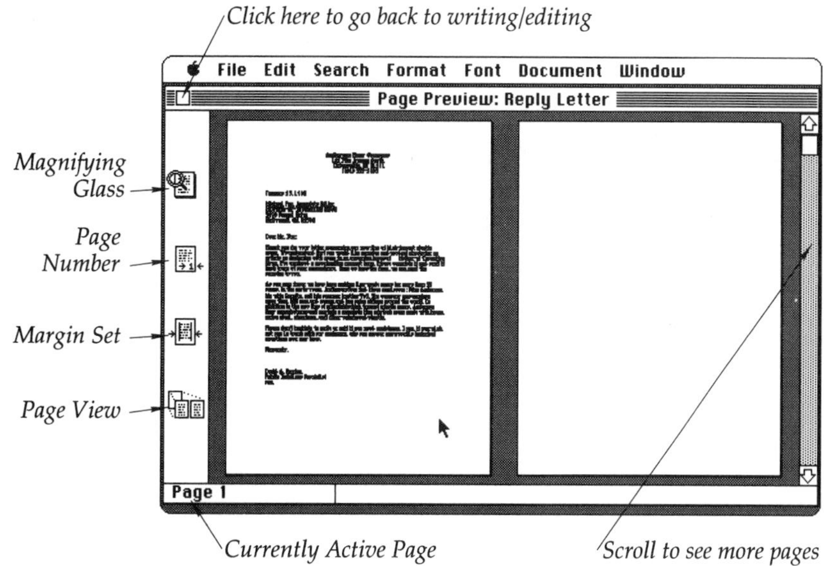

Figure 1-19
Page Preview of letter.

Now you can print the letter. Be sure the printer is on and on line; assuming you're using an ImageWriter, the SELECT light should be glowing. And of course, be sure the printer is loaded with paper and connected to the Macintosh. (Refer to your printer's instruction manual for details on setting it up and connecting it to the Macintosh.) To print the letter:

❶ Choose Print from the File menu.

❷ Click the Faster option in the dialog box that appears, as shown in Figure 1-20.

❸ Click OK or press the Return key.

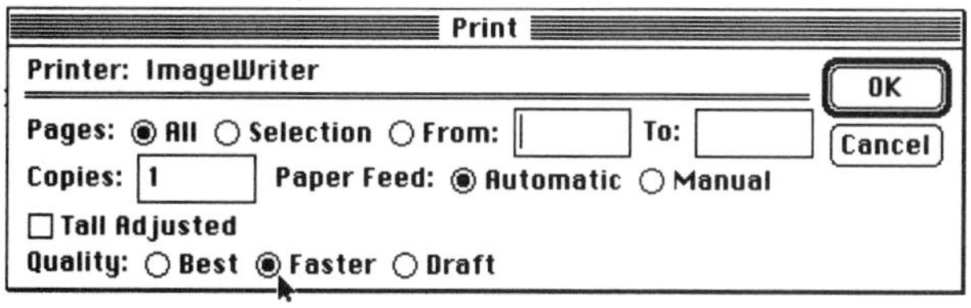

Print
Printer: ImageWriter
OK
Pages: ◉ All ○ Selection ○ From: To:
Cancel
Copies: 1 Paper Feed: ◉ Automatic ○ Manual
☐ Tall Adjusted
Quality: ○ Best ◉ Faster ○ Draft

Figure 1-20
The Print dialog box for the ImageWriter.

The letter prints in standard quality. You can stop printing at any time by clicking the Cancel button in the dialog box that appears during printing, or you can temporarily freeze printing by clicking the Pause button. Figure 1-21 shows how the letter looks when printed.

Anderson Gear Company
121 Pike Avenue South
Urbaneville, NJ 01111
(201) 555-1265

January 15, 1988

Michael Fox, Associate Editor
MOTHER-OF-INVENTION NEWS
5690 Sunset Drive
Hollywood, CA 91500

Dear Mr. Fox:

Thank you for your letter concerning our new line of high-impact plastic gears. We understand that you would like samples and product sheets for an article on designing with gears in an upcoming issue of Mother-of-Invention News. I've enclosed a merchandise request form. Please complete it and send it back to me at your convenience. Once we have the form, we can send the samples to you.

As you may know, we have been making fine-grade gears for more than 50 years. In the early years, Anderson Gear had three employees: John Anderson, his wife Loretta, and his younger brother Ted. The company now employs more than 220 men and women and has sales offices around the world. In addition to the new line of affordable high-impact plastic gears, Anderson Gear manufactures and markets a complete line of stock gears made with brass, nylon, steel, aluminum, and fiber-reinforced plastic.

Please don't hesitate to write or call if you need assistance. I can, if you wish, put you in touch with our engineers, who can answer any specific technical questions you may have.

Sincerely,

David A. Buxton
Public Relations Specialist
enc.

Figure 1-21
Final printout of letter.

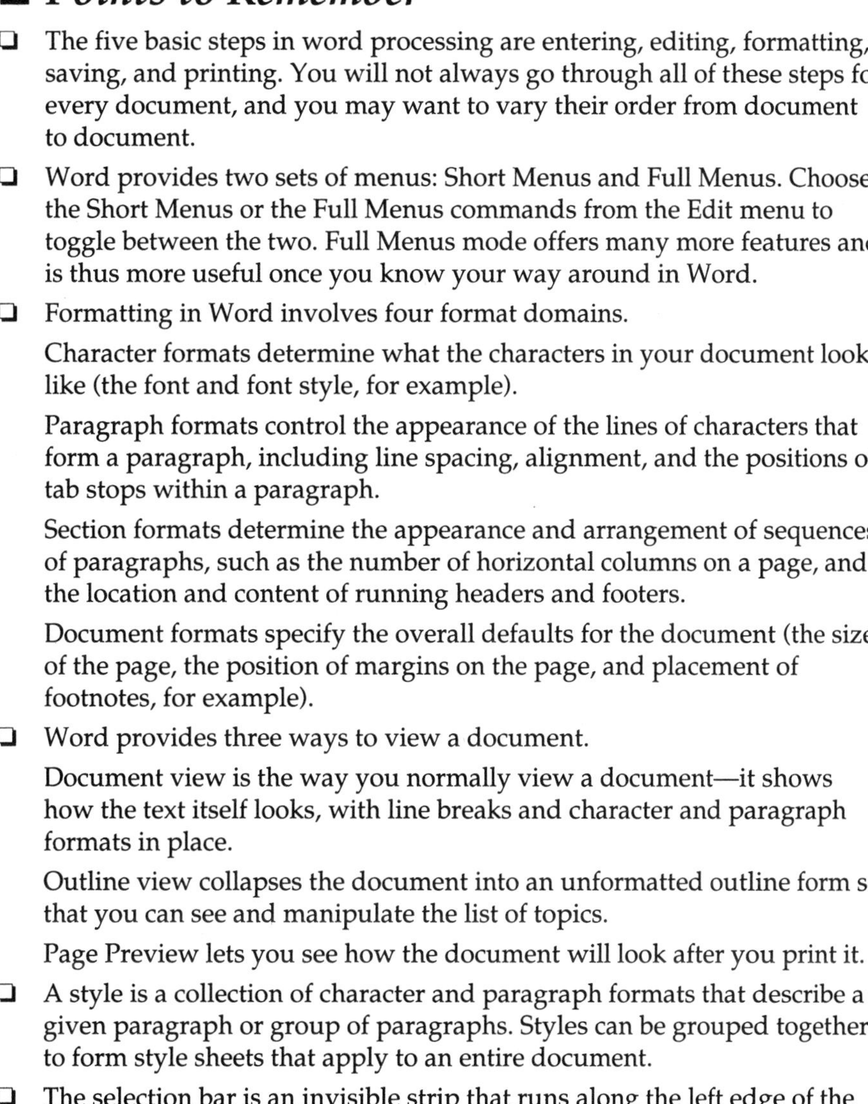

■ *Points to Remember*

- ❑ The five basic steps in word processing are entering, editing, formatting, saving, and printing. You will not always go through all of these steps for every document, and you may want to vary their order from document to document.
- ❑ Word provides two sets of menus: Short Menus and Full Menus. Choose the Short Menus or the Full Menus commands from the Edit menu to toggle between the two. Full Menus mode offers many more features and is thus more useful once you know your way around in Word.
- ❑ Formatting in Word involves four format domains.

  Character formats determine what the characters in your document look like (the font and font style, for example).

  Paragraph formats control the appearance of the lines of characters that form a paragraph, including line spacing, alignment, and the positions of tab stops within a paragraph.

  Section formats determine the appearance and arrangement of sequences of paragraphs, such as the number of horizontal columns on a page, and the location and content of running headers and footers.

  Document formats specify the overall defaults for the document (the size of the page, the position of margins on the page, and placement of footnotes, for example).
- ❑ Word provides three ways to view a document.

  Document view is the way you normally view a document—it shows how the text itself looks, with line breaks and character and paragraph formats in place.

  Outline view collapses the document into an unformatted outline form so that you can see and manipulate the list of topics.

  Page Preview lets you see how the document will look after you print it.
- ❑ A style is a collection of character and paragraph formats that describe a given paragraph or group of paragraphs. Styles can be grouped together to form style sheets that apply to an entire document.
- ❑ The selection bar is an invisible strip that runs along the left edge of the window. It lets you select lines and paragraphs quickly. When you see a right-pointing arrow, your pointer is in the selection bar.

Techniques

Basic Skills

Scroll in a document

❶ Click on the appropriate arrow in the vertical scroll bar.

Select text

❶ Move the pointer to one end of the text.

❷ Press the mouse button, drag the pointer to the other end of the text, and release the mouse button. (See also the shortcuts in the section that follows.)

Deselect text

❶ Click anywhere in the document.

Editing

Insert text

❶ Position the pointer and click to set the insertion point.

❷ Type the new text.

Replace text

❶ Select the text to be replaced.

❷ Type the new text.

Move text

❶ Select the text to be moved.

❷ Choose Cut from the Edit menu to move it to the Clipboard.

❸ Set the insertion point where you want to move the text.

❹ Choose Paste from the Edit menu.

Check spelling

❶ Set the insertion point where you want the spelling check to begin.

❷ Choose Spelling from the Document menu, and press the Return key.

❸ Click Suggest to have Word list potential correct spellings for an unknown word.

Formatting

Display or hide formatting marks

❶ Choose Show ¶ or Hide ¶ from the Edit menu.

Display or hide the Word Ruler

❶ Choose Show Ruler or Hide Ruler from the Format menu.

Change graduations in Ruler

❶ Choose Preferences from the Edit menu.

❷ In the dialog box that appears, click the button for the type of graduation you want.

❸ Click OK.

Change a character attrribute

❶ Select the text to be changed.

❷ Choose a character format from the Format menu.

Or,

❶ Select the text to be changed.

❷ Choose Character from the Format menu.

❸ Select the formatting options you want.

❹ Click OK.

Change the font and point size

❶ Select the text to be changed.

❷ Choose a font from the Font menu.

❸ Change the point size of selected text by choosing a point size from the same menu.

Center text

1. Set the insertion point within the paragraph to be centered, or select a block of text to be centered.
2. Display the Word Ruler, and click the Center icon. Any text you type while the Center icon is selected will be centered.

Preview a document before printing

1. Choose Page Preview from the File menu.

To return to Document view from Page Preview, either click the close box in the upper-left corner of the window, or choose Page Preview from the File menu again.

Saving

Save a new document

1. Choose Save As from the File menu.
2. Type a filename, and select the folder or disk to which you want to save the document.
3. Press the Return key.

Save an existing document

1. Choose Save from the File menu.

You'll see the progress of the save expressed as a percentage in the lower-left corner of the window in Document view.

Printing

Print a document

1. Choose Print from the File menu.
2. Check the settings.
3. Press the Return key.

■ *Keyboard and Mouse Shortcuts*

To	Do this
Show/Hide ¶	Command-Y (toggles)
Show /Hide Ruler	Command-R (toggles)
Copy	Command-C
Cut	Command-X
Paste	Command-V
Select a word	Double-click on the word.
Select a paragraph	Double-click in the selection bar next to the paragraph.
Select the entire document	Click in the selection bar while pressing the Command key, or press Option-Command-M.
Print the document	Command-P
Save the document	Command-S

Word Fundamentals: Creating a Two-Page Document

The exercise presented in this chapter begins where the letter tutorial in Chapter 1 left off. Now that you've worked in Short Menus mode to produce a standard block-format letter, you are ready to create a different, more elaborate kind of document while exploring Full Menus mode. Along the way, you will use some of Word's more advanced features: You'll learn how to work with outlines, add words to a personal dictionary, and create style sheets as well as how to take fuller advantage of the Ruler and formatting commands. By the end of the chapter you will have transformed two pages of raw text into a polished piece of work.

■ *Entering the Text*

If Word isn't already up and running, start it from the desktop. Check the menu and preference settings, as described in Chapter 1. This tutorial assumes that:

❑ Full Menus mode is in effect.

❑ Format marks are not displayed.

❑ The unit of measurement is in inches.

Making an Outline

Your first step in creating a document might be to stop and think about what you want to say. Suppose that you are a senior account representative for Garrett & Associates, a public relations firm doing promotional work for the New York entertainment industry. Because the company's accounts are growing at a rate that fast outstrips the staff's ability to handle them, you recently hired a new crop of junior account representatives to fill the gap. Before they can hope to succeed in the trade, however, they need to master the common jargon; toward this end, you must create a vocabulary list.

Start by using Word to organize your thoughts. When you choose Outlining from the Document menu, you see a blank window in Outline view, as shown in Figure 2-1.

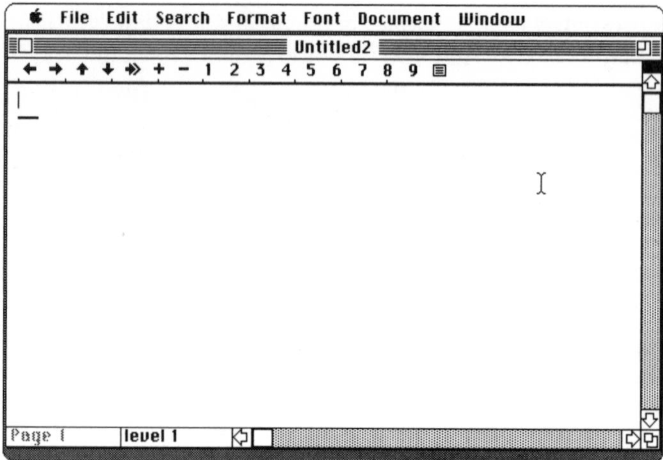

Figure 2-1
A blank window in Outline view.

You decide that first you need an introduction, then the list of jargon terms, and finally a cute closing remark. Type these three headings, or topics, in your document; where you see the ¶ symbol, press the Return key.

Introduction¶
Jargon Terms¶
Cute Closing Remark¶

As you enter these topics, the level of each one is displayed in the lower left corner of the window in an area called the *status box*. You can change the level of a topic very easily by clicking one of the first two icons in the Outline icon bar. Do this with the list of jargon terms that you enter next:

❶ Place the insertion point at the end of the *Jargon Terms* topic by clicking anywhere to the right of the line.

❷ Press the Return key to start a new line. The status box gives the level of the new heading as level 1.

❸ Click the right arrow icon in the Outline icon bar. The insertion point moves to the right, and the status box now says *level 2*. Anything you type will now be a subtopic under the level 1 topic.

❹ Enter these terms:

Boffo¶
Wipe¶
Big Dance in Newark¶
Tasty¶
RAP¶
Tenay Deejays¶
Angel¶
Breather¶
Zzz¶
Bally¶
Brodie¶
Gig¶
Four & Three¶
HIP¶
Nope¶

You typed the terms as they might occur to you, but they really should be in alphabetical order. No problem—simply use the Sort command while in Outline view:

❺ Select the list of terms by moving the pointer to the left margin of either the first or last line of the list. Move the pointer in the margin (the selection bar) until the I-beam pointer turns into a right-pointing arrow. Hold down the mouse button and drag the mouse to the other end of the list to select only the terms.

❻ While the words are selected, choose Sort from the Document menu to reorder the list instantly. Click anywhere in the document to deselect the list.

If you made a mistake—selected the wrong text, for instance—merely choose Undo Sort from the Edit menu before you do anything else, and try again. The Undo command is remarkably handy: The phrase you see when you display the Edit menu reflects the last operation performed. The outline should now look like Figure 2-2.

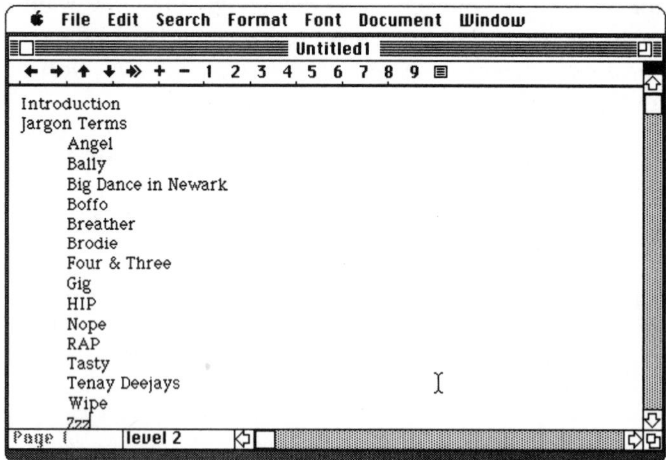

Figure 2-2
The terms after being sorted.

Editing the Outline

While you're in Outline view, change the topics so that they more fully describe their purpose:

❶ Select the first topic, *Introduction*, by clicking in the selection bar to the left of it.

❷ Type the following text, which replaces the text you selected (don't press the Return key after you type it):

Show Biz Buzzwords

Now change the second and third topics:

❸ Select the *Jargon Terms* topic, and replace it with this text:

The Lingo

❹ Select the *Cute Closing Remark* topic, and replace it with this text:

In Closing...

Now that you have edited the outline, you can move on to work with the body of the text. The finished outline is shown in Figure 2-3.

TIP

Don't Press the Return Key After You Retype a Topic in Outline View
Doing so inserts an extra paragraph mark in the style for that topic. This can cause problems when you later try to insert body text on the line after the topic. Any text you type in front of one of these extra paragraph marks will be in the same style as the topic, instead of in the *Normal* style you expect. This happens because the style attached to the paragraph mark determines the style of the entire paragraph.

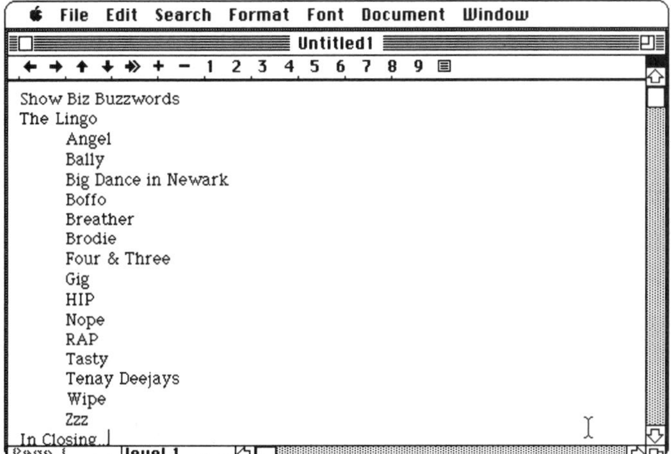

Figure 2-3
The finished outline in Outline view.

To return from Outline view to Document view, again choose Outlining from the Document menu. What you now see depends on whether or not you have the 12-point New York font installed in your System file. If you do, Word uses it as the default font for your base style, as shown in Figure 2-4. If you don't, Word uses 12-point Geneva as the default font. To see the complete list of fonts available, choose Character from the Format menu. The Font menu lists only a few of the more common fonts (unless you've already added some fonts to it).

Now, before you enter the rest of the text, save the document by choosing Save As from the File menu. Name the document *Buzzwords*, and click OK.

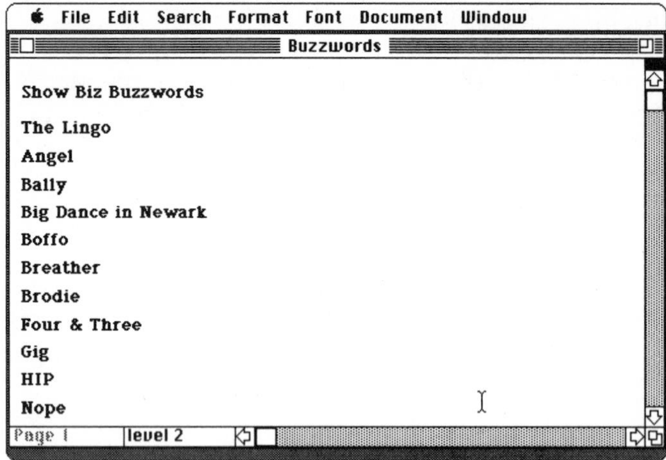

Figure 2-4
The finished outline in Document view.

Using Styles

Notice that when you return to Document view all the topics and jargon terms you entered are there, but their formatting is different than when you entered and edited them in Outline view. The text is in boldface, and the level 1 headings seem to have a little more space above them than before. If you set the insertion point in any of the headings, the name of the level you assigned to that heading becomes visible in the status box. This is the name of the style you attached to the text when you entered the topic in Outline view and assigned it a level. Every level of topic you create in Outline view has a style name, from *level 1* to *level 9*, and becomes a heading when you return to Document view.

Let's investigate this further. Click anywhere in the first heading, *Show Biz Buzzwords*, and choose Define Styles from the Format menu. A dialog box like the one in Figure 2-5 appears.

Listed are four items. Ignore the *New Style* item for now, and click on *level 1*. When you do this, the style's name pops up in the Style field, and a list of the style's formatting attributes appears below the name. Currently, the *level 1* style definition should read *Normal + Bold, Space Before 12 pt*. This means that the *level 1* style is based on the *Normal* (default) style, that it is displayed in boldface, and that an extra 12 points of line spacing is inserted before the heading to set it off from the preceding text. (Font sizes and line spacing are specified in Word in points. A point is a conventional unit of measure equal to 1/72 inch, so 12 points of extra line spacing is equal to 1/6 inch.) Each item in the list box is a style, and the collective list is called the style sheet for that document. Word stores a style sheet within each document you create.

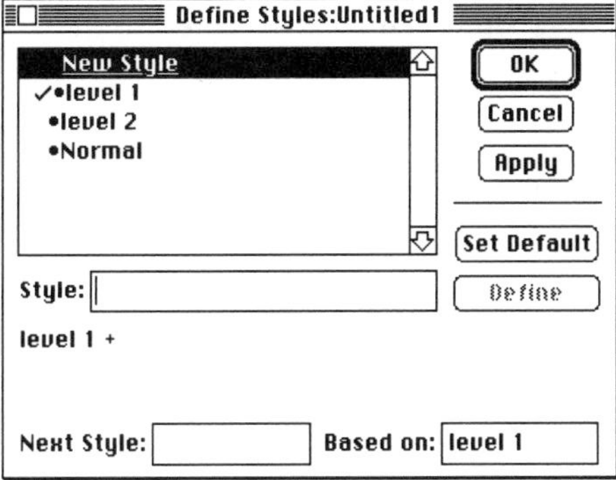

Figure 2-5
The Define Styles dialog box.

You may have noticed in looking at the *level 1* style definition that formats for two of the four format domains—character and paragraph—are represented. The boldface attribute is a character format; the extra line spacing is a paragraph format. Style definitions can contain both types of formats, but when you apply a style to some text, the formats that make up the style affect the entire paragraph that contains the text. If, for example, you change the font, font size, font style (such as bold or italic), line spacing, space before or after a paragraph, or alignment in a style definition, the change is reflected in every paragraph to which you attached the style. Thus, you can't use a style to change the format of a single word within a paragraph.

Play a bit with the *level 1* style definition so that you can see how changing the style changes your document. While the Define Styles dialog box is displayed and the *level 1* style is selected, choose Italic from the Format menu. *Every heading in your document that has the level 1 style changes at the same time.* The style definition also changes to reflect the new attribute. This is why the style feature in Word is so powerful: It allows you to establish a consistent design for a document and to refine that design until it's exactly the way you want it, without having to hunt for and reformat every piece of text. The care and feeding of style sheets is discussed later in this chapter and throughout this book, but for now make a few adjustments to the heading styles so that you can enter the rest of the text. With the *level 1* style still selected:

❶ Choose Italic again from the Format menu to return the *level 1* headings to the unitalicized typeface. (This is one of the commands in Word that toggle: Choose it once to turn it on, choose it again to turn it off.)

❷ Choose Underline from the Format menu.

❸ Click the Define button in the dialog box, and then click OK.

Now change the definition of the *level 2* style, which is attached to the jargon words in the document:

4. Click on any of the jargon words.
5. Choose Define Styles from the Format menu.
6. Select the *level 2* style.
7. Choose Bold from the Format menu to toggle off the boldface format.
8. Choose Italic to italicize all the jargon words.
9. Click the Define button, and then click OK.

At this point, your document should look like Figure 2-6. The next step is to enter the introductory paragraph, the jargon definitions, and the closing paragraph.

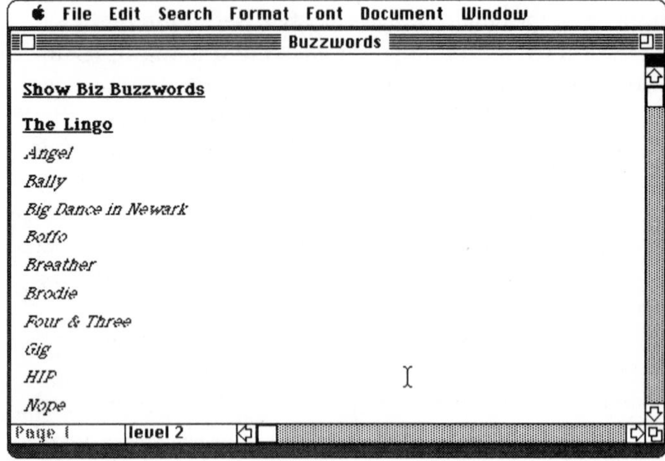

Figure 2-6
The document after the styles have been redefined.

Entering the Body Text

The body of the document consists of three distinct portions: an introductory paragraph, then a series of smaller paragraphs for the definitions, and, finally, the closing paragraph.

The Introductory Paragraph

Place the insertion point at the end of the *Show Biz Buzzwords* heading by clicking anywhere to the right of the line, and press the Return key. Type the following text:

Garrett & Associates Public Relations serves more than a dozen entertainment-industry clients, from a three-person circus act to a multibillion-dollar-a-year record company. Like all fields, the entertainment industry has its own peculiar lingo: colorful words and phrases used in conversation, news releases, and even newspaper and magazine articles. Here is a short list of some of the more common show biz terms you'll need to know in your new position as junior account representative.

At some point as you typed this text, you may have noticed that the style name in the status box for the text you entered is *Normal*. Take a quick look at the definition of this style by choosing Define Styles again and then selecting the *Normal* style. This is the style assigned to your text in the absence of any other style definition. Many people who use Word without learning about style sheets use this style constantly without ever being aware that it exists. Yet by changing the definition of this style, you can reformat all the body text in your document in one stroke (well, maybe one stroke and a couple of mouse clicks). Click Cancel to close the dialog box.

The Jargon Definitions

Each definition of a term is a separate paragraph following its *level 2* heading: Enter each definition by placing the insertion point at the end of a term, pressing the Return key, and typing the definition. Don't type the terms again, only the definitions.

Angel:

The backer of the show. During the Roaring Twenties, the term angel was used by con men to describe the victims of their swindles, so use the term carefully!¶

Bally:

A free show. Used most often in connection with a carnival sideshow to promote the main attraction inside the tent. The bally often ended up being more interesting than the real show, which is probably why the term is often used today to describe a show that promises more than it delivers.¶

Big Dance in Newark:

Everyone loves your show—the producers, the backers, the critics, even the stagehands. So why isn't anyone in the audience? There must be a big dance in Newark!¶

Boffo:

A success through and through. The word probably sprang from the phrase "good box office." See brodie.¶

Breather:

A film that has little going for it except atmosphere: the mood created by the lighting, set decoration, and camera angles.¶

Brodie:

A turkey. The term was first coined in dubious recognition of Steve Brodie, perhaps the greatest belly-flopper of all time. Disgruntled by his lack of success, poor Steve tried to end it all in 1886 by jumping off the Brooklyn Bridge. He flopped on that one, too: He survived the attempt and went on living for another 40 years. See boffo.¶

Four & Three:

A theatrical company not located in New York City. The term's origins lie with the small New York-based repertory troupes, whose casts comprised four men and three women.¶

Gig:

In the music industry, an engagement to perform.¶

HIP:

Short for high-impact priority. Any record album called a HIP hit is slated for a multimillion-dollar advertising campaign.¶

Nope:

Short for no promotion. If a record company doesn't think an album has a chance, the album is marked as a nope (usually with a hole drilled in the corner of the cover), given no advertising, and sent to the cutout bins of cheap department stores.¶

RAP:

Short for radio air play.¶

Tasty:

In the record industry, the current in word for "the greatest." Generally replaces boss, groovy, heavy, and mellow.¶

Tenay Deejays:

Radio station deejays who play only the Top Ten.¶

Wipe:

Being fired before the show ends.¶

Zzz:

A G-rated film.¶

Part of the document, with the definitions typed in, is shown in Figure 2-7.

Show Biz Buzzwords
Garrett & Associates Public Relations serves more than a dozen entertainment-industry clients, from a three-person circus act to a multibillion-dollar-a-year record company. Like all fields, the entertainment industry has its own peculiar lingo: colorful words and phrases used in conversation, news releases, and even newspaper and magazine articles. Here is a short list of some of the more common show biz terms you'll need to know in your new position as junior account representative.

The Lingo

Angel
The backer of the show. During the Roaring Twenties, the term angel was used by con men to describe the victims of their swindles, so use the term carefully!

Bally

Figure 2-7
Portion of document after definitions have been entered.

The Closing Paragraph

Now wrap up this production by entering the closing remarks. Put an insertion point at the end of the last heading, *In Closing*, press the Return key, and type this text:

Be a boffo representative of Garrett & Associates! If you pull a brodie and don't please your angel by giving these tasty terms some RAP, we'll mark you nope, and you might even need a HIP promotional to land another gig (undoubtedly with a Four & Three) after you get wiped!

■ *Editing the Text*

For the purpose of this tutorial, we'll assume that you are an inspired writer and need make no changes to your document other than to correct a few misspelled words. If you think you made a few mistakes other than incorrect spelling, take a moment to scroll through the document and make changes using the methods you learned in Chapter 1.

Even if you're an expert typist, it's still a good idea to use Word's spelling checker to locate misspelled words. This time, however, try adding words to a personal dictionary.

Creating a Personal Dictionary

The entertainment-lingo document contains numerous words not found in Word's Main Dictionary. In your role as senior account representative, you might use some of these words in future documents, in which case you should add the specialized words to a personal dictionary. (The Main

Dictionary cannot be added to or edited.) Adding words to a personal dictionary is a straightforward task:

❶ Save the document again before using the spelling checker: Choose Save from the File menu.

❷ Set the insertion point at the beginning of the document (immediately before the *S* in *Show*), and choose the Spelling command from the Document menu. A small dialog box appears briefly, telling you that the Main Dictionary is being loaded.

When the Spelling dialog box appears, note that the Open Dictionaries list box shows Main Dictionary and User 1. User 1 is a personal dictionary that Word creates for you. Later you will learn how to create other dictionaries. Both the Main Dictionary and your personal dictionaries (User 1, User 2, and so on) are loaded automatically when you choose the Spelling command if the dictionaries are in the same folder as Word when you launch the program. Otherwise, you may see a dialog box asking where they are. (Refer to Appendix A for recommendations on arranging your Word files.)

❸ Click the Start Check button.

❹ Unless you somehow misspelled *Show*, the first unknown word should be *Biz*. Click the + button to add the word to your personal dictionary.

❺ Click the Continue Check button. The next suspect word should be *Buzzwords*. Add that one to the personal dictionary, too.

❻ Continue checking until you reach the end of the document. Notice that the spelling checker differentiates between uppercase and lowercase letters: The program stops at *biz*, even though you previously added *Biz* to the dictionary. Later in this book, you'll learn how to check both uppercase and lowercase versions of words, adding only the lowercase version. When you reach the end, a dialog box appears, saying *End of document reached*. Click OK.

Reopen the Spelling dialog box by choosing the Spelling command one more time. Click on User 1 in the Open Dictionaries list box. The words you added are shown in the Words list box. If you discover that you added a word you don't want, select it and click the - (minus) button.

Saving the Dictionary

Like documents, your dictionaries should be saved before you quit Word. The easiest way to save your User 1 dictionary is simply to quit Word when you are ready to end your session; a dialog box appears, giving you the opportunity to save both your document and the User 1 dictionary:

❶ Choose Quit from the File menu.

❷ Word asks if you want to save your Buzzwords document. Click Yes.

❸ Word asks if you want to save your User 1 dictionary. Click Yes.

❹ The Spelling dialog box appears as Word verifies that it's a dictionary you're saving; then a Save As dialog box appears in front of the Spelling dialog box. Word assumes that you want to save the User 1 dictionary in the same folder as your document, but instead save it in the same folder as Word. Then, the next time you start Word and do a spelling check on another document, Word will be able to access this dictionary without having to ask you where it can be found. After you switch to the correct folder, click Save. Your User 1 dictionary is now recorded on disk.

If you or someone else used the program's spelling checker before, the actual sequence of steps may differ from that presented here. For example, if the User 1 dictionary is already in the Word folder, Word will simply ask you if you want to save the changes to User 1 rather than presenting the Save As dialog box. Click Yes to update the dictionary.

■ *Formatting the Text*

With all the text entered and corrected, now you can play with designing and formatting the document. The styles you used earlier will make this process a breeze. After you adjust the design of the document, you will finish the formatting by changing the characteristics of individual words. You can always alter the font, font size, and font style while you're writing, of course, and you will probably do this often, but for the sake of simplicity this exercise separates the entering and editing process from the formatting process.

Establishing a Design through Styles

You can establish an overall design for the document by working with the style sheet. Start Word again, and open the Buzzwords document. The first step is to adjust the style for the *level 1* and *level 2* headings:

❶ Choose Define Styles from the Format menu, and select the *level 1* style.

❷ Choose Character from the same menu. The Character format dialog box appears.

❸ In the lower left corner a list box displays the names of all the fonts that have been installed in your System file. Select Times; when you do, all the font sizes installed for that font appear in the list box just to the right. Click on the 18-point font. If either or both of these options aren't visible, simply choose another font and point size from the options available.

❹ In the upper left corner of the dialog box, both the Bold and Underlined typeface options are selected. The 18-point font is visible enough without boldfacing, so click in the Bold check box to toggle off the format. Then click OK.

❺ In the lower right corner of the Define Styles dialog box, the contents of the Based On field read *Normal*. This means that if you did not set a specific format (for the font, for instance) for the *level 1* style, then that format is taken from, or based on, the *Normal* style. This topic is explored in depth later; for now, simply double-click on the word *Normal* and press the Backspace key. (On some keyboards this key is called the Delete key.) This makes the *level 1* style independent of the *Normal* style so that the changes you will make to the *Normal* style a little later will not affect this style.

❻ The *level 1* style definition now reads *Font: Times 18 point, Underline, Flush left, Space Before 12 pt.* All the *level 1* headings in your document changed to reflect the modified style. Click Define.

❼ Now select the *level 2* style, and choose the Character command again.

❽ Change the font to Times (or whatever font you chose in Step ❸), and leave the 12-point size option as is. Leave the italic typeface, but add boldface; then click OK. The *level 2* style definition should read *Normal + Font: Times, Bold Italic, Space Before 6 pt.* Select and delete the contents of the Based On field, as you did for the *level 1* style.

❾ Now click Define and Cancel. (Clicking Define and OK would define the style and then apply it to the paragraph containing the insertion point. Clicking Define and Cancel redefines the style without applying it.)

Thus, without having to search for each heading and repeat the same steps over and over, you simply and elegantly established a design for most of the document. If you used the Times font for the headings, your document should look like Figure 2-8.

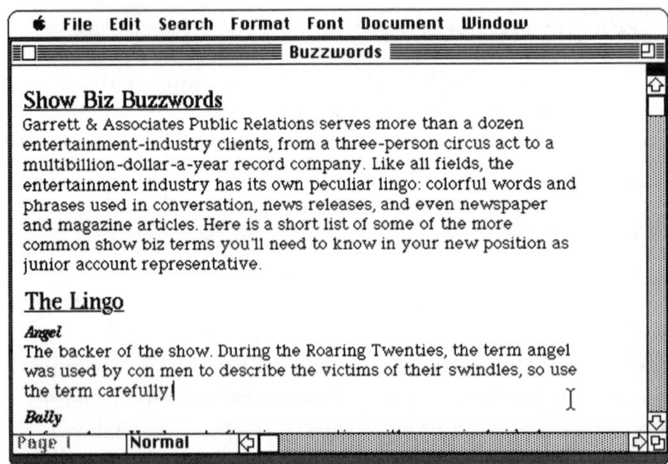

Figure 2-8
Portion of document showing reformatted headings.

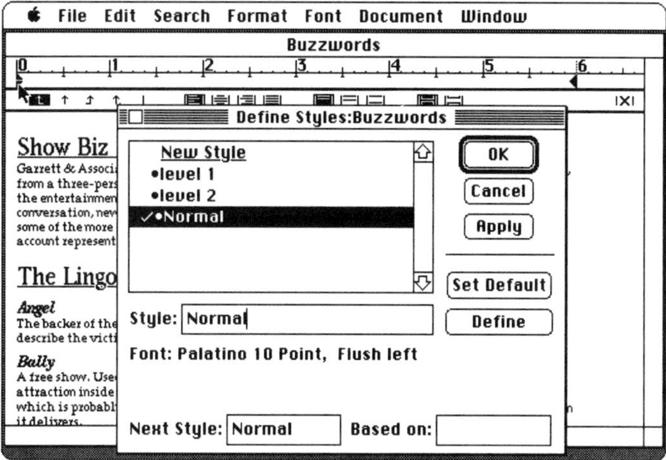

Figure 2-9
Ruler with pointer positioned over left indent marker.

Now work with the body text. This time you'll change not only the character formatting (the font and size), but also the paragraph formatting.

1. Choose Define Styles again. Select the *Normal* style. The current style definition should read *Font: New York 12 point, Flush left.*
2. Choose the Character command. Select Palatino 10 point (or any other suitable font and size). Click OK.
3. Change the position of the left indent, a paragraph format. Choose Show Ruler from the Format menu. The Ruler appears at the top of the document window, as in Figure 2-9.
4. Position the pointer over the left indent marker (the lower of the two small triangles in the Ruler), press the mouse button, and drag the marker half an inch to the right. Both triangles will move. The left indent of the body text (but not of the headings) changes to reflect the new indent.
5. Click the Justified alignment icon (the last of the alignment icons in the Ruler). In the Define Styles dialog box, click Define and Cancel.

Making Final Formatting Adjustments

Now that the overall design is set, you need to reformat a few words. Under the *Boffo* heading, look for the words *See brodie,* double-click on *brodie,* and choose Italic from the Format menu. Under the *Brodie* heading, look for the words *See boffo,* double-click on *boffo,* and choose Italic again. In the final paragraph, italicize the words *boffo, brodie, angel, tasty, RAP, nope, HIP, gig,*

Four & Three, and *wiped*. (For better word spacing after the italicized words, you could add an extra space, but italicized words almost always look better on paper than on the screen.)

Adding a Footer and Page Number

Your document should now be approximately 1 ½ pages long—that is, long enough to have a header or footer and page numbers. To see exactly where the page break occurs, choose Repaginate from the Document menu. The page break—a dotted line, as shown in Figure 2-10—should be within the *Tasty* definition. The Page Preview command also repaginates the current document. Notice that the page break occurs between a term and its definition; we'll fix this in Page Preview in a moment.

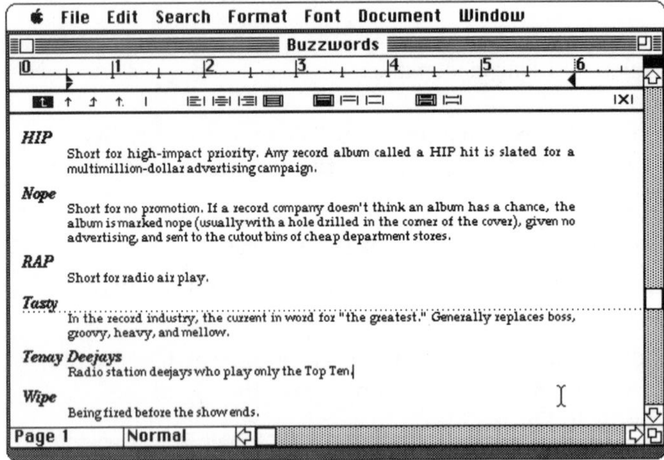

Figure 2-10
A page break produced by repagination.

To create a footer containing the page number:

❶ Choose Open Footer from the Document menu. The Footer window appears at the bottom of the screen. Choose Show Ruler from the Format menu to see the type and placement of the default tabs in the Footer window. The status area in the lower left corner of the Footer window says *footer* because the text you type in this window has this style, which is another of the automatic styles. (If you chose Define styles now, you would see this style added to the other so-called *automatic* styles in the list box.)

❷ Type the text *Garrett & Associates* into the Footer window. Press the Tab key twice to move past the center-aligned tab stop to the right-aligned tab stop superimposed over the right indent marker. Type *Page*. Press the Spacebar once to put a space after the word.

❸ Click the Page Number icon in the upper left corner of the Footer window. The numeral *1* appears. Choose Show ¶ from the Edit menu for a moment: A dotted box surrounds the number. When you clicked the Page Number icon, you inserted a special character into the footer that Word increments for each new printed page. Choose Hide ¶ to hide the formatting marks, and choose Hide Ruler to hide the Ruler.

❹ Press the Return key to move the insertion point to the start of the next line, and type *4321 5th Avenue, New York, NY 10011.*

❺ Select both lines, and choose Italic and then Bold from the Format menu to set them off a little from the body text. Choose the 12 Point option from the Font menu to make the footer text a little larger. Your footer should look like the one in Figure 2-11.

❻ Now click the close box in the upper left corner of the Footer window to save the footer.

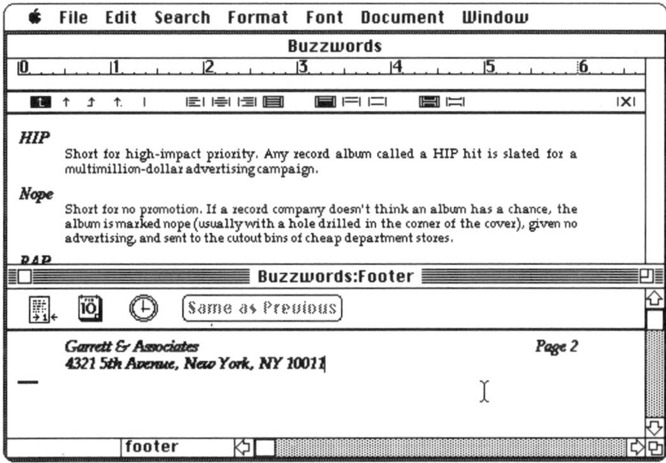

Figure 2-11
The completed footer.

■ *Previewing and Printing the Document*

In Word, looking at your document in Page Preview mode is a great way to avoid printing draft copies repeatedly. You can get immediate feedback on the overall appearance of your document, zoom in to take a closer look, and adjust margins, page breaks, and header and footer placement.

When you choose Page Preview from the File menu, you see the entire Buzzwords document in miniature. Play around a little in this mode to get a taste of how to make final adjustments to your document before printing.

Click the third icon from the top, the Margins icon. A set of guidelines appears on the second page, showing the placement of the margins and the footer for both pages of the document, as in Figure 2-12.

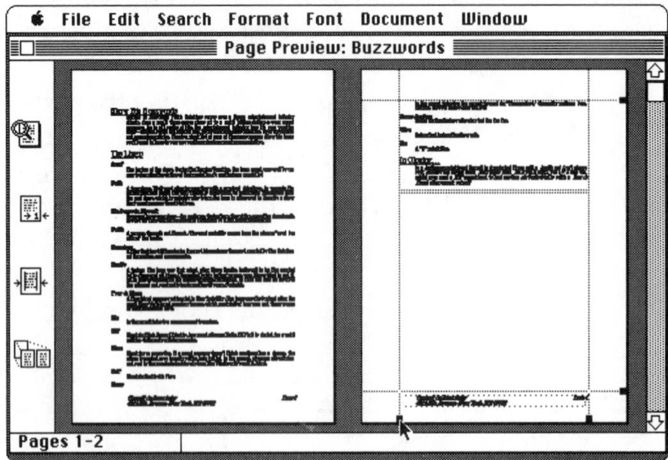

Figure 2-12
The document in Page Preview mode, showing the margin and footer guidelines.

To adjust the left margin, place the pointer on the handle of the left margin guideline (see Figure 2-12), and drag it to the right. As you do this, the status area displays the width of the left margin. Set the left margin to 1.5 inches. To have Word update the screen image using the new margin, click the Margins icon again. You can also click anywhere else on the screen except within the page that shows the guidelines. Now move the right margin toward the left so that it is set to 1.5 inches as well.

Take a look at how the page number in the footer turned out. If you are still in the margin-changing mode (that is, if the guidelines are still displayed), leave the mode by clicking the Margins icon again. Then put the arrow pointer on the page number and double-click to get a close-up. (You can also use the Magnifier icon, but the double-click method is more convenient here.) The page number is now positioned a little to the right of the right indent of the body text. This happened because the position of the page number in the Footer window is determined by a tab stop, and tab stops are measured relative to the left indent of the paragraph. (If you want, you can go back to the Footer window later to realign the page number.) Now use the scroll bars to move around the magnified page; when you are finished, simply double-click anywhere in the magnified image.

Before you print this document, adjust the page break so that the *Nope* definition moves to the top of the next page:

❶ Click the Margins icon, and then click anywhere in the first page. The guidelines will move to the first page of the displayed document.

❷ Move the pointer to the page-break line, a broken line just above the line for the bottom margin. You can tell the page-break line from the bottom margin because the page-break line appears between the side margins only, whereas the bottom margin runs across the entire page.

❸ Press the mouse button to select the page-break line (the arrow pointer changes to a cross-hair pointer), and drag the line up until it is above the word *Nope.* When you release the button, the display will be updated, and the entire *Nope* definition will appear on page 2.

Note that Word will not adjust this manual page break if you later edit the document and then repaginate it. As a result, you may end up with page breaks in odd places. If necessary, you can move the offending page breaks out of the way in Page Preview mode or simply select and delete them in Document view. Figure 2-13 shows that this type of page break, called a *manual* or *forced* page break, looks different from those produced when you repaginate a document.

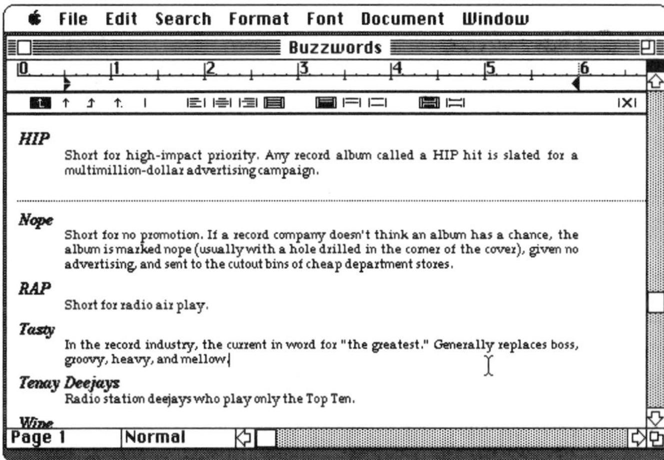

Figure 2-13
A manual page break inserted in Page Preview.

The document requires no special print settings, so print it in the usual way:

❶ Choose Print from the File menu. You can print while you are in Page Preview mode.

❷ Be sure the printer is on and is loaded with paper.

❸ Click the OK button.

If you need to stop the printing process or pause during printing, click the Cancel or Pause button in the dialog box that appears during printing.

The printed document should look like Figures 2-14a and 2-14b, which were printed on a LaserWriter.

Show Biz Buzzwords

Garrett & Associates Public Relations serves more than a dozen entertainment industry clients, from a three-person circus act to a multibillion-dollar-a-year record company. Like all fields, the entertainment industry has its own peculiar lingo: colorful words and phrases used in conversation, news releases, even newspaper and magazine articles. Here is a short list of some of the more common show biz terms you'll need to know in your new position as junior account representative.

The Lingo

Angel

The backer of the show. During the Roaring Twenties, the term angel was used by con men to describe the victims of their swindles, so use the term carefully!

Bally

A free show. Used most often in connection with a carnival sideshow to promote the main attraction inside the tent. The bally often ended up being more interesting than the real show, which is probably why the term is often used today to describe a show that promises more than it delivers.

Big Dance in Newark

Everyone loves your show—the producers, the backers, the critics, even the stagehands. So why isn't anyone in the audience? There must be a Big Dance in Newark!

Boffo

A success, through and through. The word probably sprang from the phrase "good box office." See brodie.

Breather

A film that has little going for it except atmosphere: the mood created by the lighting, set decoration, and camera angles.

Brodie

A turkey. The term was first coined in dubious recognition of Steve Brodie, believed to be the greatest belly-flopper of all times. Disgruntled by his lack of success, poor Steve tried to end it all in 1886 by jumping off the Brooklyn Bridge. He flopped on that one too: he survived the attempt and went on living for another 40 years. See boffo.

Four & Three

A theatrical company not located in New York City. The term was first coined after the small New York-based repertory troupes, whose casts comprised four men and three women.

Gig

In the music industry, an engagement to perform.

HIP

Short for high impact priority. Any record album called a HIP hit is slated for a multi million-dollar advertising campaign.

Garrett & Associates *Page 1*
4321 5th Avenue, New York, NY 10011

Figure 2-14a
First page of the printed document.

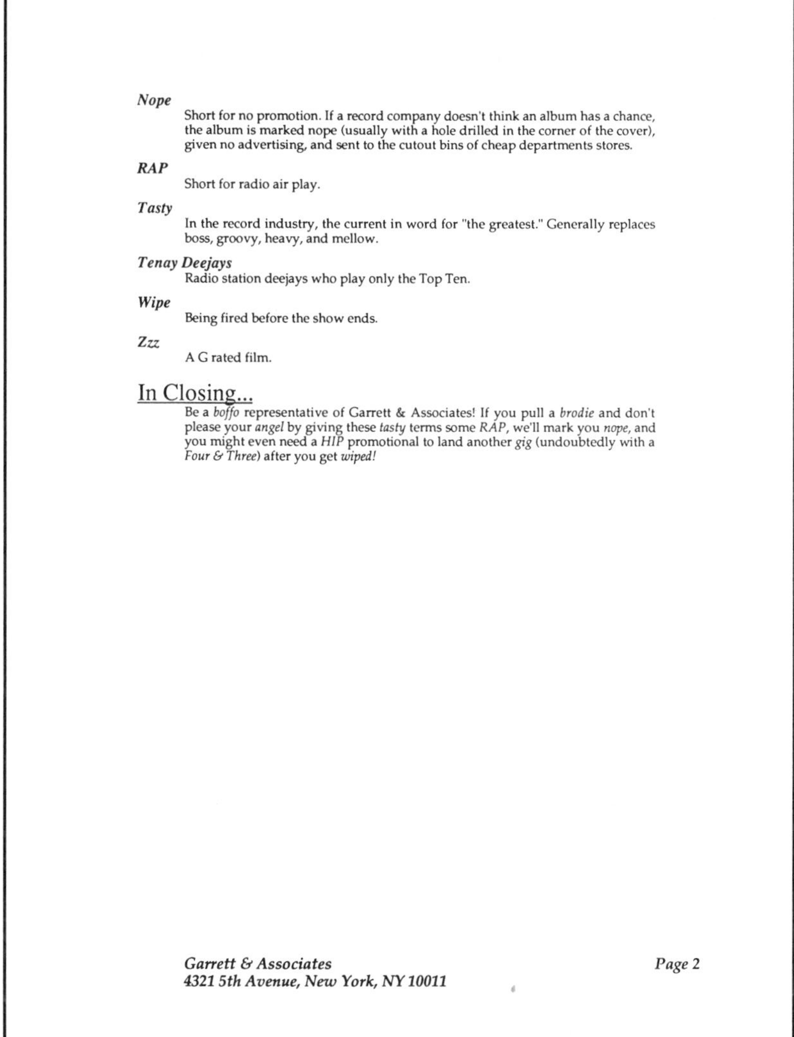

Nope
Short for no promotion. If a record company doesn't think an album has a chance, the album is marked nope (usually with a hole drilled in the corner of the cover), given no advertising, and sent to the cutout bins of cheap departments stores.

RAP
Short for radio air play.

Tasty
In the record industry, the current in word for "the greatest." Generally replaces boss, groovy, heavy, and mellow.

Tenay Deejays
Radio station deejays who play only the Top Ten.

Wipe
Being fired before the show ends.

Zzz
A G rated film.

In Closing...

Be a *boffo* representative of Garrett & Associates! If you pull a *brodie* and don't please your *angel* by giving these *tasty* terms some *RAP*, we'll mark you *nope*, and you might even need a *HIP* promotional to land another *gig* (undoubtedly with a *Four & Three*) after you get *wiped!*

Garrett & Associates
4321 5th Avenue, New York, NY 10011
Page 2

Figure 2-14b
Second page of the printed document.

You've now learned the basics of creating documents with Word. You have also begun to appreciate how easy the program is to use and have gained some sense of the variety and depth of its features. When you're ready to take fuller advantage of Word's power, turn to Section 2, "Building the Framework."

■ Points to Remember

Many of these techniques and topics are covered in much greater detail in later chapters.

- ❑ The text you see in Outline view resembles a traditional outline. The different levels of topics are indented, and none of the formatting shows; all text looks the same.
- ❑ You can have up to nine levels of topics in an outline.
- ❑ The status box in the lower left corner of the window shows, among other things, the name of the style assigned to the paragraph containing the insertion point. If no other style has been assigned, the *Normal* style is used.
- ❑ A style applies to an entire paragraph. You cannot apply a style to part of a paragraph, and you can assign only one style to a paragraph. In Word a paragraph is defined as any amount of text followed by a paragraph mark (shown as a ¶ when Show ¶ is in effect). It is possible to change the format of individual characters in a paragraph. Simply select the text to be changed and choose the attributes you want from the Font and Format menus.
- ❑ Word maintains a personal dictionary named User 1 for you. You can add words to and delete words from your own personal dictionaries, but you cannot change entries in Word's Main Dictionary.
- ❑ The first time you save a personal dictionary, be sure to put it in the same folder as the Word program so that Word will be able to find it. Otherwise, Word will save the dictionary in the same folder as the document, which may not be the right one.

■ Techniques

Basic Skills

Undo the previous command

❶ Choose Undo from the Edit menu.

The words that appear after Undo vary depending on the previous command.

Outlining

Enter Outline view

❶ Choose Outlining from the Document menu.

Return to Document view

❶ Choose the Outlining command again.

Enter outline topics

❶ Type your topics, and press the Return key after each one.

❷ Click the right arrow icon in the Outline icon bar to begin typing subtopics.

❸ Click the left arrow icon to return to the next higher level of topic.

The status box in the bottom left of the window shows the level of the current topic.

Change the level of an outline topic

❶ Set the insertion point on the topic to be changed.

❷ Click the left arrow icon in the Outline icon bar to promote the topic, or click the right arrow icon to demote the topic.

Replace an outline topic

❶ Select the topic to be replaced.

❷ Type the new topic.

Do not press the Return key after you type the new topic.

Enter body text into an outline

❶ Return to Document view.

❷ Set the insertion point after the appropriate topic.

❸ Press the Return key, and type the text.

Sorting

Arrange a group of lines in alphabetical order

❶ Select the lines to be sorted.

❷ Choose Sort from the Document menu.

Working with Styles

Display the definition of a style

❶ Choose Define Styles from the Format menu.

❷ Select the style from the list box. Its definition will appear below the Style field.

❸ Click Cancel when you are through.

Alter the character attributes of a style

❶ Choose Define Styles from the Format menu.

❷ Select the style you want to alter from the list box.

❸ With the Define Styles dialog box open, choose from the Format menu the attributes you want to assign to the style (Bold, Italic, Underline, and so on).

❹ Click Define, and then click OK.

Alter the font and point size of a style

❶ Choose Define Styles from the Format menu.

❷ Select the style you want to alter from the list box.

❸ With the Define Styles dialog box open, choose Character from the same menu.

❹ Select the font name and size from the dialog box. (You can also change the character attributes here.)

❺ Click OK to return to the Define Styles dialog box.

❻ Then click Define and Cancel.

Alter the left margin of a style

❶ With the Define Styles dialog box displayed, choose Show Ruler from the Format menu.

❷ Drag the left indent marker (the lower of the two triangles on the left) to the new margin position. (Both triangles will move.)

❸ Click Define and Cancel in the dialog box.

Alter the alignment of a style

❶ Follow the steps for adjusting the left margin, but click one of the alignment icons in the Ruler instead of moving the left indent marker.

Using a Personal Dictionary

Add a word to a personal dictionary

1. During a spelling check, click the + button in the Spelling dialog box to add the highlighted word to your User 1 dictionary.
2. Click Continue Check to check the rest of the document.

Remove a word from a personal dictionary

1. Click on the name of a dictionary in the Open Dictionaries list box.
2. The list of words in that dictionary appears in the Words list box.
3. Select the word you want to delete, and click the - button.

Page Formatting

Add a footer with a page number

1. Choose Open Footer from the Document menu.
2. Type any text that is to appear at the bottom of every page. Text you type at the center-aligned tab stop will be centered.
3. Place the insertion point where you want the page number to appear.
4. Click the Page Number icon to have Word insert page numbers.
5. Format the footer as you like.
6. Click the close box to save the footer.

Adjust margins in Page Preview mode

1. Click the Margins icon to display the margin guidelines.
2. Drag the handle of the margin you want to move to the new location.
3. Click outside the page to update the screen.
4. Click the Margins icon again to remove the guidelines.

Adjust page breaks in Page Preview mode

1. With the margin guidelines displayed, drag the page-break line (the dotted line between the side margins) to the new location. The display will be updated when you release the mouse button.
2. Click on a page to move the margin guidelines to that page, if necessary.

This process inserts a manual page break that will not be changed when Word repaginates the file.

SECTION 2

Building the Framework

Organizing Through Outlining

Whether you are writing a business letter, preparing an important speech, or churning out a spy thriller, Word's built-in outlining feature can help you transform your thoughts into a complete, well-organized document. The feature serves not only as a planning aid—that is, as a means to create a conventional outline—but also as a powerful writing and editing tool. In fact, you can use it to reorganize an entire document, freely moving blocks of text with a few clicks of the mouse.

To enter Outline view, be sure that you are in Full Menus mode, and then choose Outlining from the Document menu. If you are starting a new document, the outline window is empty. If you already entered some text in Document view, however, it appears in the window (although you see only the first line of each paragraph). This occurs because Outline view presents a different view of the same document, not a different document. Thus, any change you make to an outline is reflected in the Document view text, and vice versa.

Most menu commands are accessible in Outline view and operate the same as they do in Document view. The Footnote, Spelling, and Hyphenate commands and the contents of the Format and Font menus are unavailable. Therefore, these commands are dimmed on the menu.

■ *Creating and Manipulating Outline Text*

Across the top of the outline window, Word displays the Outline icon bar (shown in Figure 3-1), which contains the tools you use to work with outlines. Let's examine the function of each icon in the bar.

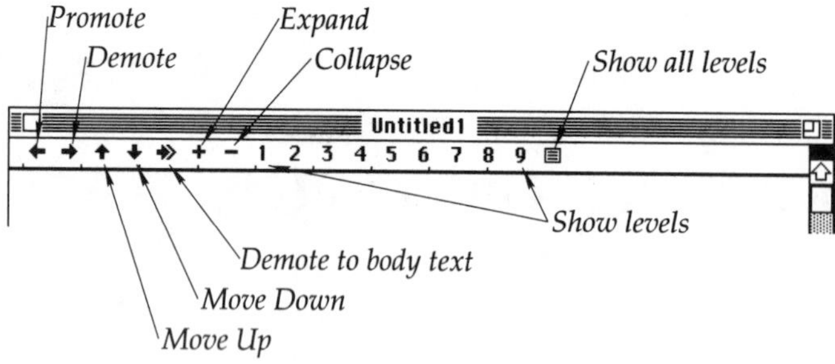

Figure 3-1
The Outline icon bar.

Setting Levels and Promoting and Demoting Topics

Like conventional outlines, Word outlines are organized according to topic or heading level, with each level distinguished from the others by the amount of indention. The main, or level 1, topics appear near the left margin; level 2 topics are indented half an inch to the right; level 3 topics are indented an additional half inch; and so on. As you learned in Chapter 2, to establish the level of a topic, you select some text or start a new line and click the Promote (🡸) icon or the Demote (🡺) icon. The left arrow "promotes" the topic to the next higher level; the right arrow "demotes" the topic to the next lower level. You can use the Promote and Demote icons before or after you enter head–ings or other text in the outline.

If your keyboard has arrow keys, you can establish topic levels by pressing the left or right arrow key. Don't try to establish levels by pressing the Tab key, however. As in Document view, it simply inserts a tab character and indents the line to the next tab stop. This means that your topic will not be associated with the appropriate style. If you think that you may have absentmindedly used the Tab key in an outline, choose Show ¶ from the Edit menu to make the tab characters visible.

The current level is displayed in the status box in the lower left corner of the window, as illustrated in Figure 3-2. Once a level has been established, you can either type some text or edit text you already entered. If the text extends beyond one line, the characters on subsequent lines are indented when the text wraps. When you finish a topic, press the Return key; the topic then becomes a separate paragraph. The insertion point stays at the same topic level. If you want to change levels, simply click the Promote or Demote icon again.

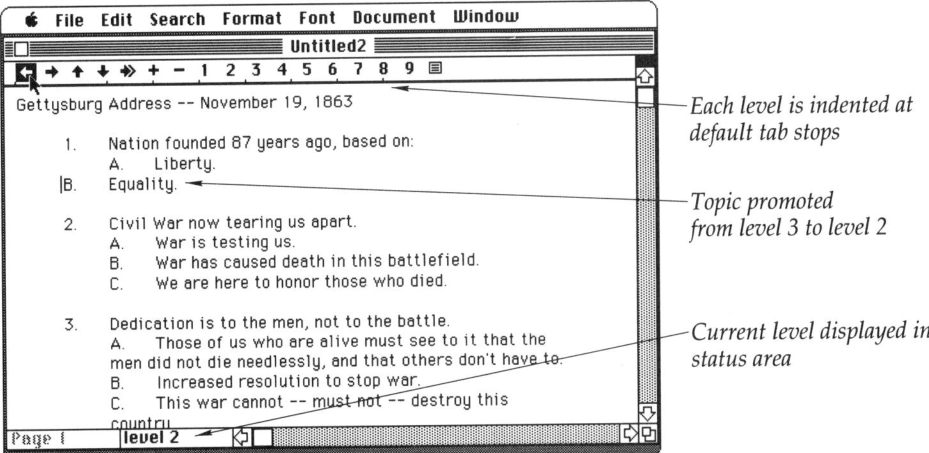

Figure 3-2
The outline window.

You insert new levels between existing ones the same way that you insert new paragraphs in Document view. Click at the end of the line above where you want to insert the new line, and press the Return key. The space you open for the new entry has the same level as the topic above it, as shown in Figure 3-3. Click the icons or press the left or right arrow key to promote or demote the new topic.

Word's outlining feature is extremely flexible: You can enter topics and establish levels in a variety of ways. For example, you can enter all the level 1 topics first, without having to switch between level settings, and then go back and insert the level 2 topics. Or you can simply type in the entire outline and then establish levels afterward. To speed up the latter approach, you can promote or demote a number of adjacent topics at the same time, even if they are on different levels, by selecting them as a group and clicking the appropriate icon. This shortcut is also handy if you want to make room for new levels or place existing topics under a newly created topic.

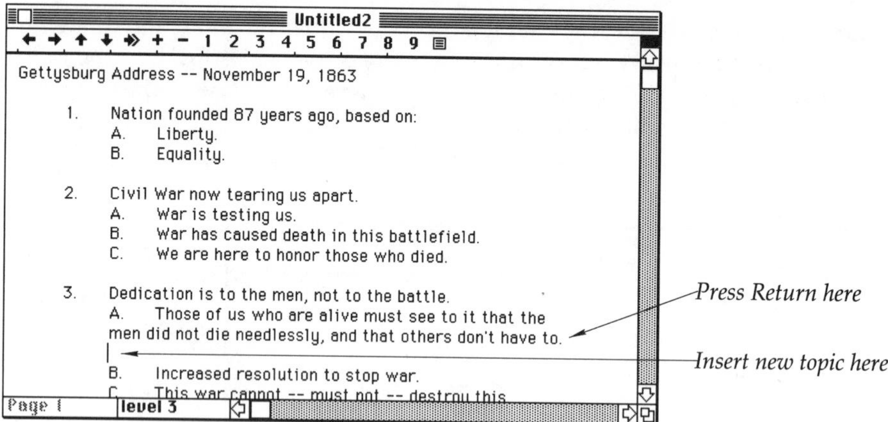

Figure 3-3
Inserting a new topic.

Moving Topics Up and Down ↑ ↓

The Move Up (↑) and Move Down (↓) icons in the Outline icon bar let you rearrange topics (headings) and the body text beneath them. Simply select the material you want to move, and click the appropriate icon. If you select two or more topics, they all move at once. If you select the first line of a paragraph of body text, the entire paragraph moves. The Move Up and Move Down icons do the same job as the Cut and Paste commands (which are also available in Outline view), but they do it more quickly. You can also use the up and down arrow keys if your keyboard has them.

You can move material within an outline in one of two ways: by line or by topic.

Moving by Line

Suppose you want to reverse the order of two topics, neither of which has any subtopics or body text. You can accomplish this most easily with a technique called *line selection*. Simply select anywhere within the first topic and then click the Move Down icon (or select the second topic and click the Move Up icon). For example, if you select topic 2 in the outline shown in Figure 3-3 and click the Move Down icon, the topic moves down one line, as shown in Figure 3-4. The level of the topics stays the same, even if the two topics you are reversing are on different levels.

If you select two or more adjacent lines, you can move them as a group. (To select multiple lines, drag in the selection bar or drag over the lines themselves.) In Outline view, Word selects the entire topic, even when you click in the middle of it.

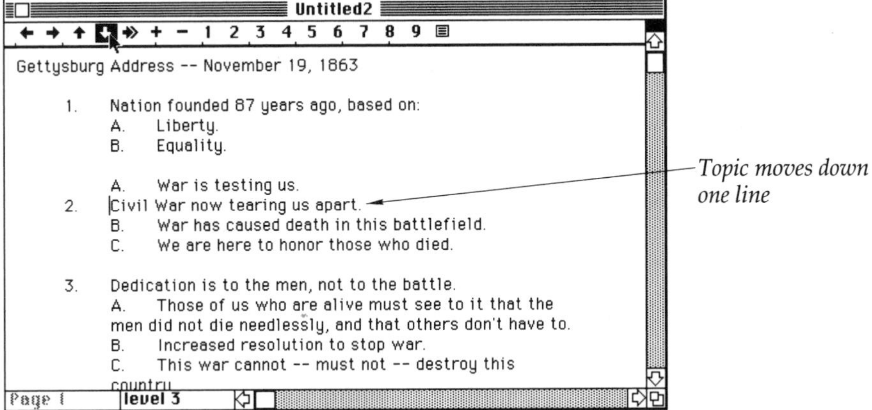

Figure 3-4
Moving a heading one line at a time.

Moving by Topic

Moving selected lines one line at a time is useful for fine-tuning an outline, but often you'll want to rearrange your document more radically, for instance, by placing all of part 3—the major topic, its subtopics, and all body text paragraphs—before part 2. You do this with a technique called *topic selection.*

To select a topic and all its associated subtext, double-click in the selection bar next to the topic. Clicking the Move Up icon now moves the selected topic up not by one line but by one topic—that is, to the point before the preceding topic of the same level as the one you selected.

For example, suppose that you double-clicked the topic for part 3 of the outline in Figure 3-3. All part 3, including its three subheadings, would be selected. If you then clicked the Move Up icon, all part 3 would move to before part 2.

A word of caution: The appearance of a block of selected text gives no hint as to how it was selected, so be sure to remember which operation—topic selection or line selection—you performed, before you move a topic.

Demoting a Topic to Body Text ➾

Normally, the text you type in Outline view consists of topics of varying levels. Sometimes, however, you may want to enter a short paragraph of body text within an outline and format it in the *Normal* style, like regular text entered in Document view. (In Outline view, *body text* is any paragraph that is not formatted as a topic.) One method is to enter the text as an outline topic (level 1 for maximum line length), and then select anywhere within the text and click the Demote to Body Text (➾) icon. To continue entering topics, simply start a new line and click the Promote or Demote icon.

You can also change body text to an outline topic by selecting anywhere within the text and clicking the Promote or Demote icon. Keep clicking until you establish the level you want.

TIP

Taking a Quick Look at a Body Text Paragraph
If you want to take a quick look at the full text of a paragraph without returning to Document view, select the paragraph and click the Promote icon to change the paragraph to a level 1 topic. Remember to return it to body text by clicking the Demote to Body Text icon when you are finished. Note that when you return the paragraph to body text, it will be assigned the *Normal* style. If the paragraph was originally in *Normal* style, this won't be a problem. If, however, the paragraph was originally in some other style, you have to return it to that style manually.

Expanding and Collapsing Subtopics and Text + –

Word lets you collapse and expand the subtopics and text under a topic so that you can view only those topics you want to see. When you select a main (level 1) topic and click the Collapse (–) icon, the levels underneath disappear; a dotted line appears under a collapsed level to indicate hidden topics. The Expand (+) icon does the reverse: When you select a topic and click this icon, all subtopics and the first line of each text paragraph appear. Word does not print collapsed text, so if you want to print the entire outline, be sure all levels are expanded. If you do print an outline with some text collapsed, the dotted line representing collapsed text does not appear in the printed version.

TIP

Moving a Main Topic by Collapsing and Moving It
In addition to the topic-selection method described above, you can also move a main topic along with all its subtopics by selecting the main topic, clicking the Collapse icon, and then clicking the Move Up or Move Down icon. Word treats the topic and its subtopics as one group.

Showing Specific Levels 1 2 3...

The Expand and Collapse icons work on topics that you select; the number icons, on the other hand, collapse and expand one or more topic levels for the entire outline. For example, if you click the number 2 in the icon bar, the outline displays levels 1 and 2; any higher numbered levels are collapsed. (See Figure 3-5.) When you use the number icons, regular text paragraphs are always collapsed, so if you want to see all topic levels without body text, simply choose an icon number higher than the number of levels in your outline. And because Word does not print collapsed levels, you can use the number icons to create a simplified outline for distribution to others while maintaining a complete version for your own use. (An alternative is to extract a table of contents from the outline, a subject covered in more detail in Chapter 13, "Creating a Table of Contents and Index.")

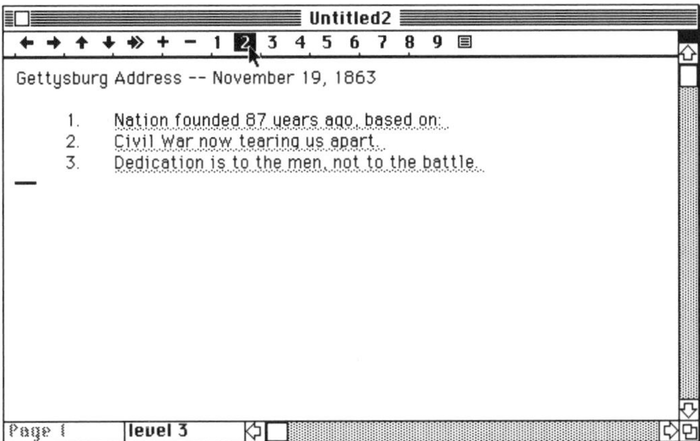

Figure 3-5
Topics collapsed with the 2 icon.

Showing All Text

The Show All icon to the right of the number icons works like a switch. Click it once to collapse the body text while displaying all topic levels. As with collapsed levels, collapsed body text is indicated by a dotted line on the screen. Click it again to display all topic levels and the first line of each paragraph of body text. If the body text is longer than one line, ellipses (...) appear at the end of the line.

TIP

Changing the Format of Outline Text
In Outline view, all text is shown in a single-spaced *Normal* style, even if the *Normal* style was defined as double spaced. This is true despite the fact that topic levels are assigned styles. The look produced by these styles becomes visible only when you go to Document view, where you see that the level styles are the same as the *Normal* style, except that they call for boldface and add a little space before each topic.

To change a *level* style, you can go through the text and format each instance manually, but it is far easier to change the format of all instances of each style by using style sheets. Simply choose Define Styles from the Format menu, click on the name of the *level* style you want to change, then choose the formats you want from the appropriate menus, and click Define and Cancel, as you learned in Chapter 2. See Chapter 9, "Working with Style Sheets," for a thorough discussion of this topic.

■ *Numbering*

You can use the Renumber command from the Document menu to number or renumber an outline with up to nine levels. The command affects all selected topics; if no text is selected, the entire document is renumbered. To select all of the outline except its title—which you probably don't want to number—use the Shift-click method: Click at the beginning of the desired selection and, while holding down the Shift key, click at the end. All topics between the first click and the second are selected.

Once the topics are selected, choose the Renumber command; the dialog box shown in Figure 3-6 appears. Click the All button beside the Paragraphs label. The Start At field probably contains a 1. If it doesn't, the first paragraph selected will start with a number other than 1. If you want to start at a number other than what Word proposes, simply select the contents of the field and type in the number.

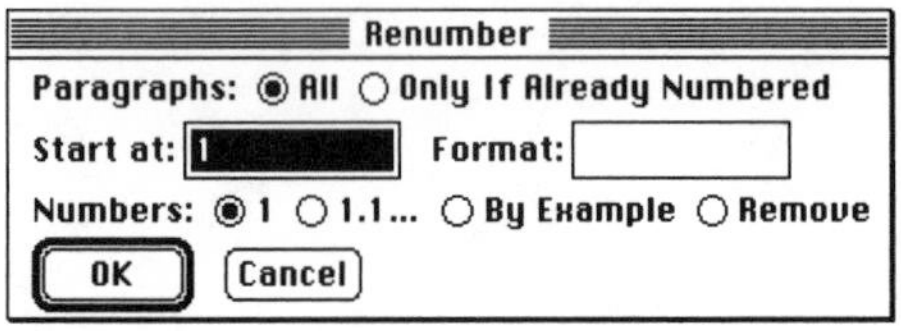

Renumber
Paragraphs: ◉ All ○ Only If Already Numbered
Start at: 1 Format:
Numbers: ◉ 1 ○ 1.1... ○ By Example ○ Remove
OK Cancel

Figure 3-6
The Renumber dialog box.

Unless you specify otherwise, Word numbers each level starting with numeral 1. The numbering repeats for each set of levels, producing a result like that shown in Figure 3-7.

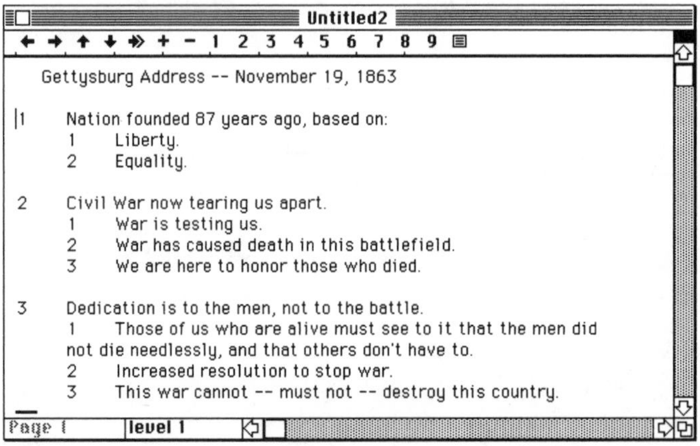

Untitled2
1 2 3 4 5 6 7 8 9

Gettysburg Address -- November 19, 1863

1 Nation founded 87 years ago, based on:
1 Liberty.
2 Equality.

2 Civil War now tearing us apart.
1 War is testing us.
2 War has caused death in this battlefield.
3 We are here to honor those who died.

3 Dedication is to the men, not to the battle.
1 Those of us who are alive must see to it that the men did not die needlessly, and that others don't have to.
2 Increased resolution to stop war.
3 This war cannot -- must not -- destroy this country.

Page 1 level 1

Figure 3-7
Portion of a numbered outline.

You are not restricted to this numbering system, however. Word provides a great deal of flexibility in outline numbering. In addition to Arabic numerals, you can use uppercase or lowercase Roman numerals, uppercase or lowercase letters, or any combination of these. Furthermore, you can follow the numbers or letters with a period, comma, parenthesis, or any other nonalphanumeric character.

For example, suppose you wanted to number a five-level outline using this standard format:

I.A.1.a.i.

That is, the level 1 topics are to be preceded by an uppercase Roman numeral, the level 2 topics by an uppercase letter, the level 3 topics by an Arabic numeral, and so on; and each number or letter is to be followed by a period. You would enter the desired format in the Format field, as shown in Figure 3-8a, and click OK. The resulting outline would resemble Figure 3-8b.

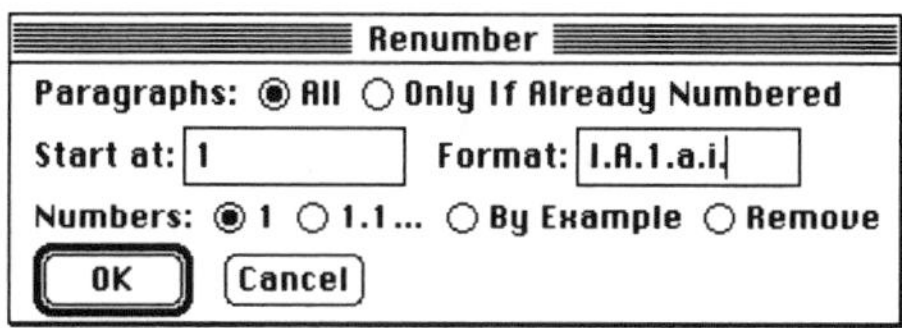

Figure 3-8a
A numbering style specified in the Format field.

Untitled1

Gettysburg Address -- November 19, 1863

I. Nation founded 87 years ago, based on:
  A. Liberty.
  B. Equality.

II. Civil War now tearing us apart.
  A. War is testing us.
  B. War has caused death in this battlefield.
  C. We are here to honor those who died.

III. Dedication is to the men, not to the battle.
  A. Those of us who are alive must see to it that the men did not die needlessly, and that others don't have to.
  B. Increased resolution to stop war.
  C. This war cannot -- must not -- destroy this country.

Page 1 level 2

Figure 3-8b
The result after renumbering.

To have each topic reflect both its own level and the levels above it, click the 1.1 option in the Numbers field. In the outline shown in Figure 3-8b, for example, this option would cause the B section of part I to be numbered *I.B.* instead of merely *B*.

Whether you use the 1.1 option or the 1 option, you can easily rearrange and then renumber topics by repeating the numbering process. Simply select the affected text, choose the Renumber command, specify the number format, and click OK.

As you can see, the numbering function is not only flexible but easy to use. If you experiment further with the Renumber command, however, you'll find that it reveals some complexities and, occasionally, offers frustrations. For example, although you might never use this information, it's interesting to know that you can have a character precede as well as follow your outline numbers. Word inserts a *starting character* before each entry if the first character you enter in the Format field is nonalphanumeric—a parenthesis, for example. Such a character is optional, as is an *ending character* such as the last period in the Format field of Figure 3-8a. But beware: If you dispense with an ending character—a period, for example—no period will appear after Arabic numerals in your outline, but one will still follow all letters and Roman numerals. Word does this to prevent confusion in a case such as the following:

A A New Way to Number Outlines

A word of warning: The Renumber command may sometimes produce results that initially surprise you. Simply experiment until you get the look you want. A few more instructions and tips follow:

- ❑ The Start At option works only for the first topic level.
- ❑ To remove outline numbering, double-click the Remove option in the Renumber dialog box. Double-clicking any of the radio buttons is the same as selecting it and clicking OK.
- ❑ If you change the order of part of the outline after numbering it, select the text and the first topic level above it that still has correct numbering. When you choose the Renumber command, the By Example option is selected, and the Start At field displays the number of the first selected paragraph. Word assumes that you want to use the numbering format of the first paragraph you selected unless you specify otherwise.
- ❑ If you want to number only some topics in an outline, place a number (any number will do) beside those topics as you create the outline. When you are done, select the entire outline and click the Only If Already Numbered option. Those topics without a number will be skipped.

- If you follow the numbering format with a space, Word follows each number in the outline with a space instead of the customary tab character. However, you must first remove the numbering before using this format.
- You can change the numbering manually and then use the Sort command from the Document menu to reorder your outline. See Chapter 14, "Documents with Tables and Lists," for more information on the Sort command.
- You can use the Renumber command on any set of paragraphs, not only outlines. Lawyers are fond of this feature, using it often in contracts.

■ *Using Outlining as an Editing Tool*

You can use Word's outlining feature as an editing tool in two ways. First, you can navigate in a document very easily in Outline view—much more easily than by scrolling manually or by searching for key words in Document view. Second, you can rearrange large sections of text more efficiently with outlining icons than with the Cut and Paste commands.

Navigating in Your Document

In Word, you can manually scroll through a document to find what you're looking for, you can use the Find command to look for key words, or you can use the Go To command from the Search menu to go to a specific page. None of these methods can take you directly to the beginning of a section of text, but the outlining feature can, through a method called *synchronized scrolling*. The procedure is simple. Display the document in Outline view, and then click in the vertical scroll bar until the heading you want is the topmost line in the window. Now return to Document view. That heading appears at the top of the window.

Synchronized scrolling works even better when you split a window into two panes and then look at the document in Outline view in one pane and in Document view in the other pane. Starting in Outline view, drag down the solid black bar (the split bar) at the top of the scroll bar to divide the window. Then click in the bottom pane, and press Command-U to change the bottom pane to Document view. Now scroll a bit through the outline in the top pane; the topmost heading in the bottom pane changes as you scroll. This synchronization makes it easy to work on the structure of a document in one pane and on the body text in the other. To remove the split from the window, click in the pane you want to keep, and then drag the split bar to the top or bottom of the window. Chapter 4 discusses split-screen techniques in more detail.

TIP

Entering Body Text in Outline View
When you enter body text in Outline view, you see only the first line, which is a problem when you write whole paragraphs because you can't see what you're typing. Synchronized scrolling can help you with this problem. Type the first line of the paragraph, scroll the window so that the line is at the top of the screen, and press Command-U: The line appears at the top of the screen in Document view. When you are finished typing, toggle back to Outline view.

Moving Paragraphs

You've already seen how to use the Move Up and Move Down icons to move topics around in an outline. You can also use this feature to move entire paragraphs within a document without having to carefully select text, cut it out, set a new insertion point, and paste it in again. Simply select the paragraphs and click the appropriate icon. (See Figure 3-9.) When you return to Document view, you see that all characters in the selected text are transported, including blank lines and forced page breaks. You can remove these if they adversely affect the layout of the document.

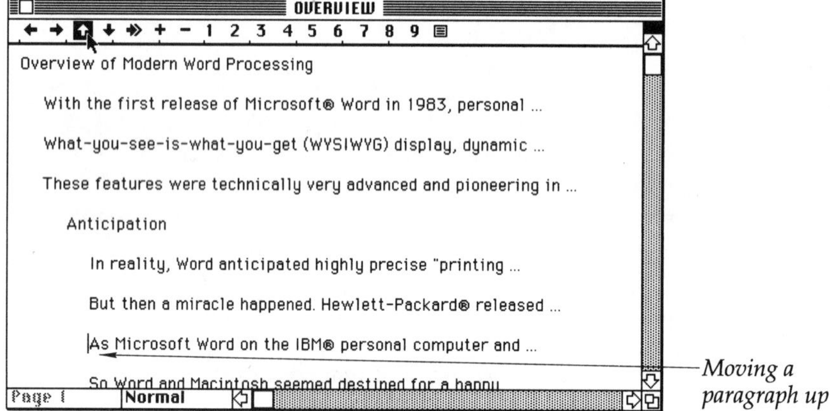

Figure 3-9
Moving a paragraph within an outline.

Points to Remember

- ❑ In Outline view, any change to the outline changes the document itself.
- ❑ Outlines can contain two kinds of paragraphs: *topics,* which are formatted as level 1 through level 9, and *body text,* all other styles of paragraphs. Only the first line of a body text paragraph is shown followed by ellipses (...).
- ❑ The way in which you select a topic determines how the Move Up and Move Down icons work. If you double-click in the selection bar, the icons move the selected topic before or after the nearest topic of the same level. With any other method of selection, the icons simply move the selected block up or down one paragraph at a time.
- ❑ The way in which you select a topic also determines how the Expand and Collapse icons work. If you click in the selection bar or otherwise select the entire topic, the icons collapse or expand all the subtopics at once. If instead you select only part of the topic or merely set the insertion point somewhere in it, each click on the icons collapses or expands one subtopic level at a time.

Techniques

See "Mouse and Keyboard Shortcuts" for an overview of the icons in the Outline icon bar.

Scroll to a specific section (synchronized scrolling in one pane)

❶ Enter Outline view.

❷ Scroll until the section you want to see is at the top of the window.

❸ Return to Document view.

Show Outline view in one pane and Document view in the other

❶ Drag down the split bar (the black bar at the top of the vertical scroll bar) as far as you want.

❷ Click in the pane you want to appear in Outline view.

❸ Choose the Outlining command (Command-U).

❹ When you scroll in one pane, the other pane scrolls accordingly.

Select a topic and all its subtopics and body text (Outline view)

❶ Double-click in the selection bar.

Promote or demote a group of adjacent topics

❶ Select the block to be affected and click the appropriate icon.

Promote body text to a topic

❶ Select the paragraph to be promoted and click the Promote icon.

Move paragraphs of body text

❶ Select the paragraphs to be moved and click the Move Up or Move Down icon.

Print a simplified outline

❶ Collapse the outline to show only the topic levels you want to print.

❷ Choose Print from the File menu.

Move a topic and its subtopics and text up or down by level

❶ Select the entire topic by double-clicking in the selection bar to the left of the topic.

❷ Click the Move Up or Move Down icon.

Or,

❶ Collapse all levels beneath the level of the topic you want to move.

❷ Select the topic and click the Move Up or Move Down icon.

The collapsed material moves with its topic.

Number or renumber an outline

❶ Select the text to be renumbered. (If none is selected, the command affects the entire document.)

❷ Choose Renumber from the Document menu.

❸ Specify the options you want to use.

The 1.1 option precedes the number for a topic with the numbers of the topics above it (for example, *1.2.1.*).

The By Example option causes Word to use the numbering format of the first selected paragraph.

❹ Click OK.

Specify a numbering format

❶ Unless you indicate otherwise, Word uses Arabic numerals followed by periods.

❷ Enter the format you want to use in the Format field of the Renumber dialog box (for example, *I.A.i.*).

Remove outline numbering

❶ Click Remove in the Renumber dialog box.

❷ Click OK.

■ *Mouse and Keyboard Shortcuts*

In Outline view, as in Document view, the keypad keys are available for moving the insertion point.

To	Mouse Click	Keyboard Press	Keypad Press
Promote topic	⬅	left arrow	
Demote topic	➡	right arrow	
Move topic up	⬆	up arrow	
Move topic down	⬇	down arrow	
Demote topic to body text	➡»	Command-right arrow	
Collapse next lower topic or text	−		–
Expand subtopics and text	+		+
Collapse selected topic			Command- –
Expand selected topic			Command- +
Display to a level	1 2 3...		
Display all levels and first line of body text (toggles)	▤		* or =

To manipulate the outline while in Document View, press Option-Command-T and then press the keys indicated below:

To	Keyboard Press	Keypad Press
Promote topic	left arrow or K	4
Demote topic	right arrow or L	6
Move topic up	up arrow	8
Move topic down	down arrow	2
Demote topic to body text	Command-right arrow	

Writing and Editing Techniques

With Word, the process of writing, or entering text, is nearly indistinguishable from rewriting, or editing. Letters, words, and entire phrases can be added easily, deleted, or moved around, even during the initial writing stages. In this chapter, therefore, writing and editing are generally treated as one concept. In the pages that follow, you'll examine in greater detail some of the features and techniques introduced in Chapters 1 and 2, and you'll cover some new ground. More specifically, you will learn about setting up Word exactly the way you like it, entering standard and special characters, selecting text you want to manipulate, moving text within a document, finding and changing text, and saving a document.

■ *Customizing Word*

Before you get into serious writing and editing with Word, you need to optimize the Word environment for your particular needs. You can do this in three ways: by making changes to the Control Panel, by recording your preferences in the Word Settings file, and by adding items to Word's menus.

The Control Panel

The Control Panel desk accessory, shown in Figure 4-1, controls several characteristics of the Macintosh keyboard and screen display. You can alter these characteristics with the Word startup disk or any startup disk on which the Control Panel desk accessory is installed. The changes to the Control Panel are stored in the Mac's Parameter RAM and are kept fresh by the Mac's clock battery; they remain in effect until you change them again or until the battery fails or is removed. Because the Control Panel is part of the Macintosh system software, any changes you make to the Control Panel affect not only Word but also any other program you work with. (Be sure you have the latest versions of the Mac system software.)

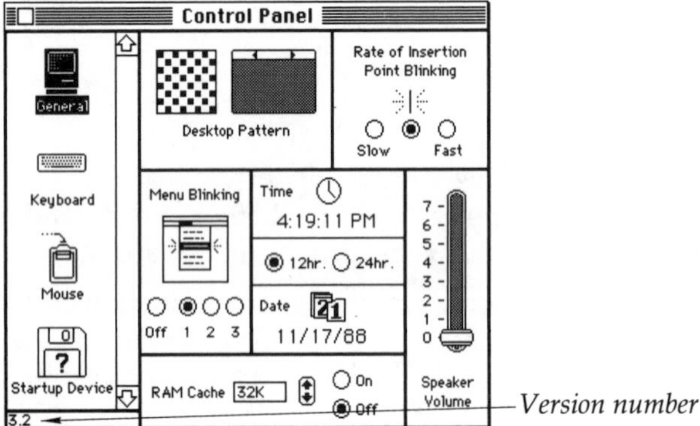

Figure 4-1
The Control Panel, version 3.2.

The Control Panel options of primary interest are these:

- ❑ Key repeat rate (displayed when you click the Keyboard icon): Varies the rate at which the character keys repeat when they are held down. Touch typists may want to set the key repeat at fast or moderately fast. Others should keep it at slow or moderate.
- ❑ Delay until repeat (displayed when you click the Keyboard icon): Varies the time interval after which the keys start to repeat. Touch typists can choose a short delay; others do best with a moderate delay.

- ❑ Double-click speed (displayed when you click the Mouse icon): Varies the interval between successive clicks that the Mac interprets as a double-click. Keep it at the slow setting if you are new to double-clicking. If you're comfortable with the mouse, you might prefer the fastest setting.
- ❑ Mouse tracking (displayed when you click the Mouse icon): Alters the tracking ratio of the mouse and pointer. When you select one of the mouse options, the pointer moves in a variable ratio depending on the speed of the mouse—the faster the mouse moves, the farther the pointer travels. If you choose the tablet option, the pointer moves in a constant 1:1 ratio with the mouse, regardless of speed. Choose this setting if you're using a graphics tablet or have trouble positioning the pointer accurately.
- ❑ Rate of insertion-point blinking (displayed when you click the General icon): Changes the rate at which the insertion point blinks. A slow blink makes the insertion point hard to locate in a full screen of text. Choose the medium or fast speed to enhance its visibility.
- ❑ Menu blinking (displayed when you click the General icon): Changes the number of times a chosen menu item blinks before the command is carried out. Most people set this at one blink to save a little time.

The Word Settings File

No word processor can please all the people all the time. Word is extremely accommodating, however, letting you personalize certain operating parameters to make your life easier. Your preferences are recorded in a file called Word Settings, which you can see in the System Folder on the Finder's desktop. If this file is erased, damaged, or renamed, Word starts over again with its "default" (normal) settings. The following chart lists categories of preferences that the Word Settings file stores, gives Word's default settings, and lays out your options. You can set new defaults for Page Setup, Styles, and Section formats by clicking the Set Default button in the relevant dialog box. Additional details on choosing new defaults are provided in the chapters that deal with these topics.

Settings Stored in the Word Settings File

	Default	**Your options**
Settings Preferences		
Full/Short Menus	Short Menus	Either Short Menus or Full Menus
Hide/Show ¶	Hide ¶	Either Hide ¶ or Show ¶
Measurements	Inches	Inches, Centimeters, or Points

	Default	Your options
Show Hidden Text	On	On or Off
Display as Printed	On	On or Off
Keep in Memory	Neither File nor Program	File, Memory, or both
Printer setup state		
Print Hidden Text	Off	On or Off
Print Quality	Faster	Best, Faster, Draft (LaserWriter only)
Print Cover Page (LaserWriter only)	Off	On or Off
Styles		
	Normal and the other *automatic* styles are set to default definitions.	You can change the *automatic* styles and add your own styles. (See Chapter 9.)
Dialog window placement		
	Standard placement	If you move a window, Word remembers the new position.
Page Setup options		
	U.S. Letter, Tall, 8.5x11 in., 1 in. top and bottom margins, 1.25 in. left and right margins, 0.5 in. default tab stops. (Choose Page Setup from the File menu to see the rest.)	Word remembers all changes made in the dialog box.
Section formats		
	New Page section start, numeric page numbering, 0.5 in. header/footer margins, 1 Column, endnotes included.	Word remembers all changes made in the dialog box.

	Default	Your options
Format menu		
	Plain Text, Bold, Italic, Underline, Outline, Shadow	Word remembers any character format you add to the menu.
Font menu		
	Boston, Chicago, Geneva, London, Monaco, New York, Venice, Zapf Dingbats if installed in your System file.	Word remembers any font you add to the menu.
Work menu		
	No menu	Add document, glossary, and style names.

Exploiting Memory-Management Options

If your Macintosh has at least one megabyte of memory, you can take advantage of the memory-management option recorded in the Word Settings file.

First, a little background—what exactly is memory management? Normally, Word loads only parts, or *segments,* of itself into memory as needed. When a segment is no longer needed, it remains in memory until Word needs to use the memory for another segment. Similarly, Word loads only part of your document at a time. As you scroll through the document, Word loads additional parts of the document while returning other parts to disk.

This memory-management system makes sense if your Mac has little memory to spare, but all the loading and unloading of program and file segments can considerably slow the program's operation. If you like, you can tell Word to load nearly all the program into memory at once. (Word will still load its printing and file-conversion segments only when they are needed.) When you launch the program, it takes a little longer for the blank document window to appear, but thereafter Word runs briskly. And you can further instruct Word to load and keep an entire document in memory. Again, you will notice a delay as a long document loads, but subsequent operations are speeded up, because Word doesn't need to access the disk drives as often.

You can even open multiple documents at once—theoretically as many as 25—and load each one entirely into memory (as long as there is enough free memory to accommodate them).

Word lets you specify whether you want to load the program or files into memory for the current session only or for all sessions; if you choose the latter, Word records the change in the Settings file when you quit. To set the memory-management options, choose Preferences from the Edit menu. The dialog box shown in Figure 4-2 appears.

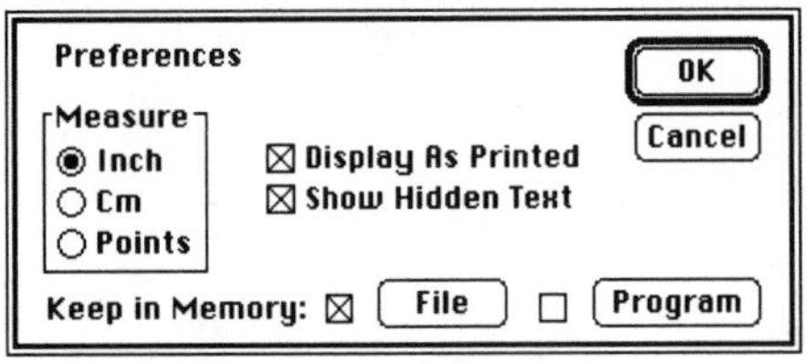

Preferences

Measure
◉ Inch
○ Cm
○ Points

☒ Display As Printed
☒ Show Hidden Text

OK
Cancel

Keep in Memory: ☒ File ☐ Program

Figure 4-2
The Preferences dialog box.

- ❑ To load all of Word for the current session only, click the Program button.
- ❑ To load all of Word for all sessions, click the check box beside the Program button and click OK.
- ❑ To load the currently open document for the current session only, click the File button.
- ❑ To load all opened documents for all sessions, click the check box beside the File button and click OK.

TIP

Using Memory-Management Options with One Disk Drive
You can particularly benefit from the memory-management options if you have only one disk drive. Normally, Word would keep asking you to swap disks in and out of the drive as you work with your documents. With both Word and the documents in memory, however, you can minimize disk swapping and thus make your work go much faster.

How well the memory-management options work depends on how much free memory your Mac has available. The options fare better with a Macintosh Plus, SE, or II than with a 512 KB Mac, because the first three machines have a lot more memory available. In addition, memory-gobbling utilities and accessories, such as Switcher, eat into the space otherwise used by Word's memory-management options and make them less effective.

Interestingly, although these memory-management options make the program more responsive, they don't affect the overall length of your editing session. This is because Word reserves a block of memory for keeping track of the changes you make to a document, and the size of this block never varies. Preloading the program into memory affects the responsiveness of the program when you issue a command, and preloading a document affects the speed of operations such as scrolling and searching and replacing.

TIP

Using Disk Caching with Word's Memory-Management Options
The Macintosh system software lets you control an aspect of memory management through a technique called *disk caching,* in which you set aside some of the Mac's memory to store frequently accessed blocks of the documents you work with; this memory then becomes unavailable for the program. (See the RAM cache option in the Control Panel shown in Figure 4-1.) Because Word does a good job of managing the memory allocated to it and to your documents, it is usually counterproductive to have both disk caching and the memory-management options set at the same time. In most cases, you'll benefit most from using Word's memory-management preferences alone.

Saving the Word Settings File

As you saw, the Word Settings file incorporates a lot of information, and if you make many changes to the file, re-creating it can be tiresome if the file is damaged or lost. To be on the safe side, you can make a backup. Alternatively, you might periodically back up your working copy of the Word disk. This saves the Word Settings file as well as any custom dictionaries or glossaries you create and place on the disk.

If you like to switch between your preferences and Word's defaults, you can make several copies of your working disk, each containing a different settings file. A more efficient approach, especially suitable if you have a hard disk, is to store several settings files on one working copy of Word. Here is how to do it:

❶ Start Word and make the desired changes to the settings.

❷ Quit Word.

❸ Locate the Word Settings file in the System Folder and give it a descriptive name, such as *Newspaper Layout* for a file geared toward desktop publishing or *Novel Prefs.* for a file to help you write your bestsellers.

Repeat the process for each settings file. (See Figure 4-3.) Remember to rename the file each time, or you'll overwrite the old preferences. To use a particular settings file, locate it on the desktop and double-click it to start Word. Word uses these settings as it loads. However, any preference changes you make during that session are still recorded in a file called Word Settings in the System folder when you quit Word. For this reason, be sure you have a duplicate copy of the original Word Settings file, and then rename the new version with the name of the settings file you double-clicked to start Word.

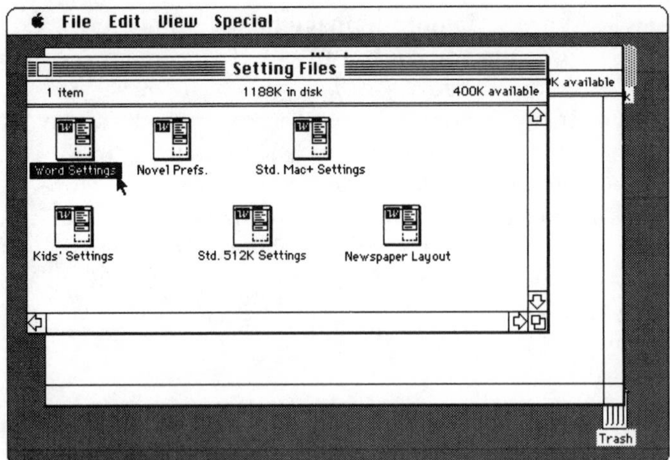

Figure 4-3
Sample settings files.

Menus

Word is one of the few Macintosh programs to let you change the contents of its menus—in effect to create custom commands! You can add character formats to the Format menu, fonts and font sizes to the Font menu, and document, glossary, and style names to a user-defined menu called the Work menu. Simply press Option-Command- + (press Option, Command, and the plus key), and then select the format, font, document, or whatever you want to add. Experiment by adding a document to the Work menu:

❶ Press Option-Command- +. The pointer changes to a large plus symbol.

❷ Choose Open from the File menu, and double-click on the filename you want to add. A new menu name, Work, appears in the menu bar, and the menu bar blinks to signal that the item has been added. Note, however, that Word does not actually open the document.

❸ Pull down the Work menu; the first item on it is the name of your document. Choosing the new "command" opens the document.

The Work menu is especially convenient for documents that you use frequently or need quick access to, such as boilerplate text or a list of ideas that you add to throughout the day. Later chapters describe how to add glossaries and styles to the Work menu. Adding to the Font and Format menus is just as easy. To add a character format, for example, simply press Option-Command- +, choose Character from the Format menu, and click on the option.

You can even add many items to a menu at the same time. Begin by calling up the appropriate dialog box—the Character dialog box, for instance. Then press Option-Command- +, click on the font or format you want to add, and repeat these two steps as many times as you want while the dialog box is displayed. Each time you add an item, the menu bar blinks. If you wish, you can also hold the Shift key down as you click on a series of items to add to the Work menu. If you try to add an item that is already on the menu, you'll hear a beep, but no harm will be done. Click Cancel when you are finished. Resist the temptation to add every conceivable option to the menus, for the amount of free memory decreases with each addition.

Removing options that you don't use from these menus is simple: Press Option-Command- – (hyphen), pull down the appropriate menu, and choose the option you want to delete. The pointer is a large minus sign when you're in the delete mode.

■ *Discovering Word's True Characters*

On your Macintosh keyboard, you'll find represented the alphabetic, numeric, and punctuation characters that appear on a typewriter keyboard. However, Word supplies many characters that a typewriter, or even other word processors, don't. And some familiar characters work, in Word, in unfamiliar ways. This section provides a brief overview of some of the program's character features. For a thorough discussion of fonts, see Chapter 7, "Character Formatting."

Special Font Characters

Word 3.0 comes with several fonts, or typefaces, that comprise standard characters as well as some additional ones. To see the standard characters in a given font, choose the Key Caps desk accessory from the Apple menu and choose the font you want to see from the Key Caps menu in the menu bar. (See Figure 4-4. In Key Caps desk accessory versions before 3.0, you can view the Chicago font only.) To see the characters available with different key combinations, hold down the shift key, the Option key, or the Shift-Option combination. Each time you press one of these, the Key Caps keyboard displays the set of characters produced when you hold down that key and press the keys on the keyboard. When you type on the Mac keyboard or click on the Key Caps keyboard, text appears in the field above the keyboard. You can cut or copy the text to paste it into a Word document.

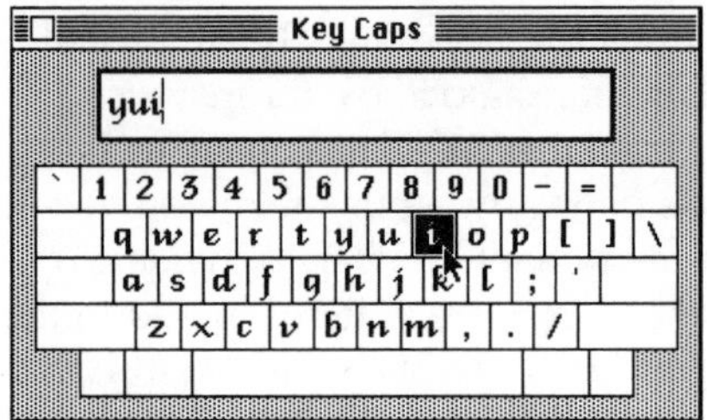

Figure 4-4
Key Caps with the Venice font.

Word is an international program that lets you add accent (diacritical) marks to characters by pressing the following key combinations. The accent is added to the next character typed; pressing the Option key combination twice creates only the accent character.

Press	**To get**
Option-`	` (grave accent)
Option-e	´ (acute accent)
Option-i	^ (circumflex)
Option-n	~ (tilde)
Option-u	¨ (umlaut)

You can also buy fonts that have special zero-width characters. Typing one of these characters produces a symbol that overlays the next character typed—useful for creating obscure accented or combined letters. And you can use font-editor programs such as Fontographer from Altsys Corporation to make adjustments to one of Word's fonts. Unless the font editor supports the LaserWriter and PostScript, however, the font changes you make may not appear when you print the document.

Almost all fonts contain not only text characters but graphic characters as well. The chart in Figure 4-5 shows some of the characters found in common fonts. To see one example of a graphic character, press Shift-Option-` (grave accent); as the chart indicates, the current font and point size determine which character is entered. Use the Key Caps desk accessory to find the key sequences for other graphic characters, such as the bullet (•, Option-8) and the paragraph mark (¶, Option-7).

You can also use fonts containing nonalphabetic images such as Cairo, Taliesin, Symbol, and Zapf Dingbats. (The last two are high-resolution fonts which print well on the LaserWriter.) The symbol font has a special significance: Word uses it to construct equations in its formula-translation feature. See Appendix D, "Mathematical Formulas in Word," for more information.

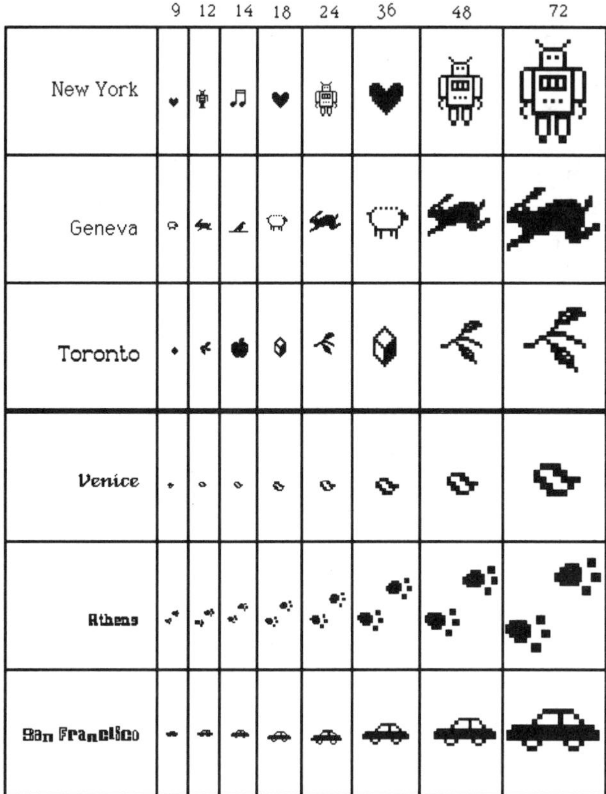

Figure 4-5
Some graphic characters available in Word fonts.

Hyphens, Dashes, and Spaces

Use hyphens to join words together, to make a compound word or phrase, such as *built-in* or *state-of-the-art*. When you press the hyphen key (located to the immediate right of the zero key), you create what is termed a *normal* hyphen. If a hyphenated word or phrase appears at the end of a line, Word may break (wordwrap) the line at the hyphen, like this:

built-
in

or this:

The new toy is a three-
wheeled cart.

If you then edit the text in a way that affects the wordwrap, Word rejoins the compound word on one line.

If you don't want Word to break a line at a hyphen, you can enter a required, or *nonbreaking*, hyphen by pressing Command- ~ (the Command key and the tilde key). And if you want a word to be hyphenated only if it falls at the end of a line, enter an *optional* hyphen by pressing Command- – (the Command key and the hyphen key). Optional hyphens have no width and usually don't appear on the screen unless the word breaks at the end of the line. Word inserts optional hyphens when you choose Hyphenate from the Document menu. To display optional hyphens (whether inserted by you or by Word), choose Show ¶ from the Edit menu. Figure 4-6 shows the appearance of the three types of hyphens when Show ¶ is on. (For more information on hyphens and the Hyphenate command, see Chapter 12, "Document Formatting and Printing.")

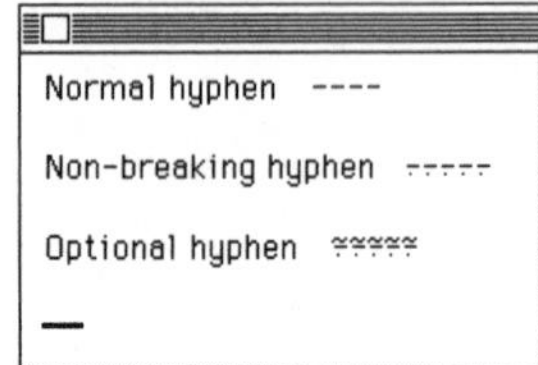

Figure 4-6
The three types of hyphens.

Similar to hyphens are the less frequently used *en* (–) and *em* (—) dashes, created by pressing Option- – and Shift-Option- –. The em dash is the typesetter's equivalent of two hyphens—the common alternative—used when you want to indicate a break in thought, for example. The en dash, which is a bit wider than a hyphen, is used primarily with ranges of numbers, as in *1987–88* or *pp. 18–24*. The en dash is also used to join two terms when one of them consists of two separate words or a hyphenated word (for example, New York–based, first-in–first-out accounting). Word will break at these dashes if they occur at the end of a line.

With Word, as with a typewriter, pressing the Spacebar creates a blank space. In Word, however, this space is a character, appearing as a small dot when Show ¶ is on. Actually, you can produce two kinds of spaces. When you press the Spacebar alone, you insert a *soft space;* Word understands that it can break a line at the space and that it can adjust the width of the space in justified paragraphs. When you press Option-Spacebar, Word inserts a *hard space,* at which it will not break the line. You might use a hard space to keep compound words, names, or addresses on the same line. You can also insert this character after the numbers in a numbered list when you're using justified alignment. That way, when Word adjusts the width of the spaces within each line, the space after each number remains unchanged. Use this type of space judiciously; too many hard spaces will make the right edge of your text look very ragged or, if you are using justified alignment, will cause unacceptably wide spaces between words.

ASCII Codes and Characters

A little-known but useful feature of Word is its dual ability to report the ASCII code of any selected character in a document and to enter any character into a document when you type its ASCII code. ASCII—the American Standard Code for Information Interchange—assigns a number for every letter, number, punctuation mark, and symbol so that different computers and different programs on the same computer can (at least theoretically) read one another's text. The letter *A*, for instance, is assigned the code 65. A complete set of ASCII codes for some common fonts, including Symbol and Zapf Dingbats, is given in Appendix B.

You can find the ASCII code for any character in a document by selecting the character and pressing Option-Command-Q. The code for that character appears in the status box in the lower left corner of the screen. If you type the ASCII code for a different character, the new code replaces the old in the status box; when you press the Return key, the new character replaces the old in text.

To enter a character without replacing another, place the insertion point where you want the character to appear and press Option-Command-Q. The word *Code* appears in the status box, and the character assigned to the number you type is entered in the document when you press the Return key. You can cancel this operation by pressing Command-(period) or by clicking in the window. Also, if you need to enter another character by its ASCII code, you can simply click in the status box without first pressing Option-Command-Q. The word *Code* appears again and you can then enter the ASCII code for the character.

■ *Basic Editing*

Of the basic actions required to enter and edit text, three of the most basic are creating paragraphs, backspacing to erase text, and selecting text before otherwise manipulating it. You practiced these actions in Chapters 1 and 2; this section gives you some additional information.

Creating Paragraphs

Pressing the Return (or Enter) key both completes a paragraph—leaving behind a paragraph mark, which is visible with Show ¶ on—and starts a new line and paragraph; this is called a *hard return*. Many of Word's formatting options, such as alignment and margins, apply to an entire paragraph; that is, the lines of text preceding the paragraph mark conform to the formatting options you chose for that paragraph. See Figure 4-7 for an example of this.

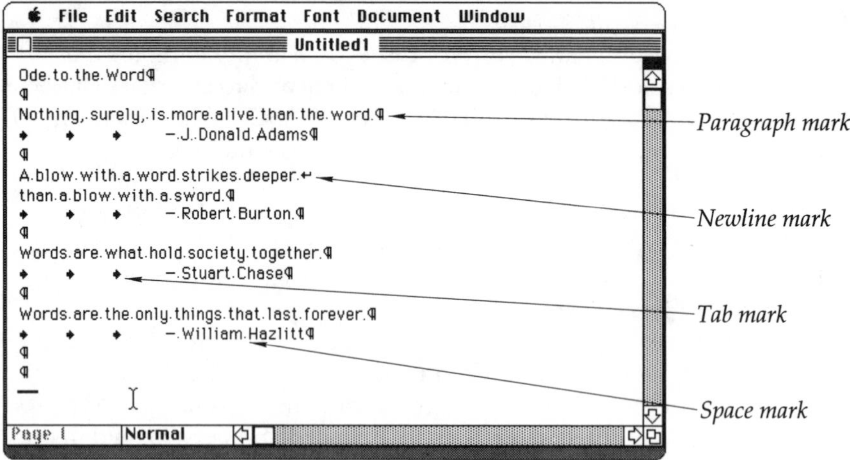

Figure 4-7
Sample text with formatting marks.

If you want to end a line without starting a new paragraph, press Shift-Return to enter a *soft return,* also known as a *newline mark.* You can use soft returns when you want to handle a series of lines as one paragraph. The paragraph formatting commands then apply to all the lines.

Finally, if you want to end a paragraph but not move the insertion point to the new line, press Option-Command-Return. This action is useful if you want to break a paragraph in the middle and then start typing at the end of the first paragraph.

Backspacing over Text

As you learned earlier, pressing the Backspace key (or the Delete key) deletes the character to the immediate left of the insertion point. If you try to backspace from one paragraph to another that has a different format, however, Word beeps when you reach the paragraph mark and refuses to backspace over it. It does this to keep you from losing any formatting. To delete the paragraph mark, you must select it (by double-clicking on it as though it were a word—although you can also double-click the pointer to the right of the paragraph mark) and then press the Backspace key.

Selecting Text

In Word, as in most other Macintosh applications, you first select the text you want to manipulate, and then you specify what you want to do with it. Most word processors for other types of computers require you to work in reverse: Choose the action first and then select the text. The latter method isn't as intuitive, and it usually requires you to reselect the same text block again and again if you want to perform a number of actions on it. Word lets you select text in a variety of ways. Some of these ways call for you to click in the *selection bar*; this is an invisible strip that runs along the left edge of the document window. The pointer becomes a right-pointing arrow when it is in the selection bar.

To select	Do this
An insertion point	Click at the desired spot.
One or more characters	Drag over them.
A whole word	Double-click on the word.
One sentence	Press the Command key, and click anywhere in the sentence.
One line	Position the pointer in the selection bar next to the line, and click.
One paragraph	Double-click in the selection bar next to the paragraph.
A range of text	Position the pointer in the selection bar at one end of the section, and drag to the other end of the section. *or* Click at one end of the section; Shift-click at the other end of the section.
Entire document	Press Option-Command-M. *or* Position the pointer in the selection bar, and Command-click.
Column of text (also called *block selection*)	Press the Option key, and drag through the column, as shown in Figure 4-8.

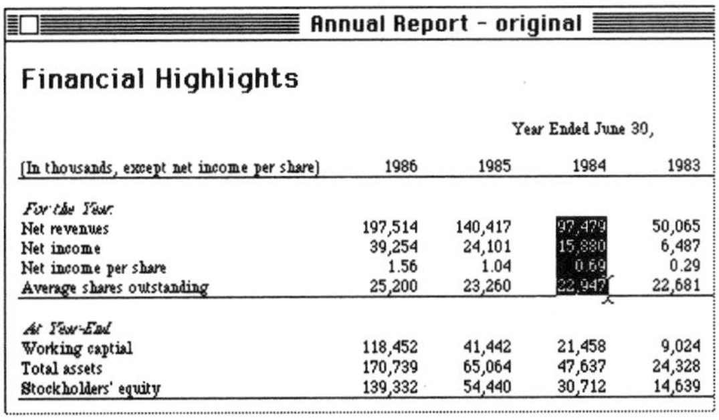

	Year Ended June 30,			
(In thousands, except net income per share)	1986	1985	1984	1983
For the Year				
Net revenues	197,514	140,417	97,479	50,065
Net income	39,254	24,101	15,880	6,487
Net income per share	1.56	1.04	0.69	0.29
Average shares outstanding	25,200	23,260	22,947	22,681
At Year-End				
Working captial	118,452	41,442	21,458	9,024
Total assets	170,739	65,064	47,637	24,328
Stockholders' equity	139,332	54,440	30,712	14,639

Figure 4-8
Selecting a column of text.

Shift-Clicking and Other Methods

Shift-clicking is one of the easiest ways to select text. You click once to set a starting point, or *anchor*, and then click again—this time holding down the Shift key—at a second point either before or after the anchor.

To see how this works, click within some text to set an anchor point, press the Shift key, click again at some other point (either before or after the anchor point), and then drag the mouse. Note that the selection is anchored where you first clicked the mouse button. When you release the mouse button after clicking the second time, the selection is set.

Another way to select text is a unit at a time. You can select text one word at a time by double-clicking on the first word and then dragging over the other words you want to select. Only whole words are added to the selection. If you press the Command key, click in a sentence, and then drag, the selection proceeds a sentence at a time. If you double-click in the selection bar and drag, you select one paragraph at a time, and clicking once in the selection bar and then dragging causes text to be selected one line at a time.

When you use this method, the unit selected becomes the anchor. For example, if you double-click in the selection bar and then drag, the entire paragraph you clicked in is always part of the selection, regardless of the direction in which you drag the mouse.

This technique can be very useful, but it can also be a bit frustrating if, for example, you are selecting paragraphs and then decide you want to end the selection in the middle of a paragraph. You won't be able to do it without deselecting the text and starting over using the Shift-click method.

Extending or Reducing a Selection

Once you have selected some text, you can extend or reduce the selection. The basic technique for doing this is to press the Shift key before you click. To extend the selection, move the pointer to the end of the text you want to add and Shift-click. To reduce the selection, move the pointer to the beginning of the text you want to deselect and Shift-click.

The original anchor that you set with your first mouse click is used as a reference point when you extend or reduce the selection. Thus, you can extend a selection in only one direction: the same direction as the original selection. If you try to extend it in the opposite direction, the text from the anchor to the new selection boundary will be selected, but text on the other side of the anchor will no longer be selected. Think of the selection as revolving around the anchor.

The unit of text that is added to or removed from the selection depends on the method you use to make the original selection. If you select text simply by dragging over it or by using the Shift-click method, you can Shift-click on a given character and extend or reduce the selection exactly to that character. If you double-click to select a word and then Shift-click in the middle of another word, the whole word will be added to the selection. Similarly, if you double-click in the selection bar to select a paragraph and then extend the selection by Shift-clicking in the middle of the next paragraph, the entire paragraph will be added. This also works for sentence and line selection.

■ *Copying and Moving Text*

Word gives you two ways to copy and move text. You can use the Cut, Copy, and Paste commands (all in the Edit menu), which use the Clipboard, or you can use the Copy To and Move To keyboard commands, which bypass the Clipboard. If you copied graphics into your document from another source, you can move or copy them with these commands; the procedure is the same as for text.

Both these methods let you move or copy text within a Word document or from one Word document to another. However, both files must be open if you want to use the Move To or Copy To command to transfer text between documents. This is not necessary with the Cut, Copy, and Paste commands.

It is also possible to use the Cut, Copy, and Paste commands to move or copy text to or from another Macintosh application, such as Microsoft Excel or Microsoft Works. This is discussed in Chapter 15, "Transferring Text and Graphics."

Using the Cut, Copy, and Paste Commands

To move or copy with the Edit menu commands:

❶ Select the block of text to be cut or copied.

❷ Choose Copy or Cut from the Edit menu.

❸ Indicate a new location for the text by selecting an insertion point (in the current document or another document).

❹ Choose the Paste command to enter the block at the insertion point. (See Figure 4-9.)

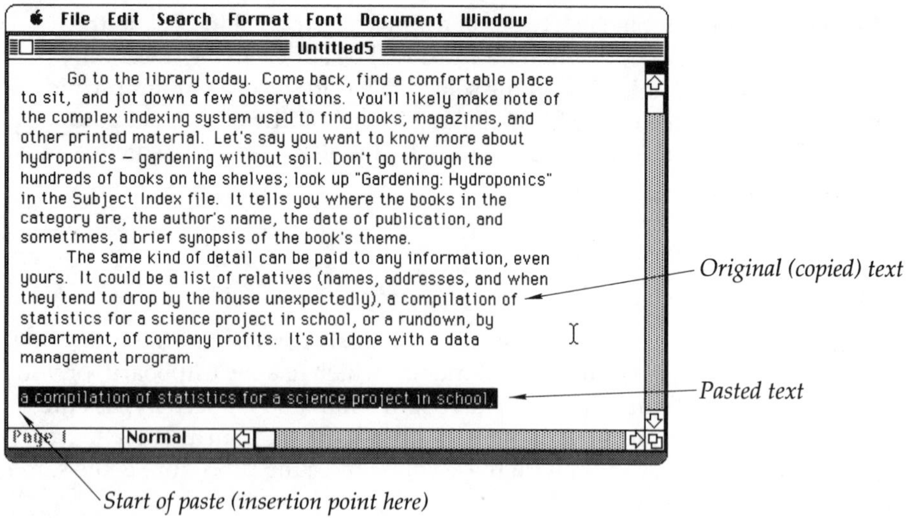

Figure 4-9
Pasted text.

Viewing the Clipboard

From time to time, it's helpful to view the contents of the Clipboard to see what you are pasting into the document. To do this, choose Show Clipboard from the Window menu. A short Clipboard window appears on the bottom of the screen. To see more of the window, enlarge it by dragging the title bar upward and then dragging the size box in the lower right corner until the window is the size you want, or expand it to full size by clicking the zoom box in the upper right corner. Click the close box when you are through.

Using the Move To and Copy To Keyboard Commands

Word includes two shortcut commands that bypass the Clipboard: the Move To and Copy To keyboard commands. In addition to saving time, these commands let you duplicate or relocate blocks of text without disturbing the contents of the Clipboard and work with large documents when free memory is scarce. To copy text:

1. Select the text you want to duplicate.
2. Press Option-Command-C. Note that the status box in the lower left corner of the window reads *Copy to.*
3. Scroll or move to the spot in the document where you want to copy the text block, and click. A dotted insertion point appears, as illustrated in Figure 4-10.
4. Press Return to copy the block. The original text block is unaffected.

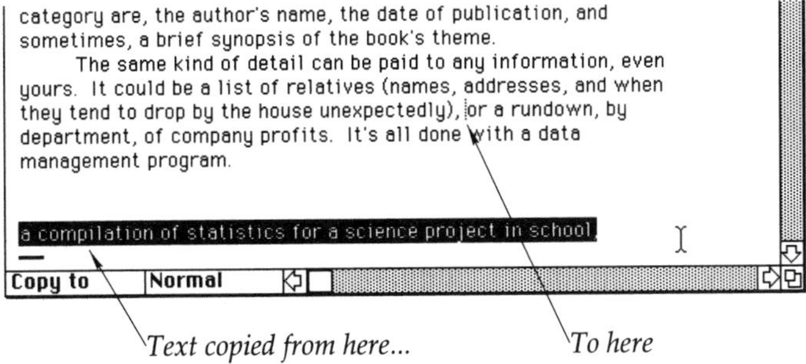

Figure 4-10
Copying text with the Copy To command.

If you change your mind or discover that you selected the wrong material, you can press Command- (period) to cancel the operation. Also, instead of simply clicking an insertion point for the destination, you can select text for replacement using any of the methods described above. You'll see a dotted underscore rather than the normal highlight, and the selected text is replaced by the copied text.

The process of moving text is nearly identical:

❶ Select the text you want to move.

❷ Press Option-Command-X. Note that the status box reads *Move to.*

❸ Scroll or move to the spot in the document where you want to move the text block, and click. A dotted insertion point appears. (See Figure 4-11.)

❹ Press the Return key to move the block. The original text block is deleted and appears in the new location.

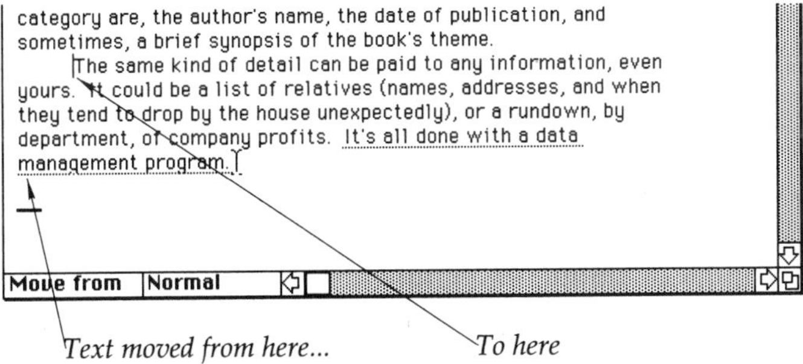

Figure 4-11
Moving text with the Move To command.

All this is fine for moving or copying material from the place in which you're working in a document to another place. But what if you're typing and suddenly decide to grab a phrase or sentence from a distant paragraph and enter it at the insertion point? It turns out that the Copy To and Move To commands magically become the Copy From and Move From commands if no text is selected when you issue the command. Simply set the insertion point and press Option-Command-C or Option-Command-X. The insertion point stops blinking, and the status box reads *Copy from* or *Move from*. Select the material you want to copy or move; as you do so, it will be underscored with a dotted line. Press the Return key after selecting the material to complete the command.

■ *Finding and Changing Text*

Want to find all occurrences of the word *halcyon* in your latest manuscript? If the document is any size at all, you'll spend a lot of time if you have to hunt down every last one. But Word can do it in a flash. And if you want to replace *halcyon* with another, easier-to-understand word, such as *tranquil* or *peaceful*, Word can do that, too.

Finding Text

Word can search a document for any character or group of characters. You can enter a part of a word, an entire word, or a phrase, and Word will find every occurrence of it. To find a word, you usually start by clicking at the beginning of the document to set the insertion point there. The search then starts from the beginning. Then do the following:

1. Choose Find from the Search menu. A dialog box like the one in Figure 4-12 appears.
2. Enter the word or words (hereinafter called a *string*) into the Find What edit field. If a string is already there, drag through the text in the field to select it, and then type the new string.
3. Set the Whole Word and Match Upper/Lowercase options, as desired. (See below.)
4. Click the Start Search button. If Word finds a match, it stops and selects the string in the document.
5. To find the next occurrence, click the Find Next button.

When you are finished, click Cancel or click the Find window's close box.

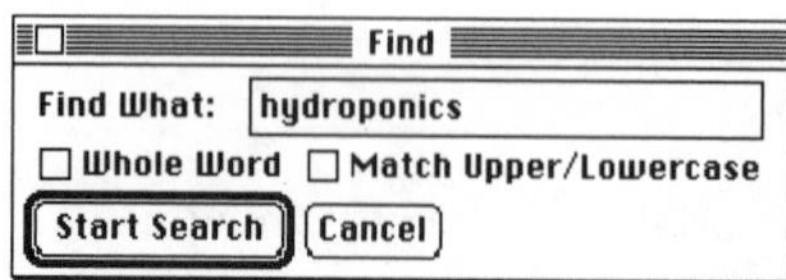

Figure 4-12
The Find dialog box.

Word helps you avoid finding matches that are not what you want by letting you set two options, Whole Word and Match Upper/Lowercase.

With Whole Word, the program selects only text strings that stand on their own, with a space on either side. When searching for *hyper*, for instance, Word normally flags *hyper*, *hyperbole*, *hyperspace*, and all other words that have *hyper* anywhere in them. Click Whole Word, and the program flags only *hyper*.

Leave the Whole Word option off when you are searching for both the root and derivations of a word. Searches work best when the root is an uncommon word. The search string *the* will select a lot of words (*these*, *other*, *their*, *thesis*, and so forth); the search string *magnet* narrows the field to only a few similar words: *magnetize*, *electromagnetic*, *magneto*, and so on.

The Match Upper/Lowercase option specifies that you are looking for words that are capitalized (or not capitalized) in a certain way. If this option is off, Word would find a word like *Eschew* in all its possible capitalizations: *eschew*, *ESCHEW*, *esChew*, and so forth. With the case option on, Word would flag only *Eschew*.

Changing Text

To replace a text string, you usually start by clicking at the beginning of the document to set the insertion point there. Then do the following:

1. Choose the Change command from the Search menu. A dialog box like that shown in Figure 4-13 appears.
2. Enter the text to be replaced in the Find What field.
3. Type the replacement text in the Change To field.
4. Set the Whole Word and Match Upper/Lowercase options as desired.
5. Click the Start Search button. If Word finds a match, it stops and selects the string. Click the Change button to replace the string, or click No Change to leave the string as it is and continue the search.
6. If you want Word to change all occurrences of the string, without having you verify them, click the Change All button instead of Start Search.

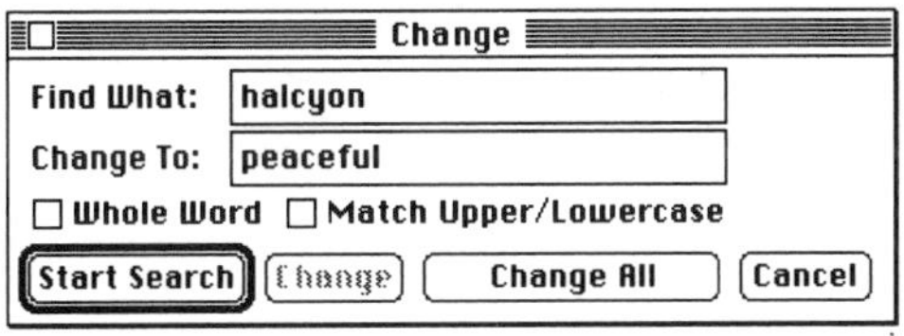

Figure 4-13
The Change dialog box.

The Change Selection button makes the change in the currently selected text and stops the search. This button has two uses. For one, you can use it to replace at once all occurrences of the search string in a selected block of text. To do this, select the block, choose Change, enter the text you want to find and replace, and click Change Selection. Because Word selects the search string when it finds it, you can also use this button to change the current occurrence of the string and then discontinue the search. Simply click Change Selection when the program stops at a word. Word will change the selection and leave the Change dialog box on the screen so that you can enter a new Find What or Change To string and begin another search.

Wildcard Searches

In card games, a wildcard is a chameleon; it can assume the identity of any card in the deck. In Word, a wildcard is a special character that assumes the identity of one or more characters in a search (Find What) string. You use wildcard characters to find variations in spelling and so forth. You cannot use wildcard characters in the Change To field.

Word supports one wildcard character: the question mark (?). The question mark substitutes a single character in that position in the search string. Here are some examples:

Type	**To find**
Budget?	*Budget1, Budget2, Budget3,* and other words that start with *Budget* and have one other character (won't find *Budget10*).
sep?rate	*separate, seperate,* and other spellings in which the fourth character is different.

Searching for and Replacing Special Characters

Word lets you search for special characters, including format marks, page breaks, and tabs. To make it easier, first display the space, tab, paragraph, and newline marks by choosing the Show ¶ command. You enter the circumflex (^) character by typing a shifted numeral 6.

Type	To find
^*w*	"White" space (as seen with paragraph formatting symbols off). It finds all formatting marks, including hard spaces, paragraph marks, tabs, newline marks, optional hyphens, section marks, and page breaks. If several marks are together, Word selects them all when found.
^*s*	Hard space.
^*t*	Tab mark.
^*p*	Paragraph (hard return) mark.
^*n*	Newline (soft return) mark.
^-	Optional hyphen.
^~	Nonbreaking hyphen.
^*d*	Section mark (including required page breaks).

Interesting Facts About Finding and Changing Text

Interesting Fact 1. Unless Match Upper/Lowercase is on, Word retains the capitalization when replacing text. This means that capitalization at the beginning of sentences is kept. For example, if you entered *hello* in the Find What field and *howdy* in the Change To field, they would come out in your document as follows:

Original word	Changed to
hello	howdy
Hello	Howdy
HELLO	HOWDY

Interesting Fact 2. The Find What and Change To fields can each contain up to 24 visible characters, but you can type as many as 255 characters in each field. The runoff text in the field scrolls left as you type.

Interesting Fact 3. You can replace a block with text that is longer than 255 characters by first copying the new string into the Clipboard (select it and choose Copy) and then typing ^*c* in the Change To field. This code does not work in the Find What field; that is, you cannot search for text that matches the contents of the Clipboard.

Interesting Fact 4. The text strings that you enter in the Find What and Change To fields remain there until you change them or until you quit Word. This saves you from having to retype the text if you use the same string over again. Further, the Find What fields of the Find and Change dialog boxes are shared. For example, if you type *dimethylnitrosamine* in the Find What field of the Find dialog box, the same word will appear if you then display the Change dialog box.

Interesting Fact 5. To search for a string with a question mark in it, precede the question mark with a circumflex character (^). Here is an example:

To find	Type
What is this thing called love?	*What is this thing called love^?*

Interesting Fact 6. To search for a string with a circumflex (^) in it, precede the character with a second circumflex; you would enter *40^^6* to find *40^6*.

Interesting Fact 7. To find any ASCII character, whether you can type it directly from the keyboard or not, enter the ASCII code for that character by typing *^n*, replacing *n* with the ASCII code number you want, from 0 to 255. You can use this technique in the Change To field as well.

Why is this so useful? Because there are some formatting characters and special graphic characters that you can't type directly from the keyboard or enter as one of the special characters described in the previous section. Specifically, you can use the ASCII code numbers to look for the following:

To find	Type
Graphics	*^1*
Page number character from header	^2
Current date character from header	^3
Current time character from header	^4
.\ (used in formulas) and footnote separator	^6
Footnote continuation separator	^7
Page Break	^12
Required hyphen	^30
Space character	^32

Other ASCII codes produce characters that either can be typed directly from the keyboard or are undefined, but undefined characters appear as small rectangles (□). Refer to the table in Appendix B for a complete list of the codes for each special character.

TIP

Removing Undefined Characters from Imported Text Files
Often, when you capture a file with a modem or transfer a file from a PC, strange characters appear in your document. The linefeed character, ASCII 10, is probably the most common of these. You can choose Show ¶ to make these characters more visible, yet often all you see is the standard Mac symbol for an undefined character, a small rectangle (□). If all you can see is this generic character, how can you search for it and replace it with nothing?

Simply select the mystery character, find its ASCII code by pressing Option-Command-Q, and enter that decimal ASCII code in the Find What field of the Change dialog box, leaving the Change To field blank. See Chapter 15, "Transferring Text and Graphics," for more information on importing text files.

■ *The Undo and Again Commands*

Mistakes happen to everyone, but when you're hurrying to perfect a term paper, report, or magazine article, accidentally deleting a paragraph you really want to keep or fouling up the formatting of an entire page can be frustrating and nerve-racking. Word lets you undo almost any action, including typing, editing, deleting, and formatting.

To undo the previous command, choose Undo from the Edit menu immediately. Word remembers only one action at a time, and thus you can undo only the last action or command. When you are typing, Word remembers all the characters you entered since the last command.

The Undo command is context sensitive; that is, it describes the command that can be undone, as shown in Figure 4-14. For example, if you typed some text, the command reads Undo Typing. If you did a paste, the command reads Undo Paste. If the previous command is one that can't be reversed, the command reads Can't Undo and is dimmed.

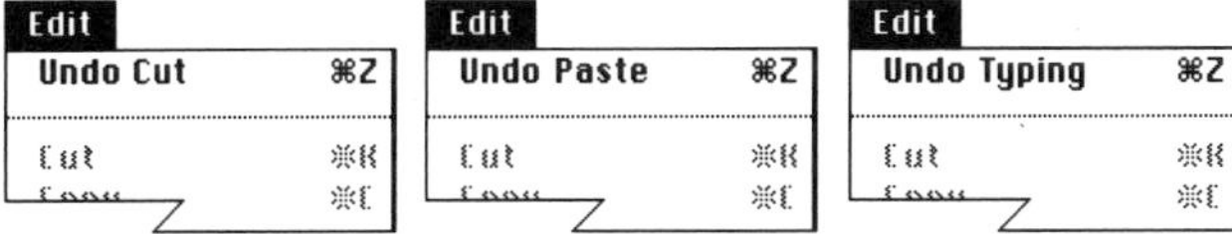

Figure 4-14
Examples of the Undo command.

TIP

Using the Undo Command to Experiment
You can use the Undo feature to test the look and feel of formatting, editing, or some other change in the document. Make the change, and then look over the document. If you like the way it looks, keep it. If not, undo the change and start over. When you've undone something, the Undo command changes to Redo. You can undo and redo changes easily by pressing Command-Z.

Word doesn't have Undo commands for the following actions. Fortunately, however, they can be reversed by clicking a Cancel button in a dialog box if it appears, by choosing the command again, or by some other action. To stop a command in progress, try pressing Command-(period).

To reverse	Do this
Starting Word	Quit Word (use Command-Q).
About MS Word	Click the OK button.
New	Close the new window.
Open	Click the Cancel button.
Close	Click the Cancel button (or reopen the document).
Save As	Click the Cancel button.
Delete	Click the Cancel button.
Page Preview	Close the Page Preview window.
Merge Print	Click the Cancel button.
Page Setup	Click the Cancel button.
Print	Click the Cancel button.
Quit	Click the Cancel button (or restart Word after you reach the Desktop).
Show/Hide ¶	Choose the command again.
Preferences	Click the Cancel button.
Short/Full Menus	Choose the command again.
Go To	Click the Cancel button.
Show/Hide Ruler	Choose the command again.
Outlining	Choose the command again.
Spelling	Click the Cancel button.
Window menu commands	Close the window (for Show Clipboard, or New Window), or reactivate the desired window.

On the other hand, there will be times when you want to use the same command repeatedly. You can do this with the Again keyboard command. Simply press Command-A to repeat your last command. To repeat the last Find command, press Option-Command-A. The Again command can save you a good number of keystrokes. Here are a few other ways to use it:

- After replacing text by typing over it, you can replace other text with the same phrase by selecting the text and pressing Command-A.
- After a copy operation done without the Clipboard (Option-Command-C), you can copy the same text to another place by setting the insertion point in another location and pressing Command-A.
- After making a set of formatting changes using a dialog box, the Ruler, or the Copy Formatting command (Option-Command-V), you can apply the changes to another selection.
- You can repeat a Print command and use the same options.
- You can mix repeated find operations with general editing, repeated text-replace commands, or formatting changes.

Navigating in Your Document

Word offers you a multiplicity of ways of finding your way around in a document. The previous chapter discussed synchronized scrolling with a split window, one pane of which was in Outline view. This chapter already explored the Find command, useful for jumping to the location of a significant phrase. If you're working on a document and need to quit for the day, you can type a unique string, such as @@@, to mark your place and use as the search string the next day.

You can also go to a specific page, jump to any of the last few places you edited using the Go Back key, or arrange your windows so that you can see more than one part of your document at a time.

The Go To Command

Choose Go To from the Search menu to jump to a specific page in your document. Keep these facts in mind when using the Go To command:

- The document must be paginated.
- If changes were made to the document since it was paginated, the page numbers in the status box will be dimmed. You can still use the Go To command, but the page numbering may not be accurate.
- If you specify a number larger than the number of pages in the document, Word takes you to the last page.

- If your document has more than one section, you can enter a section as well as a page number. For example, you can enter *2S3* to go to the second page in the third section.

The Go Back Key

The Go Back key is one of Word's most convenient features, yet it is one of the least known. The idea is simple: Word remembers the locations of the last few places where you entered or edited text. Press the 0 key on the keypad or Option-Command-Z on the keyboard to move the insertion to the last place you edited. Press it again to go to the location before that, and so on. By pressing the key repeatedly, you can rotate through the locations over and over again. Word remembers as many as four locations, although the actual number of locations is often only two or three, depending on what you did last. Every time you make a change at a different place, the location of the oldest edit is forgotten.

You can use this feature when you want to paste something into your document and then continue typing at the beginning of the pasted text rather than at the end. After you paste something into a document, the insertion point moves to the end of the pasted material. If you then press one of the key sequences for the Go Back key, the insertion point jumps back to the beginning of the pasted text, where you first placed the insertion point. Pressing the Go Back key again takes you to the place you edited before that, and eventually the insertion point ends up back at the end of the material you pasted.

Another good use for this feature is when you want to move a section out of the area in which you are working and then continue editing in that area. Simply select and cut the material, scroll to the new location, paste it, and press the Go Back key twice. The insertion point jumps first to the beginning of the pasted text and then to the place from which the material was cut so that you can continue working.

Finally, you can use the Go Back key when you've scrolled away from the area where you're working, and you simply want to return there. In this case, Word returns first to the location of the insertion point, and then to the location of the last edit.

Window Management

Depending on available memory, you can have up to 19 windows open at the same time. Most dialog boxes are not true windows, because they lack a close box, scroll bars, and in many cases a title bar. However, some dialog boxes behave like windows in many ways, and so some of the window-management techniques discussed here can be applied to certain dialog boxes as well.

Usually you will have only one window open and it will fill the screen. You can move around in the document by using any of the techniques discussed so far, but you will probably use the scroll bars most often. (See Figure 4-15.)

The horizontal scroll bar, active only when you are in Full Menus mode, lets you scan back and forth across the printable area of the document. With Word, you can create documents that are up to 22 inches wide.

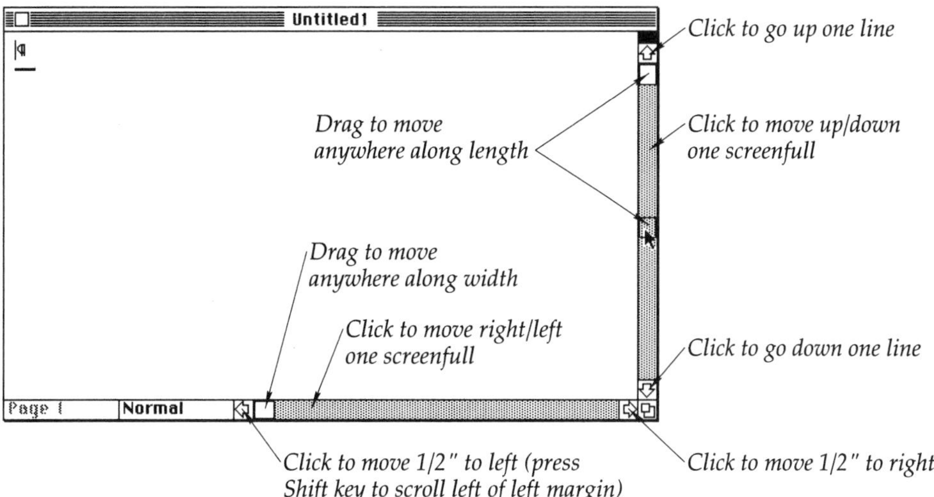

Figure 4-15
Using the scroll bars.

Resizing and Relocating Windows

Whether you have one window on the screen or many, you can freely resize and move them.

- To expand or shrink a window, drag the size box (in the lower right corner).
- To move a window around the screen, drag it by its title bar. You can't push the entire title bar off the screen. To drag an inactive window without first making it active, press the Command key while you drag it.
- To quickly expand or shrink a window, double-click in the size box or title bar, or single-click in the zoom box in the upper right corner. These actions toggle the window between a full-screen display and its previous size and location. This is handy if you need to keep a collection of windows on the screen; when necessary, you can zoom one out to take over the screen and then send it back to its original dimensions when you are finished with it.

Many dialog boxes with title bars can be moved around on the screen like windows, although they cannot be resized or scrolled. To move a dialog box when you want to see the text underneath, simply click on the title bar and drag it out of the way. To move the box back so that you can work with it, double-click on the title bar. Every time you double-click, the dialog box toggles back to its previous position. Word saves the positions of dialog boxes in the Word Settings file when you quit, so they will be in the same place when next invoked.

Handling Multiple Windows

Only one window is active at a time. Commands you choose and characters you type affect or go into the active window only. You can always identify the active window: It is the only one in which the scroll bars and title bar are visible. To make a window active, click anywhere in it. The active window is always on top; others may be hidden behind it.

Another way to activate a window is to choose it from the list that appears in the Window menu, as shown in Figure 4-16. Each window is listed by document name. Windows that have not been saved yet are named Untitled1, Untitled2, and so on. To activate a window, select it from the list.

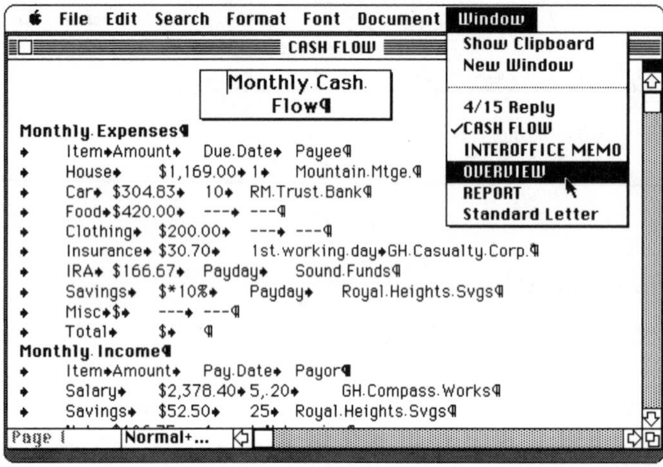

Figure 4-16
Windows listed in the Window menu.

Split Windows

All document windows can be split horizontally into two *panes* (in Full Menus mode only). The top and bottom panes have their own scroll bars so that you can selectively view any part of the document in either one. Split windows are most often used to view two separate portions of the same document—the beginning and end of a report, for example, to see how well the closing remarks summarize the rest of the document. You cannot display a different document in each pane, but, as was mentioned previously, you can display the same document in Outline view in one pane and in Document view in the other.

To split a window, drag the split bar (the black bar immediately above the vertical scroll bar) downward. You can vary the proportion of the panes by positioning the split bar exactly where you want it. As with windows, only one pane is active at a time. The active pane is the one with the insertion point. To remove the split, click in the pane you want to have take over the window and drag the split bar all the way up or down.

■ *Saving Your Work*

If you ever had something go wrong while you were working at a computer and ended up having a lot of hard work disappear forever, you know the importance of saving your files regularly and of making backup copies. If this has never happened to you, don't learn this lesson the hard way. It is a good idea to save your work after every page or so. That way, if something happens, you stand to lose only the last page, not the entire manuscript. To save your document, do the following:

❶ Choose Save from the File menu.

❷ If the document has not been saved before, Word asks for a name. Type a suitable name into the name field.

❸ Click the Save button.

Names can be up to 31 characters long, but you should keep your names short so that you can read them easily on the Finder's desktop. A name can contain any character except the colon (:). To save the file on a different disk, click the Drive or the Eject button, as usual. To save it in a different folder, select the folder you want from the list box and then click Save.

The only time you have to provide a name for a document is the first time you save it. After that, when you choose Save, Word assumes that you want to use the same name and record the document on the same disk.

Replacing a File

If the name you give a document has already been used for another document in that folder, you have three choices:

❶ Choose another name.

❷ Save it on another disk or in another folder.

❸ Save it on the current disk with the name provided.

The first two choices leave the old file alone. The third erases the old file and replaces it with the new one. Be sure that this is what you want to do. Word provides a safety feature to help you avoid accidentally erasing files. If you use a name that already exists in that folder, Word beeps and displays a dialog box. Click No if you don't want to replace (and therefore erase) the old file; click Yes if you do.

Doing a Fast Save

Word stores in RAM a list of the edits you make rather than altering the original text of the document. This is one of the secrets of Word's editing speed—it doesn't take the time to actually rearrange the text every time you make a change. What you see on the screen is a combination of the original draft and the list of corrections.

If the Fast Save option is selected when you click the Save button, the document itself is not updated; only the most recent corrections are added to the file. Fast saves are faster because it takes less time to update the list of corrections than to reorder the entire document. If you do a fast save when this list gets too long, Word rewrites the entire document anyway to empty the list and speed up subsequent editing. This complete reordering is called a *full save.* You can tell when Word does a full save because the status box shows what percentage of the document has been saved, and it increments more slowly for full saves than fast saves.

Other than deselecting the Fast Save option manually, Word also deselects the option when you save the document for the first time, when you change the name of the document, or when you save it to another disk.

TIP

When Not to Use the Fast Save Option
You may want to turn off the Fast Save option under two exceptional circumstances. First, if you need to make a large number of changes to a document (perhaps by using the Change command), do a full save first to empty the edit list. This gives Word more memory to store the impending changes. Second, some programs that can read Word files, such as PageMaker from Aldus Corporation, require that you do a full save of the document before they can successfully read the file.

Making Backup Copies

It is a good idea sometimes to preserve the last version of an important document as a backup, in case you make a mistake you can't undo and want to revert to the earlier version. You can make a copy from the Finder's desktop, but Word lets you make a backup copy without leaving the program.

❶ Choose Save As from the File menu.

❷ Click the Make Backup option.

❸ Click the Save button.

The backup is named *Backup of* (filename). Whenever you save the document from this point on, Word saves the unedited version of the document as the backup and the edited version as the actual file. However, when you use this feature, it overrides the Fast Save option and does a full save every time.

Saving in Different Formats

Word normally saves documents in Word 3.0 format. You also have the option of specifying another file format. For example, you can save a document in Text Only format so that it can be read by another word processor or transferred to a spreadsheet. To save in a format other than Word 3.0 (in Full Menus mode only):

❶ Choose the Save (for a first save) or Save As command. Before providing a name and clicking the Save button, click the File Formats button. A list of formats appears in a dialog box, as shown in Figure 4-17. Click the format you want. The available formats are as follows:

Normal: Stores the file in Word 3.0 format.

Text Only: Creates an ASCII file. Files in this format can contain text characters only; there is no formatting, including line breaks. For use with other word processors and some telecommunications programs.

Text Only with Line Breaks: The same as Text Only, but Word inserts a paragraph mark, or carriage return, at the end of each line.

Microsoft Word 1.0: Stores the file in the format used by Microsoft Word 1.0 for the Macintosh. This format is also used by Microsoft Works. When you open a document created with Word 1.0 or Microsoft Works, Word converts it to Word 3.0 format.

Microsoft Word (MS-DOS): Stores the file in the format used by Microsoft Word for MS-DOS computers. Of course, you must first transfer the file to a disk compatible with the MS-DOS computer.

MacWrite: Stores the file in the format used by Apple's MacWrite (compatible with both the RAM-based and disk-based versions). When you open an existing MacWrite document, Word converts it to Word 3.0 format.

Interchange format (RTF): RTF stands for Rich Text Format, a format used by programs that run on the IBM PC, the Macintosh, and XENIX/UNIX computers. An RTF file contains both text and Englishlike formatting instructions. Word can convert an existing RTF file into Word 3.0 format.

❷ Click the OK button in the Format dialog box.

❸ Provide a name for the document.

❹ Click Save.

This topic will surface again in Chapter 15, "Transferring Text and Graphics," which discusses the problems involved in transferring files between programs and from one machine to another.

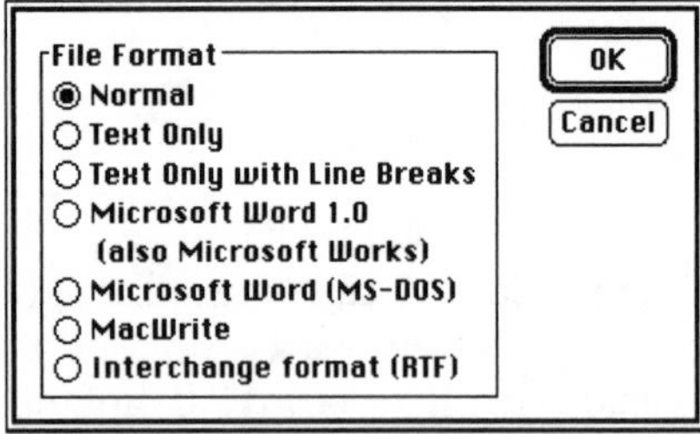

Figure 4-17
The File Format dialog box.

Points to Remember

- The Control Panel, available from the Apple menu, lets you control characteristics of the mouse, keyboard, and screen display.
- Word maintains the Word Settings file to store your preferences from session to session so you don't have to set them each time you start Word. You can have more than one settings file. To start Word with a settings file other than Word Settings, double-click on the settings file you want to use.
- If you have enough memory, Word will run faster when you load the entire program and any open documents into memory. To do this, choose Preferences from the Edit menu and click the Keep in Memory options.
- The Work menu is a user-defined menu to which you can add documents, glossary entries, and styles that you use frequently.
- You can have as many as 19 windows open at once, including those for documents, headers, footers, and dialog boxes.
- The status box in the lower left corner of a document window usually contains the current page number. In the following situations, the page number is replaced with other information:

  After an Open, the number of characters in the document is briefly displayed.

  If you open a locked file, you can read it, but not change it, and the status box displays the message *Locked File.*

  During a time-consuming operation, such as a Save, the percentage completed is displayed. After a Save, the number of characters in the file is displayed.

  When you enter a temporary mode, a prompt is displayed. For example, after you press Option-Command-C to perform a copy operation, the status box reads *Copy to.*

  During certain graphics and Page Preview operations, sizes and the pointer position are displayed.

  During repagination, printing, or table of contents or index generation, the page currently being processed is displayed.
- A document name can be 31 characters long, but short names are easiest to read in the Open and Save As dialog boxes, and on the Finder's desktop.

■ *Techniques*

View the contents of the Clipboard

❶ Choose Show Clipboard from the Window menu.

❷ Click the close box when you're through.

Repeat the previous command (the Again key)

❶ Press Command-A.

To repeat the last Find command, press Option-Command-A.

Undo the previous command

❶ Choose Undo from the Edit menu.

Customizing Menus

Add a command to a menu

❶ Press Option-Command- + (on the keyboard). The cursor changes to a plus sign. Click on the item you want to add. Use Shift-click to add more than one item.

You can add	To this menu	Items to add
Formatting options	Format or Font	Any item from the Character or Paragraph dialog boxes or from the Ruler.
Documents	Work	Any document in the Open dialog box or on the title bar of a window.
Glossary entries	Work	Any entry in the Glossary dialog box.
Styles	Work	Any style name in the Styles or Define Styles dialog box.

Delete a command from a menu

1. Press Option-Command- – (minus).
2. Choose the command you want to delete from the Format, Font, or Work menu.
3. Use Shift-click to delete more than one item.

Entering formatting characters

To enter	Press
End of paragraph	Return or Enter
Nonbreaking space	Option-Spacebar
Nonbreaking hyphen	Command- ~
Optional hyphen	Command- – (hyphen)
End of line (newline)	Shift-Return
New page	Shift-Enter (on keypad)
New section	Command-Enter (on keypad)
Formula character	Option-Command-\
Paragraph mark after insertion point	Option-Command-Return

Entering accented characters

1. Press the keys for the accent desired from the following table.
2. Enter the character to be accented.

To enter	Press
Grave accent (`)	Option-`
Acute accent (´)	Option-e
Circumflex (^)	Option-i
Tilde (~)	Option-n
Umlaut (¨)	Option-u

Entering other characters

To Enter	Press
En dash (–)	Option-- (minus)
Em dash (—)	Shift-Option-- (minus)
ASCII character codes (see Appendix B)	Option-Command-Q, then enter the character's ASCII code and press the Return key

View characters available with different key combinations

❶ Choose Key Caps from the Apple menu.

❷ Select a font from the Key Caps menu.

❸ Hold down the Shift key, the Option key, or the Shift-Option combination to see the characters available from the keyboard.

If you want,

❶ Type the characters you want.

❷ Choose the Copy or Cut commands.

❸ Paste them into the Word document.

❹ Format them in the font you desire.

Selecting Text

To	Do this
Select an insertion point	Point to where you want to insert, and then click.
Select a character	Drag over it.
Select a word	Double-click anywhere in it.
Extend a selection by words	Double-click and drag.
Select a sentence	Command-click anywhere in the sentence.
Extend a selection by sentences	Command-click and drag.
Select a line of text	Click in the selection bar to the left of the line.
Extend a selection by lines	Drag in the selection bar.
Select a paragraph	Double-click in the selection bar to the left of the paragraph.

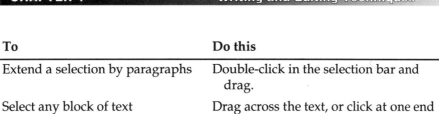

To	Do this
Extend a selection by paragraphs	Double-click in the selection bar and drag.
Select any block of text	Drag across the text, or click at one end and Shift-click at the other end.
Select the entire document	Command-click in the selection bar, or press Option-Command-M.
Select a graphics frame	Click inside the frame. A solid frame and three handles will appear.

Copying Text

Copy text using the Clipboard

❶ Select the text and choose Copy from the Edit menu.

❷ Position the insertion point where you want to place the text.

❸ Choose Paste.

Copy text without using the Clipboard

❶ Select the text and press Option-Command-C. *Copy to* appears in the status box.

❷ Set the insertion point where you want to copy the text.

❸ Press the Return key.

You can also start with an insertion point:

❶ Press Option-Command-C. *Copy from* appears in the status box.

❷ Select the text you want to copy.

❸ Press the Return key.

You can cancel this command by pressing Command-(period).

Moving Text

Move text using the Clipboard

❶ Select the text you want to move.

❷ Choose Cut from the Edit menu.

❸ Position the insertion point at the new location.

❹ Choose Paste.

Move text without using the Clipboard

1. Select the text, and press Option-Command-X. *Move to* appears in the status box.
2. Position the insertion point where you want to move the text.
3. Press the Return key.

You can also start with an insertion point:

1. Press Option-Command-X. *Move from* appears in the status box.
2. Select the text you want to move.
3. Press the Return key.

You can cancel this command by pressing Command-(period).

Finding Text

Search for text

1. Choose Find to search for specified text and select it.
2. Enter the text in the Find What field, and set options from the list below the table. Type up to 255 characters. To find a special character, type the appropriate code from the following table:

To find	Type
Any single character	*?*
A question mark	^*?*
White space	^*w*
A nonbreaking space	^*s*
A tab mark	^*t*
A paragraph mark	^*p*
A newline mark	^*n*
An optional hyphen	^-
A nonbreaking hyphen	^~
A section mark or page break	^*d*
A caret (^)	^^
Any character by its ASCII code	^*ddd*, where *ddd* is its ASCII code

Whole Word: Finds whole words only—not those embedded in other words.

Match Upper/Lowercase: Finds only the arrangement of uppercase and lowercase characters you specify. If this option is turned off, the search string will be matched regardless of capitalization.

❸ Click one of the buttons in the following list:

Start Search: Starts the search at the insertion point or the beginning of the selection.

Find Next: Continues the search.

Cancel: Stops the search.

❹ If you started the search at some place other than at the beginning of the document, when Word reaches the end, it asks if you want to continue the search from the beginning of the document. Click Yes or No.

Finding and Changing Text

Search for and replace text

❶ Choose Change from the Search menu.

❷ Enter the text to be found in the Find What field. See "Finding Text" for a list of special characters that can be used in this field.

❸ Enter the replacement text in the Change To field. If you leave this field blank, Word deletes the search text. To specify a special character, type the appropriate entry from the following table:

To replace with	Type
A nonbreaking space	^*s*
A tab mark	^*t*
A paragraph mark	^*p*
A newline mark	^*n*
An optional hyphen	^-
A nonbreaking hyphen	^~
A page break	^*d*
A caret (^)	^^
The contents of the Clipboard	^*c* (must be used by itself)
Any ASCII character	^*ddd*, where *ddd* is its ASCII code

Whole Word: Finds and changes whole words only—not characters embedded in words.

Match Upper/Lowercase: Finds and changes only the arrangement of uppercase and lowercase characters you specify. If this option is turned off, the search string will be matched regardless of capitalization, and replacement text will be adjusted to match the capitalization of found text.

❹ Click one of the buttons from the following list:

Start Search: Starts the search at the insertion point or the beginning of the selection.

No Change: Leaves the selected text unchanged and finds the next occurrence.

Change: Changes the selected text and finds the next occurrence.

Change All: Changes all occurrences of the search text throughout the document.

Change Selection: Changes all occurrences of the search text within the selection and cancels the search.

❺ If Word reaches the end of the document, it asks if you want to continue the search again from the beginning of the document. However, if you started at the beginning of the document, Word simply says it has reached the end of the document. Click Yes or No.

Find and change text in a footnote or header

❶ Open the Footnote window by pressing Shift-Option-Command-S, by pressing the Shift key while dragging down the split bar, or by choosing Open Header or Open Footer from the Document menu.

❷ Choose Change, and search for and replace the text as you would normally.

Managing Windows

Move a window

❶ Drag the title bar.

Close a window

❶ Click the close box at the left end of the title bar.

Change the size of a window

❶ Drag the size box (in the lower right corner).

Split a window into two panes

❶ Drag down the split bar (the black bar above the vertical scroll bar).

❷ Drag it up or down to restore the window to one pane.

Toggle between a small and full-size window

❶ Click the zoom box at the right end of the title bar, or double-click in the title bar or the size box in the lower right corner.

Shrink two full-screen windows to half-screen size

❶ Double-click the size box of each window.

The first is placed in the upper half of the screen, and the second is placed in the lower half.

Open a new window for the document in the active window

❶ Choose New Window from the Window menu.

Both windows will share the same name but will have a sequence number distinguishing them from each other. Changes made in one window appear in the other.

Scrolling

Scroll a line at a time

❶ Click the arrows at the ends of the scroll bars.

Scroll a screenful at a time

❶ Click the gray part of the scroll bar, above or below the scroll box, depending on whether you want to scroll forward or backward.

Scroll quickly in the document

❶ Drag the scroll box to the corresponding position.

The current page number appears in the status box, dimmed after the point where you've edited the document, to indicate that it's an estimation.

Scroll back to a previous selection or insertion point

❶ Press the Go Back key (0 on the keypad or Option-Command-Z on the keyboard).

Pressing the key repeatedly rotates through the last several edit locations.

Scroll horizontally to left of left margin

❶ Hold down Shift and click on the left arrow in the horizontal scroll bar.

Scroll to a specific page

❶ Choose Go To from the Search menu.

❷ Type the number of the page you want.

❸ Click OK.

The page numbers refer to the last repagination of the document. If each section of your document begins with page 1, you must also specify a section number. For example, *1S2* indicates page 1 of section 2. You can also use the scroll box to go to a page by following the display of page numbers in the status box as you drag the scroll box.

Saving

To save a document, glossary, or personal dictionary; rename a document; make a backup copy; save on a different disk; or save a document in a different file format for use with other programs:

❶ Choose Save As from the File menu.

Save Current Document As: Type the document name. If the document is already named, Word proposes the current name. Click Save to accept the proposed name, or type a new document name.

Fast Save: Saves your documents much faster but creates longer files that take up more disk space. When edits to a document accumulate, Word disables this option automatically and does a full save to consolidate changes.

Make Backup: Creates a backup copy of the last version you saved under the name *Backup of* (filename).

File Format: Lists options for saving your document in different file formats. After clicking this button, you can choose among the following:

File format option	Saves as this
Normal	Word 3.0 format.
Text Only	Creates an ASCII file without Word formatting; use for transferring the document to other programs.
Text Only with Line Breaks	Creates an ASCII file without Word formatting but with carriage-return characters at the end of each line.
Microsoft Word 1.0	Saves in Microsoft Word 1.0 format (for working with external programs that read only Microsoft Word 1.0 format, such as Microsoft Works).

File format option	Saves as this
Microsoft Word (MS-DOS)	Saves in PC Word 3.1 format (for transferring files from your Macintosh to a PC).
MacWrite	Saves in MacWrite 4.5 format.
Interchange format (RTF)	Converts all formatting, the style sheet, and graphics into the RTF interchange format and saves as a text file.

■ *Mouse and Keyboard Shortcuts*

Deleting Text

To delete	Mouse click	Keyboard press
Previous character		Backspace (Word stops at paragraph marks that separate paragraphs with different formats.)
Previous word		Option-Command-Backspace
Next character		Option-Command-F
Next word		Option-Command-G
Block of text	Select text and press	Backspace
And move block of text to Clipboard	Select text, choose Cut, or press	Command-X
Block of text and replace with new text	Select text and	Type replacement text

Manipulating Windows

To	Keyboard press
Make next window active	Option-Command-W
Zoom window	Option-Command-]
Split window	Option-Command-S (toggles)

Choosing Commands with the Period Key on the Keyboard

❶ Press the period on the keypad to enter into menu-selection mode. The menu bar is highlighted. In this mode, you can do any of the following from the keyboard:

To	Keyboard press	Keypad press
Choose a menu	First letter of menu, or Shift-letter to choose next menu starting with that letter, or right and left arrow keys	Number of menu—0 for Apple menu, 1 for File menu, etc. Once menu is selected, the 4 and 6 keys move left and right.
Choose a command	First letter of command, or up and down arrow keys	2 and 8
Execute the command	Return or Enter	
Cancel a command	Backspace (delete), Command-(period)	

Navigating in Dialog Boxes

To move	Keyboard press	Keypad press
To next text field	Tab	
To previous text field	Shift-Tab	
Up in list box	Up arrow	
Down in list box	Down arrow	
To next group of options	Right arrow	
To previous group of options	Left arrow	
To next option	Command-Tab	Decimal point
To previous option	Shift-Command-Tab	
Select the current option	Command-Spacebar	0
Select an option directly	Command-first letter of option, or only the letter if only buttons are present	

Automatic Text Entry with Glossaries

Microsoft Word has many features aimed at automating the writing process. One of the most important of these is its support for *glossaries*. If you have ever found yourself thinking, as you typed the same text over and over, that there must be a better way, or if you have ever wished that you could insert a letterhead at the top of a document quickly and easily, the glossary feature is for you. It allows you, with a few keystrokes, to insert a predefined block of text or a graphic anywhere in any of your documents.

In Word, a glossary is not a list of terms and their definitions but a file containing blocks of text and graphics. Each block is called a glossary entry, and each glossary entry has a name that you use when you want to insert it into a document. With glossaries you save time, not to mention many keystrokes.

Suppose that you are a lawyer or a lawyer's assistant and that you often prepare contracts for clients. Most contracts are made up of small chunks of standard text. Instead of typing these chunks each time you draw up a contract, you can record them as separate glossary entries. Then, when you want to insert one into a contract, you press a few keys in the proper sequence, and the text appears automatically.

This chapter shows how to use glossaries to drastically reduce the time you spend typing text. You'll learn how to make a glossary entry, call it up at a moment's notice, delete or edit it, as well as how to manage glossary files.

■ *Anatomy of a Glossary*

As illustrated in Figure 5-1, each block of text or graphic is a single entry. Glossary entries are similar to the cuttings you might keep in the Scrapbook desk accessory, but you can access glossary entries much more quickly.

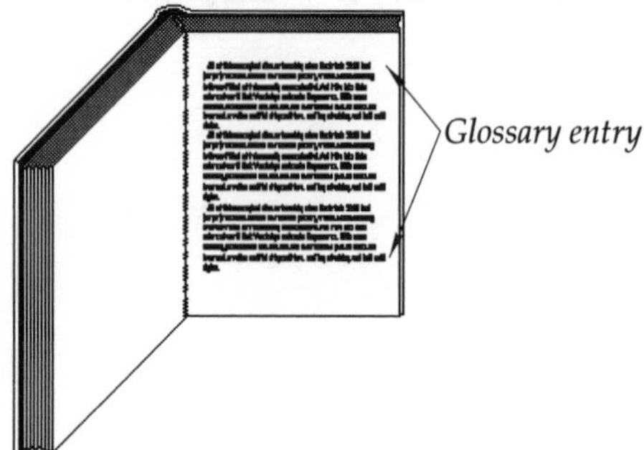

Figure 5-1
Glossary entries.

You already saw how a glossary could make assembling a legal contract easier and faster. Here are a few other items that are perfectly suited to be glossary entries:

- ❏ Letterheads (text, graphics, or both).
- ❏ Your name and return address.
- ❏ Often-used mailing addresses of friends and business associates.
- ❏ Account numbers.
- ❏ Telephone numbers.
- ❏ Names or long words, such as *Santiago de los Caballeros* and *phenylalanine.*
- ❏ Text with unusual formatting, such as the Zapf Dingbat *o* followed by a tab character that we use for the shadowed boxes in this list.
- ❏ Headers and footers that you use regularly.
- ❏ Graphic elements, such as gray rules from MacDraw or digitized logos.
- ❏ PostScript graphics elements.
- ❏ Character names, scenes, and camera directions in screenplays.
- ❏ Samples of long mathematical formulas. (See Appendix D, "Mathematical Formulas in Word.")

- The complimentary close and signature in business letters, such as:

  Sincerely,¶
  ¶
  ¶
  ¶
  David A. Buxton¶
  Public Relations Specialist¶
  enc.¶

Word comes with a glossary file called Standard Glossary. Inside this file are two default glossary entries called *time* and *date* for inserting the current time of day and date. When you enter either of these items into your document, Word inserts the appropriate text but does not continuously update it. (You can also create a time or date that is updated; see the tip that describes this in Chapter 11.) You can either add to the Standard Glossary or create your own glossary files. The Standard Glossary is accessed every time you start Word. Unlike style sheets, glossaries can be shared among all your Word documents rather than being linked to a single document.

Creating a Glossary Entry

The first step in creating a glossary entry is to select a graphic or a block of text to use. You can also paste the contents of the Clipboard into a glossary, if it is more convenient to do so. Of course, the number and size of your entries determine the size of the glossary file, and the larger the file the less room there will be on your work disk for other files. Most of your glossary entries will be a sentence or two in length, and the graphics will be relatively small. However, Word doesn't restrict the size of an entry—you could store a blank business-letter template, for example. To add an entry to the glossary:

1. Select the text or graphic in the normal way, or copy or cut something to the Clipboard.
2. Choose Glossary from the Edit menu. The Glossary dialog box appears. (See Figure 5-2.)
3. Think of a name for the glossary entry. The shorter the name the better, but it should be fairly descriptive. Type the name into the Name field.
4. If you want to use the contents of the Clipboard as the glossary entry, choose the Paste command and skip to Step 6. (Pasting something from the Clipboard automatically defines the entry.)
5. Click the Define button. The item, whether selected or on the Clipboard, is recorded as an entry in the current glossary, with the name you provided.
6. Close the Glossary dialog box by clicking the Cancel button or the close box.

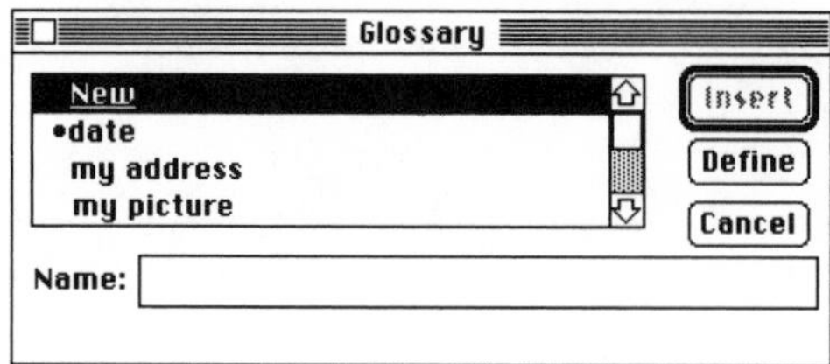

Figure 5-2
The Glossary dialog box.

If you click the Define button without providing a name, Word names the glossary entry for you. The first name assigned is *Unnamed1*, the second is *Unnamed2*, and so forth. You can change the name of a glossary entry by selecting the name you want to change in the list box, typing a new name in the Name edit field, and then clicking Define.

Like any other Word document, a glossary must be saved or any changes and additions you have made will be lost. If you don't save the glossary, Word will prompt you to do so when you quit the program. If you add several entries to the glossary, it is a good idea to save them right away, rather than waiting until the end of your Word session. However, you don't need to save a glossary in order to use entries you've just added. To learn more about your options for saving a glossary, see "Working with Glossary Files," later in this chapter. If you simply want to save your new entries in the Standard Glossary file, display the Glossary dialog box and choose Save As from the File menu. Be sure that the filename is *Standard Glossary* and then click Save.

■ *Inserting a Glossary Entry*

You can insert a glossary entry into your document in three ways: by choosing the Glossary command, by accessing the glossary from the keyboard, or by choosing a glossary entry that you have added to the Work menu.

Regardless of the method you use, you must first set the insertion point where you want the entry to appear. If, instead of merely placing the insertion point, you select a graphic or a block of text, the glossary entry will replace the selection.

Choosing the Glossary Command

To insert an entry using the mouse and the Glossary command, do the following:

1. Choose the Glossary command. The Glossary dialog box appears.
2. Scroll through the list box and click on the entry you want to use.
3. Click the Insert button, or simply double-click on the entry name.

The entry is placed at the insertion point, as shown in Figure 5-3, or it replaces the previously selected text or graphic. If you decide not to use a glossary entry, click the Cancel button or the close box. If you make a mistake and need to undo the entry, choose Undo Expand Glossary from the Edit menu. *Expanding* is the term Word uses for the action of inserting an entry.

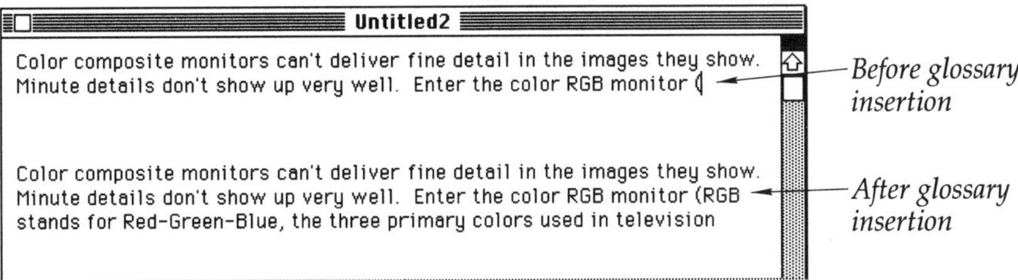

Figure 5-3
Before and after inserting a glossary entry.

Using the Keyboard

If you remember the name of the glossary entry, you can insert it more quickly by using the keyboard. Simply place the insertion point, or select the material you want to replace with the entry, and then do the following:

1. Press Command-Backspace. As Figure 5-4 shows, the status box in the lower left corner of the window will read *Name.*
2. Type the name of the entry. You can use uppercase or lowercase letters; Word doesn't care. Keeping your entry names short helps make this process more convenient.
3. Press the Return key when you're finished typing. The entry is placed at the insertion point or replaces the previously selected material.

If you misspell the entry, the program will beep at you. To cancel the insertion, press Command-(period) or click anywhere in the document.

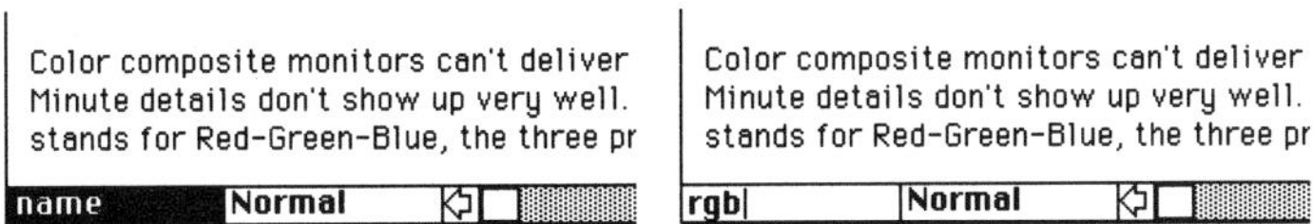

Figure 5-4
The status box during entry insertion from the keyboard.

Using the Work Menu

The third way to insert a glossary entry is to create an item for it on the Work menu and then simply choose that menu item when you want to insert the entry. To add a glossary entry to the Work menu, do the following:

1. Press Option-Command- +. The pointer changes to a large plus sign.
2. Choose the Glossary command, and double-click on the entry you want to add to the Work menu. The menu bar blinks to confirm the addition.

To test the new Work menu item, place the insertion point somewhere in your document, and then choose the new glossary menu item. It couldn't be easier. You may want to add all your glossary entries to the Work menu in this way, but restrain yourself. Once you begin using the Work menu to add documents, glossary entries, and style names, you'll realize that space on it is scarce. You can have a total of 31 entries on the Work menu, including the dotted lines that divide each type of entry.

Formats Within Glossary Entries

Any glossary entry you create contains, in addition to text or graphics, any character or paragraph formats the material may have. If the selected or copied material for the entry contains a paragraph mark, the paragraph formats that are attached to it (such as line spacing, indention, and style information) remain with the entry in the glossary. For this reason, unless you specifically want the paragraph formats to travel with the entry, select only the text inside a paragraph and not the entire paragraph before you create the glossary entry. If you do this, only the character formats of the selected material remain with the entry.

Any styles attached to the material at the time you create the entry are also recorded in an invisible glossary style sheet. These formats and styles are carried over when you insert an entry into a document, even if it is not the same document from which the entry originally came. If a style name attached to the entry already exists in the document, Word uses the document style to format the inserted entry. On the other hand, if a style attached to the entry does not exist in the document's style sheet, then Word adds it from the style sheet hidden in the glossary.

For example, let's say that a book you are working on has a heading called *For Further Reading* at the end of each chapter, listing the bibliographic references for the chapter, and that it has the *level* 2 style. In addition to using the *level* 2 style that you developed (say, 14-point Palatino bold with 20 points Space Before), you manually added italics to the *For Further Reading* heading. Then, suppose that you select this heading and create a glossary entry called *head/biblio*.

If you opened a blank document and inserted this glossary entry, you would see the italic formatting of the original but not the 14-point Palatino bold style you defined in the first document, because the *level 2* style is an *automatic* style, meaning that it is automatically predefined for every blank document. Because the default definition for the *level 2* style is the *Normal* style font in bold, with 6 points Space Before, you would see these formats plus the italic you added manually. In all probability, this is not what you expected or wanted.

This behavior may seem awkward to you, but there is a reason for it that applies to other aspects of Word as well. When you copy a style into a document—whether by inserting a styled glossary entry or by copying and pasting styled material from one document to another—the styles of the document, not of the inserted material, take precedence. This approach preserves the information contained in the document until you decide to change it. If it were otherwise, a style attached to an inserted paragraph could overwrite a style in your document's style sheet, causing all the text in that style to be changed. In other words, you can add a style that wasn't in your document before, but Word won't let you replace a style without making a conscious choice.

If you want the *level 2* headings in the two documents to match, it is easy enough to copy the styles from the source document to the new document. Simply choose Define Styles while the new document is active; then choose Open and open the source document's style sheet. All the styles defined in the source overwrite the styles of the same name in the new document. See Chapter 9, "Style Sheets," if you want to copy only a few of the styles to the new document.

The behavior of not transferring a style definition that already exists in a document when you insert a glossary entry also holds for a glossary itself. This is a consequence of the fact that a glossary has only one hidden style sheet. For example, suppose that you define a new entry in the current glossary for a paragraph having a style called *letterhead*. Suppose you now close the document from which this entry came and open a new document. In the new document you create a definition for the *letterhead* style that is different from that in the first document. If you now create a new glossary entry for a paragraph having the *letterhead* style of the new document, the new definition does not stay with the entry in the glossary because the glossary's hidden style sheet already contains a definition for that style.

TIP

Opening a Glossary as a Document

Here is an experiment for the stouthearted to demonstrate that glossaries do indeed have hidden style sheets. Note that the average user will never need to open a glossary in this way; it is easy to make almost any change to a glossary using the standard methods described in the next section.

First, close every open document for safety's sake. Then open a blank document and choose the Glossary command. Next choose Save As, naming the glossary *Glossary Test*, in order to create a copy of the glossary for your experiments. Once you've done this, quit and restart Word; this is necessary because Word lets you open a glossary as a document only if it's the first time it is being opened for any reason during that session. Now hold down the Shift key while choosing Open from the File menu. A dialog box appears, listing every file in the current folder, regardless of whether it's a Word document or not. Open *Glossary Test* as a document.

You see a list of every entry in your glossary, each ended by a paragraph mark (invisible unless Show ¶ is on). You can carefully change the material in this document—editing within an entry, reformatting text, and so on—but be careful not to delete an entry. If you do, glossary entries may no longer match their correct names or the glossary may become totally unusable.

Choose the Define Styles command to see the list of styles attached to the glossary. You can do many things with the glossary's style sheet: change style definitions, delete styles that are no longer attached to glossary entries, and even open a style sheet belonging to another document to merge its styles into the glossary's style sheet.

When you have finished editing the glossary document, save it. A Fast Save preserves the file type attached to the glossary so that you can open it as a glossary again without problems. However, if you made many edits, have many documents open (remember the suggestion to close all open documents?), or repaginated the glossary document (although you should never need to do this), Word does a Full Save and changes the document's file type and icon to that of a standard Word document.

If this happens, don't worry; you can still open the document as a glossary if you haven't changed the file too much. To do this, restart Word, choose the Glossary command, and press the Shift key while choosing Open from the File menu. When the Open dialog box appears, open *Glossary Test*. If all goes well, your edited glossary document will be reopened as a glossary. To complete the process, immediately save this glossary under a third name, such as *New Glossary*, so that Word will change the file type and icon back to those of a glossary.

Any time you open a glossary in this way, test carefully any changes you make before using it with an important document.

This technique can be helpful if for some reason (such as a problem with a glossary carried forward from version 3.0) you suspect that your glossary has been damaged and you want to recover its contents. Simply open the glossary as a document using Shift-Open, and copy its contents into a blank document. You can then reconstruct the glossary.

■ *Modifying a Glossary Entry*

You can change the contents, format, and name of any glossary entry except the two standard entries for time and date. You can also delete any glossary entry you no longer need (again, with the exception of the time and date).

Editing an Entry

Often, after creating a glossary entry, you will decide that you need to make a few changes in it. Start by inserting into a document the entry you want to change. Use a new, blank document window if necessary, to avoid messing up the one in which you are currently working. Then redefine the contents of the entry as follows:

❶ Make the desired changes in the contents and format of the material you inserted.

❷ Select the edited material.

❸ Choose the Glossary command.

❹ Select in the list box the entry to be replaced, and click the Define button.

❺ Click Cancel to resume editing.

TIP

Editing Graphics Stored in the Glossary
Word cannot edit graphics imported from programs like MacPaint or MacDraw. If you need to edit a graphic stored as a glossary entry, open the Glossary dialog box, select the entry, and choose the Copy command. Then go back to the drawing program, paste the graphic, change it, and cut or copy the new version to the Clipboard. Finally, restart Word, open the Glossary dialog box again, select the entry name, and choose the Paste command to replace the entry with the contents of the Clipboard.

Changing the Name of an Entry

To change the name of a glossary entry without changing its contents, do the following:

❶ Choose the Glossary command.

❷ Select in the list box the entry to be renamed.

❸ Enter a new name in the Name field. When you click on a glossary entry, the name appears selected in the Name field. Enter the new name.

❹ Click the Define button.

❺ Click Cancel to resume editing.

Even though you may have selected or copied something in your document, when you change an entry name, Word assumes that you don't want to store the selected or copied material under the new name. If you change your mind and decide you do want to create a new entry with the selected or copied material, click Cancel and create the new entry as described earlier.

Deleting an Entry

To delete a glossary entry you no longer need, do the following:

1. Choose the Glossary command.
2. Select in the list box the entry to be deleted.
3. Choose the Cut command.
4. Word double-checks to be sure you really want to delete the entry. Click Yes if you do or No if you don't.
5. Click Cancel to resume editing.

Once you have cut an entry, you may find it helpful to paste its contents into a document you called, for instance, *Glossary Heap*, so that you can recover it if you need it again.

■ Working with Glossary Files

Glossaries have many applications. You can, if you want, store full paragraph formatting with glossaries so that when entries are inserted in text, they use their own special formatting characteristics, rather than the characteristics of the surrounding text. You can also store only the text of a paragraph, without its paragraph formatting but retaining its character formatting. You can also print glossaries so that you have a record of the name and definition of each entry.

You are by no means limited to a single glossary. Custom glossaries are ideal for storing text and graphic entries for specialized applications. One glossary file might contain entries for use with the LaserWriter and PostScript, another might contain entries for use with business correspondence, and still another might include entries for technical and scientific papers. You can use one glossary file at a time, or you can combine them in any way you want, by cutting and pasting entries between them or by incorporating all the entries from one glossary into another.

Once you have set up glossaries to your liking, you can print them so that you have a record of the name and definition of each entry.

Word opens the Standard Glossary file the first time you choose the Glossary command. This file is included on the Word master disk and should be kept in the same folder as the Word program. If, when it starts, Word cannot find a Standard Glossary file on the disk (see Appendix A for the list of where Word looks for files), it creates a new one. Of course, you can generate your own custom glossary files and store them on any disk.

Probably the most important thing to understand about glossaries is the relationship between the Standard Glossary and the current glossary. The *current glossary* is a working area within Word; it is simply a block of memory. The Standard Glossary is a file that actually exists in your Word folder. When you choose the Glossary command for the first time in a session, Word opens the Standard Glossary file and adds its entries to the current glossary. If you add entries to the current glossary from your documents and then quit Word, Word asks if you want to save the current glossary and prompts you with the Standard Glossary filename if you haven't opened any other glossaries in the meantime.

To begin exploring glossary files, try saving any entries you've added to the current glossary in the Standard Glossary file. The easiest and the most common way of doing this is simply to quit Word and have it ask whether or not you want to save the changes to the glossary. However, often you will want to save changes you made and either begin a new glossary or open one that you already created. To save the current glossary as the Standard Glossary, do the following:

1. Choose the Glossary command.
2. Choose Save As from the File menu. A dialog box appears, requesting a filename for the current glossary.
3. If you haven't cleared the current glossary or opened one with a different name, Word suggests the obvious, *Standard Glossary*, as the filename. If that name doesn't appear, type it in.
4. Click Save. Word asks you to confirm that you want to replace the existing Standard Glossary file. Click Yes.
5. Click Cancel in the Glossary dialog box.

Note that saving a glossary does not affect the contents of the current glossary.

Clearing the Current Glossary

Every time you open a glossary file, you add its contents to all the other entries in the current glossary. To avoid this, you can explicitly clear the current glossary of entries beforehand. You should also do this when you want to create a new glossary so that you start with a clean slate before adding new entries.

For example, suppose that you start Word and begin using the glossary. The current glossary would then consist of the entries in the Standard Glossary, which Word opened when you chose the Glossary command. If you choose Glossary again and open a different glossary, you would add the contents of the second glossary to the current glossary, which already contains the entries in the Standard Glossary. Later, when you quit Word and save the current glossary under the same name as the second glossary you opened, all the entries, including those in the Standard Glossary, would be saved in the file. As you can see, it is important to clear the current glossary before opening or creating another if you want to keep the entries separate.

To clear the current glossary, you open the Glossary dialog box and choose New from the File menu, as follows:

❶ Choose Glossary from the Edit menu.

❷ Save any changes you made to the current glossary, if you want to keep them.

❸ Choose New from the File menu. The dialog box shown in Figure 5-5 appears, to verify that you want to clear the contents of the current glossary. Click Yes.

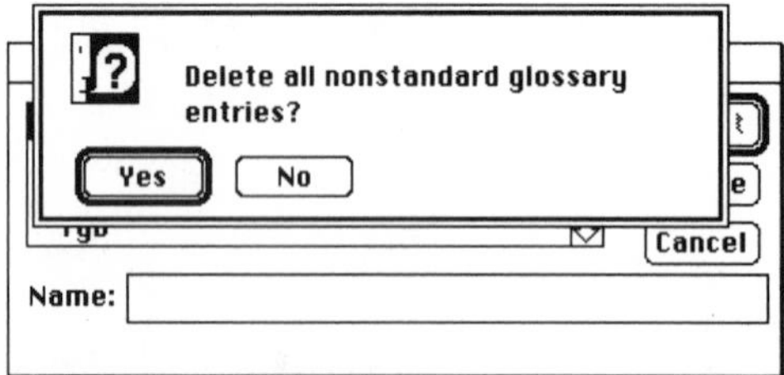

Figure 5-5
The new glossary dialog box.

At this point, the current glossary is empty of entries other than the standard time and date items. You can now either create a new glossary or open another glossary stored on disk. To start a new glossary, select each piece of boilerplate text in turn, and enter it into the current glossary with a suitable name. When you're finished, save the current glossary with an appropriate title, or quit and let Word lead you through the process.

You can also clear the current glossary and create a new entry at the same time. Simply select the material (text, graphics, or both), open the glossary, clear it, name the new entry, and click the Define button.

Opening a Glossary

Once you've created a custom glossary, you need to know how to open it so that you can use it in your documents and add, delete, or modify its entries.

❶ Choose the Glossary command to open the Glossary dialog box.

❷ Choose the New command to clear the current glossary.

❸ Choose the Open command. A list of available glossary files appears in the list box. Click the Drive and Eject buttons if you want to view glossary files on other disks. The Standard Glossary file is exactly the same as any other (except that it is the one opened by default), so you can open or reopen it if you want.

Repeat the process for as many glossary files as you like. Remember, however, that the entries from each file will be added to the others in the current glossary. If you would rather delete entries in the current glossary before opening another one, choose the New command first.

If you want, you can start Word and open a glossary file at the same time by double-clicking on the icon of the glossary file.

Combining and Extracting Glossary Entries

Because opening a glossary without clearing the current glossary first adds the glossary's contents to the current glossary, you can combine entries from many smaller glossaries into larger glossaries. Combining glossaries lets you share entries across many disks. However, because glossary entries are stored by name, trouble can arise if you merge an entry into a glossary that already has an entry of the same name. When this happens, Word gives preference to the merged glossary item, and the entry with that name in the current glossary is replaced.

To remove one or more entries that you don't want included in the combined glossary, select each entry and choose the Cut command. Word verifies your choice with a dialog box; click Yes or press the Return key to delete the entry. When you have deleted all the entries you don't want, save the current glossary under a new name.

If you mistakenly delete an entry you want to keep, don't panic. The entry isn't permanently gone; it still exists in the original glossary file on disk, and it may even exist on the Clipboard, if you haven't replaced it with other material. Choose Show Clipboard from the Window menu to see if it is still there. If it is, paste it back as though you were creating a new entry. You can also get an entry back by opening its glossary again. This will merge all the deleted entries back into the combined glossary, so if you don't want some entries, you will have to delete them again.

Another way to recover an entry or to move or copy an entry from one glossary file to another is to save the current glossary under a new name, clear it, open the old glossary, and cut or copy entries from the old glossary to the new one. To do this, first save the current glossary, and then do the following:

1. Choose the New command to clear the current glossary.
2. Choose the Open command and open the glossary from which you want to copy the entry.
3. Select the entry you want to copy.
4. Choose the Copy command to place the entry in the Clipboard.
5. Choose the New command again to clear the current glossary.
6. Choose the Open command and open the glossary to which you want to copy the entry.
7. Choose the Paste command to add the entry to the current glossary.

Before you go on to other tasks, it is a good idea to save your combined glossary. Otherwise, your hard work may be lost. If you neglect to save the glossary, Word will remind you to do so when you quit the program.

TIP

Moving Groups of Glossary Entries
If you need to move more than one glossary entry at a time, there are a few tricks you might try. The first is simply to insert all the entries you want to move from the source glossary into a document, clear the current glossary, open the destination glossary, and then add the entries to it. The second is to save a copy of the source glossary under a temporary name, such as *My Glossary/trash*, and then delete all the entries you don't want to move. With this modified glossary as the current glossary, open the destination glossary to merge the two sets of entries.

The third, not for the fainthearted, is to make a duplicate of the source glossary, clear the current glossary, open the destination glossary, and then open the copy of the source glossary *as a document* by pressing the Shift key while choosing the Open command. You can then scroll through the entries, selecting and reentering them as needed. Delete the copy of the source glossary when you're done, as it may no longer be a usable glossary file.

Printing the Current Glossary

Names of glossary entries can be as difficult to remember as names of styles. Fortunately, you can print the name and definition of every currently loaded glossary entry. A printed list of available glossary entries can serve as a helpful reference when you are working.

To print the entries in a particular glossary file, first clear the current glossary and open the glossary you want to print. If you simply want to print the entries in the current glossary, you need not bother to do this. Then do the following:

❶ Choose the Glossary command to display the Glossary dialog box, if it is not already on the screen.

❷ Choose the Print command.

❸ Select the desired options, and click OK.

If you will be printing more than one glossary file, remember to clear the slate each time before you open the next glossary file, or all the entries will be merged into one huge glossary.

The glossary entries are printed in alphabetical order. The printout includes the name of each entry and its contents. (See Figure 5-6.)

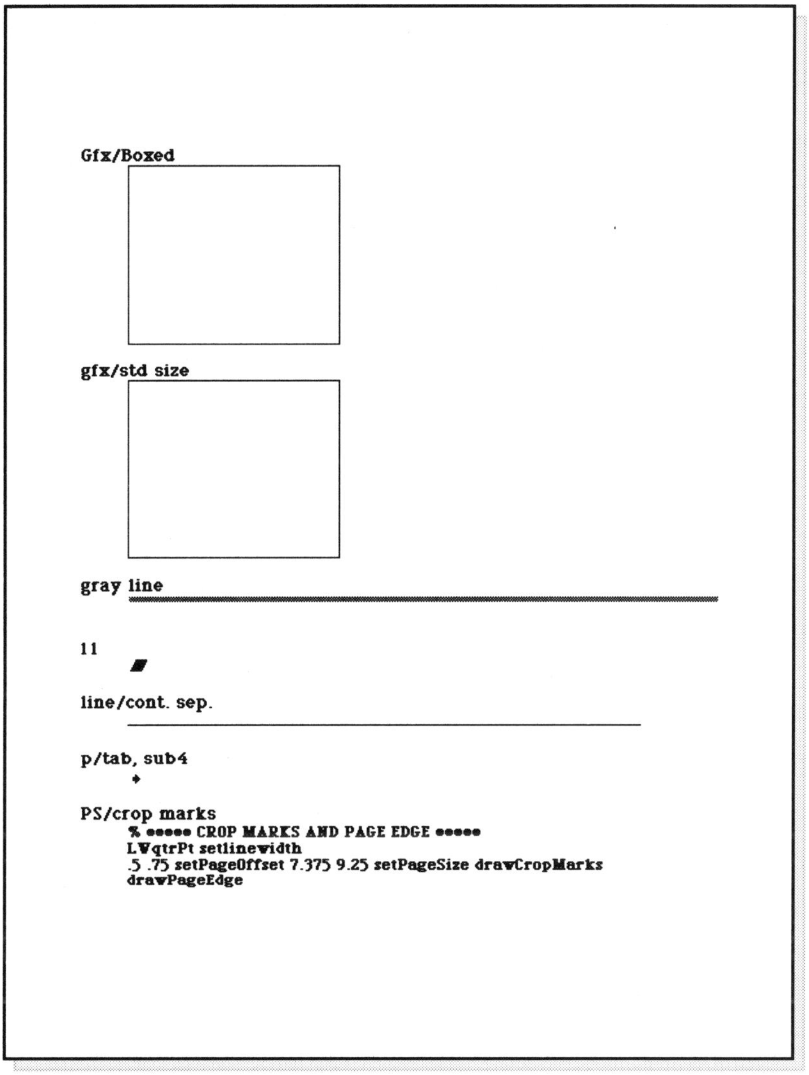

Gfx/Boxed

gfx/std size

gray line

11

line/cont. sep.

p/tab, sub4

PS/crop marks

```
% ●●●●● CROP MARKS AND PAGE EDGE ●●●●●
LWqtrPt setlinewidth
.5 .75 setPageOffset 7.375 9.25 setPageSize drawCropMarks
drawPageEdge
```

Figure 5-6
A page from a printed glossary.

Points to Remember

- A glossary is a collection of entries, each with a name, that you can insert into your documents quickly and easily. An entry can consist of text, graphics, or both.
- Unless you specify otherwise, Word stores your glossary entries in a file called the Standard Glossary. This file is provided on your Word disk and must be in the same folder as the Word program.
- Word loads the Standard Glossary when you first choose the Glossary command or otherwise access a glossary entry in a given session.
- All glossary files contain the following two standard entries, which you cannot modify or delete:

  date Inserts the date in the form MM/DD/YY

  time Inserts the time in the form HH:MM PM (or AM)
- Each glossary entry retains the style, character formats, and paragraph formats that were attached to the text when the entry was created. However, if the document into which an entry is inserted contains a style with the same name as a style attached to the entry, the inserted entry is formatted according to the document style, not the glossary style. If no style exists by that name, the glossary style is used.
- The current glossary is a work area that contains the entries belonging to the open glossaries. Each time you open another glossary, its contents are added to the current glossary. If you want to remove the current entries before you open another glossary, you must do so explicitly by choosing the New command.

Techniques

Working with Glossary Entries

Create a glossary entry

1. Select the text or graphic you want to use.
2. Choose the Glossary command.
3. Type a name for the entry.
4. Click Define.

Insert a glossary entry into a document

❶ Place the insertion point.
❷ Choose the Glossary command (Command-K).
❸ Select the name of the entry to be inserted.
❹ Click Insert, or simply double-click the entry name.

Or,

❶ Place the insertion point.
❷ Press Command-Backspace. (The status box displays the prompt *Name* .)
❸ Enter the name of the glossary entry you want to insert.
❹ Press the Return key, or cancel by pressing Command-(period).

Display an entry

❶ Choose the Glossary command.
❷ Select an entry name.
❸ The first part of the entry text appears at the bottom of the dialog box.

To see the entire entry, insert it in your document, read it, and then choose Undo (Command-Z) to remove it.

Replace an entry

❶ Select the replacement material in your document.
❷ Choose the Glossary command.
❸ Select the name of the entry to be replaced.
❹ Click Define.

The text from the document replaces the previous entry; the first part of the new entry appears at the bottom of the dialog box.

Delete an entry

❶ Choose the Glossary command.
❷ Select the name of the entry to be deleted.
❸ Choose the Cut command.
❹ Click Yes in the dialog box that appears.

The entry will be moved to the Clipboard.

Rename an entry

1. Choose the Glossary command.
2. Select the entry to be renamed.
3. Type the new name.
4. Click Define.

Add a glossary entry to the Work menu

1. Press Option-Command- +.
2. Choose the Glossary command.
3. Double-click on the entry you want to add.

This lets you insert the entry simply by choosing it from the Work menu.

Working with Glossary Files

Save the current glossary

1. Choose the Glossary command.
2. Choose the Save As command.
3. Type the name of the glossary to be saved.
4. Click Save.

Clear the current glossary

1. Save the current glossary first, if it contains changes you want to keep.
2. Choose the Glossary command.
3. Choose the New command.
4. Click Yes in the dialog box that appears.

Open a custom glossary

1. Choose the Glossary command.
2. Clear the current glossary, if you want.
3. Choose the Open command.
4. Select the glossary file you want to open.

Copy an entry from one glossary file to another

❶ Choose the Glossary command.
❷ Open the source glossary.
❸ Copy the appropriate entry to the Clipboard.
❹ Clear the current glossary.
❺ Open the destination glossary.
❻ Paste the entry into the glossary.

Print the current glossary

❶ Choose the Glossary command.
❷ Choose the Print command.
❸ Click OK.

Using the Spelling Checker

Word's built-in spelling checker is a boon to anyone who makes typing mistakes or sometimes forgets how to spell a word—and who doesn't? Because the spelling checker is built into Word, you don't have to quit the program and start up another application in order to check spelling. This means that you can call up the spelling checker at a moment's notice and quickly check text, even a single word.

This chapter shows you the nuances of the spelling checker. You will learn how to do basic tasks, such as adding words to and deleting words from one or more personal dictionaries, as well as more advanced techniques, including how to manipulate personal dictionary files.

■ *Doing a Spelling Check*

You can do a spelling check at any time, but for most documents, you'll want to wait until you're almost finished. Checking a document too early in the creative process doesn't guard you against spelling and typographical errors later on.

If you have any text in hidden format in your document, be sure it is visible before you start the spelling check; do this by choosing Preferences from the Edit menu and clicking Show Hidden Text in the dialog box if the option is not already on. Word will not check hidden text unless it is visible. (Hidden text is discussed in Chapter 7, "Character Formatting.") Then, to check an entire document:

1. Click at the beginning of the document to place the insertion point there. (Word begins checking from the insertion point.)
2. Choose Spelling from the Document menu. After a short wait while Word loads the dictionary (when this is the first time in the session that you've used the spelling checker), the dialog box in Figure 6-1 appears. If Word cannot locate the disk containing the Main Dictionary file, it asks you to insert the correct disk. Put the disk containing the Main Dictionary in the drive and press the Return key.
3. Click the Start Check button to begin the spelling check.

When Word finds a word that is not in its dictionary, it selects the word and displays it after Unknown Word, and the Start Check button now reads *No Change.* Your options at this point are many; you can do any of the following:

- ❑ Correct the word.
- ❑ Have Word suggest an alternate spelling.
- ❑ Add the word to a personal dictionary.
- ❑ Both correct the word and add it to a personal dictionary.
- ❑ Do none of the above—neither correct the word nor add it.

These options are described at length in the sections that follow. If you want to get on with your work now and learn the details later, you can use the spelling checker at its most basic level by doing one of the following: Click No Change to continue the spelling check without changing the word; type the correct spelling after Change To and then click Change to correct the word and continue the spelling check; or click Suggest to have Word display a list of proposed spellings for the word, select one, and click Change.

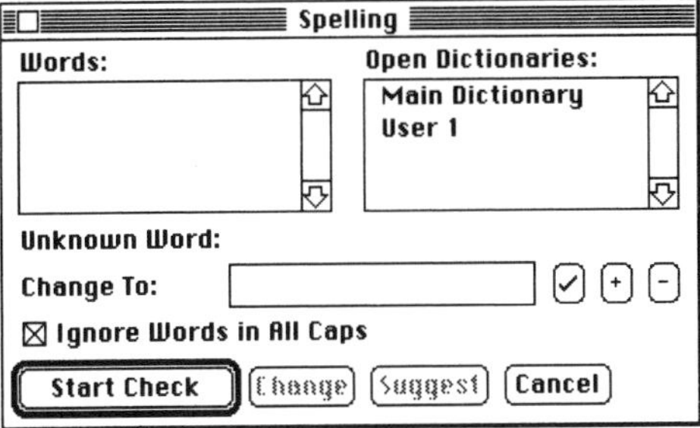

Figure 6-1
The Spelling dialog box.

You don't have to check the entire document; you can also check single words and blocks of selected text, simply by selecting the text before you choose the Spelling command. If you select only one word, Word checks that word. When it has finished checking the selection, Word displays a dialog box that says *Finished checking selection*. Click OK (or press the Return key), and you are back to editing.

You can use this feature to check the spelling of single words as you type. After entering a word that you suspect may be spelled incorrectly, double-click on it to select it, and then choose the Spelling command. If the word is spelled correctly, Word displays its *Finished checking selection* message. Press the Return key to resume editing. If the word is spelled incorrectly, Word flags it as an unknown word.

If you start a spelling check anywhere but at the beginning of a document, Word displays the message *Continue checking from beginning?* when it reaches the end. Click Yes to have Word check from the beginning of the document, or click Cancel to resume editing.

Ignoring Words in All Caps

Acronyms are words formed from the initial letters within a term and are usually capitalized. Because of their specialized nature, acronyms are not included in Word's dictionary. If you write or edit a document that is loaded with acronyms, the program will stop every few words, making the whole process a hindrance rather than a help.

For this reason, Word lets you ignore words that are capitalized. If you want to skip over acronyms and other words that are all caps, be sure that the Ignore Words in All Caps option is on (on is the default setting) before you start the spelling check. If you want to check capitalized words, click the box to turn off the option. The option turns back on again when you initiate a new spelling check.

Correcting a Word

If you're like most people, your most common mistake will be mistyping words that you know how to spell. For example, you may type *adding the term to adictionary* and want only to separate the correctly spelled words. To do this, you can either type the correct word (or words), or you can edit it.

To retype the entire text:

1. Click in the Change To edit field and type the correct spelling (*a dictionary* in the example above).
2. Click the Change button. Word replaces the text and continues checking your document.

To edit the text:

1. Click on the word displayed next to the Unknown Word label. The term appears in the Change To edit field.
2. Click in the Change To field to deselect the word and set the insertion point.
3. Edit the word. When you're finished, click Change to change the word in the document and continue the check.

Having Word Suggest a Spelling

If, while checking a document, Word finds an unknown word that you are not sure how to spell, don't reach for your printed dictionary yet. You can access Word's internal dictionary by clicking the Suggest button. The program then presents a list of words that it believes are close to the one you want. (See Figure 6-2.) These suggestions come from the Main Dictionary only, not any of your personal dictionaries. If it cannot find any alternatives, Word displays a message telling you this. Then you can grab your Webster's.

If many words are displayed in the list box, scroll to find the one you want. When you spot the right word, select it, and then click the Change button or simply double-click on the word in the list box. If you click the Suggest button by accident after Word has presented the list, you may see a dialog box that says *Word is already spelled correctly.* This happens because the program is reading the word in the Change To field, which is the word currently selected in the Words list box, and that word is spelled correctly.

Getting a suggestion for a word you typed can be very efficient, sometimes even more efficient than taking the time to remember how to spell it correctly and edit it manually. Simply double-click on the word, choose the Spelling command, click the Suggest button, and double-click on the correct spelling to replace the word in your document.

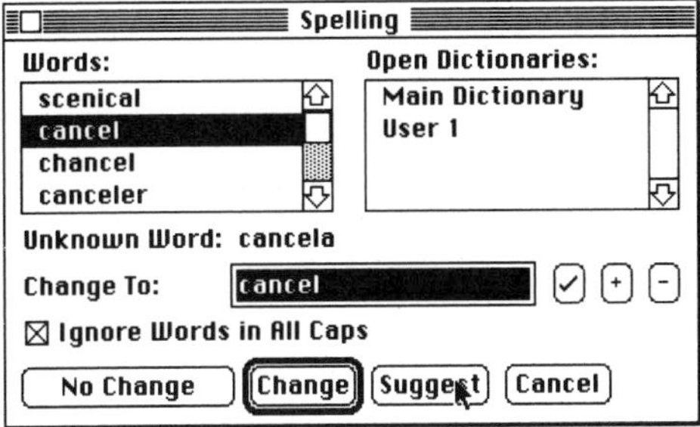

Figure 6-2
A list of suggested words.

Should you not find the word you are looking for in the list of suggestions, try this: Enter a different (probably incorrect) spelling of the word in the Change To field, and then click the √ (check mark) button located immediately to its right. Clicking this button asks Word to search for the Change To word in its dictionary. If the word is spelled correctly this time, a dialog box appears telling you so. If the word isn't found in the dictionary, the program displays it as the Unknown Word. To list a set of alternatives for the new entry, click the Suggest button again, and see if the right word is provided in the Words list box.

Adding Words to a Personal Dictionary

Often, a term that Word stops on is spelled correctly but is not in the Main Dictionary. The word might be a proper noun or a specialized term used in your field or profession. If the word is one that you are likely to use again, you will probably want to add it to one of your personal dictionaries. The words you add are recognized in subsequent spelling checks, and you usually don't have to worry about them anymore.

The Main Dictionary, which is shipped with Word, cannot be altered. The internal format of the file is designed for maximum efficiency, and adding words to it would only slow down the process. Instead, words are added to personal, or User, dictionaries. You can create and use any number of personal dictionaries, although having a large number of dictionaries open at the same time can slow down the checking process. A good rule of thumb is to keep fewer than one thousand words in each of five open dictionaries.

For example, you can create a dictionary filled with legal terms for use when you write and edit legal documents. Another dictionary can hold contractors' terms, for writing and editing home-building specifications. The smaller the dictionary, the faster the spelling checker works. It is better to have many small dictionaries and use them as needed than to have one very large personal dictionary.

Creating a personal dictionary and adding words to it is simple. Word assumes that you want to use the Main and User 1 dictionaries whenever you use the spelling checker, so Word opens them when you choose the Spelling command. (See Appendix A for a list of the folders Word looks in first to find the Main and User dictionaries.) The Open Dictionaries list box shows the dictionary files that are currently open. Unless you've already added words to it, the User 1 dictionary is empty.

To add a word to User 1 or another personal dictionary, assuming that the Spelling dialog box is displayed and the unknown word is selected:

1. If you have more than one personal dictionary open, click on the name of the dictionary to which you want to add the term. This step is optional if only the User 1 and Main dictionaries are open, because Word assumes you want to add terms to the User 1 dictionary. If more than one personal dictionary is open, Word assumes that you want to add the term to the dictionary you selected last, unless you specify otherwise.
2. Click the + (plus) button, as shown in Figure 6-3. The word is added to the selected dictionary, the contents of which appear in the Words list box. (If more than four words are in the dictionary, you may have to scroll in the Words list box to see the word you just added.)
3. Repeat the process for each additional word that you want to add to the selected dictionary.

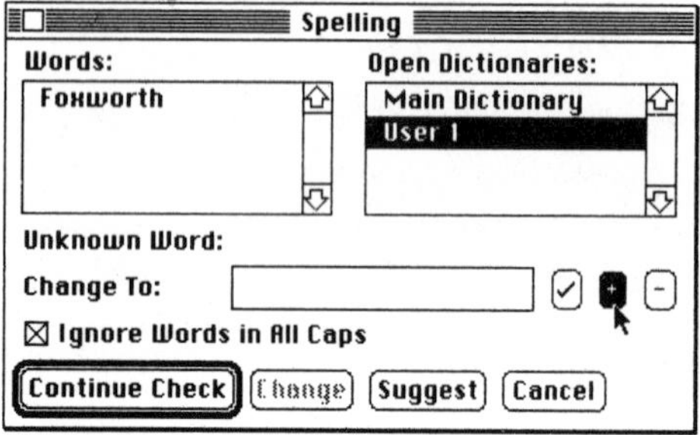

Figure 6-3
Adding a word to the User 1 dictionary.

Correcting a Word and Adding It to a Dictionary

Of course, nothing prevents you from both changing the word and adding it to a personal dictionary. You can do this as follows:

1. Click on the name of the dictionary to which you want to add the word.
2. Click in the Change To edit field and enter the correct spelling, or click on the unknown word to enter it into the Change To field, and edit it.
3. Click the + button to add the word to the selected dictionary.
4. Click the Change button. Word replaces the text.

Beware of trying to add more than one word at a time when you click the + button, as you might when separating two words joined by a typing mistake. If you do this, unpredictable results may occur; for example, the words you add might not show up in the list for the dictionary you selected.

Skipping Past Words

Very often, Word will stop on a person's name, a company name, a street name, or another word that you don't want to add to a personal dictionary. The simplest choice in this situation is to click the No Change button and continue. Once you've done this for a given word, the program remembers it, and for the rest of that session, it skips past the word, pausing on it only long enough to let you know the word may still be suspect.

However, what if you change your mind and decide to add the word or name to a dictionary after all? Because Word only pauses on the words you have skipped over, it doesn't seem as though you have the opportunity any longer. If you double-click on the word and choose the Spelling command to check its spelling, Word responds that the word is spelled correctly. The program assumes that you knew what you were doing when you skipped over the word and that, therefore, it must be spelled correctly.

There are two ways to get around this and add a word to a selected dictionary once you've skipped over it. The first is to set an insertion point in the document, choose the Spelling command, type the word into the Change To field, and click the + button.

The second way involves a trick. If you press the Shift key while choosing the Spelling command, Word forgets its list of skipped words and stops on each one again, allowing you to correct it or add it to a dictionary. Therefore, to add a word, double-click on it to select it and then press the Shift key while choosing the Spelling command. This time Word does not tell you that the word is spelled correctly, but instead presents the Spelling dialog box. Simply select the dictionary to which you want to add the word, and click the + button.

Removing Words from a Dictionary

Sooner or later, you will need to delete a word from one of your personal dictionaries. You may decide that you no longer need a word you previously added, or you may find out that *zephir* is spelled with a *y* instead of an *i* and want to remove the mistake. Here's how to do it:

1. Select the dictionary from the Open Dictionaries list box. The words in that dictionary appear in the Words list box.
2. Select the word to be deleted in the Words list box.
3. Click the – (minus) button to delete the word.

Moving a Word from One Dictionary to Another

To move a word to another dictionary, you must remove it from the source dictionary and then add it to the destination dictionary. The Change To field makes this process simple:

1. Select the source dictionary in the Open Dictionaries list box.
2. Select the word to be moved in the Words list box. The word appears in the Change To field.
3. Click the – button to delete the word from the dictionary.
4. Select the destination dictionary in the Open Dictionaries list box.
5. Click the + button to add the word to the dictionary.

■ *Working with Dictionary Files*

Using dictionary files is much like using any other file; you can open them, close them, and rename them with the commands on the File menu while the Spelling dialog box is active. You can replace the Main Dictionary with one more suited to speakers of the King's English: the UK Dictionary. You can even transfer groups of words from one dictionary to another or convert a dictionary from another word processor into one that Word can use, although these procedures are only for experimentalists.

Saving Dictionaries

Dictionaries, like documents, must be saved on a disk, or their contents will be lost. Word opens the Main and User 1 dictionary files whenever you start the first spelling check in a session. If you want your most frequently used personal dictionary opened for you each time you use the spelling checker, have it be the one named User 1, and store the file in the same folder as the Main Dictionary.

To save the User 1 dictionary, choose the Save command while the Spelling dialog box is active. (Click on the dictionary name before choosing Save if more than one personal dictionary is open.) Click the Save button in the dialog box that appears. (If you've already used the dictionary and created a User 1 dictionary, Word simply saves the file under that name without presenting the dialog box.) The file is saved on the disk as *User 1*. If you neglect to save the dictionary, Word reminds you to do so when you quit the program. If this happens, click the Yes button to save the dictionary.

Alternatively, you can save the dictionary under a different name, on a different disk, or in a different folder. With the User 1 dictionary selected, choose the Save As command and type the new name, as illustrated in

Figure 6-4. Note that the Save dialog box looks and behaves like the one you see when saving a regular document, except that you can't specify a file format or make backup copies of the dictionary file. Click the Drive or Eject button if you want to place the dictionary on another disk. A dictionary can have any name, but to help keep things straight on your desktop, why not add *Dict* to the end of its name, to differentiate it from the other documents you have on the disk?

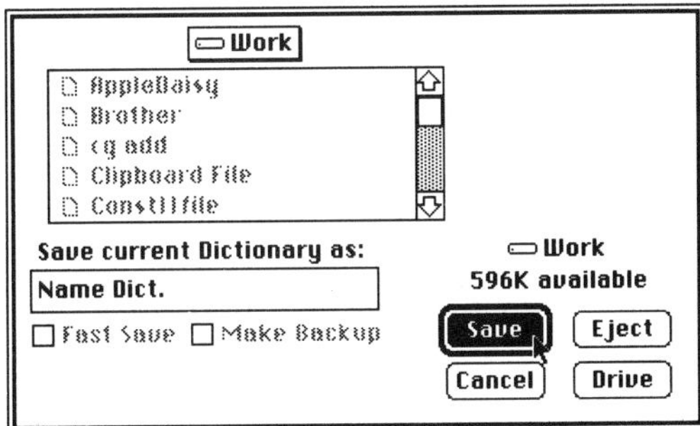

Figure 6-4
The Save Dictionary dialog box.

Creating a New Dictionary

Adding words to the User 1 dictionary is by far the most convenient approach to take if you want all your words in one place. However, if you work with documents from many different fields, you may find that your User 1 dictionary contains so many terms that the speed of the spelling check degrades. (Each personal dictionary works best when kept to fewer than one thousand words.) You may also find it convenient to keep proper names in one dictionary (called Name Dict, for instance), standard words not in the Main Dictionary in the User 1 dictionary, and special jargon in yet another (such as Apiarian Dict). To start a new dictionary:

❶ Choose the Spelling command.

❷ Choose New from the File menu. The name of the new dictionary appears in the Open Dictionaries list box. If the only dictionaries open are Main and User 1, the new name is User 2.

❸ Choose the Save As command to rename your new dictionary, if you like.

After you've created a new dictionary, add your terms to it and save the changes when you quit Word.

Opening and Closing Dictionaries

To open a previously saved dictionary:

1. Choose the Spelling command.
2. Choose the Open command.
3. A list of dictionaries in the current folder is shown in the dialog box. Select and open the dictionary you want.

Open dictionaries are displayed in the Open Dictionaries list box. They remain open until you close them or quit Word. To close a dictionary:

1. In the Open Dictionaries list box, select the name of the dictionary you no longer want to use.
2. Choose the Close command from the File menu. If you have made any changes to the dictionary, Word displays a dialog box asking whether you want to save the dictionary first. Click Yes to save it and close it.

Remember: Keep open only those dictionaries that you need. Your spelling checks go much faster that way.

Changing the Main Dictionary to the UK Dictionary

If you live in the British Isles or Canada, you'll probably be interested in spelling words the British way: *theatre, humour, realise,* and so on. You can do this by substituting the UK Dictionary (found on the Word Utilities disk) for the Main Dictionary. Simply change the name of the Main Dictionary file to US Dictionary and then change the name of the UK Dictionary to Main Dictionary. Reverse the process to switch back.

Advanced Work with Dictionaries

The normal way of adding words to a dictionary is to enter each one individually as you check a document. This can be time consuming if you want to create a dictionary from a word list or convert a dictionary from another word processor or spelling-check program to a Word dictionary.

Adding a Word List to a Personal Dictionary

The procedure for adding a large group of words to a dictionary without using tricks is straightforward. Simply open the document containing your word list, choose the Spelling command, start the check, and for each word that Word selects, press Command- + and then the Return key. If you are working with more than one dictionary, first select the dictionary to which you want to add the word. Otherwise, Word assumes that you want to add all words to the last dictionary selected.

Converting a Non-Word Dictionary to a Word Dictionary

The process just described can be time consuming for lists containing hundreds of words. There is a shortcut for converting a word list to a dictionary, but proceed with caution: Damaged dictionary files may result. Make copies of every dictionary you use beforehand, and revert to the duplicate if you damage a dictionary file. You can copy a file by quitting Word and using the Duplicate command from the Finder's File menu.

The document containing the list of words you want to convert to a dictionary must be stored as a text-only file. First be sure that the words in the document are in the proper format. Each word must be on a line of its own and should end with a paragraph mark (a Return). No extra spaces should appear before or after any word, as shown in Figure 6-5. (The best way to check this is to choose Show ¶ from the Edit menu.) The words should not have capital letters in them unless you want to require that a given word (such as a proper name) be capitalized.

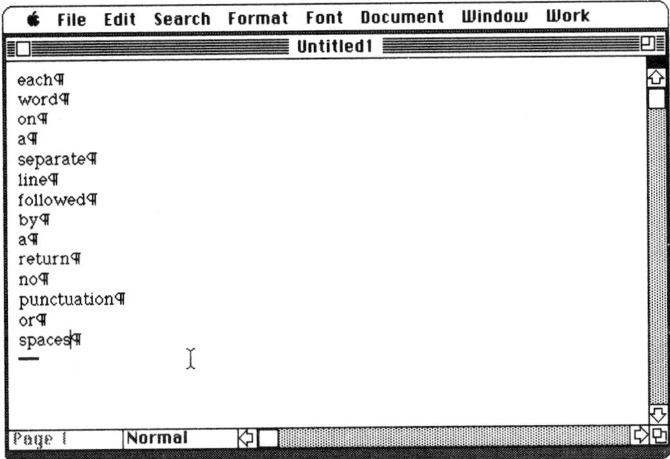

Figure 6-5
The format for converting a word list to a dictionary.

Next, organize the words into three groups, with all-capped words (such as acronyms) first, then initial-capped words (such as proper names), and finally lowercase words. Then select one group at a time and choose the Sort command. The words in each group are sorted from A to Z. When you have sorted the list, be sure there are no blank lines anywhere, including the paragraph mark at the end of the document. (Word does not let you remove the last paragraph mark in a document, so remove the one at the end of the line before it to close up the blank line.) Save the document as a text-only file. (Choose Save As, click the File Formats button, and click the Text Only option.) Then close the document. So far, so good.

To convert the document into a personal dictionary, do the following:

1. Choose New from the File menu to open a blank document.
2. Choose the Spelling command. The Spelling dialog box appears.
3. Press the Shift key and choose the Open command. (Use the mouse, not Shift-Command-O, which is the keystroke sequence for inserting open space in a paragraph.)
4. Open the previously saved document by double-clicking on its name in the list box that appears. The document's name will appear in the Open Dictionaries list box.
5. Select the dictionary's name in the list box (if it is not already selected).
6. Choose the Save As command. Type a new name, or keep the old name. When using the old name, Word asks you to verify that you want to replace the old file; click Yes.

Word converts the file into a personal dictionary, which can be used like any other dictionary. You can add words to it, delete words from it, open it (in the same way as your other dictionaries), close it, and more.

Converting a Dictionary to a Regular Document

You can open any dictionary other than the Main Dictionary as a normal document. You may want to do this, for instance, when using a Word dictionary with another spelling-check program (on the Macintosh or some other computer). The other spelling program must accept word lists that have one word per line, each line ending with a paragraph mark.

You can also use this technique if you want to print a list of the words in a personal dictionary, since Word currently doesn't offer a way to print a dictionary file. In addition, you can open more than one personal dictionary and combine, split, or transfer groups of words at a time.

To convert a dictionary to a regular Word document:

1. Make duplicates of the dictionary files you want to convert, in case something goes wrong. Do this by quitting Word and using the Duplicate command on the Finder's File menu.
2. Restart Word. If you try to open a dictionary as a document after choosing the Spelling command in a session, Word will present a dialog box saying *Not a valid Word document.*
3. Press the Shift key and choose the Open command. The names of all the documents in the current folder are shown. Open your personal dictionary file as a document. Do this for every duplicated dictionary file with which you want to work.

Avoid the temptation to open anything other than regular Word documents and personal dictionary files, unless you're opening a duplicate of the file. Even if Word can successfully open a file (like the Finder), doing so may cause Word to fail, or worse, may disrupt and permanently damage the file if you try to save it.

❹ Edit the lists; cut, copy, or paste between them; or format and print them. If you want to prepare a text-only document to be converted back into a dictionary, however, be sure that each word list you create conforms to the pattern described in the previous section.

❺ When you're finished, save each word list. If you want to convert a word list back into a dictionary, save it in Text Only file format.

Once you have opened and converted a dictionary in this way, you should quit and restart Word before using it with the spelling checker. You can then open the word lists you created as dictionaries if you want, using the methods described earlier in this section. If you don't restart the program, Word will insist that any dictionaries you converted are still open, even if you have closed all document windows.

■ *Points to Remember*

- ❑ You cannot change entries in Word's Main Dictionary, but you can create your own personal, or User, dictionaries. Each personal dictionary can have as many as 64,000 entries, and you can have as many as 16 dictionaries open at once, but for speedy spell-checking, limit your entries to 1,000 per dictionary, and do not have more than five dictionaries open at one time.
- ❑ The spelling checker will not check text that is in hidden format unless it is visible. The Preferences dialog box controls the display of hidden text.
- ❑ Word opens the Main Dictionary and the User 1 dictionary when you choose the Spelling command. You must open other dictionaries you want to use.
- ❑ When you click the No Change button for an unknown word during a spelling check, Word ignores that word for the rest of the session. To have Word "forget" its list of No Change words, press the Shift key while you choose the Spelling command.
- ❑ If you need to, you can convert a document to a dictionary file or open a dictionary file as a document. However, always be sure to make copies of any files you manipulate in this way, in case one should become damaged.

■ *Techniques*

Check Spelling

The Spelling dialog box	Action
Words list box	After you click Suggest, shows possible correct spellings; after you select a personal dictionary, shows the words in that dictionary.
Open Dictionaries list box	Shows the names of the open dictionaries.
Unknown Word area	Shows the word that caused the spelling checker to stop.
Change To field	Contains the word that is to replace the unknown word or that is to be added to the selected dictionary.
Ignore Words in All Caps option	Indicates whether Word should ignore uppercase text and acronyms.

The Spelling dialog box	Action
√ button	Checks the spelling of the word shown in the Change To field.
+ button	Adds the unknown word or the word in the Change To field to the selected personal dictionary.
- button	Removes the selected word from the selected dictionary.
Start Check or Continue Check button	Starts or continues a spelling check.
Change button	Replaces the unknown word with the word in the Change To field.
No Change button	Skips past the word for the rest of the session.

Start a spelling check

❶ Position the insertion point where you want to begin the spelling check, or select specific text. (Double-click on a word to check its spelling alone.)

❷ Choose Spelling from the Document menu. Word checks first the word containing the insertion point or to the left of it.

❸ Click Start Check.

When a word is not found in a dictionary, it appears in the Unknown Word area. If you start a check in the middle of a document, when Word reaches the end it asks if you want to continue checking from the beginning of the document. Click OK to continue or Cancel to stop.

Add the unknown word to a personal dictionary

❶ Select the dictionary.

❷ Click the + button, or press Command- +.

Correct the unknown word

❶ Type the replacement in the Change To field, or click on the unknown word to display it in the Change To field and then edit it.

❷ Click the Change button.

Correct the unknown word and add it to a dictionary

❶ Type the replacement in the Change To field, or click on the unknown word to display it in the Change To field and then edit it.

❷ Select the dictionary to which you want to add the word.

❸ Click the + button, or press Command- +.

❹ Click the Change button.

Have Word suggest a spelling for the unknown word

❶ Click the Suggest button.

❷ Select the correct word.

❸ Click the Change button.

Do nothing to the unknown word

❶ Click the No Change button. Word will not stop on that word again during the current session.

Remove a word from a dictionary

❶ Choose the Spelling command.

❷ Select the dictionary by clicking on its name in the Open Dictionaries list box.

❸ Select the word to be removed from the Words list box, or type it in the Change To field.

❹ Click the - button, or press Command- –.

Working with Dictionary Files

Create a new dictionary

❶ Choose the Spelling command.

❷ Choose New from the File menu.

❸ In the Change To field, type each word you want to add and click the + button after each. Be sure to type words as they should appear in the document; for example, type all proper names with an initial capital letter.

You can also run a spelling check on a document containing the words you want to add.

Open a dictionary

1. Choose the Spelling command.
2. Choose Open from the File menu.
3. Open the desired dictionary file.

The name of the dictionary appears in the Open Dictionaries list box.

Save a dictionary

1. Choose the Spelling command.
2. Select the dictionary you want to save.
3. Choose the Save command.
4. If you haven't saved the dictionary before, Word will ask you to specify a name. Do so, and then click Save.

Close a dictionary

1. Choose the Spelling command.
2. Select the dictionary you want to close.
3. Choose Close from the File menu.

Move a word from one dictionary to another

1. Choose the Spelling command.
2. Select the source dictionary and select the word to be moved. The word appears in the Change To field.
3. Click the - button to delete the word.
4. Select the destination dictionary.
5. Click the + button to add the word to the selected dictionary.

Use the UK Dictionary

1. Give the Main Dictionary another name.
2. Change the name of the UK Dictionary file to Main Dictionary.

Character Formatting

When you spend a lot of time getting the wording in a document just right, you want it to look good on paper. A well-designed document presents text in a format that is attractive, readable, and easy to follow. It invites the reader to delve into its pages. A document that is not formatted or that is poorly designed is likely to turn away potential readers. Reading such a document is distracting because the design elements that should serve as guideposts for readers are inconsistent or missing altogether. A poor design can intrude upon and detract from the message you are trying to get across.

Microsoft Word provides many features for enhancing the look, style, and readability of your written communications. These capabilities allow you to do much more than construct simple paragraphs or italicize a word here or there. Word's formatting features enable you to personalize your documents and make them special with little extra work on your part.

With Word, you can format your documents almost any way you like. For example, Word lets you freely adjust tabs, margins, line spacing, and character attributes. With only a handful of commands, you can precisely control the location of every character on every page. In the next several chapters, you'll learn how to control the look of your text and the shape of each paragraph, how to number pages in a variety of styles and formats, how to break documents into sections, and more.

■ *An Overview of Document Design*

Look at the sample documents in Chapter 17, "Blueprints." They were developed not to represent the ultimate in modern graphic design but to give you an idea of the range of effects you can achieve in Word and to show you how to go about creating similar designs for your own documents. As you read the next few chapters, keep in mind the following principles of good design.

Your primary goal is a document that is attractive and readable. The font you use must be easy to read, and the relationship of the font used for body text to the fonts used in headings, headers, and footers should be harmonious and balanced. The lines of text should be short enough for you to read without losing your place. You should be able to find the major sections in a document, but the design elements that give the document its order and structure should not be overwhelming or distracting.

The appearance you develop for a document must be consistent. Readers use design elements (the style of headings, for example) to orient themselves. If a main heading and a subtopic look too much alike or, worse, if the same level of heading is in a different style in two places, the reader may become confused as to the logic and structure of your thesis. Style sheets in Word are a tremendous aid for establishing a consistent design. With this feature you can attach styles to the different elements of your document and fine-tune the design before, during, and after the writing of text. When you make a change to a style definition, every instance of that style in the document changes as well.

The design you develop for a document should also be appropriate to its subject. Poetry, for example, does not consume much space on a page, and so you can be freer with margins and line spacing, and you might arrange to have each poem printed on the right side of the page, with a graphic on the left. A scientific treatise might have four or five heading levels, because its purpose is not so much to provide an aesthetic experience as to communicate information clearly.

Of course, more than anything else, you want the design of your document to present your topic clearly. After all, unless you write for yourself alone, you are writing to communicate with the reader. Every element in a document—the content as well as the appearance—should support that clarity. The reader should not have to work to extract meaning from the material you present.

The need for clarity and consistency is of such importance that in many fields documents must be formatted according to specific requirements, or they are rejected out of hand. Doctoral dissertations, for example, must be prepared using a strict set of manuscript preparation rules; the same applies to screenplays, government bids and reports, and application forms. Often you can get style guides from writer's manuals, from the editorial offices of the publication for which you are writing, or from the department where you expect to get your doctorate. Once you have received a style guide, you must then translate its rules into a set of specifications—page dimensions and margins, font choices, style sheet definitions, placement of footnotes, and so on—in Word.

The Four Format Domains

In Word, you apply formatting and design decisions by making changes within one of the four format domains. These range in scope from the smallest unit your document can contain—the character—to the largest possible—the document itself.

Character Formats

Characters to Word are what atoms are to chemists; there is no smaller unit in a Word document. You can change the appearance of almost all 256 elements in the ASCII character set by changing their *font*. Some fonts, such as Zapf Dingbats, contain few or no alphabetic letter shapes, but instead consist of geometric shapes, border patterns, specialized icons, and so on. You can change the point size, or *font size,* of characters, and you can also change their attributes, or *font style* (not to be confused with styles on a style sheet), by making them bold or underlining them. Finally, you can adjust the placement of characters on a line by superscripting or subscripting them, or by expanding or contracting the spacing of characters. These topics are covered in this chapter.

Paragraph Formats

A paragraph is any collection of characters that is delimited by the paragraph mark, which is entered when you press the Return key. The paragraph attributes you can change in Word include margins, indention, location and type of tab stops, alignment and spacing of lines, and space before and after each paragraph. You can also draw lines around paragraphs as well as change their placement on the page—printing them side by side, starting them at the top of a page, or making sure that two paragraphs are kept together on one page. The next chapter covers this subject.

You can collect a set of character and paragraph formats, give it a name, and store it in a style sheet with other style definitions. When you apply a style, you apply it to one or more whole paragraphs; each paragraph in a document is assigned a style. When you make adjustments to a style, the changes are reflected in every paragraph to which that style has been applied. Styles are discussed in detail in Chapter 9.

Section Formats

Sections are collections of paragraphs that are separated by the double-dotted line that appears when you press Command-Enter. Sections are perhaps most easily compared to chapters in a book: You can have a chapter always start on a right-hand page, or use a different running head than the chapter before it, and you can specify that footnotes be printed at the end of each chapter. In a more generic sense, sections control some of the larger design elements in a document. For example, you can change from three-column text to one-column text and back again within one page of a newsletter by defining each of the areas as a different section. Chapter 10 covers this topic, and Chapter 11, "Headers, Footers, and Footnotes," deals with more of these large-scale design elements.

Document Formats

The largest unit in your document is the document itself, composed of one or more sections. Some of the parameters that pertain to the document as a whole include the size of the paper on which you want to print your document, the overall margins of the page, whether you want to print vertically or horizontally, and whether footnotes should fall at the end of the document or at the end of sections within the document. You can change these attributes by choosing the Page Setup command from the File menu and by manipulating the document while in Page Preview mode. Document formatting, Page Preview, and all the preparations for printing are covered in Chapter 12, "Document Formatting and Printing."

■ *Working with Character Formats*

Characters consist of the letters, numbers, symbols, and punctuation marks you write with in Word. You can vary the shape, size, style, and placement of characters individually or throughout an entire document. Character formats in Word consist of the following:

- ❑ Font: You are limited only by the number and variety of fonts installed in the System file on the Word disk.
- ❑ Font size: The size of a font can range from 2 points to 127 points. The Macintosh follows typesetting standards and displays 72 points per inch on the screen.
- ❑ Font style or attribute: Choose from among underline, outline, **bold**, *italic*, and more—or combine them as you see fit. You can bury comments, editorial notes, and so on in your documents by using the Hidden character attribute.
- ❑ Position: In addition to their normal position on the baseline, characters can be either above it (as a superscript) or below it (as a subscript).
- ❑ Spacing: You can s t r e t c h or shrink the spacing of characters.

You establish a character format primarily through the Character dialog box, although you can also access some formats from the Format and Font menus. Text can be formatted either after you've entered it or as you type it.

In the first case, you simply select the text and choose one or more character formats. In the second, you set the insertion point and choose a new character format. Every character you type after that reflects the new format.

When you replace text, the characters you type retain the format of the original text. Suppose you underlined one word in a document. If you double-click on the word to select it and then start typing, the new text will be underlined. If you backspace over the word to delete it, the insertion point is still set for the underlining attribute, even after you delete the last character. Any new text you type in that spot will be underlined.

This behavior can be a little confusing; you probably don't expect to see underlining after you've deleted the word. However, Word assumes that you've just placed the insertion point there and chosen that set of formats in preparation for inserting some text. A good trick for getting around this is simply to backspace one character past the beginning of the underlined word to reset the insertion point to plain text.

When you choose Character from the Format menu, you see a dialog box like the one shown in Figure 7-1. It is divided into groups of options that reflect the character formats you can apply to text. You can move this dialog box, as you can move the others that have a title bar, by dragging it to a new position. Double-clicking in the title bar toggles the dialog box between its original position and the new position so that you can reveal the text beneath it. For your convenience, Word records in the Word Settings file the position the box is in when you quit the program.

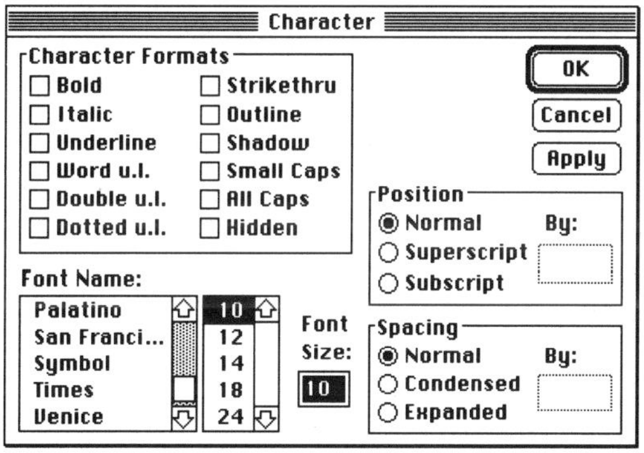

Figure 7-1
The Character dialog box.

The Character dialog box is the control center for all character formats; you can see what formats your text has by placing the insertion point and displaying this dialog box.

By definition, the insertion point is always between two characters. The format of text you type at the insertion point is almost always determined by the preceding character. The exception is when the preceding character is one of the special characters Word uses for such items as footnote references and the page and date elements in the Header and Footer windows. In these cases the format is taken from the text immediately before the special character. The reason for this should be obvious: You want any text you insert after a footnote reference to have the same format as the rest of the text, rather than the format of the footnote reference. If for some reason you have more than one of these special characters in a row (for example, the time and date elements in a Header window), Word reverts to plain text instead of taking the format from the text before the special characters.

Changing the Font

Word uses the 12-point New York font when you first start typing in the *Normal* style (if you haven't yet redefined the style), but you can choose a new font for any text in the document.

Fonts, sometimes called *typefaces*, are stored as resources in the System file on the Word disk. The Character dialog box displays the names and point sizes of all the fonts that are currently installed. All startup disks have their own System file, each of which can contain a different set of font resources. Use the Apple Font/DA Mover to install or remove fonts (as well as desk accessories). The amount of space a font consumes is not trivial, especially if you install a range of point sizes. The larger the point size of a font, the more disk space it uses. It is best to install only fonts you will use regularly.

TIP

Fonts and System Disks
If space on your working disk is tight, keep extra copies of Word, each with its own System file and font assortments, for special occasions when you need an unusual or special typeface.

Choosing Fonts from the Character Dialog Box

Word displays fonts in the Font Name list box in the Character dialog box and on the Font menu. To choose a new font from the list box:

1. Choose the Character command. The dialog box appears.
2. Scroll through the Font Name list box until you find the font you want. Select it and click OK, or double-click on the font name.

Instead of clicking the OK button, you can click the Apply button to see the effect of your font choice in the document without dismissing the dialog box. Clicking Cancel after using the Apply button does not cancel the font change; to do that, you must choose Undo Formatting from the Edit menu.

Choosing Fonts from the Font Menu

To choose a new font from the Font menu, simply pull down the menu and select the one you want. If the font isn't there, you must access it through the Character dialog box.

If fonts you use regularly are not on the Font menu, you can add them as follows: First choose the Character command; then, for each font you want to add, press Option-Command- + and click on the font name.

Word's Font, Format, and Work menus are limited to 31 items each. If you've added more fonts than your screen can display at one time, you see a triangle at the bottom of the menu. Drag the pointer below the end of the menu to scroll the menu and display the items at the bottom of the list. When you do this, the first few items on the menu are replaced with another triangle, which signals that more items are listed above the top of the menu. Unfortunately, you cannot choose these "hidden" menu items from the keyboard; use the mouse instead.

To delete a font from the Font menu, press Option-Command- – (minus), pull down the Font menu, and click on the font you want to remove.

Choosing Fonts from the Keyboard

Another useful way to set a font is from the keyboard. Press Shift-Command-E; the word *Font* appears in the status box of the window. Type the first few letters of the name of the font you want—enough to establish it as unique—and press the Return key. To change the font again, simply click in the status area. The word *Font* appears again, and you can type a new font name.

TIP

Font ID Numbers

Instead of typing the font name in the status box when you are using the Shift-Command-E key sequence, you can type the ID number for the font. The Macintosh system and some programs know each font both by a number assigned to it and by its name. This table lists some common font ID (FID) numbers:

FID	Name	FID	Name
0	Chicago	13	Zapf Dingbats
1	Geneva	14	Bookman
2	New York	15	Helvetica Narrow
3	Geneva	16	Palatino
4	Monaco	18	Zapf Chancery
5	Venice	20	Times
6	London	21	Helvetica
7	Athens	22	Courier
8	San Francisco	23	Symbol
9	Toronto	24	Mobile
10	Seattle	33	Avant Garde
11	Cairo	34	New Century Schoolbook
12	Los Angeles		

Word, however, uses only the font ID number, and not the font name, to keep track of your fonts internally. This can cause occasional problems, because the Font/DA Mover is capable of changing this number if you install a font that has the same number as a font already installed in the System file. Suspect that you are having this problem if you create a document under one System file and find that, when you reopen it under another, a font used in the document seems to have been replaced with another, even though that font is also installed in the second System file. (If a font used in your document doesn't exist in the System file, Word substitutes another font, usually New York or Geneva.)

For example, the Boston and Zapf Dingbats fonts may collide if your System file originally had Boston in it and you added Zapf Dingbats later. If you create a document containing some dingbats on another Mac and then open the document under this System file, all the Zapf Dingbats in your document change to characters in the Boston font. To correct this situation:

❶ Launch the Font/DA Mover, and open the System file's fonts.

❷ Remove the Zapf Dingbats and Boston fonts.

❸ Reinstall the Zapf Dingbats font from a copy of the original disk containing the LaserWriter Plus fonts. (If you don't have the disk, try installing the font from another System file that doesn't have Boston on it.) The original font ID number is preserved this time, since there is no collision.

❹ Reinstall the Boston font. Because the Zapf font has already been installed, the ID number of the Boston font in the System file changes instead of that of the Zapf font.

❺ Quit the Font/DA Mover.

Because there is no requirement that each font have a unique ID number, you may run into this problem more frequently with special fonts obtained from sources other than Apple.

If you don't have the option of removing and adding fonts to the System file of the Mac which prints your document, you can also try saving the file in the RTF format on the Mac that you've used to create the document. When you do this, Word encodes the fonts used in the document by their name, not by font number. Then, when you want to print the document on the Mac having a different arrangement of fonts, simply open the file from Word on that Mac to convert the RTF file back to Word format. For more information on RTF files, see Chapter 15, "Transferring Text and Graphics."

Changing the Font Size

Fonts come in different point sizes, usually ranging from 9 to 24 points. You can actually use any point size from 2 to 127 (in whole numbers); if the specific point size you want is not installed on the disk, Word scales the font to fit your request. Scaled fonts typically look jagged and uneven, as depicted in Figure 7-2, because the scaling is not always perfect. For speed and appearance, choose only font sizes that are installed on the disk. If you are using a LaserWriter, the scaling issue is not as important, because fonts are scaled smoothly when printed, regardless of what you see on the screen.

This is text in 12-point Chicago.

This is text in 14-point Chicago.

Figure 7-2
A normal font and a scaled font.

Note that when you choose a font from the Font menu, some of the sizes are outlined and others are plain. (See Figure 7-3.) The outlined font sizes are the ones installed for the current font in the System file of your Word disk. The nonoutlined sizes are not installed on the disk; choosing one of these displays the font scaled from one of the sizes that are available.

Figure 7-3
Font menu for Geneva sizes.

If you must pick a font size that is not installed on the disk, try for one that's exactly twice as large as an outlined font size. Text scaling in Word—and in other Macintosh applications, for that matter—works better when performed in even multiples of an installed font. A 12-point font scaled up to 24 points looks better than the same font scaled to 18 points.

Choosing a Font Size from the Character Dialog Box

You can choose a font size at any time, whether you pick a new font or not. Like fonts, font sizes can be selected from within the Character dialog box or from the Font menu. To change the font size from the Character dialog box, do the following:

1. Choose the Character command.
2. The Font Size list box (to the right of the Font Name box) lists the point sizes installed on the disk for the selected font. If you see the one you want, click on it. Otherwise, type the new point size in the Font Size edit field. (The number displayed in the field is the currently selected size.)

Remember that scaled fonts slow down the Mac and may look jagged and uneven onscreen and remain so when you print the document on a dot-matrix printer such as the ImageWriter. If you print on the LaserWriter this is not as important a consideration, because PostScript printers can scale fonts much more smoothly.

Choosing a Font Size from the Font Menu

To pick a new font size from the Font menu, pull down the menu and choose the one you want. Note that the Font menu is limited to 31 fonts and sizes (combined), and so it may contain only a few of the sizes you need. Like fonts, font sizes can be added to and removed from this menu. For example, if you are doing a newsletter and use 36-point Bookman for the titles of your articles (commonly called the *display font*, as opposed to the *text font* for your document), you would add the 36-point size to the Font menu as follows:

1. Choose the Character command.
2. Select the Bookman font from the Font Name list box.
3. If 36-point Bookman is installed in your System file, the 36-point option appears in the Font Size list box. If not, type *36* in the Font Size edit field next to the list box.
4. Press Option-Command- +, and click on the 36-point size in either the list box or the edit field depending on what you did in step 3. The menu bar blinks, signaling that the item has been added to the Font menu.
5. Click Cancel.

Choosing a Font Size from the Keyboard

You can't set a specific font size from the keyboard, but you can easily increase or decrease the current size. Simply select some text or set an insertion point, and press either Shift-Command- > to increase the size or Shift-Command- < to decrease the size. Word displays the new point size in the status box of the window, choosing the next size from a list of the most common font sizes (7, 9, 10, 12, 14, 18, 24, 36, 48, 60, and 72 points). Keep increasing or decreasing the size until you have what you want.

Changing Character Attributes

All characters can be assigned various *attributes*, such as boldface or underlining. These attributes are listed in the Character Formats option group in the Character dialog box, but they will be called attributes here to distinguish them from fonts, font sizes, character position, and letterspacing, which are also character formats. Most character attributes can be mixed; that is, you can both boldface and underline text if you want. Do this with caution, however; too many attributes can spoil the brew. Figure 7-4 shows the 12 possible character attributes and how they look on the screen. The first line in the figure, showing Plain Text, is for comparison. (See "The Plain Text Command," later in this chapter.)

Plain Text – ABCDEFabcdef1234567890
Bold – ABCDEFabcdef1234567890
Italic – ABCDEFabcdef1234567890
Underline – ABCDEFabcdef1234567890
Word Underline – ABCDEFabcdef1234567890
Double Underline – ABCDEFabcdef1234567890
Dotted Underline – ABCDEFabcdef1234567890
~~Strikethru – ABCDEFabcdef1234567890~~
Outline – ABCDEFabcdef1234567890
Shadow – ABCDEFabcdef1234567890
SMALL CAPS – ABCDEFABCDEF1234567890
ALL CAPS – ABCDEFABCDEF1234567890
Hidden – ABCDEFabcdef1234567890

Figure 7-4
The 12 character attributes.

When every character of a block of text you've selected has exactly the same set of character attributes (a *homogeneous* set of attributes), and you choose the Character command, you see those attributes checked in the Character Format group of the dialog box. If some of the characters in the selected text have different formats, you see all the attribute check boxes filled with gray. The check boxes are also gray if you've selected a large amount of text, roughly 500 characters if you are selecting by characters or 40 paragraphs if you are selecting by paragraphs.

If you are experienced with Microsoft Excel, you might expect Word to use a similar convention for the display of format options in the dialog box: checked if all selected text has the format and gray if only some of the text has the format. However, there are so many possible format combinations that it would take Word too long to analyze the text you've selected and display the information in the dialog box. Instead, Word shows every check box filled with gray.

A similar condition exists in the lower half of the Format menu. If you select text that has a homogeneous set of formats and then pull down the menu, you see the attributes checked on the menu. If you select text that does not have a homogeneous mixture of character formats (or if too much text is selected), none of the menu items are checked.

Choosing Character Attributes

You can set a character attribute in one of three ways. First, you can choose the Character command from the Format menu and select options from the dialog box that appears.

The second way is to choose an option from the lower half of the Format menu. You can add attributes to the Format menu by first choosing the Character command and then pressing Option-Command- + and clicking on every attribute you want to add to the menu. When you're finished adding the attributes, click Cancel to avoid changing anything in your document.

The third way to set a character attribute is to press a sequence of keys from the keyboard. It may help you remember these sequences to know that Word uses Shift-Command combinations for formatting operations and Option-Command combinations for editing operations. The complete set of keyboard sequences you need to achieve these effects is presented at the end of the chapter.

All these methods for setting a character attribute toggle. For example, if you select a word and underline it, you remove the underlining by using the same command or set of keystrokes again. If the text you select does not have a homogeneous set of attributes, the attribute you choose will be applied to all the text. Using the same command again will then remove the attribute from every character in the text.

Now let's take a tour through Word's range of character formats.

TIP

Undoing Character, Position, and Spacing Formats
While the Character dialog box is displayed and before you click Apply, you can return certain options in a changed format to their original state without resetting other options you want to keep—like a partial Undo command. Each group in the Character dialog box is surrounded by a line and has a title: Character Formats, Spacing, and Position. (The font and font size aren't marked in this way and don't work like this.) If you selected a set of changes to the options in a particular group and want to return them to their original state, simply click on the title of that group. For example, to revert to the previous character attribute settings, you would click on the Character Format title in the dialog box.

The Bold, Italic, Strikethrough, Outline, and Shadow Attributes

The bold, italic, strikethrough, outline, and shadow attributes are quite straightforward. To set one of these formats, simply select the text and apply the attribute by using one of the methods described in the previous section.

The outline, shadow, and underline formats, as well as the subscript and superscript formats, are unusual in that using them often changes the line spacing for the lines in the paragraph containing the formatted text. For example, if you underline a word in a paragraph, you may notice that the following line moves down a bit. This happens because the format has changed the dimensions of the text in the paragraph, and Word pushes down the subsequent lines to accommodate the change.

Usually you don't want this to happen, as it detracts from the appearance of your document. Choose the Paragraph command from the Format menu and check the Line edit field; when the line spacing is set to Auto or to a number close to single spacing, Word makes adjustments to the line spacing. The remedy is either to set the line-spacing number high enough to provide room to spare if a format increases the vertical dimension of the text, or to use a negative number in the Line field. A negative line-spacing number tells Word to use that line spacing regardless of the dimensions of the text in the line. This is discussed in more detail in the next chapter, "Paragraph Formatting."

Underlining Text

Word supports four forms of underlining, only one of which can be selected at a time:

- ❑ Underline: A standard underline. Underlines all characters, including spaces.
- ❑ Word Underline: Underlines complete words and punctuation marks only; spaces, nonbreaking spaces, and tabs are not underlined.
- ❑ Double Underline: Places a double underline below all characters and spaces.
- ❑ Dotted Underline: Places a dotted underline below all characters and spaces. When printed on the LaserWriter, a dotted underline looks more like a gray bar than a series of dots.

If you are experienced with Word 1.05, you may have used its tab leader feature to draw horizontal lines in your documents for elements such as dotted lines in contracts or page-number references in tables of contents. This feature exists in Word 3.0, but you don't have to use it as much because of the new version's wider range of underline attributes. When you underline text containing tabs, the tabs are underlined as well. If you want to underline only text—the headings in a table, for instance—use the Word Underline attribute.

Capitalizing Text

You can choose SMALL CAPS or ALL CAPS, but not both. Small caps are commonly used for the abbreviations A.M., P.M., B.C., and A.D., for acronyms that might be obtrusive if presented in full-size capital letters, or to give a distinctive look to display text (such as article titles). You type lowercase letters, which in small-capped format are converted to capital letters in the next smaller font size.

These attributes are interesting in that they do not really convert lowercase letters to uppercase letters; only their appearance changes. If you type lowercase letters in one of these formats, you see uppercase letters as though you had pressed the Caps Lock key. However, if you then remove the attribute, the text returns to whatever case you originally typed.

Using Hidden Text

The hidden attribute affects characters in one of two ways: When the Show Hidden Text option is turned on in the Preferences dialog box (displayed from the Edit menu), characters formatted as hidden appear with a light dotted or gray underline, as shown in Figure 7-5. When Show Hidden Text is turned off, the text disappears from view. The Show Hidden Text option affects the visual display of characters only; a similar option in the Print dialog box controls whether or not hidden text is printed.

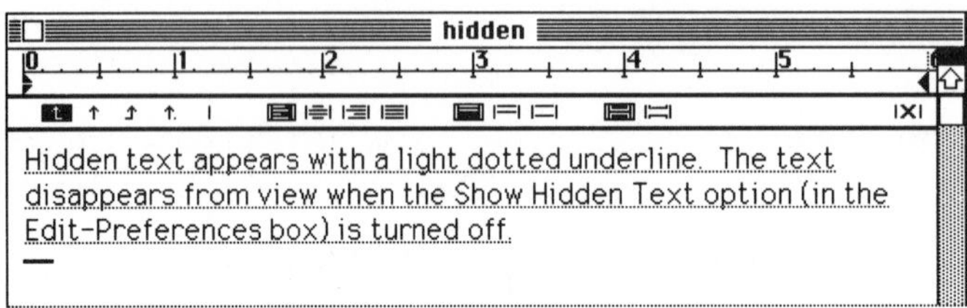

Figure 7-5
Hidden text as it appears on the screen.

Hidden text can be considered the ultimate formatting option because you can control whether text with this attribute is visible or invisible. The main uses for hidden text are as follows:

- ❑ To bury comments in a document. This is useful for documents created or edited by more than one person. You can pass remarks from person to person without changing the apparent content of the document.
- ❑ To hide PostScript commands in a document. (See Appendix C.)
- ❑ To indicate markers for tables of contents and index entries. (See Chapter 13, "Creating a Table of Contents and Index.")
- ❑ To bury a filename before material inserted when you use Word's QuickSwitch feature. (See Chapter 15, "Transferring Text and Graphics.")

Hidden text has a few properties that make it different from the other character attributes. When you do a spelling check, for instance, Word does not check the spelling of hidden text while it is invisible. To check the spelling of hidden text, first turn on the Show Hidden Text option. Similarly, you usually do not want to repaginate or hyphenate hidden text, and so you should make it invisible before repaginating or hyphenating your document. Also, you can print the hidden text regardless of whether or not it is visible in the document when you select the Print Hidden Text option in the Print dialog box.

TIP

Adding Show Hidden Text to the Format Menu
You can add the Show Hidden Text option to the Format menu by choosing Preferences from the Edit menu, pressing Option-Command- +, and clicking on the Show Hidden Text option. The menu bar blinks to signal that the option has been added to the menu. To remove the option, press Option-Command- – (minus), and choose Show Hidden Text from the menu.

Changing the Position of Text

The various characteristics of characters have been given names over time; Figure 7-6 shows some of them. Word usually prints and displays characters with their baselines aligned, even when there is more than one font, size, or character attribute on a line. You can move text up or down relative to this baseline with the Position options in the Character dialog box.

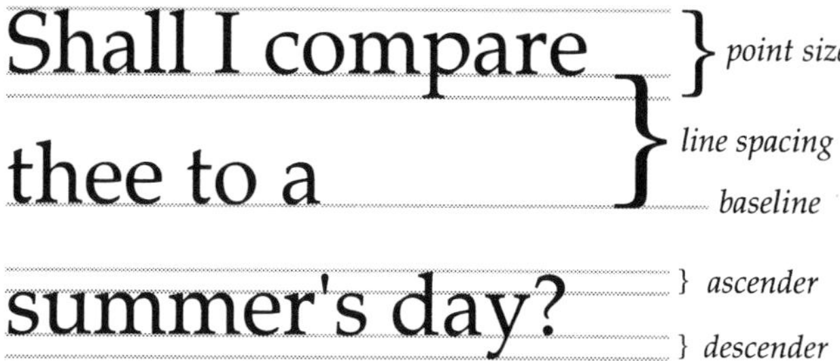

Figure 7-6
Character anatomy.

The superscript format is often used to place numbers or special graphic characters (often called dingbats) a little above the text for such purposes as marking footnote references. In fact, if you look at the automatic style definition for footnote references, you'll see that it uses the superscript position format. Here are some of the characters that are frequently superscripted:

Character	Name	Key sequence
*	asterisk	Shift-8
™	trademark	Option-2
®	registered trademark	Option-R
§	section mark	Option-6
†	dagger	Option-T
‡	double dagger	Shift-Option-7

You can use the Key Caps desk accessory to find other special characters. Another use for superscripting and subscripting is for exponents and the indices of subscripted variables:

$$r_{(n+1)}^2 = x^2 + y^2$$

Look closely at the Mac's screen and you'll see that it is composed of many lines, each of which is made up of tiny dots, or *pixels*. The standard Macintosh screen contains 342 lines with 512 dots per line (or a screen resolution of 512 by 342 pixels). Each line is equal to 1 point, or 1⁄72 inch.

In Word, you can specify both superscripting and subscripting in increments of 0.5 point, from 0.5 to 63.5 points (about 7⁄8 inch). Measurements are rounded to the nearest half point. For example, Word rounds 0.74 point to 0.5 point, and 0.76 point to 1 point. It may seem extreme to have a superscript that is as much as 63.5 points above the baseline, but it isn't when you consider that in some mathematical applications superscripts themselves can have superscripts and that large font sizes may need high superscripts to achieve the right effect.

To raise text by 1 point, select it and choose the Character command. Click the Superscript option in the Position group. Word offers the default positioning, 3 points. Change the number to 1 point and click OK. Figure 7-7 shows the effect of superscripted and subscripted text moved 2, 4, and 6 points above and below the baseline.

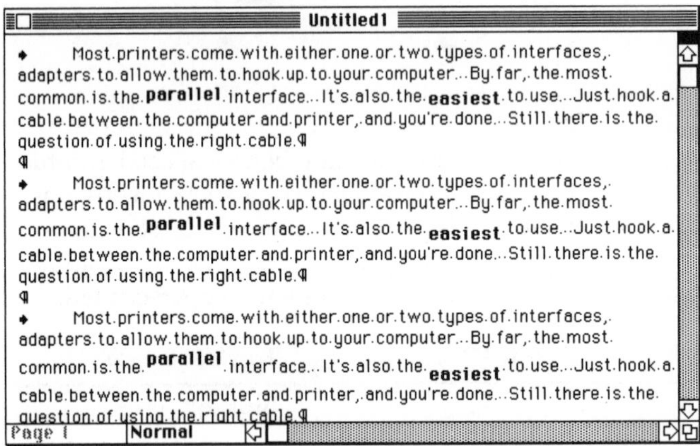

Figure 7-7
Subscripted and superscripted text.

Changing the Spacing of Text

Most fonts for the Macintosh are known as *proportional fonts*—that is, the *i*'s and *l*'s take up less horizontal space than the *m*'s and *w*'s. Characters in fixed-width, or *monospace*, fonts, including Monaco and Courier (the latter is used with the LaserWriter), are evenly spaced on the screen and on paper. The spacing properties of a font are built into it when the font is created. You can extend or contract this spacing with the Spacing options. The process of adjusting the spacing between letters or throughout a font is called *kerning* in the publishing and graphic arts trades.

To increase the spacing between characters, click Expanded and enter the number of points by which you want to increase the spacing. Word always adds the space after the character, not before. You can expand the spacing by as much as 14 points, in quarter-point increments. To decrease the spacing, click Condensed and enter a number of points from 0 to 1.75, again in quarter-point increments. Figure 7-8 shows some examples of expanded and condensed text.

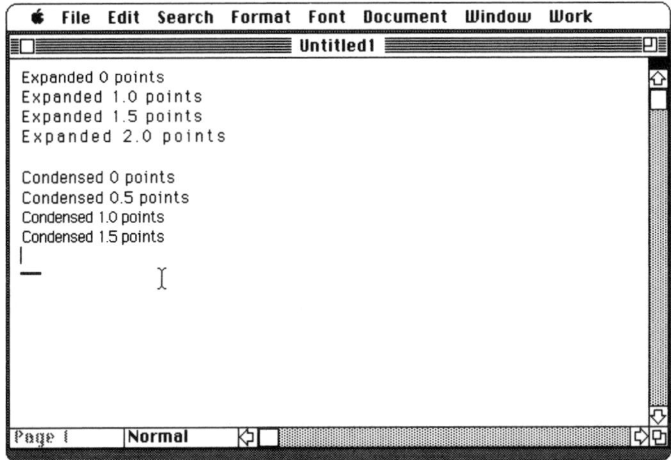

Figure 7-8
Expanded and condensed text.

Because the Macintosh screen can't display anything smaller than one pixel, or one point, you can make adjustments in the spacing of text that will be visible when the document is printed but not when it is displayed on the screen. These adjustments are more noticeable when you print expanded or condensed text on a PostScript printer such as the LaserWriter (which can position text accurately to 0.25 point) or a typesetting printer such as a Linotronic typesetter (accurate to as little as 0.03 point). However, you'll find that you have much more control over the spacing of characters when you set the Fractional Widths option in the Print dialog box before you print on a PostScript printer. See Chapter 12, "Document Formatting and Printing," for more information on the Fractional Widths option.

Generally you kern text for three reasons: to adjust specific letter pairs, to stretch or contract an entire font, and to achieve special typographic effects.

Kerning Pairs of Letters

Often, a pair of letters does not fit together pleasingly when printed, leaving either an unsightly gap or no space at all. Consider the following examples:

Unkerned	Kerned	Effect used
VA	VA	Condensed, 1.8 points
RT	RT	Condensed, 1.8 points
wC	wC	Expanded, 1.3 points
$400	$ 400	First character expanded, 3 points

These differences may be subtle, but they can have a significant impact on the aesthetics of your documents, particularly in large display text such as titles of articles or sections in a document.

To kern a pair of letters, select the first letter, choose the Character command, and enter an appropriate spacing. Because the spacing is measured from the end of each letter selected and you want to adjust the gap between two letters, be sure to select only the first letter in the pair.

TIP

Kerning Tables in Word

A kerning table in typography consists of a list of selected pairs of letters and a specification for each pair describing how much space to remove (or add) between them. Word doesn't support kerning tables yet, in that it can't look for specific pairs of letters and adjust their spacing automatically, but with some work you can achieve a similar effect. To create a "kerning table" in a certain font at a specific point size (such as that established in a style definition), do the following:

1. In a blank area of your document, type each pair of letters that needs kerning. Select the first letter in each pair, and set its spacing.
2. When you've finished, go back to the beginning of the list and copy (don't cut) the first pair to the Clipboard.
3. Choose Change from the Search menu, and enter that pair in the Find What edit field and enter ^c in the Change To field. This allows you to replace the pair with the contents of the Clipboard.
4. Search through the document, replacing each match in that font and font size with the kerned pair. Because the spacing characteristics of two letters depend on whether the letters are in uppercase or lowercase, you may want to create new pairs for uppercase and lowercase combinations.

This can be an involved task if carried to extremes, so it's best to limit the kerning replacements to obvious cases. You can also use macro-recording software, such as Tempo from Affinity Microsystems, to make this process more automatic.

Kerning a Font

The phrase *kerning a font* properly refers to the process of establishing a kerning table, often containing hundreds of character pairs, and slowly refining it until the spacing is perfect (to a typographer's eyes, which are more sensitive than those of mere mortals). Here the term describes the act of expanding or condensing every character of a font by a certain amount of space; this is known as a *tracking adjustment*.

Because a style sheet definition specifies at most one font per style, you can use this feature to stretch or compress all text in a given style. Simply choose Define Styles from the Format menu, select the style you want to adjust, choose the Character command, and alter the spacing. Click OK to add the spacing format to the style definition. If you use this method to adjust the spacing between the characters in a font attached to a style, remember that it will also apply to any text within a paragraph having that style, not only the font the style specifies.

Expanding or Contracting Selected Text for Effect

The third major use of spacing adjustments is purely for artistic effect. Consider these typographic elements:

T H E J U P I T E R

Wolfgang Amadeus Mozart

GETTING STARTED

Configuring Your Word Disk

As you can see, you can change the spacing of text in your document for reasons that have nothing to do with the legibility of the text. Simply select the text to be affected, choose the Character command, and enter the spacing you want to use. Click Apply or OK to put the spacing into effect.

TIP

Adding Position and Spacing to the Format Menu

You can add position and spacing formats to the Format menu, but the method for doing so is a little different from that for adding other character formats. To add a 2-point superscript to the menu, choose the Character command, select the Superscript option, and enter *2 pt* in the edit field. Then press Option-Command- +, click on the Superscript option again, and click Cancel. When you pull down the Format menu, you will see, toward the bottom, the *Superscript 2 pt* option. You can add a collection of formats, say 1-point, 2-point, and 3-point superscripts, to the menu. However, remember that you are limited to a total of 31 items on any of the configurable menus, including the dotted lines separating groups of options. Incidentally, you can add the Normal Spacing and Normal Position options to the menu as well.

Removing Character Formats

Once you've established a set of formats for the characters in your text, how do you go about selectively removing them if you need to? The most obvious way to remove a specific character attribute is to call up the Character dialog box and deselect the option in the Character Format group. Remember that, depending on the amount of text selected when you choose the Character command and whether it contains a homogeneous set of formats, some options in the Character Format group of the dialog box may be selected, some gray, or all the options may be gray. The Character Format group is like a master control panel for the attributes in the selected text. Clicking on a gray attribute option fills the box with an X and sets that attribute for all the selected text. Clicking on the option again clears the box and removes that attribute from the text.

To remove one of the position or spacing formats, simply click the Normal radio button in the appropriate group of the dialog box. Of course, because these groups use an edit field to specify the amount of spacing change for the format, you can't return a 3-point superscript, for example, to a previously established 2-point superscript without typing the number in the edit field.

Sometimes you will want to remove *all* the character attributes without affecting the font, spacing, and position formats in your text. One way to do this is to deselect the options in the Character Format group one by one, as has been discussed. An easier way is to use the keyboard shortcut Shift-Command-Z. This command deselects every option in the Character Format group of the Character dialog box, leaving the font, position, and spacing unchanged. It works even if these character attributes are part of a style definition assigned to the text; selecting the text and pressing these keys removes the attributes.

The Plain Text Command

If you work with styles, you'll often find it convenient to return selected text in a paragraph to the base character formats defined for the style assigned to that paragraph, removing any additional formats (attribute, font, position, or spacing) you've added. You can do this by selecting the text and choosing Plain Text from the Format menu. In Word 1.05, the Plain Text command removed only character attributes; the Shift-Command-Z key sequence does this in Word 3.0. This change can be confusing at first to users upgrading to Word 3.0 from Word 1.05.

Testing New Character Formats

The Character dialog box has three buttons: OK, Cancel, and Apply. Clicking the OK button tells Word to implement your formatting choices and close the dialog box. The Cancel button aborts your changes (as long as you haven't yet clicked Apply) and closes the dialog box. The Apply button, however, lets you test the new format without closing the dialog box. When you click this button, any selections you made in the Character dialog box are applied to the selected text without dismissing the dialog box. (See Figure 7-9.) You can move the dialog box out of the way if it covers the selected text. (Double-click on the title bar to toggle it between the two positions.) The Apply button is a timesaver when you're experimenting with a new format. Use it when you're having trouble making up your mind or simply trying out an option.

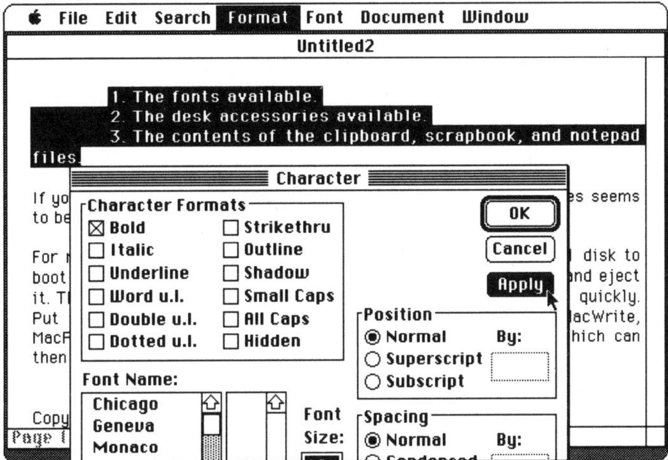

Figure 7-9
Applying a new format.

If, after experimenting with the Apply button, you want to return your text to its original state, simply click OK and then choose Undo from the Edit menu. Clicking Cancel won't remove the formats you've added with Apply.

Points to Remember

- ❑ A well-designed document is attractive and readable. Use a design appropriate to your subject matter.
- ❑ To implement the design of your document in Word, you work with four format domains: character, paragraph, section, and document. The character domain, the subject of this chapter, controls font, font size, character attributes (boldface, italic, and so on), letterspacing, and the position of characters with respect to the baseline. The other domains are described in detail in later chapters.
- ❑ The Character dialog box, displayed when you choose Character from the Format menu, is the main vehicle for altering character formats, although you can also issue certain commands from the Font menu, the Format menu, and the keyboard.
- ❑ The Character dialog box shows the formats in effect for the selected text or for the text containing the insertion point. If all the selected characters do not have the same attributes or if you've selected a large amount of text, the boxes in the Character Format group are gray and the Font Name list box does not show the current font name or point size.
- ❑ The hidden character attribute lets you create hidden text. Text in this format doesn't appear when Show Hidden Text in the Preferences dialog box is turned off, and it is not printed when Print Hidden Text in the Print dialog box is turned off. When hidden text is invisible, it is not hyphenated, repaginated, or checked for spelling.
- ❑ Because the smallest unit that the Macintosh can display is 1 point and you can make spacing adjustments of as little as 0.25 point, some adjustments you make will not show up on the screen; however, they will appear when the document is printed.

Techniques

The Character Dialog Box

Option	Action
Character Formats option group	Adds or removes character attributes. (These actions act as toggles.)
Font information group	Sets the font and font size.
Font Name	Shows the fonts currently installed in your System file; the sizes available for the selected font are listed to the right. The font selected is the current font.

Option	Action
Font Size	Shows the current font size. You can select another from the list of available sizes, or you can enter a different font size (from 2 points to 127 points). If you specify a size that is not available, Word scales the font to match the size you requested.
Position option group	Positions characters relative to the baseline. You can specify any value from 0.5 to 63.5 points, in 0.5-point increments.
Normal button	Places text on the baseline.
Superscript button	Places text above the baseline; defaults to 3 points.
Subscript button	Places text below the baseline; defaults to 2 points.
By field	Specifies how many points above or below the baseline to position text.
Spacing option group	Sets the spacing between characters (kerning).
Normal button	Uses the default spacing.
Expanded	Increases the space between characters by up to 14 points.
Condensed	Reduces the space between characters by up to 1.75 points.
By field	Specifies number of points to add to or subtract from the normal spacing between characters. Enter values in multiples of 0.25 points.
Buttons	
OK	Implements the selected formats and closes the dialog box.
Cancel	Closes the dialog box without implementing the selected formats.
Apply	Implements the selected formats without closing the dialog box.

Change the character format of existing text

❶ Select the text.

❷ Choose Character from the Format menu.

❸ Make the desired changes in the dialog box.

❹ Click OK.

(If the formats you want appear in the Font or Format menu, simply select the text and choose the desired options.)

Change the character format before typing text

❶ Set the insertion point where the text is to appear.

❷ Choose Character from the Format menu.

❸ Make the desired changes in the dialog box.

❹ Click OK.

(If the formats you want appear in the Font or Format menu, simply set the insertion point and choose the desired options.)

Undo a formatting change

❶ Choose Undo Formatting from the Edit menu immediately after you make the change.

Add a font to the Font menu

❶ Choose the Character command.

❷ Press Option-Command- +.

❸ Click on the font you want to add.

Add a font size to the Font menu

❶ Choose the Character command.

❷ Select the font for which you want to add the font size.

❸ Select the font size in the list box, or type it in the Font Size edit field.

❹ Press Option-Command- +.

❺ Click on the font size.

Add a character attribute to the Format menu

❶ Choose the Character command.

❷ Press Option-Command- +.

❸ Click on the attribute you want to add.

Add a position or spacing format to the Format menu

❶ Choose the Character command.

❷ Select the option you want to add, and enter the amount of the spacing in the By field.

❸ Press Option-Command- +.

❹ Click on the option to be added.

Remove a format from the Format or Font menu

❶ Press Option-Command- – (minus).

❷ Pull down the menu from which the option is to be removed.

❸ Choose the option to be removed.

Remove all character attributes from selected text

❶ Press Shift-Command-Z.

Restore selected text to the base style for the paragraph

❶ Choose Plain Text from the Format menu.

■ *Keyboard Shortcuts*

Changing the Font

To	Press
Set the font for selected text	Shift-Command-E, enter first letters of font name or font ID number, and then press the Return key.
Insert a Symbol font character	Shift-Command-Q, then type the character.

Use the Key Caps desk accessory to view font character sets. You can copy characters you type in Key Caps and paste them in your document. If you do, reselect the pasted characters and press Shift-Command-Spacebar to return the text to the base character format for that paragraph.

Changing the Font Size

To	Press
Increase the font size	Shift-Command- >
Decrease the font size	Shift-Command- <

The new font size appears in the status area.

Changing Attributes

These key sequences toggle; use the same keystrokes to set and remove the format.

For	Press
Bold	Shift-Command-B
Italic	Shift-Command-I
Underline	Shift-Command-U
Word Underline	Shift-Command-]
Double Underline	Shift-Command-[
Dotted Underline	Shift-Command-\
Strikethrough	Shift-Command-/
Outline	Shift-Command-D
Shadow	Shift-Command-W
Small caps	Shift-Command-H
All caps	Shift-Command-K
Hidden text	Shift-Command-X

Changing the Position

For	Press
3-point superscript	Shift-Command- + (plus)
2-point subscript	Shift-Command- – (minus)

Removing Formats

To	Press
Return to the character attributes defined for that style.	Shift-Command-Spacebar
Remove character attributes only	Shift-Command-Z

Paragraph Formatting

Chapter 7 discussed the types of formatting you can do within the character format domain, Word's smallest level of detail. This chapter explores the next horizon, the paragraph format domain. Paragraph formats control these characteristics:

- Line spacing.
- Space before and after the paragraph.
- Indention.
- Alignment.
- Type and location of tabs.
- Graphic treatment of paragraphs—lines, boxed paragraphs, and so on.
- Grouping and placement of paragraphs on a page.
- Whether the lines of the paragraph are numbered when printed.

Working with Paragraphs

Previous chapters have defined a paragraph, but it's worth repeating. In Word, a paragraph is any block of text that precedes a paragraph mark, which is created by pressing either the Return key or the Enter key. A paragraph can have one letter in it or hundreds. It can even be a blank line.

If you want to see the boundaries of paragraphs, you can do so by choosing Show ¶ from the Edit menu. With Show ¶ in effect, you see all the characters that are usually invisible, including paragraph marks, newline marks, tabs, and spaces.

To see how the paragraph mark acts as the boundary of a paragraph, type two paragraphs of sample text, and then select and delete the first paragraph mark. It's relatively easy to select a paragraph mark when it's visible; when it's not visible, a good trick is to position the mouse pointer anywhere to the right of the last line of the paragraph and double-click. You see a black rectangle representing the selected paragraph mark. When you delete the mark, the two paragraphs become fused into one.

Before launching into a full-scale exploration of paragraph formatting, you should know a few techniques for working with paragraphs.

- You can join two paragraphs by selecting the paragraph mark between them and pressing the Backspace key. (Backspacing over the paragraph mark won't work if the two paragraphs use different paragraph formats.)
- Pressing Option-Command-Return inserts a paragraph mark after the insertion point instead of before it. This is useful when you want to both break a paragraph and continue typing at the end of the first paragraph.
- Changes to the paragraph formatting of existing text affect only the selected paragraphs. If you set the insertion point or select only part of a paragraph, the formatting within all that paragraph, and in that paragraph alone, changes.
- If you alter the paragraph formatting while typing, you change the formatting for any paragraphs you type after that. (This may not apply if you use the Next Style feature of Word's style sheets, discussed in the next chapter.)
- Pressing Shift-Return starts a new line but does not end the paragraph. These *newlines*, also called soft returns, are helpful when you need to start a new line but want Word to consider the lines as one paragraph. The uses of the newline character are discussed in this and later chapters. Note that its mark (with Show ¶ on) looks like a bent arrow instead of the proofreader's paragraph mark, as shown in Figure 8-1.

¶ *Paragraph mark*

↵ *Newline mark*

Figure 8-1
Paragraph and newline marks.

■ Changing Paragraph Formats

To change a paragraph format in a document, first select one or more paragraphs, and then do one of the following:

- ❑ Choose Show Ruler from the Format menu, and make the change.
- ❑ Choose Paragraph from the Format menu, and make changes within the Paragraph dialog box.
- ❑ Choose an option that you've added to the Format menu.
- ❑ Use a key sequence to make the change.
- ❑ Set a style for the paragraph and assign it with the Styles command from the Format menu or by choosing the style from the Work menu, once you've added it. (The next chapter is devoted to this subject, so it won't be covered here.)

Some of the formats are not accessible by every method. Alignment, for example, can be set from the Ruler, from the Format menu (after you have added its options), and from the keyboard, but not from the Paragraph dialog box. Each of these methods is discussed briefly here and in more detail where we explore each of the paragraph formats.

TIP

Styles and Paragraph Formats
Changing paragraph formats through the style sheet is much easier than hunting down every instance of a text element and reformatting it manually. See Chapter 9, "Working with Style Sheets," for more information.

The Ruler

Word's Ruler controls the position of indents and tabs, text alignment, and spacing between lines and paragraphs. Many of these functions are also available through other commands in Word, but the Ruler makes them more accessible. The Ruler must be visible for you to use it. If it is not displayed at the top of the window in Document view, choose the Show Ruler command from the Format menu. Conversely, to get rid of the Ruler, choose the Hide Ruler command. You can also display the Ruler in the following windows:

- ❏ The Header window.
- ❏ The Footer window.
- ❏ The Footnote window, as well as the Footnote Separator, Continued Separator, and Continued Notice windows (all of which concern footnotes).

The Ruler is shown in Figure 8-2, with labels for the various icons and markers. The unit of measure shown in the Ruler reflects the current Measure setting in the Preferences dialog box. Any settings you change with the Ruler affect an entire paragraph. This differs from the character formats, which you can apply to a single character if you want. You can make Ruler changes while you type your document or while you edit it.

If you are using a split window and choose Show Ruler, the Ruler appears at the top of the active pane. Regardless of its location, the Ruler changes to reflect the paragraph formats of the currently selected paragraph, whether it is in the top or bottom pane or even whether the currently selected paragraph has scrolled off the screen.

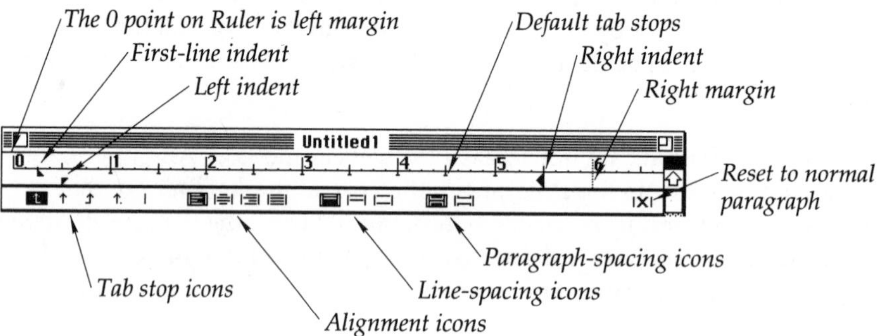

Figure 8-2
The Ruler.

Clearing the Ruler

If you make many alterations to the Ruler and then change your mind, Word lets you start over with a fresh Ruler. Clicking the X, or normal paragraph, icon located near the right edge of the Ruler restores the selected paragraphs to the *Normal* style. The preset paragraph format settings of the *Normal* style are as follows: single line spacing, no extra space between paragraphs, and flush-left alignment. The default tab stops are whatever you specified in the Page Setup dialog box, usually every 0.5 inch. However, if you redefined the *Normal* style definition, any or all of these formats may be different. Remember, that the X icon resets only paragraph formats, not character formats.

If you are using styles and want the selected paragraphs to return to the paragraph formats of the style they had before you started making changes, rather than to the *Normal* style, choose Undo Formatting from the Edit menu.

The Paragraph Command

Just as the Character dialog box is the master control panel for the character formats, the Paragraph dialog box is the primary means of controlling the layout of paragraphs. Choosing the Paragraph command brings up the dialog box shown in Figure 8-3.

The Ruler accompanies the dialog box (if it is not displayed already), as if you had chosen both the Show Ruler and Paragraph commands at the same time, and you can make adjustments in either the Ruler or the dialog box.

The Paragraph dialog box is divided into five basic sections: the Ruler edit field, Spacing options, Border options, Tab leader options, and a series of check boxes that control options for positioning paragraphs relative to one another and the page.

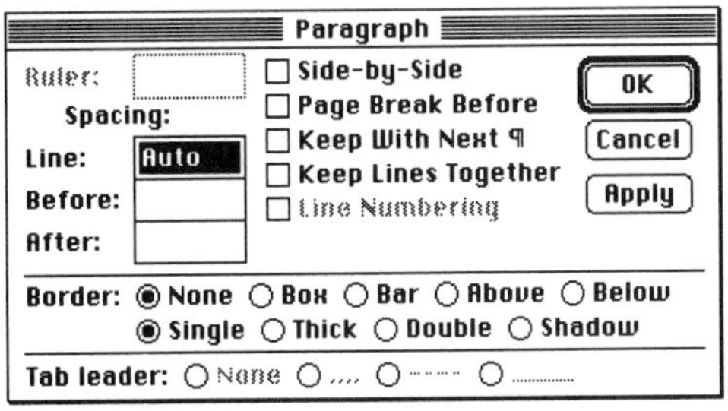

Paragraph
Ruler:
Spacing:
Line: Auto
Before:
After:
Side-by-Side
Page Break Before
Keep With Next ¶
Keep Lines Together
Line Numbering
OK
Cancel
Apply
Border: None Box Bar Above Below
Single Thick Double Shadow
Tab leader: None .... ------ ....

Figure 8-3
The Paragraph dialog box.

The Ruler Edit Field

The Ruler edit field, located in the upper left corner of the dialog box, allows you to enter the positions of the various indents and tabs without dragging icons in the Ruler. In addition, whenever you use the Ruler to adjust the position of an indent or tab, the Ruler field displays its position on the Ruler. The position is shown in inches, points, or centimeters, depending on the Measure setting in the Preferences dialog box, in increments of 1/16 inch rounded to the nearest hundredth, 0.05 centimeter, or 1 point. The 0 point on the Ruler—the left margin—is the reference point for these measurements. When neither an indent nor a tab is selected, the Ruler field is dimmed.

Control Buttons

The Paragraph dialog box has three control buttons: OK, Cancel, and Apply. These work exactly like the buttons in the Character dialog box. OK indicates that you're through fiddling with the formats and you want to implement the changes you made and get back to the document. Cancel means that you've decided not to make any changes after all.

The Apply button lets you audition format changes without closing the Paragraph dialog box. This works best when you are changing the format of previously typed text; you can't readily see the change in a blank document.

To use the Apply button, select the paragraphs to be changed, display the Paragraph dialog box, and click the options you want. Drag the box by the title bar if it obscures the text you want to see. (Double-click in the title bar to alternate between the two positions.) Click the Apply button to audition the changes. The dialog box stays open, but the text changes to the new format. Continue choosing new formats and applying them for as long as you like. When you leave the dialog box, use the Undo command to revert to the format before the last Apply only. Clicking Cancel doesn't undo an Apply.

If you need to see the effect of a massive formatting change and are afraid you may mess up the document or forget how it was originally formatted, save the document before the test. Then, if the experiment goes awry, you can close the document without saving it and reopen the original.

Adding Paragraph Formats to the Format Menu

So far in your exploration of Word, you've seen how to add documents, glossaries, and styles to the Work menu, fonts and font sizes to the Font menu, and a variety of character formats to the Format menu. You can also add all the paragraph formats to the Format menu by pressing Option-Command- + and clicking the desired paragraph format in either the Ruler or the Paragraph dialog box, but you can't add any tab stop formats.

Working with Paragraph Formats

Now that you've learned the various methods for using the paragraph formats, let's consider each format in turn. Figure 8-4 shows a typical paragraph and some of the formats you can change.

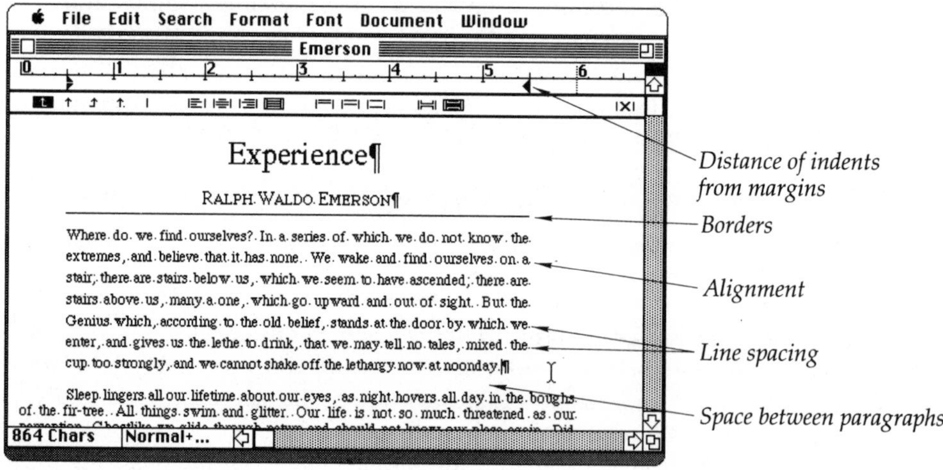

Figure 8-4
A typical paragraph.

Indents

Setting an indent is not the same as setting a margin, although many people are confused on this point. You set the margins by changing the contents of the Margins edit fields in the Page Setup dialog box (available from the File menu) or in Page Preview; you set indents by dragging an indent marker in the Ruler or by specifying an indent in the Ruler field of the Paragraph dialog box.

What is the difference between the two? The Margins settings in the Page Setup dialog box apply to your document as a whole; they specify the default boundaries of the text on the page, whether it is in *Normal* style, in another style, or in a header, footer, or other element. Until you change the margins, Word establishes them at 1 inch from the top and bottom of the page and 1.25 inches from the left and right edges of the page.

Indents, on the other hand, are a way of temporarily changing the left and right margins for selected paragraphs in your document. The three types of indent are: left, right, and first line. If you haven't explicitly changed the left or right indents (the first-line indent will be discussed in a moment), Word assumes you want your text to run to the margins.

Indents are measured from the left and right margins. The left margin is the 0 point on the Ruler, and the position of the left indent (the lower of the two triangles at the left edge of the Ruler) is relative to this point. If you change the left margin (and thus change the 0 point), the left indent changes too, remaining the same distance from the 0 point as before. Similarly, the position of the right indent is relative to the right margin, which appears as a dotted vertical line in the Ruler. (See Figure 8-2.)

Besides the left and right indents, you can control the first-line indent (the upper of the two triangles at the left edge of the Ruler). This indent applies only to the first line of the paragraph. The first-line indent is measured relative to the left indent rather than to the left margin, and the left and first-line indents are normally linked together so that moving the left indent also moves the first-line indent. The most common use of the first-line indent is to offset the first line of a paragraph, but its range of applications is much wider, as you will see in the next section.

A Small Gallery of Indention Effects

This section gives you a quick tour through the range of effects that you can achieve through different placements of the left, right, and first-line indents relative to one another in your documents.

To provide a reference point for this discussion, Figure 8-5 shows the standard format for normal paragraphs. The left and right indents are at the same location as the left and right margins, and there is no first-line indent. Many people use a tab to indent the first line of a paragraph; whether you do this or use the first-line indent is not important as long as you achieve the results you want.

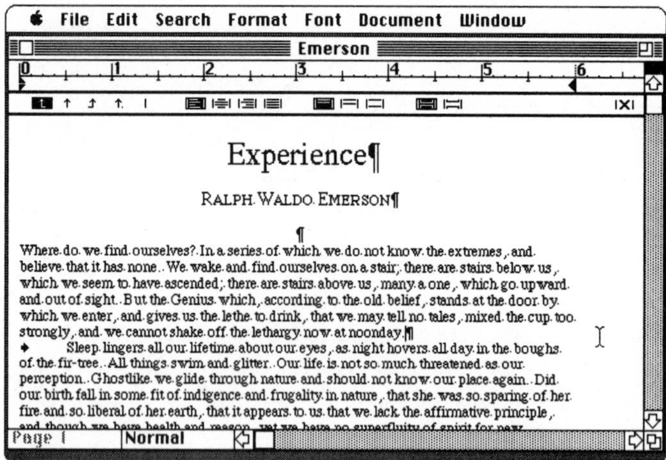

Figure 8-5
Normal paragraph indention.

You can create another indention pattern, called *nested indention*, by moving the left and right indents toward the center and away from the margins, as shown in Figure 8-6. Nested indents are often used for quotations or to set off captions for figures.

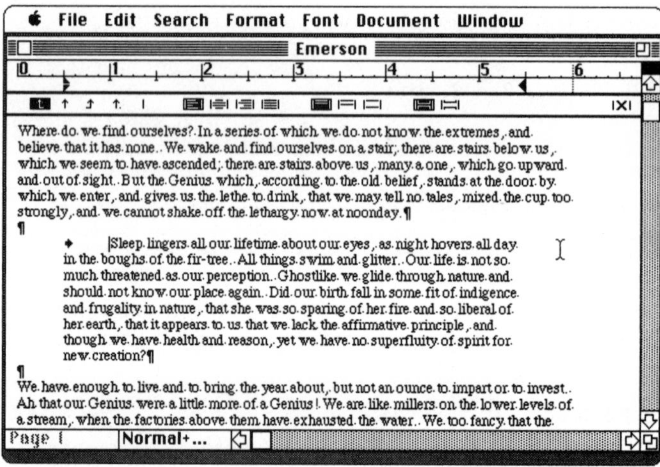

Figure 8-6
Nested paragraph indention.

A *hanging indent* occurs when you place the first-line indent to the left of the left indent, as shown in Figure 8-7. Hanging indents are very useful for lists and are often used in bibliographies. The numbered procedures in this book, each paragraph of which is preceded by Zapf Dingbat characters such as ❶ (ASCII characters 182 through 191), are called *numbered lists* and use hanging indents. The unnumbered lists in this book, each paragraph of which is preceded by the Zapf Dingbat character ❑ (lowercase *o*), are called *bulleted lists*. In both cases, a tab mark is used within the hanging indent to make the number or bullet stand out from the body of text.

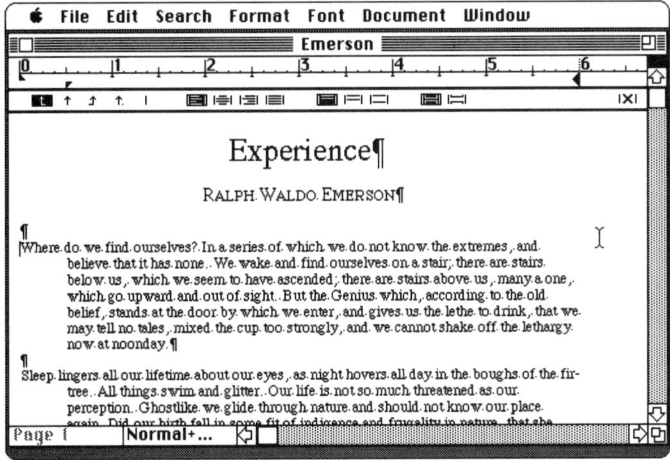

Figure 8-7
Hanging indents.

Finally, Word lets you place any of the indent markers outside the limits of the page margins. Negative indents are particularly good for the headings in a document. Such indents are called *negative indents* because they must be measured in negative numbers; otherwise, they would be confused with normal indents. (See Figure 8-8.) Since Word does not display the edges of the printable area of the page in the Ruler, when you use negative indents you run the risk of having your text run off the page. You can use Page Preview to check for this problem. Also, because negative left indents run to the left of the left margin, Word may not show them in Document view. To shift the screen to the right, as shown in the figure, press the Shift key while clicking the left arrow in the horizontal scroll bar.

You can combine these indention patterns in any way you want. For example, you can create negative hanging indents or use a nested indent for the left edge of the text and leave the right indent at the right margin.

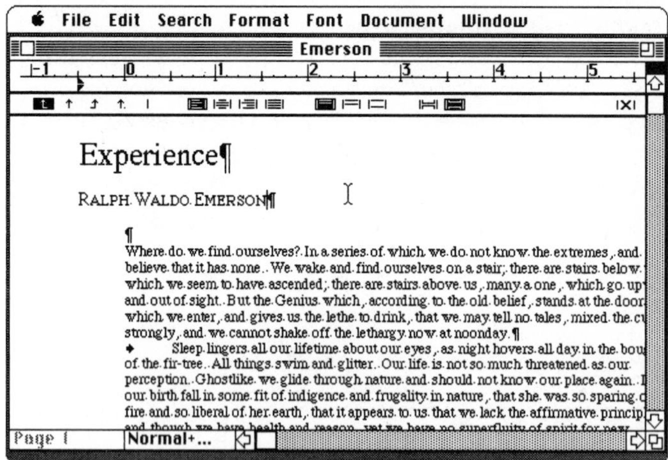

Figure 8-8
Negative paragraph indention.

Setting Indents from the Ruler

To set indents with the Ruler, first choose Show Ruler from the Format menu and select the paragraphs to be affected. If you are changing only one paragraph, simply click in it—because indention is a paragraph format, this will cause the new indents to be applied to the entire paragraph. When you click in a paragraph, the Ruler displays the current placement of the three indent markers. If you select more than one paragraph and those paragraphs use different formats or have been assigned different styles, the Ruler is filled with gray and the markers reflect the indents of the first paragraph selected.

Once you've specified the text, drag the appropriate indent marker in the Ruler to the location of the new indent. To move the first-line and left-indent markers together, drag the lower triangle. If you drag only the upper triangle, you'll move only the first-line indent. To move only the left indent, press the Shift key and then drag the lower triangle. The position of the first-line indent is always linked to that of the left indent. Even if the two indents are in different positions, moving the left indent causes a corresponding change in the position of the first-line indent. The Shift key uncouples the markers so that you can drag them separately.

Indents can be positive or negative with respect to the left and right page margins. You normally start the text at the 0 point on the Ruler, but you can also start it farther to the left or right. This 0 point is normally locked at the left edge of the screen, but you can drag the first-line or left-indent marker (or both) past the edge of the screen. After a delay of about one second, the scale in the Ruler and the contents of your document slide to the right, revealing the negative indent positions. Alternatively, you can Shift-click the left arrow in the horizontal scroll bar to move the document to the right and then move the indent markers.

Setting Indents from the Paragraph Dialog Box

When you choose the Paragraph command, the Ruler appears, so everything discussed in the previous section applies here as well. However, the Ruler limits the precision with which you can specify an indent. Depending on the unit of measure set in the Preferences dialog box (available from the Edit menu), the Ruler uses minimum increments of 0.0625 inch (1⁄16 inch), 0.05 centimeter, or 1 point. By using the Ruler field in the Paragraph dialog box, you can specify indents with an accuracy of 0.01 inch, 0.002 centimeter, or 0.1 point, again depending on the current unit of measure.

Suppose you have set inches as the unit of measure in the Preferences dialog box. If you want to set a first-line indent of 1 pica (1⁄6 inch, or 0.1667 inch), you need to use the Ruler edit field, as follows:

❶ Select the text you want to format.

❷ Choose the Paragraph command. The Ruler and the Paragraph dialog box appear.

❸ Click on the first-line indent marker. The label of the Ruler edit field changes to First.

❹ Enter the position of the indent, *0.1667 in*, or if you prefer to use measurements in points, enter *12 pt*. Click OK to implement the indent.

Remember that first-line indents are measured relative to the left indent, not the left page margin. If you want to set a hanging indent, enter a negative number.

TIP

Checking Special Indent Values

An interesting problem can occur when you want to check an indent value (or a tab value, for that matter) that you have set to an intermediate position (that is, a position between two Ruler increments). If you open the Paragraph dialog box and click on an indent marker set to a special value, it pops to the nearest interval (1⁄16 inch if you're using inches), and the Ruler edit field shows the new position, not the original value.

To read the value associated with an indent or tab marker without changing it, you can pretend that you want to create a new style and choose Define Styles from the Format menu. The *New Style* item in the list box is selected automatically, and its definition is displayed underneath; this definition describes the formats contained in the selected text, including the position of the marker.

If the selected text already has a style attached, the definition simply names the style and does not list its definition. In such cases, delete the contents of the Based On edit field and then click in the Style edit field. The complete definition for the selected text appears, as though you were starting from scratch, and you can find the position of the marker in the definition. Click Cancel when you are ready to close the dialog box.

Tabs

Tabs are characters that you can use to align text in columns without laboriously adding and deleting spaces. They are invisible, but you can use the Show ¶ command to make them appear. When you press the Tab key, the insertion point moves to the next tab stop. If you haven't changed the tab stops, Word assumes that you want them placed evenly at half-inch intervals. The four different types of tab stops, illustrated in Figure 8-9, are as follows:

- ❑ Flush left. Aligns the left edge of the text to the tab stop. This is the default tab stop.
- ❑ Centered. Centers the text directly over the tab stop.
- ❑ Flush right. Aligns the right edge of the text to the tab stop.
- ❑ Decimal aligned. Aligns the decimal point to the tab stop.

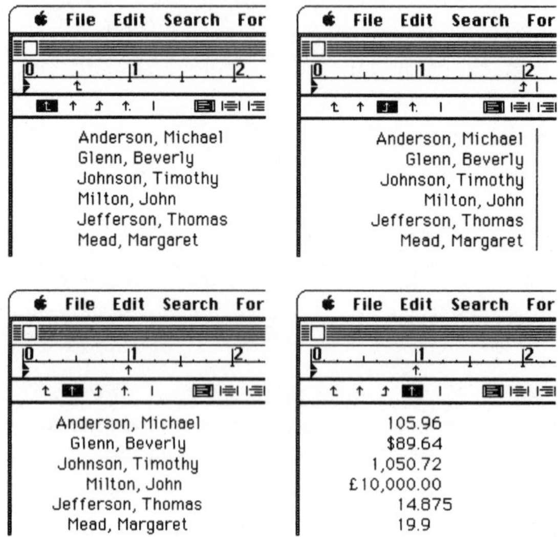

Figure 8-9
The different types of tab stops.

You will often use centered and flush-right tab stops to create smart-looking tables. The decimal tab stop is ideal for presenting numbers in an orderly fashion. You can have any number of digits to the right and left of the decimal point, yet all the decimal points line up at the tab stop.

There is a fifth icon in the Ruler next to the four Tab Stop icons. The vertical line is not really a tab stop, but it is often used to draw lines in tables and so is grouped with them. It draws a line that you can use as a separator or border. You simply select the icon and click in the Ruler where you want a line to appear; there is no need to enter any characters to create the line, and the insertion point skips past the line when you press the Tab key. The line continues down the page through each paragraph that has this format. This feature can be used for other types of formatting as well, especially multiple-column documents. The flush-right tab stop example in Figure 8-9 shows how you can use this tab stop with the vertical line format.

You can set tab stops in three ways: by changing their default positions from the Page Setup dialog box, by using the markers in the Ruler, and by specifying new positions in the Paragraph dialog box.

Changing the Default Tab Stops

Word's default tab stops are set at half-inch intervals along the length of the Ruler. The positions of the default tab stops are marked by tiny, upside-down T icons in the Ruler. Technically, these default tab stops are not in the paragraph format domain but are part of a document level format that belongs to every paragraph in the document. Even if you set some tab stops, the default tabs will remain to the right of those you've set unless you completely clear all default tab stops.

Tab markers take precedence over the default tabs, so if you place a tab marker on the Ruler, the default tab stops to the left of it disappear. To change Word's default tab stops or to eliminate them completely, do the following:

1. Choose the Page Setup command from the File menu.
2. Double-click in the Default Tab Stops edit field, and enter a new number. The measurement can be in inches, centimeters, or points. The smallest default tab stop you can set is 0.06 inch; the largest is 22 inches. If your current unit of measure is points, the stops can be 4 to 1584.1 points apart; if you are using centimeters, the permissible range is 0.15 to 55.85 centimeters. (Enter *22 in* if you want to remove all the default stops.)
3. Click OK to set this tab stop interval for the current document only. Click Set Default to store the new default tabs in the Word Settings file and use them for all subsequent documents you create.

Setting Tabs Stops from the Ruler

As with indents, nondefault tab stops can be set in two ways: with the Ruler alone or from the Paragraph dialog box. To set a tab stop from the Ruler, do the following:

- To place a tab stop on the Ruler, drag the icon for the type of tab you want to the desired location on the Ruler. You can also simply click the icon for the type of tab you want and then click at the desired location on the Ruler.
- To move a tab stop, drag its marker along the Ruler to the new position.
- To remove a tab stop, drag its marker off the Ruler and release the mouse button.

If you are moving a tab stop and you click near but not directly over it, the marker jumps to the position of the mouse pointer as though it were magnetic. This can be a problem when you are positioning tab stops close to one another or close to an indent marker—a marker you didn't want often jumps to the mouse pointer. To avoid this, click somewhere else in the Ruler to add the tab marker and then drag it to the correct position. If a tab marker is positioned directly over an indent marker and you click on them, the tab sticks to the mouse pointer, and the indent is not affected.

If you select several paragraphs having different tab settings, the Ruler is filled with gray and shows the tab markers for the first paragraph only. Because any paragraph can have up to 30 tab stops set within it, when you add a tab stop to a Ruler filled with gray, you add that tab stop to every paragraph selected. The new tab stop replaces an old one only if they are in the same position. To remove the tab stops from every paragraph and add new ones, you first have to remove all the tab markers from each paragraph. You can then reselect the paragraphs and establish the new tab stops.

Note: The Ruler is also filled with gray if any of the other paragraph formats vary among the selected paragraphs. However, because the other paragraph formats permit only one option each (for instance, a paragraph can have only one left indent and only one line spacing), changing such a format replaces that format in all the paragraphs selected.

TIP

A Quick Way to Reset the Default Tab Stops
If you are using styles in your documents, you should set the majority of the tab stops through the style sheet so that you can change all paragraphs with that style at once. Even if you are not defining your own styles, you are using at least one style without knowing it—the *Normal* style. If you haven't done much character or paragraph formatting other than setting tabs within a given paragraph, try clicking the X icon in the Ruler to reset the paragraph's format to the *Normal* style. All character and paragraph formats return to the default settings for the *Normal* style, and you can start over.

Setting Tab Stops from the Paragraph Dialog Box

Tab stops are easily set from the Ruler. Like indents, however, they can be set more precisely from the Ruler field in the Paragraph dialog box. The minimum increments for tabs set from the Ruler are the same as those for indents set from the Ruler: 0.0625 inch, 0.05 centimeter, or 1 point, depending on the unit of measure. Also, the dialog box offers several tab leaders (discussed in the next section). To set a tab stop using the Paragraph dialog box:

1. Select the paragraphs you want to format.
2. Choose the Paragraph command. The Paragraph dialog box appears.
3. Drag the desired tab stop onto the Ruler. The Ruler edit field displays its current position.
4. Enter a position for the tab stop, and click OK or press the Return key.

TIP

A Hanging Indent Sets the First Tab Stop Automatically
If you create a hanging indent by setting the first-line indent to the left of the left indent, Word establishes the first tab stop at the position of the left indent. For example, the numbered and bulleted lists in this book use a default tab stop of 18 points, or 0.25 inches. Since the first line of the text for each item in the list begins at the left indent (see ❸ above), we didn't establish an additional tab stop format for the first line.

Tab Leaders

Tab leaders are extra characters that Word uses to fill blank spaces before a tab stop. You can use a tab leader, for example, when preparing a table of contents, as shown in Figure 8-10. The tab stop on the right, for the page number, has a dotted leader. When you press the Tab key to move to the tab stop, Word inserts the leader in the line. There are three styles of leader: dots, dashes, and underlines. You can assign a different tab leader to each of the tab stops you place on the Ruler.

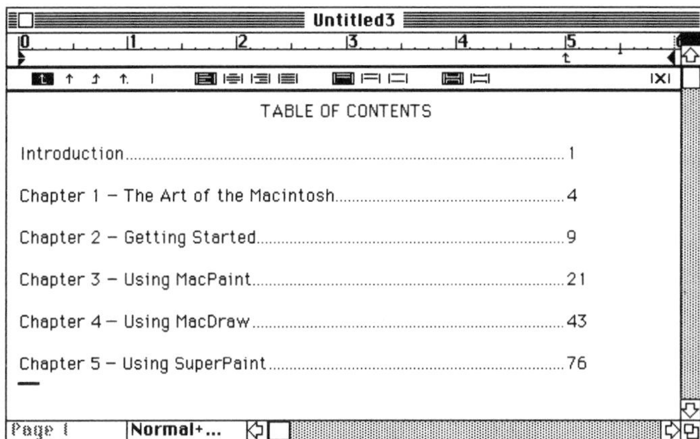

Figure 8-10
Dotted tab leaders in a table of contents.

A leader fills the space before the tab stop to which it is assigned. To assign a tab leader to a tab stop:

❶ Select the paragraphs you want to format and choose the Paragraph command.

❷ Drag the type of tab you want from the icon bar onto the Ruler at the position you want. The tab leader options are activated.

❸ Click the leader you want. Click OK to resume editing.

To add a leader to an existing tab stop, display the Paragraph dialog box, click on the tab marker to receive the leader, and then click on the type of leader you want. Click OK to implement the leader. Remember that tab leaders, like tabs, are in effect only for those paragraphs that are so formatted. If you want tab leaders to apply to all paragraphs in your document, either specify them before you start writing or select all the paragraphs and choose the tab leader for them at the same time.

TIP

Checking Tab Leaders

You can check the type of tab leader assigned to a tab and change it, if you want, by clicking on the tab marker in the Ruler (with the Paragraph dialog box displayed). When you do so, the button for the tab leader assigned to that marker is selected. Click on another option if you want to change the leader. Remember that when you click on the tab marker, it will pop to the position of the mouse pointer, so you may have to reassign its position.

You can also check tab leaders by choosing Define Styles from the Format menu to see the proposed definition, as though you were going to create a style based on the attributes of the currently selected paragraph. This technique is discussed in the tip "Checking Special Indent Values" earlier in this chapter.

Line Spacing

Word can separate lines by almost any distance that you'd like. In typesetting, the term *line spacing* refers to the distance from the baseline of one line of text to the baseline of the next or preceding line. Word does not use the same convention, but for most purposes the effects are similar. You'll learn more about this in a moment, but first let's work with setting line-spacing formats from the Ruler.

Setting Line Spacing from the Ruler

The Ruler provides three line-spacing settings: single space, one-and-one-half spaces, and double space. This lets you set the three most common line spacings quickly, without calling up a special dialog box. To change the line spacing for a selected paragraph, click the desired line-spacing icon (under the 3 in the Ruler). The effects of the three line spacings are shown in Figure 8-11. Like the other paragraph formats, the line-spacing setting affects the entire paragraph.

When you use the default single spacing, Word adjusts the line spacing to the point size of the text in the paragraph. For example, if a paragraph is in a 12-point font, the automatic line-spacing format sets the line spacing to 12 points. If, however, you insert a character (or graphic) that is taller than 12 points, the spacing around that line opens up a bit to accommodate the oversized element. This happens frequently when you use more than one font or point size in a line of text, use the outline or underline character formats, or have subscripts or superscripts in your text. If you want the line spacing to vary with the size of the elements within it, you must set it with the Paragraph command, discussed in the next section.

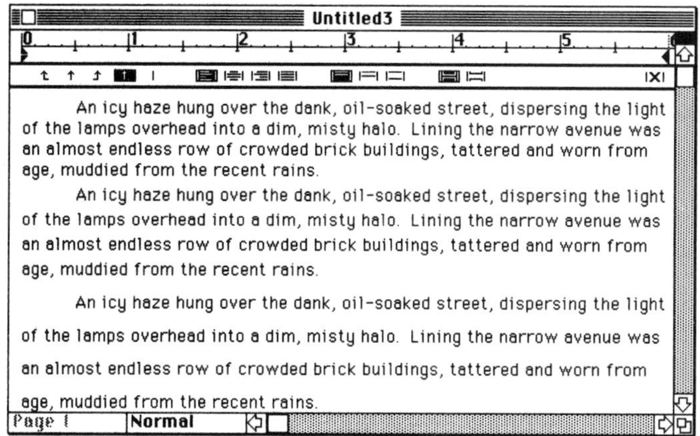

Figure 8-11
The three types of line spacing available from the Ruler.

The one-and-one-half space option sets the line spacing to 18 points per line, but Word will open up the line spacing if something in a line is larger than 18 points. The double-space option works in the same way but sets the spacing to 24 points per line. Actually, both these spacing options are misnamed: The only font size for which 24 points really is double spaced is, of course, a 12-point font. If you use the double-space option with an 18-point font, you still get 24 points of space, not 36 points.

Setting Line Spacing from the Paragraph Dialog Box

You can get much more control over the line spacing in your text by using the Line edit field in the Spacing group of the Paragraph dialog box. It lets you specify line spacing in the following measurements:

- Points. Enter *12 pt,* for instance, to single-space a 12-point font. You can enter line-spacing measurements in 0.5-point increments if you want.
- Inches. If you require a spacing of 1 inch between lines, for example, enter *1 in* into the Line field.
- Centimeters. To specify a spacing of 2 centimeters between lines, enter *2 cm* into the Line edit field.
- Lines. You can set a line spacing in multiples of lines. To triple-space your text, for example, enter *3 li* into the Line edit field. Word interprets a line as 12 points.

You can express any measurement in fractions. To express a fractional measurement, use a decimal value (for example, *1.13 in* or *2.78 pt.*) Enter the word *auto* or the number *0* to have Word adjust the line spacing automatically for the font size. Word converts all these units of measure to the nearest 0.5 point and displays the converted value the next time you open the

Paragraph dialog box. However, even though you can express line spacing to 0.5 points, Word actually measures line spacing in multiples of one point.

As was mentioned earlier, some character formats or font sizes can produce text elements that extend higher or lower than the rest of the characters in a line of text, causing Word to add extra space around the line. This can happen regardless of the line spacing, given an extreme enough combination of character formats. Whenever the Line edit field contains a measurement expressed as a positive number, Word adjusts the actual line spacing to accommodate oversized elements. To prevent this behavior and force a specific line spacing regardless of the dimensions of the text, enter the line-spacing distance as a negative number.

TIP

Line Spacing in Word

Word does not follow the standard publishing convention of measuring line spacing from baseline to baseline. Instead, it calculates the spacing from descender to descender. (See Figure 8-12.) You will recall from Chapter 7 that a descender is the part of a character that extends below the baseline of text, such as the tails of the lowercase letters *y*, *g*, and *q*. Most of the time, the descender-to-descender distance is the same as the baseline-to-baseline distance.

You can see the space allotted for a line by selecting it and observing the upper and lower limits of the highlight, as shown in Figure 8-12. To illustrate this point, the size of a word containing a descender has been increased to accentuate the effect. Notice that the highlight extends from the top of the highest character in the line to the bottom of the lowest character.

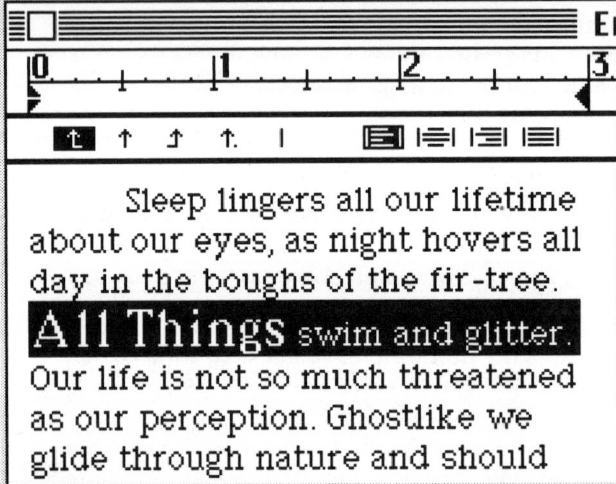

Figure 8-12
Line spacing is actually measured from descender to descender.

When you set automatic line spacing by entering *auto* in the Spacing field of the Paragraph dialog box, the spacing of each line is determined by the distance from the top of the highest ascender to the bottom of the lowest descender. If a given line doesn't contain characters with descenders, the space for the descender is still reserved. Similarly, space is also reserved for the ascender height of a font even if a character in that font within a given line doesn't have an ascender.

When you increase the line spacing to more than that set by automatic spacing, the extra space appears above each line in the paragraph, even the first line. This behavior can lead to some tricky problems if you are aiming for highly accurate paragraph formatting in a document. This is particularly true when two successive paragraphs have different line-spacing formats.

For example, the distance between level headings and the first paragraph under them will vary if the font sizes of the various types of headings are different, yielding descenders of different lengths. If the body text under each heading is in the *Normal* style with automatic line spacing, the distance between the baseline of a heading and the baseline of the first line in the paragraph depends solely on the font size of the heading, not the line spacing. To adjust the actual baseline-to-baseline distance between paragraphs with different line-spacing formats, experiment with setting negative line-spacing formats and with the Before and After paragraph formats discussed in the next section.

Paragraph Spacing

A second type of spacing within the paragraph format domain is used to separate a paragraph from the ones before and after it. The Space Before format adds space above the top edge of the interval set by the line spacing in the paragraph, and the Space After format adds space below the lowest descender in the last line of the paragraph. If a paragraph having a Space Before format falls naturally at the top of a page, Word doesn't insert the space at the top of the page. However, if you create a manual page break by setting the Page Break Before paragraph format or by inserting a page break or section mark, the Space Before format is not ignored. Figure 8-13 shows how these formats work together. The paragraph containing the title of the essay and the name of the author are separated by the title's Space After format, not a blank line. The first and second paragraphs of the essay are separated by the Space Before format of the second paragraph, as shown by the highlight in the figure.

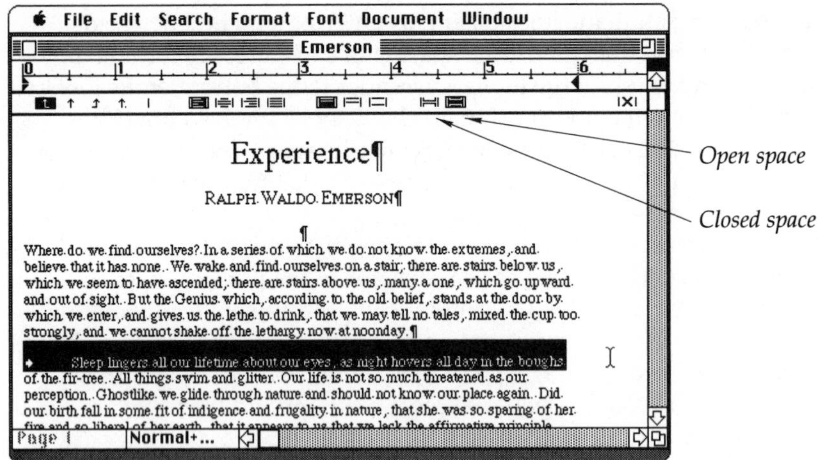

Figure 8-13
The Space Before format in relation to a typical paragraph.

The Space Before and Space After formats are useful for setting off body text, indicating a pause in the flow of a document, or setting off the headings in a document. The Space Before format is used in the default *level 1* and *level 2* styles. (Again, using the style sheet to establish space around text elements is a powerful means for developing a consistent design in a document.)

Setting Paragraph Spacing from the Ruler

The Ruler offers only two paragraph-spacing options: either no extra space (the Closed Space icon) or 12 points of space before each paragraph (the Open Space icon, which was used in the figure). If you want paragraphs to be separated by the same amount of space as the lines, click the Closed Space icon. If you want extra space between paragraphs, click the Open Space icon.

Setting Paragraph Spacing from the Paragraph Dialog Box

Use the Before and After fields in the Spacing options of the dialog box to set the spacing before and after each selected paragraph. Like the Line edit field, these fields accept spacing in inches, centimeters, points, or lines, although Word always displays the measurements in points when you reopen the dialog box. To remove extra spacing before or after a paragraph, you must enter *0 pt* in the appropriate field; simply deleting the entry won't work.

TIP

Paragraph Spacing in Word
Like line spacing, paragraph spacing is not measured from baseline to baseline. Technically, the Space Before format (for instance) indicates the distance to the bottom of the prior paragraph's Space After format.

This can lead to some confusing effects in your document, particularly when you are trying to achieve a consistent design. In a good design, the treatment of elements such as level headings, including the amount of space before each one, must be consistent. Yet the actual amount of space before a heading, measured from the baseline of the heading to the baseline of the previous paragraph, depends not only on the Space Before format of the heading, but on both the font size of the prior paragraph (especially the length of its descenders) and the prior paragraph's Space After format.

However, there are steps you can take to minimize this type of inconsistency. The most obvious of these is to use either the Space Before or Space After format, in your design. That way, you will know that any variation in the placement of design elements is caused by differences in the depth of the descenders in the prior paragraph, a function of the font size used.

The next step is to realize that the design elements in a document usually follow one another in particular patterns. For example, body text almost always follows a heading. Generally, you want to include some extra space not only before the heading but after it as well. In such cases, it's better to set both Before and After spacing formats for the headings so that you don't have to locate the first paragraph of body text after each heading and manually set a Space Before format for it. By analyzing your document, you can determine which elements follow one another and adjust your formats accordingly.

Finally, you can create special spacing elements that consist of nothing more than a paragraph mark to which you have assigned an appropriate style. For example, you can use a style called *Std. Line Space* with a specific line spacing to regularize the spacing around figures and around bulleted and numbered lists. You can store the paragraph mark in a glossary; when you insert it, if that style name exists in your document, Word uses its definition; if not, Word copies the style from the style sheet hidden in the glossary.

You can even create a complete set of spacing elements, each with its own special style, for removing the spacing inconsistencies between any two design elements in your document. In other words, you can create a spacing element for all possible pairs of paragraphs, for instance:

Sp/Norm-Level1
Sp/Norm-Level2
Sp/Norm-Level3
Sp/Fig-Level1
Sp/Fig-Level2
Sp/Fig-Level3
Sp/Norm-NumList (before a numbered list)
Sp/NumList-Norm (after a numbered list)

Then, after you've placed all the spacing elements and you're ready to fine-tune the design for the document, you can adjust the spacing throughout by changing the style definitions for these elements. This is the method used in this book. Obviously, this can lead to very complicated style sheets and is only for the most demanding of document designs.

Paragraph Alignment

The Ruler alone controls the alignment of lines within each paragraph; no alignment options are available from within the Paragraph dialog box. You can choose from four types of paragraph alignment; they are illustrated in Figure 8-14:

- Left aligned. Lines are even with the left indent, and their right edge is ragged.
- Centered. Lines are centered over the midpoint between the left and right indents.
- Right aligned. Lines are even with the right indent, and their left edge is ragged.
- Justified. Lines are even with both the left and right indents. Word expands the spaces between words to push the ends of lines to the left and right indents.

To set alignment, select some paragraphs (or set the insertion point if only one paragraph is to be affected) and click one of the alignment icons in the Ruler. To indicate the alignment of a paragraph you are about to type, set the insertion point and then click the appropriate icon.

A lone figure stood among the brick buildings, a figure accustomed to the dankness of the night and the glare of the street lamps. The eyes of the figure slowly scanned up and down the avenue, but the rest of the body was awkwardly still, as if the wetness and clinging coldness had paralyzed it.

A lone figure stood among the brick buildings, a figure accustomed to the dankness of the night and the glare of the street lamps. The eyes of the figure slowly scanned up and down the avenue, but the rest of the body was awkwardly still, as if the wetness and clinging coldness had paralyzed it.

A lone figure stood among the brick buildings, a figure accustomed to the dankness of the night and the glare of the street lamps. The eyes of the figure slowly scanned up and down the avenue, but the rest of the body was awkwardly still, as if the wetness and clinging coldness had paralyzed it.

A lone figure stood among the brick buildings, a figure accustomed to the dankness of the night and the glare of the street lamps. The eyes of the figure slowly scanned up and down the avenue, but the rest of the body was awkwardly still, as if the wetness and clinging coldness had paralyzed it.

Figure 8-14
The four types of paragraph alignment.

Borders

The Border options let you draw lines (often called *rules*) around paragraphs. They are available only from the Paragraph dialog box. The effects of the four main options, Box, Bar, Above, and Below, are shown in Figure 8-15. Any of the four options can be drawn in fine, thick, double, or shadowed lines. The border formats were originally intended to be used for setting up tables. This subject is covered in Chapter 14, "Documents with Tables and Lists"; for now, the discussion will be limited to an overview of the various effects you can achieve with borders.

These two sets of four options can be combined in 16 different ways. In addition, you can create effects with the Vertical Bar icon next to the Tab icons in the Ruler, with the tab leader characters, with any of the various underlining character formats, and even with lines and other shapes copied from drawing programs such as MacPaint or MacDraw.

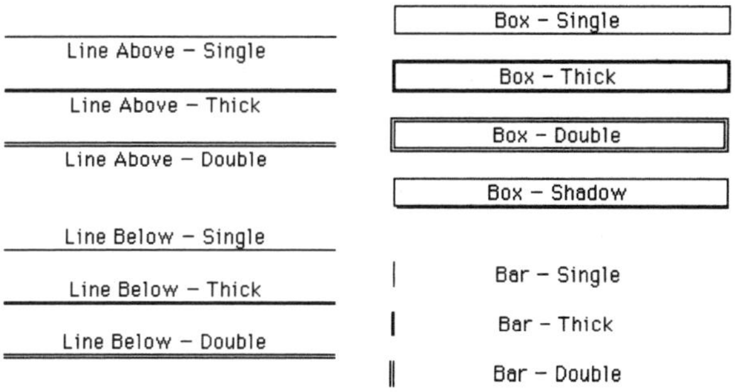

Line Above – Single
Line Above – Thick
Line Above – Double
Line Below – Single
Line Below – Thick
Line Below – Double

Box – Single
Box – Thick
Box – Double
Box – Shadow
Bar – Single
Bar – Thick
Bar – Double

Figure 8-15
Border effects.

Boxes

The Box option in the Border group draws a line around the limits of the selected paragraph. The placement of the sides of the box is determined by the following parameters:

Side	**Controlled by**
Left	Left or first-line indent, whichever is leftmost.
Right	Right indent.
Top	Highest ascender in first line of paragraph.
Bottom	Lowest descender in last line of paragraph.

Figure 8-16 shows an example of this format. You might think that the upper and lower limits of the box would be set by the Space Before and Space After formats, but this is not the case. You can use the paragraph-spacing formats instead to set off boxed text so that the lines do not run too close to the preceding or succeeding paragraph.

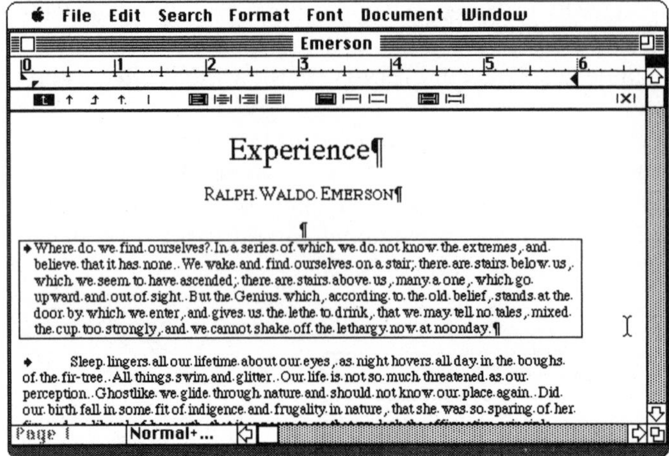

Figure 8-16
The Box border effect.

You can use a few tricks to get more space between the edges of the box and the text. Use the first-line indent and tab stops to add space between the box and the left edge of the text. To add space at the top and bottom of the text, add a newline mark (Shift-Return) at the beginning and end of the paragraph. You can then vary the space by changing the font size of the newline mark and the paragraph mark at the end. You can even put these specially formatted characters in the glossary so that you can use them consistently. It's harder to get more space on the right edge of a paragraph. You can manually break each line by inserting newline marks, but this trick does not work if you've set the right-aligned or justified formats for the paragraph.

When you box a series of paragraphs, Word puts a single line between them, even if you use the Double option. If you want a series of paragraphs to have one box around them (such as for sidebar text elements), use newline marks and tabs to create the effect of a series of paragraphs that is really one formatted paragraph. Figure 8-17 shows an example of this technique.

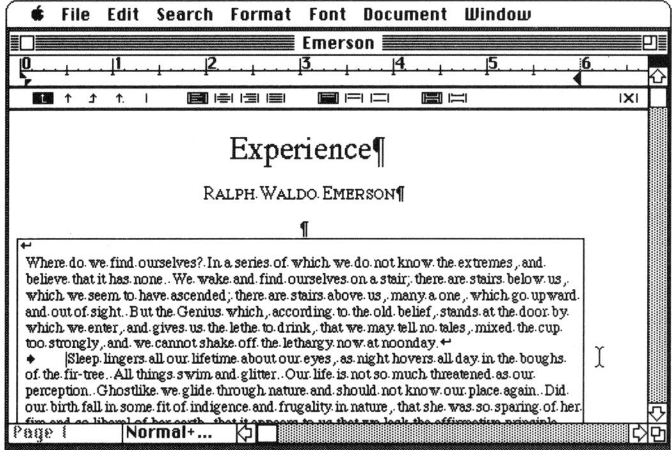

Figure 8-17
A sidebar text effect created using newline marks and tabs.

Bars

Ordinarily, the Bar option causes Word to draw a vertical line to the left of the paragraph. Unlike boxes, the bars are placed 2 points to the left of the left margin and are not affected by the first-line or left indents. This means that if you set a negative indent, the bar will run through your text. However, if you turn on the Facing Pages option in the Page Setup dialog box, Word places the bar on the left edge of left pages and on the right edge of right pages.

Lines Above and Below

The placement of lines above and below a paragraph follow the rules for boxes: The leftmost indent (first-line or left) determines the left end of the line, and the right indent sets the right end.

TIP

Special Border Effects

You have two ways of establishing designs for the elements in your documents: You can work within the normal range of the software to see what effects you can create, or you can start out with an idea and experiment to see how that design might be implemented. The first method is generally easier, whereas the latter method yields richer results at a greater expense of time. Working with the border formats in Word is no different, and to that end here is a potpourri of suggestions for special border effects:

- ❑ Remember that you can use alignment on a hanging first-line indent to set the left edges of boxes and rules. You can then set a tab stop to set the actual starting position of the first line.
- ❑ You can construct boxes from underlined tabs, tab leaders, and vertical bars, in addition to using the border formats.

- You can combine vertical bars with the paragraph border formats. The vertical bar will extend to the edge of the relevant border. This is particularly useful for setting up tables. (See Chapter 14.)
- Use newline marks (Shift-Return) and tabs to create extra space between rules and the paragraph text. If you're using justified alignment, a newline mark causes the text in that line to spread out to the right indent (if the line contains more than one word). This can happen when you use a newline mark to simulate the end of a paragraph in a series of paragraphs that you want to surround with one box. If this occurs, insert a tab character just before the newline mark to force left alignment of the last line in the paragraph.
- You can create rules and other graphic elements in MacDraw, MacPaint, or another drawing program and copy them into your document. You can then format the graphic with any of the border formats, vertical bars, and so on. The glossary is a good place to store these elements when you have perfected them.
- You can turn the formatted image of a set of paragraphs into a graphic by selecting them, pressing Option-Command-D, and pasting the image back into the document. You can then assign the Outline character format to the image to put a border around it. This border can be stretched until it is placed correctly with respect to the text. After doing this, format the original paragraphs as hidden text so that you can edit the text if you need to. See Chapter 15, "Transferring Text and Graphics," for more information on using this technique.
- Instead of using the document itself to experiment with exotic border elements, open a new, blank document and copy material from the document. Alternatively, you can save a copy of the document under a different name, such as *Test*, and experiment with the copy instead.
- Use a macro-recording desk accessory, such as Tempo, to standardize complicated formatting operations.
- Finally, you can create nearly any effect you want by adding PostScript commands before the paragraphs. This is covered in Appendix C, "Using PostScript."

Paragraph Layout Options

The paragraph layout options control how Word arranges paragraphs relative to one another and the page and whether they are numbered. The options are Side-by-Side, Page Break Before, Keep With Next ¶, Keep Lines Together, and Line Numbering.

Side-by-Side

The side-by-side format lets you arrange paragraphs in multiple columns on a page. However, instead of flowing and snaking from one column to the next, the paragraphs are placed next to each other in a controlled manner. The paragraphs to be placed side by side follow one another in the document and are meant to be grouped together horizontally. The side-by-side format is handy for design elements such as the following:

- ❑ Two-column scripts.
- ❑ Level headings in a margin, aligned horizontally with the first paragraph under them.
- ❑ Marginal annotations, references, or graphics.
- ❑ Graphics and captions arranged horizontally.
- ❑ Tables in which you want to establish comparisons by arranging blocks of text across columns.

You can either format side-by-side paragraphs while you write or select and format them after you've entered them. Most of Word is WYSIWYG (what you see is what you get), but this is not the case with side-by-side paragraphs. Instead, in Document view the paragraphs appear one after the other, properly indented so that they will not overlap when printed side by side. However, once you've set up paragraphs in this format it's a simple matter to use the Page Preview command to see what they will look like when printed.

Setting up side-by-side paragraphs involves two steps: assigning the side-by-side format to the paragraphs you want to group together and then adjusting the indents for the paragraphs so that they are placed the way you want them. It really doesn't matter which you do first. Be sure that there is only one paragraph mark between each pair of paragraphs to be formatted in this way. It will not work if you have inserted a paragraph mark between paragraphs to create a blank line.

Let's take the simplest case first—two paragraphs that are to be arranged horizontally on the page, as shown in Figure 8-18. First, assign them the side-by-side format:

❶ Select both paragraphs.

❷ Choose the Paragraph command.

❸ Click the Side-by-Side option and then click OK.

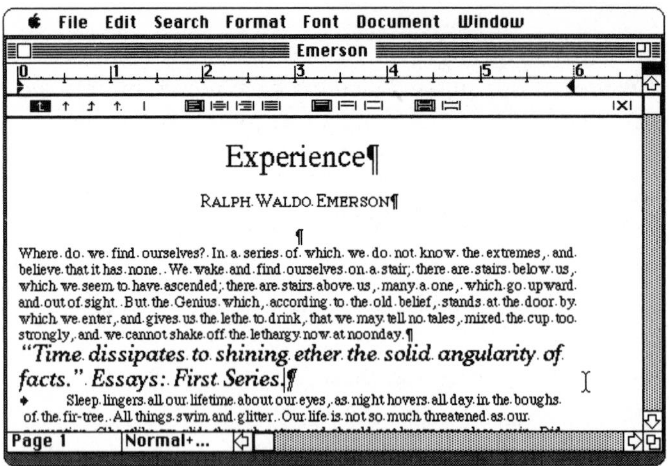

Figure 8-18
The two paragraphs to be set side by side.

At this point you see no visible difference on the screen. Next, indent each paragraph in turn, one on the left and one on the right:

❹ Select the first paragraph by clicking in it.

❺ Display the Ruler.

❻ Set the left and right indents for the first paragraph. You want the first paragraph on the left side of the page, and the left indent is undoubtedly already at 0 inches, so simply drag the right indent marker to 3.5 inches.

❼ Select the second paragraph.

❽ Set a quarter-inch interval between the paragraphs by dragging the left indent of the second paragraph to 3.75 inches.

You can also set the indents with the Ruler edit field in the Paragraph dialog box. The screen should now look like Figure 8-19. To check your work, view it in Page Preview. (See Figure 8-20.)

TIP

Using the Style Sheet to Set Margins
Going back and forth between two or more indent settings can be a chore, but you can almost eliminate the trouble by using the style sheet feature. Simply define two styles on the style sheet, one for the left paragraphs and one for the right paragraphs. You can then assign either style with a few keystrokes. See Chapter 9, "Working with Style Sheets," for more information.

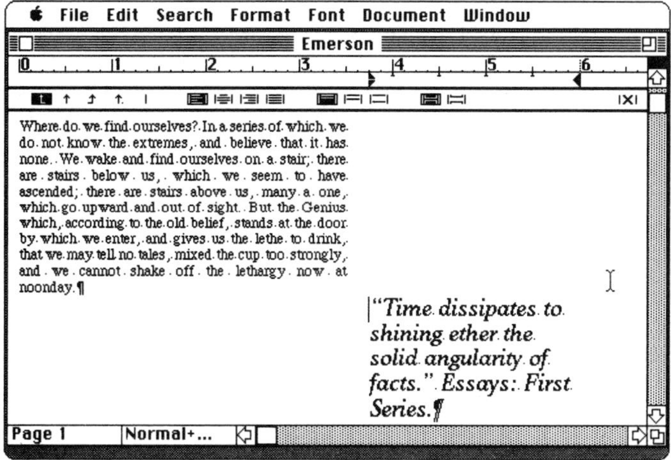

Figure 8-19
The paragraphs after side-by-side formatting, in Document view.

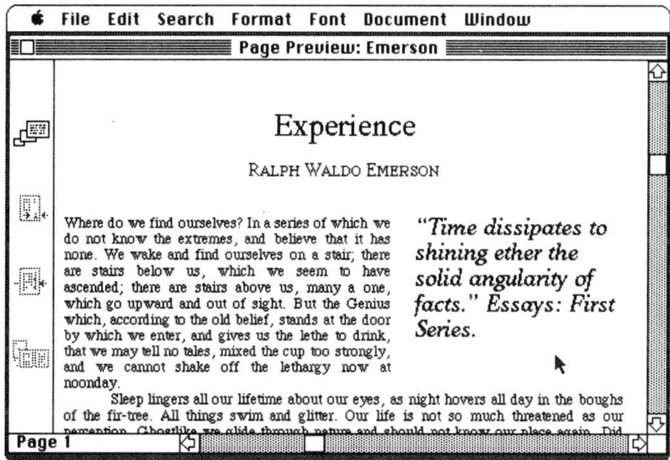

Figure 8-20
The same paragraphs in Page Preview.

Now let's consider a more complicated case, one that reveals the inner logic of the side-by-side format. Suppose you are preparing a newsletter in a single-column format but want to place a graphic in the center of the page with notes arranged around it, as shown in Figure 8-21. (The attribution of tribe names to these artifacts is whimsical.) Figure 8-22 shows the original sequence of the paragraphs. (Incidentally, the graphic is a full-screen image digitized with ThunderScan that has been compressed to 50 percent of its original size, using a technique described in Chapter 15, "Transferring Text and Graphics.")

1. Kwakiutl oil lamp, discovered by George MacDonald during his field study of North American Indian Energy Usage.

2. Sammish woven basket, circa 1921, now in our Indian Works in the Twentieth Century exhibit.

3. Burnished Salish clay pot, discovered in our Columbia River digs, found by Judith Lindsay.

4. Tlingit seal-oil lamp, found by a summer intern on MacDonald's field study.

❑ If you'd like more information on this fascinating study, contact the Museum's Patron Relations Office. Intern, vacation, and summer-study programs are also available.

Figure 8-21
A more complex side-by-side arrangement.

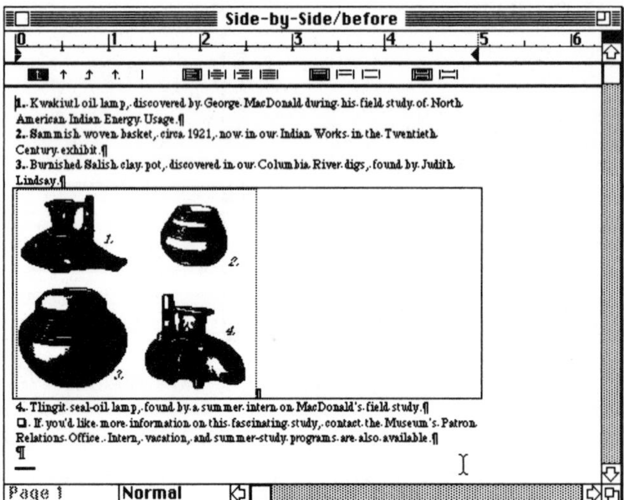

Figure 8-22
The paragraphs before being formatted.

To re-create this arrangement of paragraphs, follow the steps just listed. First, select all the paragraphs (including the graphic), and set the side-by-side format. Then, for each paragraph, set the left and right indents according to the table on the next page.

Element	Left indent	Right indent
Paragraphs 1 and 2	0 inches	1 inch
Paragraph 3 and graphic	1 1/8 inch	3 7/8 inches
Paragraphs 4 and 5	4 inches	5 inches

When you're done, the paragraphs should look like Figure 8-23. To make the group look better, add 4 points of space after each text paragraph. Also, paragraphs 1 and 2 are right aligned, paragraph 3 is justified, and the paragraph containing the graphic is centered and has the box border format.

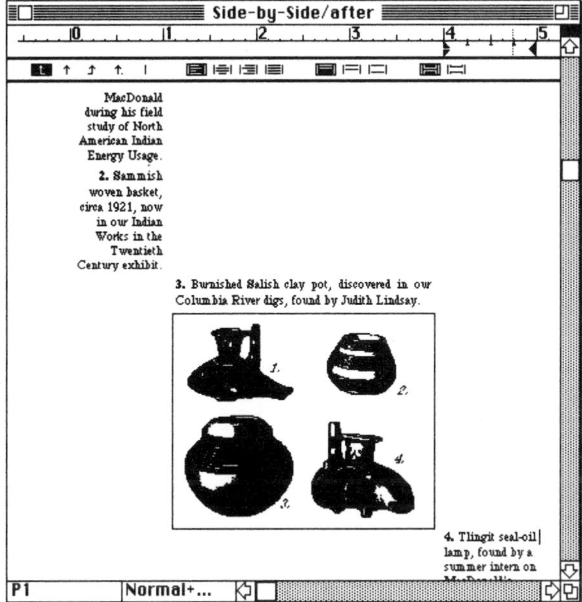

Figure 8-23
The formatted paragraphs in Document view.

Word actually places each paragraph in a chain of paragraphs having the side-by-side format according to the position of its left or first-line indent alone, whichever is leftmost. (A chain of paragraphs is any sequence of paragraphs that is preceded by and succeeded by paragraphs not in the side-by-side format.) The rules for the placement of paragraphs in the side-by-side format are as follows, assuming the left indent is left of the first-line indent:

- If the paragraph's left indent is the same as the one before it, Word places the paragraph in the same column as the one before it.
- If the left indent of a paragraph is greater than (to the right of) the left indent of the one before it, it starts a new column. The new column starts at the beginning of the Space Before setting for the first paragraph in the chain having a left indent less than that of the new column.

- On the other hand, if the paragraph's left indent is less than the one before it, Word places the paragraph in a new row. The new row starts just below the longest column in the row above it.

In the example, the first and second paragraphs are in the same column because they have the same left indents. The third paragraph starts a new column because its left indent is greater than that of the one before it; it is aligned with the beginning of the first paragraph. The paragraph containing the graphic goes below the third paragraph because they have the same left indents. The fourth paragraph starts a new column because, again, its left indent is greater than that of the graphic and paragraph 3. Finally, the fifth paragraph has the same left indent as the fourth one. Because no paragraph has a left indent less than the one before it, no new rows were started.

TIP

Experimenting with the Side-by-Side Format
Set up the following three styles to learn about this powerful feature of Word:

Style and alternate name	Indents
Col1, 1	0 and 2 inches
Col2, 2	2 and 4 inches
Col3, 3	4 and 6 inches

Assign the side-by-side format and the box format to each. The box format will make it easier to see the limits of each paragraph. Create a series of about six short paragraphs of different lengths, and number them as in the example so that you can see where they'll go. Then you can assign a column style to a paragraph easily by clicking in it, pressing Shift-Command-S, the number of the column in which you want to place the paragraph, and then pressing the Return key. Use Page Preview or print the page to see how assigning styles in different patterns changes their arrangement with respect to one another.

TIP

Drop Caps
A drop cap is a typographic element that consists of a large capital letter at the beginning of a paragraph, usually at the start of a chapter or major section in a document. The capital letter is brought down (or dropped) below the baseline of the first line in the paragraph. You can create drop caps like the one shown in Figure 8-24 in two steps. After typing the paragraph:

1. Type the capital letter by itself in a new paragraph before the paragraph in question. Set a larger font size for the capital letter, and give it and the paragraph it belongs to the side-by-side format.
2. Move the left indent of the paragraph containing the capital a bit (about 1/4 inch) to the left of the body paragraph. This makes the body paragraph start a new column to the right of the capital. Word draws overlapping paragraphs as though they were transparent—a side effect of the

side-by-side format—so neither obscures the other. In this way, you can create elements you couldn't with Word's standard range of features.

❸ Insert tabs at the beginning of the first few lines of the text paragraph to create a space for the capital, and insert a tab before the capital to position it flush left with respect to the left indent of the body paragraph.

❹ Use Page Preview to see the effect. You can lower or raise the drop cap by adding space before or after it in the Paragraph dialog box.

Figure 8-25 shows the formats used to create the drop cap in Figure 8-24.

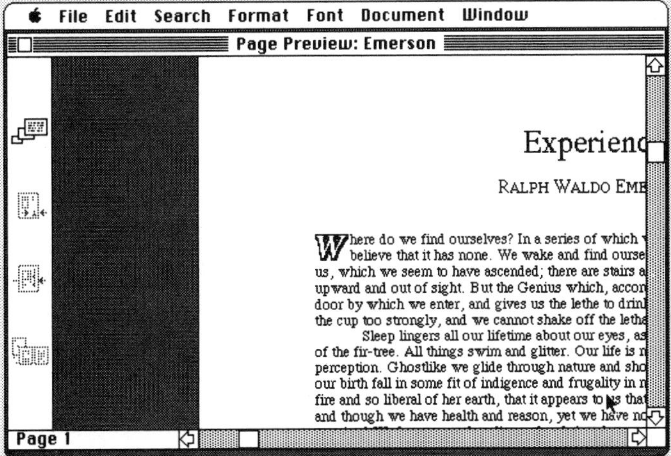

Figure 8-24
A drop cap.

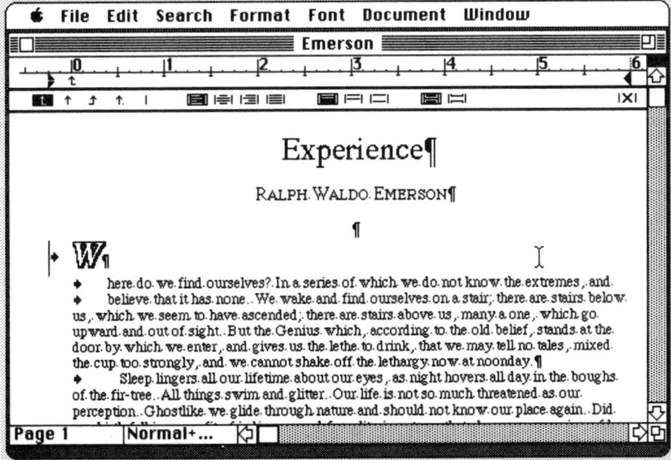

Figure 8-25
The Ruler settings for the drop cap in the previous figure.

Page Break Before

The Page Break Before option tells Word to start the paragraph on a new page. You might use this feature at the beginning of a full-page chart or to start a chapter of a book on a new page (this can also be done with section formats). In most cases, you'll preview page breaks before printing. To set a page-break format, select the paragraph, choose the Paragraph command, click on the Page Break Before option, and then click OK. This is an easy way to force a page break, because you can add the Page Break Before format to the Format menu with the Option-Command- + key sequence.

Keep With Next ¶

Use the Keep With Next ¶ option to group two or more paragraphs together on one page. You can use this feature to keep a caption with a graphic or to keep the name of a character in a screenplay with the dialogue that follows. Note that Word is still free to chop either paragraph in two to start a new page, but it will never break the page between the two paragraphs. To keep a series of paragraphs together, simply select all but the last paragraph. (Because the format keeps the paragraph to which it is assigned with the one that follows it, there is no need to select the last paragraph.) Then choose the Paragraph command, and select the Keep With Next ¶ option.

You can remove paragraphs from the series at any time by selecting one or more of the paragraphs and turning off the Keep With Next ¶ option.

Keep Lines Together

The Keep Lines Together option keeps an entire paragraph on one page, preventing Word from breaking it in the middle. Use this option with Keep With Next ¶ if you need to create an unbroken block of text.

There is a practical limit to the amount of text that can fit on one page. If you tell Word to keep lines together, yet the paragraph is longer than one page, Word fills the first page with as much text as it can and then puts the remainder on a fresh page, rather than insisting that the job can't be done.

Line Numbering

The Line Numbering option is dimmed unless you have turned on the Line Numbering option in the Section dialog box. When you set the Line Number section format, Word turns on the Line Numbering paragraph format, and you have to turn it off for the paragraphs you don't want numbered. This feature is covered in more depth in Chapter 10, "Section Formatting."

When the Line Numbering format is set for a paragraph, you don't see the numbers in Document view, but they appear in Page Preview and when you print the document. Line numbering has its own automatic style, but it doesn't support some paragraph formats, such as tabs and first-line indents. Word doesn't use these formats, even if you do add them to the definition for the *line number* style. Also, line numbering doesn't appear in side-by-side paragraphs and in headers and footers.

■ *Formatting Tricks and Tips*

This section consists of a collection of useful tips you can use while formatting your documents.

Searching for and Replacing Formats

You can search for and select text that has the same formats as the text you have just selected by using the Option-Command-R key sequence. Use this feature, along with the Again commands (discussed in a moment), to find and change all text with a specific set of formats.

What you find depends on what you have selected. For example, to find all occurrences of a particular set of paragraph formats, select a paragraph having those formats by double-clicking in the selection bar. Then press Option-Command-R. If Word finds any paragraphs after that with the same formats, it selects them, stopping at the end of the last paragraph with that set of formats.

Similarly, if you set an insertion point and use the Option-Command-R key sequence, Word selects every character beyond that point having the character formats of the character preceding the insertion point, up to the first character having a different format. Incidentally, if the selection stops at the end of a paragraph when you do this, it's because the (usually) invisible paragraph mark doesn't have the same formats. If you set an insertion point in plain text (that is, text with no additional character formats) and search for formats in this way, Word selects all text after the insertion point that has the same font.

If you select more than one word but not an entire paragraph, Word searches for the formats of the last character in the selection. The main use for this technique is to systematically replace one set of formats (character or paragraph) with another, particularly when you aren't using style sheets. However, once you have changed the formats for a given paragraph or set of characters, how do you search for further occurrences of the old formats? There is no text nearby in the old format that you can select and use as a pattern for a new search.

Simply press Option-Command-A (Again) to repeat the original format search. Notice the similarity between this key sequence and the Command-A sequence used to repeat the last action. These commands are designed to work together, as follows:

❶ Select the text having the formats you want to find and change. Press Option-Command-R to find the next segment of matching text.

❷ When Word selects the matching text, change its formats as needed.

❸ Press Option-Command-A to repeat the format search.

❹ When Word selects more matching text, press Command-A to repeat the format change.

❺ Repeat steps 3 and 4 throughout the rest of the document. If no matching text is found, when Word reaches the end of the document it asks if you want to continue from the beginning. Click Yes if you do, No if you don't. If you are changing all of a certain set of formats, you probably should click Yes, because the text upon which you based your original search has not yet been changed.

Using the Again Command for Ruler Format Changes

When using the Ruler to make formatting changes to a paragraph, you can use the Command-A key sequence to repeat the last set of format changes collectively. For example, you can set justified alignment, a range of tab stops, and double-spacing in one paragraph and then repeat the entire set of formats in another paragraph by clicking in it and pressing Command-A.

Transferring Formats Quickly

You can easily transfer the formats of a paragraph to others without using style sheets, if need be. As Figure 8-26 illustrates, you use one paragraph as the master paragraph and copy its formats to the others. This trick relies on the fact that Word connects the formats for a given paragraph to its paragraph mark. When you replace the paragraph mark of a paragraph with that of another, you also replace its paragraph formats.

First, select the paragraph mark for the master paragraph by double-clicking in the space just to the right of it. Press Command-C to copy it to the Clipboard. Next, select the paragraph mark for the paragraph you want to change and press Command-V to replace it with the one in the Clipboard.

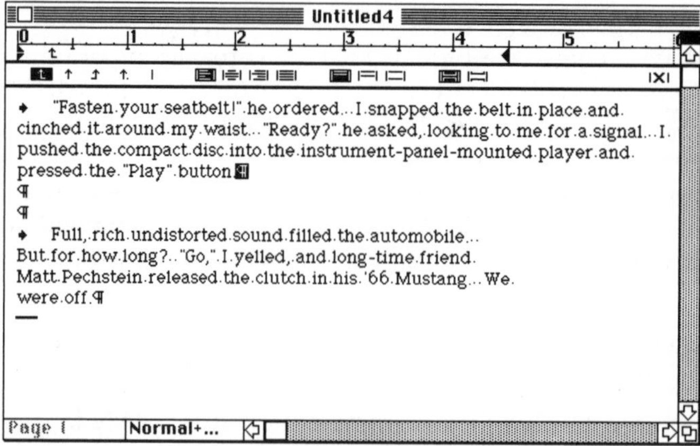

Figure 8-26
Replacing paragraph marks.

You can replace a group of paragraph marks at once by first copying the master paragraph mark to the Clipboard and then selecting the range of paragraphs you want to change. Next, choose the Change command; in the Find What field enter ^*p*, and in the Change To field enter ^*c*. Click OK to replace the paragraph marks. One final observation: The style assigned to a paragraph is also tied to the paragraph mark, so you can use this technique to assign a style to a selected range of paragraphs.

Formatting Glossary Entries

Most of the time, text you select for use as a glossary entry will not include the paragraph mark. Text without the paragraph mark is stored without paragraph formatting. If you insert that text into the middle of a paragraph, it takes on the formats of the paragraph.

However, if you specifically want to store the paragraph formats as well—for a company letterhead, for example—select both the text and the paragraph mark before creating the new glossary entry. You can even store the paragraph mark only, without the text. It helps to choose the Show ¶ command for this if the mark is not already visible on the screen.

Copying Character and Paragraph Formats

You can copy either character or paragraph formats from a sample without having to repeat a complicated set of formatting steps. Whether you copy paragraph or character formats depends on what you have selected—a series of characters or an entire paragraph.

❶ Select the sample text or paragraph.

❷ Press Option-Command-V. The status box in the lower left corner of the screen reads *Format To.*

❸ Select the text you want to reformat. The selection has a dotted underline. When all the text is selected, press the Return key to transfer the character or paragraph formats.

Points to Remember

- A paragraph is any block of text that precedes a paragraph mark (¶). It can even be a blank line. Paragraph marks are visible only when Show ¶, from the Edit menu, is in effect.
- The paragraph format domain in Word controls tabs, indention, alignment, line spacing, the spacing before and after paragraphs, the presence of rules or boxes around paragraphs, the grouping and placement of paragraphs on the page, and the numbering of lines in paragraphs.
- Paragraph formats are attached to the paragraph mark. Deleting the paragraph mark removes the formats. (The paragraph then merges with the one that follows it.) Replacing the paragraph mark changes the paragraph formats to those attached to the new paragraph mark.
- The Paragraph dialog box and the Ruler, displayed when you choose Paragraph from the Format menu, are the primary means by which you alter paragraph formats. You can display the Ruler alone by choosing Show Ruler from the Format menu, and you can also add paragraph formats to the Format menu.
- The Ruler and the Paragraph dialog box show the paragraph formats in effect for the selected paragraphs or for the paragraph containing the insertion point. If the selected paragraphs have different formats, the Ruler and the boxes for the paragraph layout options in the Paragraph dialog box are filled with gray.
- The unit of measure shown in the Ruler reflects the current unit of measure set in the Preferences dialog box, available from the Edit menu. You can choose inches, points, or centimeters.
- The Ruler edit field in the Paragraph dialog box allows you to set tabs and indents more precisely than you can with the Ruler. The minimum interval for each in the various units of measure is as follows:

Unit of measure	Ruler increment	Accuracy in edit field
Inches	0.0625 inch	0.01 inch
Centimeters	0.05 centimeter	0.002 centimeter
Points	1 point	0.1 point

- Indents are not the same as margins. Margins are in the document format domain and apply to your document as a whole; you set them with the Page Setup dialog box, available from the File menu. Indents apply to individual paragraphs and are used to override the margin to achieve a temporary effect in your document. On the Ruler, the 0 point represents the left margin, and a dotted vertical line shows the location of the right margin.
- Setting a tab stop removes all default tab stops to its left.

- ❑ Specifying a tab stop for selected paragraphs adds a new tab stop to the ones already there and replaces an existing tab stop only if set at exactly the same position.

■ *Techniques*

The Ruler

Icon	Name	Action
Indent markers		
◣	First-line indent	Sets the indent for the first line of the paragraph.
◤	Left indent	When you drag the left-indent marker, the first-line indent moves with it. To move the left-indent marker alone, press Shift and drag the marker.
◀	Right indent	Sets the right indent.
Default tab stops		
⊥2	Default tab stop	Indicates the default, defined in the Page Setup dialog box.
Tab icons		
↑	Flush-left tab	Characters begin at the tab stop.
↑	Flush-right tab	Characters end at the tab stop.
↑	Centered tab	Characters are centered over the tab stop.
↑.	Decimal-aligned tab	Decimal points are on the tab stop.
|	Vertical line	Draws a vertical line in the paragraph. Not a true tab stop.

Icon	Name	Action
Alignment icons		
|≡|	Flush-left alignment	Lines are even with the left indent and ragged on the right.
|≡|	Centered alignment	Lines are centered between the left and right indents.
|≡|	Flush-right alignment	Ragged on the left.
|≡|	Justified alignment	Lines are even with the left and right indents.
Line-spacing icons		
|=|	Single space	Sets auto line spacing.
|=|	One and one-half spaces	Lines are 18 points apart.
|=|	Double space	Lines are 24 points apart.
Paragraph-spacing icons		
|=|	Closed space	Specifies no extra space before the paragraph.
|=|	Open space	Sets a Space Before format of 12 points for the paragraph.
Normal paragraph icon		
|X|	Normal style icon	Resets the selected paragraphs to the default format (the *Normal* style).

The Paragraph Dialog Box

Ruler edit field	Shows or specifies the position of a tab or indent marker. The word *Ruler* changes to indicate the type of marker selected. Measurements can be in inches (in), points (pt), or centimeters (cm). This field is dimmed if no marker is selected.

Spacing option group	Determines the spacing before, within, and after the paragraph. Specify spacing in points (pt), inches (in), centimeters (cm), or lines (li). Fractional values are acceptable; values with more than two decimal places are truncated.
Line	Specifies spacing between lines in a paragraph. Auto (the default) sets the spacing automatically depending on the font size. The spacing within a paragraph varies, when necessary, to accommodate larger elements. Enter a negative value to prevent this.
Before	Specifies the spacing before a paragraph. Enter *0 pt* to remove the extra space.
After	Specifies the spacing after a paragraph. Enter *0 pt* to remove the extra space.

Border option group	Draws various types of borders around paragraphs.
None	No rule or box is drawn.
Box	Draws a box around the paragraph. The four sides are determined by the leftmost indent, the right indent, the highest ascender in the first line, and the lowest descender in the last line.
Bar	Draws a vertical rule 2 points to the left of the left margin. If Facing Pages is set, the bar is drawn on the outside edge of the page.
Above	Draws a horizontal rule above the paragraph between the leftmost indent and the right indent.
Below	Draws a horizontal rule below the paragraph between the leftmost indent and the right indent.
Single	The rule or box is a 1-point line.
Thick	The rule or box is a 2-point line.
Double	The rule or box is two 1-point lines.
Shadow	The box is shadowed. This option works only with boxes.

Tab leader option group	Specifies a tab leader for the selected tab stop. The chosen tab leader fills the space before the tab stop.
None	No tab leader is used.
Period, hyphen, or underscore	Uses a period, hyphen, or underscore, respectively, as the tab leader character for the tab stop.
Paragraph layout option group	
Side-by-Side option	Places the selected paragraphs next to one another. The paragraphs must be indented correctly.
Page Break Before option	Starts the paragraph on a new page.
Keep With Next ¶ option	Does not permit a page break after the paragraph. Word is still free to place a page break within any paragraph having this format.
Keep Lines Together	Does not permit a page break anywhere in the paragraph.
Line Numbering	Adds or removes line numbering in a paragraph. This option is dimmed unless the Line Numbering option in the Section dialog box is turned on.
Buttons	
OK button	Implements the selected formats and closes the dialog box.
Cancel button	Closes the dialog box without implementing the selected formats.
Apply button	Implements the selected formats without closing the dialog box.

Working with Paragraphs

Merge two paragraphs into one

❶ Choose Show ¶ from the Edit menu to display the paragraph marks.

❷ Select the paragraph mark between the two paragraphs.

❸ Press the Backspace key.

Start a new line without ending the paragraph

❶ Press Shift-Return.

Insert a paragraph mark after the insertion point

❶ Press Option-Command-Return.

Copy paragraph formats from one paragraph to another

❶ Select the paragraph mark of the paragraph whose formats are to be copied, and copy it to the Clipboard.

❷ Select the paragraph mark for the paragraph to be changed.

❸ Paste the paragraph mark from the Clipboard to the document, replacing the selected paragraph mark.

This technique can also be used to copy styles among paragraphs.

Copy character or paragraph formats from one place to another

❶ Select the text whose formats are to be copied. If the selection includes a paragraph mark, the paragraph formats are copied.

❷ Press Option-Command-V. The status box reads *Format To.*

❸ Select the text to be reformatted, and press the Return key.

Specifying Text to be Formatted

Format one paragraph

❶ Set the insertion point in the paragraph.

Format several sequential paragraphs

❶ Select the paragraphs.

Format text you are about to type

❶ Set the insertion point where you plan to enter the text.

Setting Indents

Set an indent from the Ruler

❶ Select the paragraphs to be indented.

❷ Choose Show Ruler from the Format menu.

❸ Drag the appropriate marker to the location of the indent.

If you move the left-indent marker (the lower of the two left triangles), the first-line indent moves with it. To move the left indent only, press Shift and then drag the left-indent marker.

Set the left or first-line indent to the left of the page margin

1. Drag either or both indents past the 0 point on the Ruler.
2. After a few seconds delay, the window scrolls to the right.

You can also scroll to the left of the 0 point by pressing the Shift key as you click the left scroll arrow.

Set an indent with the Ruler edit field

1. Select the paragraphs to be indented.
2. Choose Paragraph from the Format menu.
3. In the Ruler, click on the indent marker you want to set. The word *First, Left,* or *Right* replaces *Ruler* next to the edit field.
4. Click in the edit field to set an insertion point.
5. Enter the position of the indent in inches, points, or centimeters.
6. If you're setting the first-line indent, position it relative to the left indent.
7. Click OK.

Setting Tabs

Change Word's default tab stop interval

1. Choose Page Setup from the File menu.
2. Double-click in the Tab Stops field.
3. Enter a new tab stop interval in inches, points, or centimeters.
4. Enter *22 in* to remove all default tab stops.
5. Click OK.

Set tab stops from the Ruler

1. Select the paragraphs to be affected.
2. Choose Show Ruler from the Format menu.
3. Drag the appropriate tab icon to the desired location on the Ruler.

Set tab stops with the Ruler edit field

1. Select the paragraphs to be affected.
2. Choose the Paragraph command.
3. Drag the icon for the type of tab you want onto the Ruler. The word *Tab* replaces *Ruler* next to the edit field.
4. Enter the position of the tab stop in the edit field.
5. Click OK.

Delete a tab stop

❶ Drag the tab marker off the Ruler.

Move a tab stop

❶ Drag the marker on the Ruler, or click on the marker and specify a new position in the Ruler edit field.

Place a vertical line in the paragraph

❶ Select the paragraphs to be affected.

❷ Choose Show Ruler from the Format menu.

❸ Drag the Vertical Line icon to the desired location.

Assign a tab leader to a tab stop

❶ Select the paragraphs to be affected.

❷ Choose the Paragraph command.

❸ Set a new tab, or click on an existing tab.

❹ Click the option you want in the Tab leader option group. Click None to remove an existing tab leader from the stop.

❺ Click OK.

Setting Line and Paragraph Spacing

Set line spacing or paragraph spacing from the Ruler

❶ Select the paragraphs to be affected.

❷ Display the Ruler.

❸ Click the appropriate icon.

Set line or paragraph spacing with the Spacing options

❶ Select the paragraphs to be affected.

❷ Choose the Paragraph command.

❸ Enter the new spacing in the Line, Before, or After edit field.

❹ Click OK.

Specifying Paragraph Layout Options

Set paragraphs side by side

1. Select the paragraphs to be affected.
2. Choose the Paragraph command.
3. Click Side-by-Side.
4. Click OK.

Next, indent the paragraphs so that they will fit beside one another in the arrangement you want, according to the position of their left or first-line indents (whichever of the two indents is leftmost).

- If the leftmost indent of a paragraph is greater than (to the right of) the paragraph above it, the paragraph goes to the right of the preceding paragraph on the same row.
- If the leftmost indent of a paragraph is less than that of the preceding paragraph, it starts a new row below the preceding paragraph.
- If the two leftmost indents are the same, the second paragraph appears underneath the one before it and in the same column.

Force a page break before a paragraph

1. Select the paragraph to be affected.
2. Choose the Paragraph command.
3. Click the Page Break Before option.
4. Click OK.

Disallow page breaks in or between paragraphs

1. Select the paragraphs to be affected.
2. Choose the Paragraph command.
3. Click the Keep With Next ¶ or Keep Lines Together option (or both).
4. Click OK.

Remove line numbering from a paragraph

The Line Numbering option is dimmed unless you have turned on the Line Numbering option in the Section dialog box. When you do this, all lines are numbered automatically. To remove the line numbers from certain paragraphs:

1. Select the paragraphs to be affected.
2. Choose the Paragraph command.
3. Click the Line Numbering option.
4. Click OK.

Other Techniques

Change the alignment of text

1. Select the paragraphs to be affected.
2. Choose Show Ruler from the Format menu.
3. Click the icon for the type of alignment you want.

Add borders or rules to paragraphs

1. Select the paragraphs to be affected.
2. Choose the Paragraph command.
3. Click the button for the desired border (Box, Bar, Above, or Below).
4. Click the button for the type of line you want (Single, Thick, Double, or Shadow).
5. Click OK.

Return the selected paragraphs to the Normal style

1. Display the Ruler.
2. Click the X icon near the right edge of the Ruler.

Display a list of the formats for the current paragraph

1. Choose Define Styles from the Format menu.
2. If the current formats are not listed, delete the contents of the Based On field and click in the Style field.
3. Click Cancel when you are through.

Add paragraph formats to the Format menu

1. Press Option-Command- +.
2. Choose Paragraph from the Format menu.
3. Click on the option you want to add in the Ruler or dialog box.

Search for and replace paragraph formats

1. Select text having the formats you want to search for.
2. Press Option-Command-R. Word selects the next block of text with those formats.
3. Change the formats as needed.
4. Press Option-Command-A to search for the next occurrence of the formats.
5. Press Command-A to repeat the format change.

Keyboard Equivalents

Changing Indents

The following commands alter the indent by the default tab stop interval, set in the Page Setup dialog box. This interval is preset to 0.5 inch.

To	Press Shift-Command and
Increase the left indent	N
Decrease the left indent	M
Indent the first line only	F
Indent all lines except the first	T

Changing Other Paragraph Formats

To	Press Shift-Command and
Restore paragraph to *Normal* style	P
Change the style	S, type the style name, then press the Return key.
Align text flush left	L
Align text flush right	R
Center text	C
Justify text	J
Set side-by-side format	G
Double-space text	Y
Add extra space between paragraphs	O

Working with Style Sheets

The style sheet may well be Word's most powerful feature, yet it is also the least understood. Although styles can be used to produce complex effects, the basic concept behind them is quite simple: A style is merely a group of character and paragraph formats that you've given a name; a style sheet is all the styles one document contains.

You've already encountered styles many times in this book. In Chapter 2, you learned how to create an outline and use the level styles to establish a consistent design for the heads in a sample document. You've also seen numerous allusions to the fact that using styles is easier than repeating a complicated series of formatting operations for each element in a document. Finally, it should be clear by now that every document uses styles, even if you haven't assigned any explicitly, because Word assigns the *Normal* style to the text you enter in the absence of any other style.

The most important principle behind the concept of styles is that nearly every document consists of repeating design elements, such as:

- Level headings (assigned one of the *level* styles)
- Body text (assigned the *Normal* style)
- Headers
- Footers
- Figure captions

- Tables
- Lists
- Side-by-side text in columns
- Marginal annotations

Without styles, you would have to maintain a detailed list of the font, font size, line spacing, alignment, and other character and paragraph formats for each element. Experimenting with the design for a document would be difficult, as you would have to make each formatting change individually.

With styles, all you have to do is identify the unique design elements in a document and define and name each element. You can then attach a style to an element simply by selecting the element and specifying the style; the character and paragraph formats contained in the style definition are applied to the text at once. If you want to play with the appearance of a document, you merely have to modify a style, and every paragraph assigned that style changes instantly.

Moreover, once you've taken the time to work out a well-balanced and good-looking set of styles for one document, you can easily transfer the style sheet to another document. In this way, you can build on your efforts rather than repeating them. In addition to letting you transfer styles between documents, Word also supports standard operations such as the cutting, pasting, and deletion of style entries.

Style Sheet Basics

As was mentioned earlier, a style is a collection of character and paragraph formats that has a name. More specifically, a style can contain any formatting instruction available in the Character dialog box, the Ruler, and the Paragraph dialog box. Section and document formats set in the Section dialog box, Page Setup dialog box, and elsewhere cannot be stored in a style.

Each style sheet can contain a maximum of 255 styles. Many of these styles are so common that they are predefined as *automatic styles;* there are 34 of these, including the *Normal* style. You've already encountered the *level* styles in Chapter 2; others include the *header* style for headers, the *footer* style for footers, and the *page number* style, which controls the format of the page number you can place in Page Preview. That leaves 221 empty slots for your design elements. By comparison, this book uses 56 styles, 15 of which are automatic styles.

Styles affect an entire paragraph at a time and therefore might better be termed paragraph styles. The style assigned to a paragraph is tied to its paragraph mark, as was mentioned in the previous chapter. You can't, for example, double-space half a paragraph and single-space the other half. Once you assign a style to a paragraph, you can selectively alter the format for any character within the paragraph. If a style calls for bold text, for instance, you can still remove the boldface from any portion of the text. Similarly, you can override any paragraph format in a style definition by manually applying another format.

However, once you have created a style, you should generally alter the formats of text having that style through the style sheet, rather than by making extensive manual adjustments. As Figures 9-1a and 9-1b illustrate, if you change the definition of a style, all text formatted with it changes instantly.

Unlike a glossary, which can be shared by all documents, a style sheet is considered a part of a particular document. You can, however, copy style sheets from one document to another, as you'll see later in this chapter.

You do not need to save your style sheets on disk, as you do personal user dictionaries, glossaries, or documents. Because the style sheet is a part of the document, it is saved when you save the document.

Word keeps the preset definitions for the automatic styles in a default style sheet, stored in the Word Settings file. You can change the preset definitions of these styles and even add more styles to the list so that any new document you create starts with the new defaults. This, too, is discussed later in the chapter. First, you have to learn how to define and use styles.

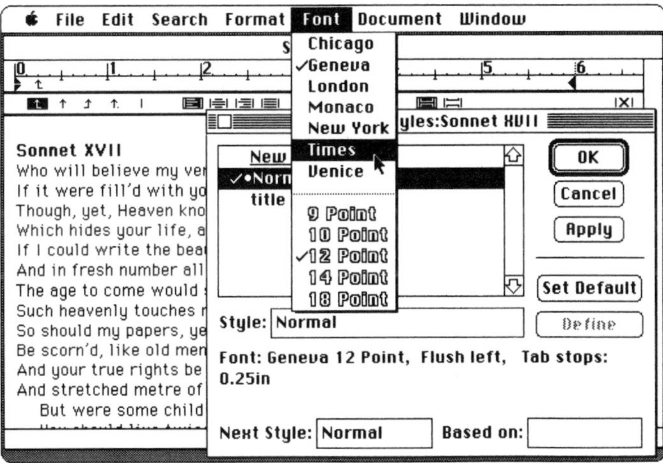

Figure 9-1a

Changing a format through the style sheet.

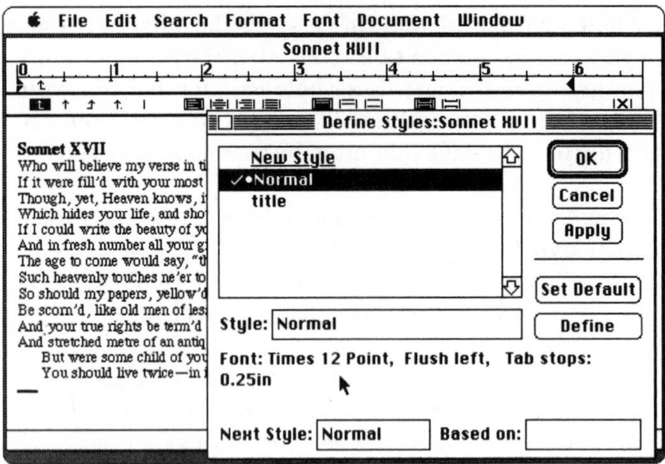

Figure 9-1b
After the the style has changed.

TIP

Multiple Word Settings Files and Default Style Sheets
Although this was mentioned in Chapter 4, it bears repeating in this context: You can create different settings files for different purposes (giving each a different name, of course). To start Word with one of these settings files, double-click its icon from the Finder. In this way you can set up different environments, each with its own default style sheet. When you double-click a document icon or the Word icon, the program uses the defaults specified in the file named Word Settings. If there is no Word Settings file, Word creates one and fills it with the preset defaults.

■ *Defining Styles*

You will probably want to become acquainted with styles by defining a few of your own and applying them in a document. This section and the next describe how to do this. You will learn how to alter the *Normal* style, define your own styles, and make changes to styles, including the automatic styles. Once you know these basic techniques, you'll see how you can assign styles to paragraphs of text. Finally, the last section of this chapter concentrates on more advanced techniques for manipulating styles.

Redefining the Normal *Style*

The easiest way to begin learning about styles, and probably the most common use for styles, is to redefine the *Normal* style, one of the 34 automatic styles that Word supports. When you choose New from the File menu and start typing, this is the style Word assigns to your text. The preset definition for the *Normal* style is as follows:

- ❑ Character formats: 12-point New York. If the New York font is not installed in your System file, Geneva is used instead.
- ❑ Paragraph formats: Single line spacing, flush-left alignment, no tabs other than the defaults established in the Page Setup dialog box, closed paragraph spacing, paragraph indents even with the left and right margins.

Each new Word document starts with the *Normal* style. The style that is assigned to the first paragraph of text you selected (or the paragraph containing the insertion point) appears in the right half of the status box, located near the lower left corner of the window. (See Figure 9-2.) When you open a new document, the box always reads *Normal.*

Figure 9-2
The style name in the status box.

Try redefining the *Normal* style by changing its font from New York to Helvetica and specifying double-spaced lines. Start by making a copy of a short document for your experiments. You can do this from the Finder by selecting the file and choosing Duplicate from the File menu, or from Word by opening the file and saving it under a different name.

Now start Word if you haven't already, open the file, and save it as Text Only by choosing Save As from the File menu, clicking the File Format button, selecting the Text Only option, clicking OK, and then clicking Save. This step removes all character and paragraph formats from your document and converts it to *Normal* style text.

Next, choose the Define Styles command. The Define Styles dialog box, shown in Figure 9-3, appears.

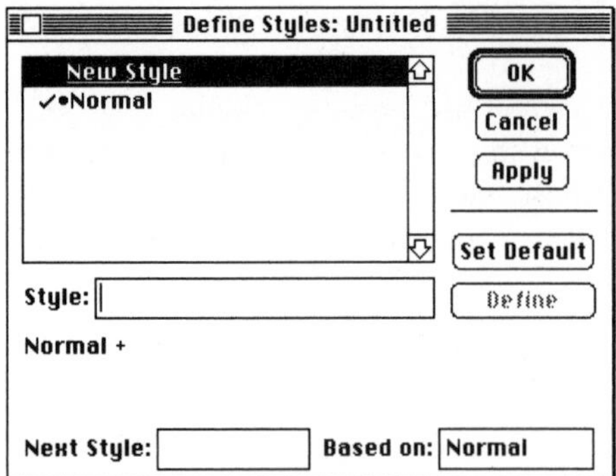

Figure 9-3
The Define Styles dialog box.

The list box showing all the styles currently defined in your document contains only two entries: *New Style* and *Normal*. The name *Normal* is preceded by a check mark, indicating that it is the style of the currently selected paragraph, and a bullet, indicating that it is one of the automatic styles. The automatic styles appear in this list box only when you use them in a document. For example, when you look at the styles for a document created with the outlining feature, you see a style name for every level your outline uses.

Notice that the *New Style* entry is underlined; this means it really isn't a style per se but a "dummy" style. Word assumes when you call up the dialog box that you want to create a new style rather than modify an old one, and so instead of highlighting the name of the style of the selected text, it highlights *New Style*.

❶ Click on *Normal* in the list box. The current definition of the *Normal* style appears in the lower part of the dialog box.

❷ Choose Character from the Format menu. Select Helvetica (or any other font) and click OK. Notice that all the text in your document changes to the new font.

❸ Press Command-R to display the Ruler. (Or choose Show Ruler from the Format menu.)

❹ Click the double-space icon in the Ruler. The text in your document changes to the double-spaced format. (Incidentally, this is a great way to set double spacing for the rough drafts of your document. You can change it back to single spacing when you're ready to print the final version.)

❺ Click the Define button to redefine the *Normal* style, and then click Cancel. If you want to both redefine the style and apply it to the currently selected text, click Define and OK (however, simply clicking OK alone also defines it too). If you want to cancel the operation, click Cancel without clicking Define.

If you wanted to, you could redefine the *Normal* style for all new documents by clicking the Set Default button just above the Define button. Both buttons redefine the style, but the Set Default button also changes the definition in the Word Settings file. The Define button changes the style for the current document alone.

Defining a New Style by Command

You saw how to redefine the *Normal* style by command. Defining a new style by command involves a similar process, except that you work with the *New Style* item instead of the *Normal* entry in the list box of the Define Styles dialog box. Here is the procedure:

❶ Choose the Define Styles command. When the dialog box appears, the *New Style* item is selected.

❷ Enter a name in the Style edit field. Style names can contain any character except the comma. Word is case sensitive when it comes to styles: It maintains a distinction between uppercase and lowercase letters. Keep this in mind when you assign style names. Also, even though you can enter names up to 254 characters long, only 24 characters fit into the Define Styles list box.

❸ Choose the character and paragraph formatting commands you want to define for the style from the Format and Font menus, or use the key sequences for the formats. As you set the formats, they appear in the definition area of the dialog box. (See Figure 9-4.)

❹ When you're done, click the Define button; then click OK to apply the new style to the currently selected paragraph or Cancel to define the new style without applying it.

It is possible to assign alternate names to a style by separating the names with commas. This is useful if you want to assign short codes that are easy to enter from the keyboard. Alternate style names are discussed in more detail later, in the section on assigning styles from the keyboard.

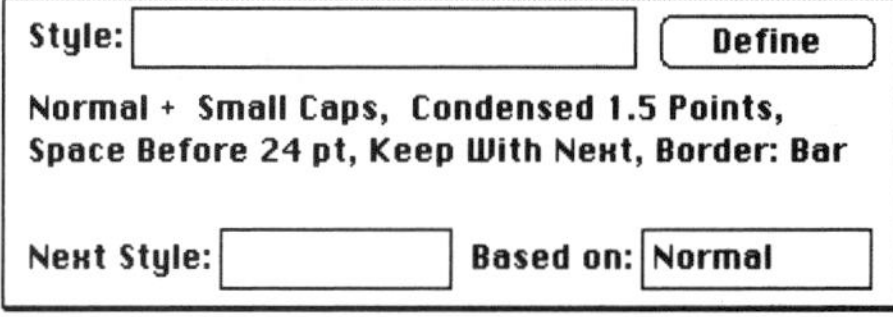

Figure 9-4
Styles in the definition area.

Defining a New Style by Example

Defining a new style by example is like defining one by command, but instead of choosing a series of formatting commands, you base the style on a sample of text that has the character and paragraph formats you want.

This technique is useful if, for example, you make some paragraph formatting changes to text in the *Normal* style and then decide to save these formats as a separate style so that you can use them again. When you change the formats in a paragraph of normal text, you see *Normal +* in the status box. You can interpret this as "This paragraph uses the *Normal* style, with some additional paragraph formats applied manually." When you display the Define Styles dialog box, the formatting changes you have made are listed in the definition area. Here's how to define these formats as a style:

1. Choose Define Styles from the Format menu. The *New Style* item is selected in the dialog box, and the current definition of the selected paragraph appears in the lower part of the dialog box. (If you selected more than one paragraph, you see the paragraph formats of the first paragraph and the character formats of the first character of the selection. If you only set the insertion point, you see the character formats of the first character after the insertion point.)
2. Click in the Style edit field, and type the name of your new style. Do not use commas in the name. See the previous section for more information on style names.
3. Click the Define button, and then click OK to apply the new style to the currently selected paragraph, because you undoubtedly want to assign the style to the paragraph you used to create the style.

The name of the new style appears in the status box.

TIP

Creating a Work Area for Styles in a Document

A good way to experiment with styles, while minimizing the effect of formatting on the actual text of the document, is to create a work area at the end of the document, as follows:

1. Copy a sample of each design element to the end of the document. For example, copy an example of each level of heading, one for the body text, a sample of each type of table or list, and so on.
2. Place the insertion point at the beginning of each paragraph and enter the name you will give to the style when you define it.
3. Format each element until you have what you want.
4. Use each formatted sample to define the style for it by example, as was just described.

Using a work area is also a good way to get all the design elements in one place so that you can see how they work together.

■ Assigning Styles to Paragraphs

Once you've named and defined a style, you can apply it before or during the typing of a paragraph or any time after you type it. When you apply a style, the selected paragraphs take on the defined formats, as though you had manually set an entire range of character or paragraph formats at once.

You apply a style in one of four ways: by choosing the Styles command or the Define Styles command from the Format menu, by choosing a style that you've added to the Work menu, or by using a key sequence to call up the style by name. Also, if certain styles tend to follow each other, you can have Word assign them as you write.

Using the Styles or Define Styles Command

The technique for applying styles is basically the same for the Styles and Define Styles commands. Either command works well for this purpose. Simply select some text, choose either command, select a style, and click OK to assign the style to the text. If you choose the command while typing or if you place the insertion point in a paragraph, the style is applied to the paragraph containing the insertion point.

You're already familiar with the Define Styles dialog box. The Styles dialog box, shown in Figure 9-5, is an abbreviated version of the same dialog box. It contains a list box showing all the styles on the style sheet. (Remember that only the automatic styles you're actually using appear in the box.) The definition of the highlighted style appears in the lower part of the dialog box, but less room is given to the definition here than in the Define Styles dialog box. Finally, you see the familiar OK, Cancel, and Apply buttons on the right side of the box. You may find it more convenient to use this dialog box for applying styles, once you've defined them with the Define Styles dialog box.

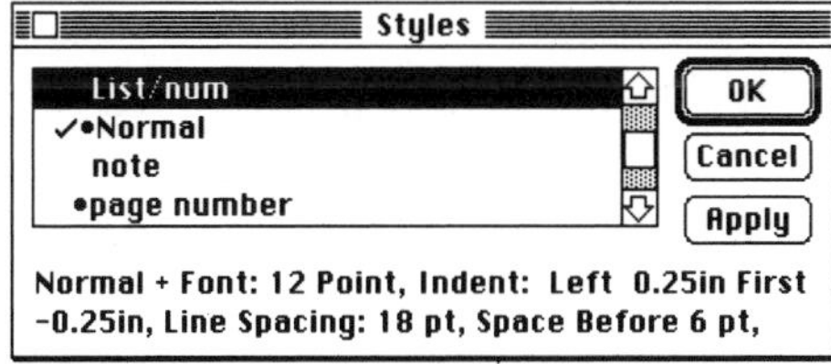

Figure 9-5
The Styles dialog box.

Applying Styles from the Work Menu

Once you are comfortable with styles, adding them to the Work menu makes applying them within your documents very convenient. The process is simple: Choose the Styles or Define Styles command, press Option-Command- +, and click on a style name in the list box. The menu bar blinks to signal the addition. If you've already added that style to the menu, the program beeps. Once you've added a style to the Work menu, you can apply it simply by placing the insertion point in a paragraph or selecting some text and then choosing the style from the menu as though it were an ordinary Word command.

As was mentioned earlier, style sheets are kept with their documents. However, Word stores the Work menu in the Word Settings file and makes the same menu available to any document you work with. If you choose a style from the Work menu that doesn't exist in the document, Word merely beeps and does nothing.

This situation suggests two approaches you can take when working with styles that you have added to the Work menu. The first approach, and by far the most powerful, is to standardize the names you give your styles. The definition assigned to a given name can vary from document to document. Remember that Word is sensitive to case in style names, so be careful to keep capitalization consistent. You can even share styles among documents you use to promote this consistency. (This topic is explored later in this chapter.)

The other approach is to maintain a series of different settings files and start Word by double-clicking on the settings file you want to use for that session. This approach is more cumbersome than standardizing the style names but can be very useful when you work with widely varying types of documents.

Applying Styles from the Keyboard

Using the keyboard to assign styles saves you from reaching for the mouse and pulling down menus. You will probably use the keyboard method once you get used to style sheets and want to work as quickly and efficiently as possible. The keyboard approach does require that you know your styles by name, because you must enter their names from the keyboard.

❶ Set the insertion point or select the text to be affected by the new style.

❷ Press Shift-Command-S. Note that the status box now reads *Style*.

❸ From the keyboard, type the name of the style you want to use, and press the Enter key or the Return key.

You do not need to type the entire name of the style you want, only enough to distinguish it from the rest of the styles in the style sheet. Also, although Word is case sensitive when you are defining styles and invoking them from the Work menu, here you can enter the name in lowercase letters if it will not conflict with another style name.

For example, suppose you wanted to apply a style you have named *Special*. None of Word's automatic styles start with *S* and, assuming that none of the styles you've created start with an *S* (whether uppercase or lowercase), you can simply press Shift-Command-S, type the letter *s* and press the Return key. Word will understand which style you want to use.

However, suppose now that you have another style called *Specification*. Both *Special* and *Specification* start with the same five letters, so to differentiate between the two, you must type at least the first six letters of the style you want to use, either *specia* or *specif*.

If you change your mind about applying the style after using this shortcut, you can abort the command by pressing Command-(period), or clicking anywhere in the document window. Word will also abort the command if you take longer than 30 seconds to enter a style name in the status area.

A Shortcut for the Keyboard Command

If you are assigning styles to text you've already entered, you will probably use the mouse to scroll through the document and select insertion points. After you've used the Shift-Command-S keyboard routine once, you can merely click in the status box to display the *Style* prompt. (See Figure 9-6.) Then type the first few letters of the style name and press the Return key.

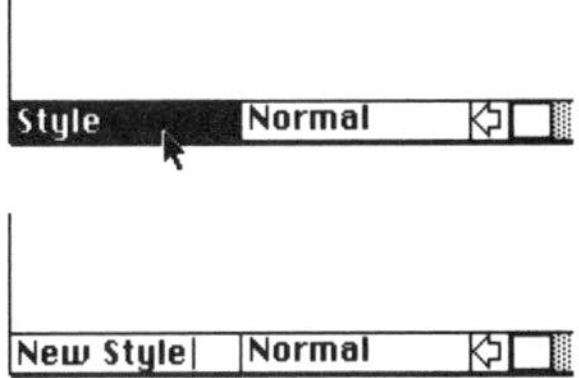

Figure 9-6
Clicking in the status box.

Note that the status box can display prompts for a variety of options, including font selection and the entry of ASCII code characters. To recall the *Style* prompt after using any other of these commands, you must press Shift-Command-S again.

Alternate Style Names

When you enter a name for a style you're defining, you can give the style one or more alternate names separated from one another by commas. The best use for these alternate names is to create code names that are easy to remember and easy to enter from the keyboard.

For example, suppose you are writing a screenplay and have created different styles for the various parts of the document, such as for the character name, dialogue, and action. The names and codes you use for these styles might resemble the ones in Figure 9-7. You can apply the *dialogue* style by pressing Shift-Command-S and typing the entire word *dialogue* to differentiate it from the *dialogue list* style, or you could simply type *d*. You can add the code when you first define the style or when redefining the style.

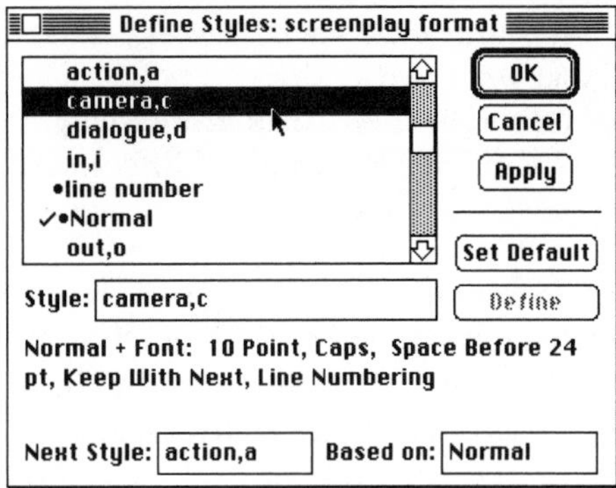

Figure 9-7
Assigning alternate names to styles.

Remember that the rules about entering a unique style name when using Shift-Command-S applies to alternate names as well as full names. For example, if you had defined another style in Figure 9-7 called *dialogue list,* and given it the alternate name *dl,* you would no longer be able to access the *dialogue* style by entering *d* alone, because *d* is shared by two alternate names. Instead, change the alternate name for *dialogue* from *d* to *di* or something similar.

TIP

Applying Styles with the Again Key
In Word, Command-A is the Again command; it repeats the previous command. You can use this command to apply the same style repeatedly to different paragraphs within your document. First, apply to some text the style you want to use. Then, set the insertion point where you want to apply the style again and press Command-A.

The Next Style Option

The Next Style option is a great help when you're entering the text for a document and expect certain styles to follow one another in a logical progression.

For example, body text usually follows a heading in a document. If you are using one of the *level* styles for the heads and the *Normal* style for the body text, this means you want to start typing in *Normal* style text after you've entered the heading and pressed the Return key.

Without the Next Style feature, you would have to change the style for the body text to *Normal* manually. However, if you enter *Normal* in the Next Style edit field when you define the style for each level head, Word switches automatically to the *Normal* style when you press the Return key after typing a heading.

The automatic styles for the level heads are preset to use the Normal style as the Next Style. For other styles, the style itself is the default; that is, text you type after pressing the Return key continues in the same style. For an example of how how this feature of Word might be used in a document, take a look at the screenplay document in Chapter 17, "Blueprints."

Applying Styles and Preexisting Character Formats

Suppose you have been writing in the *Normal* style and have put some text in italics, as in Figure 9-8a. Later, you decide you'd like to create a style for quotes that contains the italic character attribute. If you go back and apply the style to the entire paragraph, you'll see every word in the paragraph become italicized *except* the text itself, which returns to the unitalicized (often called *Roman*) typeface. Figure 9-8b shows how this might look.

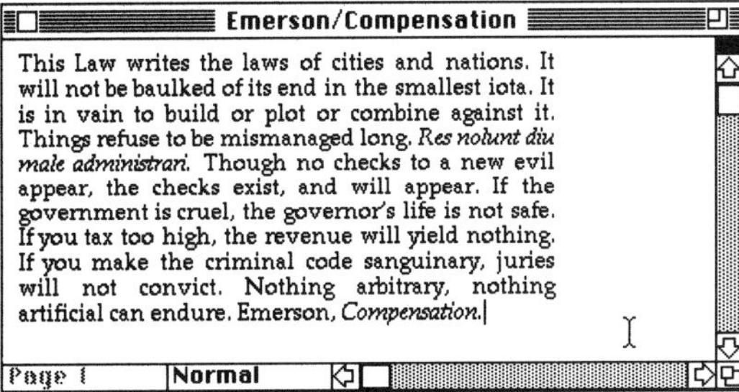

Figure 9-8a
The text as it might appear when you add italics manually.

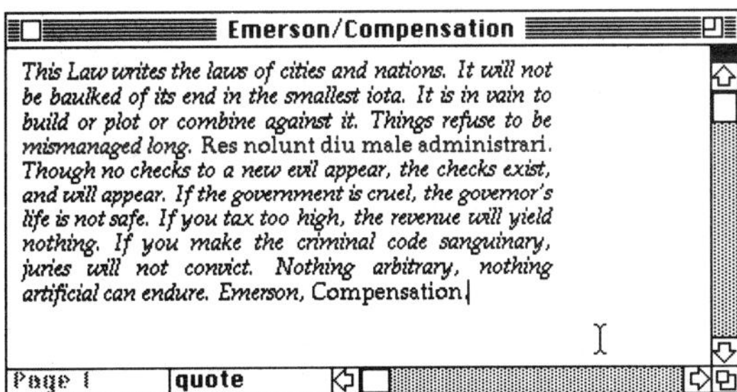

Figure 9-8b
What happens when you apply a style containing the italic character attribute.

Why does this happen? In most cases, you change the typeface of text to emphasize it or to convey a certain quality. When you apply a style containing the character format you've previously added to text in a paragraph, Word preserves the distinction between the words you've altered and those you haven't by *toggling* the character format you've added.

This can be confusing when you have formatted all the text in a paragraph with a certain character format and then decide to create a style for the paragraph containing the same character format. When you apply the style to the paragraph you've formatted manually, it appears as if that character format you added has disappeared.

For example, suppose you put a heading in boldface to make it more visible, redefine a *level* style for it, and then add the boldface attribute to its definition. When you apply the style back to the heading, the boldface attribute that was already there toggles, and the boldface goes away.

To reset the character formats for the heading to those defined in the style, do the following:

❶ Select the text, either by selecting only the text you want to reset or by double clicking in the selection bar next to the heading to select the entire paragraph.

❷ Choose the Plain Text command, or press Shift-Command-Spacebar.

■ *Redefining Styles*

You can use the technique you learned for redefining the *Normal* style, presented earlier in this section, to alter any style you want, including the automatic styles. Any change you make to an automatic style affects the current document only; the default styles are not changed. (You will learn how to reset the defaults later in this chapter.) Here is the basic procedure for redefining an existing style:

❶ Choose the Define Styles command, and select the style you want to redefine. The definition of that style appears in the definition area.

❷ Make the desired changes in the style by choosing commands from the Format and Font menus or by using their keyboard equivalents.

❸ Click the Define button, and then click Cancel, because you probably want to redefine the style without applying it to the currently selected paragraph.

If you change your mind about redefining the style and you haven't yet clicked the Define, OK, Apply, or Set Default buttons, you can restore the style to its original definition by clicking on another style name or clicking the Cancel button.

Renaming a Style

To assign a different name to a style, do the following:

1. Choose the Define Styles command. Scroll through the styles in the list box and click on the one you want to rename.
2. Edit the name in the Style edit field, and then click the Define button.
3. Word double checks to verify that you want to change the name. Click OK.
4. Click OK or Cancel to resume writing or editing.

Note that if you try to rename one of the automatic styles, Word simply assigns the new name as an alternate name. You can use this technique to assign all paragraphs in one style to another style. Suppose, for example, that you've created two styles, *A* and *B*, formatted a series of paragraphs with each style, and then discovered that you really want to group both sets of paragraphs under style *A* and not use *B* at all. You might think you'd have to find each instance of style *B* and change its style to *A*, but there's a better way. You can merge all the paragraphs in the *B* style into style *A* by doing this:

1. Choose the Define Styles command and select style *B*. Its name appears in the Style edit field.
2. Change the name to the name of style *A*, and click Define.
3. Word asks *Name matches style. Merge with A?* You want to assign style *A* to all the paragraphs now in style *B*, so click OK. The Define Styles dialog box reappears, and *A* is selected in the list box.
4. Click Cancel because you probably don't want to apply style *A* to the currently selected text.

Also, if both styles you merge have short names, both sets of short names remain. For example, suppose *styleA* has the short name *a*, and *styleB* has the short name *b*. If you merge *styleB* into *styleA*, the resulting entry in the list box will read *styleA, a, b*.

Transferring Formats with Cut, Copy, and Paste

You can copy character and paragraph formats both between styles in a style sheet and from sample text to a style in the same document. Doing so replaces the definition of the style receiving the copied formats.

To use sample text as a template for a style, select it, choose Define Styles, select a style name from the list box, and choose the Paste command. (After selecting the template text, you could choose the Copy command, but in this case it's necessary only to select the text.) Click Define to record the new definition. Instead of pasting the text you've selected (or copied), the command transfers only the formats of the text to the style, replacing the prior definition. This is similar to the process of defining a new style by example, but this method is better when you have already defined a style and want to replace its definition with another.

Similarly, you can cut or copy a definition from one style to the Clipboard and use it to replace the definition of another style. If you choose Cut instead of Copy, Word asks you to verify that you want to delete the style. Once the style is in the Clipboard, select another style in the list box and choose the Paste command to replace its definition. Then be sure to click Define to define the new style. Note that you cannot use this technique to transfer styles from one document to another.

When a dialog box is active on the screen, Word lets you click the buttons in it by pressing the Command key and the first letter of the text that shows in the button. This causes conflicts with the standard key commands for editing; for instance, the key command for Cancel is Command-C, the same as the keyboard equivalent of the Copy command. The dialog box takes precedence; therefore, in this case you have to use the mouse to choose the Copy command. However, because no button in the dialog box starts with the letter V, you can use Command-V to paste a style definition if you want.

TIP

Resetting a Style to the Definition of the *Normal* Style
An easy way to reset the definition of a style to that of the *Normal* style is to select the name of the style in the Define Styles dialog box, choose the Show Ruler command if the Ruler isn't visible, then click the X icon on the right side of the Ruler. You can also reset the style by selecting it in the Define Styles dialog box and pressing Shift-Command-P, the key sequence for resetting paragraphs to the *Normal* style.

Redefining the Automatic Styles

You can redefine the automatic styles as you can any of the styles that you create. You can also change the defaults for these styles. If you don't like the way Word formats indexes, for example, you can change the automatic index styles to your liking and use the modified styles as the new defaults.

To see an automatic style listed in the Styles or the Define Styles dialog boxes, choose the Define Styles command, and enter its name in the Style edit field. Also, you can force Word to show all its automatic styles by pressing the Shift key while choosing the Define Styles command. A bullet precedes each of the automatic styles in the list box.

To change an automatic style, do the following:

1. Select the automatic style you want to modify.
2. Change the style definition by command or by copying and pasting formats from another style or from some sample text.

❸ If you want to redefine the style without setting a new default, click the Define button, and then click Cancel. If you want to use the definition as the default, click Set Default. Word asks you to verify that you want to record the style in the default style sheet. Click OK, and then click OK or Cancel in the Define Styles dialog box, depending on whether or not you want to assign the style to the current paragraph.

When you click Set Default, the new default style is stored in the Word Settings file.

To return to the original definitions for the automatic styles, delete the Word Settings file and start Word again. However, if you do this, you will lose all other settings, including those specified in the Preferences dialog box. Refer to Chapter 4 for more information on the Word Settings file.

Following are listed the formats for Word's automatic styles. You can change any of the definitions to suit your needs.

Name	Definition
footer	Normal + Tab stops: 3 in Centered; 6 in Right Flush
footnote reference	Normal + Font: 9 Point, Superscript 3 Point
footnote text	Normal + Font: 10 Point
header	Normal + Tab stops: 3 in Centered; 6 in Right Flush
index 1	Normal +
index 2 through *index 7*	Normal + Indent: Left in multiples of 0.25 inch
level 1	Normal + Bold, Space Before 12 pt
level 2	Normal + Bold, Space Before 6 pt
level 3 through *level 9*	Normal + Bold
line number	Normal +
Normal	Font: New York 12 Point, Flush left
page number	Normal +
PostScript	Normal + Font: 10 Point, Bold Hidden
toc 1	Normal + Indent: Right 0.5 in, Tab stops 5.75 in; 6 in Right Flush
toc 2 through *toc 9*	Normal + Indent: Left in multiples of 0.5 inch, Right 0.5 in, Tab stops: 5.75 in; 6 in Right Flush

Don't use these names for your own styles unless you want to replace their definitions. In addition, it's a good idea to use names that do not begin with the same letters as any of these names. The more diverse the name, the easier you can call it up with the Shift-Command-S key sequence.

Some automatic styles have unusual characteristics that affect the way you use them.

- *Line number, page number:* These two styles are based on the *Normal* style with no additional formatting. You can set more character formats for them, but Word ignores any paragraph formats you set. The reason is that Word locks the position of line numbers on the line, and page numbers are placed in the location you specify in Page Preview.
- *PostScript:* If you intend to use PostScript in your documents, you must assign this style to each line of PostScript code in your document. You can change any format in the definition for this style, except that it must have the Hidden format. See Appendix C, "Using PostScript," for more information.
- *Footnote reference:* This is the style used for footnote reference marks in your documents. It is unusual in that you can set it for text that appears within a paragraph. This is the one exception to the rule that a style must be attached to an entire paragraph; a paragraph can have a style and also contain a footnote reference that has its own style. For this reason, the *footnote reference* style has been called a *semicharacter style*, whereas all the others are true paragraph styles. When you redefine this style, the formats of all the footnotes you entered previously do not change; this style affects only those you enter after you redefine the style. To reformat the footnote references you entered before changing the style, you must go back and reenter each footnote reference mark.

The Based On Field and Style Families

The Based On edit field in the Define Styles dialog box represents an option that you don't need to use when learning about styles but is tremendously useful when you want to use styles to their fullest. The Based On edit field lets you base one style on another and add formats to the dependent style.

The Based On option in the Define Styles dialog box allows you to define styles that are based on other styles. When you change the "parent" style, all the dependent styles change accordingly.

Good design practice typically requires the use of, at most, two or three fonts in a document. More than this tends to confuse the reader and results in a cluttered graphic style. On the other hand, most documents do have more than a few design elements. For example, in a book you might have:

- Three or four levels of headings.
- A running head style.

- ❑ A body text style.
- ❑ A figure caption style.
- ❑ A chapter title style.
- ❑ A style for marginal notes or annotations.
- ❑ A style for formatting figures.

Document designers commonly divide fonts into two classes: display fonts, such as those used for chapter titles and level heads, and body fonts, such as those used for footnotes and the body text itself. Imagine putting each style in the list above into one category or the other and being able to play with various combinations of fonts to see how they work together without having to redefine each style manually.

This is the principle behind the Based On option. With this feature you can create two parent styles called *DisplayFont* and *BodyFont*, for instance, and base each style in the list on one style or the other. Each parent style contains one or more format specifications; in this case, each would contain only the font you wanted to use for that type of style. Each dependent style would then refer to its parent for the font to use and add the other character and paragraph formats you specified in its definition.

An Example

Let's consider a typical use for the Based On option. Suppose you wanted all the *level* style headings in a document to use the same font but want to wait to decide on a font until after you've entered the text. You'd like to vary the heading styles by using different point sizes for each and making them bold to distinguish them from the body text. A good way to do this is with the work area technique presented in the tip "Creating a Work Area for Styles in a Document," earlier in this chapter. First, create a style called *DisplayFont*:

1. Go to the end of the document, start a new paragraph, and click the X icon in the Ruler to reset all paragraph formats for it to the *Normal* style.
2. Without moving the insertion point, type *DisplayFont Sample*.
3. Double-click in the selection bar next to the paragraph to select it, and give it the display font you'd like to start with. (The whole point of styles is that you can change your mind as often as you like without having to reformat everything.) Use Avant Garde or any sans serif font such as Helvetica or Geneva.
4. With the paragraph still selected, choose the Define Styles command.

When the dialog box appears, the *New Styles* item is highlighted, and you can see the current definition of the selected sample paragraph: *Normal + Font: Avant Garde*. The Based On edit field reads *Normal*. Leave *Normal* as the parent style—it's useful to base all other styles in a document on the *Normal* style. Then, if you need to apply a format across every style at once, you can apply it to the *Normal* style.

For example, you could double space your entire document by setting the double-space format in the *Normal* style. All styles based on the *Normal* style are then double spaced unless you have set new line-spacing formats in the definitions of the dependent styles. You could then change all styles back to single-spacing for the final version by redefining the *Normal* style to use the single-space format. Now define the style:

❺ Enter *DisplayFont* in the Style edit field.

❻ Click Define. Because you also want to apply this style to the sample text, click OK. The style area in the status box now reads *DisplayFont*, as you can see in Figure 9-9.

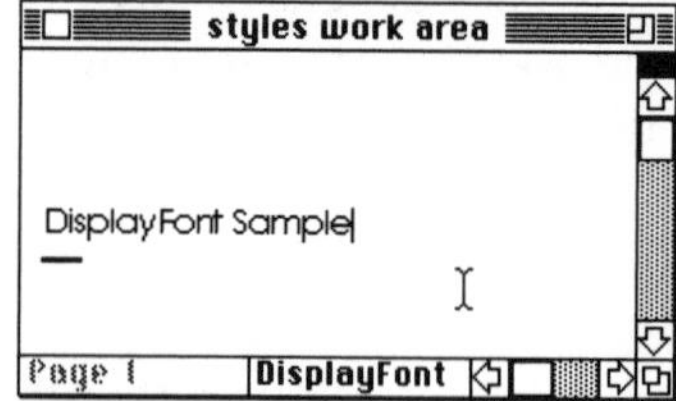

Figure 9-9
The *DisplayFont* sample after the style has been defined.

Next, redefine the *level* styles, much as you did in Chapter 2 when you created the show biz document. This time, however, base the definition for the *level* styles on the display font defined in the *DisplayFont* style:

❶ Select and copy the *DisplayFont* sample paragraph to the Clipboard. Set an insertion point about 2 lines down, and press Command-V to paste the line back into the document.

❷ Replace the name *DisplayFont* in the new sample with *level 1*.

❸ Choose the Define Styles command. Figure 9-10 shows the dialog box that appears.

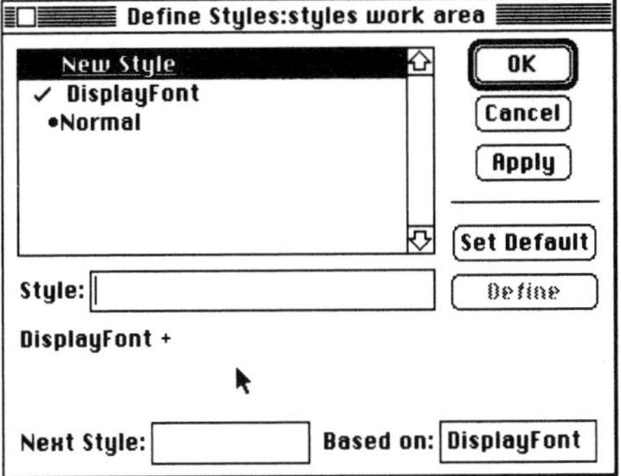

Figure 9-10
The Define Styles dialog box before a new *level* style is defined.

The *New Style* entry in the list box is selected. The Based On edit field now reads *DisplayFont,* because the paragraph containing the insertion point has been assigned that style. The definition reads *DisplayFont +,* reiterating its dependence on that style.

❹ Enter *level 1* in the Style edit field to name the style.

❺ Choose 18 Point from the Font menu, and choose Bold and Underline from the Format menu to add these formats to the *level 1* style. Choose the Paragraph command, set the Before field to 20 points, and click OK.

The definition now reads *DisplayFont + Font: 18 point, Bold Underline, Space Before 20 pt,* reflecting the changes you've made. This means that the *level 1* style uses the font defined for *DisplayFont* but in the 18-point size, boldfaced, and underlined; in addition, paragraphs in this style are set off from the preceding text. If you change the font specification in *DisplayFont,* the definition shown for *level 1* doesn't change, although *level 1* will use the new font.

❻ Click Define.

❼ Word responds by asking *Style already exists. Change its definition to match New Style?* You'll see this message because, even though the *level 1* style does not appear in the list box, it is an automatic style and therefore still defined for the document. Click OK.

❽ To assign the redefined *level 1* style to the currently selected sample text, click OK.

When you click OK, the dialog box goes away, the sample text takes on the formats of the new *level 1* style, and the status box reads *level 1,* as shown in Figure 9-11.

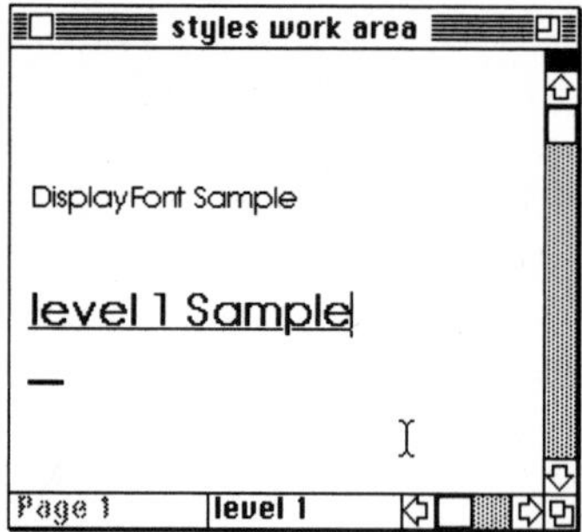

Figure 9-11
The Style work area after the *level 1* style is redefined.

Use the same process to redefine the *level 2* and *level 3* styles. Because you want to base their definitions on the *DisplayFont* sample, copy and paste it again for each of the two styles. Change the names in the samples to *level 2* and *level 3*. Then, for each style, do the following:

1. Select the sample text and choose the Define Styles command. The Based On edit field reads *DisplayFont*.
2. Enter *level 2* or *level 3* in the Style edit field.
3. Set appropriate formats for each style from this table:

Style	**Formats**
level 2	14 Point, Bold, 14 points Space Before
level 3	12 Point, Bold, 8 points Space Before

4. Click Define, and then click OK when Word asks if you want to redefine the preexisting style.
5. Click OK to apply the style to the sample text.

When you're done, the Style work area should look like Figure 9-12.

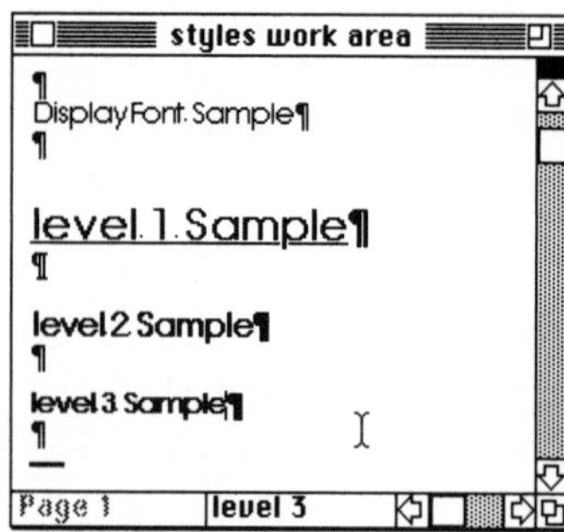

Figure 9-12
The Style work area after the *level* styles are defined.

This may seem like a lot of work, but it will save you time later. You can format the level headings in your document by assigning the appropriate style, and when you are ready to refine the design for your document, you can do so without searching for and reformatting each head. Finally, if you want to change the font for the headings, you have to redefine the *DisplayFont* style only once.

Note that you can also simply type a style name in the Based On field if you choose not to use the work area technique.

Style Sheet Strategies

If you extend the hierarchy implied by the previous example you might get a structure like that shown in this table:

Style name	Definition
Normal	Palatino 10 point, Flush Left
DisplayFont	Normal + Font: Avant Garde
header	DisplayFont + Font: 10 point, Bold, Border: Line Below
footer	DisplayFont + Font: 10 point, Bold, Border: Line Above
level 1	DisplayFont + Font: 18 point, Bold, Space Before 20 pt
level 2	DisplayFont + Font: 14 point, Bold, Space Before 14 pt
level 3	DisplayFont + Font: 12 point, Bold, Space Before 8 pt
(other styles based on *DisplayFont*)	
BodyFont	Normal +
BodyText	BodyFont + Line Spacing -12pt
footnote reference	BodyFont + Font: 9 Point, Superscript 3 Point
footnote text	BodyFont + Space After 3 pt
Table/2 column	BodyFont + Space After 4 pt, Tab Stops: 0.13 in; 2.25 in; 2.38 in
Table/3 column	BodyFont + Space After 4 pt, Tab Stops: 0.13 in; 2 in; 3.38 in; 3.5 in
(other styles based on *BodyFont*)	

The *Normal* style is at the top level, followed by the two font styles, *DisplayFont* and *BodyFont*. Based on the *DisplayFont* style are the *level* styles you just redefined, as well as the *header* and *footer* styles. Stemming from the *BodyFont* style is a style called *BodyText* for the main body text, as well as the various styles for footnotes, tables, index entries, and so on.

Word supports these dependent relationships to a depth of nine styles, including the *Normal* style. This means that if *Style1* is based on the *Normal* style, *Style2* is based on *Style1*, and so on, with the deepest style you can define being *Style8*. With a total of 255 styles and a depth of 9 styles, Word's style sheet can handle nearly any style structure you can imagine.

One interesting thing about this structure is that no text in the document is actually formatted in the *DisplayFont* or *BodyFont* styles, other than the samples in the work area. These styles are used only to enhance the consistency of the document's design and make it easier to adjust and maintain.

Your own style sheets don't have to follow this pattern if it does not suit your documents. The table on page 255 presents what is probably the most common way of arranging the dependencies in a style sheet. This is the structure Word supplies if you ignore the Based On field completely. All styles, including the automatic ones, are based on the *Normal* style. When using this arrangement, you typically enter the body text in the *Normal* style and define all other styles in relation to it. This arrangement is easy because you can create and maintain it with no special effort and because you can use the commands that reset the style of selected paragraphs, such as the X icon on the Ruler, to return the text to the *Normal* style.

Sometimes it is useful to minimize the interactions between the styles on a style sheet. You may find it helpful to do this when you're first learning about style sheets, for instance. If you remove the entry in the Based On edit field for a style, the style retains the formats of the former parent style but is no longer linked to it. You can see the definition of the style change in the Define Styles dialog box when you delete the contents of the Based On field; the definition of the parent style is added to the definition of the style that was once dependent.

Something similar happens when you change the parent of a dependent style by entering the name of the new parent style in the Based On field. If *styleA* is the name of the first parent style and *styleB* is the name of the second, the definition of the dependent style changes from *styleA* + *(formats)* to *styleB* + *(formats)*.

Subtracting Formats from Dependent Styles

If you think about the syntax of a style definition in the Define Styles dialog box, you might notice that it usually says something like *Normal + Font:*, and so on. The definition of a dependent style is either additive or replaces a format in its parent's definition. What do you do if a parent style specifies a format that you don't want in the dependent style definition?

For most character and paragraph formats, one format merely replaces another. For example, if you don't want a font, you set a different font. But the tab stop paragraph formats are different, because you can specify a list of various types of tab stops in the definition for the style. In this case, you can actually subtract a paragraph format without replacing it with another.

For example, let's say the parent definition sets a tab stop at 2 inches. When you define the dependent style, you'll see the tab stop at the expected location in the Ruler. If you drag the tab stop off the Ruler, you'll see the words *Not at 2 in* appended to the definition of the dependent style. This tells you that even though the parent style sets a tab stop, that specification doesn't hold for the dependent style.

TIP

Resetting Character and Paragraph Formats
If you've set paragraph and character formats for text to which you've assigned a style (even if you haven't, the text still has the *Normal* style), you can return either the paragraph or character formats to the base definition for the style. First, select the text. To return the text to the base character formats for the style, press Shift-Command-Spacebar. To return the text to the base paragraph formats for the style, reapply the style.

Sharing Style Sheets Among Documents

Every new document you create has its own style sheet. This can be both a hindrance and a help. You benefit from this because you can create many kinds of formats for a variety of documents—from reports, manuscripts, and outlines to screenplays, proposals, and letters—and work with only those styles that are used with the specific kind of document. The disadvantage is that it's a little more difficult to share a common style among many documents. However, Word gives you four ways of doing this:

- Merge the style sheet of another document into the current document.
- Transfer styles when you copy styled text from one document to another.
- Add styles to Word's default style sheet stored in the Word Settings file, and update a document's style sheet from that one.
- Add the styles kept with an entry stored in the glossary when you insert that entry.

Merging a Style Sheet from Another Document

You can copy an entire style sheet from another document; any styles in the current document that have the same name are replaced with the ones being copied. Here's what to do:

1. Choose the Define Styles command.
2. While the dialog box is active, choose Open from the File menu.
3. Select and open the document containing the style sheet you want to import.

The document itself won't be opened, but Word will add the styles in it to the style sheet for the current document, as illustrated in Figure 9-13. When two styles have the same name, the style being merged replaces the one in the destination document. If a style in the source document doesn't exist in the destination document, Word adds it to the destination document. If a style in the destination document has a name that doesn't exist in the source document, its definition remains intact. Therefore, if you want to preserve a style that has the same name as a style in the source document, change the name before you merge the style sheets.

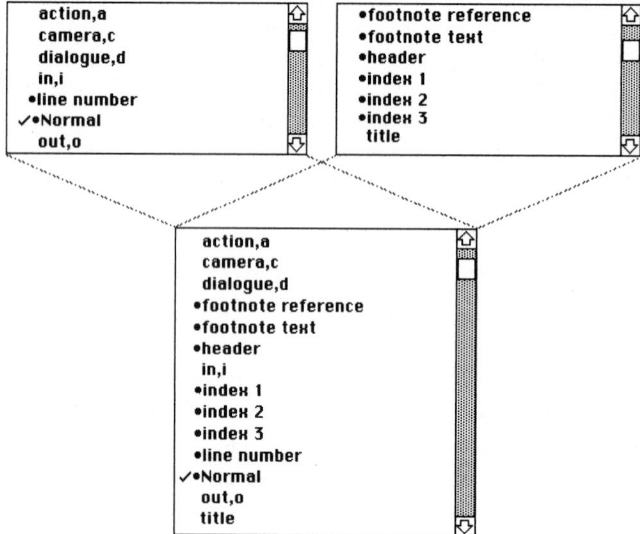

Figure 9-13
Merging style sheets.

However, there is a cost in merging a style sheet from another document. If you have added paragraph formats to paragraphs assigned a style, when you merge the style sheet, the manual paragraph formats in the destination document disappear, and you have to add them back again. If this happens frequently, try increasing the number of styles in your document (that is, make your styles more particular instead of more general) so that you aren't making as many manual formatting adjustments. You can also experiment with reducing the number of exceptional cases requiring manual paragraph formatting adjustments in your documents.

Another trick you can use to minimize loss of manual paragraph formats in the destination document is to make a copy of the source document and then remove all the styles in the copy but those you want to merge. Only those styles having the same name lose their manual paragraph formats, preserving the others.

The greatest use for merging style sheets is when you want to maintain a consistent style across many documents. You can create and maintain a reference document, or template, containing the styles that establish the design. In this document, keep at least one sample of text formatted with every style in the style sheet so that you can see how the styles work together.

This method is similar to the technique described earlier of using a style work area at the end of your document, except that you keep this work area in a separate document. You can even develop families of template documents, each of which expresses a highly refined design.

You can use these templates to create new documents. There are two ways to do this:

- Make a copy of the template file and type your new document into it. This leaves the original template document unchanged.
- Start a new document and merge the template style sheet into it, using the instructions given above.

If you enter text directly into the template document, you run the risk of accidentally saving it without first renaming it. You can avoid the extra trouble this causes by being sure you have a backup of the template in case anything happens to the original.

TIP

Protecting Template Style Sheets
If you've invested much time in developing a complex style sheet for a design, you might try locking the template document while you are in the Finder's desktop. Do so by clicking the icon for the document and choosing the Get Info command. Then click the Locked check box. This prevents the template from being accidentally thrown away or resaved. To turn the protection off, open the Get Info box again and click the Locked check box once more. If you try to save a locked document, Word offers you the chance to provide a different name.

Transferring Styles by Copying Text

When you copy styled text from one document into another, and that text has a style that is not on the destination document's style sheet, Word transfers that style and its definition. If the destination document has a style with the same name as the copied text, the pasted text takes on the formats of the same style in the destination document.

You can use this behavior to selectively transfer a few styles from a sample instead of all of them. Select a paragraph in the source document that is formatted with the style you want, copy it to the Clipboard, and paste it into the destination document. You can then delete the copied text if you want; the style will remain in the destination style sheet even if the text is removed.

Beware, however, of copying too many styles at once with this method. If you copy more than 50 paragraphs in one operation, Word will decide to copy all the styles to the destination document. This can be confusing, but you are not in any danger of losing style information in the destination document; when styles are copied into a document in this way, the definitions of the styles in the destination document are not replaced by those of the same name in the source document.

Updating Styles from Word's Default Style Sheet

You've already seen how to add styles to the default style sheet stored in the Word Settings file. Every time you create a new document, Word uses this default style sheet to establish formats for the design elements in it. However, when you change one of the automatic styles, the new style does not affect previously typed documents.

To update the style sheet of an existing document after you've changed the default styles in the Word Settings file, first create a new document. The new document uses the default style definitions. Then, copy into the blank document the contents of the document you want to update, in pieces if you want. Those styles in the pasted text having the same names as ones in the default style sheet take on the formats of the new default styles. Don't forget to copy the contents of the Header, Footer, and Footnote windows as well.

Using the Glossary to Insert a Style

Chapter 5 mentioned that the glossary contains its own style sheet for glossary entries that have styles attached. An entry can contain more than one style. When you insert a glossary entry into a document, it's as though you had pasted it into the document; the styles in the destination document take precedence. Therefore, this method works only for styles that don't already exist in the document's style sheet.

You can have glossary entries that consist of nothing more than paragraph marks to which styles are attached. Give these style glossary entries the same name as the style itself.

■ *Printing Style Sheet Definitions*

While the Define Styles dialog box is active, you can choose Print from the File menu to print a complete list of the styles you are using in a given document. Having a list of styles in front of you makes designing a system of styles easier and also reminds you of their names. Further, the definition area in the dialog box doesn't have quite enough room for complicated style definitions, such as those you might create for a table with many tabs. Word prints the styles in alphabetical order by name; the definition appears on the next line.

■ *Points to Remember*

- ❏ A style is a named collection of paragraph and character formats. A style sheet is the collection of styles for a document and is saved with the document. If no other style has been assigned to a paragraph, it defaults to the *Normal* style. A style sheet can have as many as 255 styles.
- ❏ Word includes a set of 34 automatic styles that are assigned by operations such as specifying a header, placing a footnote, or using the outlining feature. You can redefine automatic styles. A style sheet shows only the automatic styles you have used in the document. To see all 34 automatic styles, press the Shift key while choosing Styles or Define Styles.
- ❏ Only one can be assigned to a given paragraph and is tied to its paragraph mark. Some styles, such as *footnote reference*, *page number*, and *line number*, have special characteristics.
- ❏ You can override the formats in the style assigned to a paragraph by manually specifying new formats.
- ❏ A style can have more than one name; separate the names by commas. You can use a second, shorter name to make the key sequence for assigning a style (Shift-Command-S) easier to execute.
- ❏ Use the Define Styles command to create new styles and modify existing ones. When the Define Styles dialog box is displayed, all menu and keyboard formatting commands, including the Ruler, are available and apply to the style selected in the list box. Use the Define Styles or the Styles commands from the Format menu to apply styles.
- ❏ You can add style names to the Work menu, but the definitions for the styles are not attached to the names; any styles you assign from this menu must already be defined in your document.

■ *Techniques*

The Define Styles dialog box

(The Styles dialog box is an abbreviated version of the Define Styles dialog box and thus will not be described separately.)

Styles list box	Lists all styles defined for the document. A bullet precedes automatic styles. A check mark precedes the style assigned to the currently selected paragraph. Anything you do while this dialog box is displayed affects the highlighted style.

Style edit field	If *New Style* is highlighted in the list box, this field lets you enter a name for the new style. If some other style name is selected in the list box, this field lets you enter a new name for that style. A style name can contain any character except the comma. You can assign more than one name to a style by separating them with commas.
Definition area	Shows the formats used in the currently selected style or in the currently selected paragraph.
Based On edit field	Lets you define a new style by starting with an existing style as its base. Any changes to the base, or parent, style affect the dependent style. Deleting the name from the Based On field removes this link without altering either style.
Next Style edit field	Lets you specify the style that will follow by default any paragraph entered in the style you are defining. The change of style takes place during text entry only, when you press the Return key or the Enter key with the insertion point immediately in front of the paragraph mark. It does not work when the window is in Outline view.

Buttons

OK button	Applies the highlighted style to the currently selected paragraphs and closes the dialog box.
Apply button	Applies the highlighted style to the selection in the document without closing the dialog box.
Define button	Creates a new style, renames an existing style, or records changes to the formats of a style.
Set Default button	Adds the selected style to Word's default style sheet in the Word Settings file. If the style name already exists in that style sheet, the new definition replaces the old.

Working with Styles

Assign a style to text using the Styles command

1. Select the paragraphs to which you want to assign the style, or set the insertion point where you will begin typing in the style.
2. Choose Styles from the Format menu.
3. Select the style you want to assign.
4. Click OK or Apply.

Assign a style to text from the keyboard

1. Select the paragraphs to which you want to assign the style, or set the insertion point where you will begin typing in the style.
2. Press Shift-Command-S.
3. Enter enough of the name of the style to distinguish it from any other style, and press the Return key.

Define a style by command

1. Choose Define Styles from the Format menu.
2. Be sure the *New Styles* item is selected.
3. Type the name for the style in the Style field.
4. Choose the character and paragraph formats for the style. Each format you choose appears in the definition area of the dialog box.
5. Click Define to define the style.
6. Click OK or Cancel.

Define a style by example

1. Select the paragraph containing the formats you want to use in the style.
2. Choose the Define Styles command. The formats for the paragraph are listed in the definition area.
3. Type a name for the style in the Style field, and click Define, or click Apply or OK to both define the style and assign the style to the sample text.

Redefine a style

1. Choose the Define Styles command.
2. Select the style you want to redefine.
3. Change the formats in any way you like.
4. Click Define, and then click Cancel.

Rename a style

❶ Choose the Define Styles command.
❷ Select the style you want to rename.
❸ Type the new name in the Style field.
❹ Click Define, and then click OK in the dialog box that appears.
❺ Click Cancel.

Add an alternate name to a style

❶ Choose the Define Styles command.
❷ Select the style you want to rename.
❸ Click at the end of the style's name in the Style edit field, type a comma, and then type the alternate name.
❹ Click Define and then click Cancel.

Delete a style

❶ Choose the Define Styles command.
❷ Select the style you want to delete.
❸ Choose Cut from the Edit menu. Word asks for confirmation.
❹ If the style also appears in the default style sheet, Word asks if you want to delete the style there too.

Any text having the deleted style reverts to the *Normal* style.

Delete a style and assign text in that style to another style

❶ Choose the Define Styles command, and select the style to delete.
❷ In the Style edit field, replace the name of the style being deleted with the name of the style to be used instead.
❸ Click Define, and click OK in the dialog box that appears.
❹ Click Cancel.

Transfer selected styles from another document

❶ Select text having the styles to be copied, and copy it to the Clipboard.
❷ Open the document to receive the styles, and set the insertion point.
❸ Choose the Paste command to copy the text and its accompanying styles from the Clipboard. Any styles not already defined in the destination document are added to its style sheet.

Note: This works only if the styles being copied do not have the same names as styles already in the destination document.

Insert a style attached to a glossary entry

❶ Insert the glossary entry into the document. Any styles not already defined in the document are added to its style sheet.

Note: This works only if a style with that name is not already defined in the document. A glossary maintains only one common style sheet for all entries, so if you create a glossary entry for text having a style that is already defined in the glossary, the new glossary entry uses the previously defined style.

Remove a style from a glossary's style sheet

❶ Press the Shift key while choosing the Open command.

❷ Select and open the glossary. The glossary opens as a Word document.

❸ Choose the Define Styles command.

❹ Select the style you want to remove from the glossary's style sheet.

❺ Choose the Cut command. Click OK when Word asks if you want to delete the style.

❻ Click the Cancel button in the Define Styles dialog box.

❼ Save and close the glossary.

Any glossary entries having the deleted style revert to the *Normal* style.

Merge a style sheet from another document

❶ Choose the Define Styles command.

❷ Choose the Open command.

❸ Open the document containing the style sheet you want to copy.

The opened style sheet is merged with the style sheet of the active document. In case of conflict, the definition in the opened style sheet prevails.

Transfer style definitions within a document

❶ Choose the Define Styles command.

❷ Select the style you want to transfer. (It's not necessary to choose the Copy command to copy the definition to the Clipboard.)

❸ Select the style to which the definition is to be copied.

❹ Choose the Paste command.

❺ Click Define, and then click Cancel.

Copy formats from text to an existing style within a document

❶ Select the text whose formats you want to copy.

❷ Choose the Copy command to copy the text to the Clipboard.

❸ Choose the Define Styles command, and select the style receiving the formats.
❹ Choose the Paste command.
❺ Click Define, then click OK or Cancel.

Add an automatic style or change an automatic style's defaults

❶ Choose the Define Styles command.
❷ Select the automatic style you want to modify, or type the name of a new style that you want to add.
❸ Choose the character and paragraph formats to be used in the style.
❹ Click Set Default, and then click OK in the dialog box that appears.
❺ Click OK or Cancel.

Print a style sheet

❶ Choose the Styles or Define Styles command.
❷ Choose the Print command.

This is especially useful if you've created a complex style sheet or styles with complex definitions which don't fit in the Styles dialog box or the Define Styles dialog box.

Add a style to the Work menu

❶ Choose the Styles or Define Styles command.
❷ Press Option-Command- +.
❸ Click on the name of the style you want to add. If you want to add more than one style, press the Shift key while clicking on the style names.
❹ Click Cancel to close the dialog box.

■ *Keyboard Shortcuts*

To	Press
Apply a style	Shift-Command-S, and enough letters of the name to distinguish it from the other styles, or its alternate name.
Reset selected text to the base character format for style (the Plain Text command)	Shift-Command-Spacebar.
Reset selected paragraphs to the *Normal* style	Shift-Command-P.

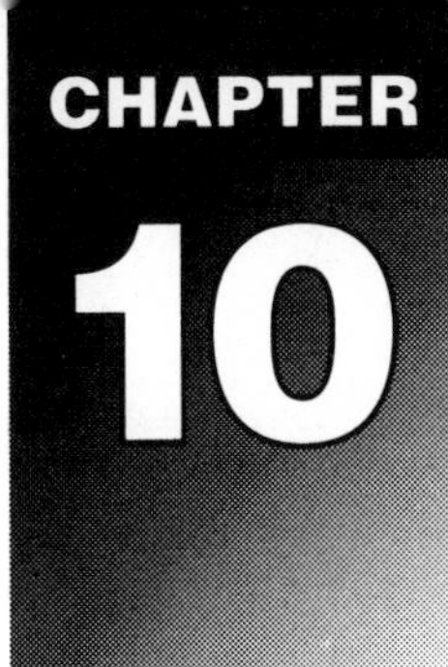

Section Formatting

So far, you've learned about two of the four format domains in Word: the character and paragraph domains. This chapter describes a third: the section domain. Sections are one of the least intuitive features of Word. (Sections were known as *divisions* in Word version 1.05.) A section can be as short as a single line or as long as your entire document. You decide where a section begins and ends. If you don't define sections, Word treats the entire document as one section. The flexibility that this feature affords you will become more apparent as you read on.

It helps to think of a section as a document within a document. A chapter in a book is a good example of a section, as is an article in a magazine or newsletter. Word lets you handle each section as a separate entity. Within each section you can control the following:

- The format and position of the page number on each page.
- The position and content of headers and footers.
- The location of footnotes.
- Line numbering.
- The number of columns and the spacing between them.
- Whether the section starts on the same page, starts a new column, or starts a new page.

■ *Dividing a Document into Sections*

Just as indents and tab settings affect an entire paragraph, section formats apply to a section—normally the entire document. If you divide a document into more than one section, you can reset these formats within each one. For example, you can change the headers in each section so that the title of the section appears at the top of each page. To create a new section, set the insertion point where you want the new section to start, and then press the Command and Enter keys simultaneously.

A double dotted line appears (see Figure 10-1), indicating the section division. The status box in the lower left corner of the document window indicates both the page number and the section number if the document contains more than one section. This is important when you are altering section formats because the insertion point must be inside the section you want to format. Note, however, that the section number in the status box indicates the section for the topmost line in the window, not the section containing the insertion point. Newly created sections take on the section formats of the preceding section.

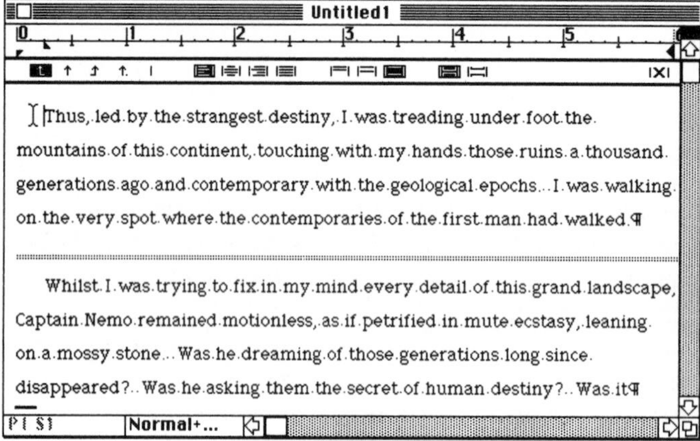

Figure 10-1
A section mark.

To apply section formats, you use the Section command, after first selecting the section mark at the end of the section, selecting any text within the section, or simply setting the insertion point anywhere in the section.

Choosing the Section command brings up the dialog box shown in Figure 10-2. The options in the box are divided into seven groups: Section Start, Page Number, Line Numbers, Header/Footer, Footnotes, Columns, and the standard buttons. You can use the Section command even if you are working with a one-section document.

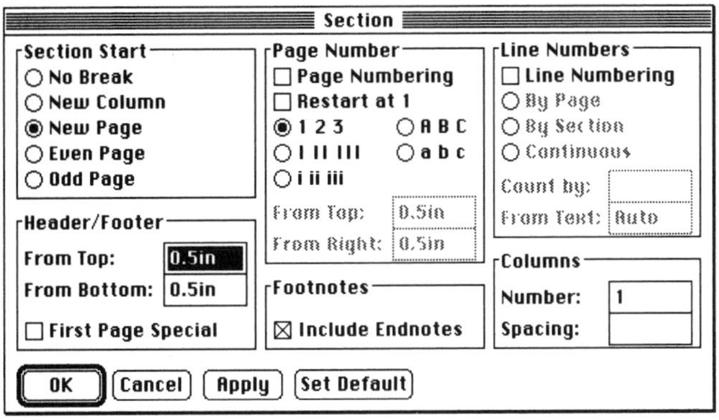

Figure 10-2
The Section dialog box.

To remove a section mark, click in the selection bar next to the mark and press the Backspace key. Just as the paragraph mark can be thought of as holding the paragraph formats for the preceding paragraph, the section mark holds the section formats for the preceding section. When you delete a section mark, the section formatting for the section that preceded the mark is replaced by the section formatting for the section that fell after the mark.

Let's take a tour of the section formats. As you read this chapter, refer to the multiple-column newsletter described in Chapter 17, "Blueprints."

TIP

Working with Section Marks
You can transfer section marks in many of the same ways that you can transfer paragraph marks. To promote the consistency of section formats within and between documents, you can select and cut or copy a section mark and paste it into another place in the document or into another document. You can even establish a range of specially formatted section marks in the glossary or archive them in your style template documents.

■ *The Section Start Options*

The Section Start options in the Section dialog box define how Word begins a new section. Normally, the New Page radio button is set, meaning that Word starts the section at the top of the next page. You can change this by choosing one of the other Section Start options described below.

No Break

The No Break option starts the section without beginning a new page; the new section begins on the page on which the preceding section ended. A primary use for this option is to vary the number of columns within a page. Look at the section layout from the newsletter in Figure 10-3. This page contains three sections that have varying numbers of columns. One of the sections, the article's title, is only one line long and is set to a one-column format that stretches across from the left margin to the right margin. To add a little space around the article's title area, Space Before and Space After formats were added to the paragraph containing the title. Multiple-column formatting is discussed further in "The Columns Options" later in this chapter and again in Chapter 17.

The header or footer for a section is taken from the section that appears at the top of the page. If a section starts somewhere in the middle of a page and continues on to the top of the next page, its header or footer (if any) begin at the top of the next page. In fact, any section format you set in a section in which the No Break option is set (except for multiple columns and numbered lines) does not take effect until the following page. If a section doesn't start at the top of a page and doesn't continue on to the next, its header or footer is not printed at all.

New Column

The New Column option causes Word to start the new section at the top of a new column. This option works only in multiple-column documents when the preceding section has the same number of columns as the section having this format. Otherwise, sections with this format start at the top of the next page.

Even Page and Odd Page

The Even Page and Odd Page options are like Word's default New Page format, except that the section starts at the top of the next even-numbered or odd-numbered page. For example, if you set the Odd Page format for a section and the preceding section ends on an odd-numbered page, Word leaves the next even page blank and starts the new section at the top of the next odd page.

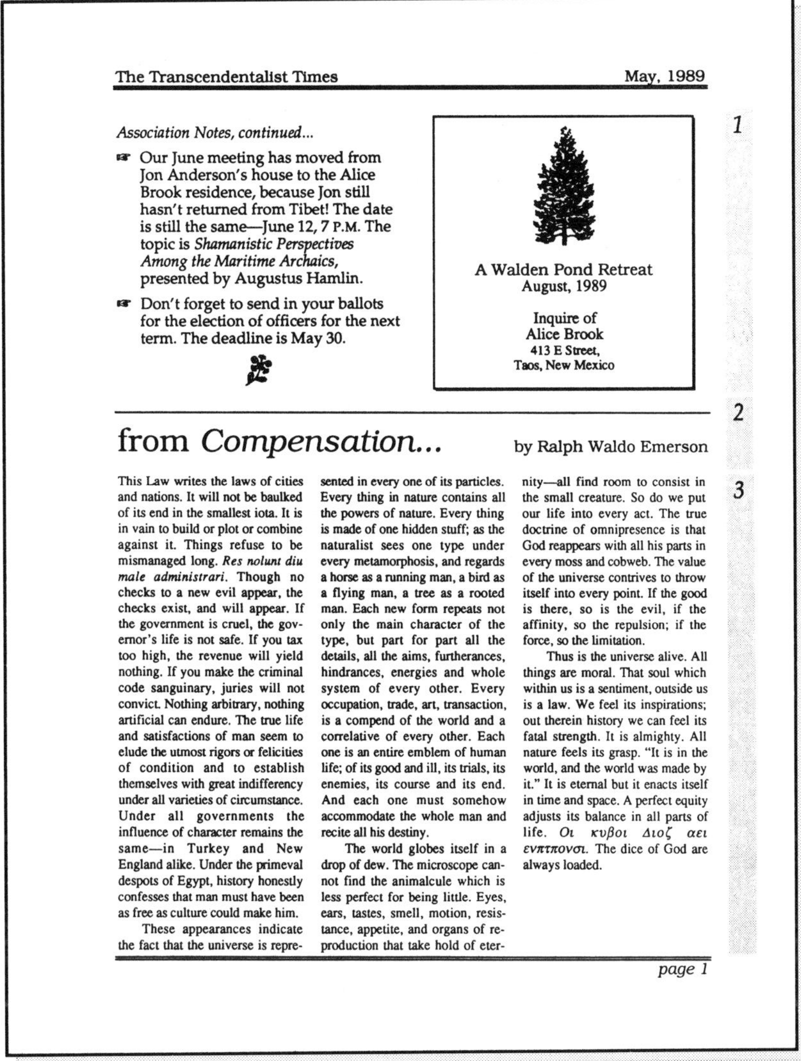

The Transcendentalist Times May, 1989

Association Notes, continued...

- Our June meeting has moved from Jon Anderson's house to the Alice Brook residence, because Jon still hasn't returned from Tibet! The date is still the same—June 12, 7 P.M. The topic is *Shamanistic Perspectives Among the Maritime Archaics,* presented by Augustus Hamlin.
- Don't forget to send in your ballots for the election of officers for the next term. The deadline is May 30.

A Walden Pond Retreat
August, 1989

Inquire of
Alice Brook
413 E Street,
Taos, New Mexico

1

2

from *Compensation...* by Ralph Waldo Emerson

3

This Law writes the laws of cities and nations. It will not be baulked of its end in the smallest iota. It is in vain to build or plot or combine against it. Things refuse to be mismanaged long. *Res nolunt diu male administrari.* Though no checks to a new evil appear, the checks exist, and will appear. If the government is cruel, the governor's life is not safe. If you tax too high, the revenue will yield nothing. If you make the criminal code sanguinary, juries will not convict. Nothing arbitrary, nothing artificial can endure. The true life and satisfactions of man seem to elude the utmost rigors or felicities of condition and to establish themselves with great indifferency under all varieties of circumstance. Under all governments the influence of character remains the same—in Turkey and New England alike. Under the primeval despots of Egypt, history honestly confesses that man must have been as free as culture could make him.

These appearances indicate the fact that the universe is represented in every one of its particles. Every thing in nature contains all the powers of nature. Every thing is made of one hidden stuff; as the naturalist sees one type under every metamorphosis, and regards a horse as a running man, a bird as a flying man, a tree as a rooted man. Each new form repeats not only the main character of the type, but part for part all the details, all the aims, furtherances, hindrances, energies and whole system of every other. Every occupation, trade, art, transaction, is a compend of the world and a correlative of every other. Each one is an entire emblem of human life; of its good and ill, its trials, its enemies, its course and its end. And each one must somehow accommodate the whole man and recite all his destiny.

The world globes itself in a drop of dew. The microscope cannot find the animalcule which is less perfect for being little. Eyes, ears, tastes, smell, motion, resistance, appetite, and organs of reproduction that take hold of eternity—all find room to consist in the small creature. So do we put our life into every act. The true doctrine of omnipresence is that God reappears with all his parts in every moss and cobweb. The value of the universe contrives to throw itself into every point. If the good is there, so is the evil, if the affinity, so the repulsion; if the force, so the limitation.

Thus is the universe alive. All things are moral. That soul which within us is a sentiment, outside us is a law. We feel its inspirations; out therein history we can feel its fatal strength. It is almighty. All nature feels its grasp. "It is in the world, and the world was made by it." It is eternal but it enacts itself in time and space. A perfect equity adjusts its balance in all parts of life. Οι κυβοι Διοζ αει ενπτπονσι. The dice of God are always loaded.

page 1

Figure 10-3
The No Break option used to start a new section on the same page.

■ *The Page Number Options*

When you add page numbers to a document, you don't see them until you enter Page Preview mode or print the document. You can number the pages in a document in one of three ways:

- ❏ By inserting the page number into a header or footer. (This is discussed in Chapter 11, "Headers, Footers, and Footnotes.")

- ❏ By dragging the page number to the desired position on the page in Page Preview. (This is described in Chapter 12, "Document Formatting and Printing.")
- ❏ By specifying the page number location and format in the Section dialog box.

The page-numbering features in Page Preview and the Section command are linked; changes you make in one affect the other. Headers and footers have their own page-numbering method, as you will see in the next chapter, although you can alter the characteristics of page numbers through the Section dialog box. To avoid duplicate page numbers, choose one method.

The Page Number options in the Section dialog box let you:

- ❏ Turn page numbering on and off.
- ❏ Force page numbering to restart at 1 at the beginning of the section.
- ❏ Specify the numbering method: Arabic numerals, Roman numerals, or letters starting at *A*. Roman numerals and letters can be either uppercase or lowercase.
- ❏ Set the exact location of the page number on the page.

To set the page number for a section, do the following:

1. Select the section, if your document has more than one, and choose the Section command.
2. Click the Page Numbering box. Word activates the From Top and From Right edit fields.
3. If you want numbering to restart at 1 at the beginning of this section, click the Restart at 1 check box.

You can override the page numbering for the first section of a document with the Start Page Numbers At option of the Page Setup dialog box. This option allows you to start the first page of a document at a number other than 1, and it affects only the first section in the document. If the Restart at 1 option is turned on in subsequent sections, their page numbers begin with 1.

You might wonder why only the edit fields become activated when you click the Page Numbering check box, whereas the Restart at 1 and number format options are always active. This happens because these options also control the numbering format for the page numbers that are inserted into headers and footers when you click the Page Number icon in a Header or Footer window.

4. Select the type of numbering you want; Figure 10-4 shows some examples. The default format is Arabic numerals. The front matter in a book, such as the preface, often uses lowercase Roman numerals. When you specify one of the letter options, Word numbers pages 1 through 26 as A through Z and then restarts on page 27 with AA, AB, AC, and so on.

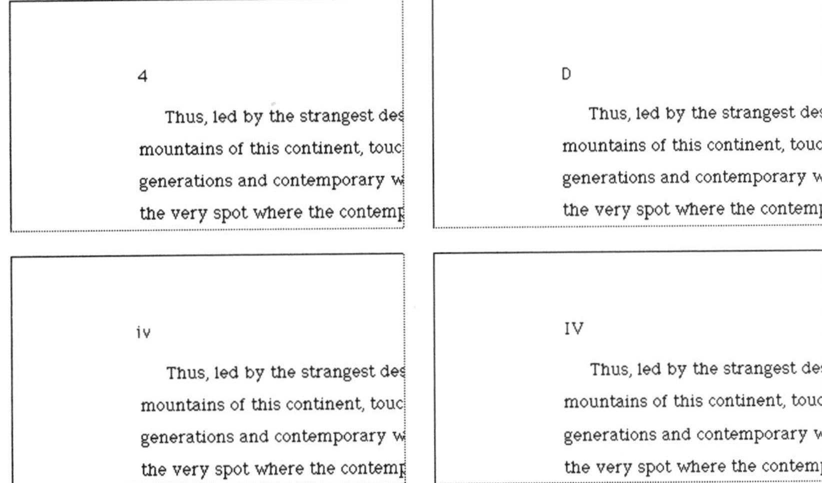

Figure 10-4
Page-numbering examples.

❺ Indicate the location of the page number on the page in the From Top and From Right edit fields. The position you enter (in inches, centimeters, or points) is measured from the top and right edges of the paper, not from the margins you set in the Page Setup dialog box. If you set the Facing Pages option in the Page Setup dialog box, Word orients the page-number placement from the top left of left (even-numbered) pages and from the top right of right (odd-numbered) pages. The Facing Pages option is discussed in Chapter 12, "Document Formatting and Printing."

The Section page-numbering feature places only a number on the page. You cannot include any other characters with the number, such as hyphens on either side or the word *Page*. If you want to print additional characters with the page number, use headers or footers instead.

When placing the page number, be careful not to put it in the middle of text, such as a header, footer, or the body of the document. Use Page Preview to check the position of the page numbers before printing the document. The default position of 0.5 inch from the top and right edges of the paper will usually not interfere with the rest of the document. If you have trouble getting it right, use Page Preview to position the number, as described in Chapter 12, "Document Formatting and Printing."

When you specify page numbers with the Section command, Word adds the automatic style named *page number* to the style sheet. You can set character formats for the page numbers by redefining this style, but Word ignores any paragraph formats you set. Even though the *page number* style pertains to all page numbers in the document, you can change the type of numbers used from section to section. You can also use the Restart at 1 and numbering options to change the page numbering in the header or footer.

Finally, suppose you've set the Page Numbering section format for a section, but later you decide you want to add a page number to a header or footer in that section instead. You only have to click the Page Number icon in the header or footer; when you close the window, Word removes the Page Numbering section format for you.

■ *The Line Numbers Options*

Many documents, such as legal briefs and contracts, have numbered lines. You can have Word insert line numbers at the left margin. The numbers do not appear in Document view, but they show up when you print the document or audition it with Page Preview. You can't edit the numbers or delete them individually, and they don't apply to side-by-side paragraphs or in headers and footers, but you can redefine their automatic style, called *line number,* if you want. As it does with the *page number* automatic style, Word ignores any paragraph formats you set for this style. A sample page with line numbers is shown in Figure 10-5.

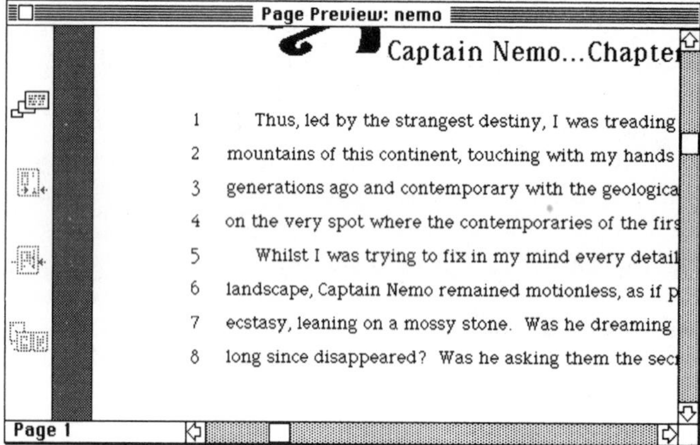

Figure 10-5
A page with line numbers.

The Line Numbers options let you do the following:

- ❏ Turn line numbering on and off for the section.
- ❏ Indicate whether the numbers should restart at 1 at the top of every page or at the beginning of the section, or whether they should continue where the previous section left off.
- ❏ Number every line, or number lines at any interval you specify. Counting by 5, for example, numbers every fifth line.
- ❏ Indicate how far from the left margin of the text the rightmost digit of the line number is to be positioned.

To specify line numbering in a section, do the following:

1. Select the section, if your document has more than one, and choose the Section command.
2. Click the Line Numbering option. Word activates the remaining options in the group.
3. Indicate where the numbers are to restart. Click By Page if you want the numbers to restart at 1 at the top of each page, By Section if the numbers are to restart at the beginning of the section, and Continuous if the numbering is to continue where the previous section ended.
4. If you want to number lines at an interval other than 1, enter the number in the Count By field. Word counts an empty paragraph as a line but does not consider space added with the Space Before or Space After paragraph formats as lines. (See Figure 10-6.)
5. Position the line numbers relative to the left margin by entering a measurement in the From Text field (or use the Auto setting to specify a position of 0.25 inch for a single-column section format and 0.125 inch for multiple columns).

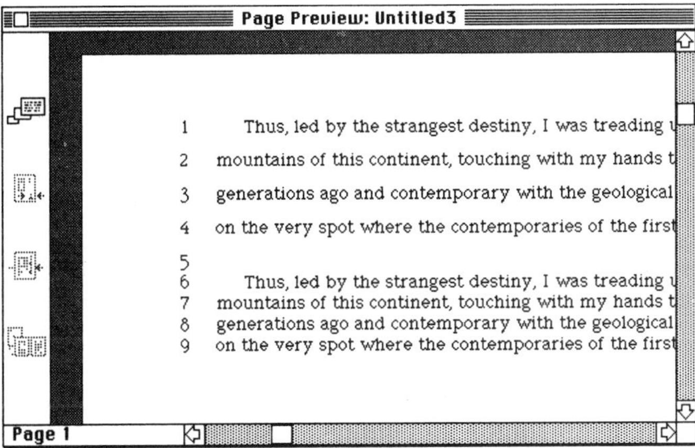

Figure 10-6
Line numbering applied to empty paragraphs and spaced lines.

As was mentioned in Chapter 8, "Paragraph Formatting," when you turn on line numbering in a section, Word activates and sets the Line Numbering option in the Paragraph dialog box. You can specify that the lines in a paragraph not be numbered by selecting it, choosing the Paragraph command, and clicking the Line Numbering option.

■ *The Header/Footer Options*

The options in the Header/Footer group let you indicate the vertical position of the header and footer and instruct Word to use a different header for the first page of the section. To specify a position for the header, enter a position in the From Top field. The measurement is from the top edge of the paper. To specify a position for the footer, enter a position in the From Bottom field. That measurement is from the bottom edge of the paper. The horizontal position of the headers and footers is determined by the margins and by any indents you set in the Header and Footer windows.

Clicking the First Page Special check box creates a new header and footer for the first page of the section only, as illustrated in Page Preview in Figure 10-7. When you turn on this option, Word adds additional commands to the Document menu for the first-page header and footer. You can leave the first-page header and footer empty for a title page, use the option to place a logo or return address on the first page of correspondence, or assign a different header or footer for the beginning of each chapter in a novel.

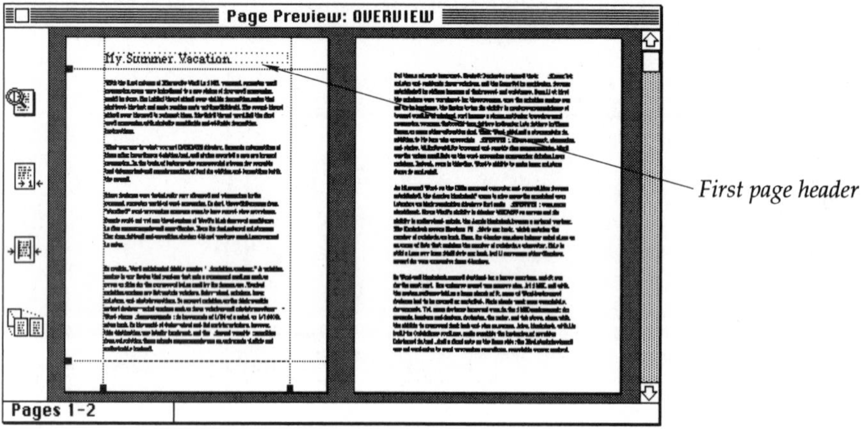

Figure 10-7
A first-page header.

If you want different headers for odd and even pages, you must set the Facing Pages option in the Page Setup dialog box. When you do this, you'll see a set of Open Header and Open Footer commands for both odd and even pages. For more information on this and other aspects of using headers and footers, see Chapter 11, "Headers, Footers, and Footnotes."

■ *The Footnotes Option*

There is only one Footnotes option among the section formats: Include Endnotes. If you click this check box, Word places at the end of the section any footnotes that have accumulated. The Endnotes option in the Page Setup dialog box must also be set.

If you don't want footnotes printed at the end of the section, turn off the Include Endnotes option. Word then collects the footnotes and prints them at the end of the next section in which the Include Endnotes option is set. If this option is turned off in every subsequent section, Word places the footnotes at the end of the document. See Chapter 11, "Headers, Footers, and Footnotes," for details on how to create footnotes.

■ *The Columns Options*

Word makes it easy to create multiple-column documents. You enter the number of columns you want in the Number field and the spacing (in inches, centimeters, or points) between columns in the Spacing field. Word then calculates the resulting column width. In Document view, the text appears as one long column, but when you examine the document in Page Preview mode, the columns are divided and arranged next to one another on the page. The multiple-column format is different from the Side-by-Side paragraph format. When you use the Side-by-Side format, you tell Word that you want selected paragraphs to be placed next to one another in a specific horizontal arrangement.

When you set a multiple-column section format, however, you tell Word that you don't care exactly where paragraphs fall horizontally on the page, only that you want the text to flow from the bottom of the first column to the top of the next. This type of format is illustrated in Figure 10-8, in which you can see three sections. In each section, the No Break format has been set and the Space Before and Space After paragraph formats have been changed to add space between the sections. The middle section on the page contains one entire three-column section, and the text flows from the bottom of one column to the top of the next within that section. Multiple-column formats are particularly useful for newsletters and magazines.

When you create a multiple-column section succeeded by a section having the No Break format, Word adjusts the lengths of the columns until they are approximately equal. This operation is called *column balancing*. If the text in a multiple-column section runs over to the next page, it flows from the end of the last column on the page to the top of the first column on the next page, and Word balances the text on that page as well. However, the columns at the end of the document are not balanced. If you want the text on the last page of a multiple-column document to be split evenly between the columns, insert one more section mark at the end of the document and set the No Break option for it.

For more information on how to format a two-column document, refer to the multiple-column newsletter project in Chapter 17, "Blueprints."

1

from *Compensation...*

by Ralph Waldo Emerson

This Law writes the laws of cities and nations. It will not be baulked of its end in the smallest iota. It is in vain to build or plot or combine against it. Things refuse to be mismanaged long. *Res nolunt diu male administrari.* Though no checks to a new evil appear, the checks exist, and will appear. If the government is cruel, the governor's life is not safe. If you tax too high, the revenue will yield nothing. If you make the criminal code sanguinary, juries will not convict. Nothing arbitrary, nothing artificial can endure. The true life and satisfactions of man seem to elude the utmost rigors or felicities of condition and to establish themselves with great indifferency under all varieties of circumstance. Under all governments the influence of character remains the same—in Turkey and New England alike. Under the primeval despots of Egypt, history honestly confesses that man must have been as free as culture could make him.

These appearances indicate the fact that the universe is represented in every one of its particles. Every thing in nature contains all the powers of nature. Every thing is made of one hidden stuff; as the naturalist sees one type under every metamorphosis, and regards a horse as a running man, a bird as a flying man, a tree as a rooted man. Each new form repeats not only the main character of the type, but part for part all the details, all the aims, furtherances, hindrances, energies and whole system of every other. Every occupation, trade, art,

transaction, is a compend of the world and a correlative of every 2
other. Each one is an entire emblem of human life; of its good and ill, its trials, its enemies, its course and its end. And each one must somehow accommodate the whole man and recite all his destiny.

The world globes itself in a drop of dew. The microscope cannot find the animalcule which is less perfect for being little. Eyes, ears, tastes, smell, motion, resistance, appetite, and organs of reproduction that take hold of eternity—all find room to consist in the small creature. So do we put our life into every act. The true doctrine of omnipresence is that God reappears with all his parts in every moss and cobweb. The value of the universe contrives to throw itself into every point. If the good is there, so is the evil, if the affinity, so the repulsion; if the force, so the limitation.

Thus is the universe alive. All things are moral. That soul which within us is a sentiment, outside us is a law. We feel its inspirations; out therein history we can feel its fatal strength. It is almighty. All nature feels its grasp. "It is in the world, and the world was made by it." It is eternal but it enacts itself in time and space. A perfect equity adjusts its balance in all parts of life. *Οι κυβοι Διοζ αει ενπτπονσι.* The dice of God are always loaded.

Figure 10-8

Using the No Break section format to change the number of columns within a page.

TIP

Starting Articles in a Newsletter

A common requirement for newsletters and similarly structured documents is to balance the columns on a page within both the ending of one article and the beginning of the next. For instance, if you set a two-column format for both articles and set the No Break format for both, you might see something like Figure 10-9. Notice that, in the absence of line spacing, Space Before, or Space After formats, the two sections run into one another.

Prudence, ***continued from page 13***

There are all degrees of proficiency in knowledge of the world. It is sufficient to out present purpose to indicate three. One class lives to the utility of the symbol, esteeming health and wealth a final good. Another class live above this mark to the beauty of the symbol, as the poet and artist and the naturalist and man of science. A third class live above the beauty of the symbol to the beauty of the thing signified; these are wise men. The first class have common sense; the second, taste; and the third, spiritual perception. Once in a long time, a man traverses the whole scale, and sees and enjoys the symbol solidly, then also has a clear eye for the beauty, and lastly, whilst he pitches his tent on this sacred volcanic isle of nature, does not offer to build houses and barns thereon, reverencing the splendor of the God which he sees bursting through each chink and cranny. 1

from *Compensation...*

by Ralph Waldo Emerson

This Law writes the laws of cities and nations. It will not be baulked of its end in the smallest iota. It is in vain to build or plot or combine against it. Things refuse to be mismanaged long. *Res nolunt diu male administrari.* Though no checks to a new evil appear, the checks exist, and will appear. If the government is cruel, the governor's life is not safe. If you tax too high, the revenue will yield nothing. If you make the criminal code sanguinary, juries will not convict. Nothing arbitrary, nothing artificial can endure. The true life and satisfactions of man seem to elude the utmost rigors or felicities of condition and to establish themselves with great indifferency under all varieties of circumstance. Under all governments the influence of character remains the same—in Turkey and New England alike. Under the primeval despots of Egypt, history honestly confesses that man must have been as free as culture could make him.

These appearances indicate the fact that the universe is represented in every one of its particles. Every thing in nature contains all the powers of nature. Every thing is made of one hidden stuff; as the naturalist sees one type under every metamorphosis, and regards a horse as a running man, a bird as a flying man, a tree as a rooted man. Each new form repeats not only the main character of the type, but part for part all the details, all the aims, furtherances, hindrances, energies and whole system of every other. Every occupation, trade, art, transaction, is a compend of the world and a correlative of every other. Each one is an entire emblem of human life; of its good and ill, its trials, its enemies, its course and its end. And each one must somehow accommodate the whole man and recite all his destiny. 2

The world globes itself in a drop of dew. The microscope cannot find the animalcule which is less perfect for being little. Eyes, ears, tastes, smell, motion, resistance, appetite, and organs of reproduction that take hold of eternity—all find room to consist in the small creature. So do we put our life into every act. The true doctrine of omnipresence is that God reappears with all his parts in every moss and cobweb. The value of the universe contrives to throw itself into every point. If the good is there, so is the evil, if the affinity, so the repulsion; if the force, so the limitation.

Thus is the universe alive. All things are moral. That soul which within us is a sentiment, outside us is a law. We feel its inspirations; out therein history we can feel its fatal strength. It is almighty. All nature feels its grasp. "It is in the world, and the world was made by it." It is eternal but it enacts itself in time and space. A perfect equity adjusts its balance in all parts of life. *Οι κυβοι Διοζ αει ενπτπουσι.* The dice of God are always loaded.

Figure 10-9
Adjacent sections in two-column format without extra formatting.

You can achieve a better-looking break between the two sections by inserting between them a one-column section containing only one blank line. You can format this blank line as needed to separate the two sections. Figure 10-10 shows how this might look. To create this special section:

1. Place the insertion point before the first character in the second section. Press the Return key and Command-Enter to start a new paragraph and section.

Prudence, ***continued from page 13*** 1

There are all degrees of proficiency in knowledge of the world. It is sufficient to out present purpose to indicate three. One class lives to the utility of the symbol, esteeming health and wealth a final good. Another class live above this mark to the beauty of the symbol, as the poet and artist and the naturalist and man of science. A third class live above the beauty of the symbol to the beauty of the thing signified; these are wise men. The first class have common sense; the second, taste; and the third, spiritual perception. Once in a long time, a man traverses the whole scale, and sees and enjoys the symbol solidly, then also has a clear eye for the beauty, and lastly, whilst he pitches his tent on this sacred volcanic isle of nature, does not offer to build houses and barns thereon, reverencing the splendor of the God which he sees bursting through each chink and cranny.

2

---

from *Compensation...* 3

by Ralph Waldo Emerson

This Law writes the laws of cities and nations. It will not be baulked of its end in the smallest iota. It is in vain to build or plot or combine against it. Things refuse to be mismanaged long. *Res nolunt diu male administrari.* Though no checks to a new evil appear, the checks exist, and will appear. If the government is cruel, the governor's life is not safe. If you tax too high, the revenue will yield nothing. If you make the criminal code sanguinary, juries will not convict. Nothing arbitrary, nothing artificial can endure. The true life and satisfactions of man seem to elude the utmost rigors or felicities of condition and to establish themselves with great indifferency under all varieties of circumstance. Under all governments the influence of character remains the same—in Turkey and New England alike. Under the primeval despots of Egypt, history honestly confesses that man must have been as free as culture could make him.

These appearances indicate the fact that the universe is represented in every one of its particles. Every thing in nature contains all the powers of nature. Every thing is made of one hidden stuff; as the naturalist sees one type under every metamorphosis, and regards a horse as a running man, a bird as a flying man, a tree as a rooted man. Each new form repeats not only the main character of the type, but part for part all the details, all the aims, furtherances, hindrances, energies and whole system of every other. Every occupation, trade, art, transaction, is a compend of the world and a correlative of every other. Each one is an entire emblem of human life; of its good and ill, its trials, its enemies, its course and its end. And each one must somehow accommodate the whole man and recite all his destiny.

The world globes itself in a drop of dew. The microscope cannot find the animalcule which is less perfect for being little. Eyes, ears, tastes, smell, motion, resistance, appetite, and organs of reproduction that take hold of eternity—all find room to consist in the small creature. So do we put our life into every act. The true doctrine of omnipresence is that God reappears with all his parts in every moss and cobweb. The value of the universe contrives to throw itself into every point. If the good is there, so is the evil, if the affinity, so the repulsion; if the force, so the limitation.

Thus is the universe alive. All things are moral. That soul which within us is a sentiment, outside us is a law. We feel its inspirations; out therein history we can feel its fatal strength. It is almighty. All nature feels its grasp. "It is in the world, and the world was made by it." It is eternal but it enacts itself in time and space. A perfect equity adjusts its balance in all parts of life. *Οι κυβοι Διοζ αει ενπτπονσι*. The dice of God are always loaded.

Figure 10-10
Inserting a one-column section to add space between two multiple-column sections.

❷ Be sure to set the No Break option in all three sections. In the new middle section, set the number of columns to 1.

❸ Click in the single blank line in the new middle section, and choose the Paragraph command. Set a double line above the paragraph, and set 18 points Space Before and 6 points Space After.

You can change the spacing formats and use graphics copied from a program such as MacDraw instead of using the boxed paragraph formats.

■ *The Command Buttons*

The Section dialog box has four command buttons: OK, Cancel, Apply, and Set Default. The OK, Cancel, and Apply buttons work as they do in the Character and Paragraph dialog boxes. You click OK to implement the format changes and close the dialog box, Cancel to close the dialog box without implementing the format changes, and Apply to implement the format changes without closing the dialog box.

When you use the Apply button to implement a section format, you can't undo the change by clicking the Cancel button. Should you decide to go back to the old format, reselect the original options and click OK (or choose the Undo Formatting command).

The Set Default button lets you record your new section formats as the defaults. If you always begin a new section on an odd-numbered page (as in a user's manual, for example), you can save time by turning on the Odd Page option and clicking the Set Default button. Word stores the new choice in the Word Settings file. This button does not apply the format to the currently selected section.

Points to Remember

- A section is any block of text that precedes a section mark (a double dotted line). If you don't divide your document into sections, any section formats you specify apply to the entire document.
- The section format domain controls page numbering, number of columns on the page and spacing between them, whether the section starts a new page or column, the position and content of headers and footers, whether footnotes are printed at the section's end, and line numbering.
- Section formats are tied to the section mark; deleting the section mark deletes the section formats for that section and merges it with the section that follows it.
- You can select and copy section marks and their formatting in the same way that you select and copy paragraph marks.
- When you have more than one section in a document, the status box indicates the section number as well as the page number of the top line in the window.
- The page numbers controlled by the Section dialog box are separate from any you include in a header or footer. The Restart at 1 and numbering options in the Section dialog box affect both types of page numbers.
- Page numbers and line numbers do not appear in Document view. You must enter Page Preview mode or print the document to see them.
- You can change the character formats of page numbers and line numbers by altering the automatic styles named *page number* and *line number*. Word adds these styles to the style sheet when you set their options.

Techniques

The Section dialog box

Section Start option group	Determines where the section begins on the page.
No Break	Begins the section without starting a new page or column.
New Column	Begins the section at the top of the next column. The section must be in a multiple-column format, and the previous section must have the same number of columns as this one; otherwise, the section begins on a new page.

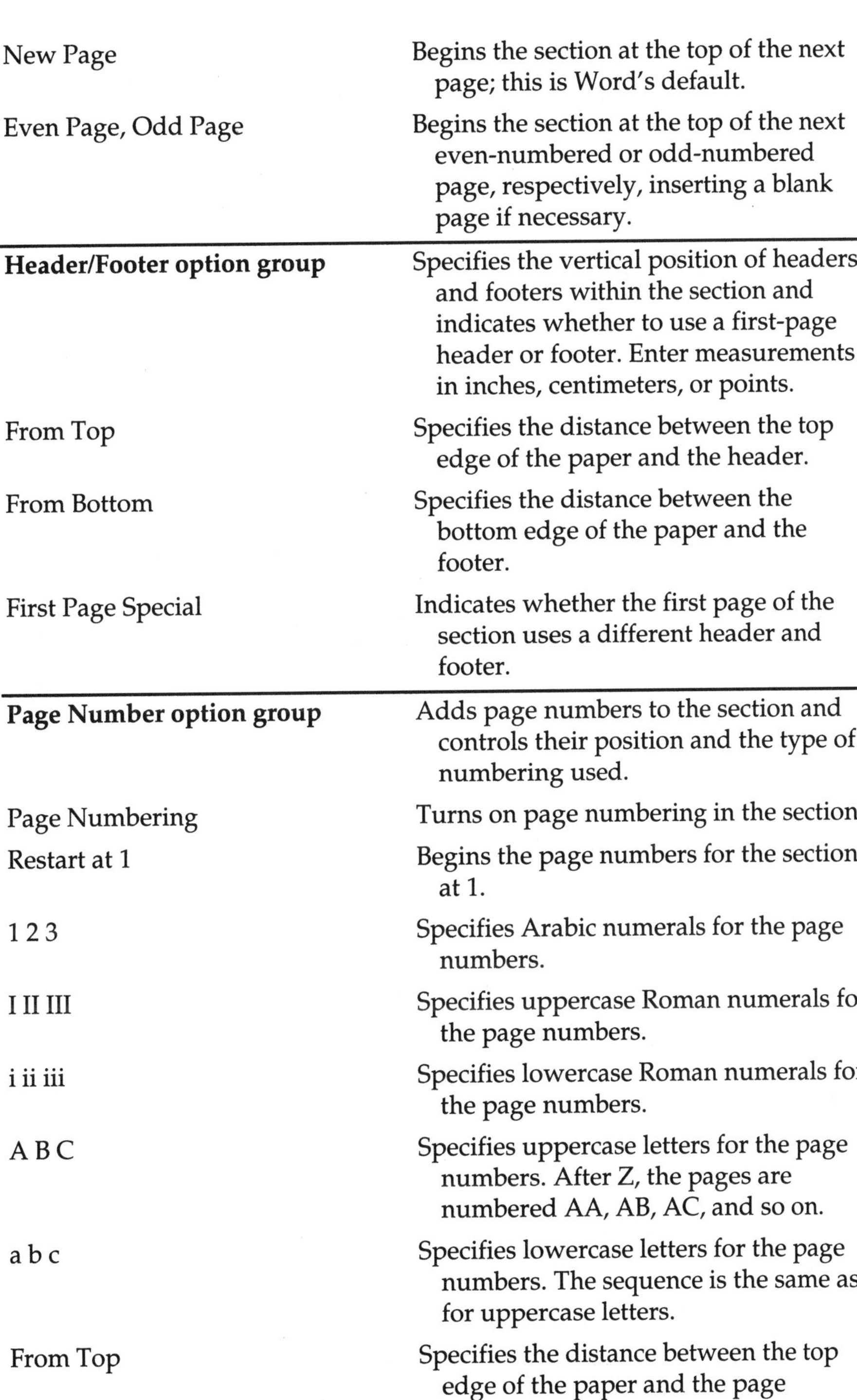

Option	Description
New Page	Begins the section at the top of the next page; this is Word's default.
Even Page, Odd Page	Begins the section at the top of the next even-numbered or odd-numbered page, respectively, inserting a blank page if necessary.
Header/Footer option group	Specifies the vertical position of headers and footers within the section and indicates whether to use a first-page header or footer. Enter measurements in inches, centimeters, or points.
From Top	Specifies the distance between the top edge of the paper and the header.
From Bottom	Specifies the distance between the bottom edge of the paper and the footer.
First Page Special	Indicates whether the first page of the section uses a different header and footer.
Page Number option group	Adds page numbers to the section and controls their position and the type of numbering used.
Page Numbering	Turns on page numbering in the section.
Restart at 1	Begins the page numbers for the section at 1.
1 2 3	Specifies Arabic numerals for the page numbers.
I II III	Specifies uppercase Roman numerals for the page numbers.
i ii iii	Specifies lowercase Roman numerals for the page numbers.
A B C	Specifies uppercase letters for the page numbers. After Z, the pages are numbered AA, AB, AC, and so on.
a b c	Specifies lowercase letters for the page numbers. The sequence is the same as for uppercase letters.
From Top	Specifies the distance between the top edge of the paper and the page number. The default is 0.5 inch.

From Right	Specifies the distance between the right edge of the paper and the page number. If the Facing Pages option is turned on in the Page Setup dialog box, this option specifies the distance from the left edge of the paper for even-numbered pages. The default is 0.5 inch.
Footnotes option group	
Include Endnotes	Prints at the end of the section any footnotes that have accumulated. Works only if the Endnotes option in the Page Setup dialog box is also set. If Include Endnotes is not set, footnotes are printed at the end of the next section in which it is set or at the end of the document if the option is turned off in all subsequent sections.
Line Numbers option group	Controls line numbering.
Line Numbering	Causes line numbers to be printed to the left of the text in the section.
By Page	Starts the first line number of each page at 1.
By Section	Starts the first line number of the section at 1.
Continuous	Begins numbering lines where the previous section ended.
Count By	Specifies an interval for the line numbers. (To number every fifth line, enter *5*, for example.)
From Text	Specifies the distance from the left margin to the line number. When Auto is set, a space of 0.25 inch for single-column text and 0.125 inch for multiple-column text is used.
Columns option group	Controls the number and spacing of columns. Word sets the column width based on the values of these options.
Number	Specifies the number of columns printed across the page.
Spacing	Specifies the space between columns.

Buttons

OK button	Implements the selected formats and closes the dialog box.
Cancel button	Closes the dialog box without implementing the selected formats.
Apply button	Implements the selected formats without closing the dialog box.
Set Default button	Records the selected formats in the Word Settings file as the new defaults. Does not implement the formats in the current document.

Create a new section

❶ Set the insertion point where you want the new section to begin.

❷ Press Command-Enter.

Assign section formats to a section

❶ Set the insertion point in the section to be affected, or select the section mark.

❷ Choose Section from the Format menu.

❸ Make the desired changes in the section formats.

❹ Click OK to apply the formats and close the dialog box.

Create a multiple-column document

❶ Insert a section mark at each point in your document where you want to change the number of columns, begin a new column, or begin a new page.

❷ Set the insertion point in the first section you want to format.

❸ Choose the Section command.

❹ Specify the number of columns for this section and the spacing between columns in the Columns option group.

❺ Indicate where the section should begin on the page by clicking one of the Section Start options.

❻ Click OK to close the dialog box.

❼ Format the next section, following the same procedure.

❽ Choose Page Preview from the File menu to see how the document looks.

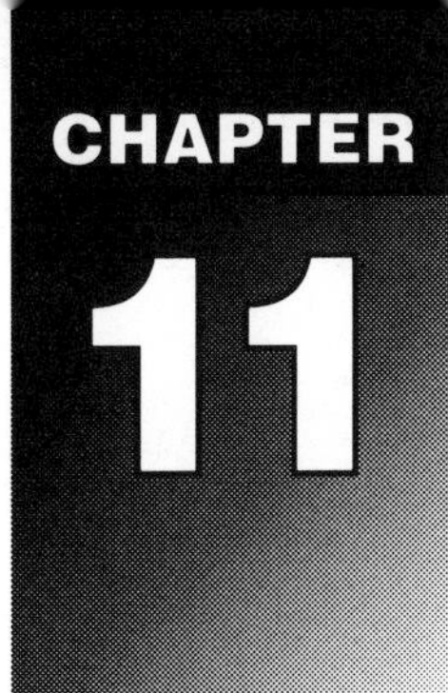

Headers, Footers, and Footnotes

This chapter gives you the information you need to work with three special elements of your document: headers, footers, and footnotes. If you've ever written a research paper, you know what footnotes are, and you may already be familiar with headers and footers if you've worked with other word processors. For the uninitiated, here are some definitions:

- A header is repeating text that appears above the top of the body text on the page. (See Figure 11-1.)
- A footer is repeating text that appears below the bottom of the body text on the page.
- A footnote provides more information about one or more statements in the text. Although footnotes can contain parenthetical asides, they usually list sources of information or provide additional comments that support assertions made in the body text. A footnote can appear at the bottom of the page containing its reference, at the end of a section, or at the end of the document.

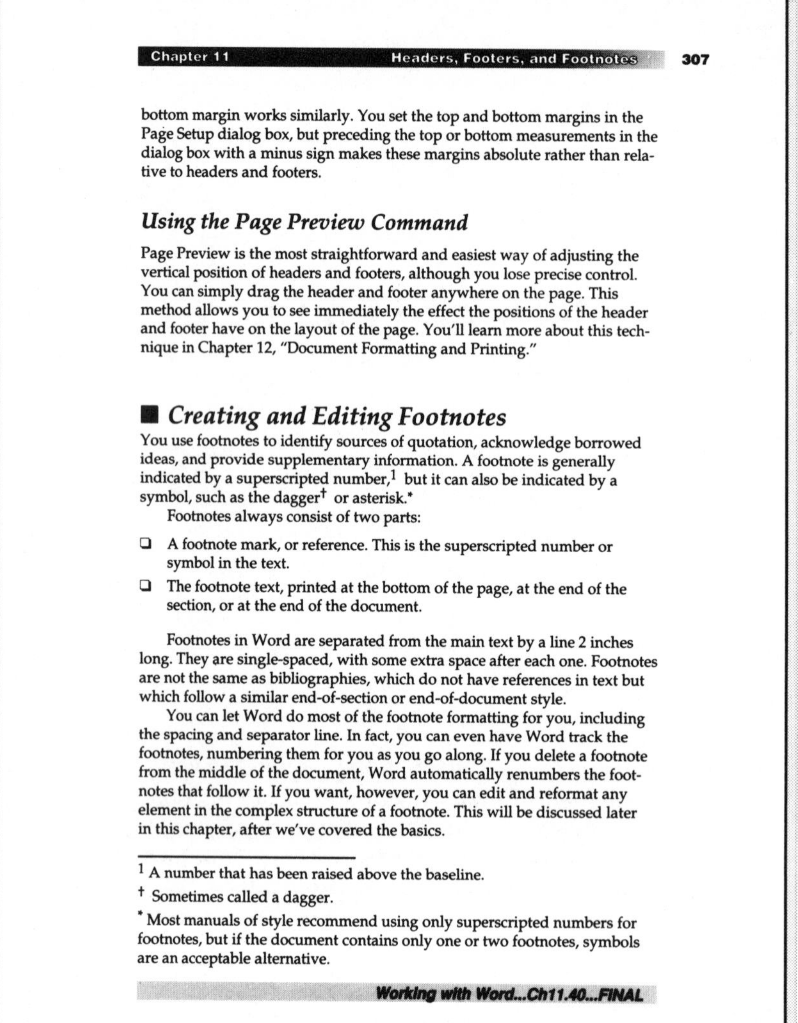

Chapter 11 Headers, Footers, and Footnotes 307

bottom margin works similarly. You set the top and bottom margins in the Page Setup dialog box, but preceding the top or bottom measurements in the dialog box with a minus sign makes these margins absolute rather than relative to headers and footers.

Using the Page Preview Command

Page Preview is the most straightforward and easiest way of adjusting the vertical position of headers and footers, although you lose precise control. You can simply drag the header and footer anywhere on the page. This method allows you to see immediately the effect the positions of the header and footer have on the layout of the page. You'll learn more about this technique in Chapter 12, "Document Formatting and Printing."

■ *Creating and Editing Footnotes*

You use footnotes to identify sources of quotation, acknowledge borrowed ideas, and provide supplementary information. A footnote is generally indicated by a superscripted number,[1] but it can also be indicated by a symbol, such as the dagger[†] or asterisk.[*]

Footnotes always consist of two parts:

- A footnote mark, or reference. This is the superscripted number or symbol in the text.
- The footnote text, printed at the bottom of the page, at the end of the section, or at the end of the document.

Footnotes in Word are separated from the main text by a line 2 inches long. They are single-spaced, with some extra space after each one. Footnotes are not the same as bibliographies, which do not have references in text but which follow a similar end-of-section or end-of-document style.

You can let Word do most of the footnote formatting for you, including the spacing and separator line. In fact, you can even have Word track the footnotes, numbering them for you as you go along. If you delete a footnote from the middle of the document, Word automatically renumbers the footnotes that follow it. If you want, however, you can edit and reformat any element in the complex structure of a footnote. This will be discussed later in this chapter, after we've covered the basics.

[1] A number that has been raised above the baseline.

[†] Sometimes called a dagger.

[*] Most manuals of style recommend using only superscripted numbers for footnotes, but if the document contains only one or two footnotes, symbols are an acceptable alternative.

Working with Word...Ch11.40...FINAL

Figure 11-1
A page with a header, footer, and footnote.

Headers and footers can be used in almost any document, even a letter. They can contain page numbers, the title of the document or chapter, and the current time and date, among other information. Once you've defined a header or footer for a section, Word applies it to all subsequent sections of the document until you change or delete it for a section.

Footnotes are generally used in academic and technical papers, journals, and books. They are never used in letters and seldom used in casual business reports and general-interest magazine articles.

■ *Creating a Standard Header or Footer*

Although headers and footers are independent entities, there is virtually no difference in the procedure you use to create each one. For the sake of simplicity, this section discusses headers only, but you use the same techniques to create and work with footers.

Think of a header that appears on every page of the document as a standard header, to distinguish it from the more specialized headers that you can define for the first page of the document, for odd pages only, and for even pages only. To create a standard header in a document composed of one section, do the following:

❶ Choose Open Header from the Document menu. (If you want to create a footer, choose the Open Footer command instead.) The Header window appears across the lower half of the window. (See Figure 11-2.)

❷ Type some text, such as the title of the document, into the Header window. This window works like the main document window; Word wraps to the next line text you type that extends beyond the right indent.

❸ Choose Show Ruler from the Format menu. Note that the tab stops for the Header window are not the same as the ones in the preset *Normal* style in the document window. The *Normal* style uses only the default tabs, but two tab stops are set in the Header window. The reason for this is that the text in the Header window defaults to the automatic style named *header*. This style contains two tab stops: a centered stop in the middle of the header area and a flush-right stop at the right indent. These tabs make it easy to position text in the header.

❹ When you are finished typing the header, click the close box of the Header window.

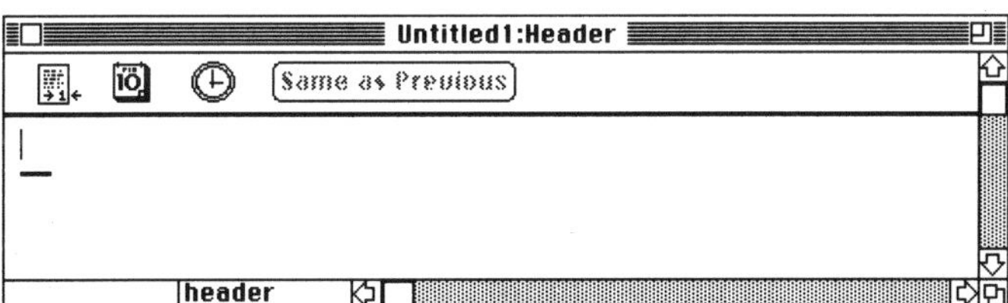

Figure 11-2
The Header window.

You can move the Header window by dragging it by the title bar, and you can resize it by dragging the size box, located in the lower right corner of the window. To quickly enlarge or reduce the window, click in the zoom box in the upper right corner, or double-click in the size box or title bar.

TIP

Keeping the Header Window Open
You need not close the Header window when you are finished with it, but doing so frees up memory and keeps screen clutter to a minimum. To return to the document without closing the Header window, click anywhere in the main document window. The Header window drops behind it and is deactivated. To reactivate the Header window, click inside it, choose the Open Header command again, or choose the Header window from the Window menu.

The header text appears only when you print the document or audition it with the Page Preview command. You may find this frustrating, but it prevents you from altering the header text during normal editing.

Theoretically, a header can contain as many lines as you can fit on a page, but most headers consist of only one or two lines. Word moves the top margin of the body text down, if necessary, to accommodate the header when you print the document. (It also moves the bottom margin up, if need be, to make room for the footer.) If this weren't done, the text in the header or footer and the body text would overlap.

At some point, however, you may need to have a header overlap with the body text in order to achieve a particular design effect. One example of this is shown in Figure 11-3. You can achieve this type of effect by specifying that the margin not be changed, regardless of the length of the header. To do this, choose Page Setup from the File menu, and enter a hyphen, or minus sign (-), in front of the Top margin measurement (or in front of the Bottom margin measurement for a footer). Doing this sets a fixed margin for the entire document, not only for a section.This technique is similar to the one of putting a minus sign in front of the line-spacing value in the Paragraph dialog box to specify a line spacing that never varies.

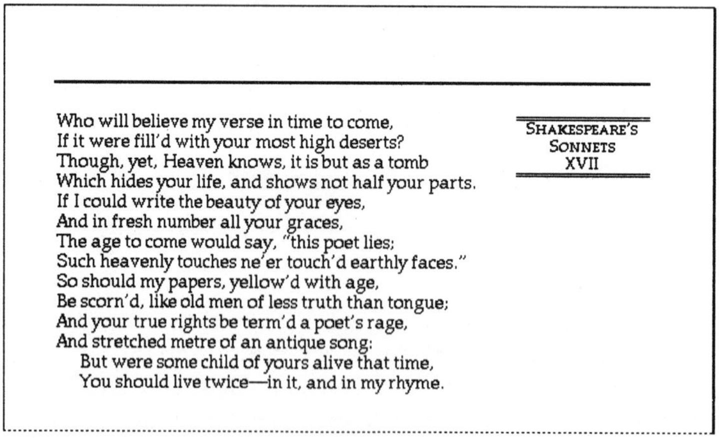

Who will believe my verse in time to come,
If it were fill'd with your most high deserts?
Though, yet, Heaven knows, it is but as a tomb
Which hides your life, and shows not half your parts.
If I could write the beauty of your eyes,
And in fresh number all your graces,
The age to come would say, "this poet lies;
Such heavenly touches ne'er touch'd earthly faces."
So should my papers, yellow'd with age,
Be scorn'd, like old men of less truth than tongue;
And your true rights be term'd a poet's rage,
And stretched metre of an antique song:
But were some child of yours alive that time,
You should live twice—in it, and in my rhyme.

SHAKESPEARE'S
SONNETS
XVII

Figure 11-3
A header overlapped with body text.

■ *Creating a First-Page Header or Footer*

Letters, title pages, and the first pages of reports and other documents generally do not contain a header, and the footer for the first page may be different from those in the rest of the document, containing a copyright notice, for instance. Word lets you remove the header or create a special header and footer for the first page of the document. To do this:

1. Choose Section from the Format menu.
2. Select the First Page Special option, located in the Header/Footer group, and click OK.
3. Pull down the Document menu. It now contains two sets of header and footer commands. (See Figure 11-4.)
4. Choose the Open First Header or Open First Footer command to create a header or footer for the first page of the currently selected section. If you want no header for the first page, press Command-Option-M to select the entire header, and then press the Backspace key to delete it.
5. Click the close box.

Figure 11-4
The Document menu after the First Page Special option has been set.

Formatting Headers and Footers

You can change the character and paragraph formatting for headers and footers in the same way that you change them for text in the document window. To change the character format, simply select the header text you want to format and choose any combination of character formats. To change the paragraph format, specify the paragraphs to be formatted in the header, and change the formats with the Paragraph dialog box or the Ruler. Try adding a rule below the header, for instance.

As was mentioned earlier, Word assigns the text you enter in the Header window the *header* style; text in the Footer window uses an automatic style named *footer*. To display the definition for this style, choose Define Styles from the Format menu and click on the *header* entry. (See Figure 11-5.) The *header* style is based on the *Normal* style, to which a centered tab stop and a right-aligned tab stop have been added. You can also format headers by redefining the *header* style, or you can insert text having any other style you have created.

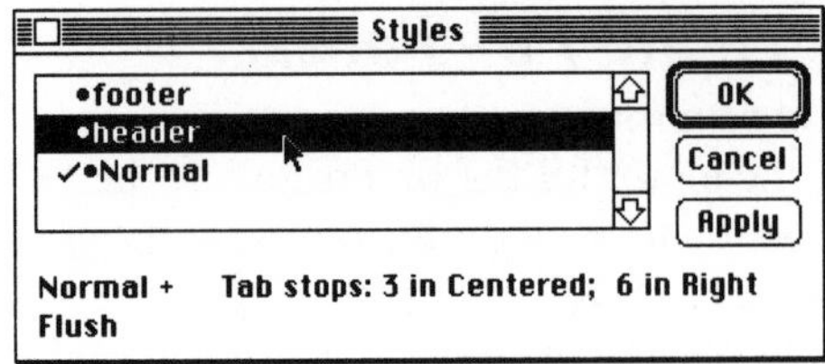

Figure 11-5
The default *header* style.

Adding Page Numbers and a Time or Date Stamp

The previous chapter described how to number pages through the Section dialog box, a method that is fine if all you need is an unadorned page number. However, if you want to include any text or symbols before or after the number, you must include the page number in a header or footer. For example, you can create a header that prints any of the following along the top of the page:

Report # 1 *Mac's Mad Movies* Page R1-103

Cascade Development Co. —43— April 15, 1988

My Summer Vacation **Page 1 of 4**

You add page numbers to a header as follows:

❶ Choose the Open Header command.

❷ Type the header text, and position the insertion point where you want the page number to appear.

❸ Click the Page Number icon in the Header window. The number of the current page appears. (See Figure 11-6.) Word places the correct number on every page when you print the document or view it in Page Preview.

To add page numbers to a footer, follow the same procedure, but choose the Open Footer command.

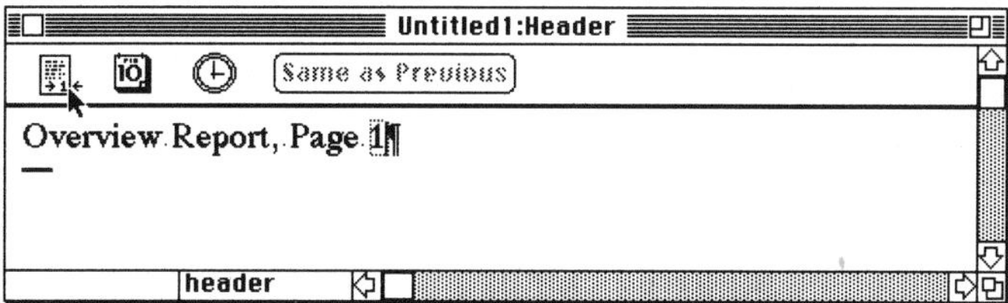

Figure 11-6
A page number added to a header.

You can readily identify a page number (or any of the other elements you insert by clicking icons in the Header or Footer icon bars) by choosing the Show ¶ command. Page numbers are then boxed with a dotted line, as shown in the figure. You can delete, cut, and paste page numbers as you would any other text, but you can't edit the number within the element.

The page number is formatted with the character formats currently in force in the header or footer. If no new character formats have been added, the number uses the formats specified in the *header* or *footer* style (not the *page number* style, used when you set page numbers through the Section dialog box). To change the format, select the page number and choose the formats you want from the appropriate menu.

TIP

Duplicate Page Numbers
You can enter as many page numbers as you like in the header and footer. In fact, both the header and footer can contain a page number. Page numbers created with the Page Preview or Section command are handled separately from the header and footer page numbers. You can use both concurrently, and Word increments both sets. There is little practical application for this, but you should be aware of it in case you change from one numbering method to the other. However, when you click the Page Number icon and close the Header or Footer window, Word turns off the Section page numbering format for you.

You add the time and date in the same way that you add page numbers: Open the Header or Footer window, place the insertion point, and click the Clock icon for the time or the Calendar icon for the date. Word uses the current time and date as set by the Alarm Clock desk accessory. The date is in the form M/D/YY, and the time is in the form H:MM PM (or AM). The time and date change whenever you open or print the document. If you want to add a fixed time or date that does not change, type it explicitly from the keyboard, or use the *time* or *date* glossary entry.

Like the page number, the time and date stamps each have a dotted box around them when Show ¶ is on and are considered one unit. You cannot edit the stamp or delete a portion of it. If you backspace over any part of the stamp, it all disappears.

TIP

Placing a Page Number, Time, or Date Stamp in the Document Window. Because the Page Number, Time, and Date icons appear only in the Header and Footer windows, it might seem that you can't insert these items into the body text of your documents, but you can do so with a little trickery.

To place the page number, time stamp, or date stamp into a document, first enter it into a header. Select it and then cut or copy it to the Clipboard. Close the Header window and set the insertion point in the document where you want the element to appear. Choose Paste, and the page number, time, or date appears. If you want, you can create entries for them in a glossary.

Word updates each of these stamps in the Document window as it does when they are placed in a header or footer. Remember that the time and date are advanced only when you print, preview, or repaginate the document.

■ *Creating Headers for Facing Pages*

Word allows a great deal of flexibility in the use of headers and footers. Even though you normally can't see the headers and footers in a document, you can set up special margins, formats, and other characteristics for them as you would for the body text in Document view. As in the previous section, the focus here is on headers, but the same techniques apply to footers as well.

If the final document will be printed on both sides of the paper and bound into a book, you may want to use facing-page headers, in which the headers on the left and right pages (the even and odd pages, respectively) are independent. How can you use this feature? You might place the page number and the name of the document on all the even-numbered pages and the name of your company on the odd-numbered pages. Figure 11-7 shows a variety of uses for facing-page headers.

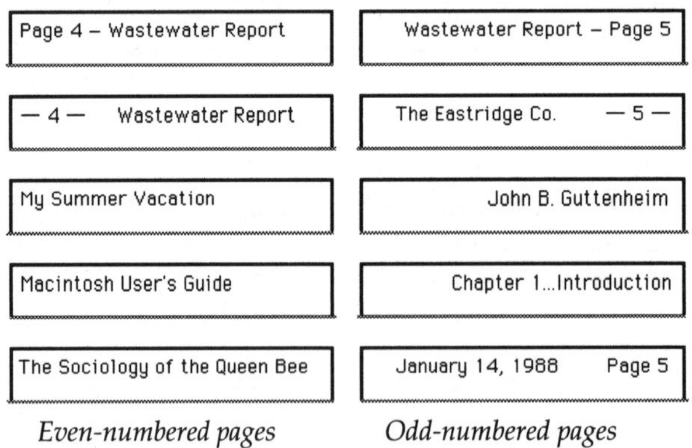

Figure 11-7
Examples of facing-page headers.

To create separate headers for odd-numbered and even-numbered pages, choose the Page Setup command and select the Facing Pages option. Word activates the Gutter edit field. The gutter is an extra margin on the left side of the right-hand (or odd) pages and on the right side of the left-hand (or even) pages to compensate for the binding. Leave the Gutter field empty if you don't want an extra margin for a binding; otherwise, enter a measurement (0.5 inch is a good start). In Page Preview, the gutters appear as gray areas along the inside margins of the facing pages. (See Figure 11-8.)

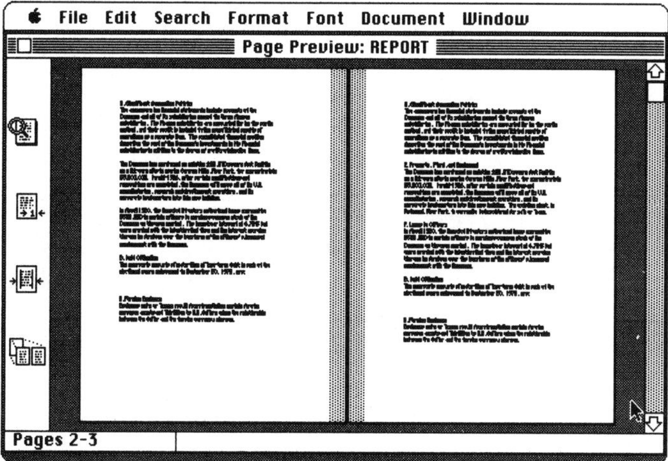

Figure 11-8
Facing pages with gutters in Page Preview.

When you pull down the Document menu after setting the Facing Pages option, you see two new sets of header and footer commands: one set for odd-numbered pages and one set for even-numbered pages. (See Figure 11-9.) Create each header as usual. You can test the layout of your headers by viewing them in Page Preview mode.

Figure 11-9
The Document menu when Facing Pages as well as First Page Special is selected.

How did odd-numbered and even-numbered pages come to be the right and left pages, respectively? In conventional publication design, the first page of a manuscript is numbered 1 and is on the right-hand side. Therefore, all odd-numbered pages are on the right and all even-numbered pages are on the left. In Word, however, you can use the Start Page Numbers At field in the Page Setup dialog box to start your document on a page number other than 1. This is useful if your document is part of a larger set of documents that must be numbered consecutively. If you do this, Word still places even-numbered pages on the left and odd-numbered pages on the right. If you start a document on page 2, for example, the first page is formatted as a left-hand page.

If you specifically need to reverse this order, putting odd pages on the left and even ones on the right, you can still use the Facing Pages option, but make sure that the Gutter field is empty. If you need a gutter, create one when you photocopy or otherwise reproduce the manuscript. (The more sophisticated copy machines have a "page offset" feature that shifts every other page either right or left.) When copying and binding the manuscript, reverse the order of the odd and even pages so that the odd pages are on the left and the even ones are on the right.

■ *Creating a Different Header for Each Section*

You now know about three different types of headers: standard headers, first-page headers, and headers for even-numbered and odd-numbered pages. You can define these headers differently for each section of your document.

As you learned in the previous chapter, you enter a section mark (a double dotted line) by pressing the Command and Enter keys. Any section formats you define for a section, including the headers and footers, are tied to the section mark that follows it.

To create a new header in a section, scroll the window so that the desired section is in view; then click in that section to place the insertion point there. Remember that the status box shows the page and section number of the top-most line in the window, not the location of the insertion point. When you open the Header window, the title bar indicates the section number for which the header is defined; check to be sure it's the right one.

Word saves you typing if you want to use the same or similar text for a new header. When you press Command-Enter to start a new section, each new header (or footer), whether it be first, odd, even, or standard, is copied from the one immediately before it. You can then open any of the Header windows and edit, delete, or replace the text.

The Same As Previous Button

A useful tool for creating new headers is the Same as Previous button in the Header or Footer window, but it is a little complicated to describe. Let's consider three cases, the simplest first.

Suppose you create a standard header—not odd, even, or first page—in a document in which you have established three sections. Before you enter text into any of the three Header windows, each header is known as a *null header*. Now enter some text into the first section's Header window. If you open the Header windows for the second and third sections, you see the text you entered in the Header window for the first section. This happens because for every null header, Word scans back through the preceding sections and uses the contents of the first non-null header it finds.

Now open the Header window for the second section, select the default header text (which comes from the first header), and delete it. You might think that this action makes the header for the second section a null header, but this is not the case. Instead, the second header becomes an *empty header* and contains only a single paragraph mark. (Every window in Word into which you enter text must have an ending paragraph mark, which you cannot delete.)

When you open the Header window for the third section, you see the second header's contents, not the first, because the second section's header is empty, not null. Because you haven't entered anything in the Header window for the third section, it's still a null header, and so its contents are taken from the second section's header. If you want to use the header for the first section again while leaving the header for the second section empty, you must open the first section's Header window and copy it, and then open the third Header window and paste it in.

Word supports the difference between empty and null headers to make it easier to have a header default to the preceding header, yet allow you to empty a header and use that as the default as well. A good use for this feature is when you have a series of large graphs or tables in a section and want to reserve as much room on the page for them as possible by removing the headers or footers for that section.

What does the Same As Previous button have to do with all this? Clicking the Same As Previous button in a Header or Footer window clears that header or footer to the null state. When a header becomes null, Word takes its contents from the first preceding non-null header it finds. When you open a Header or Footer window and the Same As Previous button is dimmed, the header is null. When you change the contents of a null header, the button becomes activated.

Now consider the second case. This time, suppose you create different odd, even, and first-page headers in only one section. If you open each of these Header windows, you see that in all but the first, the Same As Previous button is active. This happens because the odd header in a section has a special priority over the first and even headers. If you open either the First or Even Header window in that section and click the Same As Previous button, its contents are taken from the odd header in that section. The first header's Same As Previous button is dimmed because it has no predecessor.

In the third case, suppose you create three sections and enter different text into each of the three Header windows in each section. If you open the windows for the resulting nine unique headers, you'll see that only the Odd Header window for the first section has its Same As Previous button dimmed because it has no predecessor.

Now open the Even Header window for the third section. If you click the Same as Previous button, you get a copy of the contents of the odd header from the same section because the odd header has priority in that section. Finally, if you open the Odd Header window for the third section and click its Same As Previous button, Word uses the contents of the second section's Odd Header window because it is the first preceding non-null header.

■ *Positioning Headers or Footers*

You use the same character and paragraph formatting operations that you use for the text in the document window to adjust the horizontal position of the header or footer relative to the document's page margins. As for vertical placement, Word normally places the header 0.5 inch from the top edge of the page and the footer 0.5 inch from the bottom edge of the page. You can change the vertical placement of a header or footer in one of three ways:

- ❏ By adding blank lines to the top or the bottom of the text in the window.
- ❏ By specifying its placement in the Header/Footer group of the Section dialog box.
- ❏ By adjusting its position in Page Preview.

Using the Section Command

For more precise control over the header and footer margins, take advantage of the Header/Footer edit fields in the Section dialog box. Choose the Section command and enter the distance from the top of the page to the top of the header in the From Top field, and enter the distance from the bottom of the page to the bottom of the footer in the From Bottom field.

A distance of 0.5 inch is standard for both the header and footer. Most printers—including the LaserWriter—can't print much closer than this to the top and bottom edges of the paper, so don't use a smaller value. Using a larger value may make the printable area for the body of the document smaller, because for headers Word sets the actual top margin for the body of the document at the bottom of the header. The placement of the actual bottom margin works similarly. You set the top and bottom margins in the Page Setup dialog box, but preceding the top or bottom measurements in the dialog box with a minus sign makes these margins absolute rather than relative to headers and footers.

Using the Page Preview Command

Page Preview is the most straightforward and easiest way of adjusting the vertical position of headers and footers, although you lose precise control. You can simply drag the header and footer anywhere on the page. This method allows you to see immediately the effect the positions of the header and footer have on the layout of the page. You'll learn more about this technique in Chapter 12, "Document Formatting and Printing."

Creating and Editing Footnotes

You use footnotes to identify sources of quotation, acknowledge borrowed ideas, and provide supplementary information. A footnote is generally indicated by a superscripted number,[1] but it can also be indicated by a symbol, such as the dagger[†] or asterisk.[*]

Footnotes always consist of two parts:

- A footnote mark, or reference. This is the superscripted number or symbol in the text.
- The footnote text, printed at the bottom of the page, at the end of the section, or at the end of the document.

Footnotes in Word are separated from the main text by a line 2 inches long. They are single-spaced, with some extra space after each one. Footnotes are not the same as bibliographies, which do not have references in text but which follow a similar end-of-section or end-of-document style.

You can let Word do most of the footnote formatting for you, including the spacing and separator line. In fact, you can even have Word track the footnotes, numbering them for you as you go along. If you delete a footnote from the middle of the document, Word automatically renumbers the footnotes that follow it. If you want, however, you can edit and reformat any element in the complex structure of a footnote. This will be discussed later in this chapter, after we've covered the basics.

---

[1] A number that has been raised above the baseline.

[†] Sometimes called a dingbat.

[*] Most manuals of style recommend using only superscripted numbers for footnotes, but if the document contains only one or two footnotes, symbols are an acceptable alternative.

Creating a Footnote

You can insert a footnote reference and its accompanying text when you enter the text or when you edit and format it. To create a footnote, place the insertion point where you want the reference mark to be. Then do this:

❶ Choose the Footnote command from the Document menu. The Footnote dialog box shown in Figure 11-10 appears.

Auto-numbered Reference
or
Footnote Reference Mark:
OK
Cancel
Footnote Separators
Separator...
Cont. Separator...
Cont. Notice...

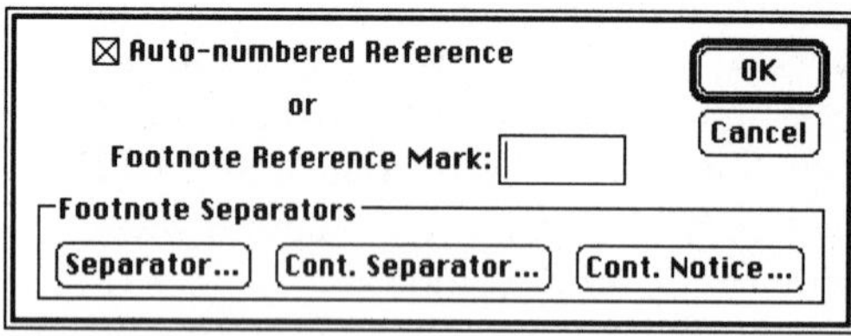

Figure 11-10
The Footnote dialog box.

❷ The Auto-numbered Reference option is already selected, so to insert a numbered footnote reference, simply press the Return key. If you want to use a footnote symbol instead of a number, type it into the Footnote Reference Mark edit field before you press the Return key. Word inserts the reference number or mark into the text, and the Footnote window (Figure 11-11) opens.

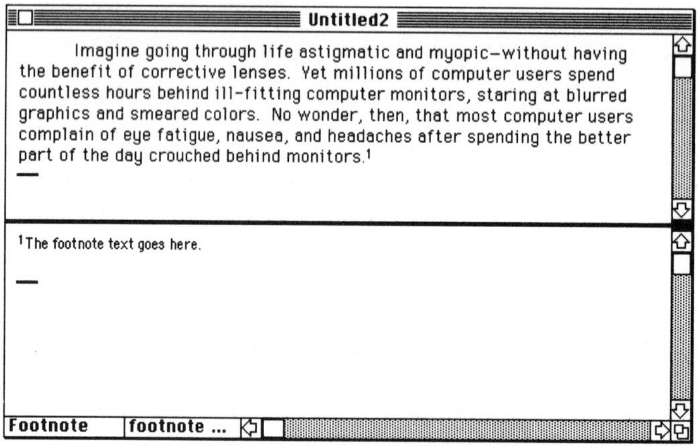

Untitled2
Imagine going through life astigmatic and myopic—without having the benefit of corrective lenses. Yet millions of computer users spend countless hours behind ill-fitting computer monitors, staring at blurred graphics and smeared colors. No wonder, then, that most computer users complain of eye fatigue, nausea, and headaches after spending the better part of the day crouched behind monitors.1
1The footnote text goes here.
Footnote
footnote ...

Figure 11-11
The Footnote window.

❸ Word inserts the same mark at the correct position in the Footnote window relative to the other footnotes. Type the footnote text after it, using any of the character and paragraph formats. Each footnote can be as long as you want; the Footnote window scrolls if you fill it with text. Word assigns the automatic style named *footnote text* to the text you enter, but you can change this style if you want.

❹ When you're finished entering the footnote, close the Footnote window by dragging the split bar down.

Speeding Up Footnote Entry

You can shorten this routine by using a few of Word's command-key shortcuts. If you're letting Word number the footnote references, you can do this:

❶ Press Command-E to open the Footnote dialog box.

❷ Don't wait for the box to appear to press the Return key. Press it while Word is drawing the Footnote dialog box on the screen, and you'll go right to the Footnote window. This cuts a second or two off the time. Many commands in this and other Macintosh programs act this way.

❸ When you've finished entering the footnote, use one of the Go Back key sequences—Command-Option-Z or the 0 key on the keypad. This places the insertion point back in the main document window at the exact place you left off. The Footnote window stays open.

The Footnote window works like a split document window. The upper pane contains the document; the lower pane contains the footnotes. You can scroll the active window up or down. (The active window is the one containing the blinking insertion point.) You can enlarge the Footnote window by dragging the split bar up, making the document window proportionally smaller. If the document window is already split when you open the Footnote window, the original panes are removed. You have to resplit the window when you're finished typing the footnote.

If you need to see the reference marks, choose the Show ¶ command to reveal all the formatting marks and special characters. The footnote references are shown boxed with a dotted line.

Automating Footnote Entry

You can enter a string of footnote references and then go to the Footnote window and type all the footnote text at once. To do this, create the first footnote as usual but don't type the footnote text yet. Instead, go back to the document and double-click on the footnote reference number to select it. Copy it to the Clipboard with the Copy command and close the Footnote window. Now go through the document and use the Paste command to insert any additional footnote references desired. Word increments each footnote number for you. Even if you return to the middle of the document and add more references, all the reference numbers will remain in the correct sequence in the document.

To type the text for all the footnotes, you must open the Footnote window, if it isn't already open. To do this, go back to the first reference number, double-click it, and then press Command-E and the Return key. Alternatively, you can open the Footnote window directly by pressing the Shift key while dragging the split bar down. Word opens the Footnote window and places the insertion point at the end of the footnote text, if there is any.

Note that the reference numbers for the footnotes you just inserted are already in the window. Scroll the window until the footnote number to which you want to add text is uppermost in the pane; Word scrolls the upper document pane to the position of the corresponding reference mark. This is called synchronized scrolling; the outlining feature works similarly. Set the insertion point between the reference number and the following paragraph mark and type the footnote text, as shown in Figure 11-12.

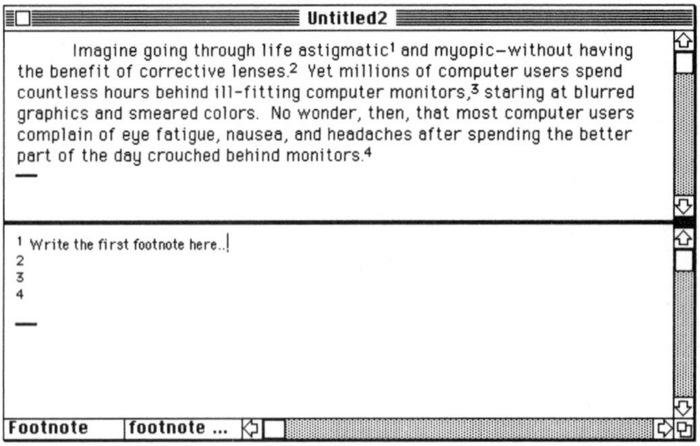

Untitled2

Imagine going through life astigmatic[1] and myopic—without having the benefit of corrective lenses.[2] Yet millions of computer users spend countless hours behind ill-fitting computer monitors,[3] staring at blurred graphics and smeared colors. No wonder, then, that most computer users complain of eye fatigue, nausea, and headaches after spending the better part of the day crouched behind monitors.[4]

1 Write the first footnote here..
2
3
4

Footnote | footnote ...

Figure 11-12
A string of footnotes.

TIP

The Special Footnote Character
Word uses a special character—ASCII code 5—to place and find auto-numbered footnote reference marks. You can verify this by selecting an auto-numbered footnote reference mark and pressing Option-Command-Q to see its ASCII equivalent. Note that you cannot find in this way other footnote reference marks you've entered in the Footnote dialog box.

You can quickly search for these references in your documents by typing ^5 in the Find What field of the Find or Change dialog box. However, you cannot create a footnote reference by inserting that character alone in a document because Word attaches a "buried" format to it that users cannot reproduce. Instead, you must copy the mark and paste it at each reference; you can also store it as a glossary entry.

Editing and Changing the Format of Footnotes

Editing a footnote is almost as easy as entering it in the first place. There are three ways of displaying a footnote for editing:

- Select a footnote reference mark and press Command-E and then the Return key. Word takes you to the end of the footnote text associated with that mark.
- Press Shift-Option-Command-S to open the Footnote window. Scroll through the footnotes; Word scrolls in the document to show you the reference marks. Edit the text, then press Shift-Option-Command-S to close the footnote pane.
- Press the Shift key while dragging the split bar down.

You can change the format of the footnote reference mark and the text in the footnote itself in several ways. You can redefine the *footnote reference* and *footnote text* styles, or you can change the formats in a reference or the text in a footnote. Also, for footnote text alone, you can insert paragraphs into a footnote containing a style other than the *footnote text* style. Remember that both styles are based on the *Normal* style, so changes you make to *Normal* may affect them.

The *footnote reference* style is not a full-fledged style: You can set Line Spacing, Space Above, and the Border formats for it, but they aren't used; only the character formats are used. A result of this is that whenever you redefine this style, the appearance of every footnote will not change. For this reason, it's best to decide on the definition of the *footnote reference* style before you enter a large number of them.

To change the appearance of the references, you must go back through the document, select each reference mark, and press Command-E to reenter it at that position. (A keyboard macro program such as Tempo from Affinity Microsystems is good for automating this process.) Even though it seems as though replacing a reference mark might replace the footnote text attached to it, the footnote text is not lost. If you're using auto-numbered footnotes, it can help to search for the magic character Word uses to mark them, as described in the previous tip, "The Special Footnote Character."

Here's another way to change all the reference marks quickly to ensure that all the footnotes in a document have the same formatting:

1. After you've redefined the style, go to the first footnote in the document and reenter it as described earlier.
2. Select and copy that reference mark alone. Press the right arrow key a few times to move the insertion point a few characters to the right of the first reference mark.

3. Choose Change from the Search menu; enter *^5* in the Find What field and *^c* in the Change To field.
4. Click Change All to replace every reference mark in the document with the reference mark you reentered.

Unfortunately, when you replace all the marks at once in this way, the footnote text is lost, so this method works best when you haven't entered any footnote text yet. Otherwise, try copying the text and pasting it into a new document to avoid losing the footnotes, then copy the footnotes back after you've replaced the reference marks in the body of the document.

TIP

Changing the Formats for References Preceding the Footnote Text
Often, you'd like to change the appearance of the references preceding the footnote text that correspond to the reference marks in the body of the document. A convenient way to do this is to select all the text in the Footnote window by pressing the Command key and clicking in the selection bar, and assigning the *footnote text* style (or any style in the document's style sheet) to everything in the Footnote window, including the reference marks. This brings the reference marks down to the baseline for the footnote text and brings together the formats for all the text in the Footnote window. When you do this, you may also have to press Shift-Command-Spacebar to return to the base character format any character formats you've given the text for the style you've just assigned.

Deleting Footnotes

When you are working with a typewriter, deleting a footnote means going back and renumbering all the ones that followed it. Word does the renumbering for you, however, so deleting unnecessary footnotes is no longer a chore. To delete a footnote:

1. Select the reference mark in the document for the footnote you want to delete.
2. Press the Backspace key.

This simple procedure erases the footnote reference, erases the footnote text in the Footnote window, and renumbers the footnote entries that follow.

Editing the Footnote Separators

Word places a single 2-inch line, known as the footnote separator, between the body text and the footnote text. You can make this line shorter or longer or do away with it altogether. You can even replace it with a double line, a row of pound signs (#), or a set of bullets. Figure 11-13 shows a few unusual footnote separators you might want to try.

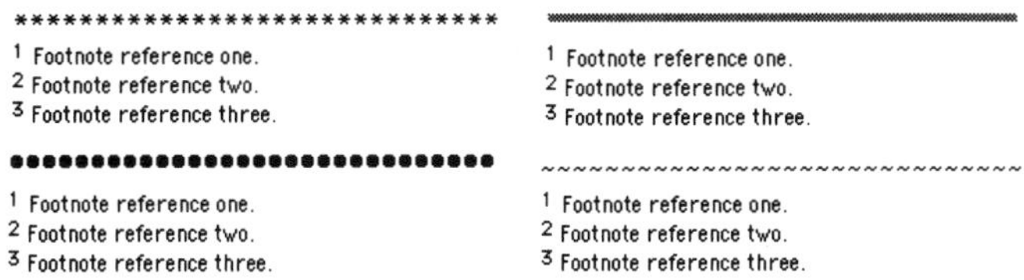

Figure 11-13
Some sample footnote separators.

When a footnote becomes too long to fit comfortably on the same page as the reference (assuming that you want it to appear on the same page), Word continues it on the next page. In such cases, Word inserts a single line that spans from margin to margin (called the continuing footnote separator) and can also provide a "continued" notice to help readers follow along. You can edit these as well; the changes affect the current document only and are not saved in the Word Settings file. To edit the footnote separator, the continuing footnote separator, or the continuation notice:

❶ Choose the Footnote command.

❷ In the Footnote Separators option group, click the separator button for the feature you want to change. A special headerlike window appears, as shown in Figure 11-14. Edit the contents of the window. The Footnote Cont. Notice window is initially empty, but you can add text such as *continued on next page.*

❸ When you are finished, close the window by clicking the close box.

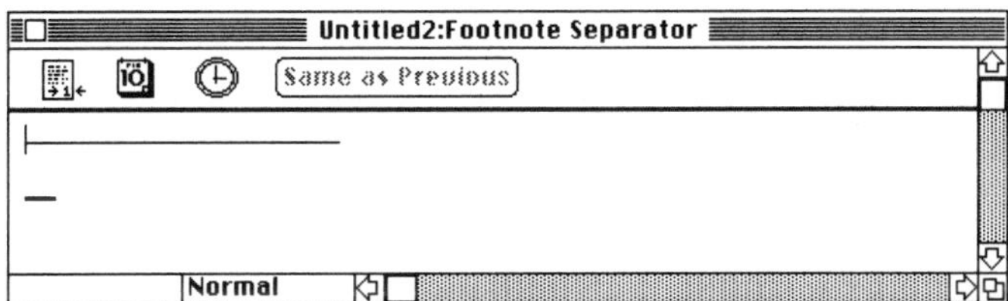

Figure 11-14
The Footnote Separator window.

Both separators are really special characters, as you can tell by turning on Show ¶ and clicking on the separator line. The line is shown surrounded by a dotted box, a telltale sign. Indeed, if you double-click on the line, all of it is selected, and pressing the Backspace key deletes all of it. If you delete one of the separators (intentionally or not), you can get it back by clicking the Same as Previous button.

Because the separator characters are like the page number, time, and date characters discussed earlier, you can also create glossary entries for them beforehand. The ASCII code for the separator character is 6, and the code for the continuing separator is 7, but, as with the other special characters, you can't simply press Option-Command-Q, and then enter 6 to get the separator character. Instead, select and copy an instance of the character itself to paste or add to the glossary. Incidentally, if you create a glossary entry for the continuing separator, it becomes an easy margin-to-margin rule for use as a special design element.

TIP

Formats in the Separator Windows

Curiously, the footnote separator and continuation notice are contained in special "header" windows that have the familiar Page Number, Time stamp, and Date stamp icons in them, although there is usually little reason why you'd want to use these.

These windows also share another feature with header windows: You can change the font, style, alignment, and position of characters within them. The footnote separator can be plain or bold, shadow or outline, 12 point or 48 point. This permits some unusual effects. Use restraint, however, so that the special effects in a document don't overshadow its content. When editing the continuation notice, you can display the Ruler to adjust the margins and alignment of the text.

■ *Placing Footnotes in a Document*

You can have Word begin numbering footnote references at any number, not only at 1. To change the starting number, choose the Page Setup command and enter a new number in the Start Footnote Numbers At field. This feature is handy if your manuscript spans several documents and you want the numbering sequence to continue where the numbering in the previous document left off. However, if you link documents through the Next File field, the process is not automatic—if you leave the Start Footnote Numbers At field blank, Word starts the count at 1.

Word lets you specify where the footnotes will be printed. Normally, Word prints them at the bottom of each page. You can tell Word to place footnotes on the page on which the footnote reference appears, either immediately below the lowest paragraph on the page or at the bottom of the page, near the margin and above the footer. You can also have Word place them at the end of a section, which in most documents is the end of the document itself. If the document has more than one section, you put them at the end of the document or at the end of every section.

❑ To place footnotes at the end of the entire document, choose the Section command and turn off the Include Endnotes option. (It is normally selected.) Do this for each section. If the document has only one section, you can ignore this step. Then choose the Page Setup command and turn on the Endnotes option in the Footnotes At option group.

- To place footnotes at the end of each section, choose the Section command and turn on the Include Endnotes option in each section. Then choose the Page Setup command and turn on the Endnotes option.
- To place footnotes at the bottom of the page, near the bottom margin, choose the Page Setup command and select the Bottom of Page option in the Footnotes At option group.
- To place footnotes at the end of the text on the page, choose the Page Setup command and select the Beneath Text option.

It may seem as if the Bottom of Page and Beneath Text options in the Page Setup dialog box do the same thing, but there is a difference. If you select the Bottom of Page option, Word places the footnotes flush with the bottom margin, as shown in Figure 11-15. If there is less than a full page of text, this can result in a big gap between the text and the footnotes. If you don't want a gap, select the Beneath Text option instead. This option causes the footnotes to be printed directly beneath the text.

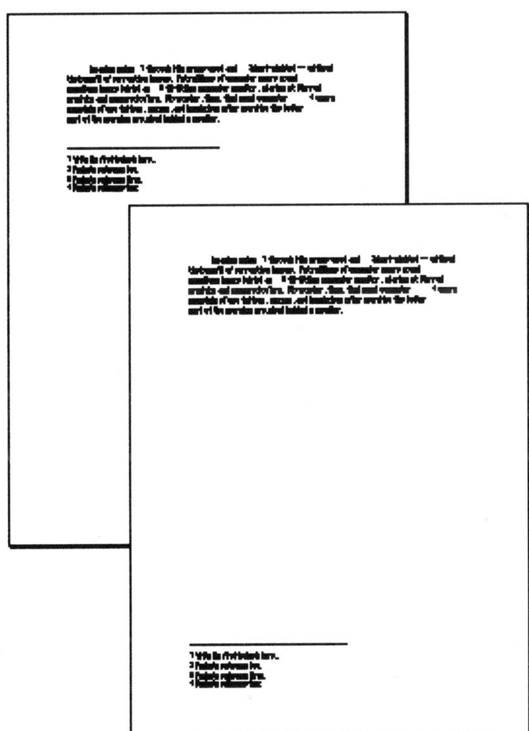

Figure 11-15
The difference between the Beneath Text and the Bottom of Page options.

If you have occasion to use both the Bottom of Page option and the No Break section format, you may be surprised by the results. Because these two options can be contradictory (for example, you might get two footnotes numbered *1* at the bottom of the page), Word ignores the Bottom of Page option and places footnotes beneath the text.

The Endnotes option in the Page Setup dialog box tells Word to save footnotes until the end of the document. However, you can have Word "dump" the footnotes it has been saving at the end of a given section, instead of at the end of the entire document, by selecting the Include Endnotes option in the Section dialog box. As was mentioned in the previous chapter, you can turn this option on and off for various sections within a document. Word saves its footnotes until it finds a section in which the Include Endnotes option is on and prints them at the end of that section.

Also, note that Footnote numbering is independent of the placement of the footnotes. To restart the numbering for each group, turn on the Restart Numbering option in the Page Setup dialog box.

Points to Remember

- A header is text that is repeated above the top margin of the page. A footer is text that is repeated below the bottom margin of the page. These elements usually contain identifying text, such as page numbers, the section or document title, and so forth.
- Three types of headers and footers are available in Word: Standard headers and footers do not vary from page to page. First-page headers and footers are printed only on the first page of the document or section. Even and odd headers and footers are printed only on even-numbered and odd-numbered pages, respectively.
- You can define a different set of headers and footers for each section in your document. If your document is not divided into sections, the headers and footers you create apply to the entire document.
- Word moves the top and bottom margins, if necessary, to accommodate the header and footer. To prevent this, enter a minus sign in front of the Top and Bottom margin measurement in the Page Setup dialog box.
- If you include page numbers in a header or footer, be sure the Page Numbering option in the Section dialog box is turned off. Otherwise, you will have duplicate numbers.
- A footnote provides supplementary information about one or more statements in the text. A footnote consists of a reference mark in the body text and the text of the footnote itself. Word can print footnotes at the bottom of the page on which their references appear, at the end of selected sections, or at the end of the document.
- Headers, footers, and footnotes do not appear in Document view. You can see them by viewing your document in Page Preview mode.

Techniques

Working with Headers and Footers

Create a standard header or footer

1. Set the insertion point in the section that is to contain the header or footer.
2. Choose Open Header or Open Footer from the Document menu. The Header or Footer window appears.
3. Type the header or footer text. These windows have two preset tabs: one centered between the indents and one flush right against the right indent.
4. Click the close box of the Header or Footer window.

Add page numbers or the time or date to a header or footer

1. With the Header or Footer window open, set the insertion point where you want the page number, time, or date to appear.
2. Click the appropriate icon in the header or footer icon bar.

Change the formatting in a header or footer

1. Open the Header or Footer window.
2. Change any of the character or paragraph formats as you would those of body text.
3. You can also redefine the *header* and *footer* automatic styles or assign any style in your document to the header or footer.

Adjust the distance between the top or bottom edge of the page and the header or footer

1. Set the insertion point in the section to be affected.
2. Choose the Section command.
3. Enter the distance in the From Top or From Bottom field in the Header/Footer option group.

You can also drag the header or footer in Page Preview; Chapter 12, "Document Formatting and Printing," discusses this.

Create a header or footer for the first page of a section

1. Set the insertion point in the section for which you want to define the header or footer.
2. Choose the Section command.
3. Select the First Page Special option, and then click OK.
4. Choose Open First Header or Open First Footer from the Document menu.
5. Proceed as you would in a standard header or footer.

Create different headers and footers for odd and even pages

Even-numbered pages print on the left facing page, and odd-numbered pages print on the right facing page.

1. Choose the Page Setup command.
2. Select the Facing Pages option.
3. Specify an additional inside margin in the Gutter field, if you want.
4. Choose Open Even Header, Open Even Footer, Open Odd Header, or Open Odd Footer from the Document menu.
5. Proceed as you would in a standard header or footer.

Define a header with the same text as the last nonempty header

This also applies to footers.

1. Open the Header window.
2. Click the Same as Previous button.

The text of the odd header for the section, if any, is used. If that header is empty, the text of the last nonempty header of the same type is used.

Working with Footnotes

The Footnote Dialog Box

Auto-numbered Reference option	Numbers footnotes sequentially. Word renumbers these reference marks when you add, rearrange, or delete footnotes. If you enter a symbol in the Footnote Reference Mark field, this option is turned off.
Footnote Reference Mark field	Sets the type of reference mark to be used. Word will not change this mark.
Footnote Separators option group	Specifies elements to be used to separate the footnotes from the body text when they are printed; also specifies the footnote continuation notice.
Separator	Presents a window for changing the separator between body text and footnotes. The default is a 2-inch line.
Cont. Separator	Presents a window for changing the separator between the text and a footnote carried over from the previous page. The default is a solid line from margin to margin.
Cont. Notice	Presents a window for changing text printed when a footnote is carried over to the next page. The default is no continuation notice.
Buttons	
OK button	Inserts the footnote reference mark and opens the Footnote window.
Cancel button	Closes the dialog box without inserting a reference mark.

Create a footnote

❶ Position the insertion point where you want the footnote reference. Choose the Footnote command.

❷ Type a reference mark, or click OK for an auto-numbered footnote.

❸ Type the footnote text in the Footnote window that appears.

❹ Drag the split bar down to close the Footnote window.

Edit a footnote

❶ Press Shift-Option-Command-S to open the Footnote window.

❷ Edit the footnote text, and close the footnote pane.

Delete a footnote

❶ Delete the footnote reference mark in the document text.

Word deletes the corresponding footnote text, and renumbers the remaining footnotes.

Specify the location of footnotes

❶ Choose the Page Setup command.

❷ Select one of the Footnotes At options.

Bottom of Page: Prints each footnote near the bottom margin of the page on which its reference appears.

Beneath Text: Prints each footnote just after the text on the page on which its reference appears.

Endnotes: Prints footnotes at the end of sections in which the Include Endnotes option is selected, or at the end of the document if this option is not selected in any section.

Change the formatting of a footnote reference mark

❶ Choose Define Styles from the Format menu, and select the *footnote reference* style.

❷ Change the formats for the style. However, only the character formats are used in the style.

❸ Then, for each reference in the document, select the reference and reenter it. Entering ^5 in the Find What field of the Find dialog box helps to locate auto-numbered references.

Change the formatting of footnote text

1. Choose Define Styles from the Format menu, and select the *footnote text* style.
2. Redefine the style as needed.

Edit the footnote separators or continuation notice

1. Choose the Footnote command.
2. Click the button for the Footnote Separators option you want to change.
3. In the window that appears, replace the separator or type text to be used as a continuation notice when a footnote is continued on the next page.
4. Note that the preset separators are special characters; you can replace them, but you can't edit them.
5. Click the close box for the window when you're through.

Document Formatting and Printing

This book presents a typical process for developing a document. First, you create the overall structure of the document with the outlining feature; then you enter the text, making use of glossaries for boilerplate text and the Spelling command. Next, you format the document at the character, paragraph, and section levels and add headers, footers, and footnotes. Of course, there are infinite variations on this theme. If you're using styles, much of the formatting you do simply involves assigning styles.

The next step is to adjust the overall shape of your opus at the page and document level and audition it in Page Preview. At this stage you often find room for further refinements and go back to change a few formats or adjust the margins. Finally, when everything is to your liking, you print the document. This whole process is the subject of this chapter. It follows a standard sequence of steps for preparing your document for printing, including hyphenation, pagination, and page layout.

One of the topics covered in this chapter is the fourth formatting domain available to you in Word: the document domain, which controls these characteristics of your document, mostly through the Page Setup dialog box:

- The size of the paper on which the document will be printed.
- The page margins, which determine the initial placement of major elements such as the left and right edges of the text, the left and right indents, and the headers and footers.

- ❏ Whether the document will be printed on both sides of the paper and therefore needs to be adjusted for left and right pages.
- ❏ The default tab stop interval.
- ❏ Whether Word should control widows (stray lines at the top or bottom of a page).
- ❏ Where to print the footnotes.
- ❏ How footnotes, lines, and pages should be numbered.
- ❏ Whether to print another document after this one.

Let's go over the process of preparing a document for printing. First, you need to choose a printer. This is necessary because the actual size of the page and the position of margins, headers, footers, and so on, are affected by the printer used. The LaserWriter, for example, cannot print closer than 0.42 inch from the edge of the page. In addition, the screen-pixel-to-printed-pixel ratio is different for the LaserWriter and the ImageWriter. You specify the printer in the Chooser dialog box, available from the Apple menu.

Next, you establish the overall shape of your document by setting formats in the Page Setup dialog box. Once this is done, you can hyphenate the document. Hyphenation is optional, but it often enhances the appearance of a document, especially if you are using justified alignment.

The next step is to control where on the page each part of the document will be printed. For example, if you're writing a book, you probably want each chapter to start at the top of a page and on a right-hand (odd-numbered) page. You don't want a major section head to be printed alone at the bottom of a page, nor do you want separate a figure and its caption. You can have Word take care of most of these page-layout decisions for you by using the Keep With Next ¶ and Page Break Before formats and the Section Start options in the Section dialog box. However, sometimes these methods aren't enough, and you have to force page breaks at certain points to get the effect you want. One of the main reasons for doing this is to achieve a good visual balance between the elements on a page. You want to maintain the clarity and proportion of the design.

The process of calculating the depth of each element (that is, its vertical dimension on the page) and deciding where to break the text and start a new page is called *repagination*. Word repaginates a document only when you specifically tell it to by choosing the Repaginate command or when you choose the Page Preview command or print the document.

The Page Preview command is an excellent way to see where Word has broken each page before you print the document. In Page Preview, you can move page breaks and adjust the margins and see the effect of these changes.

After these final adjustments, you are ready for the *coup de grâce:* printing the document. This should present few surprises (although there are several fine points you need to know about). The following sections describe each of these steps in detail.

■ Choosing a Printer

Earlier versions of Word used an internal method for setting the printer, but the Chooser desk accessory now fulfills this function. Most people use either the ImageWriter or the LaserWriter, or they use the ImageWriter in the initial stages of writing, editing, and formatting and then switch to the LaserWriter for the final version. When you print something, an application sends print commands to a special piece of Macintosh system software called a printer driver. The driver translates these commands into a form the printer can accept. Word includes the following printer drivers:

- ❑ ImageWriter.
- ❑ LaserWriter (and the Laser Prep file).
- ❑ SerialPrinter (and one or more printer resource files, such as the AppleDaisy, Brother, Diablo 630, NEC 7710, and Typewriter files).

If the driver for your printer is not already in the System Folder on the Word disk, copy it there from the Word Utilities disk. If you will be using a daisy-wheel or dot-matrix printer, you must copy the SerialPrinter driver and the desired printer resource. Remember to copy the Laser Prep file to the System Folder if you will be using the LaserWriter driver. The versions of the LaserWriter and ImageWriter drivers must be compatible with the system file you are using; you can check with an Apple dealer for the most recent system software.

When using the SerialPrinter driver, you have a choice of printer resources. The AppleDaisy, Diablo, Brother, and NEC resources are used with specific daisy-wheel printers. The Typewriter resource is generic and can be used with almost any serial dot-matrix or daisy-wheel printer.

To select a printer, choose Chooser from the Apple menu. The dialog box in Figure 12-1 appears. Icons for the available printers appear in the left side of the dialog box. Click the one you want.

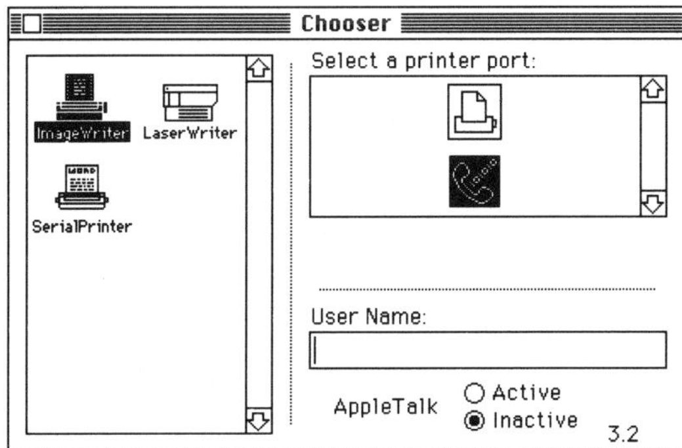

Figure 12-1
The Chooser dialog box.

Some Macintosh applications are accompanied by their own drivers, which you may also see in the Chooser dialog box. Word comes with one such driver, the SerialPrinter driver. Its icon contains the word *Word*, meaning that only Word can make use of this printing resource.

Now do one of the following:

- If you selected the ImageWriter driver, the title of the list box to the right reads *Select a printer port*, and the Telephone and Printer Port icons appear in the list box. Click the icon for the port to which your printer is connected.
- If you selected the LaserWriter driver, the title of the list box to the right reads *Select a LaserWriter*, and the laser printers available on the network appear in the list box. Click on the name of the LaserWriter to which you will be printing. Depending on the version of the Chooser that you are using (the version number is in the lower right corner of the window), the Chooser may present another dialog box telling you to be sure that AppleTalk is connected to the printer port. You may also have to click the AppleTalk Active button.
- Selecting the AppleTalk ImageWriter driver is like selecting the LaserWriter, except that you see a list of the AppleTalk ImageWriters on the network.
- If you selected the SerialPrinter driver, the title of the list box to the right reads *Select a Serial Printer*, and you must choose an associated printer resource. The resources available in the System Folder appear in the list box. Click on the one you want. Next, click the Settings button. A dialog box like the one shown in Figure 12-2 appears. Choose the pitch of the printer (the number of characters per inch), transmission baud rate (almost always 9600), and the printer port, and then click OK.

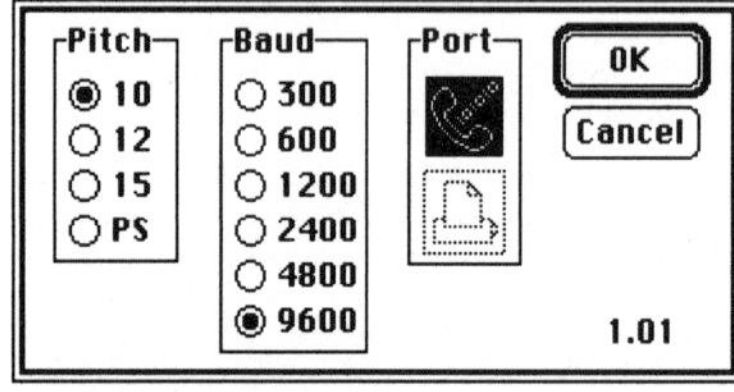

Figure 12-2
The Settings dialog box for the SerialPrinter driver.

When you are finished choosing the printer, click the close box to close the Chooser dialog box. You are now ready to print.

TIP

Choosing the LaserWriter Even If You Don't Have One
If you will eventually print your document on a LaserWriter but have only the ImageWriter, you've probably discovered that the line lengths change when you go from one printer to the other. This happens because with the ImageWriter, Word maps 80 screen dots to every printed inch, whereas with the LaserWriter (and the Wide ImageWriter), Word maps 72 screen dots to every printed inch. Consequently, the intervals in the Ruler change size when you switch printers. This can cause problems when you're trying to print a rough draft on the ImageWriter so that you can polish the formatting in your document before printing it on the LaserWriter. You get the document the way you want it only to have everything change when you print it on the LaserWriter.

You can get around this problem in two ways. First, you can do all the writing and editing and most of the initial formatting (for instance, creating style definitions or setting italics and boldface formats where desired) using the ImageWriter to print drafts. Then, you can set the final formats when you have access to the LaserWriter. If you're renting time on the LaserWriter, however, this can be expensive.

The second way is to use the Chooser to select the LaserWriter driver, even though you don't have one connected to your Mac. When you click the LaserWriter icon, no LaserWriter names appear in the list box. Simply click the close box of the Chooser dialog box; Word sets the screen dimensions for the LaserWriter. You can then use Page Preview to fine-tune the formats in your document for the LaserWriter, temporarily switching back to the ImageWriter if you need to print a draft copy.

■ *The Page Setup Command*

The first phase in preparing your document for printing is to be sure that all the options in the Page Setup dialog box are set as you would like them. You may already have set some of the options in this dialog box, such as the page margins or the placement of footnotes, discussed in previous chapters.

To display the dialog box, choose Page Setup from the File menu. A dialog box like the one shown in Figure 12-3 appears. If you don't see all these options, you are in Short Menus mode. Choose Full Menus from the Edit menu to get access to all the printing options.

Word stores the page settings you specify in this dialog box with the document, as it does all the other formats in your document. The Set Default button allows you to record these options in the Word Settings file so that they will be the default in all new documents.

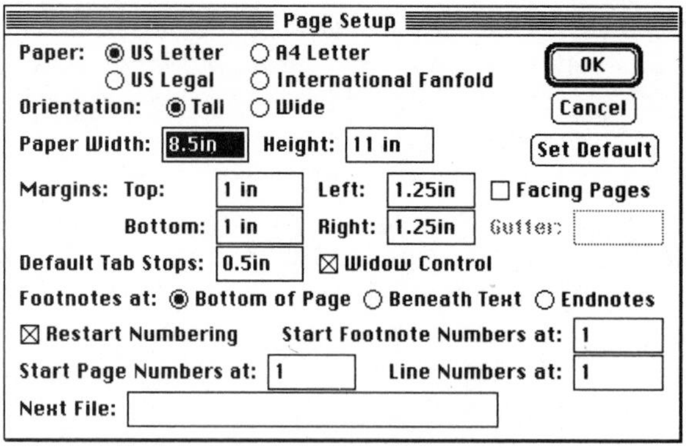

Page Setup

Paper: (•) US Letter ( ) A4 Letter [OK]
( ) US Legal ( ) International Fanfold
Orientation: (•) Tall ( ) Wide [Cancel]
Paper Width: 8.5in Height: 11 in [Set Default]
Margins: Top: 1 in Left: 1.25in [ ] Facing Pages
Bottom: 1 in Right: 1.25in Gutter:
Default Tab Stops: 0.5in [x] Widow Control
Footnotes at: (•) Bottom of Page ( ) Beneath Text ( ) Endnotes
[x] Restart Numbering Start Footnote Numbers at: 1
Start Page Numbers at: 1 Line Numbers at: 1
Next File:

Figure 12-3
The Page Setup dialog box.

Paper Size and Orientation Options

The Paper, Orientation, Paper Width, and Height options tell Word how large a canvas it has to work with and specify whether the document is to be printed normally or sideways. The four Paper options have preset dimensions. Clicking one of these options places the following dimensions into the Width and Height edit fields, depending on the unit of measurement you've set in the Preferences dialog box:

Paper	Width x Height Inches	Centimeters
US Letter	8.5 x 11	21.6 x 27.95
US Legal	8.5 x 14	21.6 x 35.55
A4 Letter	8.27 x 11.69	21 x 29.7
Intl. Fanfold	8.25 x 12	20.95 x 30.5

You can designate any other page dimension up to 22 inches wide and high in the Paper Width and Height edit fields if you want to print on a paper size not listed among the radio buttons. Obviously, your printer must be able to accommodate the paper. By choosing the Wide option with the ImageWriter I and II, you can print sideways, in order to generate documents that are wider than the print carriage, as shown in Figure 12-4 . The Tall option, Word's preset default, prints the document in normal fashion, parallel to the short edge of the paper.

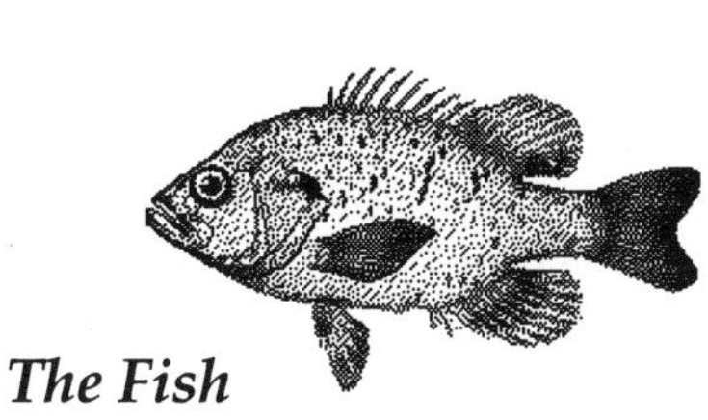

The Fish

by John Hammond

The Fish

by John Hammond

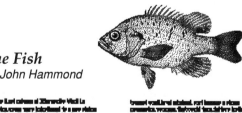

Figure 12-4

Documents printed using the Tall and the Wide Orientation options (the latter formatted for two columns).

The Margins Options

Word measures the page margins from the edges of the page set in the Width and Height edit fields. The 0 point on the Ruler indicates the left margin. A light dotted line on the right side of the Ruler shows the position of the right margin. The indents are at the margins until you change them.

The Margins options set the area for the body text of the document. (Page numbers, headers, and footers are usually printed outside this area.) To change a margin, click in the appropriate edit field and enter a measurement. You can use inches, centimeters, or points.

As was discussed earlier, the left and right indents are measured relative to the margins. You can place the indents either inside the margins—the normal case—or outside them. When you drag the first-line indent marker to the left of the left indent, you create a hanging indent. When you drag a right indent marker to the right of the right margin, you create what is known as a breakthrough indent or a margin violation. When you change the left and right margins, the indents retain their positions with respect to the margins.

Setting a Fixed Top or Bottom Margin

As was mentioned in the previous chapter, if you create a header or footer that is more than a few lines deep, Word moves the top or bottom margin of the body text to accommodate it, if necessary, so that the header or footer text does not overlap the body text.

If you want to set a top margin that remains at a constant distance from the top of the page regardless of the size of the header, enter a negative number in the Top edit field. And if you want to set a bottom margin that remains at a constant distance from the bottom of the page, enter a negative number in the Bottom edit field.

You could use this feature to place a header to the side of the body text rather than over it, as shown in Figure 11-3 in Chapter 11. Or, you can create an "electronic letterhead" when you have established a stock design on a page and want the body text to appear within the limits of the design. The electronic letterhead project in Chapter 17, "Blueprints," shows an example of this. Finally, you could put a frame around the body text in a magazine or newsletter design, for example, as shown in Figure 12-5.

You'll learn more about how to set up these design elements in Chapter 15, which describes how to copy graphics into a Word document, and in Chapter 17, which presents projects you can adapt to your own documents.

Facing Pages

Click the Facing Pages check box if you will be printing the document on both sides of the paper and assembling it in book form. When this option is set, Word creates separate headers and footers for the left and right pages (known as *even* and *odd* pages, respectively) and places page numbers in the outside corners of the paper—the upper left corner of even-numbered pages

The Transcendentalist Times
1243 Harrison Place, Duvall, WA 98702
Phone: 206-555-7532

Figure 12-5
A page frame for a magazine or newsletter.

and the upper right corner of odd-numbered ones. Also, when you give a paragraph the Bar Border format, Word places the bar on the outside of the page, just to the left or right of the paragraph.

With Facing Pages on, you can set a gutter margin, which increases the inner margin of each page to allow for the binding. Leave the Gutter field blank or enter a measurement in inches, centimeters, or points. A gutter of 0.5 inch, for example, shifts even-numbered pages ½ inch to the left and odd-numbered pages ½ inch to the right, as shown in Figure 12-6. Word still sets the 0 point on the Ruler to the left margin.

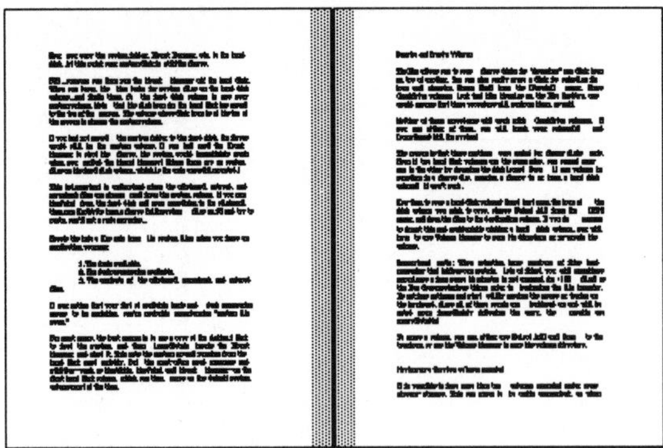

Figure 12-6
A page with a 0.5-inch gutter.

The Default Tab Stops Option

The Ruler contains default tab stops if you haven't placed any tab markers on it. Normally, Word places these at 0.5-inch intervals. Enter another measurement in the Default Tab Stops field to make the default tabs closer together or farther apart. If you don't want any default stops, enter *22 in* into the edit field. Default tab stops appear as small upside-down Ts on the Ruler.

The Widow Control Option

A *widow* occurs when the first line of a paragraph appears by itself at the bottom of a page. Widows are considered bad form because they are easy for a reader to lose. Word's Widow Control option prevents this from happening by moving the first line of a paragraph to the top of the next page. The option is normally set; click the box to turn it off. This option also causes Word to correct for *orphans*, which occur when the last line of a paragraph appears by itself at the top of a page.

The Footnote Options

As was discussed in the previous chapter, the Footnotes At options let you specify where Word prints the footnotes: at the bottom of the page containing the reference, directly beneath the text (even if the text only partially fills the page), or at the end of the document. In documents with more than one section, you can have footnotes printed at the end of certain sections by setting the Endnotes option in the Page Setup dialog box and then setting the Include Endnotes option in the Section dialog box for the section where the footnotes are to be printed. Word prints the accumulated footnotes at the end of each section in which this option is set. Set the Restart Numbering option to restart footnote numbering at 1 in each section. Use the Start Footnote

Numbers At option to set the number of the first footnote in the first section. See Chapter 11, "Headers, Footers, and Footnotes," for more details on these footnote options.

The Numbering Options

The numbering options consist of the Start Page Numbers At, the Line Numbers At, and the Start Footnote Numbers At fields. Normally, you leave the starting page number at 1, unless the document is a unit in a larger series of documents (discussed in the next section). To make Word do the numbering for you, remove the number in the Start Page Numbers At edit field, or enter a zero. If you haven't linked together a series of documents through the Next File field and still want the document to start on a specific page, enter the page number into the field. For example, if the last page of the previous document was page 24, enter *25* into the edit field. The Line Numbers At and Start Footnote Numbers At options serves much the same purpose, except that they set the starting line number and footnote number for the document.

Chaining Files

The Next File option tells Word to link another document to the end of the current one. You use this feature to chain-print two or more documents, making it easier to print them all at once. You also use chained files when compiling a table of contents or an index (described in Chapter 13, "Creating a Table of Contents and Index").

If you are chaining more than two files, open each document in the series and enter the name of the succeeding file into the Next File edit field. For example:

Filename	Enter into next file box
Front Matter	*Part 1*
Part 1	*Part 2*
Part 2	*Appendixes*
Appendixes	(Leave blank)

With chained files, even though Word continues the page numbers from one document to the next (if you've left the Start Page Numbers At field blank or entered a zero), it doesn't continue line numbers or footnote numbers. Therefore, you must enter the correct starting line or footnote number in the appropriate field if you want to continue the numbering.

Be sure to type exactly the name of the next file. Even an extra space before or after the name will confuse Word. If Word can't locate the file you've specified (because it is not in any of the current drives, is not in the same folder as the preceding file, or is spelled incorrectly), a dialog box appears, asking you to find it. Assuming you've spelled the filename correctly, locate the folder or insert the disk containing it and click OK.

■ *Hyphenation*

Once you reach a point where the line lengths in your document will no longer change, you can hyphenate it, if you want. Do this after you have chosen a printer, set the final page margins, and made final adjustments to the left and right indents. It's also a good idea to use the spelling checker first. Correcting spelling errors after hyphenation may change the lengths of words in a line of text, requiring you to do another hyphenation pass through the document.

As was mentioned earlier, hyphenation is optional. Some designers avoid it except where absolutely necessary, making the case that a hyphenated word is harder to read than an unbroken one. Most documents need only light hyphenation, especially ones with ragged right (left-aligned) text. Hyphenation can improve the appearance of justified text, particularly when long words are placed on short lines, and in multiple-column documents. Justified text (text aligned at both the right and left indents) and narrow columns may require heavier hyphenation because lines containing too few words tend to look stretched out, as Figure 12-7 illustrates.

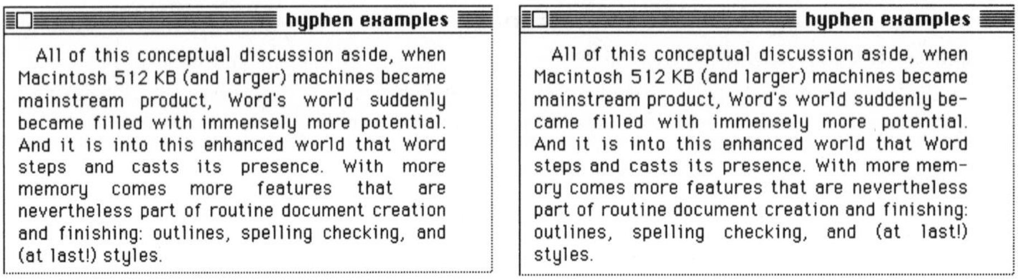

hyphen examples

All of this conceptual discussion aside, when Macintosh 512 KB (and larger) machines became mainstream product, Word's world suddenly became filled with immensely more potential. And it is into this enhanced world that Word steps and casts its presence. With more memory comes more features that are nevertheless part of routine document creation and finishing: outlines, spelling checking, and (at last!) styles.

hyphen examples

All of this conceptual discussion aside, when Macintosh 512 KB (and larger) machines became mainstream product, Word's world suddenly became filled with immensely more potential. And it is into this enhanced world that Word steps and casts its presence. With more memory comes more features that are nevertheless part of routine document creation and finishing: outlines, spelling checking, and (at last!) styles.

Figure 12-7
Spacing problems in justified text.

When hyphenating your document, keep the following guidelines in mind. Avoid hyphens at the end of more than two consecutive lines. Too many hyphenated lines can be distracting. If more than two lines out of six or seven end with a hyphen, you may be using text columns that are too narrow. Consider using a wider column or reducing the point size of the text. Don't hyphenate a word that is already part of a hyphenated compound. For example, don't hyphenate *ma-trix* in *dot-matrix*. Finally, acronyms, proper nouns, and addresses are seldom hyphenated.

There are two ways to hyphenate in Word: You can either enter hyphens manually or choose the Hyphenate command from the Document menu.

Types of Hyphens

Word allows you to enter three types of hyphens: normal, nonbreaking, and optional. (You can also enter en and em dashes; these are discussed in the next tip and in Chapter 4, "Writing and Editing Techniques.") Normal hyphens always appear in text and can fall at the end of a line, while nonbreaking hyphens always appear in text but cannot fall at the end of a line. Optional hyphens appear only when they fall at the end of a line. The hyphenation feature inserts optional hyphens into the words it divides.

Normal Hyphens

You enter a normal hyphen by pressing the hyphen, or minus, key (next to the = key). Word can break a line at a normal hyphen, as in the following:

They always thought he was a ne'er-do-
well, but he proved them wrong.

Nonbreaking Hyphens

You use a nonbreaking hyphen when you want to hyphenate two words but don't want Word to break them at the end of a line. You might use this type of hyphen in a hyphenated last name, such as *Smyth-Jones*, or to keep a unit such as an account number or other hyphenated number together on one line. To enter a nonbreaking hyphen, press Command- ~. The ~ character is called a *tilde*; the key is located in the upper left corner of the standard Mac Plus keyboard and to the left of the Spacebar on the Apple keyboard. Technically, you press Command- `; you don't press the Shift key. However, the tilde is easier to remember because it appears above a nonbreaking hyphen (⁓) when you choose Show ¶.

Optional Hyphens

You enter optional hyphens manually when you don't want to hyphenate text extensively, but simply want to fix a few problem lines, or when you want Word to break a word at a different point than it would on its own. To enter this type of hyphen, press Command- – (hyphen). Optional hyphens are normally invisible; unless Show ¶ is in effect, they appear only if Word breaks the hyphenated word at the end of a line.

Suppose, for example, that the word *countermeasure* occurs at the end of a line, and that the last four characters of the word will not fit within the indents you've set. Normally, the word would be dropped to the next line. With Word's built-in hyphenation feature, *countermeasure* would be broken as follows: *countermea-sure* . However, a more appropriate way to divide the word would be at the prefix: *counter-measure.*

This highlights an important property of Word's automatic hyphenation feature: It uses a set of rules to divide words at syllables—sometimes it divides a word at other than the ideal location. When in doubt, consult a style manual, such as *The Chicago Manual of Style* from the University of Chicago Press. Such manuals exhaustively explain the fine points of word division in the English language.

If, after hyphenating a document, you make changes to it so that some words that you hyphenated with an optional hyphen no longer occur at the end of lines, Word rejoins the words and does not display the hyphens. When you choose Show ¶, Word marks the location of each optional hyphen, whether at the end of a line or not, by a normal hyphen with a dot under it (-̣). If subsequent editing causes a word containing one of these special characters to again end a line, the word is broken at that point.

TIP

Other Kinds of Dashes
Some people use two hyphens together (--) to represent an em dash (—). This type of dash is often used to indicate a break in the flow of a sentence that isn't as extreme as that produced by parentheses. You can get this special character on your Mac keyboard by pressing Shift-Option- -(hyphen, or minus). Remember—if you want to use this character—that you leave no space on either side of the em dash.

Less common, an en dash is used to separate the beginning and end of a range, such as in *1988–91*, or in a compound, such as *Seattle–San Jose flight.* You enter this character by pressing Option- – (hyphen). Again, style manuals are good sources of information about the use of these special characters. Word treats both the em dash and the en dash as it does the normal hyphen.

Using Word's Hyphenation Feature

Word's hyphenation feature analyzes line lengths and splits words between syllables according to an internal set of rules. This set of rules is kept in a special file called Word Hyphenation. It breaks words by inserting optional hyphens, so if you edit the document or change the line lengths, the divided words are rejoined and the hyphen becomes invisible. Using the hyphenation feature is easy; you set the insertion point where you want to start hyphenating, or select a specific passage, and choose Hyphenate from the Document menu. A dialog box like the one shown in Figure 12-8 appears after a short delay as Word loads its hyphenation dictionary.

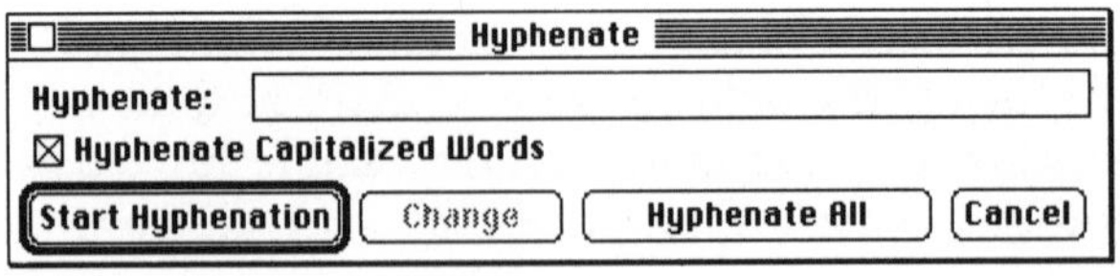

Hyphenate
Hyphenate:
☒ Hyphenate Capitalized Words
Start Hyphenation | Change | Hyphenate All | Cancel

Figure 12-8
The Hyphenate dialog box.

You can choose to have the program hyphenate words automatically, or you can review and verify each candidate for hyphenation. If you've set an insertion point within a paragraph, Word starts hyphenating at the beginning of that paragraph, not from the insertion point. Be sure to turn off Show ¶ first—Word doesn't compensate for the widths of characters that are visible only when Show ¶ is on, including the optional hyphen itself.

Automatic Hyphenation

To hyphenate words automatically, click the Hyphenate All button if you've set an insertion point, or the Hyphenate Selection button if you've selected some text. You need do nothing until the hyphenation process is complete. While Word is hyphenating, it pauses each time it inserts an optional hyphen so that you can watch the progress. When the word is hyphenated, the part before the hyphen moves to the end of the preceding line.

If you set the insertion point anywhere but at the beginning of the document, Word presents a dialog box when it reaches the end of the document and asks if you want to start over from the beginning. It's a good idea to look over the document to be sure you agree with the way words are divided.

You can change a hyphen in one word by double-clicking on the word, choosing the Hyphenate command, and clicking Hyphenate Selection. Word presents a dialog box stating that it has hyphenated the word. However, for the hyphenation to work properly, the word you selected should be the first word on the line, or else no part of the hyphenated word will move to the end of the preceding line.

You can also manually delete the existing optional hyphen; simply select it and press the Backspace key. If you edited or otherwise changed the line lengths, you can see the hyphen by turning on Show ¶. You can then enter an optional hyphen in a different place by placing the insertion point where you want the hyphen and pressing Command- – (hyphen).

Verifying Hyphenation

To verify each word before it is hyphenated, click the Start Hyphenation button. When Word finds a candidate for hyphenation, it displays it in the Hyphenate dialog box, with hyphens separating the syllables. Word highlights the hyphen it proposes to use, and in the document it highlights the hyphen that would split the word.

You'll want to pay careful attention to the dotted vertical line which appears in the Hyphenate field. (See Figure 12-9.) This line indicates where the word would break on the line if the rules for breaking between syllables were ignored. Adding optional hyphens to the right of the dotted line isn't helpful, because the word would still be too long to fit on the line.

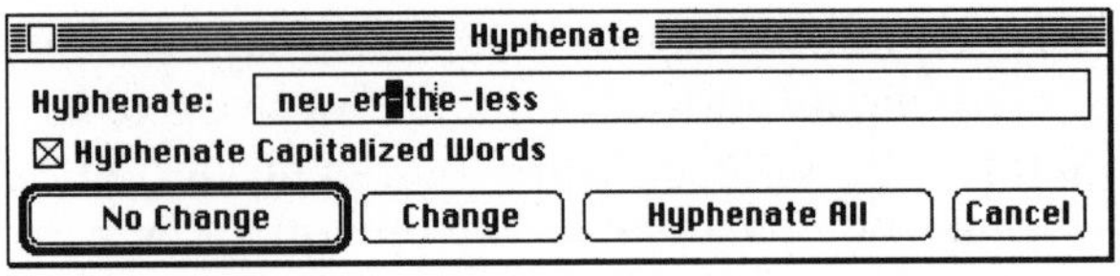

Hyphenate

Hyphenate: nev-er-the-less

☒ Hyphenate Capitalized Words

No Change | Change | Hyphenate All | Cancel

Figure 12-9
A candidate for hyphenation in the Hyphenate dialog box.

Once Word has displayed a candidate for hyphenation, you have several alternatives:

- ❑ Not hyphenate the word at all by clicking the No Change button (or pressing the Return key).
- ❑ Accept the suggested hyphenation by clicking the Change button.
- ❑ Choose one of the other hyphen points by clicking on it and then clicking the Change button.
- ❑ Choose an entirely new hyphenation point (one not shown by Word) by setting an insertion point between any two letters. After doing this, click the Change button.
- ❑ To stop hyphenation at any point, click the Cancel button.

Skipping Capitalized Words

Words in which the first letter or every letter is capitalized are usually not hyphenated. For example, proper nouns, such as names of persons or companies, are usually not hyphenated. It's also considered bad form to hyphenate the first word in a sentence or the last word in a paragraph. Acronyms should not be hyphenated unless absolutely necessary.

You can skip over capitalized words by turning off the Hyphenate Capitalized Words option (it's normally on) before you begin hyphenating. If you want to consider hyphenating capitalized words, leave the option checked and then review each candidate.

Searching for and Removing Hyphens

Unhyphenating a document is more difficult than hyphenating it. There is no "unhyphenate" command, unless you choose Undo Hyphenate immediately after you hyphenate a word. Sometimes, however, you need to remove both optional and nonbreaking hyphens for any of these reasons:

- ❑ To conform to a certain format, such as when changing from a justified and hyphenated format to one that is left aligned and ragged right.
- ❑ If you decide that your document is too heavily hyphenated and you want to remove some of the hyphens.
- ❑ To make a Word document usable by some other word processor.

For an example of the last reason, suppose that you saved a document having optional and nonbreaking hyphens as a Text Only file and then opened the file in MacWrite. Each optional or nonbreaking hyphen would appear as a square, signifying an undefined character, as shown in Figure 12-10. The same thing happens when you open Word documents with other Macintosh word processors.

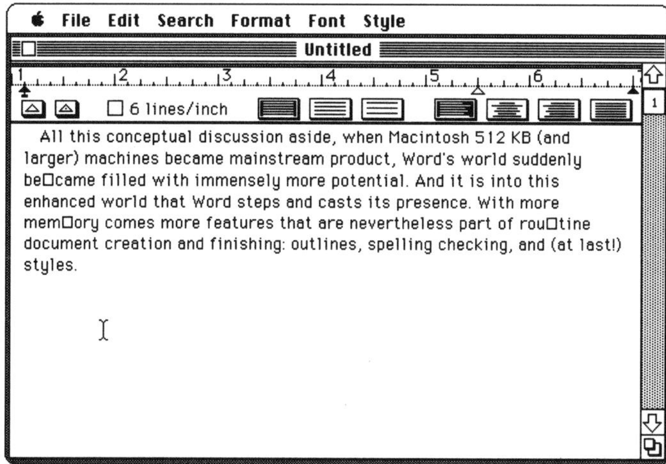

Figure 12-10
Optional hyphens as they appear in MacWrite.

You can use Word's search-and-replace feature to remove optional and nonbreaking hyphens. To start, position the insertion point at the beginning of the document. Then do the following:

1. Choose Change from the Search menu.
2. To remove optional hyphens, enter ^ - in the Find What field (the caret—Shift-6 —and the hyphen character). If you prefer, you can specify the ASCII equivalent of the optional hyphen by entering ^*31*. To remove nonbreaking hyphens, use ^ ~. (The ASCII equivalent would be ^*30*.)
3. Leave the Change To field empty.
4. Click the Start Search or Change All button, depending on whether you want to verify each change or have Word change every occurrence automatically.

Word finds all optional or nonbreaking hyphens and replaces them with nothing, thereby closing each hyphenated word.

■ *Repagination, Page Breaks, and Page Layout*

When you enter text and copy graphics into a Word document, the result is similar to a long scroll of paper. Most people use the vertical scroll bar to move up and down in a document, either a line at a time by clicking the scroll arrows, or one or more pages at a time by dragging the scroll box. Yet when you print the document, Word divides it into pages so that the text flows from the bottom of one page to the top of the next. The process of breaking a document into pages is called pagination.

Word paginates a document by adding up the line lengths, the point sizes of the text, the height of the graphics, the dimensions of the margins, and so on—a nearly endless list of factors—and calculating how much fits on each page. This calculation takes time. If Word repaginated dynamically, that is, every time you added text or made a formatting change, the amount of recalculation needed to handle the range of formatting features Word offers would cause an unacceptable degradation in performance. Therefore, Word repaginates only when necessary, as in the following instances:

- ❏ When you choose the Print or Print Merge commands. Word must do a repagination to generate an image for each page.
- ❏ When you choose Page Preview from the File menu. Word can't display the image of a page unless it repaginates the document up to the point where you chose the Page Preview command.
- ❏ When you choose Table of Contents or Index from the Document menu. Both these commands need the correct page numbers of the headings or index references in the document.
- ❏ When you choose Repaginate from the Document menu.

The page breaks that Word creates when repaginating are called automatic page breaks, and each appears as a light dotted line, as shown in Figure 12-11. When Word breaks the text into pages, each element falls on the page at the point determined by the dimensions of all previous elements combined. This arrangement is called the page layout. If Word's page layout is not to your liking, you can predetermine the position of the elements in a document in several ways:

- ❏ You can set the Page Break Before paragraph format for a paragraph that is to begin a new page. This is helpful when you want the title of a section to appear at the top of a page, especially when you are using styles to format the heads in a document.
- ❏ You can set the New Page, Odd Page, or Even Page formats for a section. This is good for starting a chapter in a book or an article in a magazine at the top of a new page, or for placing a large table on a page by itself.

- You can force a page break by clicking the insertion point where you want the page to end and pressing Shift-Enter. Word displays a manual page break as a heavy dotted line, as shown in Figure 12-11. To delete a manual page break, select it and press the Backspace key.
- You can force page breaks in Page Preview and convert an automatic page break to a manual one, but only for one-column text.

You can't delete automatic page breaks by selecting and deleting them, but you can "move" them by setting a manual page break earlier in the text. Word then recalculates automatic page breaks from the start of the new page.

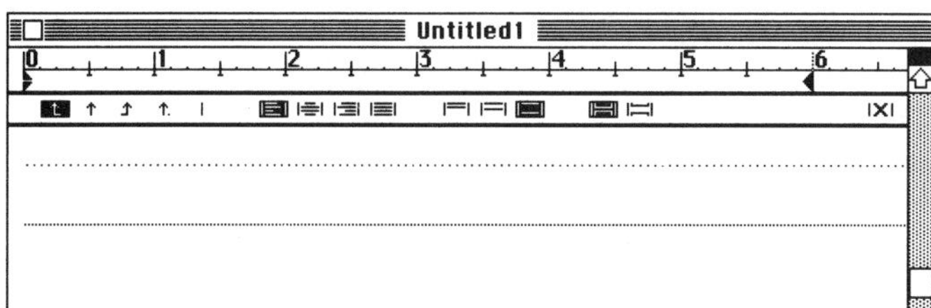

Figure 12-11
Types of page breaks, which appear on screen as dotted lines.

If you alter the text or insert manual page breaks, the length of some or all of the pages is affected. When you repaginate the document, Word places new automatic page breaks where appropriate but leaves your manual page breaks intact.

Word displays the current page and section number (if your document has more than one section) in the status area in the lower left corner of the document window. After repagination, these numbers appear in boldface and change as you scroll through the document. Word displays the number of the top line in the window. If you've made changes since the last repagination, the page numbers are dimmed, but you can still use them as an approximation (useful for traveling through the document).

TIP

Full Repagination
As was mentioned earlier, many calculations must be done to determine the size of the elements in a document and where the page breaks should occur. In order to repaginate as quickly as possible, Word skips any paragraphs that haven't changed since the last repagination. This occasionally leads to problems if you changed printers or if a document specifies a font that's not installed in your System file when you print the document. You can suspect an inaccurate repagination if page breaks seem to be in the wrong places or if lines are missing or overlap either in Page Preview or on the printed page.

To tell Word to leave no stone unturned (or not skip any paragraphs) in its recalculation of page breaks, press the Shift key as you choose the Repaginate command.

The Page Preview Command

Page Preview allows you to audition the page as it will appear on paper, manually set page breaks, and even adjust the margins. To audition a document from the beginning, click at the start of the text and choose Page Preview from the File menu. You'll see small versions of the first two pages of your document, like the screen shown in Figure 12-12. Each page is scaled proportionally to the paper size specified in the Page Setup dialog box.

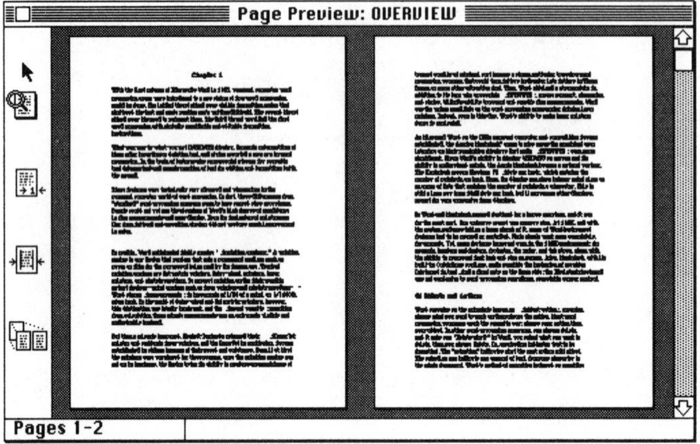

Figure 12-12
The Page Preview screen.

You cannot edit the document while in Page Preview, and most of the commands are inaccessible. You can display other pages in the document by using the vertical scroll bar. If you turned on the Facing Pages option in the Page Setup dialog box, the pages scroll two at a time, so the left page is always an even-numbered page and the right page is always odd-numbered. The four icons on the left of the window let you manipulate the document. These will be discussed in a moment.

If you need to check the page layout for an entire document, possibly setting a few manual page breaks, do so with Page Preview. With Page Preview, the document is repaginated up to the page displayed and no further. If the document is a large one, you can both repaginate it and check the layout by starting at the beginning and scrolling through it page by page.

You can return to Document view by clicking in the window's close box or by choosing the Page Preview command again. When you do this, you are returned to the last page you displayed in Page Preview. This feature also works in reverse. If you want to preview a specific page, you can scroll there in Document view and then choose the Page Preview command.

The following sections describe the icons on the left side of the Page Preview window.

The Magnifier Icon

Clicking the Magnifier icon turns the pointer into a magnifying glass. When you position the Magnifier on one of the pages and click, Word zooms in on that portion of the page, displaying it full size. Use the vertical and horizontal scroll bars to see different parts of the page. To zoom back out again, double-click anywhere in the window, or click the Page View icon, which replaces the Magnifier icon and looks like overlapping sheets of paper. If you double-click the Magnifier icon, Word zooms in on the upper left corner of the first page containing text in the display.

Actually, the icon isn't really necessary, because you can also zoom in on a portion of a page by moving the pointer to that location and double-clicking. Double-click again to zoom back out.

The Page Number Icon

Clicking the Page Number icon lets you add page numbers to the document. Click the icon (the pointer turns into a 1 with arrows on either side), and click on the location where you want the number to appear. The number is placed in that location on all pages. You can see the measurements corresponding to its location by displaying the Section dialog box. To see the position of the page number in Page Preview as you move it into place, hold down the mouse as you drag the page-number pointer. The current position appears in the status box.

The type of number used is determined by the Page Number options in the Section dialog box, and the automatic style named *page number* governs the character formats of the page numbers.

You can also include the page number in a header or footer, as described in the previous chapter. There is no relationship between the page numbers you specify in Page Preview and ones placed in the header or footer.

The Margins Icon

When you click the Margins icon, guidelines for these page elements appear on the currently selected page. Click in the facing page to move the guidelines there. Figure 12-13 shows the various types of guidelines displayed. By dragging the guidelines you can change the position of the top, bottom, right, and left margins, automatic and manual page breaks, the header, and the footer. You can also change the position of the page number if you've added one. The procedures for adjusting these will be described in a moment.

The One-Page Display Icon

Clicking the One-Page Display icon displays only one page at a time. Click it again to return to the two-page display. If you press the Shift key while clicking this icon, the page appears on the left side of the screen.

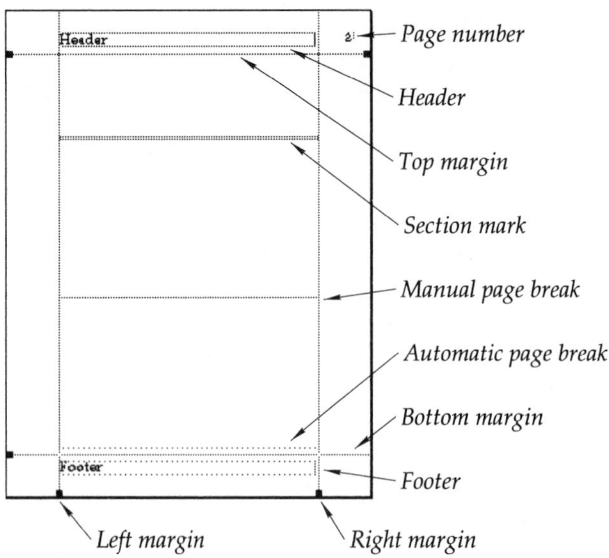

Figure 12-13
Guidelines showing elements that can be moved after you click the Margins icon.

Working in Page Preview

The Page Preview feature is the most straightforward and easiest way to adjust the placement of margins, page breaks, headers, footers, and page numbers in a document. It's not easy to create an extremely accurate design with it, however, especially on the small screen of the Mac Plus or Mac SE. You can see this when you click the Margins icon and drag an object—the current position displayed in the status box changes by jumps depending on the current unit of measure. Therefore, Page Preview is most helpful when you are setting up a design for a document or when you don't have stringent requirements for the accuracy of a design.

Adjusting Margins

To move one of the margins in Page Preview, simply click the Margins icon and drag one of the four margins by its handle (the little black box at the end of the margin guideline). Word displays in the status box the current position of the object you're dragging; the unit of measure is the one specified in the Preferences dialog box.

If you change the margins, the effect of the alteration won't appear until you either click the Margins icon again or click anywhere outside that page. The reason for this is that, again, it takes a little time to recalculate the position of each element on the page, and updating the screen every time you make an adjustment would slow down the program. If you click the close box before updating the screen, the changes you made will still take effect.

If you change the left or right margin after you hyphenate the document, you will probably have to rehyphenate it. The margin change affects the entire document. You see the new margin measurement in the document formats when you display the Page Setup dialog box.

Adjusting Headers and Footers

To move the header or footer, simply click the Margins icon (you don't have to do this again if the guidelines are already displayed), place the pointer over the header or footer, and drag it to the new position. When you're done, click outside the page to update the screen.

Even though there seems to be a little horizontal play when you drag the header and footer, you can change only the vertical placement. In addition, the range of vertical movement for the header (for instance) is stopped by the top margin, unless you have set a negative top margin in the Page Setup dialog box. If you have, you can move the header the full height of the page, or even into the area occupied by the footer at the bottom of the page. The Header/Footer options in the Section dialog box reflect the new positions and pertain only to the section in which you adjust the header.

Related to this is the behavior of headers and footers in Page Preview when you haven't set a negative margin in the Page Setup dialog box and the header is more than a few lines deep. When you switch to Page Preview and click the Margins icon, you'll see that the outline for the header overlaps the body text. If you click on the header to adjust its position, it will pop up to a position over the body text, and you won't be able to move it back down into the text. (Usually you won't want to do this, but it can sometimes create an interesting effect.) Hold the Shift key down as you drag the header down into the body text. This also has the effect of automatically entering a negative margin in the Page Setup dialog box. To reverse the effect, temporarily leave Page Preview, open the Page Setup dialog box, and remove the minus sign preceding the number in the top margin field.

As you drag the header or footer, the status area displays its vertical position. For the header, the measurement shown is the distance from the header to the top of the page. For the footer, the measurement shown is the distance from the footer to the bottom of the page.

Adjusting the Page Number

To create a page number on a given page, you must either click the Page Number icon and place the number somewhere on the page, double-click it to put the page number at the default position, or specify page numbering in the Section dialog box. To change the position of the page number, click the Margins icon and drag the page number to the new position. Also, if the document contains more than one section, the new position you set affects only that section. To find the precise position of the page number, place the insertion point in that section and look in the Page Numbering group of the Section dialog box. To remove the page number, drag its icon off the page.

Working with Page Breaks

Page Preview really shines when you have already set the margins, the line lengths, and so on, and want to adjust the layout of each page before printing. Do this by scanning through the document and checking each page layout. An automatic page break appears as a light dotted line; a manual break appears as a darker dotted line. If you click the Margins icon, drag an automatic page break up into the page, and then click outside the page, the line becomes darker, indicating that it is now a manual page break. When you convert an automatic break to a manual break, it is as though you had pressed Shift-Enter at that point. When you return to Document view, the manual page break appears where you placed it in Page Preview.

To delete a manual page break, drag it into the bottom margin of the page. If you've set a manual break by pressing Shift-Enter in Document view, you'll see it in Page Preview.

Unfortunately, Word does not let you change the page breaks in a section that has more than one column of text. If you try to drag one of the automatic breaks in a multicolumn section, Word beeps and does nothing. When you have more than one column, pressing Shift-Enter starts a new column, not a new page, and you cannot set end-of-column breaks in Page Preview. If you find a multiple-column page that isn't to your liking, you can change the layout manually by setting a new column break as follows:

1. In Page Preview, zoom in to find the spot where you want the column to break, and then switch to Document view.
2. Click the insertion point at that spot, and press Shift-Enter.
3. Switch back to Page Preview to verify that the column break is now in the correct place.

■ *Printing*

Once your document is the way you want it, you're finally ready to print it. The first part of this section describes how to set print options for the ImageWriter. Following that are instructions for using the LaserWriter.

To print a document on any printer, choose Print from the File menu, check the current settings in the dialog box, and click OK. What happens next depends on whether you are sending files across AppleTalk or printing them on a printer cabled directly into your computer. (LaserWriters connected to Macs use AppleTalk cabling and connectors.) If AppleTalk is not active, a dialog box appears, giving you the option of pausing or canceling. Clicking Pause stops the printer (the action is not immediate) until you click the Resume button. Clicking Cancel stops the printer and resets it to the top of the next page so that it is ready for another document. If you are using AppleTalk, you see a dialog box showing the status of the print job. The message in this box will change as the job progresses.

Some options you set in the Print dialog box remain in effect until you change them (even if you quit Word), and others return to their default settings each time you print a document.

Options that return to a default	Options that remain until reset
Pages: All	Print Hidden Text
Copies: 1	Quality
Paper Feed: Automatic	Tall Adjusted

The following options appear in the Print dialog box regardless of the printer you have selected.

The Pages Options

The Pages options specify the text you want to print. Normally, the All option is selected, which causes the entire document to be printed. You can also choose to print only the selected text or only certain pages and sections.

To print a selection, first select the text you want printed. It can be as little as one character or as much as the entire document. Then choose the Print command, click Selection, and click OK to print. When you print a selection, no page numbers, headers, footers, or other elements that are not part of the body text are printed.

To print a range of pages or sections, first repaginate the document, if necessary. Jot down the beginning and ending pages or section numbers for the pages you want to print. (They are displayed in the status box.) Then choose the Print command and enter these numbers in the From and To fields. If your document is divided into sections with pages that are numbered separately, you should include both the page and section numbers for the range you want to print. Figure 12-14 shows some examples of page and section numbers you can enter. If you want to print from a particular page to the end of the document, leave the To field blank. If you want to print only one page, enter its number in both fields.

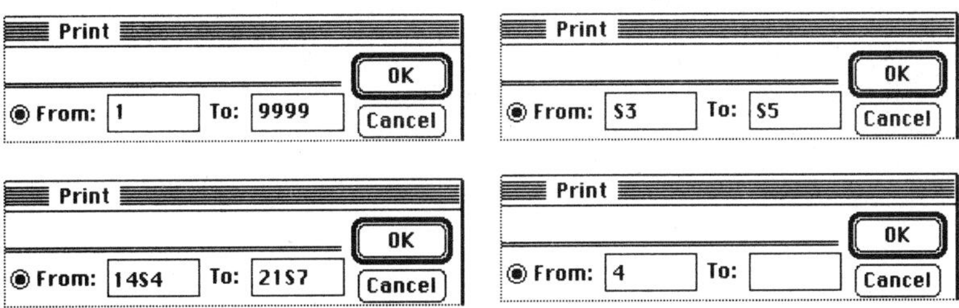

Figure 12-14
Sample range numbers for printing.

The Copies Option

The Copies option specifies the number of copies of the document to be printed. If you know you want three original copies of your document, it's faster to print them all at once rather than separately. Enter a number up to 99 in the Copies field. If you print on the LaserWriter, Word does not collate the copies but prints each page the specified number of times before moving on to the next. If you print on the ImageWriter, Word prints the entire document before printing the next copy.

The Paper Feed Options

You can tell Word to print nonstop from beginning to end or one page at a time. For nonstop printing in which paper is fed into the printer automatically, set the Automatic option. For page-at-a-time printing, when you need to hand-feed single sheets into the printer, click the Manual option. At the end of each page, a dialog box appears, telling you to insert the next sheet.

The Print Hidden Text Option

Characters formatted as hidden can be displayed or hidden independently on the screen and on paper. You can choose to print hidden text (PostScript commands, index entries, notes to yourself, and so on) by clicking the Print Hidden Text option. When hidden text is printed, it does not have the gray underline you see when you display it on the screen.

TIP

Printing Items That Are Not Documents
You can use the Print command to print Word style sheets, glossaries, and outlines as well as the contents of the screen. To print the style sheet for a document, choose the Styles or Define Styles command and then choose the Print command. You can get a full listing of the automatic styles by pressing the Shift key while choosing the Define Styles command. The automatic styles, each preceded by a bullet, print out with the others.

To print a glossary, choose the Glossary command and then choose Print. To print the outline for a document, choose the Outlining command and then choose Print. You can print the contents of the active window alone by pressing Shift-Command-4; to print the contents of the entire screen on an ImageWriter, press the Caps Lock key first. However, if you're trying to print the screen on a LaserWriter, press Shift-Command-3 instead to save a screen dump, and print the screen dump from a paint program such as MacPaint.

Printing with the ImageWriter

If you've already used the Chooser to select the ImageWriter printer driver, as described earlier, choosing the Print command displays the dialog box shown in Figure 12-15. For most printing tasks involving an ImageWriter loaded with continuous fanfold computer paper, you need only click OK to begin printing. Word prepares the document for printing and then, after a pause while Word creates a print file on disk, the printing commences. (Note that the program disk must have enough blank space on it to accommodate the print file generated by Word).

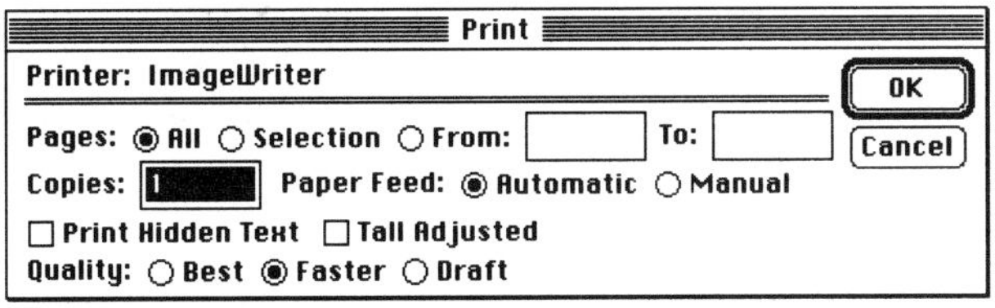

Print
Printer: ImageWriter [OK]
Pages: ◉ All ○ Selection ○ From: [ ] To: [ ] [Cancel]
Copies: [1] Paper Feed: ◉ Automatic ○ Manual
☐ Print Hidden Text ☐ Tall Adjusted
Quality: ○ Best ◉ Faster ○ Draft

Figure 12-15
The ImageWriter Print dialog box.

The following additional options appear in the Print dialog box when you choose the ImageWriter.

The Tall Adjusted Option

The Tall Adjusted option corrects the discrepancy between the horizontal resolution of the Mac's screen (72 dots per inch) and the horizontal resolution of the standard ImageWriter (80 dots per inch). (The Wide ImageWriter prints at 72 dots per inch.) This discrepancy is the reason why the size of inches in the Ruler changes when you switch to the ImageWriter after using the LaserWriter. Without the Tall Adjusted option, graphics that are round on the screen may print as ovals. With Tall Adjusted, a circle prints as a circle. Click the Tall Adjusted option whenever you must preserve the exact proportions of a graphic. This option works only in documents printed in the Tall orientation (the normal orientation).

You pay a slight price when you must use this option. With Tall Adjusted, text is squeezed slightly, although the effect is rarely noticeable. You will notice, however, that because Word can fit more text on a line, the line breaks may not be the same as they were with Tall Adjusted turned off. This can have a domino effect, throwing off paragraph and page breaks.

The Quality Options

You can select the quality of printing with the Best, Faster, and Draft options. Examples of each are shown in Figure 12-16.

- The Best option prints each character twice, giving the document a darker and neater appearance. If you have installed fonts that are twice the point size of those used in your document, Word uses these, compressing the pattern of bits that makes up each character into the point size you've chosen, which yields more detailed characters. Graphics, however, are printed in one pass.

- The Faster option is the standard setting; it prints text and graphics as they appear on the screen, but in only one pass. This option prints about twice as fast as the Best option does.
- The Draft option uses the font built into the ImageWriter to print your document, and it does not display fonts, graphics, or special paragraph formatting, such as lines and boxes. Different fonts, attributes, and point sizes affect the look of the print. (See Figure 12-16.) You get more reliable results in this mode when using a monospaced font, such as Seattle, Monaco, Courier, or Dover.

Best	Plain	Bold	Italic	Shadow	Underlined
Best	Plain	Bold	Italic	Shadow	Underlined
Best	Plain	Bold	Italic	Shadow	Underlined
Faster	Plain	Bold	Italic	Shadow	Underlined
Faster	Plain	Bold	Italic	Shadow	Underlined
Faster	Plain	Bold	Italic	Shadow	Underlined
Draft	Plain	Bold	Italic	Shadow	Underlined
Draft	Plain	Bold	Italic	Shadow	Underlined
Draft	Plain	Bold	Italic	Shadow	Underlined

Figure 12-16
Samples printed with the Best, Faster, and Draft options.

Using Shift-Page Setup to Set ImageWriter Printing Options

You may have noticed that the Page Setup dialog box isn't the standard printing dialog box offered by many Mac applications. The Page Setup dialog box in Word offers many options the standard one doesn't; the standard one offers a few items that Word doesn't. You can get to the standard dialog box by pressing the Shift key as you choose the Page Setup command. From the standard dialog box you can set the Computer Paper page size for paper on a Wide ImageWriter that is 11 inches tall and 15 inches wide. You can also set the 50% Reduction option, reducing the overall page image by 50 percent. Finally, you can set the No Gaps Between Pages option, if you need to print across the perforations between pages. You may have to reformat your document to make the best use of these options. The Tall Adjusted option is also offered in this dialog box, but it is duplicated by the same option in Word's Print dialog box, so you don't need to use it.

Printing with the LaserWriter

Apple's LaserWriter printer, probably more than any other factor, has fueled the development of high-powered word-processing programs such as Microsoft Word. Until the release of the Mac SE and the Mac II, it was said that the LaserWriter was the most powerful computer Apple made; it contains the same 68000 microprocessor as the Mac Plus but operates at a higher speed, has more internal programs (as well as fonts) stored in its 512 kilobytes of read-only memory (ROM), and has 1.5 megabytes of random-access memory (RAM). Now the newer LaserWriter Plus has even more fonts and more memory than the standard LaserWriter. The benefits of using a LaserWriter with Word are many:

- The LaserWriter prints at 300 dots per inch instead of 72 or 80. You get higher resolution text, clearer graphics, and faster text output.
- The fonts in the LaserWriter's ROM are stored in a form that makes use of this higher resolution. These fonts are registered with the International Typesetting Committee (ITC), which guarantees close conformity with the standard fonts having the same names as those used by traditional typesetters. If you format a document in any of the LaserWriter fonts, such as Times or Bookman, and then take the document to a type service bureau that has a PostScript-compatible printer, the typeset version will look very much like the LaserWriter version.
- With the LaserWriter, you can reduce or enlarge pages from 25 to 400 percent of the normal size. You can reduce a large document to fit on a small piece of paper. (An original document that is 22-by-22 inches is only 5.5-by-5.5 inches when reduced to 25 percent.)
- You can take advantage of all the benefits that PostScript offers—even if you don't know PostScript—because most of the newer graphics programs, such as Cricket Draw and Illustrator, are designed specifically to create high-quality images that can be printed only on PostScript printers. Appendix C, "Using PostScript," describes how you can insert PostScript graphics into your documents.

Since the LaserWriter's appearance, several other PostScript-compatible printers have been developed, such as the QMS-PS 800 and the Mergenthaler Linotronic 300. Although we cannot give specific recommendations for using each of these, the same issues that apply to the LaserWriter apply to most of them as well. For example, you use the LaserWriter driver to set options for PostScript-compatible printers, and many use the same fonts as the LaserWriter. The following discussion is oriented toward the LaserWriter, but it will also apply to the majority of PostScript printers.

What Happens When You Print on a LaserWriter

If you haven't already specified the LaserWriter as your printer, you should do so before setting the final margins and other document formats. Be sure that the LaserWriter is connected to the printer port of your Macintosh over AppleTalk. The LaserWriter printer driver (called LaserWriter) and the preparation program (called Laser Prep) must be in the System Folder. Choose the Chooser command, click the AppleTalk Active option, and select the LaserWriter icon. The names of the available printers are shown in the list box. Select the one you want, and then click the close box.

When you click OK in the Print dialog box, you see a dialog box showing the status of the print job and a message that the Mac is looking for the LaserWriter on AppleTalk. If nothing has been printed on that LaserWriter before, another message states that the printer is being initialized. This means that the Mac has sent the Laser Prep file to the LaserWriter. This file consists of a set of PostScript instructions that the computer inside the LaserWriter uses to decode subsequent printing commands coming from the Mac.

Once the LaserWriter is initialized, Word repaginates the document and converts it into a sequence of PostScript commands, which it transmits to the LaserWriter over AppleTalk. Word translates the elements on each page in a particular order, whether printing on the ImageWriter or the LaserWriter:

- ❑ PostScript (for the LaserWriter only).
- ❑ Header.
- ❑ Footer.
- ❑ Automatic page numbers.
- ❑ The body of the text. (If you're using line numbering in a paragraph, the paragraph is printed first, then the line numbers.)
- ❑ Footnotes.

Knowing this printing order is useful when you want to achieve special effects such as printing text over a graphic, or a header behind the body of the text in a document. For example, this is why we can put the gray tint behind the tip elements in this book.

The LaserWriter then transforms these PostScript commands (with the aid of the Laser Prep file) into a fine-grained bit-mapped image that is transferred to the paper in the form of small piles of black toner powder. The toner is fused to the paper, and the page rolls out for you to see.

Fonts

Three types of fonts are available to you when you print on a LaserWriter: bit-mapped fonts, the high-resolution fonts stored in the LaserWriter's ROM, and special high-resolution fonts stored in the Mac and downloaded to the LaserWriter when specified in one of your documents. The latter two types we can lump together under the category of PostScript fonts.

Bit-mapped fonts, also called screen fonts, are the fonts you see on the screen. Each character consists of a pattern of bits; there is a different pattern for each point size. You can use these fonts in documents printed on the LaserWriter, but printing is much slower because only the 12-point version of the font is sent to the printer, and it must scale that font to the point size specified in the document. In general, the quality of the text printed in a bit-mapped font is never as good as that achieved with the LaserWriter's own fonts. If you formatted text in a bit-mapped font, Word assumes that you did so unintentionally; therefore, the Font Substitution option in the LaserWriter Print dialog box is turned on by default. If you really want to print in a bit-mapped font on the LaserWriter, turn off the Font Substitution option.

The LaserWriter is most often used with its own internal fonts, such as Times, Palatino, and Symbol. This produces the fastest results because the fonts are built into the LaserWriter, and thus font information does not need to be transferred from the Mac to the printer. The Mac simply sends the commands to print the characters in the desired font and point size. A full page of text can be printed in less than 15 seconds.

Every font stored in the LaserWriter has a bit-mapped version, called its screen font, which you see on the screen while you're entering and formatting text in that font. If you've installed these fonts in your System file, you can use them to format a document even though a LaserWriter isn't attached to your Mac. You can print text formatted in one of these fonts on the ImageWriter as though it were any of the other bit-mapped fonts.

The third type of font is very much like the LaserWriter fonts, but the high-resolution patterns are stored in the Mac instead of the LaserWriter. These range from other ITC-registered fonts licensed by Adobe Systems to special-purpose and display fonts offered by companies such as Casady. These fonts are downloaded to the LaserWriter when needed. The downloaded font takes up memory in the LaserWriter, so you may find it impossible to print pages filled with complicated text and graphics if the LaserWriter runs out of memory.

TIP

Working with Fonts

You may have noticed that some character formats make text more difficult to read on the screen. Italics are an example of this—it often looks as if the space after an italicized word has disappeared, and it can be difficult to place the insertion point between characters correctly. Adobe Systems has released a set of screen fonts that are much easier to read.

Sometimes you need a special character that isn't available in any of the LaserWriter fonts. (Remember that you can use the Key Caps desk accessory to view the characters in a font.) You could search for the one character in the fonts offered by third-party suppliers. Instead, however, consider creating the character with a LaserWriter-compatible font editor, such as Fontographer from Altsys Corporation.

The LaserWriter Print Dialog Box

The Print dialog box you see when you choose the LaserWriter is different from the one displayed for the ImageWriter. (See Figure 12-17.) The additional options are as follows:

- Print Back to Front. Printing begins with the last page of the document and ends with the first. This is a little slower than printing front to back because Word must repaginate all the way to the end of the document before beginning to print. If your document has more than one section, specify both the starting page and section number, as in *1S1*.
- Cover Page. Prints a page identifying your document. For use when more than one Mac shares a single LaserWriter.
- Smoothing. Smooths the edges of bit-mapped graphics and fonts. This improves some graphics but blurs others. Printing is much slower with Smoothing turned on; it is on by default.
- Font Substitution. Allows the LaserWriter to substitute one of its internal fonts when it encounters a bit-mapped font in your document. Printing of text formatted in a bit-mapped font is faster when Font Substitution is on, but you may notice unsightly gaps between letters and words. Don't use a bit-mapped font on the LaserWriter unless you have a real need for it. This option is set by default.
- Reduce/Enlarge %. Lets you specify the amount by which printed material is to be reduced or enlarged. You can specify a number from 25 percent (one-fourth the size of the original you see on the screen) to 400 percent (four times the size of the original). After you have set a reduction factor other than 100 percent and printed the document, you can't change margins in Page Preview. Otherwise, the document acts just as it did before.
- Fractional Widths. This option causes Word to measure the widths of characters in LaserWriter fonts in a different way and improves the spacing of text when printed on the LaserWriter. When you set this option, you may notice that the right edge of justified text on the screen is no longer even with the right indent. This happens because the screen character widths and the printed character widths are now slightly different.

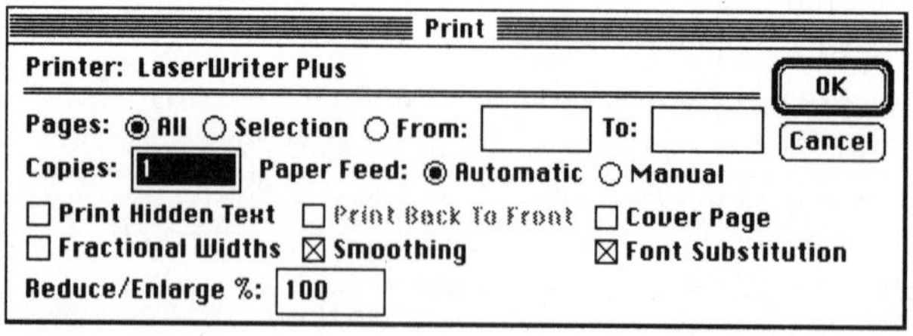

Figure 12-17
The LaserWriter Print dialog box.

The Standard LaserWriter Page Setup Dialog Box

When you press the Shift key and choose the Page Setup command, Mac's standard Page Setup dialog box appears instead of Word's. Version 4.0 of the LaserWriter driver (which comes with Finder version 5.5 and later system files) presents the dialog box shown in Figure 12-18. Every feature in this box is also in the Word Page Setup dialog box, except the Faster Bitmap Printing option, which you can use to make bit-mapped graphics print more quickly.

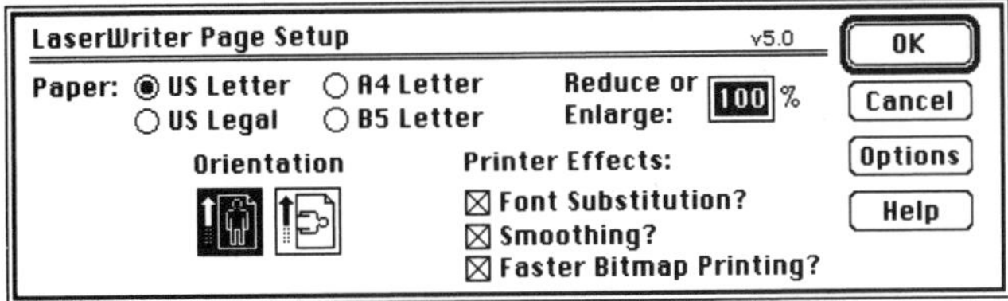

Figure 12-18
The standard LaserWriter Page Setup dialog box.

If you click the Options button, you see a dialog box like the one shown in Figure 12-19. The features in this dialog box are most useful when your Word document contains bit-mapped graphic images that you want to print with as few distortions as possible.

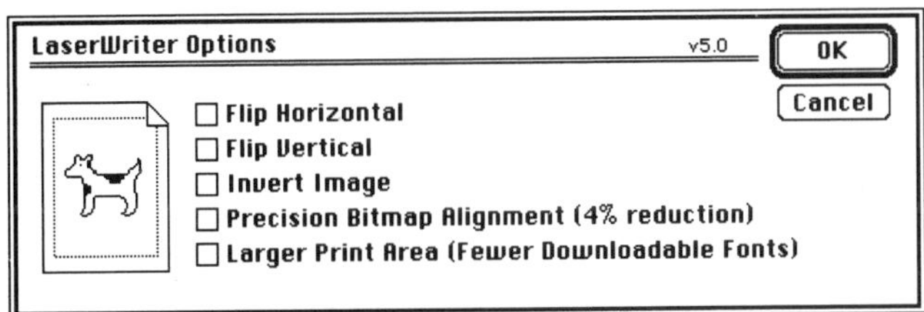

Figure 12-19
The LaserWriter Options dialog box.

The following options come with version 4.0 of the LaserWriter driver:

- Flip Horizontal and Flip Vertical let you print a graphic upside down or reverse an image.
- Invert Image turns white to black and black to white. This is handy as a special effect or if you want to create a negative image (for example, to create an image for a silkscreen).
- Precision Bitmap Alignment may be the most useful option in this dialog box. Almost every bit-mapped image created by scanners or paint programs on the Macintosh has a pixel density of 72 dots per inch. The LaserWriter prints at 300 dots per inch. Unfortunately, 72 doesn't divide into 300 evenly—if you used 4 LaserWriter dots to represent each Mac screen pixel, you'd get 288 dots per inch.

There are two ways to deal with this inconsistency. One is to shrink the image a little (to 96 percent, which is 288 divided by 300) and retain the 4-to-1 pixel-mapping ratio. This leads to a 4 percent misalignment with the other elements on a page; the larger the bit-mapped graphic, the larger the error. The second way is to scale up the bit-mapped image by an extra 4 percent so that the dimensions of the image remain accurate and the image stays aligned. However, because the pixel-mapping ratio is not exactly 4 to 1, this method produces distortions in the printed image of the bit-mapped graphic—some Mac pixels are 4 LaserWriter pixels square, some are 4 by 5 LaserWriter pixels, some are 5 by 4, and some are 5 by 5.

The Precision Bitmap Alignment option solves this problem by scaling down everything in the document to 96 percent, including the text elements around the graphic. In this way, the graphics retain the 4-to-1 ratio and everything remains aligned.

- The Larger Print Area option allows you to change the way in which the LaserWriter manages its memory. Normally, the printer reserves some memory for downloaded fonts. If you're printing very complicated pages with many elements and aren't downloading fonts, you can claim some of this memory so that the LaserWriter can store larger images. This can be useful for printing onto legal-sized paper when feeding it manually, even though you have the standard-sized paper tray loaded in the LaserWriter.

Printing with a Serial Printer

Serial daisy-wheel printers and some serial dot-matrix printers can't be used to print sideways, nor can they print at anything but 100 percent.

When using the SerialPrinter driver, you have your choice of the following printer types: AppleDaisy, Brother (any daisy-wheel model), Diablo 630, NEC 7710, and Typewriter. The AppleDaisy, Diablo, Brother, and NEC printer resources are used with specific daisy-wheel printers. The Typewriter driver is generic and can be used with almost any serial dot-matrix or daisy-wheel printer connected to the Macintosh.

If the SerialPrinter driver is not already in the System Folder, copy it there, along with the desired printer resource. Be sure that the Dover font is installed in the System file—Word uses it to represent the appearance of a letter-quality printer. Choose Chooser from the Apple menu. Click the SerialPrinter icon, and select the serial printer you want from the list. If your printer isn't listed, select the Typewriter option. Next, click the Settings button. Choose the pitch of the printer, the transmission baud rate (usually 9600), and the printer port; then click OK.

Finally, choose the Preferences command, and select the Display As Printed option. This option is useful when you want to print a standard Word document on a letter-quality printer (including, for example, graphics and formats not reproducible by the letter-quality printer, such as the outline and shadow character formats or the border paragraph formats). With this option set, you'll see only the formats the printer is able to reproduce, such as boldface and underlining.

Daisy-wheel printers cannot duplicate the various fonts and point sizes of the Macintosh, so the finished document will have only one font and one size. When the SerialPrinter driver is specified, Word displays your text on the screen in a typewriterlike font, which you cannot change unless you turn off the Display As Printed option (in the Preferences dialog box). It's best to leave this option on, however, because it gives you a more accurate assessment of how the document will look when printed on a serial printer.

The bold and underline formats print correctly on this type of printer. The others are ignored. If your document contains graphics or graphic elements (such as lines or boxes), they, too, are ignored during printing.

Points to Remember

- The document format domain represents the fourth and most global level of formatting. This domain controls the dimensions of the paper on which the document is printed, the location of the page margins, the default tab stop interval, whether even-numbered and odd-numbered pages are treated differently, where footnotes are printed and how they are numbered, whether widows should be allowed at the top or bottom of a page, and whether the document is part of a series. You set these formats through the Page Setup dialog box and in Page Preview.
- Word repaginates a document automatically when you choose the Print, Print Merge, Table of Contents, Index, or Page Preview commands. (With the last of these, it repaginates only as far as the page being viewed.) You can tell Word to repaginate the document by choosing Repaginate from the Document menu. Once a document has been repaginated, the page and section numbers in the status box are not dimmed.
- Repagination affects only the paragraphs that have changed since the last pagination. If you need to repaginate the entire document, including paragraphs that have not changed, press the Shift key while you choose the Repaginate command. This may be necessary if you have chosen a different printer, for example.
- Automatic page breaks appear as light dotted lines in the document. Manual page breaks appear as darker dotted lines. Word does not change manual page breaks when it repaginates a document.
- In addition to entering manual page breaks, you can set the Page Break Before format for paragraphs that must begin at the top of a new page and the New Page format for sections that must begin a new page.
- Word uses three types of hyphens. Normal hyphens always appear in text and can fall at the end of a line. Nonbreaking hyphens always appear in text but cannot fall at the end of a line. Optional hyphens appear only when they fall at the end of a line. The hyphenation feature inserts optional hyphens into the words it divides.
- Margin positions that you set in Page Preview appear in the Page Setup dialog box. Positions you set in Page Preview for the page number, header, and footer appear in the Section dialog box.
- The Chooser desk accessory tells Word the type of printer to be used. The printer you choose may affect the appearance of your document, so it's best to choose the printer before final formatting.
- Word supports the ImageWriter, LaserWriter, and certain serial printers. You can display and set special Print options by pressing the Shift key when you choose Print. If the printer requires its own Page Setup options as well, press Shift when you choose the Page Setup command. Choose the Print command again to start printing. Certain features of an unsupported printer's features may conflict with Word's page layout.

Printer	Driver files
ImageWriter	ImageWriter.
LaserWriter	Laser Prep, LaserWriter.
SerialPrinter	SerialPrinter and a resource for the specific printer you're using.
Typewriter	A generic printer resource.

■ *Techniques*

Choosing a printer

Choose Chooser from the Apple menu. The dialog box lists the printer drivers in the System Folder. Click Active or Inactive to indicate whether or not your printer is connected to AppleTalk. Click the icon for your printer type; the box to the right of the icons asks for specific printer information:

- ❑ ImageWriter: Click the ImageWriter icon, and select a printer port, or select an AppleTalk ImageWriter to specify that.
- ❑ LaserWriter : Click the LaserWriter icon, and select the one you want to use.
- ❑ SerialPrinter: Click the SerialPrinter icon, specify the serial printer to be used. Click Settings, and then choose the pitch that matches the print wheel, the baud rate setting, and the printer port.

Click the close box when you are done.

Page Layout

The Page Setup Dialog Box

Paper options	Specify a standard paper size for the document. When you click an option, its dimensions appear in the Width and Height edit fields, and the proportions of the page in Page Preview change correspondingly.	
	Inches	Centimeters
US Letter	8.5 x 11	21.6 x 27.95
US Legal	8.5 x 14	21.6 x 35.55
A4 Letter	8.27 x 11.69	21 x 29.7
International Fanfold	8.25 x 12	20.95 x 30.5

Orientation options	
Tall	The default option, orients the page in the usual way, sometimes called portrait orientation.
Wide	Rotates the page by 90 degrees to print each line across the length of the page; this is sometimes called landscape orientation.
Paper Width and Height	Display the dimensions of the paper size specified. Enter any dimension you want, to a maximum of 22 inches.
Margins option group	Determines the area on the printed page occupied by the body text. Enter measurements from the edge of the page in inches, points, or centimeters.
Top	Sets the top margin. Enter a negative number to set a fixed margin that does not move to accommodate the header.
Bottom	Sets the bottom margin. Enter a negative number to set a fixed margin that does not move to accommodate the footer.
Left	Sets the left margin.
Right	Sets the right margin.
Facing Pages	Causes even-numbered and odd-numbered pages to be treated differently. When this option is set, Word replaces the Open Header and Open Footer commands with Open Even Header, Open Odd Header, Open Even Footer, and Open Odd Footer commands; page numbers are placed on the left on even pages and on the right on odd pages; and bars assigned to paragraphs are placed on the left on even pages and on the right on odd ones.
Gutter	Specifies extra margin space on the right edge of even (left-hand) pages and on the left edge of odd (right-hand) pages. Enter the measurement in inches, points, or centimeters. Dimmed unless Facing Pages is set.

Default Tab Stops	Sets default tab stops for the document. Word represents these tab stops by inverted Ts in the Ruler. These tab stops are overridden by any tabs you set for a paragraph. They remain beyond the rightmost paragraph tab stop you set.
Widow Control	Prevents the last line of a paragraph from appearing alone at the top of a page and the first line of a paragraph from appearing alone at the bottom of a page.
Footnotes At options	Determine the placement of footnotes.
Bottom of Page	Prints each footnote at the bottom of the page on which its reference appears.
Beneath Text	Prints each footnote immediately beneath the last paragraph on the page on which its reference appears.
Endnotes	Prints accumulated footnotes at the end of the first section for which the Include Endnotes option is set in the Section dialog box, or at the end of the document if none of the sections have this option set.
Restart Numbering	Restarts footnote numbering at 1 at the beginning of each page or each section, depending on which Footnotes At option is set. If this option is not set, Word numbers all footnotes consecutively.
Start Footnote Numbers At	Specifies the starting footnote number for the document. This is useful when you are chaining documents with the Next File edit field.
Start Page Numbers At	Specifies the starting page number for the document. When you are chaining documents with the Next File edit field, leave this field blank.
Start Line Numbers At	Specifies the starting line number for the document. This is useful when you are chaining documents with the Next File edit field.

Next File	If you want to print a series of documents or compile an index or table of contents for a series of documents, enter the name of the next document in this edit field.
Buttons	
OK	Implements the selected formats and closes the dialog box.
Cancel	Closes the dialog box without implementing the formats.
Set Default	Stores the current formats set in the Page Setup dialog box in the Word Settings file. These formats then become the default for new documents. This option does not apply the formats to the current document.

Preview a document

❶ Scroll to the page at which you want to begin previewing the document.

❷ Choose Page Preview from the File menu.

❸ Click in the vertical scroll bar to display other pages.

❹ When done, click the close box, or choose Page Preview again.

Magnify part of a page in Page Preview

❶ Click the Magnifier icon, place the pointer where you want to magnify, and click again; or double-click, without using the icon.

❷ Use the vertical and horizontal scroll bars to see other parts of the page.

❸ Click the Page View icon (the top icon), or double-click anywhere in the window to zoom back out.

Switch to a one-page display in Page Preview

❶ Click the One-Page Display icon (the lowest icon). The display changes to show one page instead of two.

❷ Click the icon again to return to the two-page display.

Add page numbers in Page Preview

❶ Click the Page Number icon.

❷ Position the number on the page, and click to set the position. A page number is added to all pages.

Adjust the page margins in Page Preview

1. Click the Margins icon. Margin guidelines appear on the current page.
2. Drag the appropriate margin by its handle (the black box at the end of the margin) to the new location.
3. Click anywhere outside the page to update the screen.

The change affects the entire document, not only the page you've altered. You must update the screen before returning to Document view for the change to take effect.

Position a header, footer, or page number in Page Preview

1. Click the Margins icon. The elements you can move are shown surrounded by a dotted box.
2. Drag the element you want to move to its new position. The status box displays the current position as you drag it.
3. Click anywhere outside the page to update the screen. You must update the screen before returning to Document view for the change to take effect.

A change to a header or footer affects only the section containing the page you've altered. A change to the page number affects the entire document.

Insert or move a manual page break in Page Preview

1. Display the page to be changed.
2. Click the Margins icon.
3. Drag the automatic page break from the bottom of the page to the new location. The automatic page break becomes a manual page break.

The page is updated when you release the mouse button. This works only in single-column sections.

Remove a manual page break in Page Preview

1. Display the page to be changed.
2. Click the Margins icon.
3. Drag the page break into the bottom margin.

The screen is updated when you release the mouse button.

Insert a manual page break in Document view

1. Set the insertion point where you want the page to break.
2. Press Shift-Enter.

Remove a manual page break in Document view

❶ Select the page break.

❷ Press the Backspace key.

Hyphenation

Enter a normal hyphen

❶ Press the – (hyphen) key.

Enter a nonbreaking hyphen

❶ Press Command- ~. The character is displayed as ⁓.

Enter an optional hyphen

❶ Press Command- – (hyphen). The character is invisible unless it falls at the end of a line or Show ¶ is on. Then it appears as ¬.

Hyphenate the document and verify each hyphenated word

❶ Set the insertion point at the beginning of the document, and choose Hyphenate from the Document menu.

❷ To ignore capitalized words, turn off Hyphenate Capitalized Words.

❸ Click Start Hyphenation.

❹ For each candidate Word proposes for hyphenation, click No Change to leave the word unhyphenated; click Change to accept the hyphen Word suggests (the one that is highlighted).

To specify a different division for the word, click on another hyphen or between any two letters and then click Change. Do not place the division point after the vertical dotted line through the word.

Hyphenate the document automatically

❶ Set the insertion point at the beginning of the document, and choose Hyphenate from the Document menu.

❷ To ignore capitalized words, turn off Hyphenate Capitalized Words.

❸ Click Hyphenate All.

Hyphenate selected text only

❶ Select the text to be hyphenated, and choose Hyphenate from the Document menu.

❷ Click Hyphenate Selection to hyphenate the text automatically, or click Start Hyphenation to verify each word before it is hyphenated.

Printing

The Print dialog box: Word's normal options

Pages options	
All	Prints the entire document.
Selection	Prints the currently selected text. No headers, footers, page numbers, and so forth will be printed.
From and To	Set a range of pages. Indicate a section number as well if the document is divided into sections.
Copies	Indicates the number of copies to print.
Paper Feed options	
Automatic	Indicates that the paper is fed automatically.
Manual	Specifies that you will be feeding individual sheets by hand. Word stops between pages and presents a dialog box asking you to insert the next sheet.
Print Hidden Text	Prints text formatted as hidden text regardless of whether you've set the Show Hidden Text option in the Preferences dialog box.

The Print dialog box: ImageWriter options

Tall Adjusted	Prints graphics in correct proportion. Can be used only with the Tall orientation.
Quality	Specify the quality of the printing. The better the quality, the slower the printing. Best prints at highest quality, compacting fonts at twice the point size you've chosen into that point size. Faster prints at the standard quality. Draft prints at the lowest quality. Draft mode does not display fonts, graphics, or paragraph borders.

The Print dialog box: LaserWriter options

Print Back To Front	Prints documents from the last page to the first so that they appear in order in the output tray.
Cover Page	Prints a cover page identifying your document.
Fractional Widths	Prints text using the printer's internal width measurements, often producing better-looking letterspacing.
Smoothing	Smooths the edges of bit-mapped graphics and fonts.
Font Substitution	Permits the substitution of appropriate LaserWriter fonts for Macintosh screen fonts.
Reduce/Enlarge % edit field	Reduces or enlarges text and graphics on a page. Enter a percentage from 25 to 400.

The Page Setup dialog box: Extended LaserWriter options

These options are provided in version 4.0 and later of the LaserWriter driver. Press the Shift key while choosing the Page Setup command to see these options.

Flip Horizontal	Reverses the page image so that it prints backwards.
Flip Vertical	Prints the page image upside down.
Invert Image	Prints the page image as a negative. (Black is white and white is black.)
Precision Bitmap Alignment	Prints the page image at 96 percent of its original size so that bit-mapped images are mapped into the printer at a precise 4-to-1 ratio (288 dots per inch to 72 dots per inch).
Larger Print Area	Reallocates memory in the LaserWriter for storing the page image instead of storing fonts. Useful for printing pages larger than 8.5 x 11 inches.

SECTION 3

Adding the Final Touches

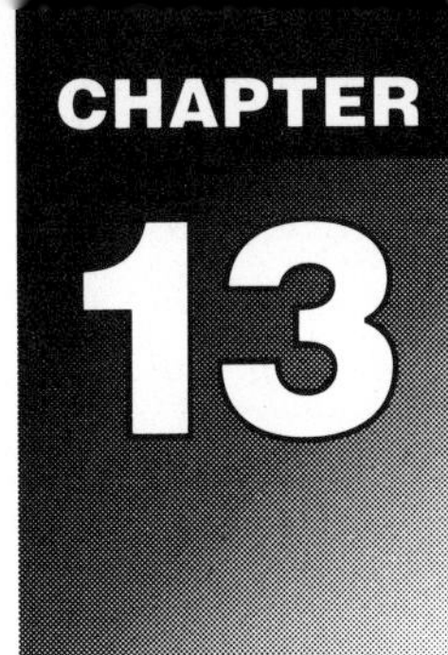

Creating a Table of Contents and Index

Two of the most useful elements in any book are the table of contents and index. If you've ever had to create and compile your own, you know how time-consuming and frustrating the job can be. And any last-minute changes in the pagination of the document mean that your original table of contents and index are off and that you have to redo all the entries. It wasn't fun the first time, and the second time isn't any better.

Once again, Word pitches in and saves you time and effort. The process of creating a table of contents and index for your documents is simple and straightforward; once you have identified the items you want to include, Word takes care of the rest.

■ *Making a Table of Contents*

If your document is longer than 10 to 15 pages and has several major topics, you'll probably want to add a table of contents at the beginning. Not only will this give the document a more professional look, but it will also help your readers find what they are looking for faster and more efficiently. You can create a table of contents in two ways: by extracting it from an outline you've created or by inserting a special code before each entry you want in the table of contents.

Generating a Table of Contents from an Outline

The levels in an outline can serve as the entries in a table of contents. The topmost level of the outline, consisting of topics formatted in the *level 1* style, produces the main headings in the table of contents. Subordinate topics are subheadings formatted in styles *level 2* through *level 9*. When you create a table of contents in this way, Word repaginates the document and then uses each heading, along with its page number if you want, as an entry in the contents. Word formats each level of entry with the corresponding style, *toc 1* through *toc 9*, which are included in Word's automatic styles.

Figure 13-1 shows part of this section and the resulting entries in a table of contents. The title of the section is formatted in the *level 1* style, which has been redefined to use bold, italic, 16-point text. The subheading uses the *level 2* style, subordinate to the main heading, and has also been redefined. Word lists the headings in the table of contents and maintains the hierarchy of the levels in the body of the document.

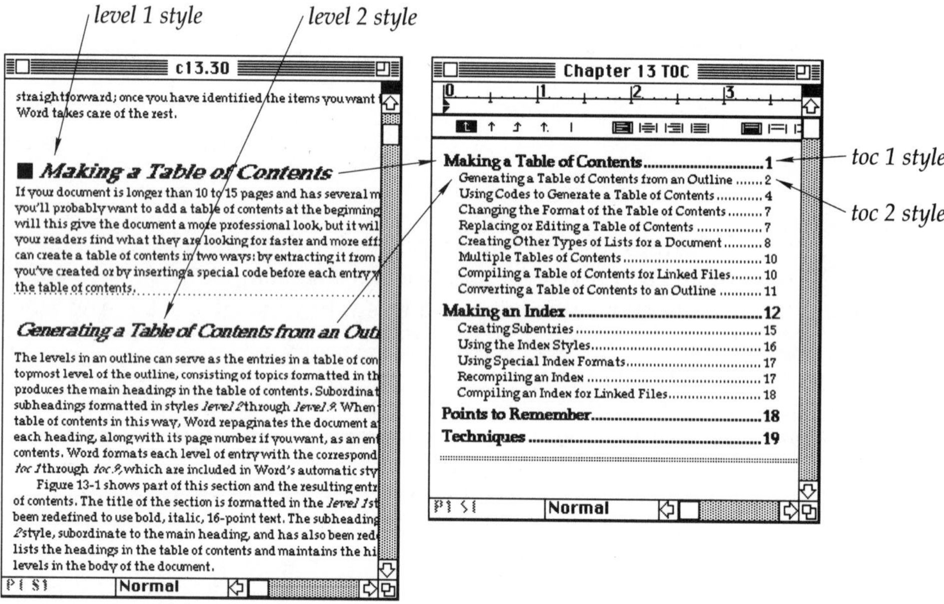

Figure 13-1
Headings in a table of contents.

To compile a table of contents based on the headings in your document, do the following:

❶ Choose Table of Contents from the Document menu. The dialog box in Figure 13-2 appears. The Outline and Show Page Numbers options should already be selected.

❷ Enter the range of levels you want in the table of contents, or let the All option remain selected.

❸ Click Start to begin.

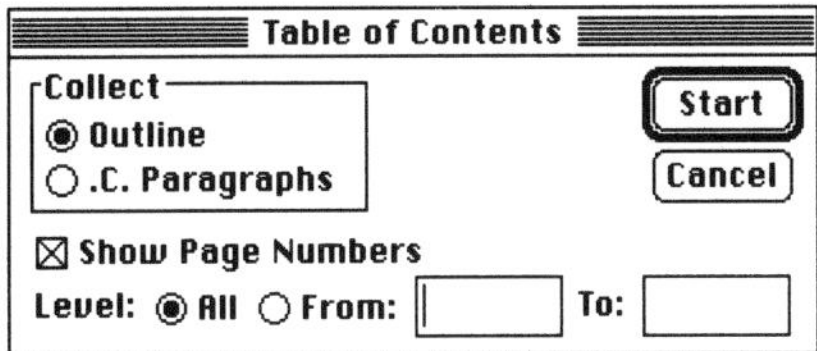

Figure 13-2
The Table of Contents dialog box.

Word first repaginates the document to ensure that the proper page numbers are used. It then goes through the document, collecting the various entries and assembling a complete table of contents. When it is finished, the table of contents is placed at the beginning of the document and is separated from the rest of the document by a section mark, so you can create a different page layout for it if you want.

The table of contents is like any other block of text; you can cut and paste it to another place in the document, and you can edit it, adding text before, after, or between the entries if you want. Most likely, you'll want to add a title page and other front matter before the table of contents. Simply set the insertion point at the beginning of the document and paste in or type the additional text.

Using Codes to Generate a Table of Contents

Another way to compile a table of contents is to insert a special code immediately before each entry that is to appear in the contents. This method gives you more control over the compilation at the expense of greater effort. You can assign up to nine levels, as you can with the outlining function, but you'll probably use only the first two or three.

Type the code *.c.* just before each entry you want on the contents page. (The *c* can be uppercase or lowercase.) You must format the code as hidden text. That way, it won't appear in the final printout of the document. Word will generate a table of contents even if the hidden text is displayed (as it is in Figure 13-3), because it temporarily turns off Show ¶ in its internal representation of the document while generating the table of contents.

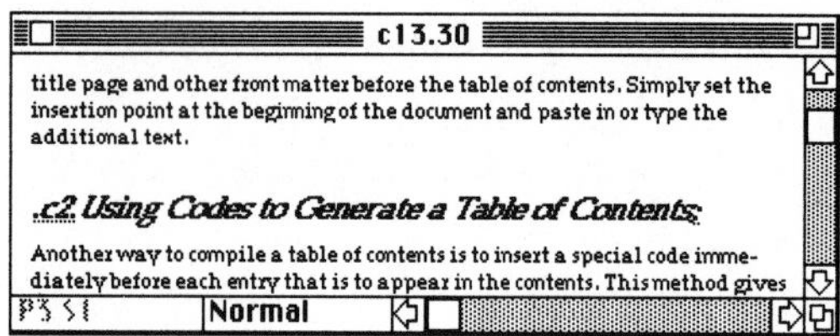

Figure 13-3
A table of contents entry. (Show Hidden Text is on.)

To assign different levels to entries, you append a number to the contents code, as follows:

For	Type
1st level	*.c.* or *.c1.*
2nd level	*.c2.*
3rd level	*.c3.*
4th level	*.c4.*
5th level	*.c5.*
6th level	*.c6.*
7th level	*.c7.*
8th level	*.c8.*
9th level	*.c9.*

How does Word know where a table of contents entry ends? In most cases, you'll be using the headings in your document as entries, and headings almost always end in a paragraph mark. In such cases, the paragraph mark signals the end of the entry. However, many tables of contents contain entries that don't appear as headings in the document; an example of this is shown in Figure 13-4.

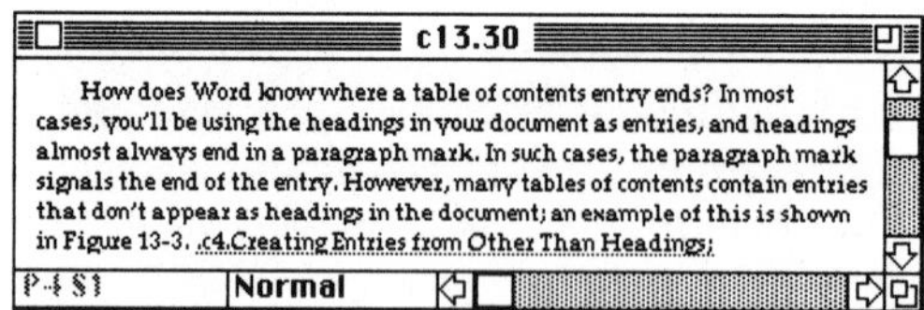

Figure 13-4
A table of contents entry that isn't a heading.

To use text taken from the middle of a paragraph as a contents entry, precede it with the .c. code and put a semicolon after it, formatted as hidden text. If you want, you can even format the entire phrase as hidden text. You can do this if, for instance, you want to include a brief description of each section in the contents. The glossary is useful for storing and inserting the codes formatted as hidden text.

You can also create subentries in the table of contents by separating the main entry from a subentry by a colon. This feature works like creating subentries for indexes, discussed later in this chapter. If you need to include a semicolon or a colon within an entry, put single quotes on both sides of the entry, and format the quotes as hidden text.

Once you have inserted the appropriate codes into your document, you are ready to compile the table of contents. You do not need to repaginate the document first; Word does it for you.

❶ Choose the Table of Contents command.

❷ Select the .C. Paragraphs option. The Show Page Numbers option should already be set.

❸ Enter the range of levels you want in the table of contents, or leave the All option selected.

❹ Click Start to begin.

Word prepares the table of contents and places it at the beginning of the document.

Changing the Format of the Table of Contents

Word's automatic *toc* styles establish the layout for the nine table of contents levels. This is the case regardless of how you generate the table of contents. You can redefine any or all of these styles. Chapter 9, "Working with Style Sheets," explains how.

Replacing or Editing a Table of Contents

Once you've compiled a table of contents for a document, you can compile another at any time and use it to replace the old one. Before recompiling the table of contents, Word asks if you want to replace the old one. Click Yes in the dialog box that appears.

Because the table of contents is standard text, you can edit and reformat it in any way you want. These changes are lost, however, if you subsequently recompile the table.

For example, if you set the Show Page Numbers option in the Table of Contents dialog box, Word adds a tab mark with leader dots and the page number to each entry in the table of contents. Some designs, however, call for the page number to appear for the major headings only and not for the subheadings. In this case, you would set the Show Page Numbers option and then manually remove the tabs and page numbers from the subheadings. You would have to do this each time you recompiled the table of contents.

Creating Other Types of Lists for a Document

You can use Word's table of contents feature to generate lists of other elements in a document as well. You can use it, for example, for a list of the illustrations and plates in a book or article. Word does not add the phrase *Table of Contents* before the table it creates, so you can type any title you like, such as *List of Illustrations, Projects,* or *Workshop Examples.* If the table or list does not require page numbers, you can easily omit them by turning off the Show Page Numbers option in the Table of Contents dialog box.

Your document can have more than one table created with the Table of Contents command, but you have to be careful that you don't erase an old table when you compile a new one. To extract an additional list, do the following:

❶ Generate the table of contents from outline levels or .c. codes, as was discussed earlier.

❷ Format the entries for the new table using .c. codes with a deeper level than any you used before—starting at .c4. or so, for example. Alternatively, you can format the entries for the new table with the outlining feature, using deeper levels.

❸ When you have identified all the entries and specified the levels, choose the Table of Contents command.

❹ Click the .C. Paragraphs option.

❺ Enter the levels for the elements you want to list in the From and To fields. You must enter numbers in both even if you are extracting only one level.

❻ Click the Start button.

If any of the levels are duplicated in another table, Word asks if you want to replace the existing table of contents. Click the Cancel button and use new numbers for the entries, avoiding any overlap. You can use this method to generate a set of different lists, each using one level of the table of contents codes. For example, if the deepest heading level in your document uses the .c4. code, you can use .c5. for figures, .c6. for tables, and .c7. for in-text hidden editorial comments.

Multiple Tables of Contents

You can create multiple tables of contents simply by clicking No in the dialog box that asks if you want to replace the existing table of contents. If you have not moved the table, Word adds the new one before it. If you have moved the table of contents, Word leaves it where you put it. You can use this feature to generate additional tables when you have run out of outline or .c. levels or when you want to create an alternate table of contents (for a teacher's copy of a study guide, for instance).

TIP

Using Both Types of Tables in One Document
You can create tables of contents from the level headings and from .c. codes in one document. This is useful in documents that have more than one type of list in the front matter, such as the table of contents proper, a list of figures, and a list of tables. Simply extract the main table of contents from the outline, and insert .c. codes for the figures and tables lists. Then extract each list separately by setting the correct options in the Table of Contents dialog box.

Compiling a Table of Contents for Linked Files

If your manuscript or other work spans several documents, you can link them together and have Word compile the table of contents from the whole group at once. The secret is in the Page Setup dialog box. For each document that is followed by another in the sequence:

❶ Choose Page Setup from the File menu.

❷ In the Next File field, enter the name of the document that follows this one. Delete the contents of the Start Page Numbers At field if you want Word to do the page numbering for you. Otherwise, be sure the starting page number in each document is correct.

❸ Click the OK button.

When you start compiling the table of contents for the topmost document on the desktop, Word repaginates and scans each document, in order, and extracts its table. If Word can't find a file in the sequence, it prompts you to locate the folder or insert the disk that contains the document. So, you'll want to have all the disks at hand when you assemble the table of contents.

A very useful application of this technique, even for smaller documents, is to put the table of contents in a "front matter" document file that precedes the main body of the document. To do this, create a new, blank document, open the Page Setup dialog box, and enter the name of the first file in the sequence in the Next File field. When you compile the table of contents, Word places it in this file. You can then put the other front-matter elements, such as the copyright page, the title page, and the acknowledgments, in the same file as the table of contents. This is a good way to set up special page layouts for the front matter without affecting the main body of the document.

Converting a Table of Contents to an Outline

Occasionally you may want to play with an outline without having to deal with the body text that goes with each heading. For example, you may be dealing with a large document that is divided into many smaller files and want to work with an outline that covers all the files. Or you may want to print a formatted outline; printing a collapsed outline from Outline view prints the outline in the *Normal* style, without formatting.

To assemble one outline for a set of documents or to print a formatted outline without the body text, first extract a table of contents for the document or series of linked documents. It's best to put this table by itself in a blank document. Then choose Define Styles from the Format menu, select each *toc* style in turn, and change its name to the appropriate *level* style. For each name change, Word asks you to verify that you want to reassign the text formatted in that style to the *level* style. After you've converted all the *toc* style text to *level* style text, you can work with the outline in Outline view or switch to Document view to reformat the *level* styles for printing.

■ *Making an Index*

When done well, an index provides a way of navigating in a document that is as useful as the table of contents. Indexing is an art, but Word makes the job of creating and maintaining one much easier for anyone.

Generating an index is only slightly more difficult than generating a table of contents with the *.c.* codes. Each index entry must begin and end with special hidden codes, which do not appear when you print the document. You type the code *.i.* at the beginning of each index entry. Format it as hidden text. The entry must end with an end-of-entry code, which can be a semicolon, a newline mark, or a paragraph mark. If you insert a semicolon to end an entry, format it as hidden text so that it won't be printed. Figure 13-5 shows a number of different index entries.

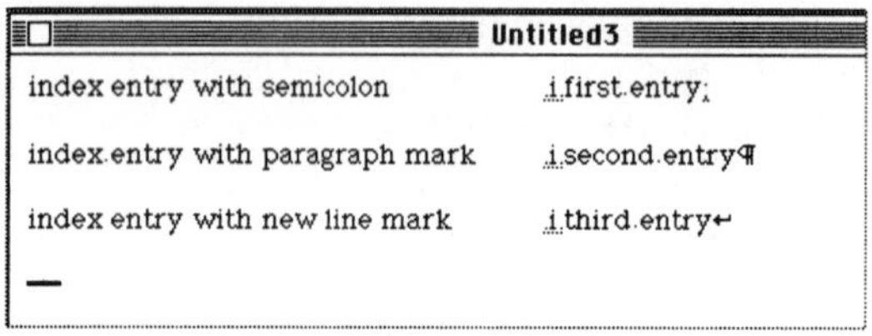

Untitled3

index entry with semicolon	.i.first entry;
index entry with paragraph mark	.i.second entry¶
index entry with new line mark	.i.third entry↵

Figure 13-5
Examples of formatted index entries.

If only the indexing codes are formatted as hidden text, the index entry will remain visible as text in the body of your document. However, if you want to link an index entry to a particular point in the document but prevent the entry from becoming part of the document, format both the indexing codes and the entry as hidden text.

You can make the job of formatting entries for the index a little easier by taking advantage of Word's glossary function. Create a generic index entry in this form:

.i.INDEX;

If most of your index entries are to be composed of text that is not actually part of the document, format *INDEX* as hidden text. Give the glossary entry a convenient name, such as *ind*. Insert the index glossary entry in text by first pressing Command-Backspace, typing *ind,* and pressing the Return key. Then, double-click on the word *INDEX,* and type the text you want for the entry.

Once you have coded all the index entries, you can compile the index. As with generating a table of contents, it isn't necessary to hide all hidden text in the document by turning off the Show Hidden Text option. Then, do the following:

❶ Choose Index from the Document menu. The Index dialog box, shown in Figure 13-6, appears.

❷ Click the Nested or Run-in option, as desired. (A description of these is given next.)

❸ Click the Start button.

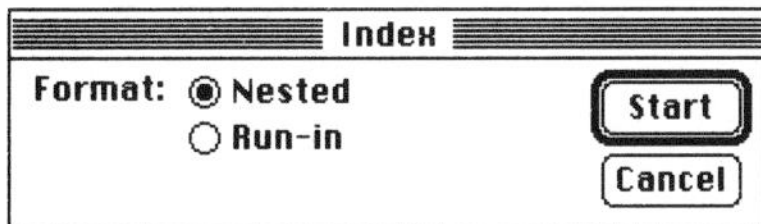

Figure 13-6
The Index dialog box.

Word's two basic index formats, nested and run-in, specify different ways of handling subentries, the subordinate entries that follow the main entry. With the nested format, subentries appear below the main entry and are indented. With the run-in format, Word places subentries on the same line as the main entry, using semicolons to separate them. Figure 13-7 shows both kinds of formats. Select the format you want by clicking the appropriate option in the Index dialog box.

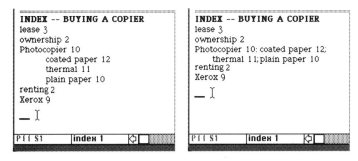

INDEX -- BUYING A COPIER
lease 3
ownership 2
Photocopier 10
coated paper 12
thermal 11
plain paper 10
renting 2
Xerox 9

P1 S1 index 1

INDEX -- BUYING A COPIER
lease 3
ownership 2
Photocopier 10: coated paper 12; thermal 11; plain paper 10
renting 2
Xerox 9

P1 S1 index 1

Figure 13-7
The two kinds of index formats.

When you click Start, Word repaginates the document and then searches through it to collect the entries you identified, along with the page number on which each entry falls. It assembles them in alphabetical order and places the index in a new section at the end of the document. The program also removes duplicate entries occurring on the same page and assembles a list of page numbers when the same entry occurs on different pages.

After Word has compiled the index, you'll probably want to go over it and edit or combine entries that aren't exactly what you wanted. The most common type of change you are likely to make is to combine entries that are phrased differently at two or more places in a document, such as *Formatting:italics* and *Character Formats:italics*. It's best to develop a consistent way of citing index entries; a style manual such as *The Chicago Manual of Style* is a good place to learn about indexing conventions.

Creating Subentries

Word assumes that all entries are main entries unless you tell it otherwise. To create a subentry, you specify the main entry first and then the subentry, separated by a colon, as in *Word:using* or *Word:printing with*. Do not insert a space after the colon. You will want to make the entire entry hidden, as shown in this example:

.i.Word:Using:Beginners;

You will also use hidden text for the entire index entry—codes and words—when you enter an expository entry. Such entries consist of words and phrases that do not occur in the text but that more accurately reflect the subject matter of the entry. Suppose, for example, that you are indexing the following paragraph:

The two main classes of cast iron are gray iron and white iron. Gray iron is inexpensive and easy to machine. It is, however, brittle and only about half as strong as steel. White iron is stronger and harder than gray iron but considerably more difficult to machine.

One way to index this paragraph might be to code the words *cast iron*, *gray iron*, and *white iron*, but those entries aren't very descriptive. A better way would be to create a new entry and format it as hidden text. Assigning the hidden format to the entry causes it to be omitted from the printed document itself. The entry you use might be something like the following:

iron, gray and white
    comparison of cost, strength, and machinability, 143

You would generate this entry by typing:

```
.i.iron, gray and white:comparison of cost, strength, and machinability;
```

You can create up to seven levels of subentries by adding more subentries and more colons. An entry such as:

```
.i.Word:using:for beginners;
```

would appear like this in the index:

```
Word
    using
        for beginners, 174
```

You can skip a level by typing two colons with nothing between, as in:

```
.i.Word::for beginners;
```

In the index, you'd find:

```
Word
        for beginners, 174
```

Using the Index Styles

When you create an index, whatever character and paragraph formats the entry has are removed, and the entry is formatted with one of the seven *index* automatic styles. The *index 1* style is for main entries; *index 2* through *index 7* are for subentries. The only difference between these styles is the position of the left indent; it moves to the right 0.25 inch at each index level. You can redefine the index styles in any way you like. See Chapter 9, "Working with Style Sheets," for more information.

Of course, you can also edit and format the index manually after it is compiled, but any such changes will be lost if you recompile the index.

Using Special Index Formats

You can change the way that Word formats the page numbers or specify text to be used instead of a page number, by including certain characters in the index entry code. Many books use boldface or italic page numbers to indicate illustrations or definitions, for example. The table on the following page shows examples of the various formatting options available.

Code	Format
.ib.*entry;*	Boldface page number; you can use either an uppercase or lowercase *b.*
.ii.*entry;*	Italic page number; you can use either an uppercase or lowercase *i.*
.i(.*entry;*	Start of multipage reference.
.i).*entry;*	End of multipage reference.
.i.*entry#text;*	*Text* replaces page number.

The following table gives some examples of how these codes might be used. As before, the dotted or gray underline signifies hidden text. If the entry is actually part of the text, do not format the entry as hidden text.

Index entry	Produces this index listing
.ib.Using Word;	Using Word **10**
.ii.Using Word;	Using Word *10*
.i(.Using Word; on the first page of the topic, and .i).Using Word; on the last page of the topic	Using Word 10-14
.iUsing Word#(See Word, Using);	Using Word (See Word, Using)

As with a table of contents, if you want to include a colon, semicolon, or other special character (such as the # character) in an entry, put single quotes around the entry and format the quotes as hidden text. For example, if you wanted to create an index entry which looks like this:

PRINT#, Using **127**

You would enter this text on page 127 of the document:

.ib.'PRINT#, Using';

Recompiling an Index

If you make changes to a document that affect the pagination, you will want to recompile the index. When you do this, Word asks if you want to replace the old index. Click Yes if you do. Word then replaces the index, even if you moved it from the end of the document to some other location. Clicking No adds a second index without deleting the one that already exists. You can use this feature, for example, if you are designing the index and want to compare different formats. To recompile the index, choose the Index command again.

Compiling an Index for Linked Files

If your manuscript spans several documents, you can link them together and have Word compile the index for the whole group all at once. You use the Page Setup dialog box to link the files. For each document to be followed by another one in the sequence:

1. Choose the Page Setup command.
2. In the Next File field, enter the name of the next document in the sequence. Delete the contents of the Start Page Numbers At field if you want Word to do the page numbering for you. Otherwise, be sure the starting page number in each document is correct.
3. Click the OK button.

When you compile the index, Word assembles the entries for all documents and places the index at the end of the last document. If Word can't find a file in the chain, it prompts you to find the folder or insert the disk that contains the document. Also, as with tables of contents, you can compile an index into a blank document at the end of the chain of linked files.

Points to Remember

- Word's Table of Contents command generates a table of contents for your document, adding the page numbers automatically. You can base the contents either on the heading levels in the document or on codes that you enter and format as hidden text.
- Word's Index command generates an index for your document, adding the page numbers and alphabetizing the entries automatically. You must code each entry to appear in the index.
- You can use the Table of Contents command to generate lists of figures and tables. Assign these elements heading levels or *.c.* codes that are deeper than any used in the document; then enter the range of levels for the list in the From and To fields in the Table of Contents dialog box before compiling the table.
- To include an entry that is not in the document in a table of contents or index, type it at the appropriate location and format the entire entry as hidden text.
- Entries in the table of contents are assigned the automatic styles *toc 1* through *toc 9*; the number corresponds to the heading level or to the number in the .c. code for the entry. Entries in the index are assigned the automatic styles *index 1* through *index 7*, corresponding to the different levels of subentries. You can redefine these styles in any way you like.
- Word places the table of contents in its own section at the beginning of the document and the index in its own section at the end of the document. You can edit and reformat these as you would any other text.
- You can create glossary entries for the table of contents and index codes to make the job of coding easier.

Techniques

Creating a Table of Contents

Generate a table of contents from the headings in the outline

1. Choose Table of Contents from the Document menu.
2. Be sure that the Outline option is on.
3. Be sure that the Show Page Numbers option is on if you want the contents to include the page numbers.

4. Specify the range of levels to appear in the contents, or leave All selected.
5. Click Start.
6. If a table of contents already exists for the document, Word asks if you want to replace it. Click Yes to replace it or No to generate a new table without deleting the old one.

Generate a table of contents from inserted codes

1. Before each entry to appear in the table of contents, insert the code *.c.* or *.c1.* for first-level entries, *.c2.* for second-level entries, and so on to the deepest level. Format these codes as hidden text. Each entry must end with a paragraph mark, a newline mark, or a semicolon. If you insert a semicolon, format it as hidden text.
2. Choose Table of Contents from the Document menu.
3. Select the .C. Paragraphs option.
4. Be sure that the Show Page Numbers option is on if you want the contents to include the page numbers.
5. Click Start.

If the entry itself is formatted as hidden text, it is still compiled in the table of contents, but does not become part of the printed document.

Creating an Index

Code index entries

1. Insert the code .i. before each index entry. Format the code as hidden text. You can vary the format of the page number by using the following codes:

Code	Format
.ib.*entry;*	Bold page number; you can use either an uppercase or lowercase *b.*
.ii.*entry;*	Italic page number; you can use either an uppercase or lowercase *i.*
.i(.*entry;*	Start of multipage reference
.i).*entry;*	End of multipage reference
.i.*entry#text;*	*Text* replaces page number

2. End each index entry with a paragraph mark, a newline mark, or a semicolon.

3. For subentries, type the usual index code; then enter the main entry, followed by a colon, and then the subentry. (Do not insert any space after the colon.) A subentry can be followed by a colon and a sub-subentry, for a maximum of seven levels.
4. Format subentries and any other index entry that is not part of the document as hidden text.

If the entry itself is formatted as hidden text, it is still compiled in the index, but does not become part of the printed document.

Compile an index

1. Choose Index from the Document menu.
2. Select the Nested option to place each subentry on its own line with a suitable indent; select the Run-in option to place the subentries on the same line as the main entry.
3. Click Start.
4. If an index already exists for the document, Word asks if you want to replace it. Click Yes to replace it or No to generate a new index without deleting the old one.

Generate a table of contents or index for linked files

1. Code the files as usual.
2. For each file in the sequence that is followed by another file, specify the file to follow it in the Next File field of the Page Setup dialog box. If you want sequential page numbering throughout the files, delete the default number in the Start Page Numbers At field in the Page Setup dialog box.
3. Open the first file in the sequence.
4. Choose the Table of Contents or Index command, set the appropriate options, and click Start.
5. The table of contents is placed at the beginning of the first document; the index is placed at the end of the last document.

Documents with Tables and Lists

It used to be that word processors and numbers didn't mix. Financial, statistical, and mathematical calculations and text were difficult, if not impossible, to format with a word processor. Tables and lists were best presented by a spreadsheet program such as Microsoft Excel or Multiplan. Microsoft Word changes all this. You can directly format tables and lists to prepare multicolumn ledger sheets, invoices, statistical tables, and more. Word even has a calculation feature, which you can use to add, subtract, multiply, and divide any group of numbers.

■ *Editing and Formatting Tabular Data*

The most rudimentary form of table contains only data or text formatted in the *Normal* style. It consists of a series of lines in which items (usually numbers) are separated by tab characters. The tabs align the items according to the tab stops you set and make the table easier to read. A sample of this type of table is shown in Figure 14-1.

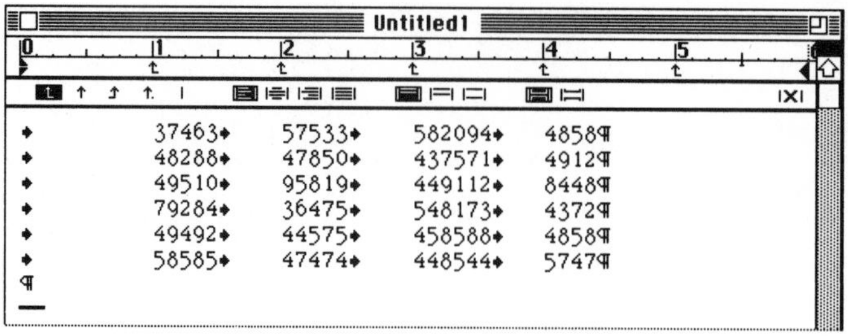

Untitled1

37463	57533	582094	4858
48288	47850	437571	4912
49510	95819	449112	8448
79284	36475	548173	4372
49492	44575	458588	4858
58585	47474	448544	5747

Figure 14-1
A simple table (Show ¶ is on).

As was discussed in Chapter 8, "Paragraph Formatting," Word supports four types of tabs, all of which are suited for tables: right-aligned, left-aligned, centered, and decimal. You can also use the vertical line "tab stop" to format your tables. The vertical line isn't actually a tab stop because it doesn't force text to align at a particular distance from the left margin, but it works well with the other tab markers for creating tables.

Of the four types of tab markers, the decimal tab is the most popular for use with numeric data. With a decimal tab, numbers are aligned on their decimal points, regardless of the number of digits that precede or follow the point. Right-aligned and left-aligned tabs are most often used to present textual data as well as numbers that don't have decimal points or fractional parts. You can, of course, mix tab types on a line.

You can arrange tab stops either before or after you enter the data for a table. If you enter the data before setting tab stops, Word assumes that you want to use the default tabs, which are placed at intervals along the Ruler. You can change this default tab stop interval in the Page Setup dialog box. To enter the data, type each number or piece of text, and then press the Tab key to move the insertion point to the next default tab stop.

Once you've entered the data, select the lines for which you want to add tab stops, and choose Show Ruler. For each column of data, you select the desired tab icon, click in the Ruler to establish an initial position away from any other tab marker, and then drag the icon to its final position. Every time you add a tab stop, the default tab stops to the left of it disappear. Several other ways of setting tab stops were described in Chapter 8. If you need to reposition any tab stops, remember to select all the lines in the table before adjusting the tab stops. (See Figure 14-2.) Otherwise, you'll end up changing only the tabs in the selected lines or in the line containing the insertion point.

TIP

Using Styles to Format Tables
Instead of setting tab stops manually, you can define a style having the tab stops you want and apply it to all the lines in the table. Then, if you need to adjust the table at any time, you redefine the style instead of manually reformatting the lines in the table. This technique is particularly handy when you have many tables in a document, all of which are formatted in the same way.

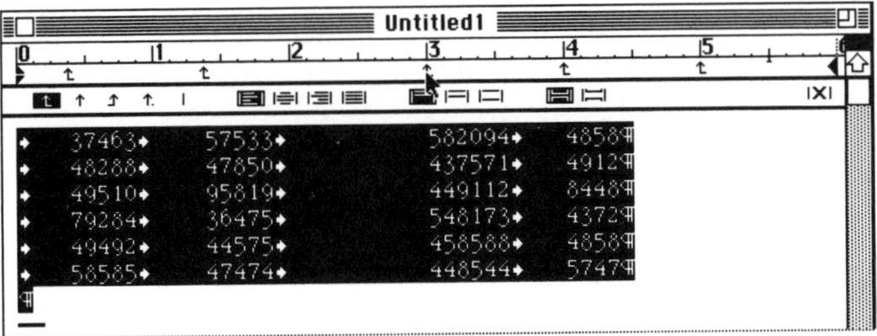

Figure 14-2
Adjusting the tab stops in the entire table.

Editing a table is only slightly more difficult than editing regular text. The point to remember is that tab characters separate the items on each line, and if you delete one of these characters, all the items to the right of it slide one tab stop to the left. You can delete the item itself if you want to have a blank space in the table, but leave the tab before it in place. It may help you to display the tab characters by choosing the Show ¶ command before you prepare or edit the table.

Cutting and Pasting Tabular Data

Word normally treats the characters in a document like one long string of beads, wrapping around from the end of one line to the beginning of the next, all the way to the end of the document. When you select text in the document, you select a string of characters that starts at one point in the text and stops at another point. All the characters between these two points are part of the selection.

Word also lets you select a portion of each line, rather than all the characters between two points. That is, you can select a column of text and leave alone the remainder of each line. This feature is particularly helpful for selecting columns of data in a table. To select a column of text, press the Option key before dragging over the column you want to select. As Figure 14-3 shows, Word skips the portions of the line before and after the column. The rule for what characters get selected is this: if half of a character or more lies within the highlighted block, it becomes part of the selection. Once you've selected the column, you can copy or move it elsewhere or format it all at once. This feature can be a tremendous timesaver; without it you would have to move individually each item in the column.

Note that if you select the tab characters along with the data in the table, cutting the column causes the columns to the right of it to slide to the left. This may not be what you want. Also, if the widths of the text in a column vary greatly or you're using the left-aligned or centered tab stop for the column, you may find it necessary to adjust the positions of the tab stops for the table so that you can select the material correctly. Once the column is in the Clipboard, you can paste it anywhere, even to another program such as Microsoft Excel or Microsoft Chart.

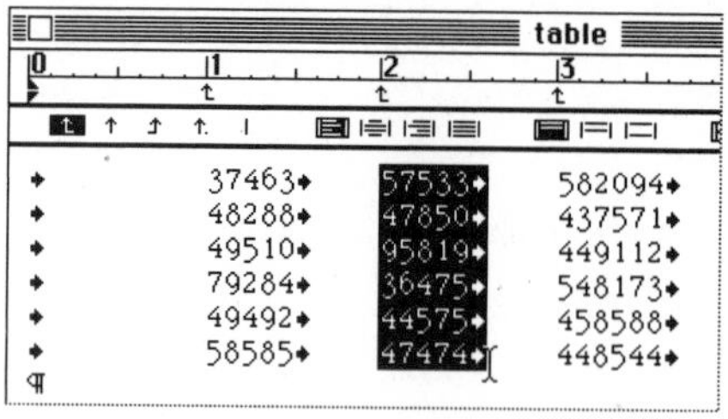

37463	57533	582094
48288	47850	437571
49510	95819	449112
79284	36475	548173
49492	44575	458588
58585	47474	448544

Figure 14-3
Selecting a column.

You can use this feature to move a column or to switch the order of two columns. Suppose, for example, you had a four-column table and you wanted to reverse the order of the second and third columns. Here's what you would do:

❶ Press the Option key and select the third column. You want to select the tab characters preceding the items in the third column, so start at the right edge of the first item in the second column, and drag down to just beyond the right edge of the third column.

❷ Press Command-X to cut the third column and place it in the Clipboard.

❸ Place the insertion point immediately to the right of the first item in the first column.

❹ Press Command-V to paste the column back into the table. The columns on the right move to the right to make room for it.

If you are pasting an extra column into a table, be sure that there's an extra tab marker to accommodate the new column. If you try to insert a fifth column into a table that has tab markers for only four columns (that is, only three tab markers per line), Word may paste in the column without separating it from the column to the left. Remember that you can undo the Paste command if the results are not what you expected. If the extra tab characters are not in the column copied to the Clipboard, you should add them to the table before you paste in the column.

This process isn't as easy if you want to copy or move a column to the far right of the table, because each line of the table ends with a paragraph mark rather than a tab character. One way to deal with this is to select and cut the tab characters preceding the text in the column instead of those succeeding the column. Another way is to add a tab character at the end of every line before you paste in the new column. You can insert a tab character at the end of each line of the last column, before the paragraph mark, by searching for the paragraph marks and replacing them with a tab character and a paragraph mark, as follows:

1. Select every line in the table.
2. Choose Change from the Search menu.
3. Enter ^*p* in the Find What field.
4. Enter ^*t*^*p* in the Change To field.
5. Click the Change Selection button. Close the Change dialog box when the program finishes.
6. Cut the column, place the insertion point between the newly inserted tab mark and the paragraph mark at the end of the first line, and paste in the column.

■ *Enhancing Tables*

Basic, unadorned tables are fine for routine work, but for a touch of pizzazz, you can enhance them by adding horizontal and vertical lines and boxes. Chapter 8, "Paragraph Formatting," discusses these formats at length. This brief recap explains how to use them with tables.

Adding Vertical Lines

You can use the vertical line tab icon in the Ruler to separate columns. With the Ruler visible, select the entire table and place a vertical line tab at each spot along the Ruler where you want a column separator to appear. Figure 14-4 shows a table to which several vertical lines have been added.

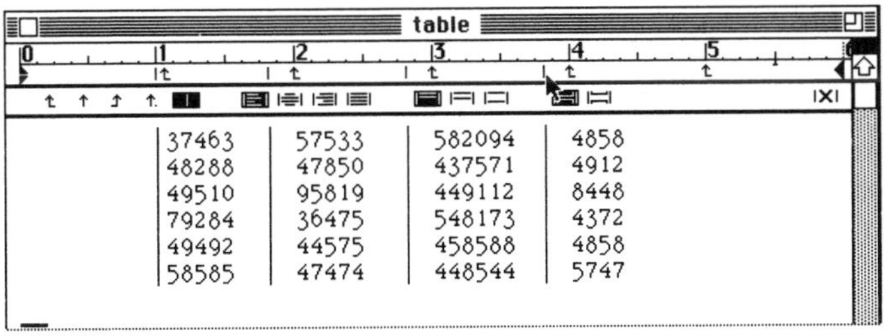

37463	57533	582094	4858
48288	47850	437571	4912
49510	95819	449112	8448
79284	36475	548173	4372
49492	44575	458588	4858
58585	47474	448544	5747

Figure 14-4
A table with vertical lines used as column separators.

Remember that the vertical line marker isn't a true tab stop. Word draws the line automatically, and when you press the Tab key, the insertion point skips past the vertical line to the next true tab stop. Thus, adding vertical lines does not affect the overall positioning of the items in a table.

Adding Horizontal Lines

Underlines and overlines stretch from one side of a table to the other and appear either above or below the text line. You might use such lines, for example, to separate column headings from the data underneath them. To add an underline to column headings, do the following:

1. Select the line containing the table's column headings.
2. Choose the Paragraph command.
3. Click the Below option in the Border group.
4. Click the OK button. Figure 14-5 shows a table to which an underline has been added.

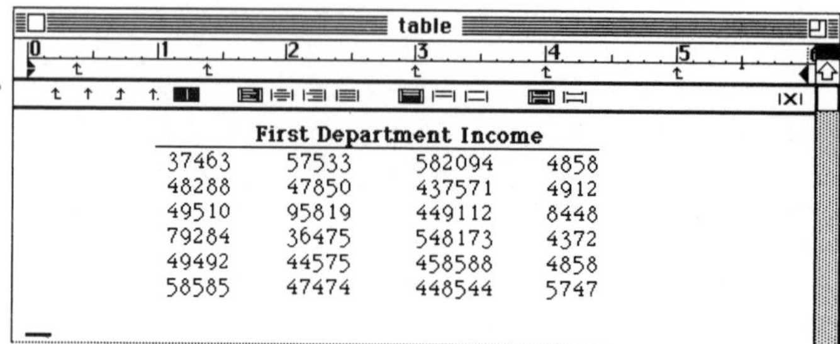

Figure 14-5
A table with the column heading underlined.

Adjust the right and left indents if the line stretches too far on either side. Other options in the Paragraph dialog box let you make the line thicker or draw a double line. You could also use the Underline or Double Underline character formats or combine these with one of the Border paragraph formats.

Boxing a Table

Boxing a table isolates it on the page. If you want one box to surround the whole table, be sure that each line ends with a newline mark instead of a paragraph mark. You enter a newline mark by pressing Shift-Return at the end of each line in the table. This causes Word to treat the whole table as one large paragraph. (See Figure 14-6.) Otherwise, each line of the table would be surrounded by its own box. The last line in the table should end with a regular paragraph mark.

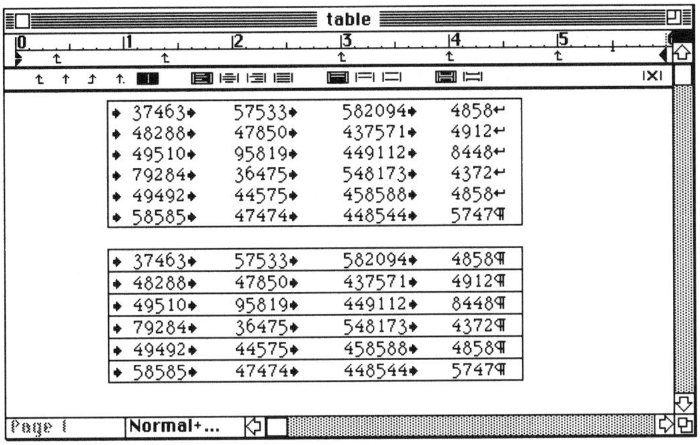

table

Page 1 Normal+...

◆ 37463◆	57533◆	582094◆	4858↵
◆ 48288◆	47850◆	437571◆	4912↵
◆ 49510◆	95819◆	449112◆	8448↵
◆ 79284◆	36475◆	548173◆	4372↵
◆ 49492◆	44575◆	458588◆	4858↵
◆ 58585◆	47474◆	448544◆	5747¶

◆ 37463◆	57533◆	582094◆	4858¶
◆ 48288◆	47850◆	437571◆	4912¶
◆ 49510◆	95819◆	449112◆	8448¶
◆ 79284◆	36475◆	548173◆	4372¶
◆ 49492◆	44575◆	458588◆	4858¶
◆ 58585◆	47474◆	448544◆	5747¶

Figure 14-6
Paragraph marks and their box effects.

To have Word draw a box around a table, change the paragraph mark at the end of each line to a newline mark (except for the last line in the table), and then do the following:

❶ Click anywhere within the table. Any paragraph formats you set apply to the entire table because it's now only one paragraph.

❷ Choose the Paragraph command.

❸ Select the Box option in the Border group.

❹ Click OK.

If the box is too wide, adjust the right and left indents in the Ruler. Other options in the Border group let you vary the line used to draw the box; it can be fine, thick, double, or shadowed. (See Figure 14-7.) You can also add space above or below the table in the box by adding blank lines ending with newline marks.

37463	57533	582094	4858
48288	47850	437571	4912
49510	95819	449112	8448
79284	36475	548173	4372
49492	44575	458588	4858
58585	47474	448544	5747

37463	57533	582094	4858
48288	47850	437571	4912
49510	95819	449112	8448
79284	36475	548173	4372
49492	44575	458588	4858
58585	47474	448544	5747

37463	57533	582094	4858
48288	47850	437571	4912
49510	95819	449112	8448
79284	36475	548173	4372
49492	44575	458588	4858
58585	47474	448544	5747

37463	57533	582094	4858
48288	47850	437571	4912
49510	95819	449112	8448
79284	36475	548173	4372
49492	44575	458588	4858
58585	47474	448544	5747

Figure 14-7
Box variations.

■ Working with Lists

A list in Word is simply a series of items, each of which ends in a paragraph mark. An item can consist of one character or a string of characters on one line, or it can extend across several lines. If two or more successive lines on the screen do not end with a paragraph mark, Word considers them one list entry. Once you have created a list, you can number its items either by using the Line Numbering paragraph format, or by actually adding numbers to the beginning of each paragraph. After you've added numbers (if necessary) you can sort the items in the list alphabetically or numerically.

Using the Line Numbering Format to Number a List

If you only want to keep track of the number of entries in the list, and if none of the entries are longer than one line, try using the Line Numbering option in the Section dialog box. The line numbers appear only when you print the document or audition it with Page Preview. See Figure 14-8 for an example. Be sure that your list is in a separate section; otherwise all the lines in the document will be numbered.

If you use this method to number a list, remember that if you sort the list the numbering is not changed—the new first item will still be number 1. In other words, the Line Numbering format is not affected by sorting, and you cannot use these numbers as the basis for sorting the list.

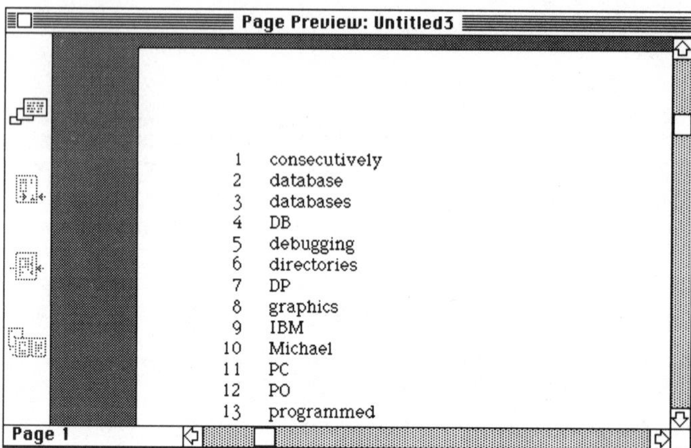

Figure 14-8
Line numbers in Page Preview.

Using the Renumber Command to Number a List

If some of the items in the list are longer than one line or if you want to precede or follow the numbers with other characters or use letters instead of numbers, use the Renumber command. Numbers are inserted at the beginning of each paragraph and appear immediately rather than becoming visible only when the document is previewed or printed. This command was discussed in Chapter 3, "Organizing Through Outlining"; only a brief review of the process will be given here. To number a list:

1. Select the items in the list.
2. Choose the Renumber command. The dialog box shown in Figure 14-9 appears.

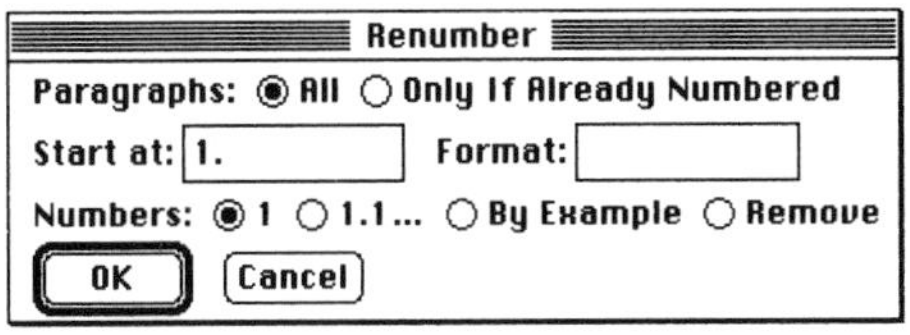

Renumber

Paragraphs: ◉ All ○ Only If Already Numbered

Start at: 1. Format:

Numbers: ◉ 1 ○ 1.1... ○ By Example ○ Remove

OK Cancel

Figure 14-9
The Renumber dialog box.

3. Click the Only if Already Numbered option if you want to renumber only those entries that already have a number.
4. Enter a number in the Start At field if you want to begin with a number other than 1.
5. Enter a numbering or lettering format in the Format field, and click By Example or select one of the other Numbers options. Figure 14-10 provides some ideas for formats you can use when numbering lists.
6. Click the OK button.

Word inserts a line number (or letter) and a tab character before each item in the list. If you subsequently add more items, delete some, or rearrange them, go through this routine again to have Word renumber the lines in the list.

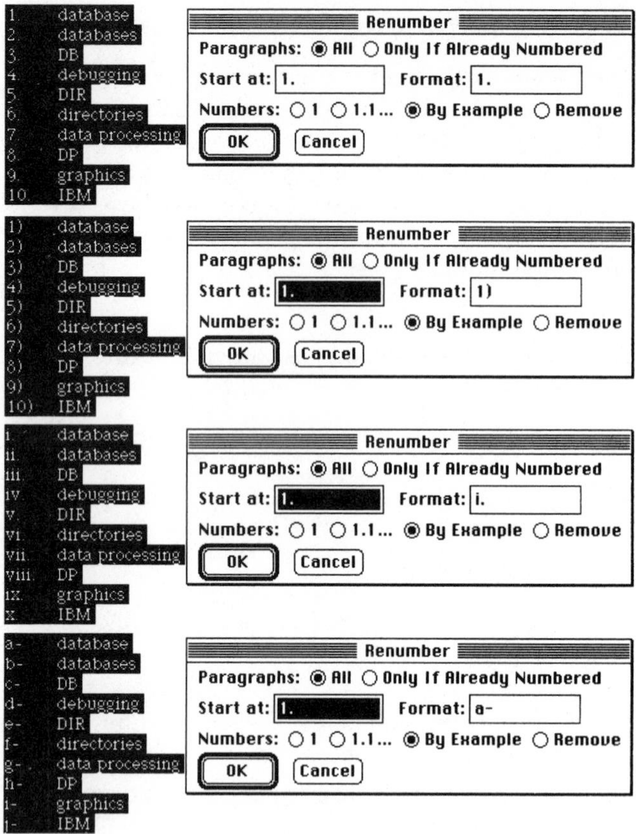

Figure 14-10
Numbering formats for lists.

Sorting the List

You can sort the items in a list alphabetically or numerically in either descending or ascending order. Each item in the list must end with a paragraph mark. To sort a list, follow these steps:

❶ Select the list. Leave out any portions (such as headings) that you don't want sorted.

❷ Choose the Sort command.

Word sorts the list by the first character of each paragraph. If a paragraph begins with double quotation marks, spaces, tabs, or diacritical characters (foreign accents alone), the program ignores them and instead uses the next character in the paragraph. However, accented characters are not ignored. The sorting sequence is as follows: punctuation marks, numbers, and letters, but the specific sorting sequence used is customized for the country in which you purchased your copy of Word. An uppercase letter will be placed before a lowercase letter, all other things being equal (Word places *Fire* before *fire*).

The following table shows the sorting sequence for single characters, in the visible ASCII character set for the Palatino font. Because the attachment of certain characters to ASCII numbers above 128 varies with the font used, Word reverts to sorting these characters in ASCII sequence.

Sorting is normally done in ascending order—smallest to largest or A to Z. If you want to sort in descending order, press the Shift key while choosing the Sort command.

"	34	>	62	f	102	q	113	¢	162	¤	219
!	33	?	63	G	71	R	82	£	163	‹	220
¡	193	¿	192	g	103	r	114	§	164	›	221
«	199	@	64	H	72	S	83	•	165	ﬁ	222
»	200	ß	167	h	104	s	115	¶	166	ﬂ	223
“	210	[	91	I	73	T	84	®	168	‡	224
”	211	\	92	i	105	t	116	©	169	·	225
#	35	]	93	í	146	U	85	™	170	‚	226
$	36	^	94	ì	147	u	117	´	171	„	227
&	38	_	95	î	148	ú	156	¨	172	‰	228
%	37	`	96	ï	149	ù	157	≠	173	Â	229
'	39	A	65	J	74	û	158	∞	176	Ê	230
‘	212	a	97	j	106	Ü	134	±	177	Á	231
’	213	á	135	K	75	ü	159	≤	178	Ë	232
(	40	À	203	k	107	V	86	≥	179	È	233
)	41	à	136	L	76	v	118	¥	180	Í	234
*	42	â	137	l	108	W	87	µ	181	Î	235
+	43	Ä	128	M	77	w	119	∂	182	Ï	236
,	44	ä	138	m	109	X	88	∑	183	Ì	237
-	30	Ã	204	N	78	x	120	∏	184	Ó	238
-	45	ã	139	n	110	Y	89	π	185	Ô	239
.	46	B	66	Ñ	132	y	121	∫	186		240
/	47	b	98	ñ	150	ÿ	216	ª	187	Ò	241
0	48	C	67	O	79	Z	90	º	188	Ú	242
1	49	c	99	o	111	z	122	Ω	189	Û	243
2	50	Ç	130	ó	151	Å	129	¬	194	Ù	244
3	51	ç	141	ò	152	å	140	√	195	ı	245
4	52	D	68	ô	153	Æ	174	ƒ	196	ˆ	246
5	53	d	100	Ö	133	æ	190	≈	197	˜	247
6	54	E	69	ö	154	Ø	175	∆	198	¯	248
7	55	e	101	Õ	205	ø	191	…	201	˘	249
8	56	É	131	õ	155	{	123	–	208	˙	250
9	57	é	142	Œ	206	|	124	—	209	˚	251
:	58	è	143	œ	207	}	125	÷	214	¸	252
;	59	ê	144	P	80	~	126	◊	215	˝	253
<	60	ë	145	p	112	†	160	Ÿ	217	˛	254
=	61	F	70	Q	81	°	161	⁄	218		

Sorting Tabular Data

You can use the same basic procedure you use to sort a list to sort tabular data, but you have an added capability: You can use any of the columns as the basis for the sort. If you want to alphabetize a list based on the contents of the third column, for instance, hold down the Option key and drag over the third column to select it, and then choose the Sort command. (See Figure 14-11.) Word moves entire lines, not only the selected column, thereby keeping each row in the table intact. Each line is considered a complete entity. Although Word normally sorts paragraphs by the first character in each line, when you use the Option key to select a column you can end each line in a newline mark as well as a paragraph mark.

table

37463	57533	582094	4858
48288	47850	437571	4912
49510	95819	449112	8448
79284	36475	548173	4372
49492	44575	458588	4858
58585	47474	448544	5747

table

48288	47850	437571	4912
58585	47474	448544	5747
49510	95819	449112	8448
49492	44575	458588	4858
79284	36475	548173	4372
37463	57533	582094	4858

Figure 14-11
Sorting a table by one of its columns.

■ *Performing Mathematical Calculations*

Word's rudimentary electronic spreadsheet function allows you to add, subtract, multiply, and divide a set of numbers. It can also calculate percentages. You can use this feature to prepare invoices, statements, and inventory reports. Typically, addition is the most common operation—you have the program add up a column of numbers and you insert the resulting total at the bottom of the column. Figure 14-12 shows a simple table in which Word has calculated the total for each column. (Each column was added separately.)

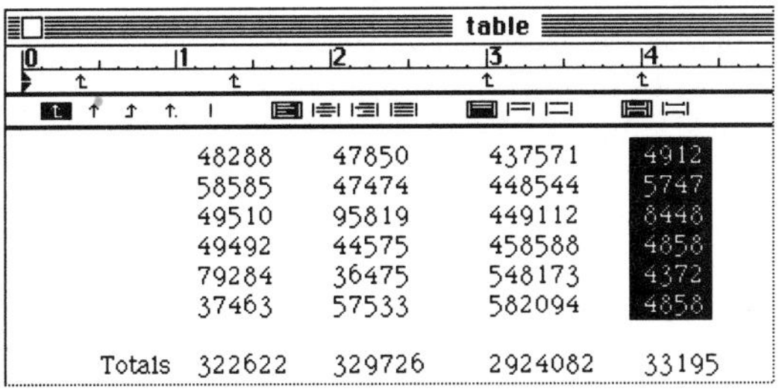

table

	48288	47850	437571	4912
	58585	47474	448544	5747
	49510	95819	449112	8448
	49492	44575	458588	4858
	79284	36475	548173	4372
	37463	57533	582094	4858
Totals	322622	329726	2924082	33195

Figure 14-12
Table with calculated totals.

With a bit of trickery, you can set up fairly complex working formulas for such tasks as calculating sales tax or figuring out a discount rate. Bear in mind, however, that Word is not an electronic spreadsheet program; using the built-in calculator requires manual intervention, but it relieves you from reaching for your calculator or switching to a program like Microsoft Excel to prepare a mere expense report. For another example of using Word's calculator, see the invoice project in Chapter 17, "Blueprints."

Doing Simple Addition

To add up a column or row of numbers, simply select them. If the numbers are in a table, you can select the column you want by pressing the Option key and dragging across the column. Blank lines or lines filled with text are treated as 0 and are not included in the calculation. Thus, you can even select a paragraph and have Word add up all the numbers it contains.

With the numbers selected, choose the Calculate command. The sum of the numbers appears in the status box. Word also places the total in the Clipboard so that you can paste it where you want it. Set the insertion point where you want the total to appear, and choose the Paste command.

Using Math Operators

To perform other types of calculations, use the following math operators:

To	Use
Add	+ (or no operator, since addition is assumed)
Subtract	- (or parentheses around the number)
Multiply	*
Divide	/
Find a percentage	%

Enter the +, -, *, and / operators before the number they are to act on; type the percent sign (%) after the number. Figure 14-13 shows some examples. Characters such as $, #, and = have no effect, but avoid using parentheses unless you want to subtract the number.

```
7*4        Seven times four
2-5        Two minus five
-3-9       Negative three minus nine
25/5       Twenty-five divided by five
23*7%      Seven percent of twenty-three
12(7)      Twelve minus seven
114(-65)   One hundred fourteen minus negative sixty-five
```

Figure 14-13
Examples of using math operators.

Word calculates a formula from left to right and from top to bottom. Unlike an electronic spreadsheet program, there is no precedence of operations. Multiplication and division are not carried out before the other operations, and calculations within parentheses are not performed first. Instead, Word assumes that numbers enclosed in parentheses are negative.

The result that Word provides contains commas and decimal points only if one or more of the numbers in the formula contains them. The number of digits to the right of the decimal point is also determined in this way. If one of the numbers has five digits to the right of the decimal point, for example, the result is also shown with five decimal places.

If you don't want the math operators to appear in the printed copy, format them (including parentheses) as hidden text, as illustrated in Figure 14-14. The operators must be visible on the screen when you perform the calculation, so be sure that the Show Hidden Text option is on.

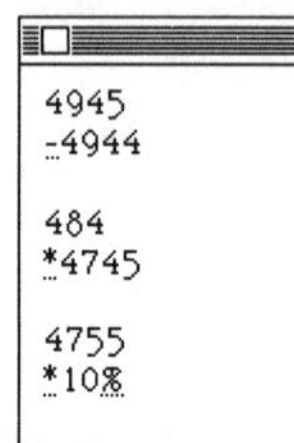

Figure 14-14
Math operators formatted as hidden text.

Constructing and Using Formulas

Figure 14-15 contains an example of how Word's calculation feature can be used effectively. The invoice it shows consists of four major parts: the number of items and their base price, the total for each item and the subtotal, the sales tax, and the grand total. To arrive at the grand total, you must make several separate calculations.

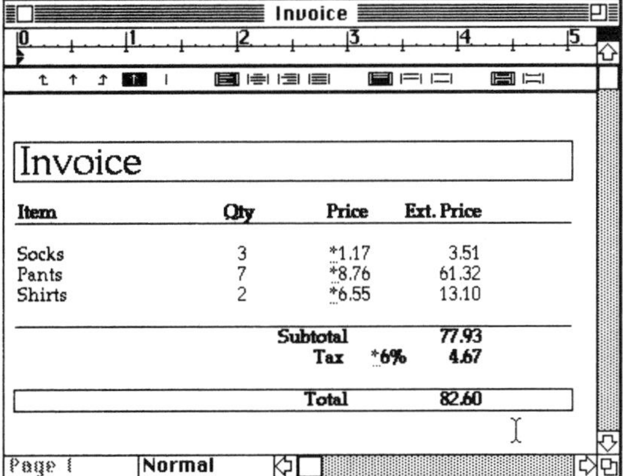

Figure 14-15
Sample invoice.

You start by calculating the total for each item, which is the base price multiplied by the quantity. After you paste in the item totals, you select them as a group and enter the sum as the subtotal. You then calculate the sales tax by multiplying the subtotal by some percentage (6 percent in the example) or by using the decimal form (**.06*); using the percent sign is a little easier. Finally, to get the grand total, you add the subtotal and the sales tax amount.

Note that in the example the operators and the sales tax formula are hidden. They do not appear in the final printout.

■ *Creating Tables from Side-by-Side Columns*

When you enter a table of numbers into Word, you type lines, not columns, although the tab characters align the entries one above another. When you transfer numbers from an on-line service such as Dow Jones or CompuServe, however, you may get them in a list, one number per line. If you want to place the columns side by side, you have to rearrange the numbers yourself, which can be quite time-consuming. One way to do this is to use the Option key to cut and paste blocks of text at a time.

Another way to format such data into columns is to use the Side-by-Side paragraph format. Each line in the column can end with either a return or a newline mark. Select all the lines that you want to put into one column and set indents for that column in the Ruler. (See Figure 14-16.) Repeat this process for each column. Then select all the columns and turn on the Side-by-Side option. Check the format in Page Preview. Figure 14-17 shows an example of columns formatted in this way. To set up separate groups of columns on a page, repeat this process for each new group.

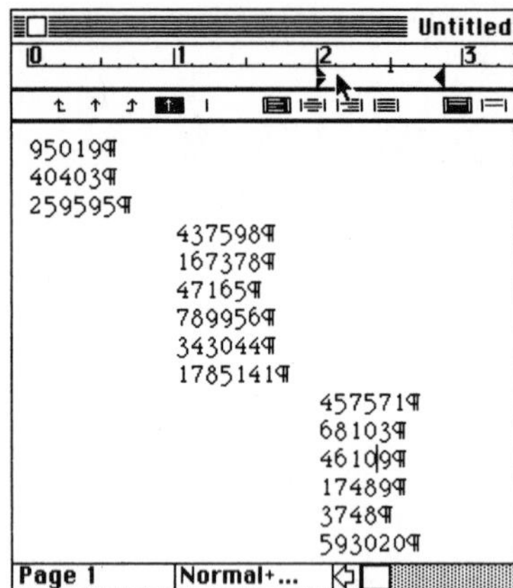

Figure 14-16
Setting Ruler indents for a column in Side-by-Side format.

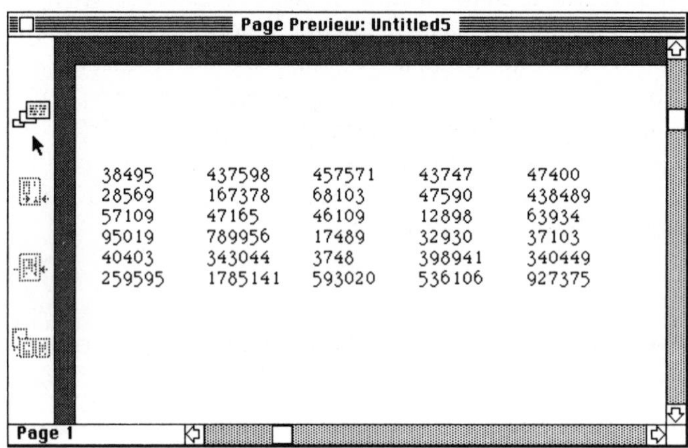

Figure 14-17
The formatted columns in Page Preview.

■ *Points to Remember*

❑ A table consists of lines containing text or data. You use tab characters to separate the elements within each line and align them vertically into columns. You can set the tab stops manually for a table, or you can define a style that has the tab stops you want.

❑ There are two ways to number items. By using the Line Numbering format you can number each line in a list; the numbering is not affected by sorting. By using the Renumber command you can insert numbers at the beginning of each paragraph in the list, and you can alter the numbering format for your needs.

❑ The Sort command arranges paragraphs in the following order: punctuation marks, numbers, and letters. It ignores double quotation marks, spaces, tabs, and diacritical characters, but not accented characters. The specific sorting order used depends on the country for which your copy of Word has been customized.

❑ The Sort command works on paragraphs only. The lines in any list or table to be sorted must end with paragraph marks, not newline marks.

If you use the Option key to select a block of text within a table, you can sort it in the order of the selected text. With this feature each line can end in either a paragraph mark or a newline mark.

❑ Word's calculation feature allows you to add, subtract, multiply, divide, and calculate percentages. It operates on the numbers in the current selection, displaying the result in the status box and also placing it on the Clipboard. The calculation proceeds from left to right and top to bottom; multiplication and division are not given precedence, and any numbers in parentheses are assumed to be negative. The result will contain commas and decimal points only if one or more of the numbers in the selection has them.

■ *Techniques*

Select a column instead of entire lines

❶ Press the Option key before dragging over the column.

You can also use Shift-clicking with this method to extend the selection.

Move a column in a table

❶ Select the column to be moved. Include the Tab character after the column in the selection, but not the one before it.

❷ Press Command-X to cut the column and place it on the Clipboard.

3. Set the insertion point where the column is to appear, before the first character of the column that will be to the right of the pasted column.
4. Press Command-V to paste the column in the specified location.

Add vertical lines between columns in a table

1. Select the entire table.
2. Using the Ruler, place a vertical line tab at each location where you want a line to appear.

Add horizontal lines to a table

1. Select the lines that are to have underlines or overlines.
2. Choose the Paragraph command.
3. Click the Below or Above option in the Border group, depending on whether you want underlines or overlines, and then click OK.

Draw a box around a table

1. End each line but the last in the table with a newline mark (Shift-Return); end the last line with a paragraph mark.
2. Set the insertion point anywhere in the table.
3. Choose the Paragraph command.
4. Select the Box option in the Border group.
5. Vary the line if you want by clicking the Thick, Double, or Shadow options, and then click OK.

Number a list by using the Line Numbering format

1. Be sure each item in the list consists of only one line of text.
2. Place the list in its own section.
3. Set the insertion point in the section.
4. Choose the Section command.
5. Turn on the Line Numbering option, and then click OK.

The line numbers do not appear until you preview or print the document.

Number a list by using the Renumber command

1. Select the list to be numbered.
2. Choose the Renumber command.
3. Set the appropriate options in the dialog box that appears, and click OK.

Word inserts the number before the first character in each paragraph.

Sort a list

1. Select the list.
2. Choose the Sort command to sort in ascending order, or press the Shift key and then choose the Sort command to sort in descending order.

Sort a table based on any column

1. Select the column that is to determine the sequence of the table. (Press the Option key as you drag.)
2. Choose the Sort command.

Word rearranges entire lines, not only the selected column.

Perform calculations on selected numbers

1. Enter math operators before each of the numbers in the calculation. The available operators are +, - (or parentheses), *, and /. For percentages, enter a percent sign (%) after the number. If you omit the operators, addition is assumed.
2. Format the operators as hidden text if you do not want them printed. They must appear on the screen when you do the calculation.
3. Select the numbers for the calculation. Any text or symbols included in the selection will be ignored.
4. Choose Calculate from the Document menu.

Word places the result in the Clipboard and displays it in the status box.

Transferring Text and Graphics

Word is a powerful program that can do much more than is commonly expected of word processors. You can extend this power by creating material in other programs and transferring it into a Word document. There are three main classes of data that you can transfer to and from a Word document: raw text, graphics, and files from certain word processors such as MacWrite and Word 3.0 for the IBM PC.

Raw text is any collection of characters without formatting such as boldface or underlining. You work with raw text when you want to incorporate into a Word document information taken from a bulletin board or information service such as CompuServe or DIALOG, tables of financial statistics from a spreadsheet, or text created with another program.

You can create illustrations and other visual elements in graphics applications, such as MacPaint, MacDraw, SuperPaint, Cricket Draw, or Illustrator, and move them into a Word document. You can also copy images from applications not ordinarily considered graphics programs. For example, you can create a chart in Microsoft Excel, copy the image of the chart to the Clipboard, and paste it into a report you're writing in Word.

Finally, Word can both read and write files in a variety of formats. The ability to read and write files in MS-DOS Word 3.0 format makes it easier to maintain common documents in an office where both Macs and PCs are used. Mac Word can also convert to the Word format files containing graphics and formatted text created with MacWrite and Microsoft Works.

You can even send a fully formatted Mac Word document through an electronic mail system such as MCI Mail by using the RTF file format.

This chapter describes how to transfer text and graphics into and out of a Word document. You'll learn how to cut and paste data, manipulate text and graphics once they are in Word, and use the Switcher and the MultiFinder for maximum efficiency.

■ *Transferring Text*

There are two ways to import and export text between Word and another program: by transferring selected text via the Clipboard or the Scrapbook and by opening and saving whole documents in a format that another program can read. Each of these will be discussed in turn.

Using the Clipboard and Scrapbook

The routines for cutting and pasting between programs are much the same no matter what program you are using. You select text or graphics in the source document and choose Cut or Copy from the Edit menu. This places the material, or a copy of it, on the Clipboard. Exit the application, and then start the program into which you want to move the material. Once you're in that application, place an insertion point and choose the Paste command.

When you cut and paste within an application such as Word, the Clipboard is maintained within an area of the Mac's memory. However, if you leave the application with something on the Clipboard, it saves the Clipboard's contents in a special file called *Clipboard File*, usually kept in the System Folder. A few programs store the Clipboard File on the disk that contains the application, and so to transfer information from one application to another, you may have to move the Clipboard File from the first disk to the second before you start the second program.

The Clipboard holds only one item at a time, but the Scrapbook can hold up to 256 items. Also, the contents of the Clipboard disappear when you copy another item to it, but items stored in the Scrapbook remain there until you remove them, allowing you to keep a collection of clip art, for instance. If you're cutting and pasting several items at a time, you can copy each item to the Clipboard and paste it into the Scrapbook before moving to the second program.

Just as the contents of the Clipboard are stored in the Clipboard File when you leave a program, the items in the Scrapbook are stored in the Scrapbook File, which is associated with the system files on the startup disk. If the application you're pasting to is on another start-up disk, copy the current Scrapbook File on it. If that disk already has a Scrapbook File, change its name before you copy; otherwise, the existing file will be erased.

You can have many scrapbook files on a given start-up disk, but each must have a different name. You can maintain different scrapbook files for different purposes; simply give each one a name that reflects its purpose, such as *Newsletter Scrapbook*, and change its name temporarily to *Scrapbook File* when you need to access its contents. The Mac always accesses the scrapbook file named Scrapbook File. If a file with that name doesn't exist on the current start-up disk, the Mac creates a new, empty one.

When you select and copy something from a program to the Clipboard, the program determines what kind of material you've copied and attaches a four-letter *data type* code to the Clipboard. If you paste the clipping into the Scrapbook, you can see this code in the lower right corner of the Scrapbook window, as shown in Figure 15-1.

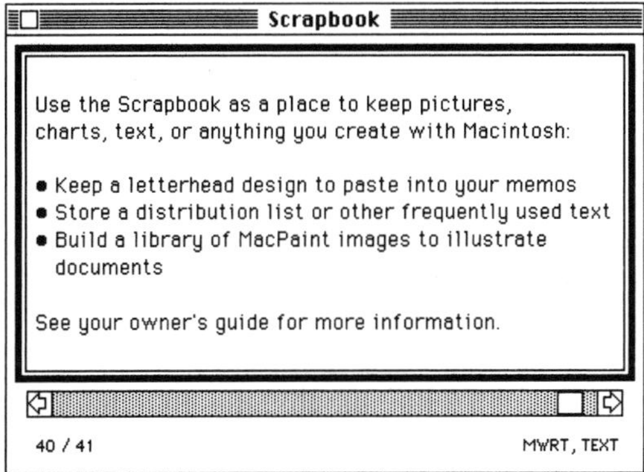

Figure 15-1
The data type code of material pasted into the Scrapbook from MacWrite.

The data type code is like a message between the routines in a program or between programs; a program uses the code to determine how to handle material stored on the Clipboard. For example, if you copy some boilerplate text from a program and store it in the Scrapbook, you'll undoubtedly see the code *TEXT* in the lower right corner of the Scrapbook window. If you paste this material into a Word document, Word checks the data type code and determines that the material on the Clipboard should be inserted into the document as text (and not, say, as a graphic).

When you copy something, the program often transfers more than one version of the selected material to the Clipboard. If you're copying formatted text, for instance, the program doesn't know whether you intend to paste the material back into a document belonging to the current application (and therefore want to retain the formatting), or whether you intend to paste it into a document that belongs to another application. Because a given program can't depend on another program to be able to interpret the internal structure it uses to format text, the program may transfer to the Clipboard both its internal version of the formatted text and a copy of the raw, unformatted text. When this happens and you paste the material into the Scrapbook, you'll see two data type codes in the Scrapbook window—one code for the internal format and the *TEXT* code for the more standard format. When you paste this material into a document belonging to the receiving program, it nearly always is able to use the unformatted version of the copied material if it is not able to handle the formatted version.

For example, if you copy text in MacWrite format to the Scrapbook, you'll see two data type codes in the Scrapbook window—*MWRT* and *TEXT*, as shown in Figure 15-1. If you start MacWrite again on another occasion and paste this material into a MacWrite document, it uses the MWRT version of the text so that the formatting is retained. If, however, you paste this material into a document within a different program, the program uses the TEXT version of the material, and the formatting does not appear.

The discussion so far has centered on how most applications handle the Clipboard and the Scrapbook. Unfortunately, Word doesn't work in quite the same way. Instead of using the standard Clipboard, Word maintains its own internal Clipboard in order to conserve memory. When you copy something, Word keeps only one version of the material—in its own internal data type—on its Clipboard. When you paste the material into the Scrapbook or switch to another application, Word converts its internal Clipboard into the standard, external Clipboard. This converts the internal data type into the standard TEXT data type, and any formatting the material had is lost.

When you paste text copied from the Scrapbook or from another program into a Word document, the result is the same, regardless of whether the text originally came from another program or from Word itself. When you place an insertion point in a document and paste such raw text, Word assigns it the style of the surrounding text but adds the New York character format. If the pasted text contains paragraph marks, the text preceding each paragraph mark takes on the *Normal* style. This happens regardless of the original style of the paragraph and regardless of whether you've redefined the *Normal* style or not.

This can be especially confusing when the definition for the *Normal* style—or any style that the pasted text has assumed—already specifies the New York font. If you then redefine that style to use a font other than New York, the text you've typed in changes to reflect the new font, but the pasted text stays in the New York font. In this situation you must select the affected text and choose Plain Text from the Format menu to return the text to the base character format defined for that style. Showing the Ruler and clicking the X icon to reassert the *Normal* style for the selected text doesn't change this character format.

TIP

Keep Formatted Text in the Glossary
Because text copied to the Scrapbook loses its formatting, if you want to store blocks of formatted text as boilerplate material, put them in a glossary or template document instead.

Transferring Tabular Data

As discussed in the previous chapter, tabular data consists of a series of lines in which each item is separated by tabs and each line ends in a paragraph mark. You can transfer raw text structured in this way between Word and spreadsheet and database programs, either by copying it from Word and pasting it into the other program or by saving the file in Text Only format (discussed in the next section).

Some programs, including Microsoft Excel, File, and Multiplan, can translate tabular data into their own file formats. In spreadsheets such as Microsoft Excel, each line of text is considered one row divided into columns by tabs. In database programs such as Microsoft File, each line of text is treated as a complete record. Commas or tabs in the table divide the items into fields. To export data from Word to a spreadsheet or database program:

1. Select and copy the desired section of data from within Word.
2. Quit Word and start the spreadsheet or file-management program.
3. Set an insertion point in the spreadsheet (or start a new record in the database manager). Choose the Paste command.

Technically, the data in Word need not conform strictly to a rows-and-columns structure for it to be transferred into a spreadsheet or database program. For example, a series of lines with no tabs in Word will become a single column in a spreadsheet program, with one paragraph per cell.

Importing data from a spreadsheet or database program to Word works along the same lines: A row in Microsoft Excel translates to a paragraph in Word. When pasted into Word, the cells within each row are separated by tabs. With a database manager, each record becomes a paragraph, and the contents of the fields are separated by commas or tabs. To import data from an electronic spreadsheet or database manager, do the following:

1. Select and copy the desired area of data from within the spreadsheet or file-management program.
2. Quit the program and start Word.
3. Set an insertion point for the data and choose the Paste command.
4. Select the data you pasted in, and set the tab stops in the Ruler to accommodate the columns. If necessary, adjust the right indent so that each row of data takes up only one line in the Word document.

If the imported data is separated by commas, you can use the Change command to replace all commas with tabs automatically:

1. Select the text you pasted into the Word document.
2. Choose Change from the Search menu.
3. In the Change dialog box, type a comma in the Find What field and type ^*t* in the Change To field. Click the Change Selection button.

Some database managers allow you to copy only one record at a time or require that you use a conversion utility or save selected records to an ASCII-format document and then open the resulting document in Word. Once a file has been converted, Word can open it as a text-only document. See the instructions that accompany the database-management program for more details on the steps you must perform to import and export data.

Transferring Text Documents

If the block of text you want to transfer is large, it's often better to bypass the Clipboard and work with the text at the document level. Word can directly read and write documents created by a variety of other word processors and programs. You see a list of these formats when you choose Save As from the File menu and click the File Format button. The use of certain of these formats involves some interesting practical issues, however. The range of formats and document structures Word 3.0 offers is extensive (multicolumn section formats and footnotes, for example), and so Word translates formats to and from other applications as best it can.

The Text Only and Text Only with Line Breaks File Formats

You could call Text Only and Text Only with Line Breaks the generic file-format options for transferring files from Word to any other Macintosh program. Both these formats save a Word document as raw text, but the Text Only with Line Breaks format puts a paragraph mark at the end of each line. This is helpful when you want to upload a Word document to an electronic mail or bulletin board service. Of course, all of the character and paragraph formats disappear from text saved in these formats. Word also converts new-line marks, section marks, and page breaks into paragraph marks, and it converts optional hyphens into normal hyphens. If you intend to transfer the document to a computer other than a Macintosh, either through a modem or via a bulletin board service, be aware that other computers do not share many of the Mac's graphic characters (such as ¶, •, ™, —, and so on); you'll have to search for these and change them manually.

Word can also read files that have been saved in a text-only format with another program. Even if the program you are using can't save the document in any of the formats that Word can translate, it probably does have some type of text-only, file-saving option. When you choose Word's Open command, you see not only the names of all the standard Word documents, but all the documents that Word is able to read and translate into a normal Word document, including ones that are text only as well as ones created with MacWrite, MacTerminal, Word 1.05, Works, MS-DOS Word, and so on.

In Microsoft Excel, for instance, you can choose Save As from the File menu and click the Text file-format option. (Incidentally, Microsoft Excel saves either the values in the worksheet or the formulas, depending on which is visible when you choose the Save As command. Choose Display from the

Options menu to switch between the two views.) Be sure to change the name so that you don't overwrite the original worksheet file. If a cell in the worksheet contains a comma, Microsoft Excel surrounds the text with quotation marks in the file saved on disk.

Once you've saved a file in this way, the name of the file appears in the list box when you choose Word's Open command. When you open the file, you can remove the quotation marks by searching for them and replacing them with nothing, but if you want to use the text in a data document for a merged form letter, you may want to keep these marks. (Read Chapter 16 for a complete discussion of form letters.)

Microsoft Word Version 1.05 and Microsoft Works File Format

Some people who don't need the power of Word 3.0 prefer the ease of use and integration offered by Microsoft Works. Works is able to read the Word 1.05 format well, so there isn't a separate option for saving a document in Works format. Use the Microsoft Word 1.05 file format to store a Word 3.0 document in a format readable by Word 1.05 or Works. Again, not all of a Word 3.0 document's formats will survive the transition. For example, Word 1.05 doesn't support style sheets, so if you save in Word 1.05 formatted text assigned a style, the text takes on the character and paragraph formats of the style without actually keeping the style.

The MS-DOS Word 3.0 File Format

Mac Word's conversion of files in the MS-DOS Word 3.0 format is perhaps the most complete with respect to the actual structure of the document. This feature is helpful in offices that use computers from both the Macintosh and the IBM PC families, because it permits the sharing of standard documents between the two types of machines. Word-specific features such as headers, footers, footnotes, and so on, transfer well between the two versions of Word.

However, certain features that the programs don't share, such as graphics, character formats such as outline and shadow, and paragraph formats such as the box options, are not translated. The transfer of style sheets depends on the direction in which the transfer is going. You can transfer a style sheet for an MS-DOS document to the Mac, but you can't transfer the style sheet for a Mac document to the PC. Also, section styles from MS-DOS documents are not converted. When you save a Mac Word document containing styles in the MS-DOS Word format, the styles are converted into individual character and paragraph formats.

Probably the main issue regarding the sharing of files is how to actually get the file from one machine to the other. One way is to use network software such as Centram's TOPS to connect Macs and PCs via AppleTalk. Another is to connect a special drive to either the Mac or the PC that can read the other machine's formats. The most common way is to connect the two machines through modems or with an appropriate cable that connects their serial ports (the Phone, or modem, port on the Mac), run telecommunication software on each machine, and use an XModem communication protocol to manage the transfer of the file. Here are some suggested communication parameters for Microsoft Access on the IBM PC and MacTerminal:

Access	
Modify settings	9600 baud, half duplex, 8-bit word length, no parity, 1 stop bit, TTY terminal, XOn/XOff protocol, ^M end-of-line character.
MacTerminal	
Terminal settings	TTY, on line, local echo, auto wraparound, new line.
Compatibility settings	9600 baud, 8 bits, no parity, XOn/XOff protocol, connection via either modem or another computer, depending on how you've connected the machines, Phone, or modem port.
File-transfer settings	No delays for pasting or sending text (but change the setting if the received text is missing characters), straight XModem protocol.

To transfer a document from MacTerminal to Access, do the following:

❶ Save the document in MS-DOS Word format. It's helpful to use a filename that conforms to the MS-DOS Word file-naming convention, up to 8 characters, ending with *DOC*. The name of the document doesn't change, because you are only saving a copy of it in the MS-DOS format.

❷ Start both communications programs, and set the programs' communications parameters if you haven't already done so. (You can save these sets of parameters to make subsequent sessions easier.)

❸ Establish a connection, and choose Send File from MacTerminal's File menu. A dialog box appears; find the MS-DOS file and double-click on the name to open it. A dialog box appears, saying *Sending the file "filename"*. At this point, MacTerminal waits for Access to respond to its attempts to send the file.

❹ On the PC, press the F10 key to activate the command menu, and use the Transfer Protocol Receive command (type *T*, *P*, and *R*). Access prompts you for a filename; enter the name of the file you are transferring. Soon Access will tell MacTerminal that it's ready to receive the file: You'll see the gauge in MacTerminal's dialog box begin to move, and the Bytes Received field in Access will increment by 128 bytes at a time. (The XModem protocol transfers data in blocks of 128 bytes.)

To send an MS-DOS file to the Mac, the process is similar, but because MS-DOS Word keeps its style sheets separate from the documents, you have to transfer the MS-DOS Word document and its style sheet in separate steps.

❶ In MS-DOS Word, save the document in the Formatted format, and quit the program.

❷ Start both communications programs and set their communications parameters if you haven't already done so. Establish a connection between the machines.

❸ On the PC, press the F10 key to activate the command menu, and use the Transfer Protocol Send command (type *T*, *P*, and *S*). Access prompts you for a filename; enter the MS-DOS Word document's name. (You may also need to supply a pathname.) At this point, Access waits for MacTerminal to respond to its attempts to send the file.

❹ In MacTerminal, choose Receive File from the File menu. A dialog box appears; enter the name of the MS-DOS file, and click the Receive button. A second dialog box appears, saying *Receiving the file "filename"*. Soon MacTerminal will tell Access it's ready to receive the file: Instead of the gauge in MacTerminal's dialog box, you'll see the Blocks Received number begin to increment in blocks of 512 bytes and the Count field in Access incrementing. When the transfer is complete, MacTerminal presents a dialog box telling you that the transfer was successful.

❺ When you've transferred the document, repeat steps ❸ and ❹ to transfer the style sheet for the document, if you have defined one.

❻ Once both the document and its style sheet have been transferred to the Mac, start Mac Word and choose the Open command. Double-click on the filename of the MS-DOS Word document to open it. When Word opens the document, it discovers its source and presents a dialog box asking if there is a style sheet file for the document. If you click Yes, you'll see another dialog box containing a file list box. Simply double-click on the name of the style sheet file; Word then uses it to create a normal Word document. If you don't have a style sheet file for the document, click No; Word then uses its default style sheet.

The MacWrite Format

If you've moved up to Word from MacWrite, you'll find that it's easy to convert all your MacWrite documents into Word documents. Simply open the MacWrite file from within Word, and the file will be converted to the standard Word format and placed in an untitled window. Some programs are able to read and save documents in MacWrite format but not in Word format, so if you need to transfer a file to or from such a program and preserve as much formatting as possible, try saving the file in this format.

The Interchange (Rich Text) Format

The Rich Text Format (RTF) file format may seem obscure, but it can be very useful when you want to transfer a fully formatted Word document to someone via an electronic communications medium that cannot handle the binary transfer of Mac files. With MacTerminal, for instance, you can transfer any Mac document, associated icon and all, by using the MacBinary file-transfer protocol. However, many bulletin boards and communications services, such as MCI Mail, cannot store and transfer such files to their destination in this format and can only accept straight ASCII, raw text files.

If you save a Word document in RTF, Word converts everything in it into sequences of standard ASCII text characters, even complicated structures such as graphics and style sheets. Word also breaks paragraphs into lines of at most 255 characters so that the long lines that make up paragraphs will not confuse the computer system. Figure 15-2 shows an example of a text file resulting from this conversion.

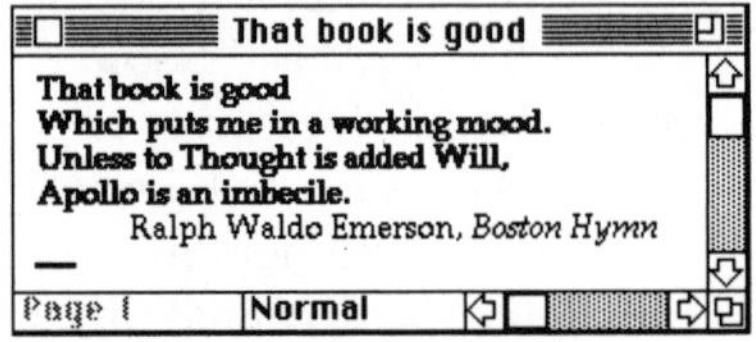

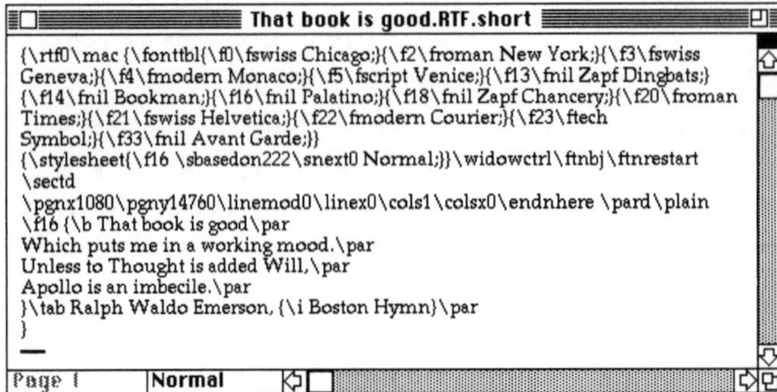

Figure 15-2
A document shown in Word format and RTF format.

If you inspect this format, you might realize that its codes are not impossible to decipher. For example, paragraph marks become *\par*, and **boldface text** becomes *{\b boldface text}*. You can upload a file in this format to an electronic mail service or a text-only bulletin board or transmit it directly to someone who doesn't have a communications program that can handle binary file formats.

When you receive an RTF file, you can capture the RTF text in two ways. The first way is to use the communication program's capture-to-disk feature (most of them have this), and save the RTF text on disk as a text file. The other way is to select and copy the RTF text within the communications program and paste it into a blank Word document. Save this document in the Text Only format, and close the document. The most important step in capturing and saving this text to a file is to be sure the actual beginning of the RTF text, *{\rtf,* starts within the first two characters in the file. This signals Word that the text in the file is in the RTF format.

Regardless of how you created the text file containing the RTF text, when you open the document in Word, the program presents a dialog box saying *Interpret RTF Text?* This gives you the option of opening the document as uninterpreted RTF codes if you want. If you click Yes, Word reassembles the formats in the document and creates a standard Word document in a new document window. After the conversion is complete, you can save it in the default format; from that point on, it's like any other Word document.

TIP

Advanced Uses for RTF Files
An earlier chapter mentioned that because Word knows a font by its ID number, rather than its complete font name, text formatted in a font on one Mac sometimes appears in a different font when opened on another Mac. As you can see in Figure 15-2, however, when a document is encoded in RTF, the fonts in it are referred to by name as well as by font ID (FID) number. If you send a document in this format, when the receiving copy of Word on the destination Mac opens the RTF document, the fonts are mapped correctly, by name rather than by FID number. If you have problems with fonts changing from one Mac to the next, try transferring the document as an RTF file.

Programmers find another interesting use for RTF files. Because in an RTF file the entire structure of the document, including graphics and styles, is encoded in a (for programmers) readable ASCII text format, it's much easier to write utility programs that manipulate RTF files to translate or otherwise operate on the internal structure of Word documents. Some examples follow:

- You can make global formatting changes by using the Change command to replace one format code with another. For example, to change every instance of boldface text in a document to underlined text, first save the document in RTF. Then, replace every instance of *\b* with *\ul*. Finally, close and reopen the document and convert it to standard Word format.
- You can write programs that automatically scale all the graphics in a document at once. To see how Word translates graphics into RTF, try pasting a simple MacDraw graphic (a circle, for instance) into a short Word document, save the document as an RTF file, and then open the file without interpreting it.
- You can perform complicated searches for combinations of text strings and formats, such as "replace all instances of *** with an incremented number that represents a bibliographic reference (from a list in another document), and put it in bold, 8-point, superscripted text." You could use this technique to number bibliographic references automatically across many chapters in a book at once.

- ❑ You can enforce one style sheet more easily across many documents by saving a document as an RTF file and then replacing its style sheet with the master style sheet. You could even extend this principle and develop document-level and section-level "style sheets" that standardize document and section properties, such as page size, margin settings, header and footer formats, and so on.

The possibilities are endless. For more information on the RTF specification, write Microsoft Corporation, RTF/Applications, 16011 NE 36th Way, Box 97017, Redmond WA 98073-9717.

The Document Content Architecture Format

The Document Content Architecture format (DCA, sometimes also called RFT or Revisable Format Text) was developed by IBM to provide a standard translation protocol between IBM mainframe and PC word processors. Most popular PC word processors provide support for this file format, including DisplayWriter, Manuscript, MultiMate, WordPerfect, and WordStar. MS-DOS Word can use this format too, although you will generally save files in the default PC Word format instead. To convert files from the DCA format to the Word format and vice versa within the MS-DOS Word environment, use the RFTOWORD and WORDTORF programs that accompany the software. (Notice that the RF in these program names refers to Revisable Format text.)

To convert a Mac Word document into DCA format, use the DCA Conversion program included on the Word Utilities disk of the Word package. This program converts DCA-format files to RTF and back again. Once you've converted a DCA file into RTF, you start Word and open the RTF file to convert it into a standard Word document. Conversely, to convert a standard Word document into a DCA format file, save the document as an RTF file; then quit Word and use the DCA Conversion program to create a DCA file.

Two-Step Conversions

As you can see, converting a standard Word document to a DCA-format file is a two-step process. Other combinations are possible. For instance, if you needed to convert a PC WordStar file into a Mac Word document, you could use the CONVWS program provided with the MS-DOS Word software package to convert the file into an MS-DOS Word file, and then transfer the file to the Mac and convert it into a standard Mac Word document.

Using Shift-Open as a Last Resort

If the program from which you want to import text can't save the file in one of the formats that Word can translate (even Text Only), you can try using Word's ability to open just about any type of document, no matter what source program was used to create it. You can also use this feature when you need to get at the contents of a document but don't have access to the program that created it. Word will not, of course, recognize the internal codes used by the source program for special formatting or graphics. These formatting codes may appear in the opened file as gibberish, nontext or symbol characters, or squares denoting undefined characters, which you must manually remove.

To open an alien document in Word, first try to save it in an ASCII or text-only format from the source program; if one is not available, use a format that is as close to raw text as possible. If you want to preserve the original copy of the file, make a duplicate of it from the Finder's desktop by selecting it and choosing Duplicate from the File menu. Then, do this:

❶ In Word, press the Shift key and choose the Open command. (Use the mouse to choose the command, not the Command-O keyboard shortcut.)

❷ In the Open dialog box, you'll see a list of all the documents on the current disk, regardless of whether or not they are in a format that Word can read. You may even see filenames you never knew existed; these may be hidden temporary files used by some programs. It's best to leave these files, programs, and system files alone, unless you're opening a copy of the file. When you find the document you want, open it.

❸ Nine times out of ten, Word opens the document successfully; if it can't, Word presents a dialog box telling you this. For example, even though you can try to open files such as the MacPaint program as a "document," Word may not be able to make enough sense of what it finds to open the file at all. Some portions of the document may include squares, odd characters, and page and section marks. Remove these manually (but first read the next section for tips on doing this).

❹ When you are finished editing, choose the Save As command, click the File Format button, and select the Normal file format. Use a new name for the opened, edited version. The document is now a standard Word document, and you can format and print it as usual.

Cleaning Up Imported Files

After you've brought text into a Word document, particularly after using Word's Shift-Open feature or after a conversion from another format, you'll often see strange characters sprinkled throughout the imported text. You can simply delete many of these characters. Others require a little more work because they're not visible when Show ¶ is off. Even when you've turned on Show ¶, you may see only empty boxes sprinkled through the document, denoting an ASCII code for which there is no corresponding character. To remove these characters, do the following:

❶ Choose Show ¶ from the Edit menu.

❷ Select one of the undesired characters in the document.

❸ Press Option-Command-Q to find its ASCII code.

❹ Choose Change from the Search menu. Enter ^ and the character's ASCII number in the Find What field. Leave the Change To field blank (or replace the character with one space if necessary).

❺ Click the Change All, Start Search, or Change Selection button as needed.

❻ Repeat steps ❷ through ❺ for each undesired character.

For example, if you've transferred a PC file to the Mac, you may have linefeed characters as well as paragraph marks (otherwise known as carriage returns) at the end of each paragraph. If you follow these steps, you will find that the ASCII code for a linefeed character is 10, and so you would enter *^10* in the Find What field of the Change dialog box.

■ *Transferring Graphics*

Word is almost as comfortable with graphics as it is with text. You can easily create images in any of the common graphics programs, such as MacPaint, FullPaint, SuperPaint, MacDraw, Cricket Draw, and Illustrator, and move them into a Word document. However, to achieve the highest quality possible from the combination of Word, the graphics program, and the printer you're using, you need to understand the kind of graphics you're transferring and some of the deeper issues involved in preparing and moving them into a Word document.

The Types of Graphic Elements

The Macintosh, and programs written for it, support a variety of formats for describing graphics. The developers of a program are, for the most part, free to represent a graphic within the program itself in any way they want in order to display it on the screen as patterns of pixels. On the other hand, the Mac environment is intrinsically an integrated system, one of the main advantages of which is the ability to share information more easily among programs than is possible with other computers.

In order for you to use an image you've created with a drawing program, for instance, in a Word document, the image must be represented in a standard format so that both programs can read it. The transfer of graphic data from one program to another usually happens so naturally in the Mac world that it's sometimes difficult to think of a graphic as anything other than simply a picture. This is a tribute to the vast amount of work the developers of the Mac have devoted to making this integration as seamless and intuitive as possible; however, every graphic image is a complicated pattern of bits and bytes.

There are three common ways of representing a graphic for transfer between programs: as a bit map, as a QuickDraw graphic, or as a set of PostScript commands that describe the graphic object.

Bit-mapped Graphics

Bit-mapped graphics are represented as pixels. A program describes an image in this format as rows and columns of bits, with each bit representing a black or white dot in the image. Programs that create bit-mapped graphics use a painting metaphor, in which you apply patterns of pixels with an image of a brush. Figure 15-3 shows a close-up of some objects in this format.

Figure 15-3
Several bit-mapped graphic objects, magnified by a factor of 2.

Bit-mapped graphics have many advantages. Most common graphics programs, such as MacPaint, FullPaint, and SuperPaint, handle bit-mapped graphics (although SuperPaint can work with object-oriented graphics as well). Often, the textures created by the patterns of bits you use in a painted image produce an artistic effect that can't be duplicated by any other means.

Another advantage is related to the fact that everything you actually see on the Mac's screen is a bit map, regardless of what that bit map represents (a circle or some text, say). For example, if you want to include a picture of a Mac screen in a document (as has been done throughout this book), you create a *screen dump* in this bit-mapped format by pressing Shift-Command-3. (This is described in more detail in the Tip, "Creating a Screen Dump," later in this chapter.)

Also, if you digitize a photograph using any of the scanners available, the program that drives the scanner can save the image either as a bit-mapped graphic or in its own internal format (which usually cannot be read by or transferred to any other program).

However, bit-mapped graphics have disadvantages as well. Most painting programs do not let you create an image based on independent objects; if you move an object in the foreground that covers something in the background, you have to reconstruct the part of the background that was hidden.

In addition, bit-mapped graphics have a lower resolution than other types of graphics because almost all bit maps are derived from the 72-dot-per-inch resolution of the standard Mac screen. Consequently, when you copy a graphic from a painting program into another program and print it, particularly on a PostScript printer such as the LaserWriter, the printed image is constructed of square pixels instead of smooth lines. You can use this to your advantage, however, as you will see a little later, because Word lets you squeeze a 72-dot-per-inch image into a smaller space, resulting in much higher resolution.

QuickDraw Object-Oriented Graphics

Object-oriented graphics consist of discrete elements—such as circles, squares, lines, and polygons—that together make up the image. The objects are created with QuickDraw, a graphics language and set of special routines built into the Mac's ROM. So-called drawing programs that create object-oriented graphics include MacDraw, Cricket Draw, and the drawing features in SuperPaint. You can also copy QuickDraw images from Illustrator, even though the program is designed to generate PostScript descriptions of graphics. Certain nondrawing programs, such as Microsoft Excel and Microsoft Chart, also provide QuickDraw graphics. Figure 15-4 shows the same objects as those in Figure 15-3, only as QuickDraw graphic objects.

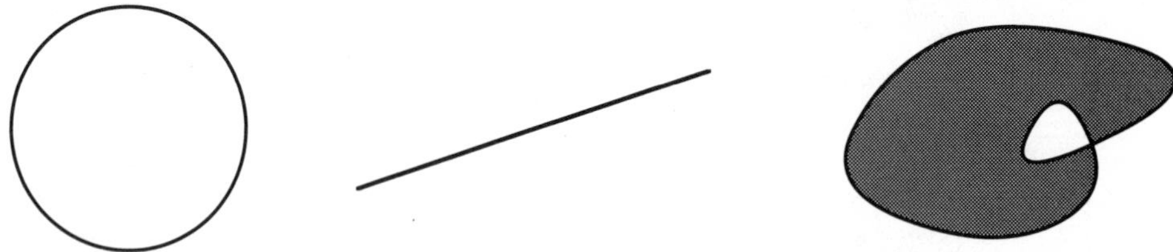

Figure 15-4
The same graphic objects as in Figure 15-3 shown in QuickDraw format.

You will want to use object-oriented graphics if the document is to be printed with the LaserWriter or other PostScript-driven output device, such as a digital phototypesetter. These devices smooth the contours of object-oriented graphics much better than they do the contours of bit-mapped graphics. The result is a sharper image.

Printing quality is only one of the advantages of QuickDraw object-oriented graphics. Because each component of the graphic is encoded in QuickDraw commands instead of having every pixel in the image set explicitly, QuickDraw graphics take up much less space than bit-mapped graphics. This can be a great help when you are working with large Word documents because it becomes more difficult to edit a document larger than a certain size, depending on the amount of memory installed in your Mac and the complexity of the document (the number of styles, paragraphs, and so on). Therefore, try to copy an image as a collection of QuickDraw objects rather than as a bit map whenever possible; charts, line drawings, diagrams, and tables are good candidates for this.

Another advantage of object-oriented graphics is that each component of such an image is independent of the others. Whereas moving the parts of a bit-mapped image usually requires repainting the uncovered areas in the image, with object-oriented graphics you can select, modify, and reposition each element without disturbing the others. For instance, suppose that you have created an image in MacDraw, pasted it into a Word document, and then discovered you need to edit the graphic. Because the graphic is in QuickDraw format, you can cut the graphic from the Word document, paste it back into a MacDraw window, and then select and move each part of the image, as you did when creating it.

The PICT Graphic Format

The PICT graphic format is a special interchange format for transferring both bit-mapped and object-oriented graphics between programs on the Mac. Technically, the PICT format is like a recording medium for calls that a program makes to the QuickDraw toolbox in the Mac ROM. The list of operations that construct an image in MacDraw, for instance, becomes a list of encoded instructions in the PICT format. You can see this when you copy a graphic from a painting or drawing program and paste it into the Scrapbook: The PICT data type code appears in the lower right corner. This format and the TEXT data type are used in the majority of data interchanges that occur through the Clipboard and Scrapbook.

When you copy something from a program that deposits two versions of the material onto the Clipboard, and then paste it into another program, if one of the data type codes attached to the Clipboard is either TEXT or PICT, you can usually count on the program's being able to interpret and use the material. For example, when you copy a chart from Microsoft Excel and paste it into MacDraw, every part of the chart becomes a separate object that you can move or alter as you wish. Figure 15-5 shows a chart copied directly from Microsoft Excel and pasted into the document that resulted in this chapter. Figure 15-6 shows the same chart after changes were made in MacDraw.

A graphic in the PICT format has all the benefits of both bit-mapped and object-oriented graphics. You can edit the object-oriented parts of the graphic in a program that uses the QuickDraw format, such as MacDraw or Cricket Draw, and then copy any bit-mapped elements it contains into a painting program such as MacPaint, FullPaint, or SuperPaint, edit it there, and copy it back into the drawing program. (Note that SuperPaint is able to handle both bit maps and a limited range of object-oriented functions.)

If you want to achieve the highest level of quality from graphics programs on the Mac, the PICT format does have one drawback: The minimum resolution any object can have is one pixel, roughly equal to one point. This means that you can position any element in a PICT graphic only to the nearest point, and the thickness of lines must be in multiples of a point. This is fine for most documents but doesn't come close to the level of refinement attainable by traditional graphic arts techniques. For that you need PostScript.

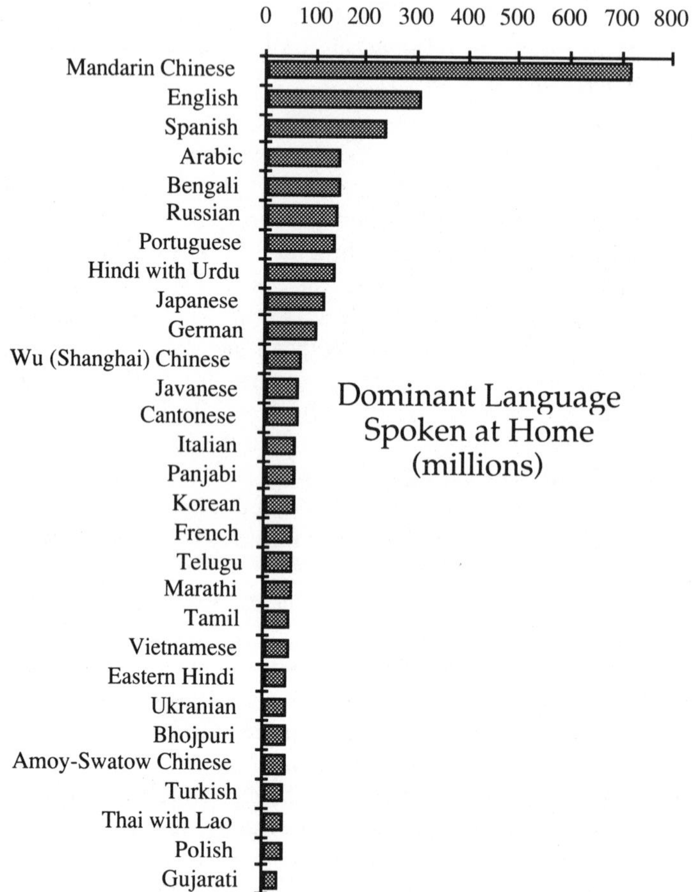

Figure 15-5
A graphic copied directly from Microsoft Excel.

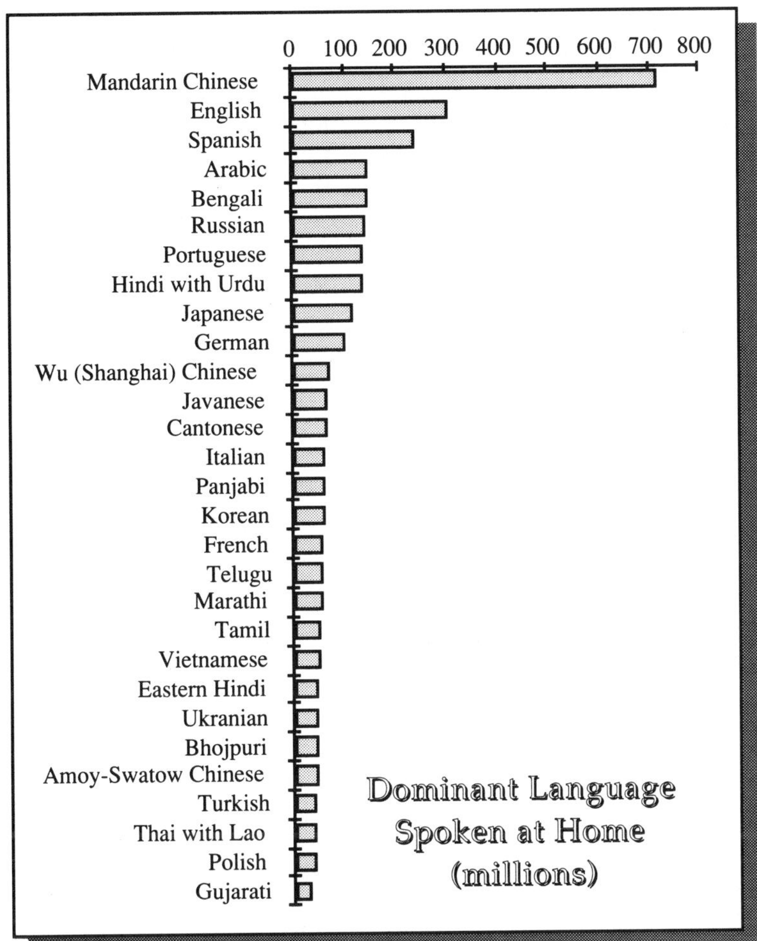

Figure 15-6
The same chart after being altered in MacDraw.

The PostScript and EPSF Formats

The third major format for encoding graphics in the Mac environment is the PostScript format. As both printers and programs become more powerful, developers are finding it increasingly difficult to support the range of printer control codes offered by a large number of printers. John Warnock, Chuck Geschke, and others of Adobe Systems, Incorporated, developed PostScript to respond to this need for a standard *page-description language* to control printers. PostScript acts as an intermediary between a program and a PostScript-compatible printer; the program needs only to translate the elements in a document into a set of operators that describe those elements. PostScript is a powerful and extensive language, but you can use it to achieve a surprising range of effects without a deep understanding of the language; Appendix C presents enough of an overview for you to get started with it.

The set of PostScript routines for creating graphics is larger than that of QuickDraw. And while the lower limit of resolution for the description of graphic objects offered by QuickDraw and the PICT format is one pixel (1/72 inch), the lower limit of resolution supported by PostScript is the lower limit of the printer, not the screen, and can be as small as 1/2540 inch. For example, the thinnest lines you can create in QuickDraw are 1 point wide. Because of this, you can create PostScript graphics that are too detailed to be represented on the Macintosh screen. Therefore, programs that generate PostScript graphics usually create two forms of the graphic—one for the screen and one in PostScript. When you make changes to the screen version, which may not show all the detail of the printed result, the program changes both versions.

Programs that support PostScript directly, by explicitly encoding their graphic objects in PostScript code that you can save or transport to another program, do so in several ways. The first way is simply to generate a text list of the PostScript commands that create each graphic object on the printer. The data type of these PostScript commands is TEXT, and you can send them directly to a PostScript-compatible printer without using Word (via Adobe's SendPS program, for instance, or from the program itself in the case of Cricket Draw).

Some graphics programs, such as Cricket Draw and Illustrator, can save PostScript graphics in the Encapsulated PostScript File, or EPSF, format. This format is identical to the raw text version of the graphic, except that it saves a PICT version of the graphic in addition to the PostScript code. (For those who have a little more background, the PostScript code is stored in the data fork of the EPSF file, and the PICT image is stored as a resource in the resource fork.) Although Word cannot open these files directly, if you press the Shift key while choosing the Open command with the mouse, you'll see the names of files stored in this format among those listed in the Open dialog box. Simply double-click on the name of a file in the EPSF format; when Word opens it, you will see the PostScript commands that correspond to the image, although you won't see the PICT-format image.

Once you get the PostScript code representing a graphic into a Word document, either by copying the PostScript code or by opening a file containing the PostScript code, select it and assign it the *PostScript* automatic style. When the document is printed, the PostScript code is interpreted to produce the graphic; you don't see the graphic until the document is printed. There are a few fine points involved in copying PostScript graphics into a Word document; Appendix C goes into these in more detail.

There is also another approach for those who want to get the benefits of PostScript without doing the work. When you copy a graphic from either Cricket Draw or Illustrator as a PICT image, the program makes use of a special feature of the PICT data format called a PICT comment. By using PICT comments, the program can bury the PostScript description of the object in the PICT image itself. If you paste this image into the Scrapbook, you will see the PICT data type but no indication that PostScript commands are buried in the image. When you paste the image into a Word document, you see the PICT graphic, but when the document is printed, the PostScript version is printed, not the PICT version. Figure 15-7 shows a graphic created in Cricket Draw as you might see it in a Word document, and Figure 15-8 on page 427 shows the same graphic when printed on an ImageWriter, a LaserWriter, and a Linotronic L300.

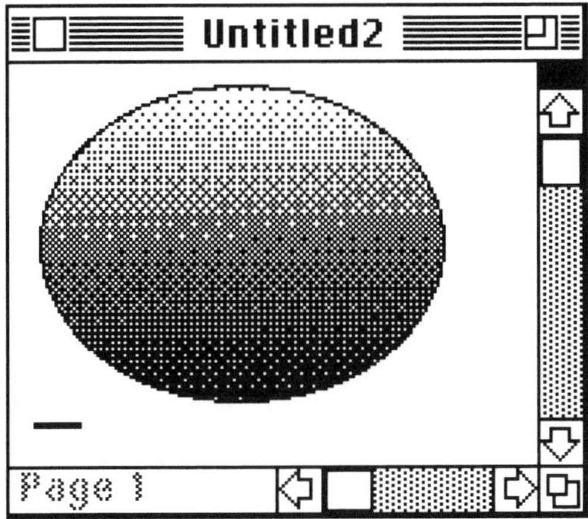

Figure 15-7
A PICT image as it appears on screen after being pasted into a Word document.

There is a drawback to this approach, however. When PostScript code is buried within a PICT image like this, the set of PostScript operators that describe the graphic can often get very large. The standard screen dumps used in this book, for instance, are usually between 10 KB and 15 KB apiece. The same image, with labels and other embellishments added in the form of buried PostScript comments, may exceed 50 KB when copied in this form. If you're using many such images in a Word document, the size of the document may grow enormously—in fact, it can get so large that Word may no longer be able to handle it effectively. Until new versions of these programs are developed that minimize the amount of PostScript code buried within a PICT graphic, you may need to either limit the number of such graphics in your Word documents or split up the document into smaller segments.

Printing Quality and the Format of a Graphic

To explore the differences between bit-mapped, QuickDraw, and PostScript graphics more fully, let's follow a simple graphic from conception to printed image. A circle, for example, is fundamentally a mathematical shape. You can describe it mathematically by stating the coordinates for its center and its radius, using a grid corresponding to a piece of paper or the screen.

A program can take that description and translate it into an image consisting of an arrangement of pixels, either on the screen or on paper. It can do this either by painting bits or by encoding the image as a series of QuickDraw object-oriented graphics commands. When you print the graphic with the latter method, the program translates it into a list of QuickDraw operations that are fed to the driver for the printer you've set in the Chooser. If you are printing with the ImageWriter, the ImageWriter driver converts the QuickDraw commands into bands of bit-mapped graphic data and sends off each band to the ImageWriter. You see the image on the page grow from top to bottom not by lines of type, but by bands of bits.

In terms of the quality of the resulting image, if the ultimate destination of the graphic is the Mac screen or the ImageWriter alone, it doesn't matter whether the graphic is in bit-mapped, object-oriented, or PICT-with-buried-PostScript format. All you see is the image in pixels, and therefore the smallest detail you'll see will be pixel sized or larger.

The situation is different, however, if you're printing on a LaserWriter or other PostScript printer. When you send the graphic to a PostScript-compatible printer, the LaserWriter driver converts the QuickDraw commands into PostScript. If the document contains PICT images, it breaks them apart and converts each component, whether it is a bit-mapped graphic or an object-oriented graphic, into the appropriate PostScript commands. Although bit-mapped graphics cannot be translated into a higher resolution than their structure in pixels, the LaserWriter printer driver converts object-oriented graphics into PostScript commands that describe every object in the image. If the document contains any PostScript commands, either as text commands assigned the *PostScript* style or as PostScript code buried within a PICT image, they are passed on to the printer unchanged.

When all these PostScript commands reach the printer, they are drawn on the paper at the highest resolution the printer is capable of producing. The resolutions of the more common output devices, expressed in dots per inch, are as follows:

Device	Resolution
Mac screen	72 DPI
ImageWriter	72, 80, and 144 DPI (When you print at 50% reduction, you can compact the image's pixels to 144 DPI.)
LaserWriter	300 DPI (for the LaserWriter and most laser printers)
Linotronic 300	635, 1270, and 2540 DPI

Thus, depending on your printer and on the graphic format, a printed graphic may have a much higher level of detail than the same image when displayed on the screen. Figure 15-8 shows an image prepared in Cricket Draw and printed on a range of printers.

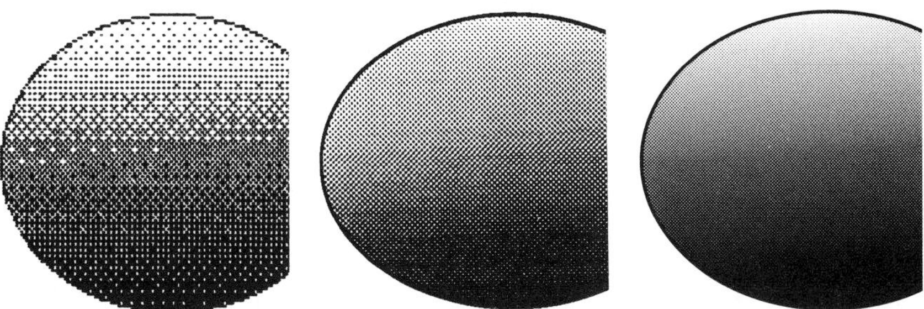

Figure 15-8
A Cricket Draw graphic printed on an ImageWriter, a LaserWriter, and a Linotronic L300.

Importing and Working with Graphics

The type of graphic format does not matter when you are importing an image to a Word document. You copy and paste both bit-mapped and QuickDraw graphics in the same way. To import a graphic:

❶ Create the graphic, if necessary, in the graphics program. Select it and copy it to the Clipboard. See the next section for specifics regarding various programs.

❷ Quit the graphics program and start Word.

❸ Set an insertion point for the graphic, and choose the Paste command. You can insert the graphic either in a paragraph by itself or in a paragraph containing text or other graphics.

When you insert the graphic, the insertion point moves to the immediate right of the graphic; it is as tall as the graphic itself. If you click on the graphic to select it, you will see the graphic's *cropping box*. You can also display the limits of the graphic by choosing Show ¶ from the Edit menu.

Copying from Various Applications

Transferring a graphic from an application is usually easy: You copy it from a document in the application and paste it into the Word document. The graphic will be in the PICT format and will be made up of some combination of bit-mapped, object-oriented, and buried PostScript elements. In certain applications, however, transferring graphics can be a little more complicated. Keep in mind that most of the following programs transfer an object-oriented version of the copied graphic to the Clipboard. Consequently, if you want to modify the graphic before copying it again and pasting it into Word, do so in a drawing program that can accept PICT graphics, such as MacDraw, Cricket Draw, or the drawing portion of SuperPaint, if possible.

- ❑ In Microsoft Chart, choose Copy Chart from the Edit menu. A dialog box appears asking if you want the image to be copied as it appears on the screen or as it appears when printed. If you're pasting the graphic into MacPaint before it goes to Word, select the As Shown on Screen option, or the chart won't fit into MacPaint's window. Most other applications, including Word, can accept the As Shown When Printed option, which creates a chart sized to the dimensions of the printed page.
- ❑ Microsoft Excel works similarly for charts. To copy a PICT image of a range within a worksheet, select the range you want to copy, then press the Shift key while choosing Copy; the command changes to *Copy Picture.* Otherwise, you'll simply copy the text contained in the range. If you paste this graphic into MacDraw, each element—every line and piece of text—becomes a separate object. Figure 15-9 shows how this range looks as a PICT image and how it might look after being cleaned up in MacDraw and copied into Word.

	A	B
1	***Dominant Languages Spoken in Home***	
2		
3	**Language**	**Millions**
4	Mandarin Chinese	720
5	English	305
6	Spanish	240
7	Arabic	150
8	Bengali	150
9	Russian	145
10	Portuguese	140
11	Hindi with Urdu	140
12	Japanese	120
13	German	105
14	Wu (Shanghai) Chinese	75
15	Javanese	66
16	Cantonese	66
17	Italian	65
18	Panjabi	63
19	Korean	61
20	French	60

Dominant Languages Spoken in Home

Language	Millions
Mandarin Chinese	720
English	305
Spanish	240
Arabic	150
Bengali	150
Russian	145
Portuguese	140
Hindi with Urdu	140
Japanese	120
German	105
Wu (Shanghai) Chinese	75
Javanese	66
Cantonese	66
Italian	65
Panjabi	63
Korean	61
French	60

Figure 15-9

Graphic copied from Microsoft Excel; the same graphic after modifications in MacDraw.

- As was discussed earlier, when you select and copy a graphic from Cricket Draw, the program buries the PostScript commands for the graphic into the PICT image. Be aware that this can dramatically increase the size of the image in bytes. To copy the PICT image only, without the embedded PostScript code, save the image as a file in the PICT format and then open the file with another application that can read the format, such as MacDraw or SuperPaint. To copy only a bit-mapped version of the selected objects, press the Option key while choosing the Copy command; note that you'll lose quality in the resulting image.
- Illustrator does not permit the pasting of graphics into any other program and does not normally support the Scrapbook. However, you can copy a PostScript-embedded PICT image from an Illustrator document by pressing the Option key while choosing Copy with the mouse.

TIP

Creating a Screen Dump
You can send the contents of an entire screen, regardless of the current program, to a file on disk by pressing Shift-Command-3. The screen shots are saved as MacPaint files with the names *Screen 0* through *Screen 9*. (The icons may not look like MacPaint documents until you edit or print them with MacPaint.) The documents are placed on the same disk as the application. The Mac beeps at you when you have used up all 10 screen shots (or if you run out of space on the disk).

The ROMs in all the newer Macs (the 512K Enhanced, the Mac Plus, the Mac SE, and the Mac II) do not allow you to create screen dumps of or print the contents of menus. If you press Shift-Command-3 while a menu is pulled down and then release the mouse button to start the screen dump, the menu disappears before the screen dump is sent to the disk. If you have to create a screen dump of a menu, you need what is called an FKEY resource, which is essentially a patch for the Mac's system software and is available from Macintosh users' groups.

Formatting Graphics

Graphics pasted into Word are treated like characters, but not all the character formats work when you apply them. You can select the graphic and give it an outline and a shadowed box, for instance, but to get a proper shadow you must use both formats, not the shadow by itself. On the other hand, the Bold format doesn't make the graphic bolder, but it does make an outline box thicker. The All Caps, Small Caps, font, and font size formats have no effect. The Position and Spacing formats do work, however, and are useful for making minor adjustments to the placement of a graphic, whether it is in a paragraph by itself or within the text of a paragraph.

If the graphic is in a paragraph by itself, you can adjust its horizontal position by moving the first-line indent. You can also place the insertion point before the graphic and press the Tab key to move it to the next tab stop, or you can choose one of the alignment icons in the Ruler.

To adjust the graphic vertically, you can add or remove lines above or below it or place it in a paragraph by itself and add a Space Before or Space After paragraph format. You can even give the paragraph a style, called *Graphic*, for instance, and change the formats for all such graphics at the same time by redefining that style. You can also select the graphic, cut it, and repaste it anywhere in that or another Word document, including into headers, footers, and footnotes.

TIP

Speed Scrolling by Hiding Graphics
Word takes longer to scroll through a document when there are graphics in view because it redraws the image every time you scroll the window. To speed up scrolling during editing, hide the graphics temporarily. You can redisplay the graphics when you need to format them and just prior to final pagination and printing. To hide a graphic, simply select the graphic, choose the Character command, and apply the Hidden character format. To display the graphic, set the Display Hidden Text option in the Preferences dialog box. If you've defined a special style for your graphics, you can add the Hidden format to all the graphics in your document at one time.

Cropping a Graphic

The term *cropping* refers to the process of removing the outer edges of a graphic, leaving only the portion that you want to have appear in the document. When you click on a graphic, the cropping box appears around it; this box has three handles, one each on the right edge, the bottom edge, and the lower right corner. The cropping box lets you either scale (magnify or reduce) the graphic to a particular size or crop off portions you don't want to show, although you can remove only the right and bottom edges of the graphic. For this reason, you should set the correct left and top edges for the graphic in the drawing or painting program from which it originated.

- To crop the graphic horizontally, drag the right handle. The status box displays the width of the graphic (in the unit of measurement set in the Preferences dialog box).
- To crop the graphic vertically, drag the bottom handle. The status box displays the depth of the graphic.
- To crop the graphic both horizontally and vertically while retaining its original proportions, drag in the lower right corner, as shown in Figure 15-10. Note that the status box shows the percentage of reduction or enlargement of the frame around the graphic. If you size the frame larger than 100%, Word centers the graphic within the frame.

Figure 15-10
Cropping a graphic.

Scaling a Graphic

You can crop or scale a graphic, but you can't do both at the same time. If you have demanding requirements for the arrangement and positioning within a graphic, try doing the scaling in a program that can handle object-oriented graphics, such as MacDraw, SuperPaint, or Cricket Draw.

- ❑ To scale a graphic horizontally, hold down the Shift key and drag the right handle. The status box displays the current width of the graphic.
- ❑ To scale the graphic vertically, hold down the Shift key and drag the bottom handle. The status box displays the current depth of the graphic.
- ❑ To scale the graphic but retain its original proportions, press the Shift key and drag the handle in the lower right corner. (See Figure 15-11.) Note that the status box gives the percentage of reduction or enlargement, rounded to the nearest whole number. The graphic is scaled by the percentage you see in the status box, even though it sometimes seems that you can drag the graphic's handles to positions between percentage points in the status box.

Figure 15-11
Scaling a graphic.

With both cropping and scaling, you can revert to the original size of the graphic by double-clicking within it.

Scaled object-oriented graphics typically look better than scaled bit-mapped graphics. If an object-oriented PICT image contains text, the text prints at the full resolution available on PostScript printers and is not converted to the bit-mapped version of the text. If an object-oriented graphic contains text, the text will be scaled along with the rest of the graphic. This can yield some interesting effects. For example, you can stretch text when you scale the image, as shown in Figure 15-12.

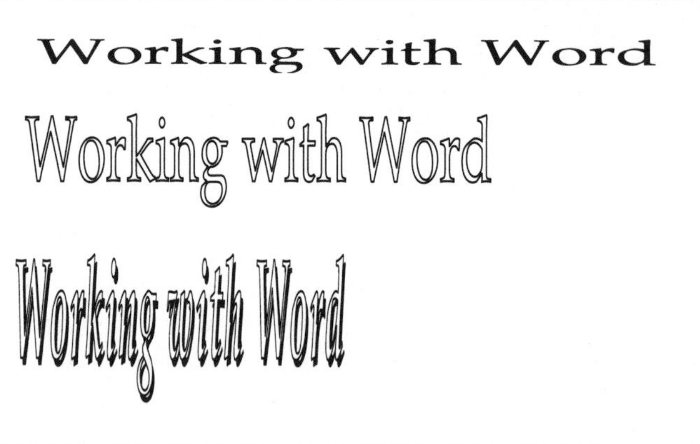

Figure 15-12
Distorted text resulting from a scaled object-oriented graphic.

When you scale down an image containing a bit-mapped component, either in a drawing program or in Word itself, the bits that make up the image are compressed into the smaller space, not lost. By using this feature, common to both drawing programs and Word, you can create an effect similar to that of a halftone image, particularly when working with scanned images, as shown in Figure 15-13. Because the pixels that make up the original image are compressed into a smaller space, the apparent quality of the image increases.

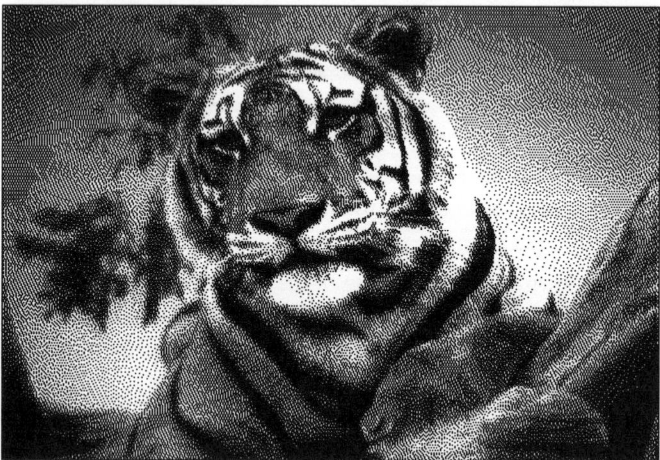

Figure 15-13
A bit-mapped graphic scanned with ThunderScan and scaled to 50%.

A scaled graphic will look considerably better when printed on a PostScript printer than when printed on the ImageWriter, due to the higher resolution. The correspondence between the scaling factor you apply to a graphic and its quality when printed depends on the ratio of the pixel density of the graphic to the pixel density of the output device.

For example, when you make a screen dump, the pixels in the image have the same density as the Mac's screen—72 dots per inch. The LaserWriter can print at a density of 300 dots per inch. Normally this results in a peculiar type of distortion in the printed image known as a moiré pattern, as shown in Figure 15-14.

Figure 15-14
Moiré pattern caused by an inexact ratio of screen resolution to printer resolution.

If you pasted the image into Word and scaled it to 50 percent of its original size, the pixel density would increase to 144 dots per inch. Whenever possible, choose a 25 percent, 50 percent, or 75 percent scaling ratio when using the LaserWriter to minimize the effects of rounding error (where certain pixels are dropped but not others). This will make items such as thin lines and even patterns look better. Most of the illustrations in this book, printed with a Linotronic L300 imagesetter, were reduced to 50 percent of their original size, but because they were printed at 1270 dots per inch, the distortions due to bit-map scaling tend to be smaller.

Inserting a Blank Graphics Frame

Sometimes it's useful to reserve space for a graphic without actually moving the graphic into a Word document. You might do this if you were in the process of writing or designing the document and didn't want to take the time to create and transfer the graphic. Also, because scrolling slows down noticeably when the graphics have been pasted into a document, you might find it convenient to do most of the writing and editing before incorporating the graphics. Finally, graphics in a document tend to increase its size dramatically; if a document is large (say, more than 100 KB), you might find it necessary to reduce its size for memory-intensive operations such as sorting and generating tables of contents.

You can insert a blank graphics frame anywhere in a Word document (including headers and footers). Do so as follows:

❶ Set an insertion point where you want the graphics frame to appear.

❷ Choose Insert Graphics from the Edit menu.

Word places a 1-inch-by-1-inch empty graphics frame at the insertion point. (It's easier to see this frame if you've chosen Show ¶.) You can leave the box empty until you're ready to paste a graphic into it. (See Figure 15-15.) If you want to resize the frame, click in it to display a cropping box, and drag the appropriate handles, as you would with a standard graphic. The size or percentage appears in the status box.

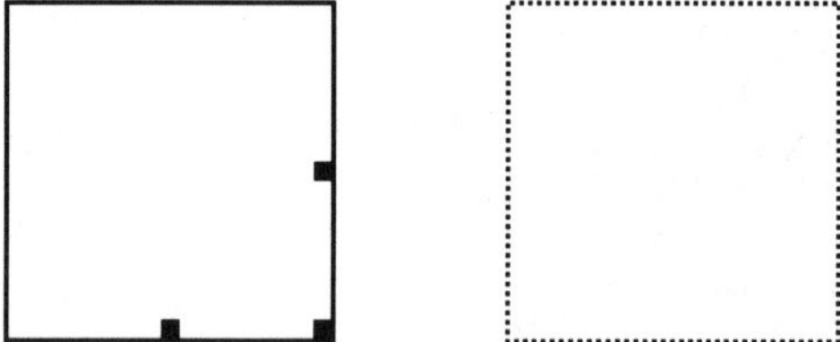

Figure 15-15
A graphics frame and the same frame with Show ¶ on.

You can also format the empty frame as you might if a graphic were actually pasted there. For example, you can assign the frame the outline character attribute to create a resizable box in your document. Simply select the box and choose Outline from the Format menu. An outline appears around the box, as shown in Figure 15-16, and remains even when the box is not selected and Show ¶ is off.

Figure 15-16
A graphics frame boxed with the Outline format.

You can use this handy trick to create small check boxes. Resize the blank box to the desired size, and give it the Outline format. The outline is always slightly larger than the box itself, so take this into consideration.

Choose various formats to see the effect they have. For example, you can create a box with a drop shadow by choosing both Outline and Shadow or make the box heavier by choosing Bold. You can even use the Strikethru format to draw a horizontal line through the graphic. You can add vertical lines within the frame by selecting the paragraph containing the frame, choosing the Show Ruler command, and then dragging a vertical-line icon in the Ruler to the desired position over the frame. The vertical-line tabs show up over both text and graphics. Figure 15-17 shows some examples.

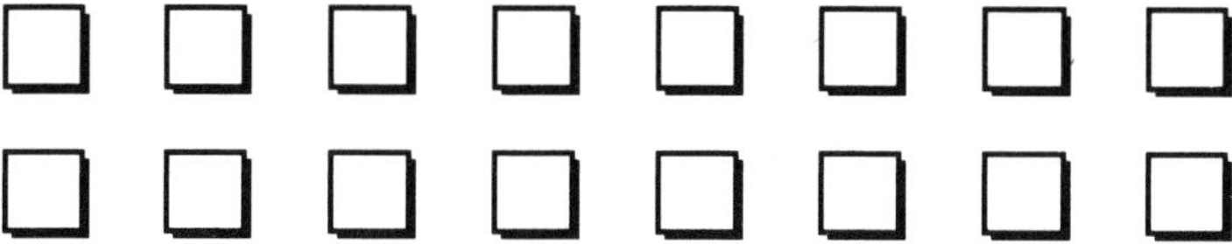

Figure 15-17
Boxes created from graphics frames.

TIP

Creating a Box Around a Group of Paragraphs
Setting one of the border paragraph formats is one way to draw a box around a single paragraph, but what do you do if you want to draw one box around more than one paragraph? One way to do this involves inserting a graphics frame before the paragraphs and using the Side-by-Side paragraph format to lay the frame over them:

1. Insert an empty graphics frame before the paragraphs. Drag out the frame until it is approximately the size it would be if it surrounded the paragraphs. Format the frame as desired, usually by giving it the Box and/or Shadow character formats or the Border paragraph formats.
2. Select the paragraphs and move their left or first-line indents (whichever is leftmost) to the right by a small amount, say 1/8 inch. Or, select the graphics frame and move its left or first-line indent 1/8 inch to the left. (Pressing the Shift key and clicking on the left scroll arrow is helpful for scrolling to the left of the left margin.)
3. Select both the graphics frame and the relevant paragraphs and give them the Side-by-Side paragraph format.
4. Finally, flipping between Page Preview and Document view, adjust the dimensions of the graphics frame until it surrounds the paragraphs evenly.

Figure 15-18 shows how this might look in Document view and in Page Preview. You can also use this same technique with a real graphic, rather than an empty frame. Figure 15-19 shows an example of this.

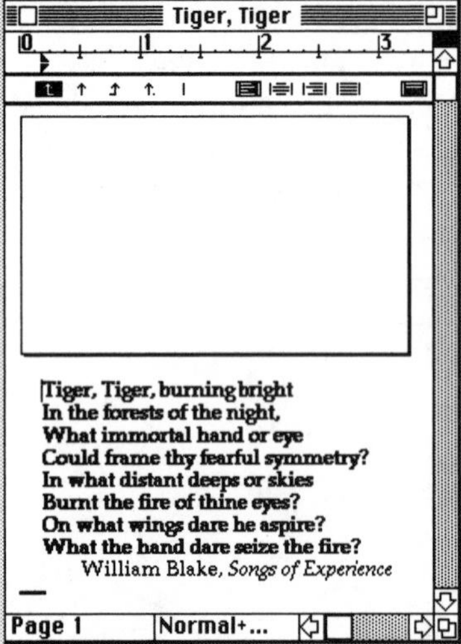

Tiger, Tiger, burning bright
In the forests of the night,
What immortal hand or eye
Could frame thy fearful symmetry?
In what distant deeps or skies
Burnt the fire of thine eyes?
On what wings dare he aspire?
What the hand dare seize the fire?
William Blake, *Songs of Experience*

Figure 15-18
Paragraphs boxed with a graphics frame and the Side-by-Side format in Document View and as they appear in Page Preview.

Tiger, Tiger, burning bright
In the forests of the night,
What immortal hand or eye
Could frame thy fearful symmetry?
In what distant deeps or skies
Burnt the fire of thine eyes?
On what wings dare he aspire?
What the hand dare seize the fire?
William Blake, *Songs of Experience*

Figure 15-19
A graphic placed behind some text with the Side-by-Side format.

Multiple Graphics on One Line

Microsoft Word is one of the only word-processing programs for the Macintosh that can place more than one graphic on the same or successive lines within one paragraph. To insert a graphic alongside an existing one (assuming that the second graphic is already on the Clipboard):

❶ Set the insertion point on the right edge of the existing graphic. You can do this by clicking on the graphic and pressing the right arrow key.

❷ Press the Tab or spacebar key, if you want, to separate the two graphics.

❸ Choose the Paste command. The graphic appears at the insertion point.

You can repeat the process as many times as you like to put any number of images on the same line. If you need to reposition the graphics along the length of the line, carefully set the insertion point and add or take out spaces. If a graphic is selected when you press a key on the keyboard, you'll delete it.

You can also place a graphic on the same line as text. To add a line of text after a graphic, for example, place the insertion point immediately after the image and type. To place the text before the graphic, set the insertion point at the front of the image and type. The bottom edge of the text aligns with the bottom of the graphic. You can use the Superscript and Subscript character formats to adjust the placement of graphics relative to the text on the line.

Exporting Graphics

Word is not a graphics program, and normally you wouldn't use it to draw pictures. Sometimes, however, it is useful to transfer an image of the text you've formatted in Word to another program. The special formatting features of Word (such as boxes and columns) are not likely to be shared by the other program, and so the only way to transfer the material with the formats intact is to first convert it to an object-oriented picture. Once the image of the formatted material is on the Clipboard, you can paste it into a document belonging to another application, or you could stay in Word and paste it to another location. Of course, the destination program must be able to accept PICT images from the Clipboard.

To transfer an image of the formatted text:

❶ Select the desired material, and press Option-Command-D. The selection is copied to the Clipboard as an object-oriented graphic.

❷ Quit Word and start the destination program.

❸ Paste the contents of the Clipboard into a document belonging to the program. Manipulate the image as you would any other graphic. Note that font formatting is retained. (The font and point size you used for the text in Word must also be present in the System file of the destination program; otherwise, the font will either be scaled or replaced with Geneva or New York.)

Word treats each line of text as a separate object. Each piece of text that changes in font, font size, or character attributes also becomes a separate object, as do any of the graphic formats, such as boxes and lines. Because the image copied to the Clipboard is a PICT image, you can transport it to an object-oriented graphics program, such as Cricket Draw, MacDraw, or SuperPaint. You can then manipulate the elements of the selection separately and copy the result to another program or even back into Word. The formatting boxes and lines are also transferred. However, because the PICT format has a lower limit of accuracy (1 point), some formats, such as compressed or expanded text, may not survive the transfer exactly.

You can use this technique to create some interesting special effects with Word. Write and initially format the text, as usual. Select the font, size, character attributes, and margins you want to appear in the final version. Copy the text block to the Clipboard using Option-Command-D, as described. Quit Word and start the graphics program (let's say MacDraw). Once you are in MacDraw, paste the selection into the window, and then use the drawing tools to embellish it. Add extra boxes, charts, or other elements as desired. The technique is particularly helpful when you've used Word's mathematical typesetting feature to create a formula—you can convert the resulting image to QuickDraw format to "lock" the formula or copy it to a document in another program.

When you are finished, select the text and added graphics, copy them, and restart Word. Delete the old text and paste in the new image from the Clipboard. If all goes well, the revised version, which you handle as you would any other imported graphic, looks like the surrounding text but has the MacDraw flourishes you added.

TIP

Creating Boxed Text Elements from Formatted Text

It's sometimes difficult to use the border paragraph formats to position a box a specific distance from some text. Instead, try converting the text to a graphic and then formatting the graphic:

1. Format the text as you would like it to appear.
2. Select the text and press Option-Command-D to transfer an image of it to the Clipboard.
3. While the text is selected, give it the Hidden character format and hide the text.
4. Paste the image of the text after the text itself. Select the image and give it the Outline character format to draw a box around the graphic, or put the graphic in a paragraph by itself and use one of the Border formats.
5. You can drag the handles of the graphic to enlarge it; the graphic remains centered within the frame.

If you need to edit the text, set the Show Hidden Text option in the Preferences dialog box, edit the text, and repeat the process.

■ *Saving Time with QuickSwitch*

Word has a unique feature called QuickSwitch that lets you partially automate the transfer of text, data, and graphics between programs. With QuickSwitch, you establish a kind of pipeline from a source program, such as MacDraw, Microsoft Chart, or Microsoft Excel, to Word. If the pasted-in data or graphics need to be changed, you can use QuickSwitch to go back to the source program and make changes. The replacement is then made for you.

To use QuickSwitch, you must use the Switcher or the MultiFinder, which is the new extension to the Macintosh system software that incorporates most of the features of the Switcher and more. The Word Utilities disk contains Switcher loading sets for use with Microsoft Excel, Microsoft File, Microsoft Works, MacDraw, and MacWrite.

If you have never used Switcher before, read the instruction manual provided with the program. When using Switcher for cutting and pasting, turn on the Always Convert Clipboard option. When you switch between programs, this option causes the Clipboard to be converted for use by each of the applications, allowing them to share cut or copied data with one another.

There is no communal Clipboard maintained by the Switcher; each program has its own independent Clipboard. When you rotate from one application to another, the contents of the Clipboard of the first program replace the contents of the Clipboard of the second program if you have set the Always Convert Clipboard option. If you don't want this to happen automatically, turn off the Always Convert Clipboard option, and press the Option key while you rotate to convert the Clipboard only when you want.

Also, when you're done with an application, quit it to remove it from the rotation. The more applications you have installed in Switcher, the less room there is for clippings. You may not have enough memory to cut and paste a large clipping if you've overloaded your Mac with applications. In any case, you cannot copy and paste a selection larger than 32 KB. If the Mac informs you that the clipping is too large, you must transfer it in smaller chunks.

Using QuickSwitch with Microsoft Excel

You can transfer two types of data between Microsoft Excel and Word with QuickSwitch: tabular text data and charts. (You have already seen how to transfer text documents and graphics.) If you are using Microsoft Excel version 1.0, be sure that the file *QuickSwitch* is on the Excel disk. QuickSwitch capability is coded into Microsoft Excel versions 1.03 and later: If you use the later releases, you won't need to use the QuickSwitch file.

Before using QuickSwitch, you need to place a line of hidden text in the Word document immediately before the table or chart you want to change or immediately before the point where you want to insert the table or chart.

If you are transferring tabular data, type the following line:

```
Excel!filename!areaname
```

In place of *filename*, enter the name of the source Excel document. In place of *areaname*, enter the named range that contains the data you want. You can also enter the cell address of the range, but it must be in R1C1 format, such as R2C2:R7C10. Format this code as hidden text.

If you are transferring a chart from Microsoft Excel, type this line:

```
Excel!filename
```

Replace the word *filename* with the name of the Excel chart document to be used. Format the code as hidden text. Assuming that you are already running under the Switcher or MultiFinder and have loaded both Word and Microsoft Excel, you can now insert or update a table or chart with QuickSwitch:

1. If you are inserting a chart or table into a Word document, place the insertion point at the beginning of the line after the hidden text code. If you are updating a table or chart that you've already inserted, select it.
2. Press Command-, (comma). You are rotated to Excel, where the data or chart to be inserted or updated is selected for you. Make whatever changes you need to the worksheet or chart.
3. Press Command-, again. QuickSwitch copies the table or chart, rotates back to Word, and pastes the updated item into the Word document, replacing the original selection.

Using QuickSwitch with MacPaint and MacDraw

You can also use QuickSwitch to edit a graphic that you have pasted into Word, but you cannot name the source document or set a range. Use the Switcher to load MacPaint or MacDraw. To avoid confusion, load only one of these programs, not both. If you're using MacPaint, it must be on the same disk as the System Folder.

1. In Word, select the graphic you want to change, and press Command-, (comma). QuickSwitch rotates to the graphics program, pastes the selected graphic into the program window, and surrounds it with a framing box. You can delete the framing box if you want.
2. Make the needed changes in the graphic. Don't move or resize the image, or some of it may not be returned to Word.
3. Select the graphic, and press Command-, again. You are rotated back to Word, where the updated graphic replaces the old one. You may need to adjust the crop box to accommodate the new graphic.

If you decide to return to Word without modifying the graphic, simply click the Switcher arrow.

Points to Remember

- You can transfer raw, unformatted text and graphics to and from Word via the Clipboard and Scrapbook. Word can also read formatted files created by Word version 1.05, Microsoft Works, MacWrite, and MS-DOS Word version 3.0; it can store files in all these formats except for the Works format, and it cannot generate a style sheet for an MS-DOS format Word file.
- All items on the Clipboard and in the Scrapbook are assigned a four-character data type code that indicates the type of material contained in the clipping. The TEXT code means that the clipping consists of raw text; the PICT code means that the clipping is either a bit-mapped or object-oriented graphic. Other codes are assigned by application programs to indicate a clipping in the program's internal format.
- You cannot keep formatted Word text in the Scrapbook; Word clippings that are copied there lose all of their formatting and are treated as raw text. Use glossary entries instead of the Scrapbook for formatted boilerplate text.
- If you will be uploading a file to a bulletin board or on-line service, save it in the Text Only with Line Breaks file format. You can also use RTF (Rich Text Format), if the person or system receiving the file can convert RTF files.
- Saving in RTF stores a Word document, formatting and all, as an ASCII file. The formats are converted into text codes.
- Bit-mapped graphics are images represented as rows of white or black pixels. Object-oriented, or QuickDraw, graphics are images that are made up of discrete elements that can be moved independently of one another. The PICT format is used to transfer both bit-mapped and object-oriented graphics from program to program.

  PostScript graphics are images represented as PostScript commands. These can be printed only on PostScript-compatible printers. Some graphics programs bury PostScript code in PICT-format images; this is known as the EPSF (Encapsulated PostScript File) format.
- Bit-mapped graphics are limited to 72 dots per inch, the resolution of the Macintosh. When sent to a PostScript-compatible printer, object-oriented and PICT-format graphics are converted into PostScript code. PostScript graphics are printed at the resolution of the printer.
- The QuickSwitch feature allows you to update a chart or table in Microsoft Excel or a graphic in MacPaint or MacDraw and transfer the changes to a Word document automatically. You must be running the programs under the Switcher or MultiFinder.

Techniques

Transferring Text

Transfer text with the Clipboard or Scrapbook

1. In the source program, cut or copy the text to be transferred to the Clipboard. From there, paste it into the Scrapbook, if you want.
2. In the destination program, set the insertion point where you want to insert the text.
3. Choose the Paste command to insert the text from the Clipboard, or open the Scrapbook, display the text clipping to be inserted, copy it to the Clipboard, and then paste it into the document.
4. Text inserted into a Word document from another program or from the Scrapbook is assigned the *Normal* style, plus the New York character format. Select the text and press Shift-Command-Spacebar to return the text to the base character format for its style.

Store a Word file for use by another program

1. Choose the Save As command, and click the File Format button.
2. Specify a file format in the dialog box that appears. If the destination program is not listed, specify Text Only.
3. Click OK, type a name for the new document, and then click Save.

Open a file created by another program

1. If the file was created in Word 1.05, Microsoft Works, MacWrite, or MS-DOS Word 3.0, simply open the file as you would a Word document.
2. Otherwise, in the source program, save the file in a text-only or ASCII format, if possible.
3. Quit the program and start Word.
4. Choose the Open command. If Word can read the file you want to open, its name will appear in the list box.

If the name of the file does not appear in the list box, try pressing the Shift key while you choose the Open command. This displays all the files on the disk, regardless of their format. Files opened in this way are likely to contain garbage characters, which you can remove manually. To save the file, choose Save As, click File Format, and click Normal. Give the file a new name before saving it.

Transfer a table in Word to a spreadsheet or database program

❶ Set up the data in the Word document so that each paragraph contains a record (for a database program) or a row (for a spreadsheet) of data. Separate the fields or cells with tabs. (You can use tabs or commas if the destination is a database program.)

❷ Select the data to be transferred and copy it to the Clipboard, or save it in the Text Only or Text Only with Line Breaks format.

❸ Quit Word and start the destination program.

❹ Set the insertion point and paste the data into a document in the program, or open the document saved in Text Only format.

Transfer spreadsheet data or database records to Word

❶ In the source program, copy the desired data or records to the Clipboard, or save it in a text format, if available.

❷ Quit the program and start Word.

❸ Set the insertion point and choose the Paste command, or open the document saved in text format.

❹ Each row or record in the resulting text is a paragraph, and the cells or fields are separated by tabs or commas.

Transferring Graphics

Copy a graphic into a Word document

❶ In the source program, create the graphic and copy it to the Clipboard.

❷ Quit the program and start Word.

❸ Set the insertion point and choose the Paste command.

❹ Format the graphic, if you want, to adjust its position or to add an outline.

Crop a graphic

❶ Click on the graphic. A cropping box with three handles appears.

❷ Drag the right handle to crop the graphic horizontally; drag the bottom handle to crop the graphic vertically. To crop the graphic both horizontally and vertically while keeping its original proportions, drag the corner handle.

Scale a graphic

❶ Click on the graphic. A cropping box with three handles appears.

❷ Press the Shift key while you drag the right, bottom, or corner handle. The right handle scales the graphic horizontally, the bottom handle scales it vertically, and the corner handle scales it but maintains the original proportions.

Insert a blank graphic frame into a Word document

❶ Set the insertion point where you want the frame to appear.

❷ Choose Insert Graphics from the Edit menu. Word inserts a 1-by-1-inch frame.

❸ To change the size of the frame, click in it to display a cropping box, and drag the handles to the desired size.

❹ Format the frame, if you want, as you would a graphic.

Create a screen dump

❶ Press Shift-Command-3. The contents of the screen are stored in a MacPaint file under the names *Screen 0* through *Screen 9*.

Copy Word text to the Clipboard as an object-oriented graphic

❶ Select the text to be copied.

❷ Press Option-Command-D. The selection is copied to the Clipboard as a PICT-format graphic.

❸ Quit Word and start the destination program. It must be able to accept PICT images.

❹ Paste the Clipboard image into the program. You can paste it into a drawing program and alter it to achieve special effects.

Using QuickSwitch

Revise a graphic with QuickSwitch

❶ Start Word and the graphics program under the Switcher or MultiFinder.

❷ In the Word document, click inside the graphic to select it.

❸ Press Command- , (comma) to switch to the graphics program.

❹ Modify the graphic. Do not move or resize the graphic.

❺ Press Command- , again to return to Word. The graphic is updated.

Don't move the mouse while switching.

Update a table from a Microsoft Excel worksheet

1. Start Word and Microsoft Excel under the Switcher or MultiFinder.
2. Type *Excel!filename!areaname* in a separate paragraph immediately above the table.
3. Format this line as hidden text.
4. Select the table.
5. Press Command- , (comma) to switch to Microsoft Excel. The worksheet with the name you typed is opened and the named area is selected.
6. Edit the worksheet.
7. Press Command- , again to return to Word.

The table you selected in Word is updated with the data from the named area on the worksheet.

Update a chart from a Microsoft Excel chart file

1. Type *Excel!filename* in a paragraph above the graphics frame for the chart, and format this line as hidden text.
2. Select the graphics frame and press Command- , (comma) to switch to Microsoft Excel. The chart is read from the chart file you specified.
3. Modify the chart as needed.
4. Press Command- , again to return to Word and update the chart.

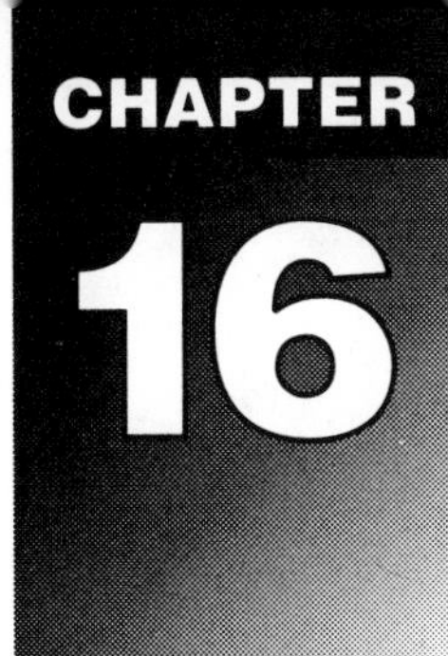

Merge Printing

The form-letter feature in Word is more commonly referred to as merge printing (or print merging). The concept involved is simple and straightforward: Names, addresses, and other data in one document are inserted—merged—into a template document. This template document can be a form letter, an invoice, or a set of mailing labels.

If your needs are straightforward, merge printing is easy to do. For example, setting up a basic form letter and having Word generate letters for a given set of names and addresses is a relatively simple task. However, if you are so inclined, you can also use this feature to achieve complex effects. You can include commands that specify that certain data be inserted only if a condition or set of conditions is met, that instruct Word to prompt you for data to be inserted, and that tell the program to include an entire file at a given point in the document. These instructions and advanced techniques are covered later in the chapter; first, you need to know the basics.

The document that contains the template—the text to appear in every letter or the mailing-list format—is called the *main document*. The document that contains the names, addresses, and other data to be inserted into the template is referred to as the *data document*. When you choose Print Merge from the File menu, Word inserts information from the data document into the appropriate locations in the main document and creates all the form documents, which it then sends to the printer, as shown in Figure 16-1.

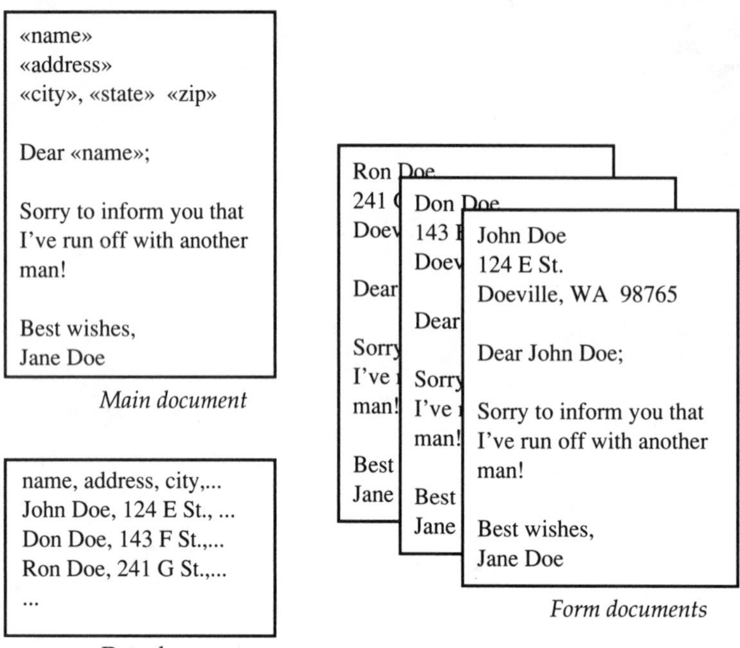

Figure 16-1
Merge printing.

Merge printing saves you the most time when there are many variables that change from one letter to the next, or when you must prepare a large number of letters. If you have only a few letters to prepare, each with only a few variables, it is easier to type in the information directly. If you use the same data over and over again (such as the names and addresses of only a few major vendors), try storing the information in the glossary. Set it up so that you can call up a complete name and address by typing in a code name.

■ *Setting Up a Data Document*

The data document contains the sets of information to be plugged into the main document. In the example used throughout this discussion, the data document contains these items:

- ❏ First name
- ❏ Last name
- ❏ Address
- ❏ City
- ❏ State
- ❏ Zip code

Of course, a data document can contain any kind of information, including account balances, phone numbers, and favorite foods. The idea is that a different set of information is provided for each person who will receive one of your form letters. The complete set of information for each person is called a *record*. Here are examples of two records:

Joe ➡	Smith ➡	123 Elm ➡	Gary ➡	IN ➡	46401¶
Mary Sue ➡	Ellison ➡	6703 Highland ➡	Santa Cruz ➡	CA ➡	95060¶

The data in a record is divided into *fields*. These example records consist of six fields: first name, last name, street address, city, state, and zip code.

The way the data is arranged is important; this is how Word knows which field goes where. Each record consists of one paragraph and ends with a paragraph mark. You separate the fields in a record by either commas or tabs. The fields must all be in the same order for each record, or Word may print a person's name where you expect to see the name of a town. Each record can have as many as 256 fields and take up as many lines as necessary, as long as it contains only one paragraph mark that falls at the end.

You can enter the data for each record by hand, or you can copy data from another program, such as Microsoft File or Microsoft Excel. Excel, for example, has a file-saving option called Text Only, and you can open files saved in this format as Word documents. Each row of a spreadsheet file is a record; it ends with a paragraph mark, and its cells are separated by tab characters.

Each record should be followed by only one paragraph mark; otherwise, Word will display a dialog box saying *Missing comma in data record.* (It will say *comma* even if you use tabs to separate the fields.) Word assumes that there is a record for every paragraph mark, and it will treat extra paragraph marks as empty—and therefore faulty—records. This isn't a serious problem, but you can avoid the dialog box by deleting blank lines between records and extra paragraph marks at the end of the document.

Special Cases

If the data in a field contains one or more tabs, commas, or quotation marks, you must surround the entire field with quotation marks. Also, you must double every quotation mark in the field. This prevents Word from seeing two fields where there should be only one. Here are two examples:

"Joe ➡ Bob" ➡	Smith ➡	123 Elm ➡	Gary ➡	IN ➡	46401¶
""Mary Sue"" ➡	Ellison ➡	6703 Highland ➡	Santa Cruz ➡	CA ➡	95060¶

If you want to leave a field blank, you must enter an extra tab or comma in its place. This tells Word to skip over the empty field and ensures that the contents of subsequent fields are associated with the correct field names. Here's an example:

♦ ♦ Resident ♦ 6703 Highland ♦ Santa Cruz ♦ CA ♦ 95060¶

The Header Record

Once you have entered your data, you still have one small task to complete in the data document. Word needs to be told the name of each of the fields. You will then enter these names in the main document where you want Word to insert their data.

To assign field names, you enter a special record containing the field names, in the exact order in which they appear in the data records, at the very beginning of the data document. This special record is called the *header record* for the data document. Separate the field names in the header record with the same character you used to separate the fields in the data records—either a comma or a tab. Tabs are more useful because they arrange the data into easy-to-read columns. Each field name can be up to 65 characters long and does not have to be one word, unlike field names in most programming languages. For example, *first name* and *street address* are legal field names.

When the header record is complete, save the document under an easy-to-remember name. A complete data document, with a header record containing field names, is shown in Figure 16-2.

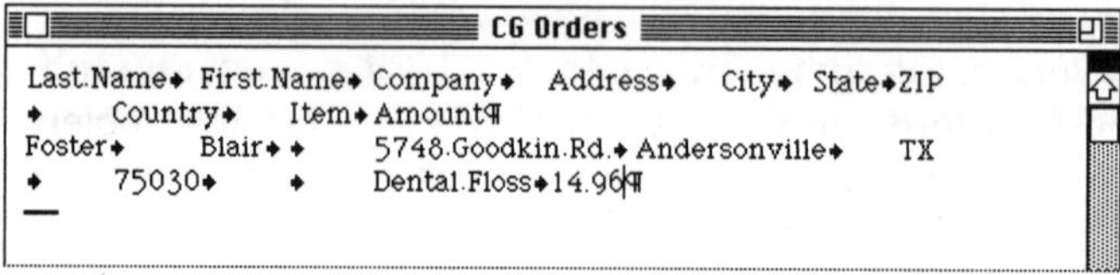

Figure 16-2
A sample data document.

■ *Setting Up a Main Document*

The main document can be almost any kind of document. In most instances, it will be a form letter of one type or another, so this section uses a simple form letter to continue the discussion of merge printing. Main documents almost always contain these items:

- ❑ The body of the document.
- ❑ Field names.
- ❑ A print merge DATA instruction.

The body text is the standard text that everyone receives. It remains the same from letter to letter. Body text requires no special formatting; you can give it any character or paragraph formats you want.

Field Names

You insert a field name wherever you want Word to insert a piece of information from the data document into the body of the main document. You can place a field name anywhere, including within a paragraph of body text. The capitalization of field names, in both the main document and the header record, must be consistent. Also, you must enclose each field name with the special characters « (Option-\) and » (Shift-Option-\). (See Figure 16-3.) If a field name appears on a line of its own, you can end it with the paragraph mark instead of the final ».

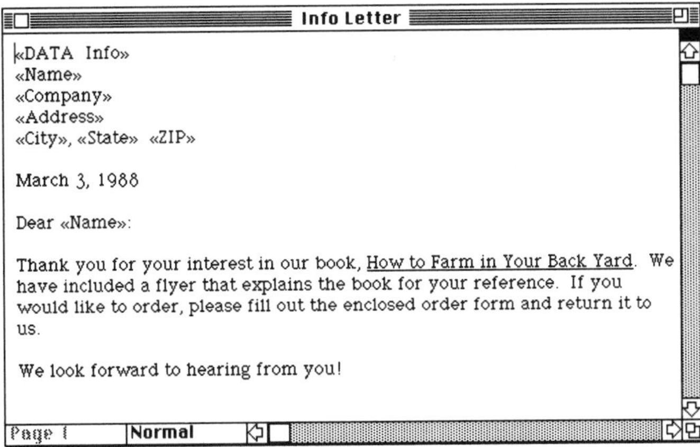

Figure 16-3
A sample form letter.

The DATA Instruction

The DATA instruction specifies the name of the data document containing the header and the data records that will be inserted in place of each field name in the main document. Other, more advanced, merge instructions are available and are discussed later in this chapter, but the DATA instruction is all you need to create a form letter. The DATA instruction must be the first merge instruction in the document, and it must be enclosed by the same « and » bracket characters that enclose the field names. Specify the name of the data document after the word DATA, before the closing » character. (See Figure 16-3.) Be sure to type the name of the data document correctly.

Using a Separate Header Document

Word lets you keep the header record and the data records in two separate documents if you want. To do this, you must use a slightly different form of the DATA instruction:

«DATA header document, data document»

In place of *header document*, enter the name of the document containing the header; this document must contain only the header record. In place of *data document*, enter the name of the document containing the data records; it must contain only data records. Separate the two names with a comma. As in a regular data document, the field names in the header document must be in the same sequence as the fields in the data document.

In most cases, you will keep your data records and header record in one file, and so the header document name is not necessary. Sometimes, however, it is helpful to keep the header record and the data records separate. You may want to use the same header record for more than one document, for example, or you may be using a data file created by saving database records from a program such as Microsoft Excel in Text Only file format. In such cases it can be more convenient to use a separate header document rather than opening the data file and inserting the header record.

TIP

Using Graphics in a Data Document

In addition to storing text in the fields of a data document, you can also store graphics. Because Word treats graphics like characters, you can insert a graphic within a paragraph and hence within a record in a data document. Here's an example:

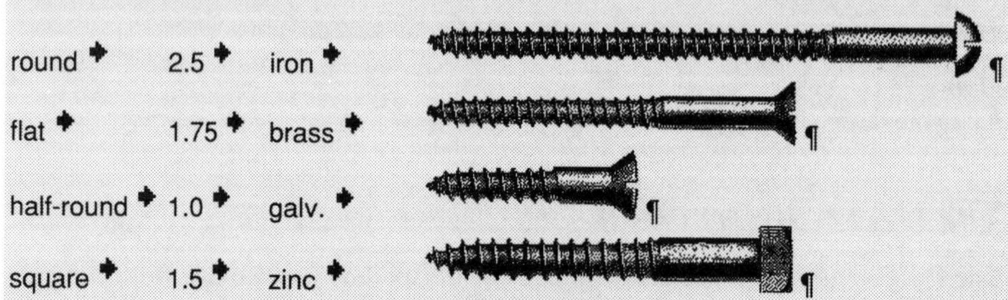

■ *Printing the Document*

To initiate printing, with the main document open choose Print Merge from the File menu. The dialog box shown in Figure 16-4 appears. Select the All option to print a form document for every record in the data document, or enter a range of record numbers in the From and To edit fields. The first data record is record 1, the second is record 2, and so on.

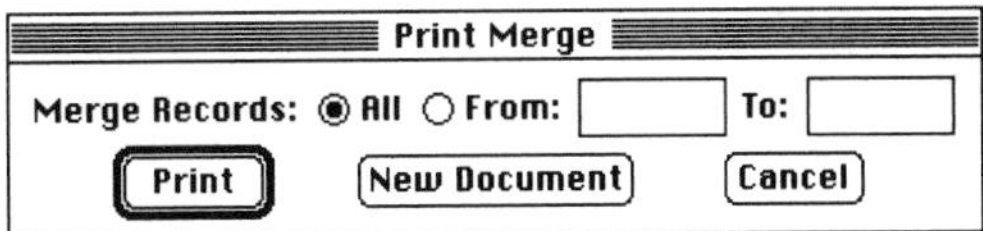

Figure 16-4
The Print Merge dialog box.

If you click the Print button, Word merges the data records into the main document according to the field names you've placed in the main document and sends each resulting form document to the printer. First, however, it presents the Print dialog box so that you can set the print quality, page range, number of copies of each form document, and so forth. Click OK when you are finished setting the options and are ready to print.

If you click the New Document button, Word opens a new, blank document and appends each merged form document to it. Section marks separate the documents. Placing the documents in a new document is useful when you want to see the results of the merge before printing or if you want to use the merge feature to synthesize new documents (from complicated sets of boilerplate text, for instance). Treat this file like any other Word document.

When merging very large files (containing more than 15 or 20 pages), Word may report that the editing session is too long and ask that you save your work. If this happens, some of the records in the data document may not be merged. To remedy this, divide the records in the data document into more sets of data documents, and merge them in more than one pass. This error condition does not occur when you are sending the merged documents directly to the printer.

When you print the merged documents, each form document is repaginated to accommodate the inserted data. Because the length of the data in any given field can vary from record to record, the finished documents may look slightly different because their lines are broken differently. If you have set up a strict page layout involving forced page breaks, this can upset your formatting and repagination. If this is a problem, try merging the form documents into a new document and then correct the formatting there. Once everything is to your liking, you can print the document by choosing Print instead of Print Merge.

■ *Using the Merge Instructions*

The DATA instruction isn't the only instruction you can include in the main document when creating a main document for merging. You can instruct Word to interact with you during a merging session, set conditions and rules for merge printing, or insert entire files into the main document. There are six types of merge printing instructions. You've already encountered the first, the DATA instruction. The others are:

- IF, ENDIF, and ELSE
- NEXT
- SET
- ASK
- INCLUDE

The IF Instruction

"If it's foggy, I'll wear my mac." That's an example of conditional branching, a basic concept in daily life as well as in computer programming. The IF instruction is like a fork in the road, and the decision to go one way or the other is made based on the answer to a question, such as: "Is it foggy?" If the answer is yes, you put on your overcoat; if the answer is no, you don't.

The question "Is it foggy?" can also be stated more completely as a condition: "Is the weather foggy?" Should the condition *weather = foggy* be met, you go off to the closet. But what do you do if it's not foggy? Then the condition is not met, and nothing happens.

The IF instruction uses the same logic. You can use it to set up your form letter in such a way that it "asks" the records in the data document a set of questions. The text inserted in the merged document for that record varies depending on whether or not the condition is met. You can set up three kinds of conditions within the IF instruction:

- Does this field contain anything at all?
- Does the text in this field match this text string?
- Does the text in this field match this number?

Checking for Text in a Field

One type of IF instruction checks to see if there is anything in a particular field and, if there is, inserts text specified in the instruction at that location in the document. If the field contains any characters at all (including numbers, symbols, or even one blank space), then the condition is met. If the field is completely blank, the condition is not met. The syntax of this type of IF instruction is as follows:

```
«IF field name» text to insert «ENDIF»
```

You place this instruction in the main document at the point where you want to insert text if the field is not empty. In place of *field name* you enter the name of the field you want to test. In place of *text to insert* you type the text string you want inserted if the condition is met. The ENDIF element signals the end of the insertion text. Incidentally, the ENDIF element doesn't have to be on the same line or even in the same paragraph; you can insert whole paragraphs, graphics, or anything you like.

Figure 16-5 shows three data records and a main document that specifies: *If there is anything in the field called Discount, print the text "Discount Given."* In the example, the field name is *Discount*. If the Discount field contains anything at all, the text *Discount Given* is inserted. If the Discount field is blank, no text is printed at that location.

Figure 16-5
An IF instruction that inserts text if there are any characters in a field.

Matching Text

Simply testing for the presence or absence of text in a field may not be enough. You may want to see whether a field contains certain characters and insert text if it does. The syntax for the IF instruction to accomplish this is as follows:

«IF field name = "text to match"» text to insert «ENDIF»

In place of *field name,* enter the name of the field you want to check. Replace *text to match* with the exact string for which you are checking. Don't forget the double quotation marks. Replace *text to insert* with the string you want printed in each document for which the specified field meets the condition.

Figure 16-6 shows a set of records and part of a form letter containing an IF instruction that tests whether the Country field contains the text *Canada.* If this condition is met, the following text is printed: *Please refer to our sales office in Canada for your supply needs.* Note that the text to be inserted can be any length. Word stops when it reaches the ENDIF instruction.

Figure 16-6
An IF instruction that inserts text if a field contains a certain string of characters.

Matching Numbers

Word provides some additional flexibility when you want to match numbers instead of text. You can test whether a field contains a specific number or a number that is higher or lower. The IF instruction for matching a number is:

«IF field name = number» text to insert «ENDIF»

In place of *field name*, you enter the name of the field to test, and in place of *number*, type the number to match. (It must be an integer.) Replace *text to insert* with the string you want printed in the merged document if the condition is met. Instead of an equal sign, you can use a greater-than sign (>) or a less-than sign (<) to determine whether the value in the field is higher than or lower than the test number.

Figure 16-7 shows a series of records and a main document containing an IF instruction that tests whether the number in the Total field is greater than 100. The condition is met when the number is 101 or greater. In the example, if Total is greater than 100, the text printed is *We are enclosing a FREE gift as our way of saying thank you for your patronage.*

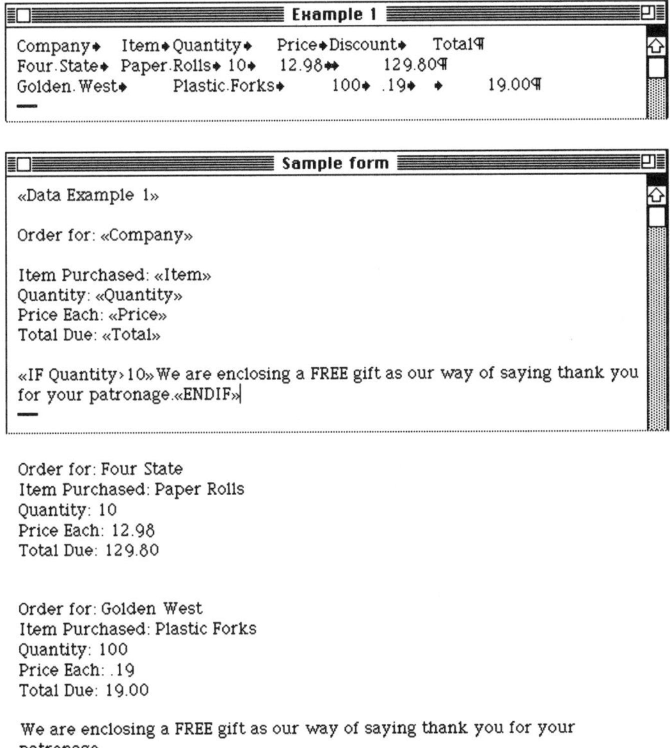

Figure 16-7
An IF instruction that tests a numeric value in a field.

Nesting IF Instructions

You can tuck IF instructions within other IF instructions. This is called *nesting*, and it provides a means of creating an elaborate tree of alternatives. Nesting allows you to refine the circumstances under which text will be inserted. Instead of having only one condition that must be met, you can specify that a record meet a number of nested IF conditions.

If you have done any programming, you will recognize the nesting scheme as a way to implement the AND logical operator. It goes something like this: *IF condition 1 AND condition 2 AND condition 3 are met, insert the text.* Should a record fail to meet any of the three conditions, the text is not inserted. A typical nested IF instruction is as follows:

```
«IF Discount» «IF Total>100» You are a valued customer, and we would like to
extend open account privileges to you. Please contact our sales office to set up a new
account. «ENDIF» «ENDIF»
```

The syntax is simple: String all the IF statements one right after another, and then enter the text to be inserted. Finish by supplying an ENDIF for each of the IF instructions. If there are two IF instructions, for example, add two ENDIFs.

Using ELSE Within an IF Instruction

In the examples of the IF instruction that you have seen so far, nothing happened if the condition was not met. If the Discount field was blank, for example, no text was inserted. But what if you need a specific response if the condition is not met? The ELSE instruction fulfills this need. You provide a condition in the IF instruction. (Any of the three types of condition will work.) You then enter the text to be inserted if the condition is met and another string to be inserted if the condition is not met. The syntax looks like the following:

```
«IF condition» text to insert «ELSE» alternative text to insert «ENDIF»
```

In place of *condition*, you enter the name of the field you want to test and also a conditional test, if desired. If the condition is met, Word prints the *text to insert*. If the condition is not met, Word prints the *alternative text to insert*. Figure 16-8 shows some examples that use the ELSE instruction.

You can also use ELSE within a set of nested IF instructions to provide an alternative when testing for more than one condition at a time. For example:

```
«IF Discount» «IF Total>100» You are a valued customer, and we would like to
extend open account privileges to you. Please contact our sales office to set up a new
account. «ELSE» Please contact our sales office for more information about open
account privileges.«ENDIF» «ENDIF»
```

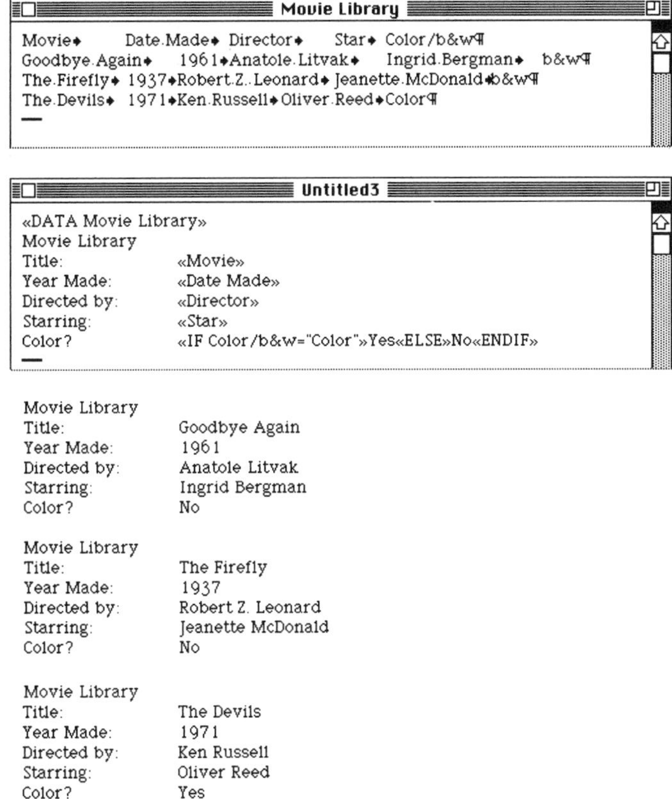

Figure 16-8
Examples of the ELSE instruction.

The NEXT Instruction

You can use the IF instruction to determine whether a form document for a certain record should be printed at all. If you know that you want to print only a certain range (from the third to tenth record, for instance), simply enter the appropriate values in the From and To edit fields in the Print Merge dialog box. If you want to print only those records that meet certain criteria, however, such as ones for past due accounts, use the NEXT instruction. You can think of the NEXT instruction as a filter: It passes (prints) only those records that meet the criteria specified in the IF instruction. The syntax for the NEXT instruction is as follows:

«IF condition» «NEXT» «ENDIF»

The *condition* can test for text in a field, matching text, or a matching number. If the condition is not met, Word skips to the next record, as shown in Figure 16-9. If the condition is met, the record is merged with the form main document and then printed. NEXT works when you are sending form documents to the printer and also when placing them in a new document.

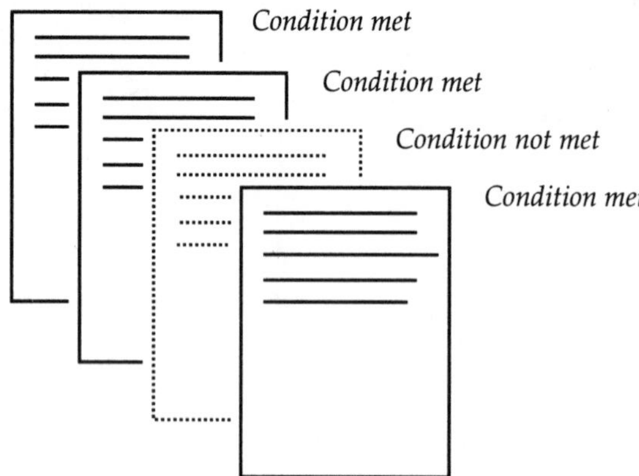

Figure 16-9
How the NEXT instruction works.

You can also use the NEXT instruction by itself. This is useful when you want to print more than one record in one document. For example, you can set up a merge document to print labels on an 8 ½ -by-11-inch sheet of labels by using a series of merge commands that look like this:

```
«name»¶
«address»¶
«city», «state»  «zip»¶
«NEXT»¶
¶
«name»¶
«address»¶
«city», «state»  «zip»¶
«NEXT»¶
¶
«name»¶
«address»¶
«city», «state»  «zip»¶
«NEXT»¶
¶
```

When you set up the merge document, create a single page of labels in this pattern, and format the document for as many columns as the labels you're using. Also, use a font, line spacing, and margin measurements that position the addresses correctly with respect to each label. When you print merge the mailing list, each time the merge document is printed, it goes on to the next set of addresses. For example, if the labels you're using are arranged three across and twelve deep, you would set up the merge document for printing 36 records at a time.

TIP

Including a Condition Test in the Record
Setting up complicated conditions using Word's merge instructions can take some work. If you prepare data documents with a database or spreadsheet program, you can take advantage of its abilities to test for conditions instead. For example, you can create a new column called PrintRecord in a database worksheet that you have created in Microsoft Excel. Enter the test condition as a formula in the worksheet, throughout the range of that column. Have the formula return *true* if the condition is met and *false* if it is not. Then, use the following instruction in the main document in Word:

«IF PrintRecord = "false"» «NEXT» «ENDIF»

In this way, you can have the data document tell the main document whether a form document should be created for that record.

The SET Instruction

The SET instruction lets you store information in a field that remains constant for every record merged. If, for example, you want to provide the current date in your monthly statements, you could include a SET instruction in the main document that asks you for the current date before merging and printing begin. Neither the data document nor the main document is physically altered by this.

You usually place the SET instruction right after the DATA instruction in the main document, although it can appear anywhere in the document as long as it falls before the field on which it acts. If you are using the SET instruction to enter the date, for instance, be sure to place the instruction before the date field, as shown in Figure 16-10.

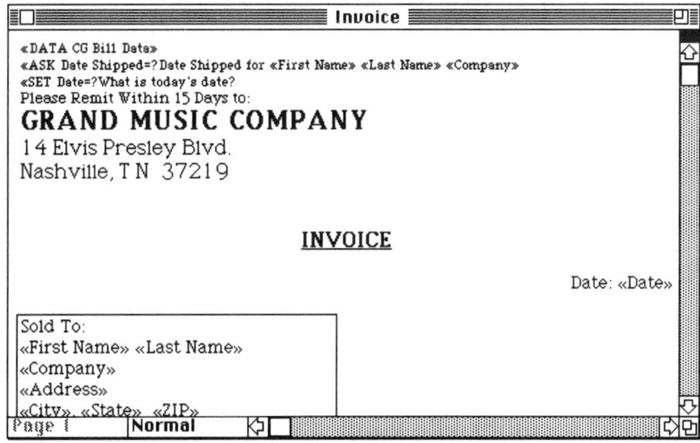

Figure 16-10
Storing data in a field with the SET instruction.

The three ways to use the SET instruction are as follows:

«SET field name = text string»
«SET field name = ?»
«SET field name = ?prompt»

The field name you specify must not be one of the names specified in the header record for the data document.

Use the first form to enter a text string into the field specified in *field name*. Word stores the characters indicated in *text string* in the field given in *field name*. Then, when you merge the document, Word replaces all occurrences of *«field name»* in the main document with the text string.

Use the second form of the instruction when you want to enter the text string for the field just before the documents are merged. When you begin merging, you will see the dialog box shown in Figure 16-11.

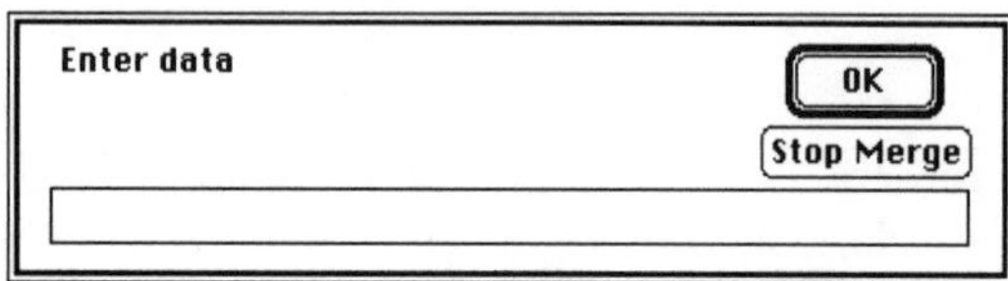

Figure 16-11
The standard SET dialog box.

If you want to provide a prompt in the dialog box, use the third form. Simply enter a message of up to 99 characters after the question mark, such as *What is the person's first name?* When Word encounters this type of SET instruction, it presents a dialog box like that shown in Figure 16-12.

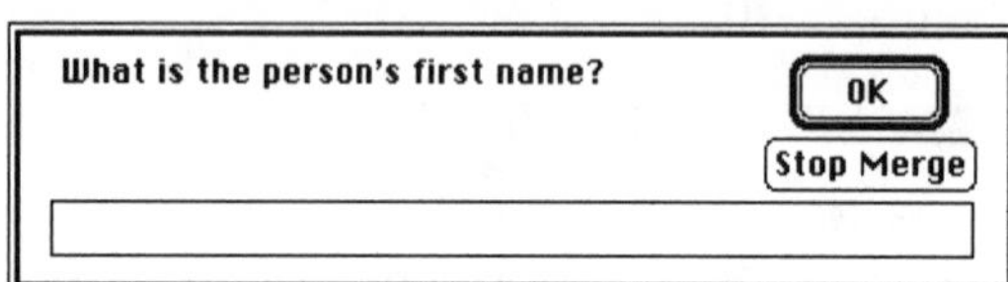

Figure 16-12
The SET dialog box with a user-specified prompt.

The ASK Instruction

The ASK instruction is like the SET instruction, except that Word presents a dialog box requesting new information for each record in the data document. Whereas the SET instruction plants the same text in all the form documents, the ASK instruction allows you to plant different text in each one.

Use the ASK instruction as you do SET: Place it right after the DATA instruction at the top of the document or anywhere before the field on which it acts. During the merge process, Word stops and asks you to enter the information for that record. The ASK instruction has two forms:

```
«ASK field name = ?»
«ASK field name = ?prompt»
```

Again, this field name must not be one of the fields in the data document.

As it does with the SET instruction, when Word encounters an ASK instruction, it presents a dialog box in which you enter the text to be placed in the field. In the first form, the dialog box lacks a prompt. So, if you have several SET or ASK instructions in the document, use the second form to have Word prompt you for the proper response.

The INCLUDE Instruction

Word's regular merge feature is useful when you want to insert individual words or sentences into the main document. But what if you want to merge entire paragraphs or pages? What if you are preparing a series of contracts in which certain paragraphs are used in some of the documents but not in others? Use the INCLUDE instruction. This instruction lets you import the contents of an entire file and place it within the merged document.

You can use INCLUDE by itself or in conjunction with an IF instruction. When used by itself, INCLUDE inserts the contents of the specified document into the main document. You can place an INCLUDE instruction anywhere in the main document; Word then inserts the document at that point.

When used with an IF instruction, INCLUDE allows you to dictate which documents receive the included text and which do not. Figure 16-13 shows a main document in which the document that is entitled *Quantity Discount* is merged into the letter if the Quantity field contains a number greater than 250. If the value in the Quantity field is 250 or less, the file is not included.

When you copy a document into the main document with the INCLUDE instruction, not all of its formats are transferred with it. The document-level formats for the included document, such as page margins, default tab stops, and the contents of the Next File field, are not transferred.

In addition, if you've defined styles in the included document that have the same names as styles in the main document, the styles in the main document take precedence. This can be convenient because you can redefine styles in the main document without having to hunt for and redefine the styles in all the documents you might include in the main document.

If a DATA or INCLUDE instruction specifies a document that is not in a disk drive when you choose the Print Merge command, Word presents a dialog box asking you to find it. Locate the folder or insert the disk that contains the document you need.

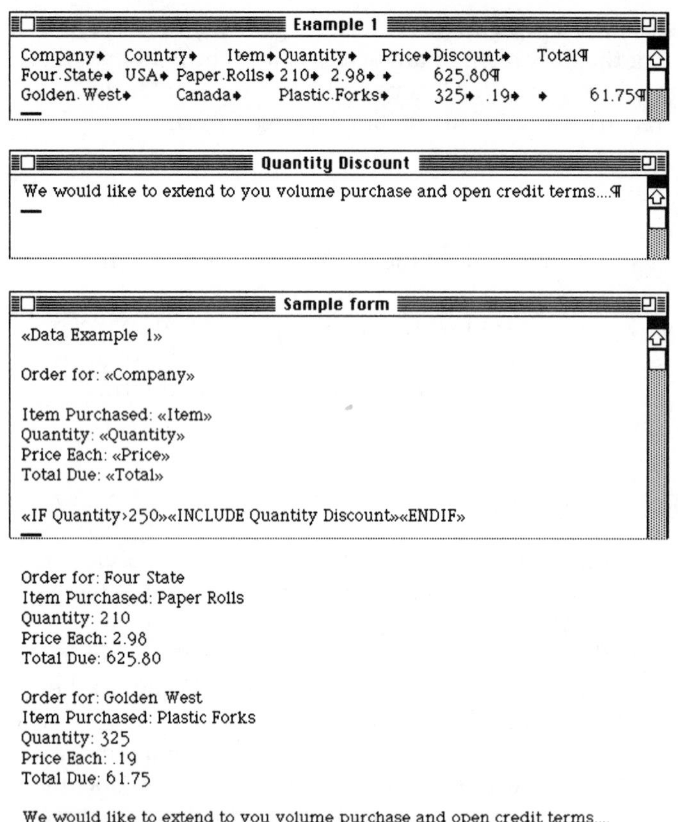

Example 1

Company◆ Country◆ Item◆Quantity◆ Price◆Discount◆ Total¶
Four.State◆ USA◆ Paper.Rolls◆ 210◆ 2.98◆ ◆ 625.80¶
Golden.West◆ Canada◆ Plastic.Forks◆ 325◆ .19◆ ◆ 61.75¶

Quantity Discount

We would like to extend to you volume purchase and open credit terms....¶

Sample form

«Data Example 1»

Order for: «Company»

Item Purchased: «Item»
Quantity: «Quantity»
Price Each: «Price»
Total Due: «Total»

«IF Quantity>250»«INCLUDE Quantity Discount»«ENDIF»

Order for: Four State
Item Purchased: Paper Rolls
Quantity: 210
Price Each: 2.98
Total Due: 625.80

Order for: Golden West
Item Purchased: Plastic Forks
Quantity: 325
Price Each: .19
Total Due: 61.75

We would like to extend to you volume purchase and open credit terms....

Figure 16-13
The INCLUDE instruction used with an IF instruction.

One further point: The number of documents that Word can have open at one time is limited to 24, and if you've added headers or footers and footnotes to a document, each counts as an additional document. For example, a main document with up to 6 headers and footers (First, Odd, and Even for each) and a set of footnotes actually counts as 3 documents. If you have opened only this document in Word, the main document could therefore contain up to 21 INCLUDE statements before running out of space.

Therefore, if you have many INCLUDE instructions in a document, close all unneeded documents. If you're using more INCLUDE instructions in the main document than Word can handle, you should do the merge in two or more passes, as follows:

❶ Replace all « characters after the twentieth INCLUDE instruction with a unique text string, such as @@@.

❷ Do the merge printing and create a new document. This merges the first 20 included documents.

3. Replace the next set of 20 @@@ strings with the « character.
4. Do another merge printing from the newly created document to insert the next 20 included documents.
5. Continue replacing @@@ strings and merging from the new document until all the included documents are in place.

Nesting INCLUDE Instructions

Normally, only the main document has an INCLUDE instruction. However, Word allows you to put INCLUDE instructions in included documents, too. This can produce a waterfall effect in which Word includes document after document, each of which contains its own INCLUDE instructions.

A document named in an INCLUDE instruction can itself contain field names and an assortment of IF, ELSE, NEXT, SET, and ASK instructions. However, it cannot contain the DATA instruction. All included documents retrieve records from the data document specified in the DATA instruction for the main document.

TIP

Using INCLUDE by Itself to Assemble New Documents

You don't have to create more than one form document to use the INCLUDE instruction effectively. The figures for this book, for example, could have been added not by copying and pasting them individually or by using QuickSwitch, but by moving each graphic into a Word file by itself and then merging all the graphics at once with the INCLUDE instruction. Each graphic file might consist of one paragraph containing one graphic. Each graphic could be merged into a chapter document by inserting an INCLUDE command in this form:

```
«INCLUDE c16 f xx
```

where *xx* is the number of that figure in the chapter, and *c16 f xx* is the filename of the document containing that graphic. The final » character was omitted to avoid having an extra paragraph mark inserted when the merging was done. (See "Omitting the Closing Bracket" below.)

There are two reasons why you might chose this way to insert graphics for a document. The first is that generally you don't need to have the figures in place until after the writing and editing is done, and having all the figures in the document would slow down scrolling, making it harder to move around and edit in the document. The second is that merging the graphics into a new document often doubles the size of the file. Working with very large files (generally in the 100 KB to 300 KB range) lessens the amount of memory left for processes such as editing and opening more than one document. We didn't use this method in this book because many chapters contain more than 22 graphics (each chapter uses headers and footers but not footnotes), and many of the graphics require special treatment (the arrows done in PostScript, for instance).

■ *Formatting Fields*

The data placed into fields in data records does not keep its original formats when merged into a form document. For example, if a name in a data record is in boldface, it loses its formatting when merged with the main document and takes on the formats in effect where it is inserted.

You can, however, have character formats applied to merged text by specifying the formats in the field names in the main document. To do this, apply the character formats you want to at least the first letter of the field name. To make the zip code in a mailing list bold, for example, format the *z* in the *zip* field as boldface. (See Figure 16-14.) You can apply any other character format in the same fashion.

«Name»
«Address»
«City», «State» «**Z**IP»

John Anderson
1423 Evergreen St.
Kansas City, MO **64142**

Figure 16-14
Specifying a boldfaced zip code.

The only way to set paragraph formats for merged text is to insert the field into a paragraph of its own and assign the paragraph formats you want to the paragraph mark in the main document.

Controlling Blank Lines

For every paragraph mark in a main document, Word places a matching paragraph mark—which starts a new line—in the form documents. This is not normally a problem, but sometimes you must control the number and placement of paragraph marks to prevent gaps in the text. You must be particularly wary of extra paragraph marks when printing mailing labels; if there are too many blank lines, the names and addresses won't fit correctly.

Even though the various merge instructions (such as DATA, SET, and ASK) don't appear in the final merged documents, blank lines will appear if you end these instructions by pressing the Return key. You can avoid these blank lines in one of three ways:

- ❑ By grouping instructions and text on the same line.
- ❑ By omitting the » character at the end of the instruction.
- ❑ By formatting the merge instruction as hidden text.

Grouping Instructions

You can put more than one instruction on a line, or you can surround an instruction with the text of the main document, as shown in Figure 16-15.

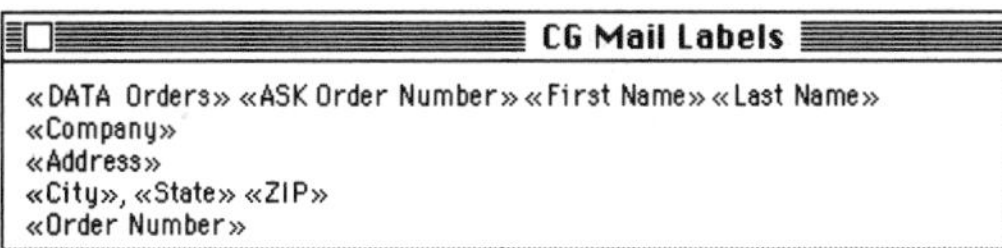
CG Mail Labels

«DATA Orders» «ASK Order Number» «First Name» «Last Name»
«Company»
«Address»
«City», «State» «ZIP»
«Order Number»

Figure 16-15
Grouped instructions and instructions with text.

A judicious positioning of the instructions (such as ENDIF) can suppress blank lines, as shown in Figure 16-16. By putting the ENDIF in the salutation, you avoid an extra line if the preceding paragraph doesn't print.

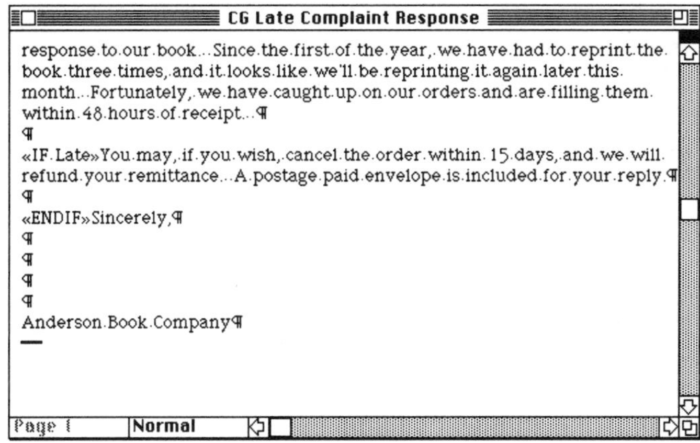
CG Late Complaint Response

response.to.our.book...Since.the.first.of.the.year,.we.have.had.to.reprint.the.
book.three.times,.and.it.looks.like.we'll.be.reprinting.it.again.later.this.
month...Fortunately,.we.have.caught.up.on.our.orders.and.are.filling.them.
within.48.hours.of.receipt...¶
¶
«IF.Late»You.may,.if.you.wish,.cancel.the.order.within.15.days,.and.we.will.
refund.your.remittance...A.postage.paid.envelope.is.included.for.your.reply.¶
¶
«ENDIF»Sincerely,¶
¶
¶
¶
¶
Anderson.Book.Company¶

Page 1 Normal

Figure 16-16
ENDIF positioned to avoid an extra line.

Omitting the Closing Bracket

If you end the instruction with a paragraph mark, you can avoid an extra line by omitting the final » symbol. Figure 16-17 shows a mailing-label document with and without the closing » character. Both documents produce the same labels, but the one with the paragraph mark and the closing bracket has an empty line at the top.

```
«DATA·Orders¶                       «DATA·Orders»¶
«First·Name»·«Last·Name»¶           «First·Name»·«Last·Name»¶
«Company»¶                          «Company»¶
«Address»¶                          «Address»¶
«City»,·«State»·«ZIP»¶              «City»,·«State»·«ZIP»¶
```

Figure 16-17
A mailing-label document without and with the closing bracket.

Hiding Merge Instructions

Because the DATA, SET, and ASK instructions don't appear when the merged documents are printed, you can make them invisible by formatting them as hidden text. As long as you also format the paragraph mark as hidden, it will not cause an extra blank line to appear in the printed document.

You cannot format as hidden the names of fields that you want to have printed in the final documents. If the fields are hidden, the merged text will be, too. You can use this to your advantage if you are using the Print Merge command to create a new document containing the merged form documents and you want to include special notes for each record. The hidden text will be merged into the documents, but unless you specify that hidden text be printed, the printed version of the document will not contain the notes. You can view the notes by opening the document and displaying the hidden text.

Points to Remember

- Word's Print Merge feature lets you create form letters and other items that combine standard text with text that is different for each document. The main document contains the standard text plus special instructions that tell Word when and where to insert the variable text. The data document contains the data to be inserted in the form documents.
- The set of data for a given form document is called a record. Each record ends with a paragraph mark. Records in the data document are divided into fields; each field contains text or data to be inserted at a certain point in the main document. A field can contain a word or even a sentence but cannot contain a paragraph mark. The fields in a record are separated by commas or tab characters. Each record can have up to 256 fields.
- A special record called the header record assigns names to each of the fields in a given data document. The header record can be either at the beginning of the data document or in a separate file.

Techniques

Create a data document

1. Type the header record at the beginning of a new document. Enter the name of each field you will use, separated by commas or tabs. A field name can have up to 65 characters and can include spaces.
2. Type the data records. Separate the fields with the same character you used in the header record. End each record with only one paragraph mark. If a field contains tabs, commas, or quotation marks, enclose the entire field in quotation marks. To leave a field blank, enter an extra tab or comma.

Create a main document

1. Place the instruction «DATA filename» at the beginning of the document; replace *filename* with the name of the data document. (Press Option-\ to enter the « character; press Shift-Option-\ to enter the » character.)
2. Type the standard text for the form documents.
3. At each point where you want to insert a field from the data document, enter «field name», replacing *field name* with the appropriate name.
4. If a field is to be inserted on its own line or at the close of a paragraph, omit the final » character to avoid generating an extra blank line.

Merge and print form documents

❶ With the main document open, choose Print Merge from the File menu.
❷ To merge a specific range of records, enter the beginning and ending record numbers in the From and To edit fields.
❸ Click Print.
❹ Choose the appropriate options in the Print dialog box that appears.
❺ Click OK.

Merge form documents into one file

❶ With the main document open, choose Print Merge from the File menu.
❷ To merge a specific range of records, enter the beginning and ending record numbers in the From and To edit fields.
❸ Click New Document. The form documents are placed one after another in a document. They are separated by section marks.
❹ When you are ready to print the form documents, choose Print.

The Print Merge Instructions

You include these instructions in the main document to specify conditions for the printing of text and so forth. Only the DATA instruction is required. You can use any combination of uppercase or lowercase for field names or instructions, but the capitalization of field names must be consistent with each other. The italicized elements are optional.

«ASK field name = ?*prompt*»

Causes Word to present a dialog box requesting text for each form document. It stores the text you enter in the specified field. If you specify a prompt, Word displays it in the dialog box.

«DATA *header document*, data document»

Specifies the data document. If the header and data are in one file, you need only specify the name of that document.

«IF field name » text to insert *«ELSE» text to insert* «ENDIF»

If the specified field contains text, Word inserts the specified text at that point in the document. If you use the ELSE element and the field is empty, Word inserts the text after the ELSE element.

«IF field name = "text string"» text to insert *«ELSE» text to insert* «ENDIF»

Word inserts the text if the contents of the field match the text string enclosed in quotation marks. If you use the ELSE element and the field does not match the text string, Word inserts the text after the ELSE element. To include a quotation mark in the text string, enter two quotation marks.

«IF field name = number» text to insert *«ELSE» text to insert* «ENDIF»

Word inserts the text if the contents of the field equal the integer number. If you use the ELSE element and the field is not equal to the number, Word inserts the text after the ELSE element. Instead of the equal sign, you can use the greater-than (>) or less-than (<) operator.

«INCLUDE document name»

Replaces the INCLUDE instruction with the file named. Omit the » character to avoid an extra paragraph mark. Styles in the main document take precedence over styles of the same name in the included document. An included document can itself contain an INCLUDE instruction, up to 64 levels deep. This instruction does not require a DATA instruction at the beginning of the main document.

«NEXT»

Causes Word to jump to the next data record without creating a form document for the current record. Usually used in an IF instruction, in place of text to be inserted.

«SET field name = text»

Specifies the contents of a field to remain constant in every form document.

«SET field name = ?*prompt*»

Displays a dialog box, with an optional prompt, requesting text that Word uses for that field in every form document.

SECTION 4

Blueprints for Projects

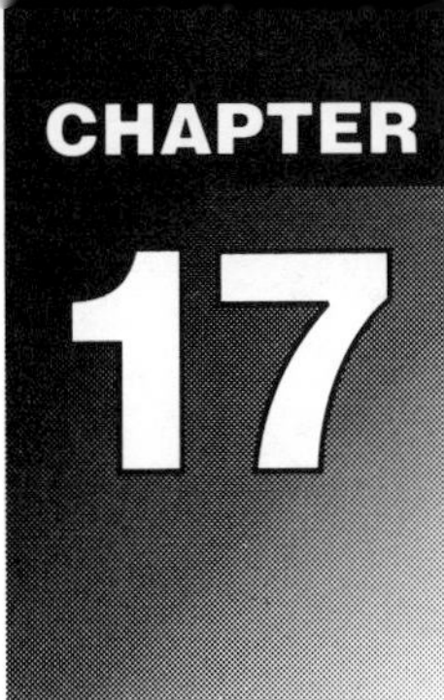

Blueprints

This chapter features sample documents that show you how the various features of Word work together in real situations. The examples are arranged in approximate order of complexity, culminating in a description of some of the elements that went into the construction of this book.

The first two sample documents are accompanied by a detailed description of the steps needed to construct each element in the design; you can recreate the design exactly or adapt parts of it to your own documents. As the documents progress in complexity, only the trickier parts will be highlighted; a complete specification for a newsletter, for example, might take an entire chapter. If a procedure looks unfamiliar, take a moment to review the relevant material in the preceding chapters.

Once you have reproduced or adapted one of these models, be sure to save it in its original state so that you can use it as a template for further alterations. A good way to do this is to add a note, such as *.template,* to the document's filename; that way you'll know it's the original.

■ *Electronic Letterhead*

You can use Word not only to print the text of your letters, but to print your letterhead as well. You may want your letterhead to consist of formatted text alone. If so, you will probably want to use a special font for it, or at least a unique font size or style. Your letterhead can also contain graphics in bit-mapped, object-oriented, or PostScript format, or some combination of any of these. Remember that object-oriented and PostScript graphics reproduce better when printed on a PostScript printer such as the LaserWriter.

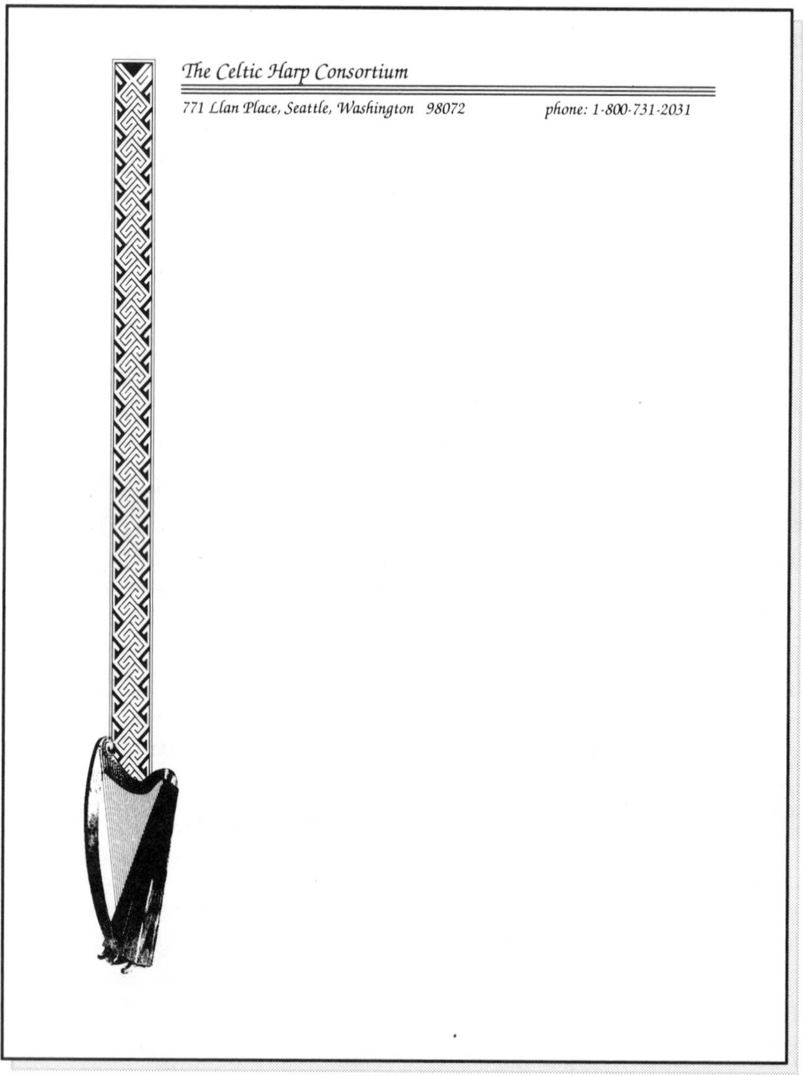

The Celtic Harp Consortium
771 Llan Place, Seattle, Washington 98072
phone: 1-800-731-2031

Figure 17-1
Sample electronic letterhead.

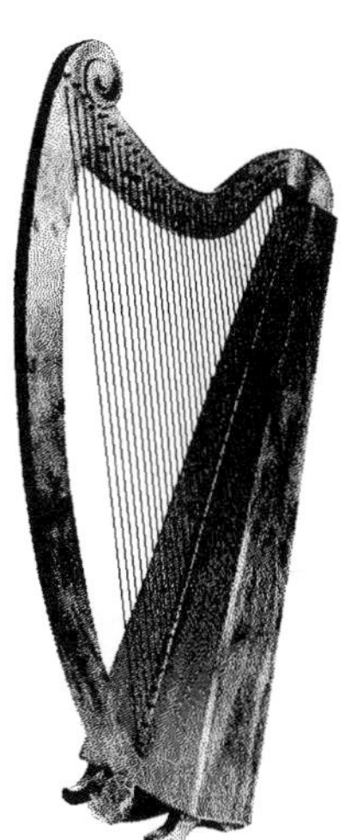

The letterhead shown in Figure 17-1 contains an image digitized by the MacVision video scanner running under the control of MoreVision, and then combined with some object-oriented graphics created with Cricket Draw. The combined image was transferred into Word, and the name and address of the company were added at the top, next to the logo.

Both the graphic and the text are stored in the header for the document, leaving the body of the document blank. Thus, everything shown in the figure is actually the header for an otherwise blank document. Normally, a large header such as this would push the body of the document down below it on the page. To avoid this, set a negative top margin in the Page Setup dialog box. This tells Word that you want the top margin to start at the location specified regardless of the size of the header.

The main reason for setting up the letterhead in this way is so that you can open the document and start typing a letter without having to pay much attention to the formatting of the header. You need only be sure that the left margin and left indent are set far enough to the right to avoid printing over the graphic.

Preparing the Letterhead

The first step is to create the graphic you want to use for your logo. You can, of course, use any program or method you like to get the effect you want; you're not limited to the programs used to create the sample. However, for the purposes of this discussion, it would be best to create a graphic of the same approximate dimensions as those of the example: roughly 1 inch wide and 9 inches tall.

When you're done, select and copy the graphic to the Clipboard and start Word. You will see the usual blank document window.

Next, paste the graphic into the header of the blank document and add the name and address of the company, following the steps given here. (You could use the footer instead, setting a negative bottom margin rather than a negative top margin, but this project uses the header.)

❶ Choose Open Header from the Document menu, and then choose the Paste command. The insertion point should be blinking at the right edge of the pasted graphic in the Header window.

❷ Display the Ruler, if it isn't already visible. Press the Shift key and click the left arrow in the horizontal scroll bar twice to shift the Ruler and the graphic to the right in the Header window.

❸ Drag the left indent for the graphic to the left to place it 1.25 inches left of the left margin for the body of the document.

Now that you've pasted the graphic into the header, the next step is to add the company's name and address and format the text appropriately.

❶ The insertion point should still be at the right edge of the graphic. Press the Return key once to start a new line, and reset its left indent to the left margin (the zero point on the Ruler).

❷ Enter the following text. Press the Return key where you see the ¶ mark and press the Tab key where you see the ➧ mark.

The Celtic Harp Consortium¶
¶
¶
¶
771 Llan Place, Seattle, Washington, 98072 ➧ ➧ phone: 1-800-731-2031¶

❸ Select the line containing the name of the company, and set the font to 18-point Zapf Chancery (or any other font you like).

❹ Select the line containing the address, and set it to 14-point Zapf Chancery. Notice that this line is still in the *Header* style, so the two tabs move the phone number past the center-aligned tab stop to the right-aligned tab stop at the right margin.

❺ To add the three rules below the company's name, select the three lines separating the company's name and address, and choose the Paragraph command. Set the Border Below option, and enter *-3pt* in the Line Spacing edit field.

❻ Select everything in the Header window. (To do this, press the Command key and click in the selection bar, or press Option-Command-M), and choose the Paragraph command. Set the Side-by-Side format, and click OK.

Because the left indent of the company's name and address is to the right of the left indent of the paragraph containing the graphic, the address aligns with the top of the graphic. The final step is to position both the letterhead and the body of the document on the page.

❶ Close the Header window, and then choose the Page Setup command. Enter *-1.5* in the Top edit field and enter *1.5* in the Left edit field. Click OK.

❷ Choose the Section command, and position the header vertically on the page by entering *1* in the From Top edit field.

Of course, if you are using a graphic with different dimensions, you will have to experiment with these specifications until everything is arranged in the way you want it. You can use Page Preview to check the positions of the different elements.

Tips and Techniques

It's a good idea to keep the letterhead in a template file. When you need to create a letter, open the template and immediately save the document under a new name. You can then type the letter and print it or save it as you want. To avoid accidentally editing the template letterhead, lock the file in the Get Info box. (You'll have to quit to the Finder for that.) Word will not let you edit a locked file.

To prevent the letterhead from appearing on the second and subsequent pages, click the First Page Special option in the Section dialog box. Or, you could create a variation of the letterhead to use on the subsequent pages.

The time required to print a letter on electronic letterhead stock varies with the complexity of the graphic you create. Graphics composed solely of QuickDraw objects take the least amount of time to print, whereas graphics containing PostScript or compressed bit-mapped images take considerably longer to print.

To avoid lengthy printing times, you can print many copies of the letterhead as blank stock, without any body text, and then later enter the body of the document into a blank window for printing on the letterhead stock. This is also more convenient if you have infrequent access to a LaserWriter or other PostScript printer and you would prefer the higher printing quality for the letterhead. If you use a letterhead like the one laid out in this blueprint, be sure to adjust the top and left margins of the document accordingly, to avoid printing over the letterhead.

■ *Reply Memo*

With a reply memo like the one shown in Figure 17-2, you can quickly prepare memos for distribution to clients, customers, associates, and business prospects. It contains an area that the recipient can use, if necessary, to respond to the message.

Memo

From:
To:
Date:
Subject:

Reply Please respond ☐ No response needed ☐ Please telephone ☐

Date:

Figure 17-2
Sample reply memo.

The reply memo is divided into four areas:

- A heading, composed of the memo title and four spaces for the sender's name, the name of the recipient, the date, and the subject of the message.
- An area for the message.
- Another heading for the reply, with instructions for the recipient.
- An area for the reply.

In addition to the areas in the memo proper, the entire page has been surrounded with a box, entered into the Header window so that it overlaps the body of the memo. Now let's construct the document.

Building the Memo Form

First, choose New from the File menu. The first step is to set the margins for the document. Choose the Page Setup command, and set the page margins to 1 inch on all sides. Enter a minus sign (hyphen) in front of the Top margin measurement to overlap the contents of the Header window with the body of the document. Click OK. Then select a standard font and font size for the blank document, as follows:

❶ Choose the Define Styles command, and select the *Normal* style.

❷ Choose a font—Bookman, for example, and the 12-point font size. Click OK, and in the Define Styles dialog box, click Define and then Cancel.

Next, type the following text. (Don't enter the line numbers; they are for reference purposes only.) Where you see the ¶ mark, press the Return key; where you see the ➧ mark, press the Tab key.

```
Memo¶
¶
 ➧ From:¶
 ➧ To:¶
 ➧ Date:¶
 ➧ Subject:¶
¶
¶
¶
¶
¶
¶
¶
¶
¶
¶
¶
¶
¶
¶
Reply ➧ Please respond ➧ No response needed ➧ Please telephone¶
¶
 ➧ Date:¶
¶
 ➧ ¶
 ➧ ¶
 ➧ ¶
 ➧ ¶
 ➧ ¶
 ➧ ¶
```

```
31  ➧ ¶
32  ➧ ¶
33  ➧ ¶
34  ➧ ¶
35  ➧ ¶
36  ➧ ¶
37  ➧ ¶
38  ➧ ¶
39  ➧ ¶
40  ➧ ¶
41  ➧ ¶
```

Next, format the header and the first few lines of the memo sheet:

❶ Select the first line by clicking in the selection bar to the left of the word *Memo*.

❷ Choose the Character command, change the font size to 24 point, and click the Italic option from the Character Formats group. Click OK.

❸ Choose the Paragraph command, and click the Below and Double Border options. Click OK.

❹ Select lines 3 through 6 (the *From* through *Subject* lines).

❺ Choose Show Ruler from the Format menu, click the Right-aligned tab stop icon (the third from the left), and drag a tab marker to 0.75 inch from the left margin. If you entered tab markers at the beginning of each of these lines as shown, each word is now right aligned at 0.75 inch.

Leave the second area unchanged. You can enter the message when you actually type a memo. Next, format the Reply heading:

❶ Double-click on *Reply* to select it, and then press Shift-Command-> three times to increase its size to 24 point. Choose Italic from the Format menu.

❷ Choose the Paragraph command, and add a double border below the paragraph.

❸ Place the insertion point immediately after *Please respond*, and press the Spacebar once to add a space.

❹ Choose Insert Graphics from the Edit menu. Select the resulting graphics frame by clicking on it, and choose Outline from the Format menu to create a resizable box. The graphics frame appears as a 1-inch-square box. Drag the right and bottom handles in the graphics frame until the box is 0.25 inch square.

❺ While the box is selected, copy it to the Clipboard. Place the insertion point after *No response needed*, press the Spacebar once, and paste in the box. Paste another box after *Please telephone*.

❻ Select the phrase *Please respond*, and choose Character from the Format menu. Change the font size to 10 point. Click the Superscript option, and enter *5pt* in the By field. This raises the phrase so that it is centered vertically with respect to the box. Repeat this for the *No response needed* and *Please telephone* phrases.

❼ To format line 23, which contains the reply date, select line 5, copy it, select line 23, and paste in the copied line, replacing the original.

The lines for the reply are underlined tab leaders, which produce lines that are thinner and more appealing for this purpose than those achieved with the Border Below paragraph format. You've already entered the tabs for lines 23 through 39. To adjust their corresponding tabs stops and add the underlined leaders, do the following:

❶ Select lines 23 through 39 (the lines containing only tab characters). Choose the Paragraph command. The Paragraph dialog box and the Ruler (if it's not visible already) appear.

❷ Click the Left-aligned tab stop icon, and then place a tab stop on the Ruler at 6.5 inches. Click the underline Tab leader option, and click OK.

All that remains is to add the box surrounding the text of the memo and then adjust the page dimensions so that the elements on the page are positioned correctly.

❶ Choose Open Header from the Document menu. If the Ruler isn't visible at the top of the Header window, choose the Show Ruler command.

❷ Choose the Insert Graphics command to insert an empty graphics frame. Select the frame and give it both the Outline and Shadow character attributes. Drag the frame out to 7.5 inches wide and 10 inches long. (The current position appears in the status box when you drag a handle.) Unless your Mac has a large screen, you will have to alternate between dragging the graphics frame and shifting the document by clicking the horizontal and vertical scroll arrows.

❸ Press the Shift key and click the left scroll arrow to shift the document ½ inch to the right until you can see the first half inch past the left margin in the Ruler. You need to do this before you can move the left edge of the graphics frame to the left of the left margin. If the graphics frame isn't selected, click on it to select it, and then drag the left indent marker in the Ruler to the left until it's ½ inch beyond the left margin. Click the Header window's close box.

Now you have it: the finished memo form. Be sure to save this form with a name that reflects its use, such as *Memo Form Template*. To avoid accidentally editing and resaving the template, lock the document from the Finder's desktop. (Use the Get Info box and click the locked check box.) Word will not let you alter a locked file.

Although the steps for constructing this document have been presented as though it was clear from the beginning how to get the desired result, in practice it's necessary to experiment and make many adjustments as you refine the design for a document.

Often, there are many ways to achieve a certain effect. For example, instead of using a graphics frame in the header, you could create a box of the proper dimensions in MacDraw and paste it into the Header window. The advantages of this approach include being able to create boxes with rounded corners and in patterns and different densities of gray instead of black.

Using the Memo Form

To use the memo form, open the document and save it under a new name that describes the memo you want to write, such as *Memo to Clients, 870823*. Fill in the information at the top of the memo (From, To, Date, and Subject). You can easily enter text at these points by clicking immediately following the word *Date:*, for example, pressing the Tab key once to move to the next tab stop, and entering the current date. Because the next tab stop is a default left-aligned tab stop, the field names and the text you enter will stay correctly aligned. If you want, change the character format for the information you enter to distinguish it from the form itself.

To enter the message, type it in the sender's message area. Keep the message short, or the memo may spill onto a second page. If necessary, you can adjust the lengths of the message and reply areas by deleting lines or copying and pasting lines within the appropriate area. Save the completed memo if you want to keep a record of it.

When printing the memo, choose the Print command, as usual, but enter *1* in the To field to print only the first page.

■ *Calculated Invoice*

The blueprint provided in this section is an invoice template designed to allow you to enter the items and then have Word calculate the extended prices, subtotal, tax, and grand total for you. Figure 17-3 shows a blank invoice, and a completed one is shown in Figure 17-4.

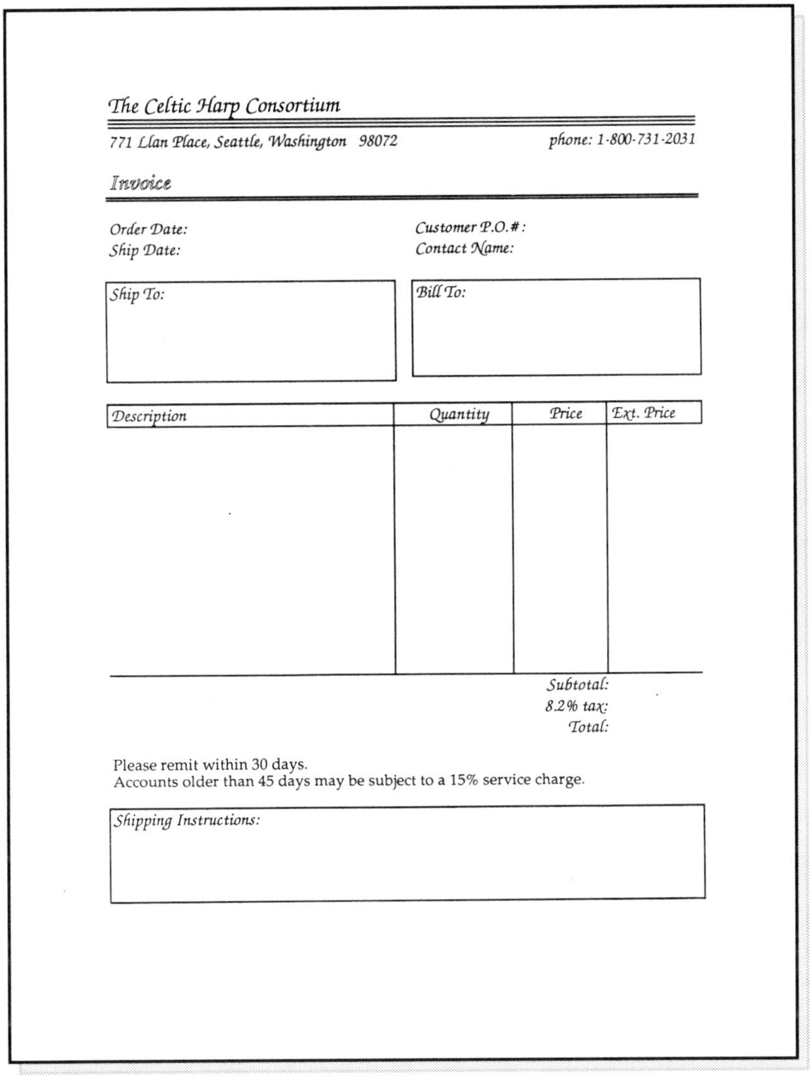

The Celtic Harp Consortium

771 Llan Place, Seattle, Washington 98072 phone: 1-800-731-2031

Invoice

Order Date: Customer P.O.#:
Ship Date: Contact Name:

Ship To:

Bill To:

Description	Quantity	Price	Ext. Price

Subtotal:
8.2% tax:
Total:

Please remit within 30 days.
Accounts older than 45 days may be subject to a 15% service charge.

Shipping Instructions:

Figure 17-3
Sample blank invoice.

Setting Up the Invoice

Instead of giving exhaustive directions for reproducing this template, we will describe only the main features; use these as a starting point for your own invoice form.

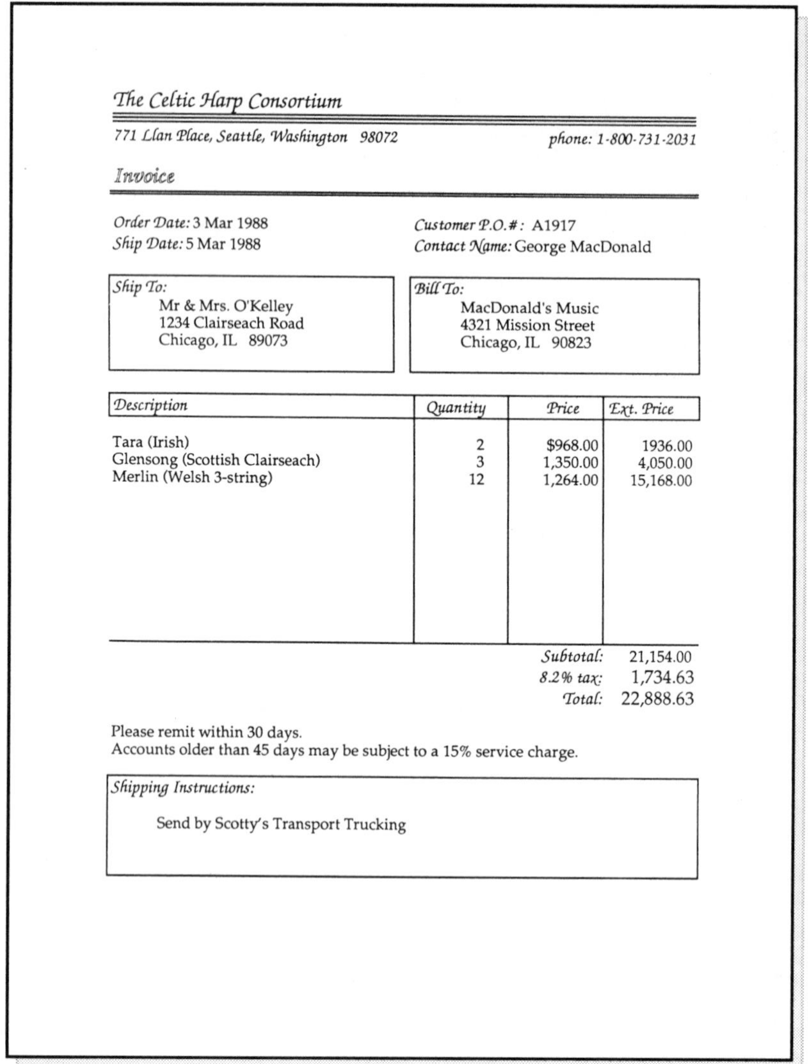
The Celtic Harp Consortium

771 Llan Place, Seattle, Washington 98072 *phone: 1-800-731-2031*

Invoice

Order Date: 3 Mar 1988
Ship Date: 5 Mar 1988
Customer P.O.#: A1917
Contact Name: George MacDonald

Ship To:
Mr & Mrs. O'Kelley
1234 Clairseach Road
Chicago, IL 89073

Bill To:
MacDonald's Music
4321 Mission Street
Chicago, IL 90823

Description	*Quantity*	*Price*	*Ext. Price*
Tara (Irish)	2	$968.00	1936.00
Glensong (Scottish Clairseach)	3	1,350.00	4,050.00
Merlin (Welsh 3-string)	12	1,264.00	15,168.00
		Subtotal:	21,154.00
		8.2% tax:	1,734.63
		Total:	22,888.63

Please remit within 30 days.
Accounts older than 45 days may be subject to a 15% service charge.

Shipping Instructions:
Send by Scotty's Transport Trucking

Figure 17-4
A completed invoice.

You can copy the title of the invoice from the electronic letterhead template described earlier. Alternatively, you can start over and enter the name of the company and the address and put it all in the Zapf Chancery font: use 18 point for the name and 14 point for the address. Use a right-aligned tab stop to position the phone number.

The three horizontal rules beneath the name of the company are actually three paragraphs with the Border Below paragraph format set. To create the lines, press the Return key three times, select the empty lines, and choose the

Paragraph command. Enter *-3pt* in the Line Spacing edit field to bring the lines close together, and then select the Below option in the Border group.

Skip a line after the address, enter the *Invoice* label in 18-point outline type, and add a double border line below the paragraph containing the label.

Next, enter the lines containing the *Order Date* and *Ship Date* areas, and make them boldface. Use boldface for all the labels attached to the areas to be filled in by the person typing the invoice. Set the tab stop for the second column at 3.25 inches.

The two boxes for the shipping and billing addresses are probably the trickiest elements in this template. They are each single side-by-side paragraphs and make use of a little-known characteristic of the Box Border format: The left edge of the box border is determined by the first-line indent, if it is to the left of the right indent. Figure 17-5 shows these boxes as they would appear on the screen.

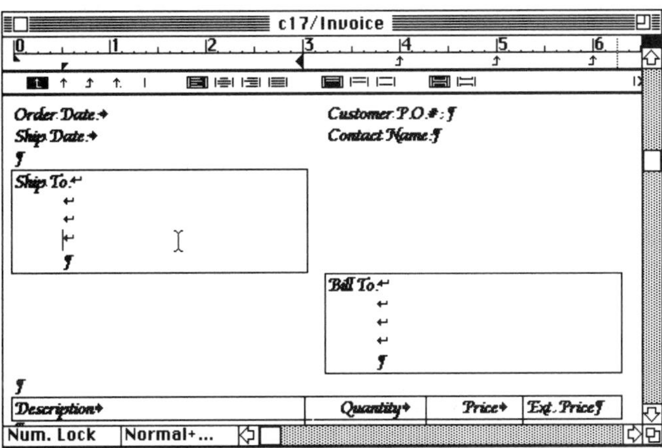

Figure 17-5
The boxed address areas as they appear on the screen.

It's a good idea to confirm the Page Setup dialog box options at this point so that the boxes you establish by changing the indents have the correct dimensions. For this invoice, the top, bottom, and right margins are all set at 1 inch, and the left margin is set at 1.25 inches, to allow the invoice to be bound, if necessary.

Notice the positions of the addresses shown in Figure 17-5. The first line of the first boxed address is a hanging indent set at the left margin (0 inch), the left indent is set at 0.5 inch, and the right indent is set at 3 inches. The first line of the billing address area is set at 3.25 inches, the left indent is set at 3.75 inches, and the right indent is set at the right margin, or 6.25 inches. Each line of an address ends with a newline character, created by pressing Shift-Return. This causes Word to treat the lines as one paragraph so that a single box surrounds each address.

The table listing the items on the invoice is more straightforward. The line containing the headings is formatted in 12-point bold Zapf Chancery and given the Box Border format.

To set the tab stops and the positions of the vertical lines, add several empty paragraphs after the heading to make room for the invoice items, and then select both the heading and the empty lines. Choose the Show Ruler command if the Ruler isn't visible, and set vertical lines at 3.25, 4.25, and 5.25 inches. Set decimal tab stops (use the fourth tab stop icon in the Ruler bar) at 4, 5, and 6 inches so that the numbers entered in their columns will align at the decimal point.

To add the horizontal rule at the bottom of the list, first enter the *Subtotal, 8.2% tax,* and *Total* labels, and then select the line containing the *Subtotal* label and give it the Above Border format. To finish the itemized list, select all three lines and set a right-aligned tab stop at 5.25 inches and a decimal tab stop at 6 inches. Add tabs at the beginning of each line to move the labels to the correct position. The two lines citing the payment instructions are in 12-point Palatino.

Finally, set up the box for the shipping instructions as you did the one for the shipping address. Copy the paragraph for the shipping address, substitute *Shipping Instructions* for *Ship To,* and move the right indent from 3 inches to 6.25 inches, the position of the right margin.

Using the Invoice

To use the invoice, enter the appropriate text after the labels for the order date, the customer's purchase order number, and so on. You can select these entries and give them a different font to differentiate them from the labels. In the shipping and billing address areas, be sure to end each line with a new-line mark (Shift-Return) so that the box surrounds the address correctly.

Next, enter the description, quantity, and price for each item on the invoice. If you need more lines, simply press the Return key at the end of a line to create another line having the same tab and vertical-line formats. If the list gets too long, however, you may need to make other adjustments to keep the invoice to one page.

You calculate the extended price by multiplying the quantity by the price, so when you enter the price, precede it with an asterisk and give the asterisk the Hidden character format. To determine the extended price for an item, select both the quantity and the price and press Command-=, as shown in Figure 17-6. Word stores the value in the Clipboard, making a guess as to the format you want for the result based on the formats of the numbers you entered. Paste it into the extended price column; you may have to press the Tab key first to move the insertion point to the last column. Continue to calculate the extended price for each of the other items in the list. When you're done, remove the asterisks if you want.

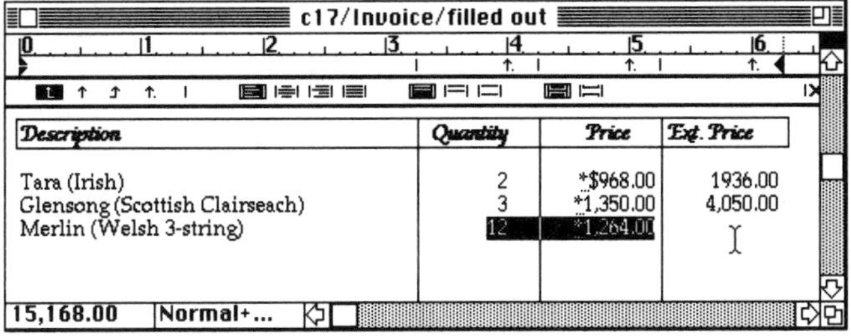

Figure 17-6
Calculating an extended price.

To arrive at the subtotal, select only the numbers in the extended price column by pressing the Option key while dragging over the numbers in the column. Press Command- = to calculate the sum of the extended prices, and then paste the number on the subtotal line. Instead of using Zapf Chancery, you may want to format the totals in a more legible font. Palatino was used for the example in Figure 17-6.

The invoice is also set up to calculate sales tax. The sales tax percentage is included in the label for the tax line: *8.2% tax*. If you insert an asterisk before this label, select the tax and subtotal lines, and press Command- =, Word calculates the percentage for you and puts the result on the Clipboard. Word understands the percent sign at the end of the tax rate; note also that you can "bury" a value in text instead of putting it in a column by itself. Paste the result after the label in the tax line, and format it as needed.

Calculate the grand total by using the Option key to select the subtotal figure and the tax figure and then pressing Command- =. Notice that you can't simply select the two lines by dragging in the selection bar, because then you would also select the tax rate. Paste the result into the *Total* line.

Tips and Techniques

You can hide the math operators if you want to clean up the appearance of the invoice. Select each asterisk in the Price column, and format it as hidden text. You can set a tab stop between the quantity and the price (for example) and put a hidden operator at this position on every line so that you don't have to go through the process of adding and then deleting them when you fill out the invoice.

Word requires that hidden text be showing when you do calculations, but after the calculations are finished you can hide the text. Remember that Word won't print hidden text unless you tell it to, even if it is showing on the screen. To be sure that hidden text won't print, check that the Print Hidden Text option (in the Print dialog box) is turned off.

Word ignores such symbols as $ and ¢, so even if you have them in the *Price* and *Ext. Price* columns, they will not be included in the result. If you want the symbols to appear, you must type them yourself.

With Word's calculator, the value with the most decimal places determines the number of decimal places in the result, so some of your invoices may not be fully accurate unless the numbers you're calculating have enough decimal places. For example, *75.90 * 6%* is calculated as *4.55* by Word. On a floating-point calculator, the value is shown more accurately as *4.554*. Typing *75.900 * 6%* produces the correct result.

Presentation Graphics from an Outline

You can use Word's outliner to order your thoughts by entering items in Outline view and then switching to Document view to add the body of the text. When you switch to Document view, all the *level* style entries turn into headings within the document. You may later turn some of these *level* style entries back into text in the *Normal* style or another style. As you develop the document, you can adjust the formats for the headings that remain by redefining their styles through the Define Styles dialog box.

This is, of course, not the only way you can use Word's outliner. In this project, we've turned an outline prepared for a presentation into a set of transparencies to be used for the presentation itself, as you can see in Figures 17-7a through 17-7d.

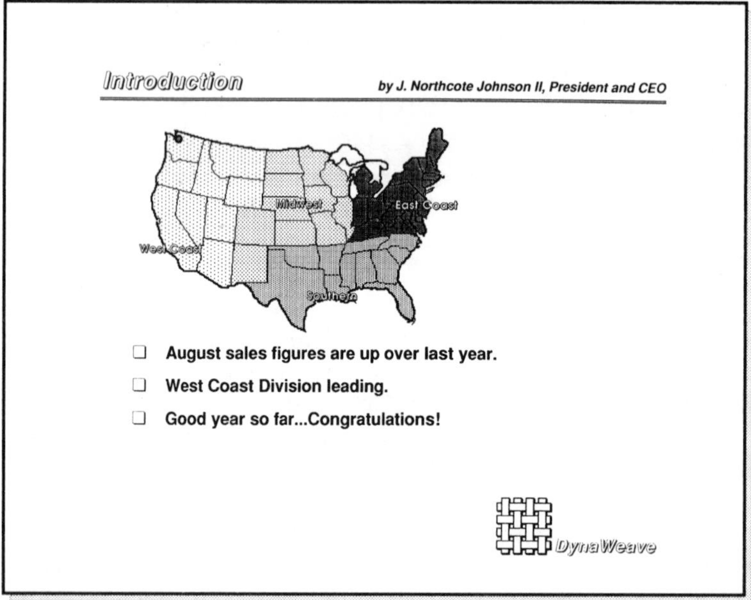

Figure 17-7a
First page of the presentation outline.

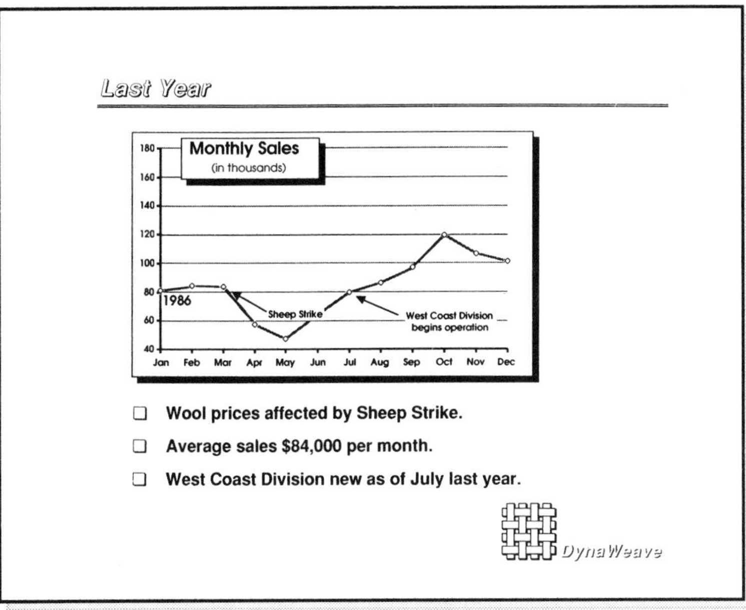

Figure 17-7b
Second page of the presentation outline.

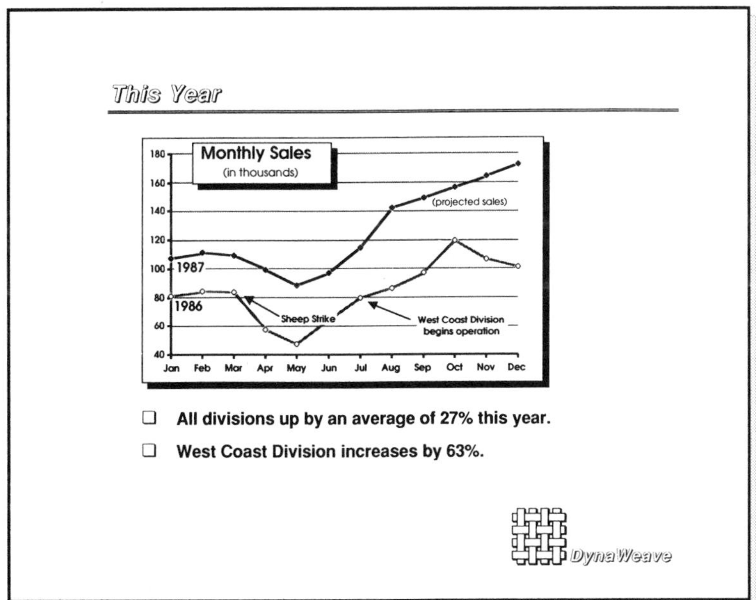

Figure 17-7c
Third page of the presentation outline.

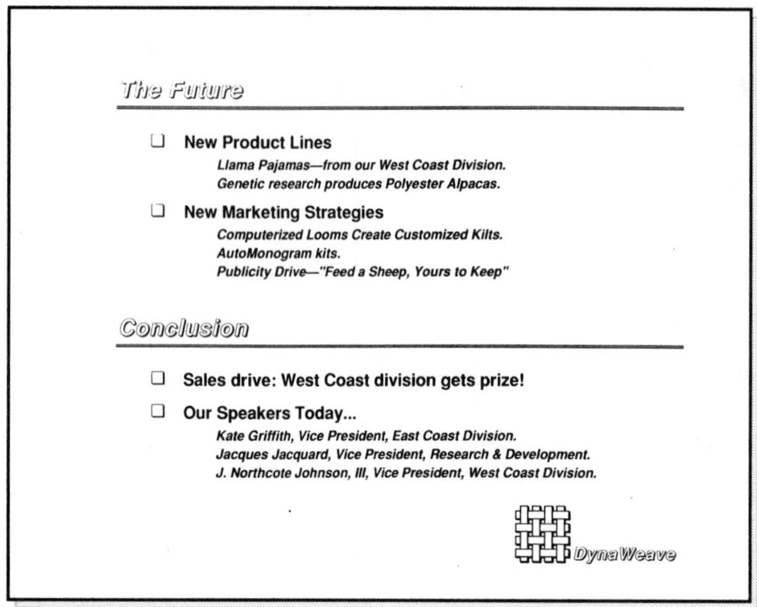

Figure 17-7d
Fourth page of the presentation outline.

Preparing the Outline

This set of presentation transparencies had a humble beginning as the outline shown in Figure 17-8. Each topic for the presenter's speech has a level in the outline and is assigned one of the *level* styles, from *level 1* through *level 3*.

c17/Presentation.before

1 2 3 4 5 6 7 8 9

Introduction by J. Northcote Johnson II, President and CEO
    August sales figures are up over last year.
    West Coast Division leading.
    Good year so far...Congratulations!
Last Year
    Wool prices affected by Sheep Strike.
    Average sales $84,000 per month.
    West Coast Division new as of July last year.
This Year
    All divisions up by an average of 27% this year.
    West Coast Division increases by 63%.
The Future
    New Product Lines
        Llama Pajamas—from our West Coast Division.
        Genetic research produces Polyester Alpacas.
    New Marketing Strategies
        Computerized Looms Create Customized Kilts.
        AutoMonogram kits.
        Publicity Drive—"Feed a Sheep, Yours to Keep"
Conclusion
    Sales drive: West Coast division gets prize!
    Our Speakers Today...

Page 1 Normal

Figure 17-8
The outline for the speech in Outline view.

After you've entered the main topics, you can write the actual speech in Document view. When you switch to Document view, the outline should look something like Figure 17-9, depending on how you've customized your default style sheet.

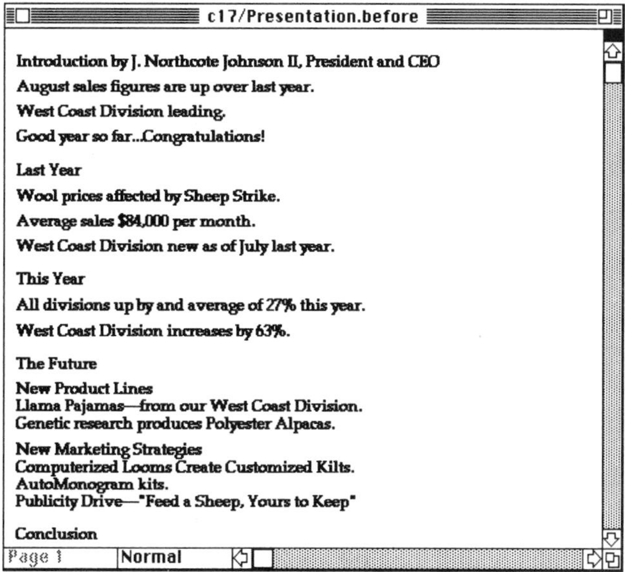

Figure 17-9
The outline for the speech in Document view.

The next step is to transform this outline into a set of "screens" or pages, with each major topic on its own page. Start by choosing the Wide option in the Page Setup dialog box to change the orientation for the document. Then, redefine the styles for the document according to this table:

Style Name	Definition
footer	Normal + Tab stops: 3 in Centered; 6 in Right Flush
level 1	Normal + Font: Helvetica 24 Point, Bold Italic Outline Shadow, Space After 12 pt, Page Break Before, Border: Double Line Below
level 2	Normal + Font: Helvetica 18 Point, Bold, Indent: Left 0.5 in, Space Before 12 pt
level 3	Normal + Font: Helvetica 14 Point, Bold Italic, Indent: Left 1 in, Space Before 4 pt, Keep With Next

As the table shows, each of the major topics—those in the *level 1* style—starts a new page and thus constitutes the title at the top of each slide. Each slide title has a double-line border beneath it to set off the title from the points to be covered in the slide. Also, each level of topic is indented one-half inch to the right of the one before it in the standard outline format.

Once you finish redesigning the document through the style sheet, the next step is to add the graphics. In the example, the map of the United States is a bit-mapped image altered in SuperPaint's paint layer to show the various sales regions and copied to the program's drawing layer. Then the labels were superimposed on the map as text, and the collection was selected, copied, and pasted into the presentation outline, in a new paragraph inserted between the title on the first page and the first topic below the title.

The sales statistics were prepared first as a table in Microsoft Excel and then converted into two charts showing the company's growth in sales. To transfer the charts into the Word document, choose Copy Chart from the Edit menu, and then paste them into new paragraphs below the titles on the second and third pages. To make the graphics align with the level 2 topics on the page, select the graphics and assign them the *level 2* style.

You can add the logo in the lower right corner of each page by creating the logo in a graphics program, copying it, and pasting it in the Footer window for the presentation document. To right-align the logo with the bar underneath the title on the page, give the paragraph containing the logo the Flush Right paragraph format by clicking the appropriate icon in the Ruler.

The name of the company, *DynaWeave*, could have been added from within the graphics program. However, Word does a better job of kerning the letters in the name (manually or by using the Fractional Widths option in the Print dialog box, or both), so we added the name in Word. To position the company's name, put the insertion point at the right edge of the logo, press the Spacebar twice, and then type the name. Format the name in 18-point Helvetica, shadow, italic, and 3 points superscript to align it with the logo.

Tips and Techniques

Generally, you would develop the presentation with a more comprehensive set of notes than was detailed in this example. A good way to go about this is to continue developing the outline, adding the charts and the body text for your speech, without redefining the styles. When everything is to your liking, print a copy of the presentation for you to use; the headings in your copy of the document will match those in the slides you will use as visual aids.

After you've printed your copy of the document, format as hidden text your comments under each topic and turn off the Show Hidden Text option in the Preferences dialog box. Now that your part of the presentation is hidden, continue converting the document into the actual images you want the audience to see in the presentation.

Another way to achieve the same effect is to develop the full text for your presentation from the outline, then use the Table of Contents command to extract the headings from your speech. Then, instead of redefining the *level* styles, redefine the *toc* styles. This method has the advantage of separating the styles for your part in the presentation and those for the visual aids. You can even print both the slides and your speech from the same document.

■ *Screenplay Format*

Movie studios and producers expect screenplays to be in a specific format. Thanks to style sheets, Word is ideally suited for preparing scripts in this format. The example shown in Figures 17-10a and 17-10b is a simplified version of a Hollywood-format screenplay.

Setting Up the Screenplay

The sample screenplay uses automatic line numbering, so first choose Section from the Format menu, click the Line Numbering and Continuous options, and click OK. Next, choose the Page Setup command. The screenplay uses standard 8 ½-by-11-inch paper with 1-inch margins on all sides except for the left, which uses a 1 ½-inch margin to accommodate the binding.

Six styles other than *Normal* are needed for the basic script format; all are based on the *Normal* style. This allows you to change the font for all the other styles simply by redefining the *Normal* style, even though *Normal*-style text isn't used anywhere in the document. Define or redefine the following styles:

Style Name	**Definition**
action,a	Normal + Space Before 9 pt, Not Line Numbering. Next Style: *action,a*
actor,x	Normal + Bold Caps, Centered, Space Before 12pt, Keep With Next, Not Line Numbering. Next Style: *dialogue,d*
camera,c	Normal + Bold Caps, Space Before 14 pt, Keep With Next. Next Style: *action,a*
dialogue,d	Normal + Indent: Left 1.25 in Right 1.25 in, Not Line Numbering, Tab Stops: 2 in. Next Style: *actor,x*
footer	Normal + Bold, Border: Double Line Above, Tab stops: 3 in Centered; 6 in Right Flush
line number	Normal + Bold
Normal	Font Palatino 12 pt, Flush left

1 EXT. DARK STREETS—NIGHT

SEVERAL SHOTS. Rex and Nixie are running down some streets. At first, only the SOUNDS of their FOOTSTEPS are heard. Gradually, SOUNDS of POLICE SIRENS can be heard approaching from the distance.

2 STREET CORNER—NIGHT

They spot a cab, its lights on and motor running. They jump in.

3 INT. CAB—NIGHT

Relieved, out of breath, they lean back, exhausted.

REX
(matter of factly)
Gotta go.

CARL
If you gotta go, you gotta go.

He puts the car in gear and they drive off.

NIXIE
We better hurry.

REX
You're following us. You were following us all day. Then you weren't there. Now we're here. How do you explain that?

CARL
(disinterestedly)
Coincidence.

Rex and Nixie sit back and look out the window of the moving cab. Lights reflect off their faces.

4 INT. LARGE APARTMENT—NIGHT

The apartment consists of a large loft, offering various possibilities for complex CAMERA SETUPS and a variety of LOCATIONS within the APARTMENT SCENES.

SAILOR, JOJO, SCOTT, and NADIA are gathered around a table on which are a bundle of dynamite sticks, some guns, hand grenades, alarm clocks, spools of wire, etc. They are listening intently to a shortwave radio.

RADIO
(sound of a prize fight)

Five Minutes to Doomsday **1/16/88** **page 1**

Figure 17-10a
First page of sample screenplay.

Notice that the only element in the template that actually uses line numbers is text assigned the *camera* style. All others have had line numbering turned off in the Paragraph dialog box (except for the *footer* style; text in the footer isn't numbered anyway). This allows you to number and refer to the camera shots in the screenplay without having to use the Renumber command. Also, the *next* style has been set up to make it easier to shift from one style to the next.

One two three four five six seven eight nine ten
you're out.

SCOTT
They've got it backwards. Turn it off.

Jojo changes the station on the shortwave. After some noises, SOUNDS of a DEMONSTRATION are heard.

5 **EXT. INDUSTRIAL LANDSCAPES—DAY**

SEVERAL SHOTS of Rex and Nixie walking through desolate industrial settings: LARGE FACTORIES, AUTO JUNKYARDS, POWER PLANTS, DIRTY ALLEYS, and so on. They are the only ones in the SHOTS.

REX (VOICE OVER)
(whispering)
It all comes together. Each of us carries a stick of dynamite. That does several things. One. It forms a bond. Two. It makes you feel special. Three. It's how we live today. Not only us, but everyone. And it keeps you in touch with reality, the human condition....

NIXIE (VOICE OVER)
(whispering)
Never stop talking. Make words, make sounds. It's the connection between body and head. All you can do is keep track...

They keep walking.

6 **EXT. STREET CAFE—DAY**

A street scene, a sidewalk cafe, tables and EXTRAS sitting at the tables and walking on the sidewalk. In the distance down the street the DYNAWEAVE FACTORY emits columns of white steam. Rex and Nixie sit at a table on the street, nervously glancing down toward the factory.

NIXIE
We are only particles of change, floating in a beam of sunlight. Soon the sunlight fades, the wind moves, and no one sees us.

REX
Lighten up, OK?

In the distance, bursts of black cloud rise up through the steam rising from the factory. Flickers of ORANGE FLAME in the clouds. In the distance, figures of small EXTRAS run from the factory. MUFFLED BOOM. Suddenly SUPERMAN

Five Minutes to Doomsday 1/16/88 page 2

Figure 17-10b
Second page of sample screenplay.

This is a simple document; the only step remaining is to add an appropriate footer showing the name of the screenplay, the date, and the page number, as shown in Figure 17-11.

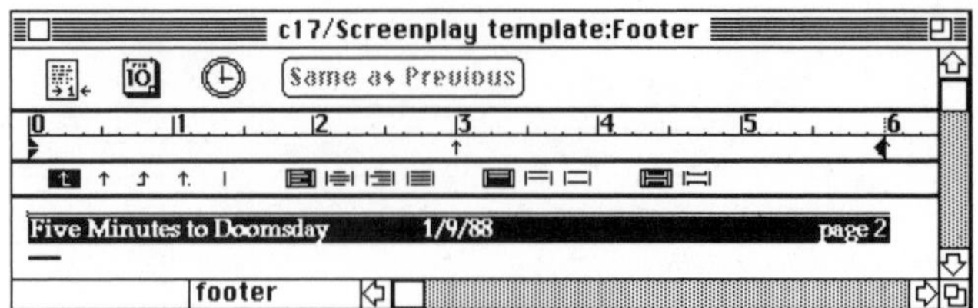

Figure 17-11
The footer for the screenplay format.

Using the Screenplay Format

Save the screenplay style sheet in a document named *Screenplay Template*. Open the document whenever you want to start a new screenplay, but save it immediately under a new name. You may want to lock the template document (call up the Get Info box from the Finder's desktop) so that you don't accidentally modify it.

When you start typing the screenplay, you can use the default *Normal* style for the title and introductory comments, if desired. To enter the first camera shot for the screenplay, press the Return key to begin a new line, and assign it the *camera* style. You can do this by choosing the style name from the Styles or Define Styles dialog box or by pressing Shift-Command-S and typing the name directly from the keyboard. With the latter method, you can type *camera* or the shortcut letter *c*. Then enter the text for the camera location. You do not need to capitalize the text; Word does it for you because the style has the All Caps character format.

When you press the Return key, Word switches to the *action* style, because after a camera shot you might want to describe what is happening in the scene. If you don't want to use the *action* style, choose another style.

When it is time for a character to speak, choose the *actor* style. Again, you do not need to capitalize the character name. When you press the Return key after typing the name, Word assumes that you want to enter dialogue, so it shifts to the *dialogue* style for you. If you need to indicate a manner of speech for the character, press the Tab key once to indent the text, and then press the Return key again to start the dialogue.

Word provides the required spacing between the camera, action, actor, and dialogue elements for you, and so under most circumstances, you do not need to add extra blank lines by inserting paragraph marks.

Both the *camera* and *actor* styles use the Keep With Next ¶ paragraph format. This keeps the camera direction and action together and the actor's name and dialogue together; Word will not separate them with a page break. However, if the dialogue or action description is more than two lines long, Word may break the page between the lines.

■ *Multiple-Column Newsletter*

Preparing a two-column or three-column document takes more time than preparing a single-column document, but the results are much more striking, especially if the text is printed on a PostScript printer such as the LaserWriter. The sample newsletter described here and depicted in Figures 17-12a and 17-12b is designed after a page format in a typical news magazine.

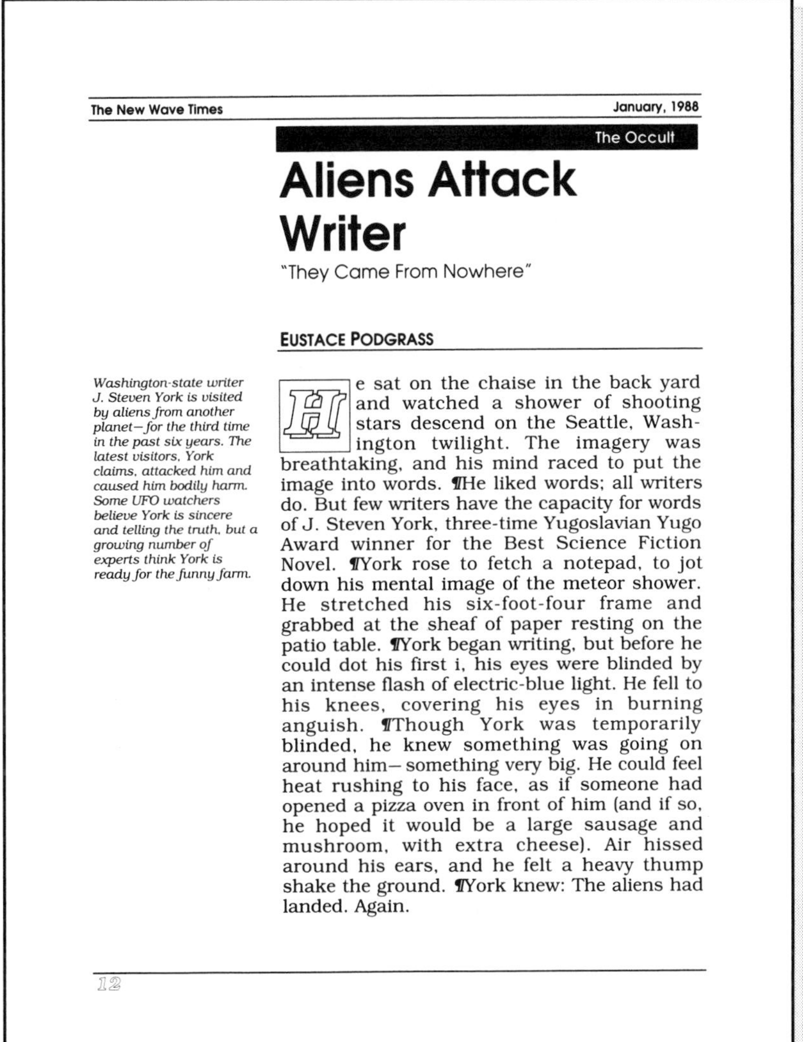

The New Wave Times January, 1988

The Occult

Aliens Attack Writer

"They Came From Nowhere"

EUSTACE PODGRASS

Washington-state writer J. Steven York is visited by aliens from another planet—for the third time in the past six years. The latest visitors, York claims, attacked him and caused him bodily harm. Some UFO watchers believe York is sincere and telling the truth, but a growing number of experts think York is ready for the funny farm.

He sat on the chaise in the back yard and watched a shower of shooting stars descend on the Seattle, Washington twilight. The imagery was breathtaking, and his mind raced to put the image into words. ¶He liked words; all writers do. But few writers have the capacity for words of J. Steven York, three-time Yugoslavian Yugo Award winner for the Best Science Fiction Novel. ¶York rose to fetch a notepad, to jot down his mental image of the meteor shower. He stretched his six-foot-four frame and grabbed at the sheaf of paper resting on the patio table. ¶York began writing, but before he could dot his first i, his eyes were blinded by an intense flash of electric-blue light. He fell to his knees, covering his eyes in burning anguish. ¶Though York was temporarily blinded, he knew something was going on around him—something very big. He could feel heat rushing to his face, as if someone had opened a pizza oven in front of him (and if so, he hoped it would be a large sausage and mushroom, with extra cheese). Air hissed around his ears, and he felt a heavy thump shake the ground. ¶York knew: The aliens had landed. Again.

12

Figure 17-12a
First page of sample newsletter.

January, 1988 The New Wave Times

York's photograph of the spaceship that wanted to cart him off to another galaxy.

At least that's how J. Steven York, author of 17 best-selling books and three blockbuster movie scripts, claims he was visited by extra-terrestrials. "This time, they wanted more than just directions to the nearest In-N-Out Burger restaurant. They wanted me!"

A day after he was visited by the aliens from Tau Upsilon IV, York held a press conference and told reporters from around the globe that he was asked to accompany the green-faced aliens, but he had to disrobe before he could enter the space ship.

"I knew these guys could melt my brain if they wanted to, so I decided to go along with their request," York said. "But when my neighbor saw me taking my clothes off, she went into laughing hysterics, ran off into the street screaming at the top of her lungs, and finally was struck and killed by a dark green 1959 Bel Air."

At this, the aliens became nervous, York recounted, so they grabbed him with their giant pincher claws, apparently intending to wrestle him inside their intergalactic space ship. "See this?" York exclaimed, rolling up his right shirt sleeve. "I received this gift from their giant claws."

York's arm was completely bandaged, but no injury could be seen.

If York is indeed telling the truth, what did the aliens want from the hulking writer from Dothan, Alabama? Were they, as York insists, taking him back to their home planet for a bold repopulation experiment? And if so, would they give him Coke and peanuts along the way, as they do in airplanes?

"I think this Steven J. York (sic) has flipped," claimed noted parapsychologist Ephraim Schwartz. "I think this whole attack thing exists only in his twisted imagination."

University of Maryland film and literary criticism professor Trent Johansonn, agrees. "J. York Steven (sic) no longer has the ability to separate the worlds of reality and science fiction," Johansonn said after the press conference. Despite the criticism against him, York holds steadfastly to his account.

Shortly after the visitation, U.S. Air Force Colonel F. L. A. Hood investigated the sighting and made tests of the area surrounding the landing site. "Something was there," Hood told reporters, "but I can't be certain beyond doubt that it was a space craft."

York offered an artifact to Hood that he claimed was left by the aliens when they made their hasty retreat, immediately following the automobile death of the next-door neighbor and York's struggle to escape. "It's either an honest-to-goodness alien artifact," Hood said, "or a week-old pizza crust. Our lab is working on it right now. We should have the test results in a week or two."

This is not the first time York has been visited by aliens. His first "close encounter" occurred more than five years ago, in February 1981, while working as a sales clerk for Radio Shack. York claims he was visited by the same aliens two months later. ❍

Figure 17-12b
Second page of sample newsletter.

Preparing the Newsletter

Depending on the size and sophistication of the group publishing a newsletter, the person doing the writing may or may not be the person who transforms the articles into the formatted result. Typically, the people responsible for a newsletter establish a design first and then take articles from writers and format them according to the design specifications to construct each issue. It's best if the writer works on the content of the article first, either leaving the refinement of its appearance until later or letting others do it.

Therefore, it will be assumed that a design for this newsletter has already been set up in a template document containing a style sheet for the various elements. The style sheet that follows is for an article. A complete newsletter would use many more styles, of course, for such items as the table of contents, advertisements, the masthead, and so on. As you tour this document, refer back to this table to find exact specifications for each element.

Style Name	Definition
Byline	Display + Font: 14 Point, Bold Small Caps, Indent: Left 2 in, Space Before 36 pt After 18 pt, Border: Line Below
Display	Font: Avant Garde 10 Point, Flush left
Drop Cap	Font: Bookman 14 Point, Indent: Left 1.94 in Justified, Side-by-Side
Fig caption	Normal + Font: 9 Point, Bold Italic, Space Before 2 pt After 12 pt, Border: Line Below
Figure	Normal + Space Before 2 pt, Border: Box
First Page	Normal + Font: 14 Point, Indent: Left 2 in, Side-by-Side, Tab stops: 2.81 in
footer	Normal + Tab stops: 3 in Centered; 6 in Right Flush
header	Display + Bold, Line Spacing -14 pt, Space After 2 pt, Border: Line Above, Tab stops: 6.5 in Right Flush
Normal	Font: Bookman 10 Point, Justified
Reading Line	Display + Font: 14 Point, Indent: Left 2 in
Synopsis	Normal + Indent: Right 4.75 in Flush left, Side-by-Side
Title	Display + Font: 36 Point, Bold, Indent: Left 2 in, Space Before 2 pt
Title Bar	Display + Font: 36 Point, Bold Indent: Left 1.94 in Right -0.5, Space Before 2 pt

Because the newsletter uses a single-column format for the first page of an article and for figures and a two-column format for the remainder of an article, the design makes extensive use of sections and section formats. The template document contains a set of sample sections; the person composing the document would copy them and replace the text they contain with the actual contents for that part of the article. The sample shown in Figures 17-12a and 17-12b contains three sections: one for all of the first page, one for the graphic at the top of the second page, and one for the two-column text in the body of the article.

The measurements for the design elements in the template document depend on the settings in the Page Setup dialog box. For this article, the following settings were used:

Option	Measurement
Top margin	-1.25 inch
Bottom margin	-1 inch
Left margin	.75 inch
Right margin	.75 inch
Facing Pages	Set
Gutter	0.5 inch
Default Tab Stops	0.25 inch

The minus sign before the top and bottom margin measurements prevents any interaction between the size of the header in a section and the top and bottom margins for a page.

Section One: The First Page

The first page of the article comprises three main areas: the header and footer, the title area for the article, and the first few sentences of the article with the synopsis in the Side-by-Side format.

The Header and Footer

As you may remember, each section in a document can contain a separate header and footer for its odd and even pages (if you set the Facing Pages option in the Page Setup dialog box) and for its first page (if you set the First Page Special option in the Section dialog box). The newsletter uses two headers, one for odd pages and one for even pages. Because inflexible top and bottom margins have been set in the Page Setup dialog box, the From

Top and From Bottom measurements specified in the Section dialog box are placed relative to the edge of the page; adjust these values so that the headers will be 1 inch from the top of the page and the footers will be 0.5 inch from the bottom.

Every sample section in the template document has the same set of odd and even headers, so the person composing the newsletter can assume that the headers will be there until they are explicitly removed (for example, on a page consisting only of one graphic or of advertisements). When you create a new section, its initial formats come from the section after it. Thus, if all or most of the sample sections in the template document use the standard headers, you have to adjust only the headers for pages that are different in some way.

The set of headers used in the article is shown in Figure 17-13. Because the article starts on a left-hand page, it uses the even header. The status area in the Header window indicates that the two lines of the header have the *header* style. You can see by referring to the table containing the style sheet that this style has the Above Border paragraph format, and the line spacing is set to -14 points so that the text in the header is evenly spaced with respect to the two lines.

Like the headers, the footers for each section consist of odd and even versions, but they contain only one line, which has the Above Border format.

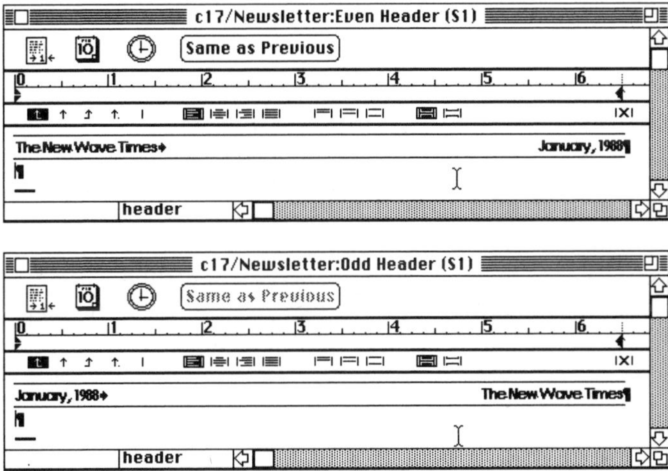

Figure 17-13
The set of odd and even headers for the newsletter.

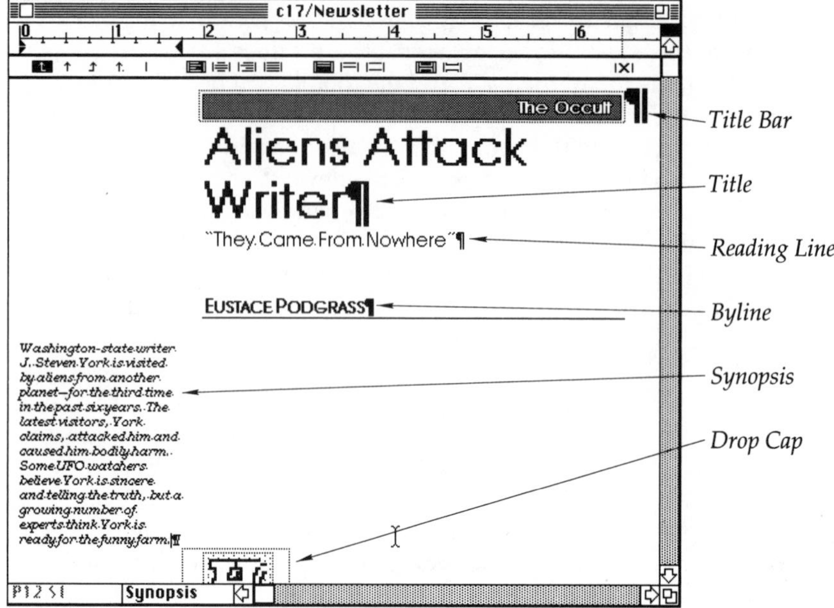

Figure 17-14
The article title in Document view.

The Title

The title of the article is very straightforward; Figure 17-14 shows how it looks in Document view. Each element in the title has its own style so that all the corresponding elements in other articles will be consistent. Heavy use is made of the Space Before and Space After paragraph formats; there are no blank lines between elements.

Even though the bar above the title is a graphic copied from MacDraw, it has a style, which is used only for positioning the graphic relative to the running head and the title. As you can see by referring back to the table that describes the document's style sheet, the rule under the byline is done with the Below Border format, and the text for the author's name is in the Small Caps character format.

The Synopsis, Drop Cap, and First-Page Text

The synopsis of the article in the left margin, the drop cap that starts the article, and the decorative treatment for the first-page text are all single paragraphs having the Side-by-Side format. Figure 17-15 shows how they look on the screen.

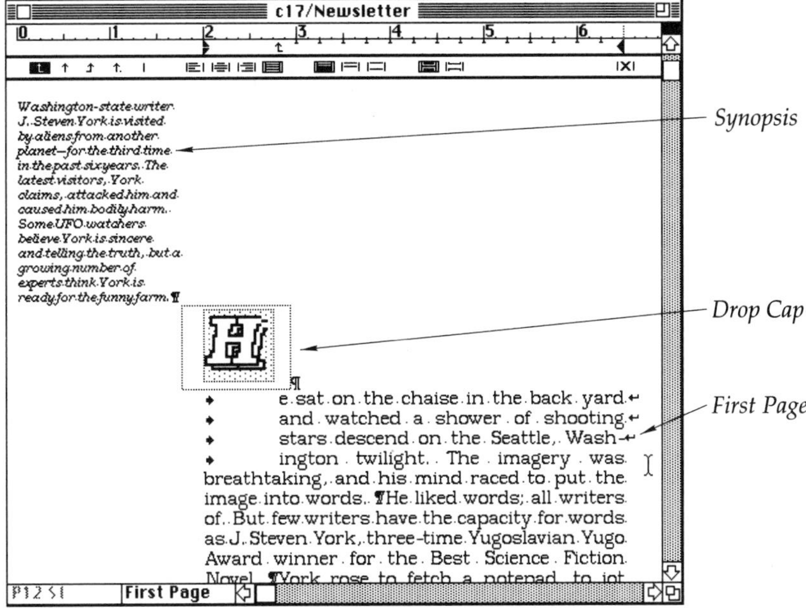

Figure 17-15
The three paragraphs in Document view.

When the newsletter is printed, Word arranges the three paragraphs in one row because their styles contain the Side-by-Side format and the left indent of each is to the right of the one before it. The drop cap is another graphic created in MacDraw, although Word could have been used to create a large capital letter in a paragraph by itself.

Notice the space for the drop cap in the first paragraph. Even though the First Page style specifies a tab stop at 2.81 inches—just enough room for the superimposed drop cap—in practice you'd probably have to adjust the exact position of the tab stop manually for the width of the particular letter being used. Also, because the design for the newsletter specifies that the first paragraph be justified, newlines were added at the end of the first four lines; they cause Word to force each line to align at the right indent. If tab stops alone had been used, the first four lines would be ragged right, and the rest of the paragraph would be justified.

Section Two: The Figure and Caption

The graphic in the figure was digitized at 200 percent by MacVision from photographs of the alien spacecraft and the house, and then squeezed down to 100 percent using the methods described in Chapter 15, "Transferring Text and Graphics." The graphic and its caption, two paragraphs, reside in a one-column section, as shown in Figure 17-16.

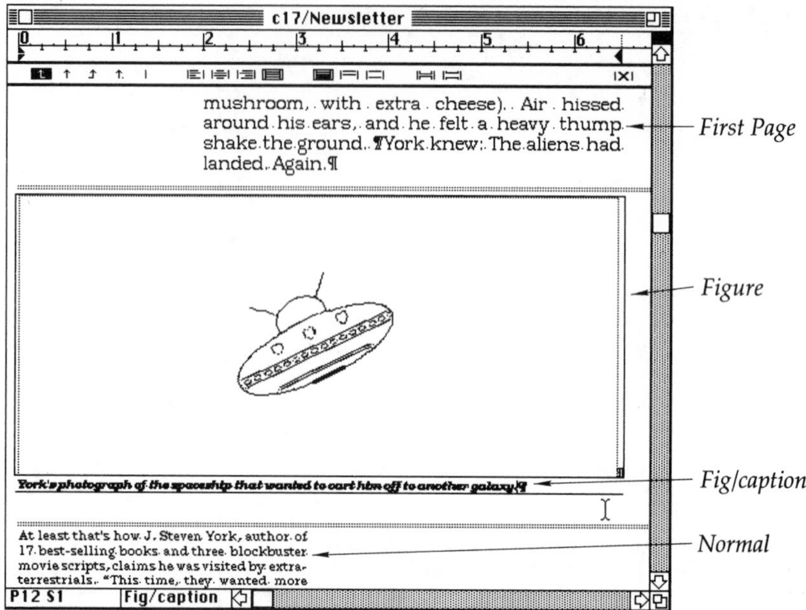

Figure 17-16
The graphic and its caption in Document view.

The style for the figure, simply named *Figure*, adds only two formats to those it inherited from the *Normal* style. The paragraph containing the graphic has 2 points of Space Before, which leaves a small gap between the top border of the graphic and the running head.

It also has the Box Border format, which creates a frame for the graphic. In practice, instead of putting a box around the entire paragraph, you could select the graphic and give it the Outline character format, which would place a tight black outline around whatever was in the graphic. The Box Border format was used here because in general it's difficult to say what kind of graphic will be in the figure: a halftone picture, an object-oriented line drawing, or simply a graphic that you will paste in after printing the document. The Box Border format draws a box around the paragraph that goes from indent to indent, regardless of what's in the paragraph.

The caption underneath the graphic has its own style, the *Fig caption* style, which uses the Below Border format to separate the figure from the text below it. It also uses the Space After format to leave a space between the figure and the two-column section beneath it.

Headers and Footers in the Second Section

The second section uses an interesting property of sections: namely that the headers and footers for a page are to be taken from the section at the top of the page. Because the section containing the figure is at the top of the second page of the article, the header and footer attached to it are the ones Word prints. Therefore, both the odd header and the odd footer on the second page belong to the second section. The structure of the odd header has already been discussed, but the odd footer for this section is special because it creates both the footer and the vertical line separating the two columns of the third section. Figure 17-17 shows this footer.

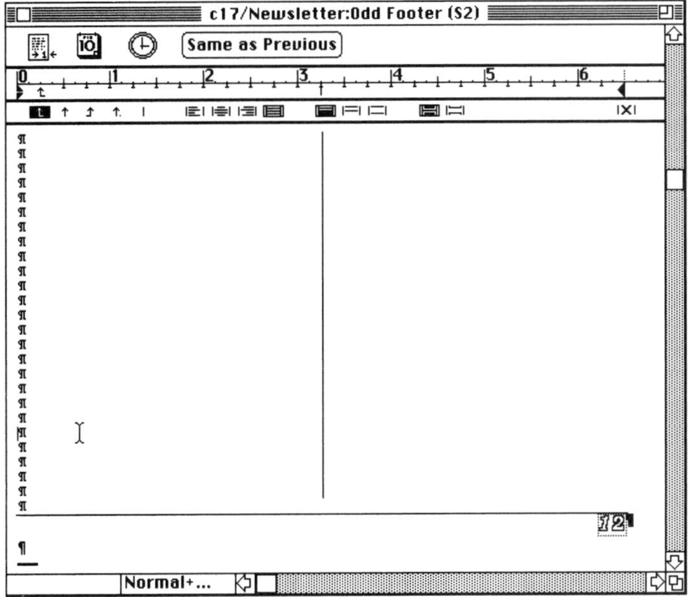

Figure 17-17
The footer for the second section.

This footer interleaves with the two-column section in the second half of the page. Every line in the footer has the *Normal* style, with a vertical-line tab stop set midway between the two columns. To adjust the length of the line between the two columns, simply add empty paragraphs in the Footer window until the length of the line matches the length of the column. You can work between Page Preview and the Footer window to do this.

Another way to do this would be to insert a paragraph mark at the bottom of the first column in the third section and add the vertical-line format for every line in the second column, but if you then had to edit or rearrange the article's text, rebreaking the column and reformatting the text in the second column would be unnecessarily time-consuming. By laying the contents of the Footer window over the text in the third section (remember that setting a negative bottom margin in the Page Setup dialog box lets you do this), you can adjust the size of the figure so that the text in the third section fits exactly in the space provided.

If, however, you wanted to create something other than a 1-point line, you would have to either create a graphic in a program such as Cricket Draw or insert a few PostScript commands in the header or footer of a section in the document. The latter method isn't difficult at all; for more information, see Appendix C, "Using PostScript."

Section Three: The Second-Page Text

This section offers few surprises; it's simply a two-column section with 0.25 inch of space between the columns. You could use the Section dialog box to set these values. As was discussed, the size of the figure in the second section determines how much space is left on the page for the text. The remaining text for the article doesn't go beyond the article's second page, so the figure was cropped vertically to adjust its size until the text filled out the bottom of the page exactly.

Incidentally, the moon symbol that ends the article is a Zapf Dingbat *m*. A few tab characters were inserted between it and the end of the sentence to right-align the symbols. This forces the text in the last line of a justified paragraph to align at both left and right indents. Ordinarily, it would align at the left indent alone.

■ *Creating This Book*

At last we come to the Big One: the creation and development of this book as a set of Word documents. In a sense, a full description of the methods used to produce this book fills a book itself—the one you're reading. However, many of the design elements used in this book are the result of a fair amount of work because we wanted not only to develop methods of achieving certain effects but to achieve those effects in the easiest, most economical way possible in a publishing environment.

We believe that Word is preferable to any other desktop publishing program for large projects such as books because it lets you automate processes. Instead of hand-placing columns of text and graphics on a page-by-page basis, we simply pasted in each graphic and assigned it a style. Instead of finding and manually reformatting every instance of text elements, such as level headings and figure captions, every time we wanted to experiment with or refine the design, we simply adjusted the style sheet and merged it into the other documents. This allowed us to play with the design until quite late in the production cycle for the book.

Because we could print proofs for the chapters on the LaserWriter before final output on a Linotronic L300 imagesetter, we could fold the production of the book into the editorial cycle and do both the editing and the design development concurrently. We like to call this method a *sculptural paradigm* for developing a document, because it is refined in small increments until the result is ready to be printed; at every stage the document is readable and is continuously better looking.

We call the standard method of document production a *transformational paradigm* because the writers and production people are separated from one another in their approach to the document, and the process of taking the document from the draft to the printed version requires what often seems like a miraculous conversion that consumes much time and energy.

With Word, everyone involved in a project works only at the level of training and expertise required for his or her role. For example, a writer's understanding of styles needn't extend much beyond using the outlining feature. The persons implementing the design, on the other hand, can exercise style sheets, import graphics, and use PostScript to achieve the look they want for the document. And they all work within the same environment.

Now let's take a tour of some of the prominent features of this project.

The Style Sheet

The style sheet for a typical chapter in this book is as follows:

Style Name	Definition
Body	Normal
Chap/Space After Head	Normal + Line Spacing: 0 pt, Space Before 136 pt
Chap/Title	Display + Space Before 96 pt
Display	Normal + Font: Helvetica 18 Point, Bold, Line Spacing: 0 pt
F/caption,fc	Font: Helvetica 9 Point, Flush left, Line Spacing: 11 pt
F/filename	Font: Times 9 Point, Bold, Indent: Left 5.25 in Right -1.63 in Flush left, Space Before 2 pt, Side-by-Side
F/gfx	Font: Palatino 10 Point, Flush left, Side-by-Side, Keep With Next
F/name,fn	Font: Helvetica 9 Point, Bold Italic, Flush left, Line Spacing: -10 pt, Space Before 10 pt, Keep With Next, Tab stops: 5 in
footer	Normal + Font: Helvetica, Bold Italic, Indent: Right -1.25 in, Tab stops: 4.75 in Right Flush
footnote reference	Normal + Font: 9 Point, Superscript 4 Point
footnote text	Font: Palatino 10 Point, Indent: Right -2 in Flush left

Style Name	Definition
header	Display + Font: LB Helvetica 9 Point, Outline, Line Spacing:12 pt, Side-by-Side, Tab stops: 0.08 in
index 1	Normal +
index 2	Normal + Indent: Left 0.25 in
index 3	Normal + Indent: Left 0.5 in
index 4	Normal + Indent: Left 0.75 in
level 1,1	Normal + Font: 16 Point, Bold Italic, Line Spacing: 0 pt, Space Before 30 pt, Keep With Next, Tab stops: 0.25 in
level 2,2	Normal + Font: 14 Point, Bold Italic, Line Spacing: 0 pt, Space Before 20 pt After 5 pt, Keep With Next
level 3,3	Normal + Font: 12 Point, Bold Italic, Line Spacing: 0 pt, Space Before 15 pt, Keep With Next
level 4,4	Normal + Bold, Side-by-Side, Keep With Next
List/num	Normal + Indent: Left 0.25 in First -0.25 in, Space Before 3 pt
margin note,m	Font: Times 9 Point, Indent: Left 5.25 in Right -1.75 in Flush left, Space Before 2 pt, Side-by-Side
Normal	Font: Palatino 10 Point, Flush left, Line Spacing: -12 pt
note	Normal + Font: Helvetica 9 Point, Indent: Left 0.25 in First -0.25 in Right 0.39 in, Line Spacing: -10 pt
page number	header + Not Outline, Indent: Left -1 in, Tab stops: -0.17 in Right Flush; 4.93; Not at 0.08 in
PostScript	Font: Courier 9 Point, Hidden, Indent: Right -1.3 in Flush left, Side-by-Side, Keep With Next, Tab stops: -0.11 Vertical Line; -0.08 Vertical Line; -0.06 Vertical Line; 0.25 in; 0.5 in; 0.75 in; 1 in; 3.5 in
s/fig>fig,s/ff	spacing,s/ + Space Before 12 pt
s/fig>lev1,s/f1	spacing,s/ +

Style Name	Definition
s/fig>lev2,s/f2	spacing,s/ +
s/fig>lev3,s/f3	spacing,s/ +
s/fig>lev4,s/f4	spacing,s/ +
s/fig>norm,s/fn	spacing,s/ + Space Before 2 pt
s/fig>num,s/f#	spacing,s/ +
s/lev4>norm,s/4n	spacing,s/ +
s/norm>fig,s/nf	spacing,s/ +
s/norm>lev4,s/n4	spacing,s/ +
s/norm>norm,s/nn	spacing,s/ +
s/norm>num,s/n#	spacing,s/ + Line Spacing: -3 pt
s/norm>user,s/nu	spacing,s/ +
s/num>fig,s/#f	spacing,s/ +
s/num>lev4,s/#4	spacing,s/ +
s/num>norm,s/#n	spacing,s/ +
s/num>user,s/#u	spacing,s/ +
s/user>norm,s/un	spacing,s/ +
s/user>num,s/u#	spacing,s/ +
spacing,s/	Normal + Font: Times 9 Point, Line Spacing: -10 pt, Tab stops: 5.25 in
T/2 col	Normal + Space After 4 pt, Tab stops: 0.13 in; 2.25 in; 2.38 in
T/2 col/wrap	T/2 col + Indent: Left 2.38 in First -2.38 in
T/3 col	Normal + Space After 4 pt, Tab stops: 0.13 in; 1.88 in; 2 in; 3.38 in
T/4 col	Normal + Space After 4 pt, Tab stops: 0.13 in; 1.75 in; 1.88 in; 2.75 in; 2.88 in; 3.75 in; 3.88 in
T/6 col	Normal + Font: 9 Point, Indent: Right 0.25 in, Line Spacing: 0 pt, Tab stops: 0 in Vertical Line; 0.19 in; 0.44 in; 0.75 in Vertical Line; 0.94 in; 1.19; 1.5 in Vertical Line; 1.69 in; 1.94 in; 2.25 in Vertical Line; 2.44 in; 2.69 in; 3 in Vertical Line; 3.19 in; 3.44 in; 3.75 in Vertical Line; 3.94 in; 4.19 in; 4.5 in Vertical Line; 5.75 in; 6.88 in; 7.88 in

Style Name	Definition
Tab	Font: LB Helvetica Black 14 Point, Outline, Superscript 3 Point, Flush Left, Line Spacing: -18 pt
Tab/chap	Tab + Indent: Left -0.5 in, Tab stops: 0.67 in Centered
Tab/summary	Tab + Indent: Left -0.25 in, Tab stops: 0.65 in Centered; 4.22 in Centered
Tip	Font: Helvetica 12 Point, Bold Italic Outline, Indent: Left -1 in Right 4.81 in Flush Right, Side-by-Side, Keep With Next
toc 1	Normal + Indent: Right 0.5 in, Tab stops: 5.75 in ...; 6 in Right Flush
toc 2	Normal + Indent: Left 0.5 in Right 0.5 in, Tab stops: 5.75 in ...; 6 in Right Flush
toc 3	Normal + Indent: Left 1 in Right 0.5 in, Tab stops: 5.75 in ...; 6 in Right Flush
toc 4	Normal + Indent: Left 1.5 in Right 0.5 in, Tab stops: 5.75 in ...; 6 in Right Flush
User Entry	Normal + Font: Helvetica 9 Point, Line Spacing: -10 pt

Probably the most noticeable aspect of the style sheet is the large number of styles devoted to spacing, all of which begin with *s/*, such as *s/fig>norm*. Because Word doesn't measure the space before and after a paragraph from baseline to baseline, we created these special styles to get the most control over the elements in the book. Many of these styles are simply based on the *spacing* style, but we added them in case we wanted to adjust globally the spacing between certain elements. A single line having one of these styles goes between each element in the book and the next; for example, *s/fig>norm* would go between a figure caption and body text having the *Normal* style.

Figure 17-18 shows how a typical page looks, including the crop marks, spacing elements, and margin notes. Each line that has a spacing style contains a label formatted with the hidden character attribute, making it easy to verify that the spacing elements have been placed correctly. We added one line for each of the spacing styles to the Standard Glossary so that it would be easy to insert them where needed.

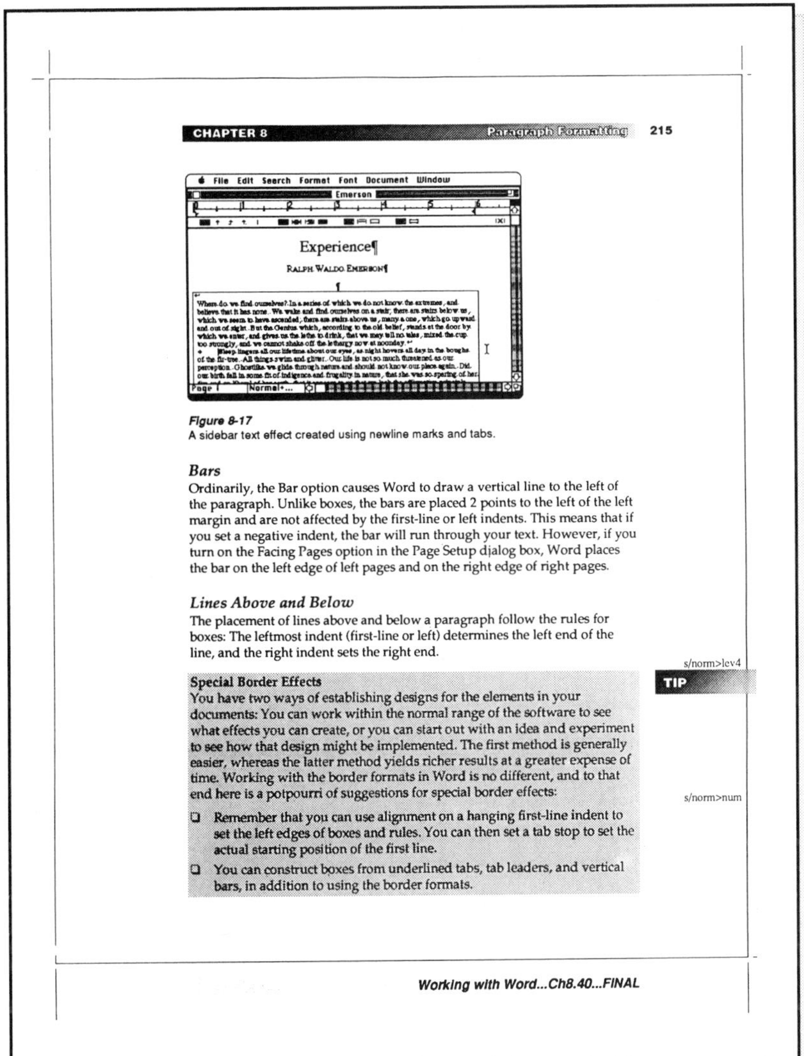

CHAPTER 8 Paragraph Formatting 215

Figure 8-17
A sidebar text effect created using newline marks and tabs.

Bars
Ordinarily, the Bar option causes Word to draw a vertical line to the left of the paragraph. Unlike boxes, the bars are placed 2 points to the left of the left margin and are not affected by the first-line or left indents. This means that if you set a negative indent, the bar will run through your text. However, if you turn on the Facing Pages option in the Page Setup dialog box, Word places the bar on the left edge of left pages and on the right edge of right pages.

Lines Above and Below
The placement of lines above and below a paragraph follow the rules for boxes: The leftmost indent (first-line or left) determines the left end of the line, and the right indent sets the right end.

s/norm>lev4

TIP

Special Border Effects
You have two ways of establishing designs for the elements in your documents: You can work within the normal range of the software to see what effects you can create, or you can start out with an idea and experiment to see how that design might be implemented. The first method is generally easier, whereas the latter method yields richer results at a greater expense of time. Working with the border formats in Word is no different, and to that end here is a potpourri of suggestions for special border effects:

s/norm>num

- Remember that you can use alignment on a hanging first-line indent to set the left edges of boxes and rules. You can then set a tab stop to set the actual starting position of the first line.
- You can construct boxes from underlined tabs, tab leaders, and vertical bars, in addition to using the border formats.

Working with Word...Ch8.40...FINAL

Figure 17-18
A typical page from this book.

Preparing the Graphics

All the images of screens in the book were produced by using the Shift-Command-3 key sequence to create screen dumps on disk. SuperPaint was used to clean up the images, reduce them to 50 percent of their original size, and add labels where needed. We could have added lines running from each label to the item it references, but because 1 point is the smallest increment that the PICT data format represents for object-oriented graphics, we decided instead to use special arrows drawn with PostScript commands. (Appendix C, "Using PostScript," discusses the commands you can use to create arrows and other special effects.)

Several of the full-page graphics in this book were produced with Glue from Solutions Incorporated, a utility that converts a printed page into a bit-mapped graphic. When you send a page to a printer, Glue intercepts the printing commands and converts the page image into a bit-mapped graphic. We then treated the resulting bit-mapped graphic like a screen dump and reduced its size with SuperPaint.

However, because we wanted to give high-quality samples for Word's formatting options, we prepared many of the full-page graphics by printing them on the LaserWriter, photographically reducing the result, and pasting them by hand into appropriately sized boxes on the final L300 output.

Design Elements

The design elements for the running heads, the Tip tabs, the chapter opening headings, and the section openers were prepared by a designer who used FreeHand from Aldus. These elements were then converted into PostScript, and a PostScript programmer modified them so that they could be printed from a Word document. This was done more as a feasibility study than because it was the only way to create sophisticated effects in this book. For example, you can create graphics in Cricket Draw and copy them into a Word document with much the same effect, because PICT-type graphics copied from Cricket Draw carry embedded PostScript commands, as was discussed in Chapter 15, "Transferring Text and Graphics."

Much of the custom PostScript developed for this book was added to the Word program itself, using the method described in Appendix C, "Using PostScript."

Word's table of contents feature was used to create the table of contents. We did not use the indexing feature extensively, however, because the creation of a good index for a book of this size is something of an art and is often best done by human hands.

Statistics

For the curious, some statistics on the size of this book as a set of files:

- ❑ 1.3 MB of source material in the form of Word documents was used, including specifications, bug reports, and recommendations from the developers of Word.
- ❑ 1.4 MB of test documents were generated to explore every feature of Word we could manage.

- Each screen dump in the book was stored in its original, cleaned-up, and final form—once for each of these three forms. The figures took up 4.9 MB.
- The actual text of the book totals about 1.3 MB in 17 chapter files, 4 appendix files, 5 section opener files, and 7 other files for items such as the index, the table of contents, and the introduction.
- The total size of one "electronic" copy of this book including text, figures, PostScript, and so on, comes to about 8.9 MB.

The full-time team that produced this book consisted of two writers, an editor, and a copy editor. We also used a designer, a PostScript programmer, a layout person, and two part-time proofreaders, for short-term projects. The final page proofs were printed on a LaserWriter Plus, and when each chapter was finished it was printed on a Linotronic 300 Laser Imagesetter by a typographic specialist in the production department of Microsoft Press.

SECTION 5

Appendixes – Toolbox

Setting Up Word

Before you start working with Word, you should prepare working copies of the Word Program and Word Utilities disks. You can optimize these working copies for the type of Mac you have and the size of your disk drives. You can use Word on any Mac except the 128 KB Mac, which does not provide enough memory in RAM. Your Mac must have at least one double-sided disk drive (800 KB capacity), or two single-sided disk drives (400 KB capacity each). The Word program and its associated files come on double-sided disks, which a single-sided drive cannot read. If you have only 400 KB drives, you can order single-sided replacement disks from Microsoft or take your disks to someone who has 800 KB drives to make single-sided copies.

■ *Preparing Working Copies of Word*

Before you use Word, you should make copies of the Program and Utilities disks. Then use the copies and store the original disks in a safe place. Using a copy reduces the chance of a serious loss of data if something catastrophic should ever happen to a disk. If you have a hard disk, you might prefer to copy the files you need from the originals to the hard disk. Making working copies of Word and its support files is easy; because they aren't copy-protected, you won't ever have to insert a master disk to start the program.

It's a good idea to begin by sliding open the write-protect tabs in the corners of both the Word Program and Word Utilities disks. This prevents accidental erasure or modification of the disks' contents when they are inside the Macintosh.

After you prepare working disks (or copy the files you need to your hard disk), store the original disks until you need them again. Word and its support files come on two 800 KB disks. If you have 400 KB drives or only one 800 KB drive, you can still use Word, but you need to take special precautions to prevent running out of disk space. The following is a list of the files on the Word distribution disks:

Disk and Files	Contents
Program Disk	
Microsoft Word	The Word application itself.
Switcher 5.1	The Switcher application.
Standard Glossary	
Read Me First	Last-minute information.
System Folder	The System, Finder, ImageWriter, and Clipboard files.
Word Utilities	
Word Help	Word's help file.
Main Dictionary	Word's main dictionary.
UK Dictionary	British spellings: To use this dictionary, name this file *Main Dictionary*.
Word Hyphenation	File containing hyphenation rules.
PostScript Glossary	Sample PostScript code you can add to your documents.
DCA Conversion	Converts between DCA and Word file formats.
Printers Folder	Contains the AppleDaisy, Diablo630, Brother, NEC7710, Typewriter, SerialPrinter, LaserPrep, and LaserWriter drivers.
Sample Documents	Various sample documents.
Switcher Sets	QuickSwitch (copy this to the same folder as Excel versions before 1.03), Word/Draw, Word/Excel, Word/File, Word/Paint, Word/Works.
LaserWriter Samples	Video/dialog script, Text + Graphics, Math Typesetting.

Of course, you don't need to transfer all these files to your working disks or your hard disk. At a minimum, to write with Word you need only the Word program file and the Word Settings File. The other files, including the dictionaries, Help file, Standard Glossary file, and so forth, are required only when you specifically access them. When Word needs to access these supplementary files, it will prompt you to insert into the drive the disk that contains them. In the next sections we'll discuss how to best arrange the files you need in the space you have.

Mac 512 KB with Two 400 KB Drives

You cannot use Word with only one 400 KB drive; two 400 KB drives is the minimum configuration. To use Word effectively on a Mac with two 400 KB drives, you should prepare three disks, as shown in this table:

Disk	Drive	Files on disk
System disk (400 KB)	Internal drive	System Folder, your documents.
Program disk (400 KB)	External drive	Microsoft Word, Standard Glossary, and custom glossaries or the User 1 dictionary.
Utilities disk (400 KB)	Internal drive	Main Dictionary, Word Hyphenation, Word Help. Any other files you may need, such as the UK Dictionary, DCA Conversion, and Printer Folder.

When setting up your Word files in such limited space, you should look for every economy possible. Use the Font/DA Mover to remove from the System file all fonts and desk accessories except those you really need. Retain in the System Folder only the printer drivers you need. For example, if you rarely use the LaserWriter, remove the LaserPrep and the LaserWriter drivers, which together count for more than 50 KB. (You could prepare more than one system disk, each containing a different set of printer resources.)

Also, if you keep many items in the Scrapbook, consider copying the Scrapbook file in the System Folder onto another disk and removing everything in the first Scrapbook. You can replace the Scrapbook desk accessory with one that can open a Scrapbook from a disk other than that containing the System Folder, such as SmartScrap from Solutions International.

For example, if you use the System Folder from the original Word Program disk and remove the Boston, Dover, and Venice fonts and every font size over 18 points, you should free up about 98 KB on the system disk for your documents. A good strategy for using this space is to copy your documents from a data disk to the system disk to work on them, and then copy them back to the data disk when you are done.

To use Word more effectively in this environment, choose Preferences from the Edit menu and click the check box to the left of the File button. Then, when you open a file, Word loads as much of it as possible into memory. When you are using the dictionary, accessing Help, or hyphenating the document, eject the system disk and insert the Utilities disk.

Mac with One 400 KB and One 800 KB Drive

Using a 400 KB internal drive with a double-sided external drive is almost the same as using two 400 KB drives. The following table shows a good disk layout for this environment:

Disk	Drive	Files on disk
System disk (400 KB)	Internal drive	System Folder, your documents (depending on the size of your System Folder).
Program disk (800 KB)	External drive	Word program, Standard Glossary, Main Dictionary, Word Hyphenation, custom glossaries and dictionaries, your documents.

You need to be careful with the space on the system disk, but you can put as many files as you need on the program disk, without fear of running out of room. However, if you don't use the spelling or on-line help features of Word often, move them onto a third disk, leaving roughly half the disk for your documents. If you do this, you can add more fonts and drivers, if needed, to your system disk.

Mac with One 800 KB Drive

If you have only one 800 KB drive, either you can try to fit Word and a small collection of system files on one disk, or you can have a large set of Word and system files on two disks and do a lot of disk swapping. This table shows a disk layout for one 800 KB drive, assuming you're using two disks:

Disk	**Drive**	**Files on disk**
System disk (800 KB)	Internal drive	System Folder, your documents (depending on the size of your System Folder).
Program disk (800 KB)	Internal drive	Word program, Standard Glossary, Main Dictionary, Word Hyphenation, custom glossaries and dictionaries, your documents.

When you are using two disks, it's often useful to start Word (this may require a few disk swaps) and click the check box next to the Program option in the Preferences dialog box. This loads almost all of Word into memory, so you can eject the program disk and replace the system disk. You can use the extra space on the system disk for your documents.

You can strip your System file of all but the most useful fonts and restrict the contents of your System Folder to only the drivers and resources that you really need. If you do this, you can fit a small System Folder (300 KB, say) and Word (350 KB) onto one disk, with around 150 KB left for the Standard Glossary or personal dictionaries. Then, when you start Word, click the check box next to the File button in the Keep in Memory group so that when you open a file from a data disk, Word loads the file into memory, letting you replace the combination system and Word disk. This method is better if your 800 KB drive belongs to a Mac 512 KB Enhanced; in this case, it's better to load a small document into memory rather than the large Word program.

Mac with Two 800 KB Drives

Having two 800 KB drives offers the most options— short of having a hard disk—of any of the environments we've discussed. A good arrangement for your files is as follows:

Disk	Drive	Files on disk
System disk (800 KB)	Internal drive	System Folder, your documents (depending on the size of your System Folder).
Program disk (800 KB)	External drive	Word program, Standard Glossary, Main Dictionary, Word Hyphen- ation, custom glossaries and dictionaries, your documents.

You have the same kind of decision to make as those with only one 800 KB drive. If you can live with a small System file and a slim System Folder, you can put both the System Folder and Word on the system disk, leaving the external drive for your data documents or another application disk such as Microsoft Excel.

If you'd rather have many fonts and desk accessories in your System File, you can also lay out your disks as in the table and use the excess space on the system disk to temporarily store documents from data documents. Eject the program disk and load the data disk to transfer the document to the system disk, and then replace the program disk to use Word with the copy of the document on the system disk.

Any Mac with a Hard Disk

You can load the entire contents of both Word disks onto your hard disk if you want, but you don't need to use every file that is distributed with Word. The best way to install Word on a hard disk is to create a new folder called something like *Word Folder*, and then copy Word and its support files to it. If you keep the Standard Glossary, Word Help, and Word Hyphenation files in the same folder as Word, Word will open them without presenting a dialog box asking you to find them. However, if you want to split up Word's files, read the information in the next section.

It's also a good idea to keep your documents in a folder other than the one containing the Word files. This makes it easier to keep track of documents. The following table shows a good arrangement of files for a hard disk:

Folder	Files in Folder
System Folder	Normal system files plus any drivers needed, from the Word Utilities disk.
Word Folder	Word program, Word Help, Standard Glossary, Main Dictionary, Word Hyphenation, custom glossaries and dictionaries.
Word Documents Folder(s)	Your documents.

■ *How Word Finds Files*

Word must be able to find its files when it needs to access one of them. You open the vast majority of files in Word by choosing the Open command and locating the file on a disk or in a folder. However, Word opens the Standard Glossary, the User 1 dictionary, the Help file, and the Word Hyphenation file by following a search path through a list of certain folders on the disks that you've mounted. If Word can't find the file, it presents a dialog box asking you to find the file by inserting a disk or opening the correct folder.

If you have more than one file named *Standard Glossary*, for example, Word opens the first one found, and it may be difficult to determine exactly which of the files was opened. This issue is important if you have a hard disk, because with the extra space it's easier to develop a multiplicity of files and folders and easier to lose track of their names and locations.

The following list shows the search path Word uses to find files. If you keep this list in mind when saving the Standard Glossary or User 1 files, you can avoid creating secondary version of these files. You can't modify the Help or Hyphenation files as you can the Standard Glossary and User 1 files, but you can avoid the dialog box asking you to find them if you ensure that Word can find them. To do this, make sure the files are in one of the following locations. Word searches through disks and folders in this order:

1. The folder containing Word.
2. The root, or topmost, folder of the disk containing Word.
3. The System folder.
4. The root, or topmost, folder of all other disks.
5. The last folder that was displayed in an Open or Save dialog box.

However, when you do a print merge, Word looks first in the folder containing the main document before looking in the folders listed above.

Table of Character Sets

ppendix B presents a table of the complete character sets for six common Macintosh fonts. The character sets for three different types of fonts are represented:

- Two standard Mac screen fonts—Geneva and New York.
- Two standard LaserWriter fonts—Times and Courier.
- Two special LaserWriter fonts—Zapf Dingbats and Symbol.

Several types of characters comprise each font, and the way you enter a character depends on its type. You can look up the key sequence for a given character in the Keystrokes column in the table. To save space, we condensed the words *Shift*, *Option*, and *Command* to single letters. For example, we represent the keystrokes for creating an em dash (Shift-Option- -) as *SO-*. For clarity, we represent an uppercase letter or symbol as Shift-*letter*.

There is often more than one way to enter a character found in the table. You can enter its key sequence from the Keystrokes column in the table. Or you can place an insertion point, press Option-Command-Q, enter its ASCII code from the table, and press the Return key. You can enter a paragraph mark, for example, either by pressing the Return key, or by pressing Option-Command-Q, entering *13*, and then pressing the Return key (although this is a roundabout way to enter a simple paragraph mark).

Both methods do not work for all characters. For example, you can insert a graphics frame by choosing Insert Graphics from the Edit menu or by pressing Command-I, but you cannot get the graphics frame by pressing Option-Command-Q, entering *1*, and then pressing the Return key. On the other hand, you could remove every graphic from a document at once by searching for *^1* and replacing it with nothing.

Normal characters: Those you use in everyday writing—the uppercase and lowercase letters from A to Z, the numbers, and the punctuation marks. You enter one of these in the expected way, by pressing a key on the keyboard or by pressing the Shift key at the same time as you press the key for the character. For example, in the table we represent an *A* as *Sa*.

Dingbat and symbol characters: Supported in many Macintosh character sets, such as the standard bullet • (Option-8) or the paragraph symbol ¶ (Option-7). You enter these by pressing the Shift or Option keys in conjunction with a key. In the table, Option-8 is represented as *O8*.

Accented characters: These are normal characters with added accents, such as *é* and *ö*. You enter these by first pressing, at the same time, the Option key and a key for the type of accent you want, and then press, alone, the letter you want accented. For example, to enter *ö*, first you press Option-u, and then press *o*. This sequence is represented in the table as *Ou,o*.

Control characters: Assigned to ASCII characters between 0 and 30, such as the tab, paragraph, and newline marks. You can enter only a few of these from the keyboard. For example, enter a tab mark by pressing the Tab key, a paragraph mark by pressing the Return or Enter keys, and a newline mark by pressing Shift-Return. In the table these keys are spelled out in a small point size, such as *SReturn* for a newline mark.

Word's reserved characters: These are set aside for marking some of the internal structures in a document, such as section marks, page breaks, and graphics. Some you can enter with a key sequence, such as Command-Enter for a section mark or Command-I for a graphics frame. Others, such as the character produced when you click the Page Number icon in a Header window, cannot be entered from the keyboard, because even though Word uses a character to represent a component of a document, it also adds other internal attributes you cannot add from the keyboard. If you want to enter one of these special characters, start by entering it in the normal way (by clicking an icon, for instance), and then create a glossary entry for it that you can enter by pressing Command-Backspace and a code you have chosen.

Many of the special characters Word uses to place items such as graphics, paragraph marks, and so on, are visible only when Show ¶ is turned on. The Comments column in the table identifies some of these special characters by name and offers some other notes where needed. Some ASCII characters in a given font are undefined and have no unique shape. When you turn on Show ¶, you see either a box (☐) or nothing at all. Because PostScript printers don't print these boxes, we have added boxes to the table as graphics to show you which are visible and which are not.

ASCII	Times	Geneva	New York	Courier	Zapf Dingbats	Symbol	Keystrokes	Comments
0	□	□	□	□		□		
1	□	□	□	□			Ci	Graphic (either an Insert Graphic box or an actual graphic)
2	□		□	□				Page number in header or footer
3	□		□	□				Date in header or footer
4	□		□	□				Time in header or footer
5	□		□	□				Footnote reference
6	\	\	\	\	✲	∴		Formula character (^\) and footnote separator
7	□	□	□	□				Footnote continued separator
8	□	□	□	□				
9							Tab	Tab (^t)
10								Linefeed
11							SReturn	Newline (^n)
12							SEnter CEnter	Page break and Section mark (^d)
13							Return	Carriage return or paragraph mark (^p)
14	□	□	□	□				
15	□	□	□	□				
16	□	□	□	□				
17	□	□	□	□				
18	□	□	□	□				
19	□	□	□	□				
20	□	□	□	□				
21	□	□	□	□				
22	□	□	□	□				
23	□	□	□	□				
24	□	□	□	□				
25	□	□	□	□				
26	□	□	□	□				
27	□	□	□	□				
28	□	□	□	□				

ASCII	Times	Geneva	New York	Courier	Zapf Dingbats	Symbol	Keystrokes	Comments
29	□	□	□	□				
30	-	-	-	-	✍	–	C~	Nonbreaking hyphen
31							C-	Optional hyphen (^_)
32							Spacebar	Normal space
33	!	!	!	!	✁	!	S1	
34	"	"	"	"	✂	∀	S'	Double quote, inches, or seconds (see also ASCII 210-213)
35	#	#	#	#	✃	#	S3	
36	$	$	$	$	✄	∃	S4	
37	%	%	%	%	☎	%	S5	
38	&	&	&	&	✆	&	S7	
39	'	'	'	'	✇	∋	'	Single quote, feet, or minutes (see also ASCII 210-213)
40	(	(	(	(	✈	(	S9	
41	)	)	)	)	✉	)	S0	(zero)
42	*	*	*	*	☛	*	S8	
43	+	+	+	+	☞	+	S=	
44	,	,	,	,	✌	,	,	
45	-	-	-	-	✍	−	-	Normal hyphen
46	.	.	.	.	✎	.	.	Period
47	/	/	/	/	✏	/	/	
48	0	0	0	0	✐	0	0	Zero
49	1	1	1	1	✑	1	1	
50	2	2	2	2	✒	2	2	
51	3	3	3	3	✓	3	3	
52	4	4	4	4	✔	4	4	
53	5	5	5	5	✕	5	5	
54	6	6	6	6	✖	6	6	
55	7	7	7	7	✗	7	7	
56	8	8	8	8	✘	8	8	
57	9	9	9	9	✙	9	9	
58	:	:	:	:	✚	:	S;	(semicolon)
59	;	;	;	;	✛	;	;	
60	<	<	<	<	✜	<	S,	(comma)

ASCII	Times	Geneva	New York	Courier	Zapf Dingbats	Symbol	Keystrokes	Comments
61	=	=	=	=	✝	=	=	
62	>	>	>	>	✞	>	S.	(period)
63	?	?	?	?	✟	?	S/	(slash)
64	@	@	@	@	✠	≅	S2	
65	A	A	A	A	✡	Α	Sa	
66	B	B	B	B	✢	Β	Sb	
67	C	C	C	C	✣	Χ	Sc	
68	D	D	D	D	✤	Δ	Sd	
69	E	E	E	E	✥	Ε	Se	
70	F	F	F	F	✦	Φ	Sf	
71	G	G	G	G	✧	Γ	Sg	
72	H	H	H	H	★	Η	Sh	
73	I	I	I	I	☆	Ι	Si	
74	J	J	J	J	✪	ϑ	Sj	
75	K	K	K	K	✫	Κ	Sk	
76	L	L	L	L	✬	Λ	Sl	
77	M	M	M	M	✭	Μ	Sm	
78	N	N	N	N	✮	Ν	Sn	
79	O	O	O	O	✯	Ο	So	
80	P	P	P	P	✰	Π	Sp	
81	Q	Q	Q	Q	✱	Θ	Sq	
82	R	R	R	R	✲	Ρ	Sr	
83	S	S	S	S	✳	Σ	Ss	
84	T	T	T	T	✴	Τ	St	
85	U	U	U	U	✵	Υ	Su	
86	V	V	V	V	✶	ς	Sv	
87	W	W	W	W	✷	Ω	Sw	
88	X	X	X	X	✸	Ξ	Sx	
89	Y	Y	Y	Y	✹	Ψ	Sy	
90	Z	Z	Z	Z	✺	Ζ	Sz	
91	[	[	[	[	✻	[	[	
92	\	\	\	\	✼	∴	\	Backslash
93	]	]	]	]	✽	]	]	
94	^	^	^	^	✾	⊥	S6	Caret (^^)
95	_	_	_	_	✿	_	S-	Underscore

<table>
<tr><th>ASCII</th><th>Times</th><th>Geneva</th><th>New York</th><th>Courier</th><th>Zapf Dingbats</th><th>Symbol</th><th>Keystrokes</th><th>Comments</th></tr>
<tr><td>96</td><td>`</td><td>`</td><td>`</td><td>`</td><td>❀</td><td>‾</td><td>`</td><td>Grave accent; however, in the Symbol font pressing ` produces a NOT operator over the succeeding character. For example, pressing ` and then a in Symbol results in $\overline{\alpha}$.</td></tr>
<tr><td>97</td><td>a</td><td>a</td><td>a</td><td>a</td><td>❁</td><td>α</td><td>a</td><td></td></tr>
<tr><td>98</td><td>b</td><td>b</td><td>b</td><td>b</td><td>❂</td><td>β</td><td>b</td><td></td></tr>
<tr><td>99</td><td>c</td><td>c</td><td>c</td><td>c</td><td>❃</td><td>χ</td><td>c</td><td></td></tr>
<tr><td>100</td><td>d</td><td>d</td><td>d</td><td>d</td><td>❄</td><td>δ</td><td>d</td><td></td></tr>
<tr><td>101</td><td>e</td><td>e</td><td>e</td><td>e</td><td>❅</td><td>ε</td><td>e</td><td></td></tr>
<tr><td>102</td><td>f</td><td>f</td><td>f</td><td>f</td><td>❆</td><td>φ</td><td>f</td><td></td></tr>
<tr><td>103</td><td>g</td><td>g</td><td>g</td><td>g</td><td>❇</td><td>γ</td><td>g</td><td></td></tr>
<tr><td>104</td><td>h</td><td>h</td><td>h</td><td>h</td><td>❈</td><td>η</td><td>h</td><td></td></tr>
<tr><td>105</td><td>i</td><td>i</td><td>i</td><td>i</td><td>❉</td><td>ι</td><td>i</td><td></td></tr>
<tr><td>106</td><td>j</td><td>j</td><td>j</td><td>j</td><td>❊</td><td>ϕ</td><td>j</td><td></td></tr>
<tr><td>107</td><td>k</td><td>k</td><td>k</td><td>k</td><td>❋</td><td>κ</td><td>k</td><td></td></tr>
<tr><td>108</td><td>l</td><td>l</td><td>l</td><td>l</td><td>●</td><td>λ</td><td>l</td><td></td></tr>
<tr><td>109</td><td>m</td><td>m</td><td>m</td><td>m</td><td>❍</td><td>μ</td><td>m</td><td></td></tr>
<tr><td>110</td><td>n</td><td>n</td><td>n</td><td>n</td><td>■</td><td>ν</td><td>n</td><td></td></tr>
<tr><td>111</td><td>o</td><td>o</td><td>o</td><td>o</td><td>❏</td><td>ο</td><td>o</td><td></td></tr>
<tr><td>112</td><td>p</td><td>p</td><td>p</td><td>p</td><td>❐</td><td>π</td><td>p</td><td></td></tr>
<tr><td>113</td><td>q</td><td>q</td><td>q</td><td>q</td><td>❑</td><td>θ</td><td>q</td><td></td></tr>
<tr><td>114</td><td>r</td><td>r</td><td>r</td><td>r</td><td>❒</td><td>ρ</td><td>r</td><td></td></tr>
<tr><td>115</td><td>s</td><td>s</td><td>s</td><td>s</td><td>▲</td><td>σ</td><td>s</td><td></td></tr>
<tr><td>116</td><td>t</td><td>t</td><td>t</td><td>t</td><td>▼</td><td>τ</td><td>t</td><td></td></tr>
<tr><td>117</td><td>u</td><td>u</td><td>u</td><td>u</td><td>◆</td><td>υ</td><td>u</td><td></td></tr>
<tr><td>118</td><td>v</td><td>v</td><td>v</td><td>v</td><td>❖</td><td>ϖ</td><td>v</td><td></td></tr>
<tr><td>119</td><td>w</td><td>w</td><td>w</td><td>w</td><td>◗</td><td>ω</td><td>w</td><td></td></tr>
<tr><td>120</td><td>x</td><td>x</td><td>x</td><td>x</td><td>❘</td><td>ξ</td><td>x</td><td></td></tr>
<tr><td>121</td><td>y</td><td>y</td><td>y</td><td>y</td><td>❙</td><td>ψ</td><td>y</td><td></td></tr>
<tr><td>122</td><td>z</td><td>z</td><td>z</td><td>z</td><td>❚</td><td>ζ</td><td>z</td><td></td></tr>
<tr><td>123</td><td>{</td><td>{</td><td>{</td><td>{</td><td>❛</td><td>{</td><td>S[</td><td></td></tr>
<tr><td>124</td><td>|</td><td>|</td><td>|</td><td>|</td><td>❜</td><td>|</td><td>S\</td><td>(backslash)</td></tr>
<tr><td>125</td><td>}</td><td>}</td><td>}</td><td>}</td><td>❝</td><td>}</td><td>S]</td><td></td></tr>
<tr><td>126</td><td>~</td><td>~</td><td>~</td><td>~</td><td>❞</td><td>~</td><td>S`</td><td>Tilde</td></tr>
<tr><td>127</td><td>□</td><td></td><td></td><td></td><td></td><td></td><td></td><td></td></tr>
<tr><td>128</td><td>Ä</td><td>Ä</td><td>Ä</td><td>Ä</td><td>❨</td><td></td><td>Ou,Sa</td><td>Zapf Dingbats and Symbol characters from ASCII 128 to 160 are undefined.</td></tr>
</table>

ASCII	Times	Geneva	New York	Courier	Zapf Dingbats	Symbol	Keystrokes	Comments
129	Å	Å	Å	Å	❩		SOa	However, even though characters in Zapf Dingbats from 128 to 141 are undefined (i.e., have no screen image), when printed on a PostScript printer they produce the images shown here.
130	Ç	Ç	Ç	Ç	❪		SOc	
131	É	É	É	É	❫		Oe,Se	
132	Ñ	Ñ	Ñ	Ñ	❬		On,Sn	
133	Ö	Ö	Ö	Ö	❭		Ou,So	
134	Ü	Ü	Ü	Ü	❮		Ou,Su	
135	á	á	á	á	❯		Oe,a	
136	à	à	à	à	❰		O`,a	
137	â	â	â	â	❱		Oi,a	
138	ä	ä	ä	ä	❲		Ou,a	
139	ã	ã	ã	ã	❳		On,a	
140	å	å	å	å	❴		Oa	
141	ç	ç	ç	ç	❵		Oc	
142	é	é	é	é			Oe,e	
143	è	è	è	è			O`,e	
144	ê	ê	ê	ê			Oi,e	
145	ë	ë	ë	ë			Ou,e	
146	í	í	í	í			Oe,i	
147	ì	ì	ì	ì			O`,i	
148	î	î	î	î			Oi,i	
149	ï	ï	ï	ï			Ou,i	
150	ñ	ñ	ñ	ñ			On,n	
151	ó	ó	ó	ó			Oe,o	
152	ò	ò	ò	ò			O`,o	
153	ô	ô	ô	ô			Oi,o	
154	ö	ö	ö	ö			Ou,o	
155	õ	õ	õ	õ			On,o	
156	ú	ú	ú	ú			Oe,u	
157	ù	ù	ù	ù			O`,u	
158	û	û	û	û			Oi,u	
159	ü	ü	ü	ü			Ou,u	
160	†	†	†	†			Ot	Dagger
161	°	°	°	°	❡	ϒ	SO8	Degree
162	¢	¢	¢	¢	❢	′	O4	Cent
163	£	£	£	£	❣	≤	O3	Pound Sterling

ASCII	Times	Geneva	New York	Courier	Zapf Dingbats	Symbol	Keystrokes	Comments
164	§	§	§	§	❤	⁄	O6	Section symbol
165	•	•	•	•	❥	∞	O8	Standard bullet
166	¶	¶	¶	¶	❦	ƒ	O7	Paragraph mark (the symbol itself, not the Word marker)
167	ß	ß	ß	ß	❧	♣	Os	
168	®	®	®	®	♣	♦	Or	Registration mark
169	©	©	©	©	♦	♥	Og	Copyright mark
170	™	™	™	™	♥	♠	O2	Trademark symbol
171	´	´	´	´	♠	↔	Oe,Oe	Acute accent
172	¨	¨	¨	¨	①	←	Ou,Ou	Umlaut or diaeresis
173	≠	≠	□	≠	②	↑	O=	
174	Æ	Æ	Æ	Æ	③	→	SO'	(single quote)
175	Ø	Ø	Ø	Ø	④	↓	SOo	
176	∞	∞	□	∞	⑤	°	O5	Infinity symbol
177	±	±	□	±	⑥	±	SO=	
178	≤	≤	□	≤	⑦	″	O,	(comma)
179	≥	≥	□	≥	⑧	≥	O.	(period)
180	¥	¥	¥	¥	⑨	×	Oy	Japanese Yen symbol
181	µ	µ	□	µ	⑩	∝	Om	
182	∂	∂	□	∂	❶	∂	Od	
183	∑	∑	□	∑	❷	•	Ow	
184	∏	∏	□	∏	❸	÷	SOp	
185	π	π	□	π	❹	≠	Op	
186	∫	∫	□	∫	❺	≡	Ob	Integral
187	ª	ª	ª	ª	❻	≈	O9	
188	º	º	º	º	❼	…	O0	(zero)
189	Ω	Ω	□	Ω	❽	⏐	Oz	
190	æ	æ	æ	æ	❾	⎯	O'	(single quote)
191	ø	ø	ø	ø	❿	↵	Oo	
192	¿	¿	¿	¿	①	ℵ	SO/	(slash)
193	¡	¡	¡	¡	②	ℑ	O1	Inverted exclamation point
194	¬	¬	□	¬	③	ℜ	Ol	
195	√	√	□	√	④	℘	Ov	
196	ƒ	ƒ	□	ƒ	⑤	⊗	Of	

ASCII	Times	Geneva	New York	Courier	Zapf Dingbats	Symbol	Keystrokes	Comments
197	≈	≈	□	≈	⑥	⊕	Ox	
198	Δ	△	□	Δ	⑦	∅	Oj	
199	«	«	«	«	⑧	∩	O\	(backslash) European open parenthesis, math *much less than,* also the symbol starting a merge language command
200	»	»	»	»	⑨	∪	SO\	(backslash) European close parenthesis, math *much greater than,* also the symbol ending a merge language command
201	…	…	…	…	⑩	⊃	O;	Ellipsis
202					❶	⊇	Cspace	Nonbreaking space
203	À	À	À	À	❷	⊄	O`,Sa	
204	Ã	Ã	Ã	Ã	❸	⊂	On,Sa	
205	Õ	Õ	Õ	Õ	❹	⊆	On,So	
206	Œ	Œ	Œ	Œ	❺	∈	SOq	
207	œ	œ	œ	œ	❻	∉	Oq	
208	–	–	–	–	❼	∠	O-	En dash
209	—	—	—	—	❽	∇	SO-	Em dash
210	“	“	“	"	❾	®	O[	Open double quote
211	”	”	”	"	❿	©	SO[	Close double quote
212	‘	‘	‘	'	➔	™	O]	Open single quote
213	’	’	’	'	→	∏	SO]	Close single quote
214	÷	÷	□	÷	↔	√	O/	
215	◊	◇	◇	◊	↕	·	SOv	
216	ÿ	ÿ	ÿ	ÿ	➘	¬	Ou,y	
217	Ÿ	[illegible]	[illegible]	Ÿ	➙	∧	SO`	
218	/	□	□	/	➚	∨	SO1	
219	¤	□	□	¤	➛	⇔	SO2	
220	‹	□	□	‹	➜	⇐	SO3	
221	›	□	□	›	➝	⇑	SO4	
222	ﬁ	□	□	□	➞	⇒	SO5	
223	ﬂ	□	□	□	➟	⇓	SO6	

ASCII	Times	Geneva	New York	Courier	Zapf Dingbats	Symbol	Keystrokes	Comments
224	‡	□	□	‡	➠	◊	SO7	
225	·	□	□	·	➡	〈	SO9	
226	‚	□	□	‚	➢	®	SO0	(zero)
227	„	□	□	„	➣	©	SOw	
228	‰	□	□	□	➤	™	SOe	
229	Â	□	□	Â	➥	∑	SOr	
230	Ê	□	□	Ê	➦	⎛	SOt	
231	Á	□	□	Á	➧	⎜	SOy	
232	Ë	□	□	Ë	➨	⎝	SOu	
233	È	□	□	È	➩	⎡	SOi	
234	Í	□	□	Í	➪	⎢	SOs	
235	Î	□	□	Î	➫	⎣	SOd	
236	Ï	□	□	Ï	➬	⎧	SOf	
237	Ì	□	□	Ì	➭	⎨	SOg	
238	Ó	□	□	Ó	➮	⎩	SOh	
239	Ô	□	□	Ô	➯	⎪	SOj	
240		□	□				SOk	
241	Ò	□	□	Ò	➱	〉	SOl	(letter "ell")
242	Ú	□	□	Ú	➲	∫	SO;	
243	Û	□	□	Û	➳	⌠	SOz	
244	Ù	□	□	Ù	➴	⎮	SOx	
245	ı	□	□	ı	➵	⌡	SOb	
246	ˆ	□	□	ˆ	➶	⎞	SOn	
247	˜	□	□	˜	➷	⎟	SOm	
248	¯	□	□	¯	➸	⎠	SO,	
249	˘	□	□	˘	➹	⎤	SO.	(period)
250	˙	□	□	˙	➺	⎥	Oh	
251	˚	□	□	˚	➻	⎦	Ok	
252	¸	□	□	¸	➼	⎫		no keyboard equivalent
253	˝	□	□	˝	➽	⎬		no keyboard equivalent
254	˛	□	□	˛	➾	⎭		no keyboard equivalent
255	□	□	□	□				no keyboard equivalent

Using PostScript

PostScript is a deep and beautiful language. In some ways, however, it shares the reputation of languages based on the syntax of FORTH, namely, that it is difficult to read and to learn. It has been said that you can tell a program in FORTH is well written if you can't read it at all!

But nothing could be further from the truth. Programs written in PostScript can be as clear and self-documenting as those in any other computer language. While the depths of PostScript require as much study as any language, you can achieve many special effects in your Word documents, such as thin lines, gray-scale text, and boxes, without great effort. This appendix is by no means a complete introduction to the language, but it should give you enough background to get started. We assume that you've had some exposure to at least one other programming language. For further study, the *PostScript Language Reference Manual* and *PostScript Language Tutorial and Cookbook,* by Adobe Systems Incorporated and published by Addison-Wesley, are highly recommended.

■ *Understanding PostScript Syntax*

The PostScript language is easy to understand, once you become accustomed to its inverted syntax. If you've ever used a Hewlett-Packard calculator, you've already had a taste of this syntax, in which you enter the numbers for the calculation first, and then enter the operator for the calculation. When you enter the numbers, they go into a special structure within the calculator called a *stack*—the last number entered becomes the topmost entry on the stack. When the operation is performed, it acts upon one or more of the topmost entries in their order of entry and puts the result on the stack for the next calculation. Here's an example of some PostScript:

```
2 3 add       % This enters two numbers and then adds them together
```

The two numbers precede the *add* command—most commands, known as *operators* in PostScript, are spelled for ease in reading rather than being represented by symbols. Other math operators include *sub* for subtraction, *mul* for multiplication, *div* for division, and *neg* for reversing the sign of a number. Here, the two numbers are pushed onto the stack, and the *add* operator adds them, putting the result—*5*—back on the stack. Finally, the % character signifies that whatever follows on the same line is a comment and is to be ignored by the PostScript interpreter.

Writing a Simple Program

PostScript commands in a Word document act upon one of three rectangular areas: one page, one paragraph, or one graphics frame. The drawing commands your program issues are measured relative to the lower left corner of one of these areas, depending on which you specify. The coordinate system PostScript uses sets the origin at the lower left corner and measures positive distances in points (1/72 inch) to the right and in an upward direction of the origin. For example, the coordinates of the origin are (0,0), and the coordinates of a point one inch to the right and two inches upward from the origin are (72,144). Where this origin is placed on a page depends on which area you set in your PostScript program.

Let's create a simple shape and show how it looks when applied within the area of the page. Here's a short program for drawing a box in the lower left corner of a page:

```
.page.               % Draw relative to the page rectangle
newpath              % Start the path to be drawn
72 72 moveto         % Move to bottom left corner of box
72 144 lineto        % Draw to top left corner of box
144 144 lineto       % Draw to top right corner
144 72 lineto        % Draw to bottom right corner
closepath            % Close path (draw back to first point)
.5 setgray           % Set a 50% gray level for the box
stroke               % Draw lines on the path just defined
```

To experiment with this PostScript, enter these lines into a blank document window. (You don't have to type the comments.) Then select all the lines from beginning to end, choose the Styles command, and give the lines the *PostScript* automatic style. If the style doesn't appear in the dialog box, press the Shift key while choosing the Styles command to make all the automatic styles appear. Because the definition of the *PostScript* style contains the Hidden attribute, you need to select the Show Hidden Text option in the Preferences dialog box so that you can see code assigned to the style. If you click the Set Default button while the *PostScript* style is selected, the style will appear in the Define Styles dialog box for any new document you create.

Word knows that any text in the *PostScript* style is to be sent on to a PostScript printer, such as the LaserWriter, as PostScript code instead of document text. When the PostScript interpreter inside the printer receives this series of operators, it executes each in the order received, creating patterns of pixels, which are then printed on paper or film.

The final step is to choose the Print command, make sure the Print Hidden Text option is not selected, and Click OK. The printed page should look like Figure C-1 (allowing for the 75% reduction in size that was used to represent the image of the page).

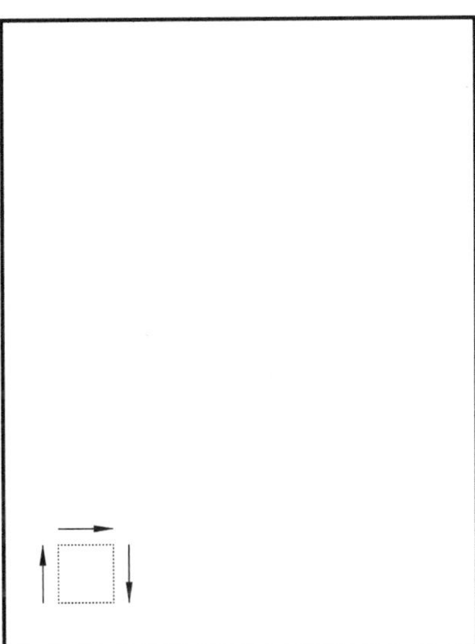

Figure C-1
The PostScript code as it looks when printed (at 25%, without the arrows).

Let's look at this code more closely. The first PostScript operator, *.page.*, tells Word that the PostScript that follows is to be drawn relative to the rectangle of the page. The next operator, *newpath*, expresses a peculiarity of PostScript relative to other languages that contain graphics commands.

In other languages, when you draw a line, that line is drawn immediately. In PostScript, however, you create a *path* first, and then you tell the PostScript what to do with the path. It's as if the PostScript interpreter first outlines a pattern with an empty pen, creating a template, and then waits for subsequent commands to draw the pattern in the way you want.

Here, the *newpath* operator tells PostScript to create a new, empty path, and the *moveto* operator moves the location of the imaginary pen to the first point in the new path. The *lineto* operators add line segments to the path after the last point specified in the path. There are three of these *lineto* operators in the program, which create the left, top, and right edges of the box. The arrows in Figure C-1 show the direction of this path. The *closepath* operator is a convenience; it tells the PostScript interpreter to add a line segment to the current path leading from the last point in the path back to the first point, without requiring that you specify the coordinates of the path. The line not marked by an arrow is the line segment created by the *closepath* operator.

Because PostScript uses the point system to set measurements, these instructions specify a path for a box that is one-inch square and starts one inch up from and to the right of the lower left corner of the page. The *setgray* operator sets the gray level of any subsequent drawing. It takes the number that precedes it on the stack; this can go from 0 (black) to 1 (white), so this box is drawn in 50% gray.

Finally, the *stroke* operator tells the PostScript interpreter to draw the path as a series of lines. This may be confusing at first, because you may have thought that this is what the program was doing all along—the use of the *lineto* operators seems to imply that actual lines are being drawn.

Modifying the Program

To understand the difference between a path and the lines drawn on the path with the *stroke* operator, let's repeat the program but replace the *stroke* operator with another, the *fill* operator:

```
.page.              % Draw relative to the page rectangle
newpath             % Start the path to be drawn
72 72 moveto        % Move to bottom left corner of box
72 144 lineto       % Draw to top left corner of box
144 144 lineto      % Draw to top right corner
144 72 lineto       % Draw to bottom right corner
closepath           % Close the path back to first point
.5 setgray          % Set a 50% gray level for the box
fill                % Fill the path with a gray level
```

When you change the one line in boldface in the code and print the document, the page you'll see should look like Figure C-2.

Figure C-2
The same path drawn with the *fill* operator instead of the *stroke* operator.

Now let's define a new operator called *squarePath,* which we can use to draw either a filled or unfilled box.

```
.page.                % Draw relative to the page rectangle

/squarePath
   { newpath          % Start the path to be drawn
   72 72 moveto       % Move to bottom left corner of box
   72 144 lineto      % Draw to top left corner of box
   144 144 lineto     % Draw to top right corner of box
   144 72 lineto      % Draw to bottom right corner
   closepath          % Close the path back to first point
   }  def             % Define the operator

.5 setgray            % Set a 50% gray level for the box
squarePath fill       % Draw the box as a filled path
0 setgray             % Set the color to black
squarePath stroke     % Draw the box as a series of lines
```

We pulled out the part of the PostScript that sets the path for the box and defined it as an operator. When you do this, you must precede the name for the new operator with a slash and surround the commands that define it with curly braces. Finally, end the definition with the *def* operator. When you print the page containing this code, it should look like Figure C-3.

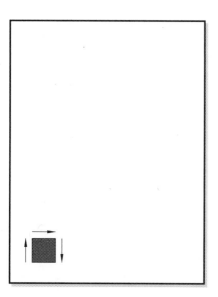

Figure C-3
Using both *fill* and *stroke* with the *squarePath* operator.

■ *If an Error Occurs*

If your PostScript program contains an error, your LaserWriter or other PostScript printer does almost the worst thing possible (other than blowing up): nothing. The yellow light blinks as the page is processed, and when the error happens, the blinking stops. You may get a partially completed page, letting you determine where in the page the problem occurred, but it's likely that you won't even get this. Errors that occur in the PostScript sent to the printer may not be reported to you by Word or by the printer.

Fortunately, there are steps you can take. If you get either a blank page or nothing at all instead of the results you expected, first check your typing. Also, in the last program, notice the blank lines between the groups of code. All the lines in a group of PostScript code must have the *PostScript* style, with no lines inadvertently assigned another style such as the *Normal* style—even the blank lines. This can happen easily, because the Next Style set in the definition for the *PostScript* style is the *Normal* style, which means that whenever you press the Return key after entering a line of PostScript, the next line reverts to the *Normal* style.

To prevent this from happening, redefine the *PostScript* style, setting the contents of the Next Style field to *PostScript*. Also, it's easier to read your code if you remove the Bold character attribute and set the font to Courier so that the spaces between operators are easier to see. In fact, you can change the *PostScript* style to anything you want, but leave the Hidden attribute set; your programs won't work without it.

There is a set of routines, called an *error dictionary*, running to about 30 lines of PostScript. (Groups of programs in PostScript are called dictionaries because you define operators that act like words in a sentence.) Error dictionaries, when sent to the printer ahead of your code, tell the printer to eject a page containing text describing what kind of error occurred and what was on the stack at the time of the error. From this you can usually discover the bug. You can get error dictionaries from user groups or from CompuServe; some are included with graphics programs that support PostScript.

You can use an error dictionary in two ways. First, you can download the dictionary to the PostScript printer before starting Word, making the dictionary *resident* on the printer until you reset it or turn it off. Cricket Draw has this ability, as does the SendPS utility from Adobe Systems. Using a resident error dictionary is handy because once you've sent it to the printer, you don't have to worry about including it before every piece of PostScript code you place in a document.

Second, you can include the dictionary in your Word document before the PostScript code you're writing and want to test. This type of dictionary is called a *nonresident* dictionary because it is cleared from the printer's memory after the printing is done. When your code works, remove the preceding error dictionary; including the error dictionary before every occurrence of your PostScript in a document can become unwieldy. (Later in this appendix we'll describe a method that lets you add your own PostScript dictionaries to the Word program itself.)

TIP

Saving a Printed Document's PostScript to a File

When you begin to plumb the depths of using PostScript in Word, you may find it useful to take a look at exactly what PostScript code is being sent to the printer. As discussed in Chapter 12, "Document Formatting and Printing," when you print a document on a PostScript printer, Word sends the document to the LaserWriter driver, which translates the graphics commands that comprise it into PostScript commands and sends them on to the printer. It precedes this stream of PostScript with a file called the Laser Prep file, consisting of about 25 KB of PostScript definitions for many of the operators used by the LaserWriter driver when it translates the document.

You can intercept this translation process and send the PostScript to a file rather than to the printer. This file can take two forms. If you choose the Print command and immediately press Command-K, the PostScript is sent to a file called PostScript0 (or PostScript1, and so on) with the 25 KB of PostScript in the Laser Prep file. However, if you press Command-F instead, the file is saved without the header. The file is saved in the same folder as the Word program, and you can open it as a text file from Word to see the PostScript commands it contains.

■ *Working with Operators and Variables*

Earlier we defined a new operator by giving a group of operators a name. You can define other objects in the PostScript environment as well. For example, consider this operator for converting inches to points:

```
/inch
   { 72 mul } def
```

The *inch* operator takes a number from the stack and multiplies it by 72, returning the result to the stack. You could use it in this way to change the definition of the *box* operator:

```
/inch
   { 72 mul } def

/squarePath
   { newpath
   1 inch 1 inch moveto
   1 inch 2 inch lineto
   2 inch 2 inch lineto
   2 inch 1 inch lineto
   closepath
   }  def
```

The number of inches to be converted precedes each instance of the *inch* operator in *squarePath.* When the PostScript interpreter encounters the number, it puts the number on the stack. When the interpreter reads the *inch* operator, it looks up the definition and executes its code. The code in the definition first puts the number 72 on the stack, pushing the number representing the inches to the second position on the stack. The *mul* operator multiplies the first two numbers on the stack and puts the result on the stack.

Defining Variables

In PostScript, variables are almost identical to operators. If you wanted, you could define the number of points per inch as a constant, as in this code:

```
/pointsPerInch
   { 72 } def

/inch
   { pointsPerInch mul } def

/squarePath
   { newpath
   1 inch 1 inch moveto
   1 inch 2 inch lineto
   2 inch 2 inch lineto
   2 inch 1 inch lineto
   closepath
   }  def
```

In the above code, *squarePath* uses, or calls, the *inch* operator and passes it the number to be converted on the stack. The *inch* operator in turn calls *pointsPerInch* to find its value and puts that number on the stack. The *mul* operator multiplies the numbers and puts the result on the stack. When control returns to *squarePath,* the number returned becomes a value passed to either the *moveto* or *lineto* operators. By defining values as constants in this way, you can make your code easier to read and to change.

Setting Values Outside a Routine

You can make a routine more useful, and therefore more general, by passing it values, which the routine uses internally. You can make the *squarePath* operator more general, allowing you to specify the coordinates of the lower left corner and drawing the sides of the square relative to that point. The complete code you need to draw this square on a page is as follows:

```
.page.
/inch
   % Usage: number inch
   % Take: number in inches to be converted to points
   % Return: number converted to points
   { 72 mul } def

/squarePath   % Draws a one-inch square
   % Usage: xLeft yBottom squarePath
   % Take: coordinates of lower left corner
   % Return: nothing
   { newpath                % Start new path
   moveto                   % Move to x and y coordinates on stack
   0 inch 1 inch rlineto    % Draw up 1 inch
   1 inch 0 inch rlineto    % Draw right 1 inch
   0 inch -1 inch rlineto   % Draw down one inch
   closepath                % Draw back to beginning of path
   }  def

1 inch 1 inch squarePath stroke
3 inch 3 inch squarePath fill
.5 setgray
5 inch 5 inch squarePath stroke
7 inch 7 inch squarePath fill
```

These lines of PostScript code may seem heavily commented for such short routines, but the style presented here is good for maintaining your work in as understandable a format as possible. Notice that *lineto* has been replaced with *rlineto;* whereas *lineto* adds a line to the current path in absolute coordinates, *rlineto* adds a line relative to the preceding point specified. In this version of the *squarePath* routine, you specify the first point in the path—the lower left corner of the square, outside the *squarePath* routine. The first *rlineto* operator measures from that first point zero inches in the *x* dimension and 1 inch in the *y* dimension. Figure C-4 shows how these squares look when printed.

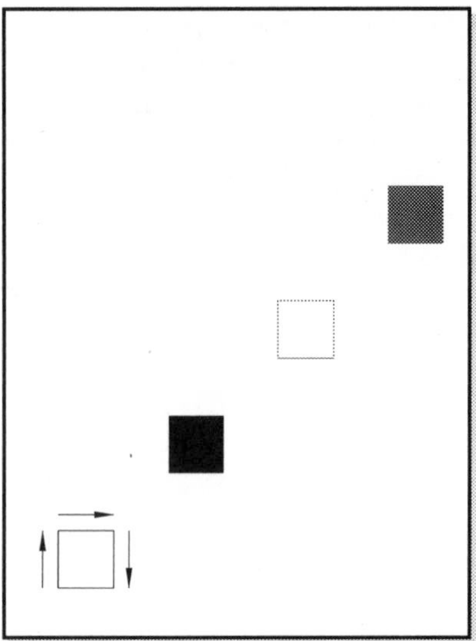

Figure C-4
Specifying the starting point of the square outside the *squarePath* routine.

Defining Variables Within a Routine

Often, it's helpful to give names to the values passed to a routine, making them variables to be used within the routine itself. You can make *squarePath* even more useful by passing it the size of the square as well as the position of its lower left corner.

```
.page.
/inch
    % Usage: number inch
    % Take: the number in inches to be converted to points
    % Return: the number converted to points
    { 72 mul } def

/squarePath   % Draws a variable-sized square
    % Usage: xLeft yBottom size squarePath
    % Take: coordinates of lower left corner and size
    % Return: nothing
    {
    /size exch def          % Store first number on stack
                            %   in variable size

    newpath                 % Start new path
    moveto                  % Move to x and y coordinates on stack
    0 size rlineto          % Draw up size points
    size 0 rlineto          % Draw right size points
    0 size neg rlineto      % Draw down size points
    closepath               % Draw back to beginning of path
    }  def
```

```
1 inch 1 inch 3 inch squarePath stroke
3 inch 3 inch 2 inch squarePath fill
.5 setgray
5 inch 5 inch 1 inch squarePath stroke
7 inch 7 inch .5 inch squarePath fill
```

In this version, *squarePath* takes three values; two numbers representing the coordinates of the lower left corner and one number for the size of the square in points. Because the size value is the last one set before *squarePath,* it is the first value on the stack when the routine is executed.

Notice the first line in the *squarePath* routine: */size exch def*. This is a special construction in PostScript; first the label */size* is pushed onto the stack, making the size the second value. The *exch* operator exchanges the positions of the first two values on the stack, and the *def* operator then assigns the value representing the size to the label *size.* Subsequently, every instance of the variable *size* is replaced with the number the label contains.

Creating variables in this way is very useful because you can use values over again or set a variable to a value at the beginning of a routine and change the value at various points within the routine. In the *squarePath* routine, the *size* variable sets the amount by which all the relative movements are added to the current path through the *rlineto* operators. Figure C-5 shows how this code looks when executed.

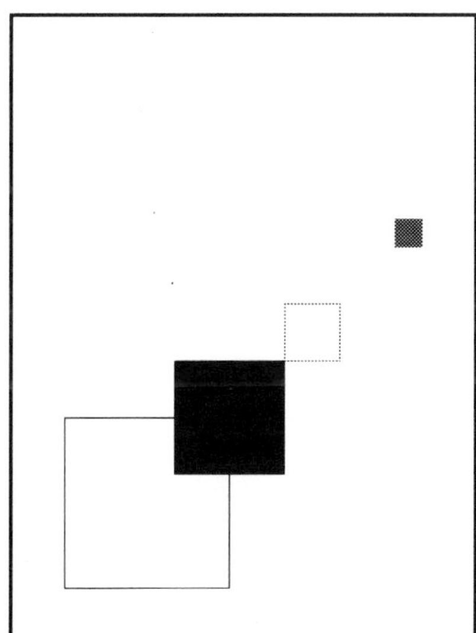

Figure C-5
Specifying both the starting point and size of the square outside the *squarePath* routine.

Drawing Rectangles

Earlier we mentioned that the PostScript commands you group together in a document are placed on the page relative to one of three areas. You've already encountered one of these areas—the page. You can also draw within the limits of the first paragraph following the PostScript and within the limits of a graphics frame. To specify an area, precede the group with one of the following operators:

.page. The limits of the printable area on the page. If you don't specify an area operator, Word defaults to this area.

.para. Vertically, from the top of the Space Before value for the paragraph to the bottom of the Space After value. Horizontally, from either the first-line or left indent (whichever is leftmost) to the right indent.

.pic. The limits of the graphic frame within the first paragraph following.

Let's look at a few examples of how you might apply PostScript within these areas. We've already discussed drawing within the page. You might use *squarePath* within a paragraph to create an interesting effect in this way:

```
.para.
/inch
   % Usage: number inch
   % Take: the number in inches to be converted to points
   % Return: the number converted to points
   { 72 mul } def

/squarePath   % Draws a one-inch square
   % Usage: xLeft yBottom size squarePath
   % Take: coordinates of lower left corner
   % Return: nothing
   {
   /size exch def          % Store first number on stack
                           %   in variable size
   newpath                 % Start new path
   moveto                  % Move to x and y coordinates on stack
   0 size rlineto          % Draw up size points
   size 0 rlineto          % Draw right size points
   0 size neg rlineto      % Draw down size points
   closepath               % Draw back to beginning of path
   }  def

0 setgray
0 inch 1.5 inch .5 inch squarePath fill
.25 setgray
.25 inch 1.25 inch .5 inch squarePath fill
.5 setgray
.5 inch 1 inch .5 inch squarePath fill
.75 setgray
.75 inch .75 inch .5 inch squarePath fill
```

Figure C-6
Using *squarePath* within the rectangle of the paragraph.

The paragraph in Figure C-6 containing the text was indented from the left margin and has 1 inch of Space After; all the x values are measured from the left margin of the paragraph, and all the y values are measured from the bottom of the Space After format. We added a Border Above format to the paragraph after the one the PostScript was applied to, providing a reference point. Notice that the squares were drawn behind the text; all PostScript on a page is drawn before any Word text is printed, regardless of where on the page it is placed or which drawing rectangle it applies to.

Applying PostScript to graphic frames is similar to applying it to pages and paragraphs, but there is one difference. To draw on a page, put the code anywhere on that page. If you want to draw within the rectangle of a paragraph, put the code immediately before that paragraph. If, however, you want to draw within a graphics frame that is itself within a paragraph, place the code before that paragraph. Also, if there is more than one graphics frame in the paragraph, you can apply PostScript to each in sequence by preceding each group of PostScript operators with a *.pic.* operator, as shown below. You can see the resulting output in Figure C-7.

```
.pic.         % graphics frame 1
/squarePath
   {/size exch def
   newpath moveto
   0 size rlineto size 0 rlineto 0 size neg rlineto
   closepath
   } def
0 setgray 0 0 9 squarePath fill
.pic.         % graphics frame 2
/squarePath
   {/size exch def
   newpath moveto
   0 size rlineto size 0 rlineto 0 size neg rlineto
   closepath
   } def
.25 setgray 9 9 9 squarePath fill
```

```
.pic.          % graphics frame 3
/squarePath
   {/size exch def
   newpath moveto
   0 size rlineto size 0 rlineto 0 size neg rlineto
   closepath
   } def
.5 setgray 18 18 9 squarePath fill
.pic.          % graphics frame 4
/squarePath
   {/size exch def
   newpath moveto
   0 size rlineto size 0 rlineto 0 size neg rlineto
   closepath
   } def
.75 setgray 27 27 9 squarePath fill
```

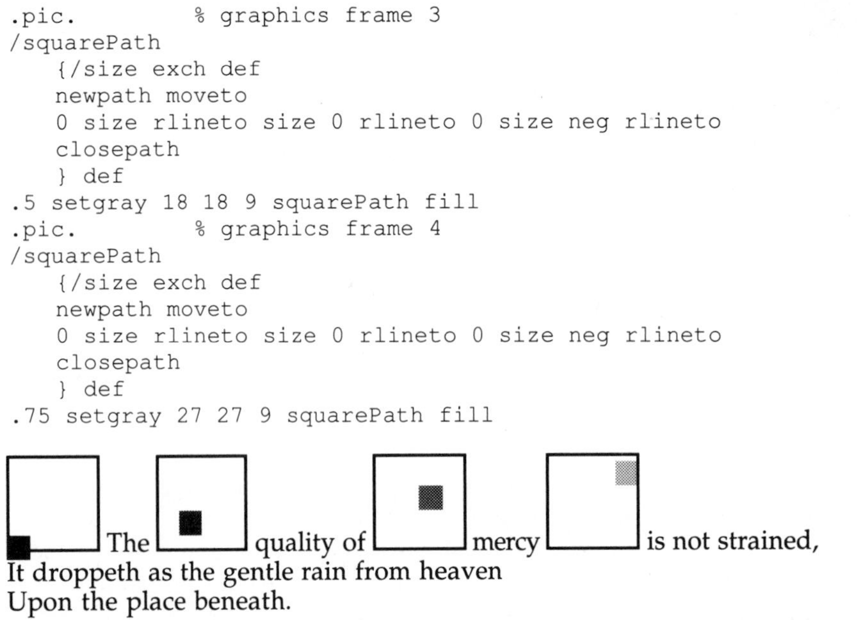

The quality of mercy is not strained,
It droppeth as the gentle rain from heaven
Upon the place beneath.

Figure C-7
Using *squarePath* within the rectangle of four graphic frames.

As you can see, you must repeat the definitions of every operator used for each instance; to shorten the resulting code, we reverted to the point system instead of using the *inch* operator. We also removed the comments and compacted the remaining code. Each graphics frame has the Outline attribute, so you can see the position of the squares relative to the frame.

When you apply PostScript to graphics frames, be sure to turn off Fractional Widths in the Print dialog box, because the actual spacing of text on the paper changes when this option is turned on, and Word cannot adjust for the difference. Also, PostScript placed with the *.pic.* operator appears in a slightly different position than the graphics frame itself. The graphics frame aligns on the baseline of the text, whereas the PostScript is placed relative to the descender of the text. You can see where the bottom will be placed when Show ¶ is on; regardless of the vertical placement of the graphics frame, the PostScript aligns with the bottom edge of the dotted outline that surrounds the frame.

Drawing Rectangles and Clipping

Word's drawing rectangles have an additional property that can be both a help and a hindrance, depending on the effect you want to achieve. Whenever you draw within one of Word's three types of drawing rectangles, the images drawn on the page are limited to the edges of that rectangle. The edges of the rectangle within which your commands are drawn is often called its *bounding box*. The path of the box that clips the image beyond its borders is called its *clipping path.*

This behavior is useful when you want to limit, for example, the extent of a PostScript effect you're adding to a certain paragraph. But what do you do if you want to draw something immediately outside a paragraph? For example, if you want to place a shaded square to the left of a paragraph by using the *squarePath* operator described earlier, you might use code such as the following:

```
.para.
/inch { 72 mul } def
/squarePath
   {/size exch def
   newpath moveto
   0 size rlineto size 0 rlineto 0 size neg rlineto
   closepath
   } def

.5 setgray
-1 inch 0 inch .25 inch squarePath
```

The last line in this code will start the lower left corner of the square one inch to the left of the left indent. Because the width of the square is 0.25 inches, the square is positioned outside the paragraph's clipping path.

You can empty the clipping path that Word automatically attaches to the drawing rectangle for the region associated with a group of PostScript commands by using the *initclip* operator. This reinitializes the clipping path, allowing you to draw anywhere on the page relative to the lower left corner of the drawing rectangle you've specified. To draw the square in the last example correctly, you would use code such as this:

```
.para.
/inch { 72 mul } def
/squarePath
   {/size exch def
   newpath moveto
   0 size rlineto size 0 rlineto 0 size neg rlineto
   closepath
   } def

initclip
.5 setgray
-1 inch 0 inch .25 inch squarePath
```

Word's Variables

Word makes it easier to position PostScript effects relative to the current drawing rectangle by passing certain variables to the PostScript printer before each group of code you place in a document. Some of these variables contain the same contents regardless of which drawing rectangle is being used, and some change. The following is a table of these variables:

Variable	Type and unit	Applies to	Contains
Variables that remain constant for all drawing rectangles			
wp$page	string	all	Current page number in the format set in the Section dialog box.
wp$page	number	all	Current page number.
wp$date	string	all	Current date.
wp$time	string	all	Current time.
Variables that change depending on the drawing rectangle specified			
wp$box	path	all	Defines a path containing the current drawing rectangle.
wp$x	number in points	all	Height of the drawing rectangle.
wp$y	number in points	all	Width of the drawing rectangle.
wp$top	number in points	*.page.*	Top margin.
		.para.	Space Before value.
wp$bottom	number in points	*.page.*	Bottom margin.
		.para.	Space After value.
wp$left	number in points	*.page.*	Left margin, including the gutter, if any.
		.para.	Distance between left margin and left indent.
wp$right	number in points	*.page.*	Right margin, including the gutter, if any.
		.para.	Distance between right margin and right indent.
wp$col	number	*.page.* only	Number of columns.
wp$xcol	number in points	*.page.* only	Width of each column.
wp$xcolb	number in points	*.page.* only	Space between columns.

Notice that in the second section of the table the four entries *wptop, wpbottom, wp$left,* and *wp$right* contain measurements that are defined for either pages or paragraphs, but not graphic frames. Using a variable in a group of code for an area in which the variable isn't defined creates an error.

Let's look at a few examples of how you might use these variables in your PostScript code. If you want to put a gray box behind the text in a paragraph, as we've done with the tip design elements in this book, use this code:

```
.para. .9 setgray wp$box fill
```

Here, the *wp$box* variable defines a path for the *fill* operator, in much the same way that we used the *squarePath* operator above.

If you want to draw a box around a paragraph, use this code:

```
.para. wp$box stroke
```

This produces an effect much like using the Box Border paragraph format. However, whereas the Box format does not take into account the Space before and Space After values, the PostScript version does. If you want to change the width of the line used to draw the box, use the *setlinewidth* operator, which takes a value in points:

```
.para. .5 setlinewidth wp$box stroke
```

Finally, if you want to draw a half-point line around a paragraph that takes into account both the Space Before and Space After formats and starts at the margins rather than at the left and right indents, you might use code such as this:

```
.para.
initclip                        % Reset the clipping path
.5 setlinewidth                 % Draw half-point wide lines
newpath                         % Start a new path
wp$left neg 0 moveto            % Move to first point
wp$left neg wp$y lineto         % Draw left side of box
wp$x wp$right add wp$y lineto % Draw top of box
wp$x wp$right add 0 lineto      % Draw right side of box
closepath                       % Return to beginning
stroke                          % Draw the path as a series of lines
```

The possibilities for PostScript in your Word documents are limitless, and this book can only hint at the range of the effects you can produce. The two books cited at the beginning of the chapter are great aides for extending your knowledge of PostScript.

■ *Adding PostScript Operators to Word*

You can add your own PostScript operators to Word by modifying the Word program itself. This is not difficult, but you should take a few preliminary steps. First, make a copy of Word to use in your experiments. Next, find the SerialPrinter driver file; if it isn't in your System Folder already, copy it there from the Word Utilities disk.

If you're using a hard disk, put a copy of ResEdit on the hard disk. If you're using floppies, put a copy of the ResEdit program on the startup disk. The 1.1b3 version of the program is about 170 KB, so you may have to remove or rearrange some files to get the System Folder, the SerialPrinter driver, and Word to fit on one or two disks.

Finally, you'll need the definitions for the PostScript operators you want to add to Word. For this example, suppose you've developed the following code, inventing two new operators. The PostScript in boldface contains the operators you want to add.

```
.para.
/inch
    % Usage: num inches
    % Take: a number in inches
    % Return: the number converted to points
    { 72 mul } def

/grayBoxFill
    % Usage: num grayBoxFill
    % Take: the graylevel, from 0 (black) to 1 (white)
    % Return: nothing
    {
      setgray                  % Takes the graylevel from the stack
      wp$box fill              % Fills the path with that graylevel
    } def
.5 grayBoxFill
0 setgray
0 0 moveto 2 inch 1 inch lineto stroke
```

A good way to go about developing this code is to first write and debug it as text given the *PostScript* style in a Word document. When everything works the way you want, select and copy every line of the code between the *.para.* operator and the commands that execute the operators you've defined. Then paste them into the Scrapbook where they will remain until needed. Also, save the Word document you used to develop the code so that you can make further refinements later.

1. Start ResEdit. You'll see a small window for each volume you have open, as in Figure C-8.

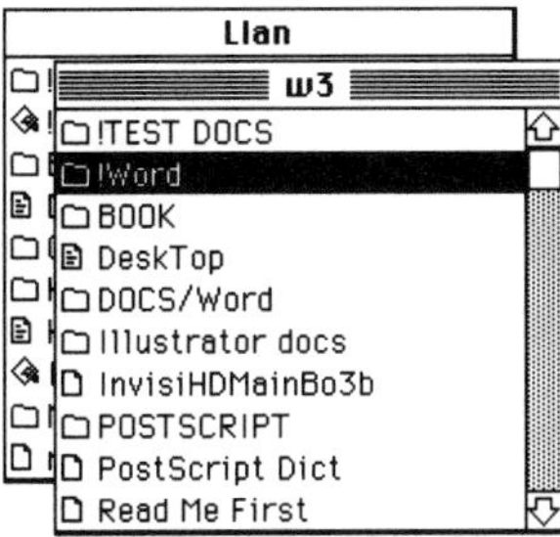

Figure C-8
The windows you see when you first launch ResEdit, one for each volume.

2. Click on the window of the startup volume to bring it to the front. Find the entry for the System Folder and double-click on its name. Another window opens, listing all the files in the System Folder.
3. Find and double-click on the entry for the SerialPrinter driver. Another window opens, listing the file's resources, as shown in Figure C-9.

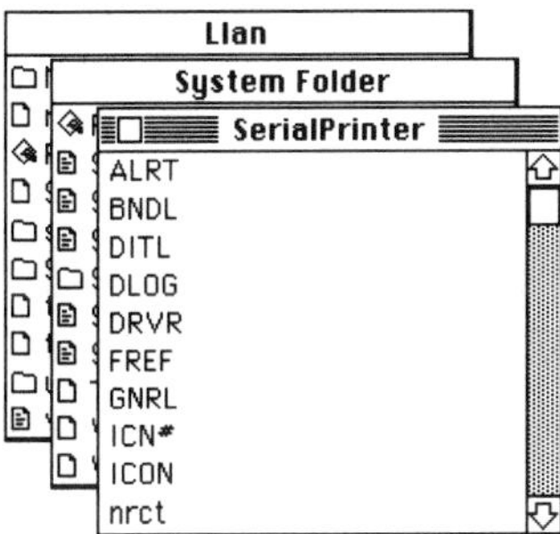

Figure C-9
The window listing all the resources of the SerialPrinter file.

4. Find and double-click the entry containing the SerialPrinter driver's PREC resources. Yet another window opens, listing the file's PREC resources, as shown in Figure C-10. Close the window.

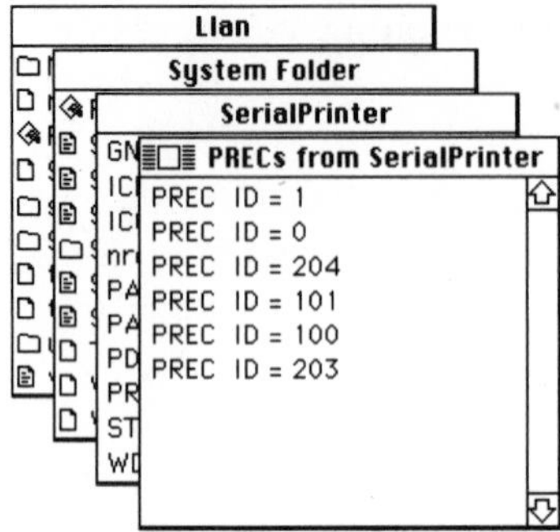

Figure C-10
The window showing all the PREC resources of the SerialPrinter file.

5. The PREC entry in the window labeled *SerialPrinter* should still be selected. If not, select it and choose Copy from the Edit menu to copy all the PREC resources to the Clipboard.
6. Close all windows of the SerialPrinter driver by clicking the close boxes of the windows labeled *PRECs from SerialPrinter* and *SerialPrinter.*

Now that copies of the SerialPrinter driver's PREC resources are on the Clipboard, the next step is to paste them into Word and transform PREC 101 into a PREC 103 resource containing the PostScript operators you want to add to the Word program.

1. Double-click the entry for the copy of Word you made. The window that opens looks like Figure C-11. If you scroll down the list of the Word resources, you'll see that Word doesn't have an entry for PREC resources.

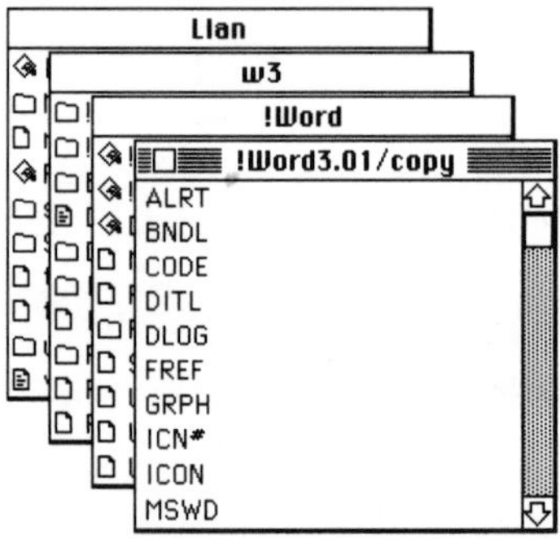

Figure C-11
The window listing all the resources of Word.

2. Choose Paste from the Edit menu to paste the SerialPrinter's resources into Word. If you scroll through Word's resources now, you'll see a new entry for the PREC resources. Open the PREC resources by double-clicking on its entry.

❸ Remove each PREC resource except PREC 101 by selecting it and choosing Clear from the Edit menu. When you are done, only the entry for PREC 101 should remain.

❹ Find and double-click on the entry for PREC 101 to see what it contains. Another window opens, as shown in Figure C-12, displaying the contents of the resource in both hexadecimal and text format. (We'll change both the ID number and the contents of the resource next.)

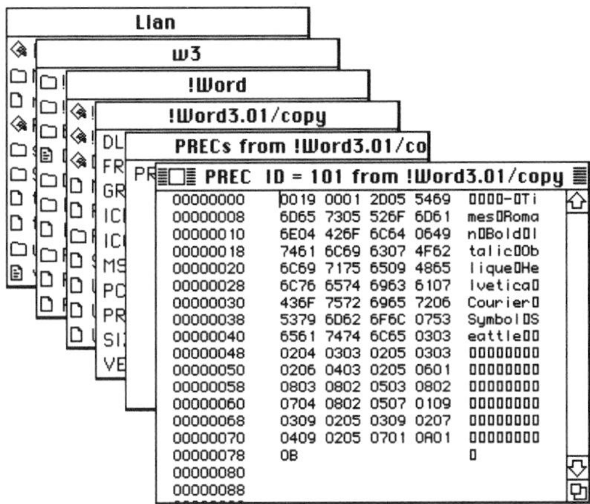

Figure C-12
The SerialPrinter driver's PREC 101 resource, in both hexadecimal and text format.

❺ Select all the text in the text area of the resource by dragging from just before the first character to beyond the last character, as shown in Figure C-13. Choose Clear to delete the text, leaving only the insertion point.

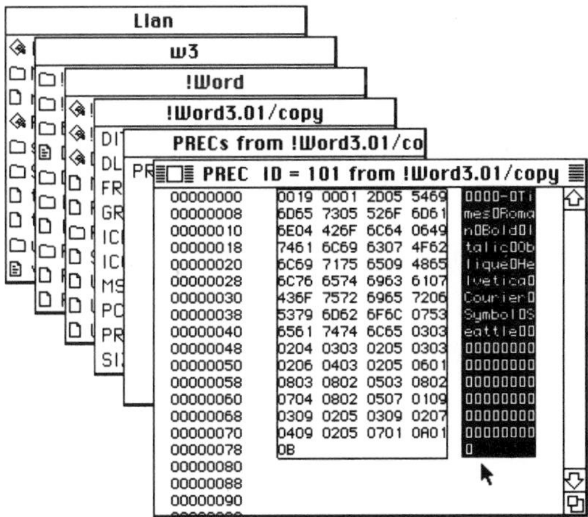

Figure C-13
How the PREC 101 window looks after selecting all its text.

❻ Copy the PostScript code from the Scrapbook where you pasted it earlier. Paste it into the PREC 101 window at the insertion point. The window should now look like Figure C-14. Close the window for the PREC resource by clicking its close box.

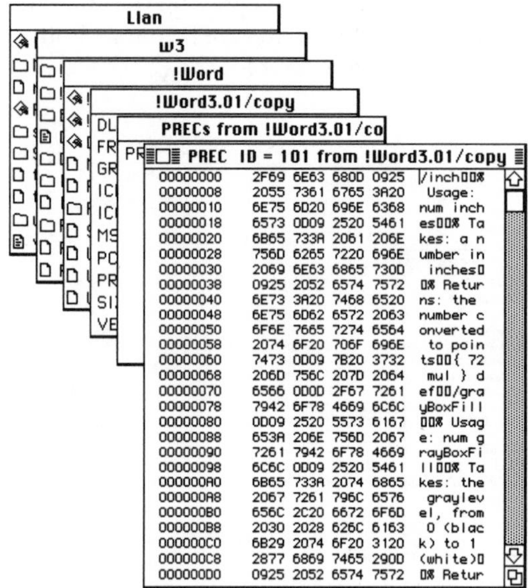

Figure C-14
The PREC 101 resource after pasting in the PostScript code.

❼ Finally, change its ID number from 101 to 103 by selecting PREC 101 and choosing Get Info. The ID edit field should contain *101;* change this to *103.* Close the Get Info dialog box by clicking its close box.

❽ Quit ResEdit. A dialog box appears asking if you want to save the edited copy of Word. Click Yes.

To verify that you've successfully added new PostScript commands to Word, start the copy of Word to which you've added the PREC 103 resource, and enter the same PostScript code as before, but this time leave out the definitions for the commands you've added:

```
.para.
.5 grayBoxFill
0 setgray
0 0 moveto 2 inch 1 inch lineto stroke
```

If the operators you've added don't work correctly or don't seem to work at all, try the following suggestions:

- Be sure you've fully debugged the code in the Word document you first used to develop the code.
- Even though you've moved the definitions for the new PostScript commands into the PREC 103 resource, you still need to precede each group of PostScript code in your document that uses the commands with a *.page.*, *.para.*, or *.pic.* operator. If you don't use one, *.page.* is assumed.
- Make the first block of code in the PREC 103 resource an *error dictionary,* which you can get from user groups, CompuServe, or from some software packages that support PostScript, such as Cricket Draw. The various forms of these error dictionaries can report certain types of errors, such as the following: when an operator needs more values on the stack to work properly; when a procedure generates so many entries on the stack that the stack overflows; or when a value on the stack is not in the form the operator needs (for example, a character string instead of a number).

Mathematical Typesetting

If you work with mathematical formulas frequently, you'll appreciate Word's math typesetting feature. However, it is a feature that requires study and a fair amount of practice to master, because it diverges from the philosophy of What You See Is What You Get. To use this feature, you encode mathemetical terms in a special language instead of entering text and arranging the terms with the mouse. For example, to express the equation for the length of the hypotenuse of a right triangle, you could create an equation such as this:

$$r = \sqrt{x^2 + y^2}$$

It's easy to superscript the number 2 in this example and to change the point size from 9 to 8. But how do you create the square root, or radical, symbol? For effects like this, you must use the math typesetting feature. The same equation expressed in math typesetting code looks like this:

r = .\R(x^2 + y^2)

This equation has only one component that isn't part of the text of the formula: the backslash with a dot under it, called the *formula character*, and the capital *R* that follows it. The *R* command draws a radical around whatever is enclosed in the parentheses. Word's typesetting commands typically use one or more *arguments,* listed inside parentheses; in the example above, the text $x^2 + y^2$ is an argument used by the *R* command. You can format the contents of an argument as you would any other text in Word.

You enter the formula character by pressing Option-Command-\. You must have Show ¶ on, or you will see only a normal backslash. Each typesetting command begins with.\ and a letter specifying the command. After you construct the formula, press Command-Y again to turn Show ¶ off. Word converts the typesetting codes into the actual formula; the formula characters, typesetting codes, and the parentheses surrounding the arguments disappear. You can select parts of the formula to format when Show ¶ is off, but remember that the placement of the parts is determined by the typesetting codes and not by Word's standard routines for arranging text, so the results can be unpredictable. Do all your formatting and editing within the typesetting code, when Show ¶ is on, or format an entire line containing the formula at once.

Most of the typesetting commands have options that alter their effects. You enter an option immediately after a command and precede each option with the formula character. For example, if you want to draw brackets around the name of a variable, you might use typesetting code such as this:

```
.\B.\BC.\{(X)
```

to create this:

{X}

Some additional points to remember:

- ❑ When typesetting formulas, avoid putting a negative sign in front of the Line Spacing measurement in the Paragraph dialog box, because this may cause parts of a formula that extend beyond the limits of the line spacing to be cut off. Often, however, the text will reappear when the document is printed.
- ❑ Use a glossary to store fragments of formulas. Give each entry a name you can remember. Select only the fragment you want to record, not an ending paragraph mark, for instance, because you want the fragment inserted from the glossary to take on the character and paragraph formats of the surrounding text. When you insert the glossary item, use it as a template, replacing its parts as needed.
- ❑ You can use many of the characters in the Symbol font to represent special characters in formulas. For example, to get the symbol for pi (π), switch to the Symbol font and type the letter *p*. A special key sequence exists for using the Symbol font: Press Shift-Command-Q, and the next letter you type will be in the Symbol font. Text you enter after the first character returns to the base character format for the style.

- Often, it's easier to use Word's standard character formatting features to create an effect, rather than construct complex arrangements of typesetting code. For example, you can superscript by using the *S* command, but you can also simply superscript by using the Character command.
- Once you create a formula, you can prevent changes to it. To do this, select the formula, press Option-Command-D to copy an image of the selection to the Clipboard as a PICT graphic, and paste the image over the original selection. Or, you can keep the original formula in a separate place, and transfer only the finished image of the formula to the main document. Also, you can transfer images of formulas to programs other than Word by copying the PICT version and pasting it into a document opened from within the other application.
- If you rarely need to create formulas, remember that you can create the image of a formula as an arrangement of text objects in an object-oriented drawing program such as MacDraw and then copy the image into Word.
- You can also use the typesetting commands to create other effects besides mathematical formulas. For example, you can position characters with the D, or Displace, command, as shown below.

The codes and options for each command and some examples showing their use are listed below:

A, Array

The A command creates a two-dimensional array from a series of arguments.

Usage .\A.*options*(*argument1*, ...)

Options

AL, AR, AC	Alignment: left, right, or centered.
CO*n*	Formats for *n* columns.
VS*n*	Sets line spacing to *n* points.
HS*n*	Sets column spacing to *n* points.

Examples

$$\begin{pmatrix} 1\,2\,3 \\ 4\,5\,6 \\ 7\,8\,9 \end{pmatrix}$$

Draw a 3-by-3 matrix.

.\B.\BC.\((.\A.\AC.\CO3(.\S.\AI4(1),.\S.\AI4(2),.\S.\AI4(3), 4, 5, 6 , 7, 8, 9))

$$\begin{bmatrix} x_{11} & \cdots & x_{1n} \\ \cdot & & \cdot \\ \cdot & & \cdot \\ \cdot & & \cdot \\ x_{n1} & \cdots & x_{nn} \end{bmatrix}$$

Create an *n*-by-*n* array.

.\B.\BC.\[(.\A.\AC.\CO5(x.\S.\DO3(11) , ., ., ., x.\S.\DO3(1n) , . , , , , . , . , , , , . , . , , , , . , x.\S.\DO3(n1), ., ., ., x.\S.\DO3(nn)))

B, Brackets

The B command places brackets on one or both sides of an argument.

Usage \B*options*(*argument*)

Options LC*c*, RC*c*, BC*c* Sets brackets on left, right, or both sides with character *c*. If *c* is {, [, (, or <, the corresponding closing character is used on the right side.

Example

| f(x) | Absolute value of f(x).

\B\BC\ | (f(x))

D, Displace

The D command positions the next character horizontally. It doesn't take an argument, but you must supply the parentheses anyway.

Usage \D*options*()

Options FOn, BAn Moves to the right (FO) or to the left (BA) *n* points.

LI Draws a line from the end of the preceding character to the starting position of the next character.

Examples

X Y Draw *Y* 30 points to the right of *X*.

X\D\FO30()Y

Y X Draw *Y* 40 points to the left of *X*.

X\D\BA40()Y

F, Fraction

The F command creates a fraction from two arguments (numerator and denominator) centered above and below the line.

Usage \F(*argument1*, *argument2*)

Example

$\frac{a + b}{c + d}$ Fraction *a* + *b* over *c* + *d*.

\F(a + b,c + d)

I, Integral

The I command creates an integral from three arguments: The
lower limit; the second sets the upper limit; the third sets the inte

Usage \I*options*(*argument1*, *argument2*, *argument3*)

Options

SU, PR — Changes the integral symbol to a summ symbol (SU) or the product symbol (PR

IN — Inline format, with the limits printed to the right of the symbol.

FC*c*, VC*c* — Changes the integral symbol to *c*. FC creates a fixed-height character, and VC creates a variable-height character that matches the height of the integrand.

Examples

$$\int_a^b f \, d\alpha$$

Integral of *f* from *a* to *b*.

\I\IN (\S\DO5(a),\S\UP15(b),*f*) dα

The symbol α is the letter *a* in 14-point Symbol font.

$$\prod_{i=1}^{n} x_i$$

Product of x_i from 1 to n.

\I\PR (i =1,n, x \S\DO3(i))

L, List

The L command creates a list of values from any number of arguments, without requiring the use of \ before each value.

Usage \L(*argument1*, ...)

R, Radical

The R command draws a radical symbol. If one argument is supplied, it appears under the radical. If two arguments are supplied, the first appears over the radical.

Usage \R(*argument1*, *argument2*)

Examples

$\sqrt{x}$

Square root of x.

\R(x)

$\sqrt[n]{x}$

Nth root of x.

\R(n, x)

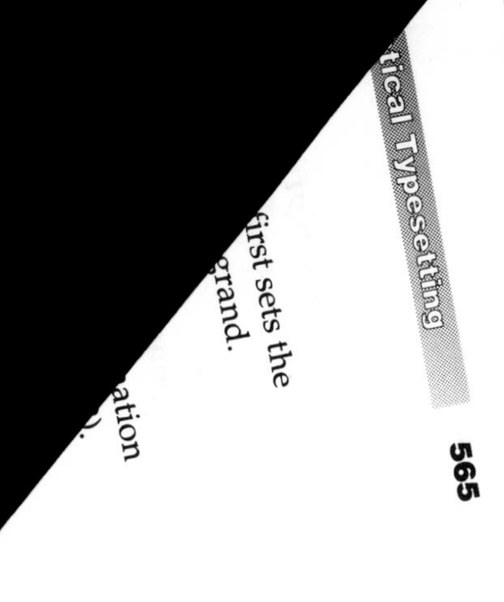

y one or more arguments.

2, ...)

ves the argument up or down *n* points.

s space in points above the ascender or ow the descender of the argument. You use this with the X command to adjust cing around bordered elements. These ons are affected by "negative" line ng measurements.

Function *f* sub 1.

f\S\DO3(1)

The subscript is in 7-point Palatino font.

O, Overstrike

The O command draws arguments over each other, in the order given by the arguments.

Usage \O(*argument1*, *argument2*, ...)

Options AL, AR, AC — Aligns the characters on their left or right edges, or centers them (the default option).

Example

\ — Simulate the formula character.

\O\AL(.,\)

X, Box

The X command draws borders around an argument. If you don't supply an option, it draws borders on all four sides.

Usage \X(*argument*)

Options

TO	Top border.
BO	Bottom border.
LE	Left border.
RI	Right border.

Example

abc — Draw a box around *abc*.

\x(abc)

Index

, (commas, in transferred data) 409
. (period) 124
: (index subentries) 378
< > (numerical values in data fields) 457
? (wildcard search) 100
^ (search for special characters) 100–101, 102

■ A

accent marks. *See* diacritical marks
Access, transferring text from MacTerminal to 412
Adobe Systems 353, 423
Again command
  applying styles with 250
  changing Ruler paragraph formats with 226
  editing with 105, 114
Alarm Clock 301
alignment
  icons 230
  paragraph 10–11, 58, 212
All Caps 175–76
  ignoring words in 147
Always Convert Clipboard option 439
anchor point 94
AND logical operator 458
Apple Font/DA Mover 168, 521
AppleTalk 346, 411
ASCII codes and characters 91, 414
  finding 102–3
  finding footnote characters with 310
  saving as 111
  sorting sequence for Palatino font 395
  table for six Macintosh fonts 527–36
ASK instruction 462–63, 470
automatic styles 240. *See also Normal* style
  footnote text 309
  formats for 255
  redefining 254–56
auto numbering 13, 224

■ B

Backspace key 18, 92, 192
Based On field in style definition 256–62
Beneath Text option *315*, 320
Best print option 349, *350*
bit-mapped graphics 419–20
  fonts 353
  scaled *432*
blueprints. *see* Template(s)
body text
  demoting outline topics to 67–68
  entering, in Outline view 74
  looking at, with Promote 68
  overlapping headers with *298*
boilerplate 7
boldface character attribute 41, 174–75, 188
borders, 213–16, 231
  special effect tips 215–16
Bottom of Page option *315*, 316, 320
bounding box 538, 551
boxes 213–15
  around tables 390, *391*, 402
  created from graphics frame *435*
  creating, around a paragraph group 435, *436*
  creating boxed text from formatted text 438
bulleted lists 199

■ C

calculate command 397
Cancel button 104, 346
capital letters
  capitalizing text 175–76
  drop caps 222–23
  skipping, in hypenation 338
.c. codes, generating tables of contents with 371–73
center text 32
chaining files 333–34
Change command 409
  dialog box *99*
change text 99–100, 101–3, 119–20
character(s)
  ASCII codes and 91, 529–37
  changing attributes (*see* character formats)
  graphics (*see* graphics)
  hyphens, dashes and spaces 89–90, 115–16
  position 166, 188
    changing 177-78
    undoing formats 174
  removing undefined, from imported text files 103
  search for/replace special 100–101
  special font 87–89, 115
  string 98
  table of character sets 527–36
Character command dialog box *167*, 184–85
  choosing fonts from 168
  choosing font size from 172
  testing new character formats from 182–83
character formats 9, 24, 31, 41, 163–89. *See also* style(s); style sheets
  applying styles and preexisting 251–52
  document design overview 164–66
    four format domains 165–66
  keyboard shortcuts 187–89
  points to remember 184
  subtracting/resetting, from styles 263
  techniques summary 184–87
  undoing 174
  working with 166–83
    changing character attributes 173–77, 188
    changing fonts 168–70
    changing font size 171–72
    changing text position 177–78
    changing text spacing 178–81
    removing character formats 182
    testing new character formats 182–83

Chooser 356
  dialog box *325*
Clipboard
  automating footnote entry with 309–10
  copy/move text with 95, 117
  cut/copy styles to 254
  transferring data with 406–8, 421, 437–38, 442
  viewing contents of 96, 114
clipping path 550–51
Clock icon 301
codes, hidden
  generating indexes with 376
  generating tables of contents with 371–73
Collapse icon 68
column(s) 13, 278, 285–89, 293, 401
  newsletter 287–89
  tables constructed from side-by-side 399–400
column balancing 285
command(s)
  choosing, with period key 124
  defining a new style with 245
  repeating (*see* Again command)
  undoing/canceling 104 (*see also* Cancel button; Command-(period); Undo command)
  user-defined 86–87, 114–16, *462*
Command- . 97, 104
Command- ~ 90, 335
Command- – 90, 335
Command-A 105
Command-F 543
Command-K 543
Command-U 73, 74
CompuServe 405
conditions tested on fields 459, 461
control characters 528
Control Panel 80–81
CONVWS program 416
Copies option 348
Copy command
  copy/move text with 95–96
  transferring formats between styles with 253–54
copying character/paragraph formats 227
copying graphics 427–29
copying text 95–98, 117, 266
Copy To command 96–98
Courier font character set 527–36
Cover Page option 354
Cricket Draw 351, 405, 420, 421, 424, 477
  copying graphics with *425*, *427*, 429
cropping box 427
cropping graphics 430, *431*
current glossary 134
  clearing 135–36
  combining/extracting entries 137–38
  opening 136–37
  printing 138–39
Cut command
  copy/move text with 95–96
  tabular data 387–89
  transferring formats between styles with 253–54

■ D

daisy-wheel printers. *See* serial printers
dashes 89–90. *See also* hyphenation
database managers, transferring data from 409–10
data document (merge print) 447, 448–50, 469
  header record 450
  special cases 449–50
  using graphics in 452
DATA instruction 451–52, 471
DATA type code *407*, 421, 424
date. *See* time and date
default settings 81–83
Define Styles 40, 47
  Based On field 256–63
  dialog box *41*, *244*, 268–69
  in outlines 69
  using to assign styles 247
Delete key 18
delete text 123. *See also* editing text
Demote icon 64–65
Demote to Body Text icon 67–68
descender 208
diacritical marks 88, 115, 528
  character sets for 528, 532–36
DIALOG 405
dialog boxes
  navigating in 124
  window placement default 82
dictionary. *See* error dictionary; Main Dictionary; personal dictionary
disk(s), backup copies 110-11, 122
disk caching 85
Display As Printed option 357
display font 172, *258*
DisplayWriter 416
document(s)
  converting a dictionary to a 156–57
  creating a styles work area in 246
  creating a two-page 35–59
  dividing into sections 276–77
  format (*see* document formatting)
  header 452
  merging (*see* merge printing)
  placing footnotes in 314–16
  printing (*see* printing text)
  tables and lists in (*see* lists; tables)
  transferring text 410–18
  using INCLUDE to assemble new 465
Document Content Architecture (DCA) format 416
document design 164–66, 508–15. *See also* formatting text
document formatting 13, 166, 323–66
  choosing a printer 325–27
  hyphens (*see* hyphenation)
  Page Setup command (*see* Page Setup command)
  points to remember 358–59
  repagination/page breaks/page layout 340–46
  techniques summary 359–64

Document view window *4*
  columns in 285
  outline in *40*
  page breaks inserted in 363–64
  placing page numbers, time/date in 302
  side-by-side paragraph in *219*
  switching outlines to, for graphics template 490
dot-matrix printers. *See* serial printers
Draft print option *350*
drawing rectangle 548. See also bounding box
drop caps 222, *223*, 504–5

■ E

editing text 7–8, 19–23, 45–47, 91–109
  adding paragraphs 20
  copying/moving text 95–98
  editing words 20–21
  error checking 22–23
  finding/changing text 98–103
  glossary entries 132–34
  moving paragraphs 21–22
  navigating in documents 105-9
  in outlines 38–39
  personal dictionary and 45–47
  points to remember 113
  tables of contents 373
  technique summary 30–31, 114–22
  using outlines for 73–74
  using Undo/Again commands for 103-5
ELSE instruction, used within IF instruction 458, *459*, 470
en (–) and em (—) dashes 90, 116, 336
ENDIF instruction 456, 470
  avoiding extra lines with *467*
Endnotes option 316, 320, 332
entering text 6–7, 18, 36–45, 79–91. *See also* editing text
  automatically (*see* glossaries)
  body of the document 42–45
  character features and 87–91
  customizing Word 80–87
  outlining 36–40
  points to remember 113
  techniques summary 114–16
  using styles 40–42
Enter key. *See* Return key
EPSF (Encapsulated PostScript File) format 423–25
error checking 22–23. *See also* Spelling checker
error dictionary 543, 559
Even Page option 278–79, 340
Expand icon 68

■ F

Facing Pages option 330–31, *332*
Faster print option *350*
Fast Save 110, 122
  when not to use 110
FID (font ID) numbers 169–70, 415
field(s)
  checking for text in, with IF 454–55
  conditions tested on 459
  data document 449
  formatting 466–68
  inserted into main documents 451
  matching numbers in 457
  matching text in 456
field name 462
file(s)
  chaining 333–34
  cleaning up imported 103, 417–18
  how Word finds 525
  saving in different formats 111–12, 122–23
  transferring (*see* transferring graphics; transferring text)
file formats 111, *112*, 122–23
filenames 109-10
Find dialog box *98*
find text 98–99, 101–3, 118–20
first page
  headers/footers on 284, 299–302
  multiple-column newsletter 502–5
First Page Special 479
  headers/footers with, 284, 299, 502
Flip Horizontal option 355
Flip Vertical option 355
font(s) 9, 58, 166. See also character(s); character formats
  bit-mapped (screen) 353
  changing 31, 168–70
    keyboard shortcuts 187
  character sets for 527–37
  ID numbers 169–70, 415
  kerning (*see* Kerning)
  LaserWriter 351, 352–53, 527
  monospace 178
  proportional 178
  scaled *171*
  special font characters 87–89 (*see also* Appendix B)
Font menu
  choosing fonts from 168–69
  choosing font size from 172
  default 83
Font Name list box 168
Fontographer 88, 353
font size 9, 165, 166
  changing 171–72, 188
font style (character attribute) 9, 24, 165, 166
Font Substitution option 354
footers 240, 284, 295–96
  adding page numbers/time-date stamp 300–302
  adjusting from Page Preview 345, 363
  creating first page 299–302
  creating standard 297–98
  formatting 299–300
  newsletter 502–3, 506–8
  with page numbers 50–*51*, 59
  points to remember 317
  positioning 306–7
  techniques summary 317–19
footer style 299

footnote(s) 284–85, 295–96, 307–14
automatic style and references to 256
automating entry of 309–10
changing references format 312
creating 308–9
deleting 312
editing/changing format of 311–12
editing footnote separators 312–14
find/change text in 120
finding special footnote characters 310
numbering 333
Page Setup options for 332–33
placing in documents 314–16, 332–33
points to remember 317
speeding up entry of 309
techniques summary 319–21
Footnote dialog box *308*, 319
Footnote Reference Mark 308
footnote reference style 311, 312, 320
Footnotes At option group 314, 315, 332
Footnote Separator window *313*–14
formats in 314, 321
footnote text style 311, 312
format(s)
changing outline 69
domains 8, 9–13, 165–66
footnote 308–9, 311–12
within glossary entries 130–32
graphics 425–30
index *376*, *377*, 379–80
saving in different 111–12
table of contents 373
tabular data 385–89
text (*see* formatting text)
Format menu 169
adding paragraph formats to 196
adding position and spacing to 181
adding Show Hidden Text to 177
default 83
formatting text 8–13, 24–25, 47–51
character (*see* character formats)
display/hide marks 9, 31
document (*see* document formatting)
footers (*see* footers)
headers (*see* headers)
merge print fields 466–68
paragraph (*see* paragraph formats)
sections (*see* section Formats)
techniques summary 31–32
WYSIWYG user interface 9
form letter. *See* merge printing
formulas
constructing/using 398–99
math 561-66
Fractional Widths option 354
FreeHand 514
Full Menus 4, *5*, 421
FullPaint 419

■ G

Geneva font character set 527–36
Get Info, locking templates in 479
glossaries 7, 125–43
anatomy of 126–27
creating entries for 127–28, 140
dialog box *128*
formats within entries 130–32
formatting paragraph entries 227
inserting entries into 128–32, 141
using the mouse 128–29
using the keyboard 129
using the Work menu 130
inserting styles with 266–67
modifying entries 132–34, 141–42
changing entry names 133
deleting 134
editing 133
opening as a document 131–32
points to remember 140
storing formatted text in 408
techniques summary 140–43
working with glossary files 134–39, 142–43
clearing current glossary 135–36
combining/extracting entries 137–38
moving groups of entries 138
opening a glossary 136–37
printing current glossary 138–39, 348
Glossary command, choosing 128–29
Go Back key 106
Go To command 105–6
graphics
bit-mapped 419–20, 353, *432*
boilerplate 7
caption 505–*6*
characters 88, *89* (*see also* Appendix B)
cropping 430–*31*
in data documents 452
editing, in glossaries 133
exporting 437-38
format of, and print quality 425–27
formatting 429–30
inserting, with INCLUDE 465
multiple, on one line 437
PICT graphic format 421–23
PostScript and EPSF formats 423–25
preparation of, for this book 513–14
QuickDraw object-oriented 420–21, 431–32, *432*
scaling *431*, *432*, 431–33
speed scrolling by hiding 430
template for presentation 490–95
transferring (*see* transferring graphics)
graphics frame
inserting a blank 433–34
using Fractional Widths 550
using PostScript with 548–49
gray level 540
gutters, facing pages with *303*, 330–31, *332*

■ H

hard return 91, *92*
header record 450
  using a separate document for 452
headers 13, 240, 284, 295–96
  adding page numbers/time-date stamp 300–302
  adjusting from Page Preview 345, 363
  creating different, for each section 304–6
  creating first page 299–302
  creating for facing pages 302–4
  creating standard 297–98
  empty 305
  find/change text in 120
  formats for footnote window separators in 314
  formatting 299–300
  keeping header windows open 298
  newsletter 502–3, 506–8
  null 305
  points to remember 317
  positioning 306–7
  techniques summary 317–19
header style 299, *300*
hidden text 146, 176–77
  merge instruction 468
  print 348
Hide ¶ command 17
horizontal lines in tables 390, 402
Hyphenate command 15, 334, 336–38
  dialog box *336*, *338*
hyphenation 15, *16*, 89–90, 334–39
  automatic 337
  searching for/removing 338–39
  skipping capitalized letters 338
  techniques summary 364
  types of hyphens *90*, 335–36
  using Hyphenation command 336–38
  verifying 337, *338*

■ I

IBM PC word processors 416
.i. codes, generating indexes with 376
IF instruction 454–59, 470
  checking for text in a field 454–55
  inserting text *455*
  matching numbers 457
  matching text 456
  nested 458
  using ELSE with 458–*59*
Illustrator 351, 405, 424, 429
ImageWriter 324
  choosing 325–26
  Print dialog box *27*, *349*, 365
  printing with 348–50
  screen resolution 426
Include Endnotes option 284, 314–15, 332
INCLUDE instruction 463–65, 471
  nested 465
  using to assemble new documents 465
indents 197–201
  automatic *10*
  checking special values for 201
  hanging 10, *199*
  first tab stops set by 205
  keyboard alteration of 238
  vs margins, 197, 330
  negative 199, *200*
  nested *198*
  Ruler markers 229
  setting, from the Paragraph dialog box 201
  setting, from the Ruler 200
  standard/normal *10*, *198*
  techniques summary 233–34
index 340
  creating 376–78
  dialog box *377*
  for linked files 381
  points to remember 382
  recompiling 380
  special formats 379–80
  styles for 379
  subentries 378–79
  techniques summary 383–84
insertion point 19, 167–68
  blinking 81
  moving back 106
  moving in outlines 77–78
instructions, print merge 451–52, 453–65, 470–71
  grouping 467
  hiding 468
  omitting closing bracket to save lines 467
Invert Image option 355
invoice, template for calculated 484–90
italic character attribute 41, 174–75, 188
  added manually *vs* in a style sheet *251*, 251–52

■ K

Keep Lines Together option 224, 232
Keep With Next ¶ option 224, 232, 324
kerning 179
  fonts 181
  pairs of letters 180
  tables, in Word 180
keyboard. *See also* keyboard shortcuts
  applying styles from 248–49
  changing, with Control Panel 80–81
  choosing fonts from 169–70
  choosing font size from 172
  inserting glossary entries with 129
  paragraph format alteration with 238
  Word characters not supplied on 87–91
Keyboard icon 80
keyboard shortcuts 33
  character formats 187–89
  entering/editing text 123–24
  outlines 77–78
  style sheet 273
Key Caps 88, 116

■ L

labels, mailing 460, 466, *468*
Larger Print Area option 356
Laser Prep file 325, 352, 521, 543
LaserWriter 88, 324, 419, 420, 508
  choosing 325–27
  Page Setup dialog box *355*, 355–56, 366
  print dialog box *354*, 366
  printing with 351–56
  screen resolution 426
layout
  page 340–46, 359–64
  paragraph 216–24, 236
letterhead 24, *25*
  electronic template for 476–79
letters, form. *See* merge printing
letterspacing 9
level 1 style 40, 41, 47, 48, 240, 258–60
level 2 style 42, 47, 48, 260
level 3 style 260
line(s)
  above and below text 215
  alignment 10–11
  automatic style line number 256
  controlling blank, in merge print fields 466
  horizontal, in tables 390, 402
  keeping together 224
  lengths, in ImageWriter *vs* LaserWriter 327
  moving outline 66–*67*
  numbering 13, 224, 282–83, 333, 495 (*see also* Renumber command)
  vertical, in tables 390, 402
Line Numbering option 224, 232, 282–83
  to number a list 392, 402
Line Numbers At option 333
line spacing 41, 206–9, 235
  icons 230
  measured from descender to descender 208–9
  setting from the Paragraph dialog box 207–8
  setting from the Ruler 206–7
Linotronic 300 Laser Imagesetter 351, 508
  resolution 426
lists 392–96
  creating, with Table of Contents feature 374
  Line Numbering to number 392
  points to remember 401
  Renumber to number 393–94, 402
  sorting 394–95
  techniques summary 401–3

■ M

MacDraw 405, 420
  Excel data altered in *423*, *428*
  using QuickSwitch with 440
Macintosh computer, setting up Word on 519–25
Macintosh screen resolution 426
MacPaint 405, 419, 421
  using QuickSwitch with 440
MacTerminal, transferring text to/from 412–13
MacWrite 405
  converting to Word 413
  data type code pasted into Scrapbook from *407*
  optional hyphens in *339*
  save in format of 111
Magnifier icon 343, 362
Magnifying Glass pointer 26
Main Dictionary 45–46, 146
  changing, to UK Dictionary 154
main document (merge print) 447, 469
  printing 452–53
  setting up 450–52
Make Backup option 110, 122
Manuscript (software) 416
margin(s) 26
  vs indents 197, 330
  in Page Preview mode *52*, 59, 344–45
  from Page Setup 330–31
    facing pages 330–31, *332*
    setting a fixed top/bottom 330, *331*
Margin Set icon 26
Margins icon 52, 343, *344*, 345, 363
mathematical calculations 396–99, 403
  addition 397
  constructing/using formulas 398–99
  on invoices (*see* Invoice, template for calculated)
  math operators 397–98
mathematical typesetting 561-66
memory-management options (Word Settings file), 83–85
menu(s)
  blinking 81
  customizing commands in 86–87, 114–16
merge printing *16*, 447–71
  formatting fields 466–68
  points to remember 469
  printing the document 452–53
  setting up a data document 448–50
  setting up a main document 450–52
  techniques summary 469–71
  using merge instructions 453–65, 470–71
merge style sheets 264–65, 272
Microsoft Chart 420, 428
Microsoft Excel 405, 409, 410, 420
  data transferred from 421, *422*, *428*
  using QuickSwitch with 439–40
Microsoft File 409
Microsoft Word 1.0 format, save as 111
Microsoft Word 1.05 411
Microsoft Word 3.0 3–6, 519–25
  customizing 80–87
    Control Panel 80–81
    menus 86–87
    Word Settings file 81–86
  how Word finds files 525
  MS-DOS format 411–13
  preparing working copies of 519–25
  techniques summary 30–32
  tutorial 16–28
  word-processing concepts and 6–16, 29
Microsoft Word (MS-DOS) format, save as 111

Microsoft Works 405, 411
mouse, Control Panel changes of 81
Mouse icon 81
mouse shortcuts 33
  entering/editing text 123–24
  outlines 77–78
Move Down icon 66–67, 74, 76
move text 95–98, 117–18
  in outlines 66–67, 74, 76
Move To command 96–98
Move Up icon 66–67, 74, 76
MS-DOS format
  data transfer 411–13
  save as 111
MultiFinder 439
MultiMate 416
Multiplan 409

■ N

New Column option 278
newline marks 192, *193*
  sidebar text effect with 214, *215*
New Page option 340
newsletters, multiple-column 287–89, 499–508
New York font character set 527–36
Next File option 333–34
NEXT instruction 459–61, 471
Next Style field 250–51
No Break option 278, *279*, 316
  columns and 285, *286*
No Gaps Between Pages option 350
Normal style *12*, 408
  in outlines 69
  paragraph format 194, 204
  redefining 243–45
  resetting a style to 254
  in screenplays 495
null header 305
numbered lists 199
numbered outlines 70–73, 76, 77

■ O

Odd Page option 278–79, 340
one-page display 26
One-Page Display icon 343, 362
Open command 525
Open Dictionaries 46, 150
Open First Header/First Footer 299
Open Header/Open Footer 297–98, 477
Operators, mathematical 397 (table), *398*. *See also* mathematical typesetting
Option-Command-+ 86, 174, 196
Option-Command-A 105, 225. See also Again command
Option-Command-C 96, 98
Option-Command-D 437, 438
Option-Command-Q 91, 103, 310, 527
Option-Command-R 225
Option-Command-Return 192
Option-Command-X 97, 98
Option-Command-Z 106
outline(s) 6, 36–38, 63–78
  changing format of text in 69
  converting a table of contents to 375–76
  creating/maintaining 64–69
    demoting topics to body text 67–68
    expanding/collapsing subtopics and text 68
    moving topics up/down 66–67
    setting levels, promoting/demoting topics 64–66
    showing all text 69
    showing levels by number 68–69
  editing 38–39
  generating a table of contents from 370–71
  icon bar *64*
  numbering 70–73
  points to remember 75
  printing 348
  techniques summary 57, 75–77
  using, as an editing tool 73–74
  using to create presentation graphics (*see* presentation graphics template)
outline character attribute 174–75, 188
Outline view *6*, *36*, *39*
  entering body text in 74

■ P

page(s)
  first (*see* first page)
  format techniques summary 59
  headers/footers for facing 302–4
  margins for facing 330–31
page break(s) 14, 324
  automatic 340
  manual/forced *53*
  in Page Preview *53*, 59, 341, 346, 363
  produced by repagination *50*, 340, *341*
Page Break Before option 224, 232, 324, 340
page-description language 423
PageMaker 110
page number(s) 15. *See also* Repagination
  added to header/footers 300–302
  adjusting from Page Preview 345, 363
  automatic style 256, 281
  duplicate 301
  footers with 50–51, 59
  placing in Document window 302
  specifying in the Section dialog box 279–82
  start at 333
Page Number icon 26, 51, 300–01, 343, 345, 362
page number style 240, 343
page offset 304
Page Preview command 14, 15, 20, 21, 26–28, 32, 51–53, 342–46
  columns in 285
  facing pages with gutters in *303*
  formatted columns in *400*
  Magnifier icon 343, 362
  margins from 52, 59, 343, 344–45

Page Preview command (continued)
  One-Page Display icon 343
  page breaks 52, *53*, 59, 341, 346
  page numbering in 279–80, 343, 345
  positioning headers/footers with 307
  repagination and 340–41
  techniques summary 362–63
  working in 344–46
Page Setup command 327–34
  chaining files 333–34
  changing default Tabs 203
  default 82
  default tab stops 332
  dialog box 323–24, *328*, 359–62
    LaserWriter *355–56*
  footnotes 314, 332–33
  margins set from 197, 330–31
  numbering page/line/footnote 333-34
  paper size/orientation options 328–29
  Shift-Page Setup to set ImageWriter 350
  widow control 332
Pages option 347
Page View icon 362
pagination. *See* page number(s)
Palatino font, ASCII sorting sequence 395
Paper Feed options 348
paper orientation/size/width/height 328, *329*
paragraph(s)
  adding 20
  assigning styles to 247–52
  creating 91–92
  creating boxes around a group of *435*
  moving in documents 21–22
  moving in outlines 74
  spacing icons 230
Paragraph command dialog box 195–96
  borders 213
  changing header/footer formats from 299
  choosing indents from 201
  setting line spacing from 207–9
  setting paragraph spacing from 210
  setting tabs stops from 204–5
  techniques summary 230–32
Paragraph formats 9–12, 41, 165, 191–238
  adding to the Format menu 196
  Again command to change Ruler 226
  alignment 10–11, 58, 212
  borders 213–16
  changing 193–96
  copying character and 227
  glossary entry 227
  indents 10, 197–201
  keyboard alteration of 238
  layout options 216–24, 236
  line spacing 206–9
  paragraph spacing 209–11
  points to remember 228–29
  search for/replace 225–26
  styles and style sheets 12
  subtracting/resetting from styles 263
  tabs 202–6
  techniques summary 229–37
  transferring 226–27
  working with *196*, 196–224, 232–33
Paste command
  copy/move text with 95, *96*
  tabular data 387–89
  transferring formats between styles with 253–54
path 539
Period key, choosing commands with 124
personal dictionary
  adding a word list to 154
  adding words to 149–50
  converting a non-Word to a Word 155–56
  converting to a document 156–57
  correcting words/adding to 150–51
  creating 45–47, 153
  moving words from one dictionary to another 152
  opening/closing 154
  removing words from 151
  saving 46–47, 152–53
  skipping past words 151
  techniques summary 59
photographs, digitizing 419
PICT data type code 421
PICT graphic format 421–23
pixels 178, 419
Plain Text *173*, 182
point size, change 31, 58
PostScript 88, 351, 352, 508, 514, 537–59
  adding to Word program 554–59
  code, shortening 550
  commands (*see* PostScript operators)
  coordinates 538
  defining new operators 541, 544
  defining variables in 544–47
  encoding graphics with 423–25
  error dictionaries in 543, 559
  errors in programs 542
  hiding commands of 176
  interpreter 538, 539
  measurements in 540
  saving document as 543
  special effects in 537
  stack 538
  syntax 537
  variables 552–53
PostScript operators
  % for comments 538
  .page. 539
  .para. 548
  .pic. 549
    alignment of PostScript with 550
    Fractional Widths option and 550
  add 538
  closepath 538, 540
  def 541
  div 538
  exch 547
  fill 540
  initclip 551
  lineto 538, 540

PostScript operators (continued)
moveto 538, 540
mul 538
neg 538, 546
newpath 538, 539–40
setgray 538, 540
stroke 538, 540
PostScript style 256, 539, 542
hidden character attribute in 539
Precision Bitmap Alignment option 355–56
Preferences command 357
dialog box *84*, 201
presentation graphics template 490–95
preparing 492–94
tips and techniques 494–95
preview text. *See* Page Preview command
Print Back to Front option 354
Print command dialog box 340, 346–47
Copies option 348
Pages options 347
Paper Feed options 348
Print Hidden Text option 348
techniques summary 365–66
printer, choosing a 325–27, 359. *See also* ImageWriter; LaserWriter; serial printers
print glossary 138–39
Print Hidden Text option 348
printing graphics, quality of, and graphic format 425–27
printing style sheet definitions 267
printing text 14–16, 26–28, 51–55, 346–57. *See also* merge printing
cancel/pause, 54
Copies option 348
default setting 82
with ImageWriter 348–56
with LaserWriter 351–56
main (merged) documents 452–53
merge printing *16*
non-documents 348
Pages options 347
pagination 15
Paper Feed options 348
points to remember 358–59
previewing before (*see* Page Preview command)
Print Hidden Text option 348
with a serial printer 356–57
techniques summary 32, 359, 365–66
Print Merge command 340, 452
dialog box *453*
Program disk 519, 521–24
Promote icon 64–65, 76
looking at body text with 68

■ Q

QMS-PS 800 printer 351
Quality print options 349–*50*
QuickDraw object-oriented graphics 420–21, 479
scaled 431, *432*
QuickSwitch 7, 439–40
techniques summary 444–45
using Excel with 439–40
using MacPaint and MacDraw with 440

■ R

Reduce/Enlarge % option 354
Renumber command
to number a list 393, *394*
to number/renumber outlines 70–73, 76, *77*
repagination 324, 340–41
full, 341
page break produced by *50*, 340, *341*
reply memo template 479–84
building the memo form 481–84
sample *480*
using the memo form 484
Return key
avoiding when retyping outlines 39
creating a hard return 91
ending paragraphs with 192
soft 192
RFT format. *See* Document Content Architecture (DCA) format
RFTOWORD program 416
RTF (rich text format)
advanced use for 415–16
save as 111
text transfer with 414–15
Ruler *9*
changing header/footer format from 299
clearing 194
controlling paragraph alignment from 212
display/hide 31
drop caps setting *223*
edit field 195
intervals in ImageWriter *vs* LaserWriter 327
paragraph formatting with *49*, 193–95
setting indents from 200
setting line spacing from 206–7
setting paragraph spacing from 210
setting tabs from 203–4
techniques summary 229–30
three graduations *17*
units of measurement 228

■ S

Same As Previous option, creating new headers with 305–6
Save Current Document As option 122
saving text 14, 25–26, 109–12
dictionaries 152–53
in different formats 111–12
fast save 110
full save 110
making backup copies 110–11
replacing a file 109–10
techniques summary 32, 122–23
Word Settings file 85–86

- Scrapbook, transferring text with 406–8, 421, 442
- screen dump 419
  - creating a 429
- screen graphics. *See* bit-mapped graphics
- screenplay format template 495–98
  - setting up styles 496–98
  - using 498
- screen resolution 426, *433*
- scrolling 18, 30
  - speed, by hiding graphics 430
  - synchronized 73, 74, 75, 310
  - techniques summary 121–22
  - vertical *19*
- search and replace 7–8, 98–103, 118–20
  - hyphens 338–39
  - paragraph formats 225–26
- Search menu 98
- section(s) 275
  - dividing a document into 276–77
  - format (*see* section formats)
- Section command dialog box *277*, 290–93
  - command buttons 289
  - positioning headers/footers with 306
- section formats 12–13, 165–66, 275–93
  - auto numbering 13
  - columns options 13, 285–89
  - command buttons 289
  - default 82
  - footnotes 13, 284–85
  - Header/Footer options 13, 284, 304–6
  - Line Numbers options 282–83
  - Page Number options 279–82
  - points to remember 290
  - Section Start options 277–79
  - techniques summary 290–93
- Section Start options 277–79, 324
- select/deselect text 30, 92–95
  - extending/reducing a selection 94–95
  - with shift-clicking 94
  - techniques summary 116–17
- Selection bar *21*, 93
- SendPS program 424, 543
- serial printers
  - choosing 325–26
  - printing with 356–57
- Set Default button 81, 289
- SET instruction 461–62, 471
- Shadow character attribute 174–75, 188
- shift-clicking
  - to select text 94
- Shift-Command-> 172
- Shift-Command-< 172
- Shift-Command-3 419, 429, 513
- Shift-Open, transferring files with 416–17
- Shift-Option-`(grave accent) 88
- Shift-Page Setup 350
- Short Menus 4, *5*, 17
- Show All icon 69
- Show ¶ command 9
  - showing paragraph boundaries 192
  - soft *vs* hard spaces and 90
- Show Hidden Text, adding to Format menu 177
- side-by-side paragraph format 217–22, 232, 502, 505
  - creating boxes around paragraphs with 435, *436*
  - Document view of *219*
  - experimenting with 222
  - Page Preview view of *219*
  - tables constructed from side-by-side columns 399–400
  - using the style sheet to set margins 218
- Small Caps option 175–76
- Smoothing print option 354
- soft returns 192
- Sort command
  - lists 394–95, 403
  - in Outline 37, *38*
  - tabular data 396, 403
  - techniques summary 57
- space(s) 9
  - soft *vs* hard 90
- Space After 209, 210–11
- Spacebar 9, 90
- Space Before 209, *210*, 211
- spacing, line. *See* line spacing
- spacing, paragraph 209–11, 231, 235
- spacing, text characters 166
  - changing 178–81
  - undoing 174
- spelling checker 8, 22, *23*, 31, 145–61
  - dialog box *147*, 158–59
  - doing a spelling check 146–52, 158–60
    - correcting words/adding to a dictionary 148–51
    - ignoring All Caps option 147
    - moving words from one dictionary to another 152
    - removing words from a dictionary 151
    - skipping past words 151
    - Word's suggested spellings 148–49
  - points to remember 158
  - techniques summary 158–61
  - working with dictionary files 152–57, 160–61
    - advanced work with 154–57
    - changing Main Dictionary to UK Dictionary 154
    - creating a new dictionary 153
    - opening/closing 154
    - saving 152–53
- split windows 73, 75, 108–9
- Standard Glossary 127, 134
- Start Footnote Numbers At option 314, 332–33
- Start Page Numbers At option 333
- status box 37
  - displaying *Style* prompt in *249*
  - during keyboard glossary insertion *129*
  - style name in *243*
- Strikethrough character attribute 174–75, 188
- string 98
- style(s) 40–42, 82. *See also* style sheets
  - Again command application of 250
  - alternate names for 249, *250*, 271
  - automatic 240, 254–56
  - creating a work area for 246

style(s) (continued)
- defining new, by command 245, 270
- defining new, by example 246, 270
- establishing a design with 47–49
- families of, and Based On field 256–63
- glossary insertion of 266–67, 272
- index 379
- keyboard application of 248–49, 270
- Next Style option 250–51
- *Normal* (*see* *Normal* style)
- preexisting character formats and 251–52
- renaming 253, 271
- *semicharacter* 256
- setting left margins of 58
- for tabular data 386
- techniques summary 58
- for this book 509–13
- transferring by copying text 266
- transferring formats between 253–54, 271
- updating, from Word Settings default 266
- using Styles or Define Styles commands 247
- Work menu application of 247–48

Styles dialog box *247*

style sheets 12, 239–73
- assigning styles to paragraphs 247–52
- Based On edit field and style families 256–63
- changing paragraph formats with 193
- defining styles 242–46
- document sharing of 263–67
- keyboard shortcuts 273
- points to remember 268
- printing 267, 273, 348
- protecting templates for 265
- redefining styles 252–56, 270
- techniques summary 268–73

subscript 174, *178*, 188

suggest spelling *23*, 148–49, *149*

SuperPaint 405, 419, 420, 421, 513

superscript 174, 177, *178*, 188

Switcher 7, 439

symbol(s)
- font character sets 88, 528, 529–37
- indicating footnotes with 307

synopsis, newsletter article 504–5

System Folder 81, 356, 406, 521–23, 524

■ T

tab(s) 9, 202-6, 232
- checking values of 201
- default 332
  - changing 203
  - resetting 204
- hanging indents and 205
- Ruler icons 229
- setting, from the Paragraph dialog box 204–5
- setting, from the Ruler 203–4
- sidebar text effect with 214, *215*
- tab leaders *205*–6
- tabular data and 386
- techniques summary 234–35

Table of Contents 340, 369–76
- changing the format of 373
- compiling, for linked files 375
- converting, to an outline 375–76
- dialog box *371*
- generating additional lists 374
- generating from an outline 370–71
- generating from codes 371–73
- multiple 374–75
- points to remember 382
- replacing/editing 373
- techniques summary 382–83

tables 385–91
- constructed from side-by-side columns 399–*400*
- editing and formatting 385–89
  - cutting/pasting tabular data 387–89
- enhancing 389–91
  - adding horizontal lines 390, 402
  - adding verical lines 389, 402
  - boxing tables 390–91, 402
- mathematical calculations on 396–99
- points to remember 401
- sorting tabular data 396
- techniques summary 401–2

tabular data
- cutting/pasting 387–89
- edit/format 385–89
- sort 396, 403
- style 386
- tabs and 386
- transferring 409–10

Tall Adjusted option 349

template(s)
- calculated invoice 484–90
- creating this book with 508–15
- electronic letterhead 476–79
- multiple-column newsletter 499–508
- presentation graphics from an outline 490–95
- protecting template style sheets 265
- reply memo 479–84
- screenplay format 495–98

Tempo (software) 311

text
- body (*see* Body text)
- boilerplate (*see* Boilerplate)
- boxed text, created from formatted 438
- center 32
- copying (*see* Copying text)
- editing (*see* Editing text)
- entering (*see* Entering text)
- formatting (*see* Formatting text)
- hidden (*see* Hidden text)
- plain (*see* Plain Text)
- printing (*see* Printing text)
- saving (*see* Saving text)
- select/deselect (*see* Select/deselect text)
- spacing problems in justified *334*
- transferring (*see* Transferring text)

TEXT data type code 407, 421, 424

Text Only format
save as 111
transferring text with 410–11
Text Only with Line Breaks format
save as 111
transferring text with 410–11
time and date
added to headers/footers 301
placing in Document view window 302
Times font character set 527–37
title, newsletter *504*
topic(s), outline
demoting to body text 67–68
expanding/collapsing 68
moving by 67
promoting/demoting 64–66
showing numbered levels of 68–69
topic selection 67
TOPS 411
tracking adjustment 181
transferring graphics 405–6, 418–38
exporting graphics 437–38
importing/working with graphics 427–37
points to remember 441
saving time with QuickSwitch 439–40
techniques summary 443–44
types of graphic elements 418–27
transferring text 405–18
cleaning up imported files 417–18
document content architecture (DCA) 416
MacWrite format 413
points to remember 441
resorting to Shift-Open 416–17
rich text format (RTF) 414–16
saving time with QuickSwitch 439–40
tabular data 409–10
techniques summary 442–43
Text Only/Text Only with Line Breaks format 410–11
two-step conversions 416
using Clipboard and Scrapbook 406–8, 442
Word 1.05 and Works formats 411
Word 3.0 format 411–13
tutorial 16–28
editing text 19–23
entering text 18–19
formatting text 24–25
previewing and printing 26–28
saving work 25–26
setting up 17
typefaces. *See* font(s)

■ U–Z

UK Dictionary, changing to 154, 161
Underline character attribute 41, 175, 188
Undo command 37–38, 56
editing with 103–5
Utilities disk 519, 521
vertical lines in tables 389, 402
widow control from Page Setup 332
wildcard searches 100
window management 106–9
handling multiple 108
keyboard/mouse shortcuts for 123
resizing/relocating 107–8
split 108–9
techniques summary 120–21
Word Hyphenation file 336–38
WordPerfect 416
word-processing concepts 3–33
editing 7–8
entering 6–7
formatting 8–13
points to remember 29
printing 14–16
saving 14
techniques summary 30–32
tutorial 16–28
Word Settings file 81–86
exploiting memory-management options 83–85
saving 85–86
settings stored in 81–83 (table)
updating styles from 266
WordStar 416
WORDTORF program 416
Word Underline 175
wordwrap 8
Work menu 169
assigning styles with 247–48
customized commands in 86–87
default 83
inserting glossary entries with 130
WYSIWYG (what you see is what you get) user interface 9
Zapf Dingbat characters 199, 527–36

The manuscript for this book was prepared and submitted to Microsoft Press in electronic form. Text files were processed and formatted using Mac Word 3.02 on an Apple Macintosh II.
Graphics were prepared on a Macintosh II and modified in SuperPaint, Cricket Draw, ThunderScan, MacVision, FreeHand, and Canvas. Certain effects were produced by custom PostScript routines. Graphics were printed on the ImageWriter, LaserWriter, and Linotronic 300 Laser Imagesetter.
Cover design by Williams & Helde, Inc.
Interior text design by the staff of Microsoft Press
Typographers: Lee Thomas and Chris Kinata
Text composition by Lee Thomas and Chris Kinata in Palatino with display in Palatino Italic and Helvetica Black. The book was typeset from a Macintosh Plus to a Linotronic 300 Laser Imagesetter.